1992

EARTH

JOURNAL

ENVIRONMENTAL ALMANAC
AND RESOURCE DIRECTORY

1992 EARTH JOURNAL

ENVIRONMENTAL ALMANAC AND RESOURCE DIRECTORY

FROM THE EDITORS OF BUZZWORM MAGAZINE

BUZZWORM BOOKS
BOULDER, COLORADO

1992 EARTH JOURNAL

Editor-in-Chief
Joseph E. Daniel

Editor
Ilana Kotin

Editorial Staff
Elizabeth Darby Junkin
Julie Hellerud
Ann Carey
Deborah Houy
Nicolle Pressly
Clare Corcoran

Design & Production Staff
Karen Oldenburg
Steve Harley
Joe Pezzillo

Editorial Interns
Thomas Mould
Juliet Serenyi
Andrea Merson
Joe Dilschneider
Jennifer Guggenheim

BUZZWORM BOOKS

Founder & Publisher
Joseph E. Daniel

Co-Founder
Peter Stainton

Earth Journal is published annually in November.

Copies of *Earth Journal* may be ordered directly by mail. Special pricing available for premium, gift and fundraising bulk orders. Call toll-free (800) 333-8857 for price and shipping information.

Distributed to the trade in the United States by Publishers Group West.

1992 EARTH JOURNAL—ENVIRONMENTAL ALMANAC AND RESOURCE DIRECTORY
ISBN 0-9603722-9-6
ISSN 1059-6488

BUZZWORM BOOKS is an imprint of BUZZWORM Magazine

Earth Journal is a trademark of BUZZWORM, Inc.

BUZZWORM, Inc.
2305 Canyon Blvd., Suite 206
Boulder, CO 80302
(303) 442-1969

♲ Printed on Recycled Paper with 10% Post-Consumer Waste

PRINTED IN THE UNITED STATES OF AMERICA
10 9 8 7 6 5 4 3 2 1

"One final paragraph of advice: Do not burn yourselves out. Be as I am—a reluctant enthusiast...a part time crusader, a half-hearted fanatic. Save the other half of yourselves and your lives for pleasure and adventure. It is not enough to fight for the land; it is even more important to enjoy it. While you can. While it's still here. So get out there and hunt and fish and mess around with your friends, ramble out yonder and explore the forests, encounter the grizz, climb the mountains, bag the peaks, run the rivers, breathe deep of that yet sweet and lucid air, sit quietly for awhile and contemplate the precious stillness, that lovely, mysterious and awesome space. Enjoy yourselves, keep your brain in your head and your head firmly attached to the body, the body active and alive, and I promise you this much: I promise you this one sweet victory over our enemies, over those desk-bound people with their hearts in a safe deposit box and their eyes hypnotized by desk calculators. I promise you this: You will outlive the bastards."

—*Edward Abbey*

TABLE OF CONTENTS

TABLE OF CONTENTS

Preface

- By Joseph E. Daniel -

THE IDEA FOR THIS BOOK CAME TO ME ten years ago while photographing a story on radical new conservation methods being attempted in Kenya, East Africa. A writer and I had traveled extensively throughout what was left of that historic wilderness, and everywhere we went we discovered signs that traditional conservation practices were in flux. The Western ideal of "preservation for preservation's sake" was no longer viable in those developing countries where the need for survival simply took precedent over efforts to protect the environment—countries beset by burgeoning populations and a shortage of natural resources. It was instead being replaced with economic arguments for sustainable development and a shift toward a "utilizationist" theory of conservation. Nowhere was this trend more in evidence than in Kenya, where the population growth rate had reached 4 percent—the highest in the world!—and where farming and grazing needs of indigenous peoples were in direct competition for lands being considered for new national parks and wildlife preserves. Controversial environmental strategies were already underway there, ranging from commercial game ranching to native management of wildlife and tourist concessions.

Our article eventually became the cover story for *The New York Times Sunday Magazine* on September 12, 1982. The *Times* received a large volume of mail about the piece, and it was evident from the way readers reacted that this was new stuff. It was also becoming clear that there was a need for some type of "independent" reporting on the subject, due to several reasons.

First, the handful of environmental magazines that existed at the time were all house organs of environmental advocacy organizations. While they were pretty to look at, they did not (could not) always report on environmental issues in a truly unbiased manner.

Second, since these environmental organizations were all nonprofit, they were also all competing with each other for the same donated dollars, using slick mailers with cute, fuzzy "celebrity species" to tug at the heartstrings and wallets of sympathetic members. While this is an effective way to raise money, it often overshadows more serious or timely environmental issues that do not have as much emotional impact. But the competition for membership was fierce, for as these organizations grew they required more and more money just to fund their infrastructures. Unfortunately, the very reason for a group's existence sometimes became lost in its struggle to exist.

Third, environmental conservation was becoming big business. That made it increasingly difficult for the average person to contribute time or money to environmental causes in an informed, responsible manner. How were we to know how our donations would be spent? Was the money funding a worthwhile project that had a chance of doing some good, or was it being used only to raise more money?

It seemed the time was right for a consumer guide to the environment, and I set out to produce just such a publication. My original plan was to publish a yearly "almanac" of the environment that would inform readers about the complex issues challenging our global environment and the new strategies being developed to meet those challenges. Its voice would be neutral and it would have no affiliation with any environmental organization. It would become a clearinghouse of information and resources, promoting personal involvement.

But it was not that easy. After two years of pitching my book proposal to every publisher I could think of, there were no takers. Editors liked the idea but felt that mainstream America did not have a high enough level of environmental awareness or commitment. None of us knew at the time just how wrong that impression was.

When the book idea failed to develop, I changed the concept to a quarterly magazine published as a nonprofit entity. This too was thwarted when new tax laws were passed eliminating certain attractive deductions for people wishing to give large donations to nonprofit causes. This, combined with a crash in the domestic oil market (a major benefactor to many private foundations), effectively dried up the private philanthropic marketplace. Running a magazine on donations was going to be very tough.

Eventually, led by blind ambition and a gut hunch that just would not go away, I decided to take a leap of faith and publish my idea as a for-profit consumer magazine. Fortunately, I knew nothing about magazine publishing or I never would have attempted such folly. The odds of launching a new magazine successfully at the time were ten to one. (They are even worse now!) Nonetheless, I managed to convince a few generous souls to invest enough money to get a prototype issue out in the Summer of 1988.

We named our new magazine BUZZWORM, which is an old southwest term for rattlesnake. Since a rattlesnake can be thought of as symbolizing a very effective form of communication—it buzzes a warning and you react—we thought it an appropriate name for an independent environmental publication warning of threats to our natural environment.

At about that same time, raw garbage started washing up on New York beaches, forest fires nearly burned down America's favorite national park, and a few months later the worst oil spill in history fouled the crystalline water and wild beaches of Prince William Sound. Americans and the world were shocked, and the outcry was deafening. What were these horrible symptoms of environmental disease our Mother Earth was suffering? How had we gone so far in our abuse of our fragile planet? The 20th anniversary of Earth Day on April 22, 1990, was celebrated by tens of millions of people in over 120 countries.

In the past three years this new environmental awareness has taken firm hold worldwide. A true eco-culture is emerging that injects environmental responsibility into every aspect of our lives. BUZZWORM magazine has not only survived, but has grown to a circulation of 100,000 and has won three major national awards for editorial excellence. The time is again right for an annual almanac of the environment, and the editors of BUZZWORM are very proud to bring you this first edition of *Earth Journal.* We have spent the past year reading hundreds of environmental books, magazines, newsletters, a dozen national and international newspapers and countless reports from journalists, scientists and environmental experts around the world. We have digested all this material into a comprehensive compilation of environmental updates, news briefs, resources, forecasts, essays and ecotips. It *has* taken ten years, but the end result is the most useful, interesting and fun environmental book ever produced. Good reading!

Joseph E. Daniel is the founder, editor and publisher of BUZZWORM *Magazine.*

Foreword

- By Dr. Jane Goodall -

ACROSS THE FACE OF THE GLOBE, wherever we look, we find evidence of a large scale destruction and fouling of the natural world. Everywhere, rainforests are being felled; wild places are being cultivated and built over; the Earth and the waters of rivers, lakes and the seven seas are polluted; vast quantities of noxious substances are loosed into our precious air. We are daily warned about the danger of holes in the ozone layer and the greenhouse effect.

And we all know the tragic consequences of human overpopulation. Already we are suffering from the effects of our mindless exploitation of natural resources and burgeoning numbers. Countless millions live on the verge of starvation. AIDS runs rampant, and diseases such as influenza have become ever more lethal. Thousands of people are victims of drug abuse. Crime flourishes in our cities all over the world. There are the unemployed and the homeless. There is racial discrimination. And everywhere there is evidence of human violence and cruelty. There are riots and revolutions and wars. Maimed bodies and maimed minds.

And it is not only we humans who are suffering. Wild animals are losing their habitats faster and faster, as a result of the expansion of human populations and human greed. The creatures of the wild places are forced into smaller and smaller areas, and even when these are designated as sanctuaries, seldom are the animals absolutely safe from their human enemies. Governments betray them, selling huge concessions in supposedly protected areas to timber companies, miners, petroleum companies. Poaching is rife. Animals are slaughtered for their tusks,

their hide and their flesh. Men—and women—buy permits to kill them for "sport." They are captured and exploited in various kinds of entertainment. And it is not only wild animals whom we persecute—our domestic animals suffer as much, or more, at our hands. Cows and pigs and chickens are confined ever more cruelly and injected with hormones in attempts to produce more meat per square inch of space and per hour of time—to feed the ever growing human population. Even our so called "friends," our companion animals, are often abused. And millions of animals are horribly tortured in the name of scientific research.

This broad picture is so shocking, so grim, that when we start to think about it, we are utterly overwhelmed, utterly depressed. We feel so small, so insignificant, so helpless. Even if we flung our whole selves into attempts to resolve these issues, what difference could we possibly make? It seems that nothing can halt the relentless march toward total destruction that was set in motion at the time of the industrial revolution. Or can it? Is there hope for the future of human and non-human beings on planet Earth?

If we take an evolutionary perspective, if we view our activities today against our prehistoric past, then we see that, after all, there is hope. Our earliest ancestors lived in a hostile world. To survive, they had to fight the environment. But they were few in number and their tools were simple. For all their efforts to tame the world around them, to bend nature to their will, they made but little impact. They used tools to make clothes and dwellings, to cut down a few trees, and to kill—for food, for skins, in self-defense.

Our world was never a paradise—from the start we knew disease and hunger, pain and misery. There were hard times—times of drought or flood. And there were many creatures better armed than puny humans, animals with sharp claws and gleaming fangs. Nevertheless, early humans multiplied. And so it became necessary for some of them to move out into increasingly inhospitable land, and this posed new challenges. Intelligence, including the use of tools, became ever more important for survival. And we went on developing these skills. Today we have technology that, until recently, belonged in the realms of science fiction. Modern technology has led to some magnificent achievements, and has been used to the great benefit of human and non-human beings alike. How unfortunate that it has also been used to destroy the very environment that brought us into existence. How tragic that human greed and selfishness—and our arrogant assumption that the world is our oyster and everything in it created for us to use for our own good—has, by and large, played a greater role in our history than concern and respect for each other and for other life forms. Else, by now, we might have entered the golden age of humanity.

Today, humans straddle the globe. We have perfected all manner of destructive skills. Trees that took hundreds of years to mature can be killed in a few minutes. And hundreds of people can be annihilated at the push of a button. Rich and fertile land can be transformed, covered by mile upon mile of concrete. We have learned how to tame all but the most inhospitable wilderness. We have plundered the riches of mother nature without thought for the future. And so, relentlessly, the desert has inched forward. Water tables have dropped. Gradually, the lush forests, the beautiful savannas,

have given place to harsh and barren wasteland where human and non-human beings alike find it harder and harder to survive. Countless plant and animal species have vanished already. Revelations of the devastation, the horrendous pollution, inflicted by the communist regimes of Eastern Europe have, recently, shocked the world. But that is no worse than the damage inflicted by the greedy West on the developing world.

But we must remember that much of the destruction of the environment took place before people understood the appalling damage being done. Only recently are we beginning to understand. Five hundred years ago, the wild places of the world seemed immense, never ending. The pioneers who invaded new continents from Europe were heroes, and the fact that they swept in and subdued the savage beings who already lived there was taken as their right. They were only doing what their Stone Age ancestors did, but their tools and their weapons were more powerful, and the destruction they caused was more devastating. Now we are seeing the results of the thoughtless rape of mother Earth. And now, at last, in the light of our growing awareness, we are taking the first steps along a path that could lead us out of the desolation and misery that we have created for ourselves and for the other living beings with whom we share the Earth.

Thanks to the growing power of the green movement, governments are being forced into creating and enforcing laws to protect the environment. It was our intellect that enabled us to inflict such horrifying wounds on the planet. Now our intellects face the hardest challenge yet: Can we use existing technology, develop new technology, try to heal, as far as possible, the terrible damage we have inflicted? I believe we can—but we do not have much time.

I have great faith in our species. One hundred years ago, the average person in the street, asked if he or she thought humans would ever land on the moon, or fly in a machine around the world, or hear someone speaking who was on another continent, would have laughed. "Science fiction," would have been the thought. But we have done those things—and more. There seems to be no end to our ingenuity once we set our minds to something. And so the very fact that more and more people understand the horrifying nature of the threat that hangs over us, that more and more scientists are devoting themselves to reducing the threat, should give us hope. The "greening" of industry, although it is, in many cases, just a public relations exercise, is slowly happening—because, though too slowly, governments are promulgating and enforcing legislation that forces compliance.

But what about us? You and me? Does this all mean that we can sit around and wait for our world to be cleaned up and made a more beautiful place for our children, and theirs? Absolutely not! It is only with the active support and cooperation of each one of us that change can come about. Unfortunately, greed and selfishness are traits that are deeply embedded in human nature. Industries will do nothing for the environment unless they are forced to do so by law. And governments will not make and enforce such laws unless there is a ground swell of popular opinion behind them. That means that you and I must make our voices heard.

That is the easy part. The hard part is to make changes in our lives so that our behavior is in harmony with our words. Otherwise we are nothing but whitened sepulchers—surely a horrible thing to be! We may not be able to have a direct impact on slowing the destruction of the tropical rainforests—though letters and fundraising efforts will help, as would a lobby to prohibit the importation of hardwoods. We cannot, individually, make much impression on the amount of chemicals escaping into the air and the water. But if we all do our part, we can. If one person refuses to buy a product because of unethical behavior on the part of the producer, it will make no difference. If we all make the same stand, our protest will be powerful.

Similar arguments can be applied to human suffering. It is true that we live in a cruel world, but, at least in the West, social wrongs are addressed. The slave trade is a nightmare of the past. We no longer execute criminals in public, gloating over their dying struggles. Society, as a whole, abhors the abuse of women and children, is concerned about the unemployed and the homeless, sinks huge amounts of money into medical research and health care. We still have a long way to go with regard to our attitudes toward non-human animals. Indeed, many people ask whether I feel it is right to spend so much effort in trying to make a better world for animals when there is so much human suffering that needs to be addressed. I believe that cruelty is one of the worst human sins, and whether it is directed toward animals or humans makes little difference. We know, today, that animals are not little bundles of stimulus and response; we know that there is a continuity of mind as well as physical structure. Non-human animals can think and reason, and they feel emotions that are, almost certainly, similar to ours. Certainly this is true for the chimpanzee, the being who resembles us most closely. My 30 years with wild chimpanzees have taught me humility. We humans are not as different from the rest of the animal kingdom as we used to think. The chimpanzee, like us in so many ways, sharing over 98 percent of human DNA in genetic make up, helps us to bridge the gap, once supposed unbridgeable, between

"Man" and "Beast." And this leads to a new respect for all the wonderful living beings with whom we share the planet. Only when we humans set love and compassion above materialistic greed and competitiveness can we hope to attain our human potential.

Once we recognize that each individual being matters, be it human or non-human, we look around us with new eyes. We recognize our kinship with the rest of the animal kingdom and realize that humans and non-humans are part of an ethical whole. Our effort to save wildlife in an African rainforest takes into consideration not only the individual animals who live there, but the individual humans as well. We cannot ignore the needs of people who have, perhaps, depended on the land for their livelihood for generations. In economically poor countries, it is desperately important that we link conservation projects with rural development projects, such as agroforestry; that we try to develop foreign exchange benefits, as with carefully controlled tourism; and that the local people are deeply involved in the protection of the areas, and in any research that may be planned.

When industry becomes truly environmentally responsible, we shall see great change. In Congo I have seen, with my own eyes, the difference in techniques of different petroleum companies on the environment. One company not only has a policy of net environmental gain—improve things elsewhere if an operation causes some destruction—but it also pays large amounts of money in order to explore for petroleum so as to cause as little damage as possible. Other companies in the area, operating far from Western scrutiny, do not show similar concern. If all large companies could be forced to act in a similar way, the environment would benefit enormously.

During the past year I have been immensely encouraged by the attitude toward conservation shown in so many African countries. Typically, major conservation efforts need to be linked to economic gain—if a government can sell concessions in a forested area to a major logging company for a large sum of money, clearly alternative sources of foreign exchange must be found—such as carefully controlled tourism. It is particularly important that the local people be involved in any such project, and learn to feel pride.

There is a little verse, originally a German children's story, that provides a wonderful message for those of us who care about our planet, giving us a message of hope:

Two frogs, strange as it may seem,
once fell into a dish of cream.
One was a pessimist by nature,
an optimist the other creature.
At first both struggled round and round,
hoping an outlet could be found.
One quickly lost all hope, grew tired,
sank in the cream and thus expired.
The other battled bravely on
till in the end persistence won
For after hours of splash and splutter,
he sat upon a mound of BUTTER.

Keep this book in a handy location and refer to it often. Use it as your guide to environmental activism and, together, let us all join the persistent frog and raise our beautiful planet from the frightening depths of decline.

Jane Goodall's 30 years of research on wild chimpanzees is one of the most significant scientific achievements of modern times. She continues her work in Gombe, Tanzania, and has expanded its breadth to include environmental conservation and animal welfare issues worldwide. These programs are facilitated through the Jane Goodall Institute, 2200 E. Speedway Blvd., Tucson, AZ 85719, (800) 999-2446.

PART I
EARTH DIARY

YEAR IN REVIEW

The time between October 1990 and September 1991 saw change and revelation concerning our environment. These months brought the Middle East conflict home to the west—and with it a different world view—and documented the beginning of the Soviet Union's division. These months also brought the issue of the environment to the forefront. Legislation making the news revealed opposing attitudes on the environment: An energy bill contained provisions for drilling in the Arctic National Wildlife Refuge, Japan agreed to ban the importation of hawksbill turtles and "wetlands" were redefined. The Year in Review documents these environmental events as they happened and expands on several important issues. Cartoons and unusual comments from those in the news lighten and enlighten the load. And the country's leading conservation groups detail the worst and best environmental events of the year.

DIARY

The entries in this column document daily environmental events around the world for one year starting in October 1990. They are presented in chronological order to provide a record of the significant environmental happenings on our planet. These news briefs are culled from a variety of sources, including *The New York Times* (NYT), Associated Press (AP), Reuters (R), *The Los Angeles Times* (LAT), *International Herald Tribune* (IHT), *The Wall Street Journal* (WSJ), *The Washington Post* (WP) and United Press International (UPI). The source and date are provided for ease in consulting the original story for more information (—*NYT 10/4* would indicate an article in *The New York Times* on October 4, 1990).

OCTOBER 1990

4 ATHLIT, Israel—Possibly the world's **oldest water well** was discovered in an 8,000-year-old village overtaken by the sea. This discovery hints that prehistoric people were aware of underground water tables, claims Ehud Galili, the archaeologist who found the well. —*NYT 10/4*

7 ANCHORAGE—Alaskans received copies of the 335-page sale catalog which

Journal

Journal offers more detailed information about environmental issues that continually appeared in the news throughout the year.

NORTHERN SPOTTED OWL DILEMMA

Portland, OR—The Department of the Interior officially declared the northern spotted owl a threatened species on June 26, 1990. Federal officials estimate that saving the remaining 2,000 to 3,000 owl pairs would cost 93,000 logging jobs in the Pacific Northwest over the next 10 years, and would protect 4 million acres of ancient forest.

While acknowledging that logging old-growth forests has driven the raptor close to extinction, the government delayed recommending specific steps to save the raptor and instead, established a study group to further analyze the economic impact.

The Bush Administration sought changes in the Endangered Species Act that would allow some endangered species to disappear if preserving them would cause "severe economic disruption." In this case, federal officials may invoke a rarely used provision of the Endangered Species Act known as the "God Committee" to allow the owl to die in a given area.

In August 1991, the government scaled back by more than 25 percent the amount of Northwest forest land that it believes must be protected to save the spotted owl from extinction. But Mark Rey, executive director of the American Forest Resource

Q: *How many acres of old-growth US forests are clearcut each month?*

Alliance, said the US Fish and Wildlife Service's new proposal to protect 8.2 million acres "would still constitute the largest land grab in the nation's history." The new proposal covers 3.8 million acres in Oregon, 2.7 million acres in Washington and 1.8 million acres in California.

US OFFSHORE OIL DRILLING

Washington, DC—President Bush announced on June 26, 1990 that he would continue the postponement of offshore oil and gas drilling in several environmentally sensitive areas on the US Outer Continental Shelf. The freeze on drilling off the coasts of Florida and California would continue for at least 10 more years, the President said. The policy will not stop development in coastal areas that are already being drilled and new leases may be sold in the waters off Alaska, the Gulf Coast, North Carolina and the Mid-Atlantic off New York and New Jersey. Nor will the policy permanently protect areas as coastal communities and environmentalists wanted.

In response to US dependency on foreign oil and the Persian Gulf crisis, the Senate quietly passed an amendment to the defense authorization bill to allow drilling in any public land area the President sees fit, including wilderness areas and other lands previously protected by law. The bill was sent to conference committee in October 1990. The Murkowski Amendment, named after author Senator Frank Murkowski (Rep.-Alaska), calls for the President to submit to Congress recommendations to increase domestic

---

"I am not prepared to have this country's energy future be based upon the principle of 'In Fahd we trust'. I believe we should take control of our own energy future and we can do that by a more fuel efficient economy."

Senator Bill Bradley (Dem.-New Jersey)

---

energy reserves and list, in order of priority, the public lands to be drilled. The President must also submit a schedule for leasing. Murkowski sought the amendment to highlight the Arctic National Wildlife Refuge as an attractive new domestic oil reserve. Senators

inventoried the surplus gear left over from the cleanup of the **Exxon Valdez** oil spill and were invited to attend the auction. Everything from duct tape to generators was auctioned off. —*NYT 10/8*

8 PORTLAND, OR—A 10-mile stretch of 10 **new volcanoes** has been discovered on the ocean floor about 300 miles off the Oregon coast. —*WP 10/8*

11 WASHINGTON—A report released by the Congressional Office of Technology Assessment warns that at the current rate of about 240 items a year entering Earth's orbit, the orbital path could become so clogged with **space debris** by the year 2000 that satellites and spacecrafts would be in danger of collision. —*NYT 10/12*

12 FLORIDA KEYS— **Coral reefs** around the world, which biologists say may serve as an early warning system for environmental degradation, are suddenly starving and in many cases dying because of abnormally warm seas. —*WP 10/12*

12 EDENHOPE, Australia—As wool prices hit rock-bottom, Australian farmers prepared for the summer by herding their sheep into burial pits and shooting them. Many in the wool industry say up to **20 million sheep** will either die of starvation or have to be killed by April. Australia

A. **6,000 acres**
Source: Saving Our Ancient Forests *by Seth Zuckerman with The Wilderness Society*

now has a sheep population of 175 million, over 10 for every person. — *IHT 10/12*

18 BANGOR, ME— Donald Rogerson was found **not guilty of manslaughter** in the shooting of Karen Ann Wood. While out hunting, Rogerson mistook Wood's white mittens for the tail of a deer and fatally shot her. —*WP 10/22*

24 WASHINGTON— Congress approved the first comprehensive legislation on **food labels** in two decades. The bill is expected to end a three-year period of confusion about what claims food manufacturers can make about their products. — *NYT 10/25*

26 TOULON, France— Hundreds of dead and **dying dolphins** washed ashore in Spain, France and Italy. Scientists believe the dolphins were the victims of a virus that is linked to the heavy pollution of the Mediterranean. —*NYT 10/28*

26 TORONTO—The Canadian Government announced plans to **slaughter 3,500 buffalo** in Wood Buffalo National Park, partly to assure disease-free beef exports. — *WP 10/26*

27 NEW YORK—A large barge carrying 31,000 barrels of kerosene struck a reef in the Hudson River and **spilled 163,800 gallons of fuel** into the water. —*WP 10/28*

Tim Wirth (Dem.-Colorado) and Bob Graham (Dem.-Florida) and several other members of Congress have written a formal letter opposing the amendment. As of October 1991, the Murkowski bill had not been introduced on the Senate floor.

In August 1991, the Bush Administration announced that it intends to ban oil and gas drilling from about half the Washington state coast. Under this new proposal, the administration would consider lifting the drilling prohibition in the year 2000, but the burden of the repeal would be placed on drilling advocates.

HANFORD NUCLEAR NEWS

Richland, WA—The Department of Energy acknowledged for the first time that doses of radiation created by the Hanford nuclear reservation during the 1940s and 1950s may have caused serious illnesses in as many as 13,500 residents of the Pacific Northwest. The DOE's findings were released in a July report which was part one of a five-year, $15 million study begun in 1988.

Hanford reactors produced plutonium fuel for use in the first US atomic bombs. Radioactive iodine was released from facilities reprocessing spent fuel rods. The extent of iodine emissions first became public as a result of a lawsuit by environmentalists four years ago which prompted the release of 19,000 pages of classified documents from the government. Energy Secretary James D. Watkins stressed that dangerous

Photo: AP/Wide World Photos

Aerial view of Hanford nuclear reservation, Highland, Washington.

. In tropical rainforests, what mammal species constitute over one half of all mammal species?

releases took place during a time when scientists and engineers had not yet comprehended the gravity of nuclear safety problems.

The study states that between 1944 and 1947, 1,400 children drinking milk from cows grazing in the countryside immediately west of the complex were most affected. These residents were exposed to radiation levels of 70 rads (a rad is a measure of radiation equal to the amount absorbed in about a dozen chest X-rays).

Headed by nuclear engineer John E. Till, the study is seeking for the first time to zero in on exposure levels and identify the surviving individuals still at risk. In addition, a study by the Centers for Disease Control in Atlanta seeks to estimate the number of thyroid cancers and other radiation induced diseases.

Watkins insists that Hanford's future will be devoted to waste management and environmental restoration rather than fuel production for warheads. Although most of the complex has been closed since 1988, it still stores some 600,000 cubic yards of waste, which according to a new Department of Energy report, may overheat and cause a chemical reaction, creating a radioactive geyser as it breaks through the crust.

In February 1991, the Department of Energy announced a delay of one to two years in stabilizing the radioactive waste problem at Hanford. The state of Washington and the EPA are accusing the department of violating a cleanup agreement reached two years ago.

A ditch cleanup project, begun in June by Hanford Restoration Operations, was halted temporarily in August by a pair of Swainson's hawks. Project workers created a 100-yard buffer around the nest tree and will continue the cleanup around the buffer zone and resume within the buffer when the hawks leave.

DIRTY GERMANY

Bitterfeld, Germany—Senior officials at the Bitterfeld Chemical Combine, the largest chemical plant in east Germany, say that for the last decade the government has fined the complex millions of dollars for dumping its dangerous wastes into nearby waterways. But, they charge, the fines were used on "other things," not on cleanup.

Eberhard Grahn, the official in charge of developing new technology at the plant, said the Industry Ministry and the planners in East Berlin were regularly

28 NEW YORK—Fifty women from around the world met at the United Nations Church Center to establish a worldwide network for bringing their agenda into the environmental debate. Their immediate goal is **equal representation** at the United Nations Conference on Environment and Development in Brazil in 1992. —*NYT* 10/28

29 DENPASAR, Indonesia—The Association of Southeast Asian Nations is taking tough countermeasures against a European Community campaign to **ban tropical forestry products**. —*IHT (AP)* 10/30

30 NEW YORK—In a series of bold experiments, scientists created **laboratory mice** with tiny human organ structures. The purpose is to study the viruses of human diseases in living human tissues. —*NYT* 10/30

31 ANCHORAGE—Nine underground sections of the **Trans-Alaska Pipeline** are being unearthed and examined as a result of allegations that workers who checked routinely for rust and cracks lacked training, used drugs and alcohol on the job and filed inaccurate test results. —*NYT* 11/1

31 AUGUSTA, ME—The Maine Caribou Project, Inc. announced it was abandoning the four-year effort to **restore caribou** to the wilds of Maine where the animal has been largely

A. **Bats**
Source: Natural Resources Defense Council

extinct for about 80 years. Project officials said they doubted that they could raise the money needed to transplant the caribou. —*NYT (AP) 11/4*

NOVEMBER

1 LONDON—Sixty-four nations signed a measure which calls for a **global ban on dumping** industrial waste at sea and restricts the volume of marine pollution discharged on land. —*NYT (AP) 11/3*

1 CHICAGO—McDonald's announced that it will do away with its plastic foam "clamshell" hamburger boxes and **switch to paper packaging.** —*NYT 11/2*

1 NEW DELHI—Because of the death of the Chief Justice who was hearing the case, India's Supreme Court has said that it will rehear the arguments challenging the $470 million settlement of the 1984 **Bhopal** gas disaster. —*NYT 11/2*

3 SAO PAULO, Brazil—An **alligator species**, commonly called "yellow snouts," has begun to rise from the polluted waters off Brazil and invade its coastal cities. Tourism and loss of the species' native habitat, the Atlantic rainforest, have been blamed for the invasion. —*NYT 11/5*

3 WASHINGTON—A new repatriation law signed by President Bush allows Native American tribes and other native groups to

informed of the plant's lethal emissions and of ways to remedy them. But whenever plant managers asked for money to build anti-pollution devices, they were overruled. According to Grahn, for years the chemical plant has poured an average of 200,000 cubic meters of untreated waste water a day into the Mulde River. More than half the waste contained heavy metals such as mercury, cadmium and lead, acids and other toxic compounds.

Preliminary studies of the Bitterfeld area indicate that the milk, food and soil have been contaminated to uninhabitable levels. "We have not published the results because we do not want to drive thousands of people crazy," said Rainer Fromman, the chemical plant chief.

Wismut, the company that ran uranium mines surrounding Aue, Germany, until the last one was closed in February 1991, is designing a $3.6 billion cleanup program. Financed by the Bonn government, the program will require the filling in of mine shafts and the cleanup of radioactive waste left behind by 45 years of production. The German government has sent teams of physicians and other experts to study disease rates and map the polluted areas. Bonn is seeking to acquire the 50 percent of Wismut that is owned by the Soviet Union. In exchange, Moscow will be released from the liability of cleaning up the environmental mess which includes mounds of extraction wastes, unused silver mines emitting radon and pools of mining waste slush.

In August 1991, it was announced that the eastern German chemical belt around Leipzig, Halle and Bitterfeld will be the focus of an environmental research center to open in January 1992. The research center, the first in Germany dedicated solely to the environment, is to form modernization and cleanup plans and make recommendations for polluted industrial regions. The Leipzig center's first-year budget will be 50 million to 60 million Deutsche Marks ($28.9 million to $34.7 million), 90 percent of which will be provided by the federal government and 10 percent by the eastern states of Saxony and Saxony-Anhalt.

DREAM HOUSE FOR SALE

Niagara Falls, NY—Twelve years after the once peaceful neighborhood around the Love Canal was evacuated because of discharges from the nation's

Q: *What percentage of the world's tropical rainforests are part of a park or reserve system?*

House for sale in Love Canal neighborhood, Niagara Falls, New York.

most infamous toxic waste dump, the state Disaster Preparedness Commission has approved plans to allow families to move back in.

Jim Carr of the State Love Canal Revitalization Agency is selling the property. As of October 1991, 27 out of 230 homes had been sold for between $55,000 and $65,000. The Love Canal houses are appraised to be worth about 20 percent less than homes in nearby but less famous areas. "The perceived stigma accounts for 10 percent [of the cost reductions]," said Carr. The revitalization agency also recommended developing a commercial zone in an area still unfit for habitation. The plan was rejected. The interfaith Ecumenical Task Force of the Niagara Frontier brought a lawsuit against the agency and the state of New York.

The town is not entirely vacant; some 60 families decided to stay instead of accepting the government's offer to buy their property and have remained since the area was evacuated in 1978.

SADDAM'S TREASURES

New York, NY—The ancient civilizations between the Tigris and Euphrates rivers—today known as Iraq—produced the first writing and earliest experiments in agriculture and urban living. The Persian Gulf crisis clouded the prospects for further explorations into the lands where civilization began.

Dr. Elizabeth Stone of the State University of New York at Stony Brook said Iraq is the "centerpiece in archaeology, with tremendously rich sites." In early

make broad **claims to religious and ceremonial artifacts** that are sometimes among the most valued objects in museum collections around the country. —*NYT 11/4*

3 RYE, NY—A **rare wood sandpiper**, which breeds in Scandinavia and northern Russia, and winters in southern Africa and Australia and has not been seen in North America outside Alaska since 1907, was spotted in the Marshlands Conservancy, a nature preserve in New York. —*NYT 11/4*

4 NEW BRAUNFELS, TX—Lafarge Corp., based in Resto, Virginia, and its subsidiary, Systech Environmental Corp., has found a loophole under which the company can burn toxic waste for fuel without heeding rigorous federal regulations that apply to incinerators. According to the EPA, if a **toxic waste is used for fuel,** it is no longer classified as waste but as a product used for recycling. —*WP 11/4*

5 SILVER LAKE, WA—Mount St. Helens exploded, sending **a plume of ash** 30,000 feet into the air. —*NYT (AP) 11/6*

5 GENEVA—European nations agreed to **freeze emissions** of the gases from fossil fuels that are most responsible for global warming. The US refused to join in the commitment. —*WP 11/8*

A. *Less than 5 percent*
  Source: Natural Resources Defense Council

5 WASHINGTON—As a result of budget cutbacks, an Department of the Interior audit report said, the Bureau of Land Management **lost 94 million board feet of timber growth** in the fiscal years 1986 to 1989 by failing to perform thinning, fertilization and other maintenance. — *WP 11/5*

6 ROME—Italy's Green Party is holding up a tax change to gain concessions on environmental safeguards for nuclear power and on the **ingredients of unleaded gasoline**. The Greens' filibuster tactics have driven all but one of the major foreign oil refiners from the country. —*IHT (R) 11/6*

6 TOKYO—Japan's Foreign Ministry denied reports that local fishery workers recently **slaughtered about 600 dolphins** to protect fishing grounds. —*NYT 11/7*

7 NEW YORK—The chemical "seeds" for life on earth may have arrived on dust that fell from **disintegrating comets**, a new analysis by National Aeronautics and Space Administration scientists suggests. —*WP (AP) 11/8*

11 SINGAPORE—Prime Minister Michel Rocard of France said his country had decided to reduce the number of **nuclear tests in French Polynesia**. —*IHT 11/12*

11 RIVERSIDE, CA— Federal officials have decided to allow a

1989, Dr. Stone and her colleagues discovered the "lost city" of Mashkan-shapir and had just set up a research base there—a base she hasn't been able to work in since the crisis began. Archaeologists also expressed concern that the outbreak of war would jeopardize priceless remains of the Sumerian, Babylonian and Akkadian cultures, which extend back 5,000 years. As of October 1991, no one has been allowed back at the sites, but early reports from Iraq indicate that most sites received only minor damage.

ANTI-ENVIRONMENT VOTE

Los Angeles, CA—Environmentalists suffered several setbacks in the November 1990 elections as legislation to protect air, land and water from pollution and the effects of commercial development was rejected by voters.

Groups on both sides of the ballot agreed that much of the reason for the losses could be found in the reluctance of voters to initiate sweeping changes or enact any measure that would raise taxes or create debt for future generations. Another reason for the losses, according to Jim Maddy, executive director of the League of Conservation Voters, was that the proposals were "unbelievably long and complicated, with pages and pages of fine print."

Despite the support of numerous celebrities, California legislation, dubbed Big Green, was one of the casualties. It would have banned many pesticides, mandated reduction in carbon dioxide emissions and banned offshore oil drilling. Big Green received only 37 percent of the vote. However, the rival measure,

---

"President Bush is making a wrong turn and he's trying to take the country with him. This is a dead-end energy policy, headed into a brick wall…. [It's] breathtakingly dumb."

Senator Al Gore (Dem.-Tennessee)

---

dubbed CAREFUL, that would have locked existing pesticide regulations into place, was also defeated, receiving only 30 percent of the vote. Senator Pete Wilson, a Republican who won the state's gubernatorial race, promised to create a California environmental

---

Q: *If the current rate of deforestation continues, what percentage of the Earth's species could be extinct by the mid 21st century?*

protection agency and to transfer pesticide regulation to that body. Wilson has also been strong in opposing offshore oil drilling.

In New York, the proposed 21st Century Environmental Quality Act, that would have authorized nearly $2 billion in bonds for land acquisition, met defeat. The measure was narrowly defeated 49 percent to 51 percent.

Despite having been the first state in the nation to enact a recycling bill for beverage containers in 1971, Oregon voters rejected a measure that would have required the producers of packaging materials to use more recyclable and recycled materials. The measure lost 57 percent to 43 percent.

Environmentalists applauded the defeat of Representative Denny Smith (Rep.-Oregon) who ran on a pro-logging platform, but were discouraged in the Alaska Governor's race by the loss of Tony Knowles, a Democrat and a moderate on the issue of development of oil reserves in the Arctic National Wildlife Refuge. The victor, Walter Hickel, former Secretary of the Interior, is known for his strong stand in favor of development.

A proposal to preserve forests in California, a stream-protection referendum in Missouri and a land use planning measure in Washington state also were defeated.

ATLANTIC COASTAL FOREST RESERVED

Ceará, Brazil—The Atlantic Coastal Forest of eastern Brazil, extending along Brazil's Atlantic coast from the northeastern states of Ceará and Rio Grande del Norte to as far south as the Uruguay border, is considered one of the most endangered tropical rainforests. The rainforest is expected to be saved from further destruction with a new landmark decree by President Fernando Collor de Mello.

The decree, issued in September 1990, is designed to halt all deforestation of native vegetation in the 13 states containing the Atlantic Forest. The declaration came as a result of recommendations issued by an international panel of field scientists working throughout the Atlantic Forest.

In June 1991, de Mello dismissed the head of Brazil's Indian Protection Agency and unveiled a program to allow foreign financing of Brazilian environmental projects. De Mello also abolished tax subsidies that made it profitable to cut down

controversial gold mine, called "heap leach" mine, to open in a sensitive area of the eastern Mojave Desert. The project's operator has agreed to comply with a set of strict environmental conditions. —LAT 11/11

13 TOKYO—A US-Japanese-French consortium has won a contract worth close to $350 million to build a coal-fired power plant in the Philippines. —IHT 11/13

14 WASHINGTON—Construction of a pipeline that will carry natural gas from western Canada to six northeastern US states, eventually replacing 100,000 barrels of imported oil a day, was given final approval by the Federal Regulatory Commission. —NYT 11/15

14 LAS VEGAS, NV—An underground test of a British nuclear weapon was delayed when four members of Greenpeace were sighted near the detonation site minutes before the bomb was to go off. — NYT (AP) 11/15

15 ALBANY, NY—New York State purchased one of the most important bald eagle habitats in the eastern US, just 80 miles northwest of New York City. —NYT 11/18

18 MONTEREY, CA—California sea lions, once hunted to the brink of extinction, have made such a comeback that

A. *25 percent*
    Source: Natural Resources Defense Council

they are becoming a nuisance by invading city marinas, sinking tug-boats, damaging docks and even biting German shepherds. —*LAT 11/18*

20 CORVALLIS, OR— The **rare Fender's blue butterfly** that was believed to be extinct for more than 50 years has been rediscovered in a remote area of Oregon's Willamette Valley. —*NYT 11/20*

22 MALE, Maldives—If the **worst-case projections of global warming** become reality, rising waters of the Indian Ocean could drown Maldives, a nation of 1,190 low-lying islands, within a hundred years. —*NYT 11/26*

22 WASHINGTON—A bill introduced in Congress would make it a Federal crime to obstruct hunters or scare their prey away. **Hunter harassment laws** are the latest effort to kill a growing animal rights movement. —*NYT 11/23*

22 UPLAND, CA—Two **Mediterranean fruit flies** were found in California just two weeks after the state said it had wiped out an infestation that lasted nearly 16 months and cost $52 million to fight, agriculture officials announced. —*NYT (AP) 11/23*

22 LAWRENCE, KS— The largest remaining stretch of **virgin prairie in northeast Kansas** was plowed up after attempts by The Nature Conservancy and local

Amazon rainforest for farming and ranching. In July, in a meeting of the seven leading industrial democracies, Brazil submitted a proposal for $1.5 billion in grants for a five-year program for rain-forest conservation.

ENVIRONMENTAL STANDARDS SOUGHT

Washington, DC—Big business, environmentalists and state governments are squaring off over commercial use of terms like "recyclable," "environmentally friendly" and "green." Many large consumer groups are confused and frustrated by state laws regulating the use of environmental claims and they are seeking to nationalize standards. Businesses want a rule which enables them to assert that their products, within a particular state, can be recycled, even if recycling operations do not exist. Environmental groups, saying such assertions are misleading, oppose the rule.

At issue is whether or not manufacturers can seek a marketing advantage for their products by labeling them as "recycled" or "degradable" and also what standards should be set for using these terms. Recently a group of 10 state Attorneys General investigated environmental marketing practices and called for the federal government to "enact a comprehensive regulatory scheme for these practices."

Manufacturers have increasingly used "environmental friendliness" claims to gain a competitive edge with concerned consumers. Three-quarters of consumers surveyed in June 1990 by Gerstman & Meyers, a package design firm, said they would pay as much as 5 percent more for products with an environmental advantage.

Officials from many states, as well as several environmental groups, are calling for federal action on environmental claims, seeking tougher standards for manufacturers. However, an official of the Federal Trade Commission said the agency was likely to favor more general guidelines. Two private companies, Green Cross Certification Co. and the Green Seal, are also trying to regulate green terms and make companies conscious that people are concerned. Both plan, for a several thousand dollar fee each, to examine manufacturing plants, test goods submitted by manufacturers, then affix labels to those that pass.

Q: *In central Europe, how many square miles of forests have been destroyed due to air pollution?*

MENDES MURDER TRIAL

Xapuri, Brazil—On December 12, 1990, the opening day of his trial, Darci Alves Ferreira confessed to the murder of Brazilian rubber tapper Francisco (Chico) Mendes. Ferreira's father, Darli Alves da Silva, was found guilty of masterminding the murder. Each received a 19-year jail sentence.

Mendes came to international recognition by representing about 2,000 people who make a living collecting latex, nuts, resins and other natural, sustainable products of the Amazon forest. He organized other rubber tappers in a campaign to save the forests from the encroachment of cattle ranchers and farmers, whose slash and burn method of converting jungle into pasture and cropland has destroyed large portions of the Amazon rainforest. Mendes's activities upset ranchers and other pro-development interest

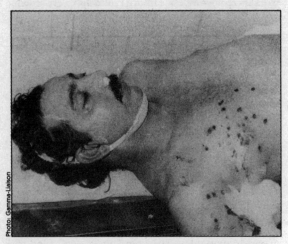

Photo: Gamma–Liaison

The body of the slain rubber tapper, Chico Mendes.

holders. Mendes was gunned down December 22, 1988, in the backyard of his home in Xapuri.

Ferreira's confession has not alleviated concerns about the safety of current rubber tapper leaders and their families. Osmarino Amancio Rodrigues, current president of the Rural Workers Trade Union of Brasiléia and secretary of the Brazilian National Council of Rubber Tappers, has received numerous death threats. According to the National Council of Rubber Tappers, landowners have been plotting the murders of peasant leaders and have hired gunmen in Xapuri and Brasiléia.

environmentalists to buy it failed. —*NYT 11/23*

23 WASHINGTON—The Administrator of the EPA, William K. Reilly, said he would veto construction of the proposed $1 billion **Two Forks Dam in Colorado.** —*NYT 11/24*

26 NEW YORK—Evelyn Berman Frank, the 75-year-old head of the barge and ship-tank cleaning companies accused of polluting New York Harbor, was sentenced to five years of probation for her role in **illegal sewage sludge dumping.** —*NYT 11/27*

27 LOS ANGELES—Chevron Corp. said that it would **begin producing oil** from a large reserve off the central California coast. —*NYT 11/28*

28 BUENOS AIRES—Presidents Fernando Collor de Mello of Brazil and Carlos Saul Menem of Argentina denounced the manufacture of nuclear weapons and promised that their **nuclear potential**, the most advanced in Latin America, would be used for "exclusively peaceful ends." —*NYT 11/29*

28 HELENA, MT—The annual fall gathering of **bald eagles at Glacier National Park** did not occur this year because the population of salmon has been nearly wiped out by the introduction of mysis shrimp into nearby Flathead Lake. The dwindling salmon population is due to food competition with the mysis. —*NYT (AP) 11/29*

A. *23,000 square miles*
Source: The Wilderness Society

DECEMBER

6 SAN FRANCISCO— The Rhone-Poulenc Basic Chemicals Co., a French-owned company, believes California will have an overflow of **500,000 tons of liquid hazardous waste** by the year 2000. —*LAT 12/6*

8 WASHINGTON— Scientists at the German pharmaceuticals group, Boehringer Ingelheim, reported that they have developed an experimental drug, known as BI-RG-587, that **prevents the AIDS virus from reproducing** in laboratory animals. —*IHT (R) 12/8*

8 STOCKHOLM— Winners of the 1990 Nobel Prize in Medicine defended the practice of using animals in medical research, saying their life-saving discoveries in transplantation depended on **animal experiments**. —*IHT (R) 12/8*

11 LOS ANGELES— The Metropolitan Water District of Southern California voted to approve the first **mandatory water conservation plan** in California since the drought of 1976-1977. —*WP 12/12*

11 TORONTO— The Canadian government announced a $3 billion program to clean and **protect the country's air, water and land** over the next five years, calling it the most comprehensive environmental plan in the world. —*WP 12/12*

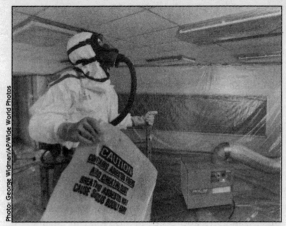

Workers remove asbestos from a Philadelphia classroom.

ASBESTOS LITIGATION UPDATE

Brooklyn, NY—A panel of federal judges, appointed by Chief Justice William H. Rehnquist to study the role of the courts in resolving asbestos cases, urged Congress to find a "national solution" to the large number of lawsuits, the delays in settlements and depletion by large legal fees of the money available for victims. The panel recommended that Congress grant courts greater powers to consolidate cases.

Until Eagle-Pitcher Industries filed for bankruptcy in January, Federal District Judge Jack B. Weinstein of Brooklyn, New York, had hoped to use his proposed class-action settlement against the former asbestos-producing company as the basis for resolving tens of thousands of asbestos claims against other hard-pressed companies. The company instead filed for bankruptcy. The proposed class-action settlement was opposed by most plaintiffs' lawyers, who said asbestos victims would get more money in a bankruptcy proceeding, in which all unsecured creditors would be treated equally and would have priority over shareholders. Federal appeals courts around the nation have also discouraged class-action suits in asbestos cases because they often do not have sufficiently common elements of fact and law.

CALIFORNIA DROUGHT

Los Angeles, CA—With little relief felt from a wet 1991 summer, the California drought is entering its

Q: *How much of the earth's tropical forests exist in Brazil, and how much in Latin America?*

fifth year and Californians are wondering where their next drink will come from and who will be asked to pay the price.

California and the Colorado River Board have been negotiating with other Colorado Basin states about obtaining a larger portion of Colorado River water. Representatives of both sides said an agreement is likely. Other solutions, like conservation, desalting sea water, seeding clouds and piping in water from Texas flood plains, have also been discussed. California Governor Pete Wilson has offered plans to encourage voluntary transfers of water to a "water bank." The new water bank would then buy water from "willing sellers," pool it in reservoirs and resell to areas most in need. The most obvious source of such water is farmers, who enjoy historic legal rights to cheap water and whose supplies cannot be arbitrarily reduced by state legislation. Over the last two generations, California built vast water projects to channel water from the mountains and streams of northern California to create the nation's largest farm industry in the Central Valley.

California farmers use 85 percent of all available water in the state. Alfalfa alone, which is sold mainly

Photo: Walt Zeboski/AP/Wide World Photos

Drought conditions at Camanche Reservoir, east of Lodi, California.

11 BERKELEY, CA—A novel experiment with fish, insects and algae in the Eel River has uncovered new evidence that plants are suppressed when there are even numbers of levels in the food chain of a given habitat, but flourish when there are odd numbers. —*NYT 12/11*

13 WASHINGTON—Richard Mitchell, an employee of the US Fish and Wildlife Service and a former Smithsonian Institution researcher, is under investigation for illegally bringing animal carcasses into the US and using his position at the Fish and Wildlife Service for his own benefit. Mitchell is **accused of hunting endangered animals** and animals whose status has not been determined. —*WP 12/13*

13 PARIS—Gilbert Caye, an oceanographer at the University of Nice, said that if **Posidonia oceanica**, a seagrass, were to disappear completely from the area, so would about 80 percent of other sea life in the Mediterranean. —*IHT 12/13*

13 PARIS—The European community has proposed the creation of an **official "green label"** to grade products for their effect on the environment. —*NYT 12/14*

13 CAPE COD, MA—Marine scientists said **43 whales failed to survive** more than a day stranded on a Cape Cod beach. The mammals

A. *30 percent and 57 percent respectively*
   Source: The Wilderness Society

were from a pod of 53 pilot whales that swam ashore for unknown reasons near Hyannisport, Massachusetts. —*WP* 12/13

15 ROCKVILLE, MD— The Nuclear Regulatory Commission approved a regulation that tightens radiation-exposure limits for nuclear plant workers and residents near atomic power installations. The **revised standards** are the first in more than 30 years. —*NYT (AP)* 12/16

15 BERLIN—Workers began shutting down eastern Germany's last **Soviet-designed nuclear power reactor**. The four-reactor power station near Greifswald on the Baltic Sea coast had supplied 10 percent of the electricity used by the 16 million people of former East Germany. —*WP* 12/16

17 BOULDER, CO—Citing New Zealand's problem with interbreeding, Colorado officials plan to kill all European red deer in Colorado and any hybrids with American elk in order to **stop interbreeding** before it starts. So far, biologists in Colorado say, no red deer or hybrids have interbred with any of the state's wild elk herd. —*WP* 12/17

17 WASHINGTON—In a report on the *World Prodigy* oil tanker accident in Narrangansett Bay in June 1989, the National Transportation Safety Board blamed the spill on the ship's captain, Iakovos Georgudis,

as hay for cattle and horses and requires more water per acre than any major crop except rice, uses more water than the combined household needs of 30 million Californians each year. Last year more than 20 percent of the state's farmland was planted with alfalfa, which used 16 percent of all available water. The California cotton harvest took another 16 percent of acreage and 8 percent of water.

Farm interests defend the growing of alfalfa, which brought receipts of $869 million to California farmers in 1989. It is considered essential to the state's $2 billion dairy industry, second only to Wisconsin's. California Farm Bureau Federation officials believe it would not be economical to import hay from distant states.

THE COST OF BIRTH CONTROL

Washington, DC—The new birth control device, Norplant, approved by the Food and Drug Administration on December 10, 1990, has become the focus of a heated debate over how much pharmaceutical companies should charge state agencies for products provided free of charge to the poor.

Norplant prevents pregnancy for up to five years and consists of several soft, matchstick-sized rubber tubes that are surgically implanted under the skin of

Photo: Richard Drew/AP/Wide World Photos

Norplant, the new five-year contraceptive device.

Q: *What percentage of plant species do people depend on for 60 percent of their calories and 56 percent of their protein?*

the woman's upper arm, where they slowly release the hormone progestin. When the implant is removed, fertility is restored. Full price in the US for the Norplant device is $350, but it is also sold in 17 other countries. In some, it is priced as low as $23.

For decades, drug companies have discounted drugs to charitable groups, public health agencies, the Veterans Administration and health maintenance organizations. Wyeth-Ayerst Laboratories, makers of the new contraception, have decided not to discount Norplant because of the unusual costs associated with training physicians on how to implant the devices.

In September 1991, Wyeth-Ayerst Laboratories said that Medicaid officials in 43 US states and the District of Columbia have added the Norplant contraceptive system to their list of drugs and devices approved for reimbursement by the program.

Gable, Canada © 1991. Cartoonists and Writers Syndicate.

GABLE
Globe and Mail
Toronto
CANADA

VALDEZ LITIGATION

Anchorage, AK—On April 24, 1991, Federal District Court Judge H. Russel Holland rejected part of the $1 billion settlement in the case of the *Exxon Valdez* oil spill of March 24, 1989, saying the record $100 million criminal fine was inadequate. This plea agreement, reached March 12, 1991, was rejected by Holland who said the $100 million in criminal fines did not reflect the environmental damage done to Prince William Sound.

Judge Stanley Sporkin, who ruled on the civil portion of the agreement, was not satisfied that the rights of 5,000 native Alaskan villagers were protected in the additional $900 million civil settlement for natural

saying he was **exhausted from lack of sleep**. —*WP* 12/18

18 WASHINGTON—A network of **instruments to monitor radiation** arriving and leaving the Earth is being set up to help scientists understand threats to the climate, said National Oceanic and Atmospheric Administration officials. —*NYT (AP)* 12/19

18 REDWOOD CITY, CA—The San Mateo County Board of Supervisors approved the nation's first law requiring nearly **all pets be neutered** to prevent unplanned litters. The ordinance imposes a moratorium on all breeding by private dog and cat owners for six months beginning in July 1991. —*NYT (AP)* 12/19

18 GALVESTON BAY, TX—The owners of the five vessels involved in the July 1990, 700,000-gallon **oil spill in Galveston Bay** have agreed to pay $156,000 for a study of the impact on the area's fishing grounds and marshes. —*WP (AP)* 12/18

20 MOSCOW—In a precedent-setting referendum, the people of the city of Odessa have **voted to shut down** ecologically "dangerous" facilities at a huge fertilizer complex built by Occidental Petroleum Corp. —*LAT* 12/20

20 MINEOLA, NY—The chairman of the Long Island Power Authority,

A. *3 percent*
   Source: Natural Resources Defense Council

Richard Kessel, proposed a $186 million plan for the **final dismantling of the Shoreham Nuclear Power Station.** —*NYT 12/21*

21 SACRAMENTO, CA—Siding with environmentalists who want to **save the redwoods**, California Governor-elect Pete Wilson urged the state Board of Forestry to reject plans for logging two parcels of the Headwaters Forest. — *LAT 12/21*

24 AUGUSTA, ME—Maine's **bottle deposit law** was expanded to include nearly all nondairy beverage containers. — *WP (AP) 12/25*

26 KISSIMMEE, FL—In an attempt to repopulate Alabama with bald eagles, teams of **nest raiders removed bald eagle eggs** from their nests in Kissimmee. The eggs were taken to Bartlesville, Oklahoma, to be hatched by chickens and then released in Alabama. —*WP 12/26*

27 NEW YORK—Researchers at the University of Iowa College of Medicine assert that symptoms of the syndrome known as "**environmental illness**" may be the result of a mental disorder. —*IHT (NYT) 12/27*

27 BALTIMORE—Baltimore's new marine mammal pavilion, a $35 million addition to the National Aquarium, is the subject of an **animal-rights controversy** involving the capturing and

resource damages. Alaskan natives sought to prevent the settlement, concerned that the agreement barred their right to sue Exxon and other companies linked to the oil spill. On May 4, 1991, Exxon and the state of Alaska withdrew the proposed civil settlement. Exxon withdrew its guilty pleas to criminal charges on May 24.

In August, the Justice Department and the state of Alaska sent a warning to Exxon Corp. that they are willing to go to trial to resolve the criminal and civil claims.

In papers filed in federal court in Anchorage, the federal government and Alaska agreed to set aside their differences over who has authority to bring claims against Exxon for damages to natural resources. Federal officials expect to file a similar agreement with native Alaskan groups. The Justice Department and Alaska said they would act as co-trustees in spending any money recovered to compensate for environmental damage caused by the oil spill.

On September 30, 1991, the US, Alaska and Exxon announced an agreement almost identical to the one reached in March. The new agreement includes $900 million for natural resource damages, a $125 million criminal fine—$25 million more than the first agreement—and an assurance that native villagers and other groups will have access to all scientific data compiled by the state and federal government concerning the environmental effects of the spill. In October 1991, the Exxon Corp. filed suit against Sperry Marine Inc. claiming that a steering system the company designed malfunctioned and caused, or helped cause, the *Exxon Valdez* tanker to run aground.

CHERNOBYL 1991

Chernobyl, Ukraine, USSR—The Soviet Union has identified 500,000 people contaminated by radiation from the Chernobyl nuclear plant explosion five years ago. Some 300,000 citizens per year are being treated for radiation exposure. Moscow has not increased the official number of deaths resulting directly from the Ukrainian power plant explosion. Soviet and Western researchers dispute the death toll, which has stood at 31 for three years, asserting that at least 500 to as many as 10,000 people have died of cancer and other illnesses caused by the accident.

An additional 120,000 Soviet citizens will be

 Q: *How long does it take a logger to cut a 33-foot wide, 1,000 year old tree?*

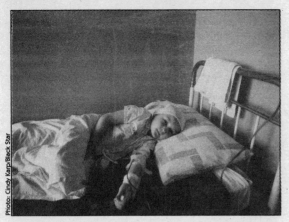

Photo: Cindy Karp/Black Star

A child from Chernobyl receiving a blood transfusion for leukemia.

evacuated during 1991 from areas near the power plant, increasing the resettlement total to approximately 325,000.

United Nations officials have begun setting up a program to provide financial and technical aid, focusing on construction materials, medical equipment and treatment, radiation monitoring and agricultural and industrial expertise.

In October 1991, the Ukranian Legislature voted to close the only two operating reactors at the plant, Nos. 1 and 3, by 1993. A fire early in October permanently disabled reactor No. 2 and No. 4 was encased in concrete following the 1986 disaster.

TAXOL

Williamette Forest, OR—Taxol, produced from the bark of the yew tree in the Pacific Northwest, is a new cancer drug that is thought to deplete and dissolve tumors that resist all other treatments. The drug has been found effective in treating advanced cases of ovarian, breast and lung cancer. But the amount of taxol now available is enough to treat fewer than 1,000 patients this year: It takes the bark of six 100-year-old Pacific yews to treat one patient, and supply is limited.

Cutting of yew trees—found growing sparsely throughout 4.3 million acres of old growth forests in the Pacific Northwest—currently is restricted by several laws, including the Endangered Species Act,

taking of animals from their natural environment and using them for entertainment purposes. —*WP 12/27*

27 BETHESDA, MD—In **a case of mistaken identity,** Maryland's state highway crews, summoned to Arun Vohra's home to cut down an ailing tree, ended up destroying seven trees, including a redwood that stood 100 feet tall. —*WP 12/27*

27 INDIANAPOLIS— Key provisions of Indiana's new law regulating **out-of-state trash** are unconstitutional because they inhibit commerce among states, US District Judge John D. Tinder ruled. —*WP 12/28*

28 MINNEAPOLIS— Minnesota's first **bicycle freeway,** a 17-mile trail from suburban St. Paul to downtown St. Paul, is to be completed in 1992. The plan begins a nine-year strategy to make bike trips easy and safe. —*WP 12/28*

28 BOSTON—Massachusetts Governor Michael Dukakis signed a clean air bill that goes beyond new federal requirements for auto emissions. The measure is based on California's **tough new standards**. —*WP 12/28*

JANUARY 1991

1 NEW YORK—In heavy fog, a 375-foot barge collided with a **tanker carrying molasses,** opening a hole in two of the barge's 10 sewage

A. *10 minutes*
* *Source: The Wilderness Society*

sludge tanks. A spokesman for the EPA, James Marshall, said he did not expect the leak to have a lingering environmental impact. —*NYT 1/1*

3 WASHINGTON—Representatives of Matsushita Electric Industrial Co. accused Interior Secretary Manuel Lujan of **inciting public fears of Japanese control of Yosemite** National Park in order to "intimidate and coerce" the company into donating park tourist facilities valued at more than $100 million. —*WP 1/3*

3 WASHINGTON—The US Postal Service is investigating the origins of a box received by People for the Ethical Treatment of Animals that contained the **bloody remains** of a small animal and a note declaring "Happy Holidays, PETA!" —*WP 1/3*

4 NEWARK—In what the authorities called the largest **illegal ivory seizure** ever in the US, Pacemark Corp. pleaded guilty to importing 13 elaborate carvings made from banned African Elephant tusks. —*NYT 1/4*

4 NEW YORK—Because it cannot account for the presence of recently discovered superstructures, a team of British and Canadian scientists concluded that the **Big Bang theory**, in its present form, must be abandoned. This announcement has thrown the field of cosmology into turmoil. —*NYT 1/5*

Photo: Gary Payne/Gamma-Liaison

Yew tree bark harvested for taxol in Willamette Forest, Oregon.

which proscribes any action that threatens the existence of the spotted owl. Bristol-Myers Squibb Co., the company licensed to carry out the development of taxol, increased its goal to obtain about 760,000 pounds of bark, requiring that 38,000 yew trees be cut this year.

Environmentalists want Bristol-Myers Squibb to switch from yew bark to yew needles, which could be pruned and regenerated. But, compared to bark, needles contain only about one-eighth as much taxol. In addition, the FDA has already approved for clinical tests the process by which taxol is manufactured from bark. The process by which taxol is made from foliage is not yet FDA approved for clinical tests. Even if switching to needles proves feasible, it could take two to four years for testing and production. Yew advocates are also asking that Bristol-Myers Squibb phase in a variety of cultivated yew shrubs grown in nurseries for possible cell culture or chemical synthesis of taxol.

VOLCANO ERUPTIONS

Manila, Philippines—Within days of each other, two long-dormant volcanoes in the Pacific erupted.

Mount Unzen, near Nagasaki in southwest Japan, first erupted the morning of June 3, killing 38 and seriously injuring 20. The first eruption of Mount Unzen, which is about 4,500 feet above sea level, was among the largest volcanic eruptions in Japan in

: *Who is the biggest road construction agency in the world?*

at least half a century. The volcano erupted again a week later and no injuries were reported. Mount Unzen last erupted in 1792 and killed as many as 15,000 people.

Mount Pinatubo in the Philippines erupted in a series of blasts on the morning of June 12, throwing a huge column of ash and smoke 50,000 feet into the air and sending thousands of people fleeing from nearby areas. The volcano erupted again late in the evening. Seismologists said that the evening eruptions were significantly larger than the morning explosions. Two people were killed by the first eruptions.

Although most geologists believe the nearly

Photo: Tim Alipello/Reuters/Bettmann

Mt. Pinatubo erupts in the Philippines.

simultaneous eruptions of the two volcanoes were a coincidence, some are investigating the possibility that the eruptions may be linked to movement by a shared tectonic plate.

HOT BANANAS

Los Angeles, CA—When unusually high pesticide residues were found in a shipment of bananas exported to California from Central and South America, banana importers agreed to monitor every shipment of bananas entering the US over a period of 90 days. Use of Aldicarb on bananas, said a California health official, constitutes "an accident waiting to happen."

Aldicarb is an acutely toxic chemical that can cause diarrhea, blurred vision and disorientation. Still used widely on citrus, soybeans, sugar and several

5 BALTIMORE—A jury in Baltimore found William Ellen, a Virginia contractor, guilty of violating the federal Clean Water Act by **filling in 86 acres of wetlands** on Maryland's eastern shore. —WP 1/5

6 TACOMA, WA—An underground pipeline used to transfer oil off a ship docked near Puget Sound ruptured, leaking an estimated **400,000 gallons of Alaskan crude** into a drainage ditch. —NYT (AP) 1/7

7 GUATEMALA CITY—A well exploded at an unfinished **geothermal power station** in western Guatemala, throwing rocks and earth and killing at least 21 people. —WP 1/7

11 WASHINGTON—The average temperatures on earth in 1990 were the highest since record keeping began in the late 19th century, **continuing a warming trend** first detected in the 1980s. —IHT (WP) 1/11

13 NEW YORK—An October mishap at the Indian Point 3 nuclear generating plant was caused in part by inadequate management by the New York Power Authority, the plant's owner. Two 1,500-pound **fuel bundles were left dangling** over the nuclear core, compromising safety. —NYT 1/13

13 PORT JERVIS, NY—The owners of Coachman Carting Inc., a

A. **The US Forest Service**
   Source: The Wilderness Society

garbage-hauling company, have been indicted on charges of illegally storing more than 160,000 pounds of blood vials, fluid samples, used hypodermic needles and other **medical waste.** —*NYT 1/13*

16 SEATTLE—Citing budget concerns, the Navy said it had canceled a program to use **dolphins to guard nuclear-armed submarines** based on Puget Sound. —*NYT 1/17*

17 SACRAMENTO, CA—In an unprecedented settlement of an act of enforcement of **Proposition 65**, DowBrands, Inc. agreed to remove the cancer-causing chemical within their K2r Spotlifter product and to contribute $50,000 to help environmentalists pursue violations of the state's toxic chemical laws. —*LAT 1/17*

20 WASHINGTON—The National Center for Health Statistics estimates that there were **4.1 million live births worldwide** in the 12-month period ending September 30, 1990, a jump of 4 percent from the previous year. —*WP 1/20*

29 WASHINGTON—Concerned that war efforts could be hampered, the White House **waived the requirements of the National Environmental Policy Act**, which calls for the assessment of the effects of Pentagon projects on the environment. —*NYT 1/30*

other foods, the insecticide is systemic and enters the fruit through the root. Although no health problems were reported from eating the bananas, the manufacturer, Rhone-Poulenc AG Co., voluntarily withdrew Aldicarb from the banana market.

CLEANING THE EVERGLADES

Everglades National Park, FL—In settling a two-and-a-half year old federal lawsuit against Florida, accused of ignoring its own water-quality laws by allowing polluted farm runoff to drain into the Everglades National Park, state and federal officials have planned an Everglades Park project. The project is likely to cost more than $700 million and take at least 10 years to implement. It is intended to reverse years of destruction due to population and industrial growth and to recover the natural flow of the Everglade waters.

However, in August 1991, legal action by sugar growers, a water control district and the Miccosukee Native Americans is threatening to delay or block the Everglades lawsuit settlement. A state appeals court must decide whether the water district is a "public entity" and has a right to be heard on the issue. If the court agrees that the drainage district has legal standing in the dispute, it could freeze efforts to carry out the agreement. Growers charge the cleanup plan would force them to give up growing sugar and vegetables in the Everglades Agricultural Area that drains into the park and Palm Beach County Refuge. The Miccosukee praised the cleanup plan but said they want to be

> *"We abuse land because we regard it as a commodity belonging to us. When we see land as a community to which we belong, we may begin to use it with love and respect."*
>
> Aldo Leopold, *A Sand County Almanac*

represented on a panel overseeing the research and monitoring programs outlined in the agreement.

With the agreement, several steps are planned: The Army Corps of Engineers has proposed dismantling much of the 98-mile canal it built to return the Kissimmee River north of Lake Okeechobee to its

 Q: *What percentage of all species are larger than a bumblebee?*

original meandering channel and filling in or re-designing several miles of two deep canals; the South Florida Waste Management District has proposed building 25,300 acres of experimental marshes to cleanse water of agricultural pollution; and the federal government is planning to add 107,000 acres to the Everglades National Park's 1.4 million acres.

OZONE LOSS

Washington, DC—Over the US, ozone loss is proceeding more than twice as fast as scientists had expected. The EPA said the ozone decline measured 4.5 percent to 5 percent in the last decade. The data show that ozone depletion extends farther south of the Arctic circle than had been thought, reaching the southernmost parts of the US, and lasts longer, starting in spring and lasting through the summer.

The National Aeronautics and Space Administration reported in October 1991 that a satellite passing over Antarctica had measured the lowest stratospheric ozone level on record, an indication of potential global health risks.

The weakened ozone shield lets in more ultraviolet light, a cause of skin cancer. EPA calculations based on the new ozone findings predict that over the next 50 years about 12 million Americans will develop skin cancer and more than 200,000 of them will die. Under previous assumptions, only 500,000 cancer cases and 9,300 fatalities were forecast.

Toles © 1991 Buffalo News. Reprinted with permission of Universal Press Syndicate.

A. *1 percent*
Source: *Natural Resources Defense Council*

30 BETHESDA, MD—In an attempt to defeat otherwise incurable tumors, two cancer patients became the first humans to receive **gene therapy**. —*NYT 1/30*

31 WASHINGTON—The EPA imposed strict controls on the Navajo Generating Station, which is 16 miles from Grand Canyon National Park and is considered the main contributor to the **haze over the canyon**. —*NYT (AP) 2/1*

FEBRUARY

2 NEW YORK—New York City is **suing the US Postal Service** to halt construction of a proposed $100-million mail center in Westchester County, which the city says would pollute Kensico Reservoir, the central receiving point for water from upstate Catskill and Delaware watersheds. —*NYT 2/3*

3 WASHINGTON—Chairman John E. Frohnmayer of the National Endowment for the Arts changed his mind and now will approve a $10,000 grant to Mel Chin, an artist who has proposed an **environmental art project**. Chin proposes to collaborate with a Department of Agriculture research agronomist on a project using plants that absorb toxic metals to clean a waste site. —*NYT 2/4*

3 LOS ANGELES—Unocal Corp. and Southern California Gas Co. announced that they will sell **compressed**

natural gas to the public from two Unocal service station sites which will be announced by the end of the year. —*LAT* 2/3

5 TULSA, OK—Ranchers inspecting fences on a ranch in Osage County found the **carcasses of four bald eagles** and 28 eagle feet, most of them missing two claws. — *NYT (AP) 2/6*

6 WASHINGTON— President Bush signed the bill designed specifically to compensate Vietnam War veterans exposed to the herbicide **Agent Orange**. The measure permanently extends disability benefits to Vietnam veterans suffering from non-Hodgkins' lymphoma and soft-tissue sarcoma which are presumed to be caused by Agent Orange. —*NYT (AP) 2/7*

6 WASHINGTON—The Department of Energy proposed **shutting down all but five of its weapons plants** permanently and letting private companies buy the closing factories. The weapons produced at the privately owned, newly acquired plants would be required to be nonnuclear only. —*NYT* 2/7

7 NEW YORK—Analysis of tiny glass fragments from Haiti, presumably produced in the extreme heat of an asteroid or comet impact, has encouraged geologists to proclaim that a massive object from outer space **smashed into Earth** 65

EARTH FIRST! TRIAL

Tucson, AZ—In December 1990, a Federal Grand Jury issued a second, superseding indictment based on FBI charges against Dave Foreman and other Earth First! members. Foreman is alleged to have conspired in eco-sabotage by providing "a cooperating witness with two copies of a book," *Ecodefense, A Field Guide to Monkeywrenching*, published by Ned Ludd books, which encouraged acts of "illegal sabotage." Foreman was further charged with allegedly providing funds to acquire the materials with which to carry out sabotage of federal nuclear power plants. The five were arrested in 1989.

On June 19, 1991, the trial of the five Earth First!ers accused of conspiring to cut power lines to three nu-

Dave Foreman and Earth First!ers escorted from a US federal court building, Phoenix, Arizona.

clear plants began. Mark Davis, Ilse Asplund, Margaret Millet and Marc Baker, four of the defendants, were also charged with cutting a ski lift pylon and the electric poles into a uranium mine and a pumping station.

On August 13, 1991, the trial suddenly and tentatively was concluded with a plea-bargain agreement. US District Court Judge Robert Broomfield first refused to accept the agreement and continued the trial into September. On September 10, Judge Broomfield accepted the agreement which called for all five guilty pleas to be accepted as a package or they would be withdrawn and the trial would resume.

Foreman pleaded guilty to one count of conspiracy.

Q. *How many acres of forest do a pair of northern spotted owls, which live only in old-growth forests, need to survive?*

Under the agreement, sentencing on the felony charge will be delayed five years. Foreman then could enter into an alternative plea agreement or plead guilty to a misdemeanor, deprivation of government property. Mark Davis pleaded guilty to one count of malicious destruction of property and received a sentence of six years in prison and a $250,000 fine. Margaret Millet pleaded guilty to one count of aiding and abetting the malicious destruction of property and was sentenced to three years in prison and a $250,000 fine. Marc Baker and Ilse Asplund each pleaded guilty to one count of failure to report a felony. Baker was sentenced to six months in prison, minus time already served, and five years' probation. Asplund received 30 days in jail and five years' probation. Both are to pay fines and perform community service.

NUCLEAR REGULATORY COMMISSION

Washington, DC—On June 28, 1991, the Nuclear Regulatory Commission approved a rule under which nuclear reactors whose 40-year operating licenses are expiring may apply for renewals for up to 20 more years. If the rule had not been approved, at least 66 of the country's oldest nuclear plants, which began operation in the 1960s, would have had to begin planning to shut down.

A crucial question in the rule was how carefully reactor owners would have to review the efficiency of

million years ago and caused the extinction of the dinosaurs. —NYT 2/7

7 NEW YORK—Dr. T. M. L. Wigley, a climatologist at the University of East Anglia in England, has proposed that reducing the **burning of fossil fuels could actually worsen global warming** in the short run. The burning of fossil fuels emits sulfur dioxide particles which reflect sunlight, cooling the earth and partly offsetting whatever warming may be taking place. A reduction in the burning of fossil fuels would reduce this cooling effect, says Wigley. —NYT 2/7

9 WASHINGTON—The Department of the Interior is proposing to open thousands of miles of the outer continental shelf to **offshore oil and gas exploration**, calling for new lease sales off the east coast, the Florida Panhandle, parts of southern California and vast areas of Alaska. —NYT 2/10

10 TOKYO—A pipe broke in a 19-year-old nuclear plant located in Mihama and touched off a series of events that ultimately forced the **emergency flooding** of the plant's reactor to cool its nuclear fuel. Officials say no radiation escaped and no one was injured. —NYT 2/11

11 WASHINGTON—The Congressional Office of Technology Assessment concluded after an 18-month investigation

Toles © 1990 Buffalo News. Reprinted with permission of Universal Press Syndicate.

A. 5,000 acres
Source: The Wilderness Society

that the Energy Department has yet to reach a realistic assessment of the magnitude and cost of cleaning up wastes and contamination from **40 years of weapons production.** —*LAT 2/11*

11 IDAHO FALLS, ID—A mechanism for dissolving unused nuclear fuel malfunctioned and **sprayed radioactive acid over three workers** at the Idaho National Engineering Laboratory's chemical processing plant. —*NYT (AP) 2/12*

14 RIO DE JANEIRO— Seeking to contain an **outbreak of cholera** in Peru, health authorities across Latin America halted food imports. — *NYT 2/15*

15 WASHINGTON— The EPA ruled it will permit the continued use of agricultural chemicals that find their way into processed foods and that pose no more than a **one-in-a-million risk of cancer** over a lifetime of regular consumption. —*WP 2/16*

16 WASHINGTON— The Defense Department has decided against giving US troops an **experimental chemical warfare drug** after new tests suggested it posed potentially life-threatening hazards and might be less effective than originally thought. —*WP 2/17*

20 ANCHORAGE—Federal and state officials are investigating allegations that Exxon Corp. **illegally shipped hazardous**

their equipment and procedures. The commission asserted that existing licensing arrangements assured that the plants were safe, but there is disagreement over how carefully this would have to be reexamined for license extension. The current licensing plan is plant-specific, differing with each of the 110 reactors in commercial operation. The document approved does not lay out precisely what must be evaluated, but instructs the commission's staff to draft the final language.

A new licensing procedure is also underway. Under the new system, reactor plans would be preapproved as meeting government safety standards. Then the plants could be given permission to operate as long as they were built as designed.

WANDERING MONTANA BISON

Yellowstone National Park, WY—In the fall of 1990, Yellowstone National Park rangers agreed to join forces with Montana game wardens to shoot any buffalo wandering outside the park's boundary. The plan of action involves three methods: Cow bison will be shot by Montana game wardens and Yellowstone park rangers, bulls will be shot in a "harvest-type" hunting season and calves will be neutered and sold at a public auction. All attempts to keep bison in the park have been unsuccessful in the past but are again being tried this year. A long-term plan is being investigated for future winters.

In late December 1990, Montana wildlife officials temporarily delayed the decision to kill bison wandering outside Yellowstone National Park. Then, on

---

"God ordained the killing of animals. He himself killed animals to provide skins for Adam and Eve after they sinned."

District Judge Warren Litynski of St. Peter, Minnesota, on why he fined a local man only $1 for leaving five puppies to die in a trash can. *Newsweek*, April 8, 1991

January 1, 1991, the state decided that Montana game wardens and federal park rangers would join hunters in killing any bison that stray. Montana livestock owners maintain that the park's bison carry brucellosis, a disease that causes cattle to abort their fetuses.

Q: *Out of the 75,000 edible plant species on earth, how many have people used for food?*

Photo: Christian Simonpietri/Sygma

In a January 1991 federal court action which was denied, the Fund for Animals, the most vocal of the animal rights groups opposing the interim plan to kill bison, asked the National Park Service to develop an alternative plan in which no bison will be killed. The Fund for Animals is appealing their case.

Yellowstone park officials are attempting to draw up a long-term plan which would help keep bison inside park boundaries, eliminating the need for a hunt. Several options being considered include drawing up temporary extended boundaries as a bison wandering "right-of-way," buying land surrounding the park area, directly reducing the number of bison within the park and cancelling specific westside grazing rights which border the park. Recently, during hearings and in written comment, the National Park Service has been criticized for not controlling bison movements or cleansing the herds of brucellosis.

In July 1991, a new angle emerged on the Yellowstone bison hunt controversy. The Medicine Wheel Alliance, an organization that seeks to preserve Native American lands and culture, has issued a proposal to donate the park's excess bison, either live or slaughtered, to nearby Native American tribes. To most tribes, the buffalo is considered a sacred animal, one that links present to past, and is therefore a valuable component in tribal ceremonies. One of the objectives of this proposal is to establish self-sustaining populations of bison on tribal lands. To follow this objective, bison migrating north of Yellowstone would be trapped and then herded to Native American land. But bison migrating into grazing lands or toward nearby cattle would still be slaughtered; the meat and carcasses would be auctioned off or donated to Native American tribes.

wastes in the ballast water of its oil tankers to a treatment plant in Alaska. —LAT 2/20

21 NEW YORK—A rare fish species, *opal allotoca*, that was **believed for 20 years to be extinct,** has been rediscovered in a pond near a dried lake bed in Mexico where it once flourished. The species dates back to before the last ice age and was believed to have existed only in Lake Magdalena, a landlocked lake in an arid region 100 miles west of Guadalajara. —IHT (NYT) 2/21

24 NEW ORLEANS— Louisiana has enacted a new tax rule that ties the amount of business property taxes a company pays to its **environmental record.** —NYT 2/27

25 DETROIT—The General Motors Corp. and the Gas Research Institute said they would spend $39 million to develop **trucks that run on cleaner-burning natural gas** and would begin production by the mid-1990s. —NYT 2/26

25 NEW YORK—The Food and Drug Administration has approved the first American tests on humans of a **purified blood product from cattle.** The experiments may lead to safer and cheaper blood transfusions, says the product's manufacturer, Biopure Corp. of Boston. —NYT 2/25

25 ANACORTES, WA— An estimated 210,000

A. *5,000*
Source: *Natural Resources Defense Council*

gallons of oil spilled as a tanker unloaded at a Texaco refinery, and 8,400 gallons reached Fidalgo Bay. Some **35 dead birds** have been found and 36 others are being treated. —*NYT (AP) 2/26*

25 TORONTO—Bowing to nearly four years of pressure from animal rights advocates and a plunge in sales and profits, the Hudson's Bay Company of Canada announced that it was **closing the last fur salons** in its Hudson Bay department stores. — *NYT 2/26*

27 MEXICO CITY—In one of the **largest private "debt-for-nature"** exchanges yet negotiated, Mexico has accepted an agreement, negotiated by the private American ecological group, Conservation International, that would reduce its foreign debt by $4 million in return for a Mexican government commitment to help preserve the country's tropical rainforests and other fast-disappearing natural resources. —*IHT (NYT) 2/27*

28 WASHINGTON—The **concentration of nitrous oxide**, "laughing gas," in the atmosphere appears to be rising at the rate of approximately 1 percent every five years. The preparation of adipic acid used in making nylon fiber may account for as much as 10 percent of the input, according to two chemists at the University of California at San Diego. — *IHT (WP) 2/28*

The alliance's proposal has been incorporated into the Environmental Impact Statement currently being drafted by the National Park Service and US Forest Service. However, no decision will be made until late fall 1991 when alternatives to the current policy will have been studied.

FARM BILL

Washington, DC—The $41 billion, five-year farm policy that introduces changes in the structure of commodity price supports and includes the strongest environmental provisions of any farm legislation in history was signed by President Bush on November 28, 1990.

Since the farm program was established in the 1930s, the supply of grain, cotton, rice and other commodities has been controlled by the government through contracts with farmers. In exchange for letting 5 percent to 15 percent of their tillable land lay fallow each year, farmers who signed up for the program were guaranteed payment and price for every bushel of grain, bale of cotton or pound of rice they produced. Under the new bill, the amount of land on which farmers can grow price-guaranteed crops will be reduced by 15 percent. A limit of $100,000 on payments to any farmer was set. Given the new limitations, farmers may choose to leave the program.

Under the new environmental provisions, the Department of Agriculture has been authorized to

Q: *What percentage of the Earth's plants and animals are believed to live in the tropical forest?*

spend $80 million per year on research into cultivation practices that use little or no toxic chemicals. Only $5 million was spent on research in fiscal year 1990. However, the organic farming portion of the bill had not received funding as of fall 1991. Farmers will also now be required to keep records on how they use 125 toxic pesticides. The records must be made available for review by the department for studies and by medi-cal specialists in the investigation of poisoning acci-dents. A provision to bar the export of pesticides out-lawed for use in the US was dropped from the bill.

CIVIL RIGHTS ACT PROPOSED

Washington, DC—On October 20, 1990, Congress sent a significant anti-discrimination bill, The Civil Rights Act of 1990, to the White House. Since 1976, the courts have allowed damages to be awarded to anyone who could prove intentional job discrimina-tion on the basis of race.

On October 22, 1990, President Bush vetoed the act after an unsuccessful effort to persuade Congress to modify it. President Bush stated that he vetoed the bill because it "employs a maze of highly legalistic language to introduce the destructive force of quotas into our national employment system."

"The environmental crisis is an outward manifestation of a crisis of mind and spirit. There could be no greater misconception of its meaning than to believe it to be concerned only with endangered wildlife, human-made ugliness, and pollution. These are part of it, but more importantly, the crisis is concerned with the kind of creatures we are and what we must become in order to survive.

Lynton Keith Caldwell, UNEP publication for the United Na-tions Environmental Sabbath/Earth Rest Day, 1-3 June, 1990

Richard Moore, co-director of SouthWest Organizing Project (SWOP), an empowerment group for regional environmental activists, sees the veto of the Civil Rights Act as "one more slap in the face" to environmental community-based organizations representing minorities trying to preserve "the integrity of their communities

MARCH

4 GRAND RAPIDS, MN—A pipeline carrying crude oil, owned by Lakehead Pipeline, **spilled an estimated 630,000 gallons of oil** onto the ground and into the nearby Prairie River. Some 200 to 300 people who lived within half a mile were evacuated. *—NYT 3/5*

7 NEW YORK—Halley's comet unexpectedly erupted with an immense dust cloud that made it hundreds of times brighter. Energy from the sun is thought to trigger such outbursts. *—IHT (AP) 3/7*

11 TOKAHOMA, Japan—High pressure readings forced a nucle-ar fuel reprocessing cen-ter in Tokahoma, 71 miles northwest of Tokyo, to automatically **shut down.** The incident was at least the third since the Mihama Nucle-ar power plant accident on February 10. *—WSJ 3/11*

12 NEW YORK—The EPA accidentally discov-ered what it believes is a safe and inexpensive way to destroy large amounts of polychlori-nated biophenyls, or PCBs. The treatment process involves **quick-lime**, a common mineral used to make cement, which, when mixed with oily sludge residues con-taining large amounts of PCBs, produces a chemical reaction that destroys the toxic mate-rial and leaves three rela-tively safe by-products—

A. *50 percent*
   Source: Natural Resources Defense Council

calcium chloride, water and carbon dioxide. —WSJ 3/12

12 CHARLOTTE, NC—The Coca-Cola Company's North Carolina bottling operation began a limited market introduction of the **first soft drink bottles made with recycled plastic.** The two-liter bottles of Coca-Cola Classic are made with a blend of 25 percent recycled plastic and 75 percent virgin resin. —NYT 3/13

19 NEW YORK—The Exxon Corp. will pay a **$5 million penalty** as part of a deal to settle claims over a 567,000-gallon oil spill that occurred over a year ago in New York Harbor. —NYT 3/20

19 WASHINGTON—Researchers studying workers' exposure to low levels of radiation at the Oak Ridge National Laboratory in Tennessee say they found a clear link between the rate of deaths from cancer and levels of radiation exposure: As radiation exposure increased, so did the **number of deaths from cancer.** —NYT 3/20

22 DENVER—T. S. Ary, the head of the US Bureau of Mines, told miners, loggers and others who advocate development of federal land, that environmentalists are **"a bunch of nuts"** and that he does not believe in endangered species. He later qualified his comments on endangered species. —NYT (AP) 3/23

and the land where they work."

The Senate failed to overturn the President's veto by one vote.

After its defeat the bill was revised. When presented again in July 1991, the House approved the bill. The vote came after the House defeated two alternative bills—a more sweeping version supported by women and black legislators and a more restrictive one backed by the White House.

In October 1991, the Senate also approved the compromise civil rights bill. President Bush has promised to sign it, saying it is "not a quota bill." The new bill will offer individuals, for the first time including Senate employee and White House staff, protections from intentional job bias and sexual harrassment. The bill includes a provision that any Senator found guilty of discrimination and sexual harrassment will have to pay damage awards from his or her own pocket.

URANIUM MINERS COMPENSATED

Washington, DC—In the fall of 1990 as part of a formal apology to US citizens, Congress passed a bipartisan bill creating a $100 million trust fund to compensate uranium miners and others who lived downwind from Cold War atomic tests and were later stricken with radiation-related illnesses. In August 1991, the Justice Department issued regulations under which claimants would be awarded $50,000 or $100,000 depending on the illness contracted and the area and years they lived in the Four Corners region of the Southwest.

MOUNT GRAHAM RED SQUIRREL

Phoenix, AZ—Arizona's 10,720-foot Mount Graham, home of the endangered Mount Graham red squirrel, was proposed in spring 1990 as the site for the University of Arizona's $200 million international observatory complex. The project, biologists said, would further diminish the squirrels' habitat and threaten the remaining population of less than 100 squirrels. After nearly a year long legal battle fought among the Sierra Legal Defense Fund, the university and the US Fish and Wildlife Service, the federal court has indicated it will rule that the university may build, without further legal action against it, three of its seven telescopes on 8.6 acres, plus two miles of road. Construction of the telescopes began in fall 1991. When the three

Q: *What is the best selling solar powered device in America?*

telescopes are completed, the US Fish and Wildlife Service will evaluate the impact of the observatory to determine if the project should continue or if it severely threatens the Mount Graham red squirrel. University of Arizona officials said construction of the telescopes would not be completed until spring 1993.

PERSIAN GULF WAR DAMAGE

Bahran, Kuwait—The fighting has stopped but environmental damage continues in Kuwait and surrounding areas. As of fall 1991, areas of Kuwaiti desert were covered with oil from wells and reservoirs, in some cases in lakes six feet deep, that destroyed roads and blocked access to the source of the leak. Oil slicks appeared on the Persian Gulf coast; environmentalists believe the source has been ground spills. Oil could be seen leaking from storage reservoirs in many places, cutting channels in the sand and forming black pools. Flowers that bloomed before the war were spotted with oil and soot. Once dry and granular, the sand became crusted with ash mixed with rain blackened as it passed through heavy soot from burning oil wells.

Since the end of the war on February 28, 1991, shepherds began walking in front of their herds of sheep and goats instead of behind, to try to protect the flocks from mines. But the animals were being led to oil-covered grass, where they appeared to poison themselves. Many showed respiratory congestion, stopped eating and died quickly. In each flock, at least one or two sheep were nearly bare of wool and appeared weak. The tanker trucks that used to bring

27 SACRAMENTO, CA—Headwaters Forest, a stand of redwoods on 2,900 acres in Humboldt County, may be preserved by millions of dollars in junk bonds seized by federal regulators in January when the Columbia Savings and Loan of Beverly Hills failed. Maxxam Inc., the conglomerate which owns the land, may **sell the forest to the state** to escape environmental protests and lawsuits over logging rights. — *NYT 3/27*

APRIL

2 SEATTLE—The federal government proposed that the **Snake River sockeye salmon be listed as endangered.** The Snake River sockeye is a type of Pacific salmon that spawns near the Continental Divide in Idaho. A formal listing could require broad changes in the dams on the Columbia River, which provide most of the electricity used in the Pacific Northwest. —*NYT 4/3*

2 BEIJING, China— China will not let foreign companies take an equity stake in **oil drilling in western Xinjiang**, the nation's most promising region for exploration, Energy Minister Huang Yicheng said. —*IHT (R) 4/2*

3 WASHINGTON—The Pentagon developed a nuclear-powered rocket for hauling giant weapons and other **military payloads into space** as part

A. *Solar powered calculators (2 million sold in 1990)*
Source: The Next Step: 50 More Things You Can Do To Save The Earth, *by the Earth•Works Group*

of the "Star Wars" program. The secret program was disclosed by the Federation of American Scientists and confirmed by internal government documents obtained by *The New York Times*. —*NYT 4/3*

4 WASHINGTON—According to the Bush Administration, the operators of nearly half the nation's underground coal mines have been **tampering with the dust samples** they send to federal safety inspectors who determine the risk of black lung disease to miners. —*WP 4/4*

5 LONDON—The Natural History Museum in London opened what it describes as the **world's first permanent exhibition** on global ecology. —*IHT 4/5*

6 JOHANNESBURG—Nelson Mandela posed as a hunter for a picture on the front page of the *Weekly Mail* to show that he supports **wildlife management in South Africa**. —*IHT 4/7*

9 LOS ANGELES—Southern California officials testified that **construction of a peripheral canal** or similar facility in the Sacramento-San Joaquin Delta is vital to preventing future water shortages. —*LAT 4/9*

11 NEW YORK—The five-year-old, $1.1 billion North River sewage plant serving most of the West Side of Manhattan is treating almost **as much sewage as it can handle**, raising questions

water for the animals were carrying it only to people. Where sheep were able to find water, it was polluted from black rain.

As of fall 1991, oil spill cleanup efforts had only a limited effect. Since July 1991, an estimated 3,000 barrels of oil a day were still being spilled into the Persian Gulf from ground spills, leaking terminals and sunken Iraqi tankers. About half the oil from the original spill was believed to have evaporated. More than 1.5 million barrels of oil were reclaimed and 2 million barrels of oil and water were collected into lagoons, awaiting separation.

Kuwait faced an air-pollution catastrophe as normal summer weather conditions concentrated the smoke of the then still burning 400 oil wells. Local climate experts warned of even greater risks to human health and reduced crop yields resulting from hot-weather temperature inversions. Inversions occur when cool air at the surface is trapped by a layer of warmer air above. In summer, the inversions are more pronounced, and the cap of warm air is very low, less than 500 feet. While inversions in Kuwait City are normally broken within a day, they can last for days in the summer; last summer, fires and inversions sustained each other, with the inversions concentrating the smoke, and smoke making the inversions last longer.

A team of British scientists said serious smog could build in the following months in the region, but there was little evidence to support dramatic warnings

Photo: Peter Menzel

Smoke and flames erupt from a burning oil well in war-torn Kuwait.

Q: *In the United States, how much of the old-growth forests have been destroyed?*

about possible long-term climatic effects. For climate change to take place, these scientists believe, sufficient soot and gases would have to rise more than eight miles into the air and enter the stratosphere.

Weather specialists who have followed the

> *"Seventy percent of the edible animals have been eaten by soldiers, especially antelope and deer."*
>
> World Society for the Protection of Animals director Victor Watkins, describing the scene at the Kuwait Zoo in the wake of the Iraqi invasion

---

smoke's trajectory by satellite said oil fires caused acidic rain at distances of 1,200 miles from Kuwait and had reached the Black Sea to the north and Pakistan to the east. Most at risk, according to meteorologists, were the agricultural regions of Iraq and Iran where highly acidic rain can corrode forests and crops. British researchers said they collected evidence of pollution from the fires as far as 1,000 miles from the wells.

By November 1991, all of the 700 burning wells, storage tanks and refineries had been capped. A team of US atmospheric scientists expect that the smoke and soot generated from the Kuwaiti oil fires will have a "minimal effect" on global climate and limited effects in the Persian Gulf region. Early speculations that the massive oil fires could lead to a nuclear winter are proving unfounded, these scientists now say.

Other studies haven't yet determined why the smoke from many of the fires was white. Environmentalists and oil-field geologists fear that white smoke indicates that water was mixing with oil underground. Some scientists contended the white smoke suggests that there were unidentified minerals mixed in with oil or that the oil is rich in sulfur oxide.

Only a few turtles and no dolphins or dugongs were reported to have died from the effects of the spill. Green and hawksbill turtles returned to their breeding islands. The sea grass beds apparently remained intact. A wildlife rescue project at Jubail, Saudi Arabia, treated 1,300 oil-mired birds of which about 500 survived. An estimated 20,000 birds perished since the spill began.

about the future water quality of the Hudson River and the future of West Side development. —NYT 4/12

12 CAPE TOWN— South Africa's Environmental Minister Louis Pienaar declared the **great white shark a protected species** within 200 miles of the South African coast. South Africa claims it is the first country to ban the killing of great white sharks and trading in great white jaws or other souvenirs. —IHT (R) 4/12

12 NEW ORLEANS— Two **laboratory monkeys,** that for a decade had been the center of an animal rights battle, were put to death, hours after medical researchers received the US Supreme Court's clearance to conduct one final set of experiments. —NYT (AP) 4/14

14 PARIS—The burning supertanker *Haven*, which spilled millions of gallons of crude oil into the Bay of Genoa after a series of explosions, sank in shallow water 2,000 yards off the northwest coast of Italy. Italian officials said most of the estimated **11 to 17 million tons of oil spilled** had burned and the leaking had stopped. —NYT (IHT) 4/15

14 AIKEN, SC—The Department of Energy is spending at least $2.2 billion to repair and modernize the Savannah River Site's **bomb-making equipment.** —NYT 4/14

A. *85 percent*
Source: The Wilderness Society

16 JERUSALEM— Israeli water reservoirs are at their lowest levels ever and top government officials blame the abundant availability of cheap water to farmers for what is described as ranging **from crisis to catastrophe**. The Israeli government is considering plans to import fresh water from Turkey, Yugoslavia or Bulgaria. — *NYT 4/21*

16 PORT ANGELES, WA— The National Park Service, unsuccessful in nonviolent efforts to **remove mountain goats from Olympic National Park**, proposed shooting the 400 goats eating the high elevation plant life. Other alternatives are being investigated. — *WP 4/16*

19 OSLO— The International Whaling Commission has banned Norway and other nations from **commercial whale hunting** for the next five years, but has allowed them to kill an undetermined number of whales per year for scientific purposes. —*WSJ 4/19*

19 REHOVOT, Israel— Scientists have created **mice with fully functioning human immune systems** by replacing the mice's bone marrow with human bone marrow. Researchers expect that the mice will be able to make human antibodies and could be testing grounds for vaccines and AIDS drugs. —*NYT 4/19*

20 BRASILIA—Brazil's

HAWKSBILL TURTLE

Washington, DC—Backing down in a wildlife conservation and trade battle with the US, Japan agreed to ban the import of endangered hawksbill sea turtles by the end of 1992. Last year Japan imported close to 20 tons of the turtles; and in 1992, Japan has promised to import only 7.5 tons. The hawksbill turtle is protected by 107 of the 110 nations that agreed to the 1973 Convention on International Trade in Endangered Species.

Photo: W. Gregory Brown/Animals Animals

An endangered hawksbill turtle in the ocean near Fiji.

The US had threatened trade sanctions to protect the turtles, barring a number of Japanese products including pearls. In June 1991, Japan agreed to put a stop to a centuries-old industry near Nagasaki where shells of hawksbills are carved into jewelry, combs and eyeglass frames. Japanese government officials say they will compensate the more than 2,000 workers formerly employed in the turtle business.

GASOLINE SUBSTITUTES

Detroit, MI—Just a few years ago consumers and companies alike were very reluctant to use anything in the family vehicle except that which was regularly pumped from the local gas station. Now, in the 1990s, consumers are demanding a more clean-burning alternative and companies are beginning to take notice. Nine oil companies in the last two years have introduced reformulated gasolines

Q: *US citizens consume how many millions of tons of paper and cardboard annually?*

MIDDLE EAST

REGULAR BODY COUNT

SUPER BODY COUNT

PREMIU BODY COUNT

Carol Simpson © 1990

in selected grades on a voluntary basis, and several car companies, including the big three, are redesigning their cars' engines to accommodate alternative fuels. Here is a brief look at a few of 1991's inventors and their inventions.

ARCO has announced that it has developed a gasoline as clean-burning as methanol that would cut some pollutants by more than a third. The new fuel, which would not affect a car's performance, is a more radical change in formula than other companies are using, says ARCO, and would be available in all

> "We SHELL not EXXONerate Saddam Hussein for his actions. We will MOBILize to meet this threat to vital interests in the Persian GULF until an AMOCOble solution is reached. Our best strategy is to BPrepared. FINAlly, we ARCOming to kick your ass."
>
> A statement circulating among office workers at oil companies

grades. The company does not, however, plan to produce this more expensive fuel, dubbed EC-X, unless it is ordered to.

Detroit Diesel Corp. won formal approval from federal and California regulators to begin selling a

President Fernando Collor de Mello has revoked a series of decrees that had sharply reduced the Amazon **lands reserved for the Yanomami**, one of the world's largest traditional tribal peoples. — *NYT (AP) 4/21*

21 WASHINGTON— The US banned feeding wild marine mammals at sea in an attempt to **halt dolphin-feeding cruises**. The cruises disrupt natural feeding habits and the timing of normal migrations, the National Oceanic and Atmospheric Administration said. —*IHT 4/21*

22 WASHINGTON— The federal government is allowing eight regional councils dominated by **local fishing interests** to hand out exclusive rights to the multibillion dollar harvest of fish off the US coast. —*NYT 4/22*

23 LAS VEGAS, NV—In an attempt to find new water supplies, **Las Vegas is looking to harvest water** underneath vast, sparsely populated rural Nevada. The multibillion dollar undertaking would pump water from an ancient aquifer in an area nearly as large as West Virginia and ship it south through more than 1,000 miles of pipelines. —*NYT 4/23*

24 WASHINGTON— The EPA has proposed rules for an **air-pollution permit system** that are the first major regulations submitted under the Clean Air Act. The regulations would

A. *69*
Source: The Recycler's Handbook, by the Earth•Works Group

establish a framework for later rulings that will deal with specific pollutants. —*WSJ 4/24*

25 HACKENSACK, NJ—Bergen and Essex Counties signed a regional garbage-disposal agreement intended to eliminate a **trash shortage** at a new $340 million incinerator in Newark and end reliance on shipments of Brooklyn garbage that have been easing the shortfall. —*NYT 4/26*

26 WASHINGTON—The Procter & Gamble Company agreed to change the name of a brand of **orange juice concentrate** from Citrus Hill Fresh Choice to Citrus Hill. The Food and Drug Administration believed the word "fresh" to be misleading. —*NYT 4/27*

26 SEOUL, South Korea—President Roh Tae Woo dismissed South Korea's environment minister in reaction to a scandal in which tap water in millions of homes was polluted with **toxic phenol waste**. —*IHT (AP) 4/26*

28 NEW ORLEANS—Archeologists say they have made the first discovery of catacombs known to have been used by Native Americans 800 years ago as **tombs for the dead** and chambers for sacred rites. —*NYT 4/28*

methanol-fueled version of its Series 92 engines for use in transit buses and trucks. This marks the first alternative-fuel heavy engine ever certified to meet both federal clean air standards and California's stringent environmental regulations. It is also the first methanol fueled engine to go into regular production for either heavy or light vehicles.

A new refinery in Pueblo, Colorado, will turn methane gas into diesel fuel. The fuel will be far cleaner, but no more expensive, than what is now available at filling stations.

General Motors Corp. said it will build 50 variable fueled vehicles in 1992 that will be calibrated to use ethanol. GM said the cars will be delivered to Wisconsin and Illinois for fuel efficiency and emissions tests in early 1992. Ethanol-powered cars will also be offered to the US Department of Energy.

In a move to greatly expand the use of natural gas, Southern California Gas Co. announced its plans to spend $18 million to establish 51 new service stations in the Los Angeles area by 1993. The company applied for approval from the California Public Utilities Commission to raise residential utility rates by about 5 cents a month to fund the program. The utility estimates that greater use of natural gas could eventually save rate-payers as much as 50 cents a month.

A joint venture of Unocal and San Diego Gas & Electric Co. opened southern California's first public natural gas station in Vista. Some 30 more fueling stations are expected to crop up in the next five years. Northern California's Pacific Gas and Electric Co. has eight facilities selling natural gas to the public. Some 19 more are to be added.

Conoco has announced it will start selling propane from pumps next to gasoline pumps at some of its stations in the Denver, Colorado, area. Conoco said it would be the first big oil company to sell propane at the service islands of its stations. Stations around the US sell propane, but mostly at separate fueling locations, for use in barbecue-grill tanks or other equipment. Conoco says cars can be converted to operate on propane only, or to use either propane or gasoline, for between $1,800 and $3,000. Conoco believes a car or truck running on propane will perform the same as one running on gasoline, while emitting 70 percent to 80 percent less carbon monoxide.

Q: *How many acres of tropical forest are destroyed each hour?*

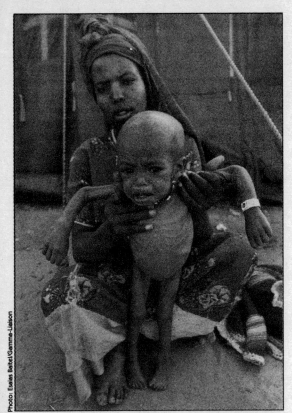

Photo: Eselas Baite/Gamma-Liaison

Mother and child in Kebri Bayah refugee camp in Ethiopia.

FAMINE 1991

Washington, DC—The new interim Ethiopian Government, dominated by former rebels of the Ethiopian People's Revolutionary Democratic Front, says famine relief is the top priority, and it intends to eliminate many formalities that have hampered past emergency operations. Still, the country is bankrupt, and its two major ports, from which international relief supplies enter, were, as of fall 1991, in the hands of Eritrean separatist rebels. The rebels established a separate provisional government in their province and held only a loose agreement with the Democratic Front to reopen the ports to relief efforts.

In August 1991, international relief officials said up to 7 million Ethiopians, or 15 percent of the population,

1 WASHINGTON—Washington initiated a two-week program to spray six national parks in the Washington area with the biological pesticide, Bt (Becillus thuringiensis), **to eradicate gypsy moths.** —WP 5/1

5 DAYTON, TX—Hunter Environmental Services, Inc. is seeking a permit from federal and Texas authorities to **build a hazardous waste disposal site** in the natural caverns within a 60 million-year-old salt dome 30 miles from Houston. —IHT 5/7

6 MEXICO CITY—Some 500 people were injured and 1,600 were evacuated for one day from their homes after **explosions at a chemical plant** in Cordoba, Mexico, released a toxic cloud. —IHT (AP) 5/6

7 BRASILIA—The last part of the **Itaipu hydroelectric dam**, a $20.5 billion project begun in 1974 on the Brazil-Paraguay frontier, was activated. The dam can generate 12,600 megawatts of electricity, nearly one-third more than its nearest competitor in size, the Grand Coulee Dam in the US. —WSJ 5/7

8 NEW YORK—Approximately 75 million gallons of **raw sewage flowed into Jamaica Bay** and threatened a wildlife refuge when a pipe burst at the Rockaway Sewage Treatment Plant. —NYT 5/9

A. **5,800 acres**
  Source: Natural Resources Defense Council

9 DENVER—Adolph Coors Co. **spilled over 150,000 gallons of beer** into Clear Creek, killing more than 17,000 fish. — *WSJ 5/13*

10 PHILIPPINES—The Philippine government announced that **logging in virgin forests will be banned** beginning on January 1, 1992. The ban affects 63 logging companies that have concessions to cut timber in areas to be restricted. —*IHT 5/10*

11 WASHINGTON—The Energy Department agreed to pay a **$100,000 fine to the EPA** for failing to meet cleanup schedules at a nuclear weapons plant in Ohio. —*NYT (AP 5/12*

12 SAN DIEGO—The California Coastal Commission approved a proposal by Santa Barbara to **build the state's first large-scale desalination plant**. The proposed plant will use enough sea water to produce 132,000 gallons of fresh water per day. —*NYT (AP) 5/13*

13 SACRAMENTO, CA—The California Department of Health Services has filed suit against Safety-Kleen, Inc., a hazardous waste recycler, charging that it **committed nearly 100 violations** of state and federal environmental laws in California. In a first-ever action, the state is demanding that Safety-Kleen sell new stocks in order to pay the fines. —*WSJ 5/13*

may need emergency food assistance. More than 5,000 people died of hunger during the spring months of 1991. Although officials believe that the current crisis will not be as devastating as the 1984-1985 famine, which took an estimated 300,000 lives, the drought situation in many parts of the country is desperate.

Ethiopian diplomats and relief officials say their efforts have been complicated by competition with more publicized disasters such as the Kurdish refugee crisis and the cyclone in Bangladesh. The crisis has been made worse by the influx of more than a half million Sudanese and Somalis fleeing war and famine in their countries.

ARCHEOLOGICAL AWAKENINGS

New York, NY—In the past year, an unusual amount of new discoveries has provided new insights into our past.

British biologists found evidence that one of the first four-legged animals known to walk on land retained its gills and seemed to live more like fish than land-dwellers. Fish-like gills were identified in fossils of a 360-million-year-old salamander-like creature found in Greenland. The species, *Acanthostega gunnari*, was one of the earliest known four-limbed creatures. These findings support previous suggestions that aquatic characteristics of four-limbed animals with digits evolved first for use in water, rather than for walking on land.

Live bacteria believed to be 11,000 years old were found in the intestines of a fossilized mastodon. It was the first documented discovery of live bacteria in an extinct species.

American scientists have found dinosaur bones on a windswept mountain near the South Pole, a discovery scientists say proves that dinosaurs were cold-weather as well as warm-weather creatures.

A team of scientists from the Carnegie Museum and the Denver Museum of Natural History uncovered four skulls of a primitive version of a tiny primate, a tarsier, that lived in Wyoming. Until this discovery, the evolutionary tree had tarsiers and anthropoids splitting apart 35 million years ago. Scientists now believe tarsiers split from the family tree at least 50 million years ago.

Paleontologists have assembled the nearly

 Q: *How much does it cost to build a major logging road?*

complete skeleton of a 135-million-year-old bird. They have discovered that the earliest known modern birds were skilled fliers, not gliders or land-dwelling animals, as some have contended.

In China, paleontologists have discovered 70 fossil species of trilobites, worms, sponges and various ancestors of crustaceans, spiders and insects in sediment of what was a sea floor 570 million years ago.

Scientific researchers believe 3-foot-long footprints from a prehistoric giant ground sloth found in an ancient lake bed in southwest Virginia are only the second set of the animal's footprints ever discovered. The prints are believed to be 13,500 years old.

A 4,000-year-old body found in the Tyrol mountains.

Scientists say they have made significant discoveries among at least 3,000 fossils dug up in Mission Viejo, California, including previously unidentified species of whales, crabs and fish. The fossils, experts say, are 10 million to 15 million years old and confirm theories that the shoreline once extended from inland Camp Pendleton northeast to Chino and that southern California once was a region of tropical temperatures.

A jawbone of an animal that could prove to be a "missing link" between apes and humans has been found in southern Africa. Preliminary evidence from surrounding rock showed the fossil is 10 million to 15 million years old. This is the first South African discovery of a hominoid, a member of the zoological family comprising apes and humans.

For the first time, scientists have firmly established

14 HOUSTON—The Exxon Corp. said that it has made a potentially large **oil and gas discovery** in the Gulf of Mexico. —*NYT (AP)* 5/15

16 NEW YORK—A gray dolphin-like creature found in the Pacific Ocean off the coast of Peru has been identified as the first **new species of whale** to be discovered in 28 years. —*IHT (NYT)* 5/16

22 LOS ANGELES—A group of oil companies led by the Chevron Corp. filed a federal lawsuit opposing a **ban on using tankers to ship crude oil** from the offshore Point Arguello oil field to Southern California refineries. —*NYT (AP)* 5/23

26 PHOENIX—Arizona's gas chamber cannot be used again until the Department of Corrections obtains a permit from the Department of Environmental Quality for **releasing cyanide gas** into the air after each execution. —*NYT (AP)* 5/27

29 WASHINGTON—The Magellan space probe completed its **first survey of Venus**, producing detailed images of a surface composed of lava flows, cracks and craters and numerous features indicating volcanic activity, scientists said. —*NYT* 5/30

31 OTTAWA—The Canadian government is opening a record amount of far northern **acreage**

A. **$45,000 per mile**
   Source: The Wilderness Society

JUNE

1 MURMANSK, USSR—Shtokman field, a large **offshore natural-gas field in the Soviet Arctic**—the largest in Europe—should be on line by 1997, according to Anatoly Malinin, head of the Murmansk regional council. —*IHT (R) 6/1*

4 LOS ANGELES—In the largest settlement yet in a long-running **legal battle over toxic dumping** at the Stringfellow Acid Pits, Alumax Inc., an aluminum manufacturer, has agreed to pay $18 million to 3,800 residents of the nearby Riverside County community of Glen Avon. —*LAT 6/4*

6 CHESAPEAKE BAY, MD—High water temperatures brought on the early appearance of **jellyfish** in the Chesapeake Bay. —*WP 6/7*

7 ROANOKE, VA—The **skeletons and carcasses of more than 40 dogs and cats** were found in an abandoned house once owned by George and Phyllis Harmon, two former board members of the local Society for the Prevention of Cruelty to Animals. The couple moved five years ago. —*WP (AP) 6/8*

9 BALTIMORE—The 203rd General Assembly of the Presbyterian Church approved a statement, in the form of an 80-line prayer, which

for oil exploration. —*WSJ 5/31*

that Neanderthals lived in Western Europe as recently as 36,000 years ago, several thousand years after the first modern humans are believed to have appeared there. The finding lends support to the view that anatomically modern people did not evolve from Neanderthals but rather co-existed with and eventually supplanted them through superior intellect and culture.

The discovery of a 4,000-year-old mummified man in a glacier in Austria is the most complete Bronze Age find in Europe and may also provide new insight into ancient weather conditions, scientists say. The body was first sighted on September 19, 1991, by German mountain climbers at 10,500 feet on the Similaun glacier in the southwestern Austrian province of Tirol near the Italian border. The body's estimated age is based on the ax found at his side. The ax is a well-known type that appears exclusively in the Early Bronze age, which started in Europe about 2000 BC.

Engineers digging the Channel Tunnel between Britain and France turned up a giant mollusk fossil believed to be 95 million years old. The fossil weighs approximately 60 pounds and is nearly a foot long.

LEADED WINE

Washington, DC—More than 600 domestic and imported wines tested by federal officials were found to contain lead, some at potentially dangerous levels for high risk individuals, according to a report released by the US Bureau of Alcohol, Tobacco and Firearms.

The report pointed to lead foil capsules that cover table wine corks as a chief cause of the toxic metal found by the researchers. The results showed that domestic wines typically had far lower amounts of lead than imports. But when the wine was poured over the lip of the bottle, where deposits from the foil capsule could have accumulated, both imported and domestic wines exceeded the lead standard for water, in some cases up to three times.

John DeLuca, president of the Wine Institute, said California wineries had already decided to phase out use of lead foil capsules voluntarily by the end of 1992. In the meantime, consumers can reduce the risk of lead consumption by removing the foil and wiping the lips of wine bottles with a damp cloth or paper towel.

Q. *In 1988, what energy source produced electricity in America that prevented the release of 1 million tons of CO_2 into the atmosphere?*

WIPP

Carlsbad, NM—The Department of Energy has carved a network of caverns into the rock salt near Carlsbad, New Mexico, to create a repository for plutonium wastes from the nation's network of nuclear weapons factories. After more than a decade of planning and excavation and more than $1 billion in expenses, the department says it is nearly ready to move the first drums of waste from its Idaho National Engineering Laboratory to the subterranean vaults of the Waste Isolation Pilot Plant, or WIPP. For the first time, the US would have a permanent disposal site for some radioactive nuclear by-products.

WIPP still faces a host of legal, environmental, administrative and political hurdles that could delay its

---

"If you are thinking a year ahead, sow seed. If you are thinking ten years ahead, plant a tree. If you are thinking 100 years ahead, make people aware. By sowing seed once, you will harvest once. By planting a tree, you will harvest tenfold. By opening the minds of people, you will harvest 100-fold."

Chinese proverb

---

opening for many months, possibly years. Several members of Congress are strongly opposed to the way the Department of Energy is handling the matter, and any attempt to ship wastes to WIPP before all hurdles are tackled is likely to result in court challenges from environmental groups.

WIPP is designed to be a permanent disposal site for nearly 300,000 55-gallon steel drums of what is known as "transuranic waste," referring to solid materials such as tools, clothing, laboratory instruments and scrap materials contaminated by plutonium during manufacture and storage of nuclear warheads. The drums would be shipped by truck in specially designed sealed containers licensed by the Nuclear Regulatory Commission. At WIPP, the drums would be unloaded in a room with negative air pressure, to prevent the escape of any emissions, then loaded onto an elevator for the five-minute descent into the

demands greater concern for the environment and **makes abusing the planet a sin**. —*WP 6/9*

11 WASHINGTON—Three air carriers—Northwest, Lufthansa and Federal Express—announced they will no longer accept wild birds destined for the **pet trade**. —*WP 6/11*

12 MOSCOW—The Russian Republic **slaughtered** 10 percent of its cattle for lack of feed. —*WP (AP) 6/13*

13 BOSTON—The US Coast Guard's *Polar Star*, the German *Polarstern* and the Swedish *Oden* will carry approximately 100 scientists, six helicopters and tons of scientific gear on a 70-day **mission to the North Pole**. The journey will be the first ever to the North Pole by Western ships. —*WP (AP) 6/13*

14 SPRINGDALE, UT—The Springdale town council has given final approval to plans for a **giant-screen theater** to be built next to Zion National Park. —*LAT (AP) 6/14*

14 PAHOA, HI—The **blowout of a geothermal drilling well,** releasing toxic sulfuric steam and stench for more than 30 hours, prompted Hawaii state officials to order the drilling company to shut down. —*LAT 6/15*

15 MANTUA, WA—More than 100,000 **gallons of fuel** have

A: *Wind turbines*
Source: *American Wind Energy Association*

mysteriously seeped into the Mantua area of Fairfax County. The source of the seepage is still unknown. —*WP 6/15*

16 ROWE, MA—A lightning strike set fire to one of the transformers at **Yankee Rowe**, a nuclear plant in western Massachusetts, knocking out both power lines that bring in electricity for safety systems and shutting down its telephone switchboard. There was no reported release of radiation. —*NYT 6/17*

17 NEW YORK—Using genetic engineering techniques, biologists have **created pigs** that produce human hemoglobin. —*IHT (NYT) 6/17*

18 BROUGHTON ISLAND, Canada—Inuit villagers who live, hunt and fish on Broughton Island, have learned from scientists that they have **higher levels of PCBs** in their blood than any known population on earth, excluding the victims of industrial accidents. —*LAT 6/18*

18 WASHINGTON—The **marbled murrelet**, a robin-size coastal seabird, is being threatened by northwest logging and should be designated a threatened species, US Fish and Wildlife Service officials say. —*WP (AP) 6/18*

20 BEIJING, China—Some 41 developing nations at the Ministerial Conference of Developing Countries on Environment and Development said the

salt caverns. The department's plan is to put up to 8,500 drums of waste into WIPP for a five-year test, monitoring the stored waste to see what gases build up in the drums. If the tests show that the site is safe, the vaults would be refilled with excavated rock salt and sealed. In approximately 100 years, the rock salt formation would close back in on itself, crushing the drums and entombing the waste.

Faced with growing political opposition in New Mexico, the Department of Energy postponed the opening of WIPP at least until the end of November, 1991.

CLEAN AIR ACTED ON

Washington, DC—House Democrats have accused Vice President Dan Quayle and other White House officials of secretly but systematically trying to undermine efforts to implement the new Clean Air Act. The accusation involves proposed EPA rules to implement an air pollution permit system that should make it easier to monitor and enforce compliance with major provisions of the Clean Air Act. Under the proposal, all major sources of pollution except for motor vehicles would have to obtain permits from state authorities specifying their obligations under the law, including the levels of pollution they are allowed to emit.

The Democrats, led by Representative Henry A. Waxman (Dem.-California), released copies of an 83-page memo from Quayle's office that contained more than 100 changes to the original EPA proposals. Among the most controversial changes proposed by Quayle's office was a provision that would give

Mike Luckovich ATLANTA CONSTITUTION

By permission of Mike Luckovich & Creators Syndicate

Q. What number of US plants face a risk of extinction in five years, according to a recent survey of American botanists?

industries "operational flexibility" to make changes in their operations by increasing their emissions of pollutants, provided state authorities did not object within seven days of receiving written notice.

BORDER POLLUTION

Washington, DC—The US and Mexico released a draft plan on August 2 to improve the quality of the environment along the border. The detailed document calls for extra investment in wastewater treatment plants, greater restrictions on hazardous-waste shipments across the border and hiring of more officials to enforce environmental laws in Mexico.

William K. Reilly, administrator of the EPA, sent letters to some 150 US companies that operate manufacturing assembly plants in northern Mexico. The letters ask that the companies voluntarily reduce their emissions of 17 toxic chemicals from these plants by one third before the end of 1992 and by 50 percent before the end of 1995. Similar letters were sent to 600 companies in the US last year.

The EPA is also conducting an environmental review that will focus more directly on issues related to free-trade, such as pesticide regulation and assurances that the two countries are operating under comparable environmental standards. Opponents of a free trade agreement contend that the increased economic activity would worsen border pollution and weaken existing US regulations. The Bush Administration contends that opening trade would have the opposite result, generating wealth for Mexico that it could invest in cleaning up the environment.

ARCTIC REFUGE

Washington, DC—When the Interior Department's Bureau of Land Management estimated that Alaska's pristine Arctic National Wildlife Refuges' coastal plain held as much as 9.2 billion barrels of oil—the bureau's median projection is 3.6 billion barrels—the fight to keep oil rigs off the refuge began.

Controversy developed over drilling for oil in the refuge because it is the last piece of Alaska's North Slope still protected from oil development. Its coastal plain is the springtime calving ground of some 180,000 caribou that migrate from Canada and bring with them wolves and brown bears. In the summer, more than 150 types of birds nest in the marshy

industrialized world has a duty to give them money and technology for environmental protection with **no strings attached.** They also maintained that the West was mainly responsible for pollution. —WSJ 6/20

20 CANBERRA, Australia—The Australian Labor Party turned down a **proposal to mine precious metals** in a remote section of the Northern Territory because the Jawoyn Aboriginal tribe said such activity would disturb the god Bula. —IHT (R) 6/20

23 LONDON—Scientists at the London Zoo said that **the wart-biter**, an endangered grasshopper used to bite off warts, had been raised successfully in captivity for the first time. —LAT (R) 6/24

24 WASHINGTON—Researchers at the US Fish and Wildlife Service's Office of Scientific Authority say a genetic discovery may prove the **red wolf** is not in fact a distinct species, but a hybrid of the grey wolf and the coyote. —WP 6/24

25 WASHINGTON—The Environmental and Occupational Health Sciences Institute in New Jersey reports that reusing **plastic bread bags** by turning them inside out to rewrap other foods may be causing lead to escape from the painted labels and may contaminate food stored in the bag. —WP 6/25

A. *253*
Source: Natural Resources Defense Council

25 KING CITY, CA—A Monterey County husband and wife were **convicted of leading sport hunts** for big cats, including two Bengal tigers, a black jaguar, a spotted leopard and two mountain lions, which they had purchased from a breeder and brought to their 4,000-acre ranch. —*LAT 6/26*

26 WASHINGTON—The House approved a $12.9 billion natural resources bill advocating increased fees for Western ranching and mining interests and seeking to expedite the reintroduction of wolves into Yellowstone Park. The measure would continue the current **moratorium on offshore oil drilling** on most of the east and west coasts of the nation. —*WSJ 6/26*

26 RIO DE JANIERO—Brazilian President Fernando Collor de Mello took steps to **improve environmental conditions in the Amazon rainforest**, including the expulsion of gold prospectors from Yanomami lands, cancellation of tax incentives for clearcutting trees and the dismissal of the head of the government's agency for Indian affairs. —*WP 6/27*

26 AUGUSTA, ME—The state of Maine announced it would end the practice of selling containers held together by plastic fasteners, such as **six-pack rings**, because of the danger posed to birds, other small animals and the environment. —*LAT 6/26*

coastal plain and in the fall polar bears come ashore to den. It is home to a large variety of wildlife which supply native tribes with food.

> *"We are tired of those who distort the arguments about ANWR's coastal plain. It is barren, marshy wilderness in the summer, infested with uncountable mosquitoes, and locked in temperatures of 60 and 70 degrees below zero for up to nine months of the year."*
>
> Governor Walter J. Hickel of Alaska

Alaskan citizens, state officials and major oil companies took part in a large lobbying campaign to persuade Congress to open the northern portion of the Arctic National Wildlife Refuge for oil and gas exploration. In May, the Senate Energy Committee passed legislation that would allow drilling in the refuge; but, in November, the Senate failed to overcome a filibuster by lawmakers who oppose drilling in the refuge and the bill was effectively killed.

WETLANDS

Washington, DC—President Bush's new wetlands policy, announced in August, calls for steps to increase federal acquisition of wetlands, expand satellite monitoring to identify wetland areas and strengthen wetland research. The plan also promises

Q: *What is the largest single crop produced in the world each year, over 1 billion tons of it?*

to streamline the regulatory process and relax criteria for federal protection of certain marginal wetlands that are not as wet, or are not wet as often, as more obvious swamps, bogs and marshes. The new definition of wetlands leaves unprotected one-third of the 100 million acres currently protected in the contiguous 48 states, including 500,000 acres of the Florida Everglades. "Wetlands" has been a catchall term for the wide variety of coastal marshes bordering such estuaries as the Chesapeake Bay, southern swamps and the prairie potholes of the midwest that flood seasonally and become waterfowl breeding grounds.

Bush believes the plan "seeks to balance two important objectives—the protection, restoration and creation of wetlands, and the need for sustained economic growth and development."

CALIFORNIA TOXIC SPILL

Sacramento, CA—Efforts to clean up a toxic pesticide spill from a derailed Southern Pacific train were hampered by lack of information on the shipping manifest, which was supposed to list hazardous chemicals aboard the train. On July 14, a tank car carrying pesticides jumped the tracks and fell from a bridge, beginning a spill which destroyed wildlife and vegetation along a 45-mile stretch of the Sacramento River.

For several hours after the derailment, state emergency workers were unsure what chemical they were handling and lacked the safety equipment needed to assess the damage. The pesticide was later identified as metam-sodium which can be deadly when it reacts with water and may cause serious birth defects in the children of pregnant women exposed to its vapors.

"...we're praying more since the CSX train derailment..."

Official testimony, Ohio Governor's Commission on Storage and Use of Hazardous and Toxic Materials, December 1990

No deaths were recorded as a result of the spill, but an estimated 300 local residents and emergency workers sought medical care.

By the first few days of August, officials declared the spill cleaned up; however, who is to pay the cost

27 NEW YORK—Olin-Hunt Specialty Products Inc., which makes chemicals for the electronics industry, agreed to pay New York state $325,000 following an October 1990 truck spill that released several hundred gallons of **ammonium hydroxide into nearby streams** and left 30,000 fish dead. —*WSJ 6/27*

27 WEST VALLEY, NY—The town board of Ashford voted to allow the federal government to **construct a low-level radioactive waste site** in return for $4.2 million in community benefits, including a new town park, road improvements and funds for the town library, fire department and a scholarship program. —*NYT 6/28*

28 WASHINGTON—A team of French scientists concluded in their report that **Modern Man coexisted with Neanderthal Man** for several thousand years in Europe, possibly exchanging tools, ideas and genes. —*IHT (WP) 6/28*

30 MOSCOW—Some 32 miners were killed when a **coal mine fire** in the Donbass region of the Ukraine released toxic gas into the tunnels. —*WP 7/1*

JULY

1 GENEVA—A United Nations meeting to discuss global warming and **proposals to limit or cut carbon dioxide pollution** ended in stalemate as the US, Soviet

A. *Sugar cane*
  Source: World•Watch August 1989

Union and Japan opposed changes in policy offered by many European nations. —*WSJ* 7/2

4 NEW YORK—The ice in the Arctic Ocean receded toward the North Pole by about 2 percent from 1978 to 1987, scientists say, indicating that a **warming climate** has affected the northernmost regions of the globe. —*IHT (NYT)* 7/5

7 WASHINGTON—The **bowhead whale**, hunted to near-extinction, is making a comeback in Alaskan waters, scientists say. —*NYT* 7/8

8 BEIJING, China—Unusually heavy downpours have caused **severe flooding** in eastern and central China, killing more than 1,700 people. —*NYT* 7/9

8 GIBRALTAR—Six parakeets, recruited to serve on board the British destroyer *HMS Manchester* as part of the ship's chemical detection system, received **bronze medals for bravery** for their role in the Persian Gulf War. —*WP (AP)* 7/9

10 VIENNA—In exchange for promises from the West to help it find alternative sources of power, Bulgaria agreed to **shut down two Soviet-built nuclear reactors** that experts say have developed leaks in emergency equipment and are in danger of flooding and exploding. —*WP* 7/10

of clean up and restoration of the damaged environment is still in question. The California Legislature last year created an offshore oil-spill response fund to be used to prevent as well as respond to accidents. Days after the Sacramento River spill, a bill was drafted that would address inland spills of toxic materials.

MOUNTAIN LION ATTACK

El Toro, CA—Laura Small, an El Toro girl who was mauled by a mountain lion five years ago at age 10 at Ronald W. Caspers Wilderness Park in Orange County, California, was awarded more than $2 million by jurors who said the county was to blame for the attack.

Jurors deliberated two days before finding the county liable for the March 23, 1986 attack. Wylie A. Aitken, the Smalls' attorney, contended that county officials were negligent because they knew mountain lions in Caspers Park presented a potential danger, but failed to take any direct action. Aitken maintained that it wasn't the cougar's action that was questioned in the lawsuit, but rather the county's failure to act, knowing a cougar was in the area. Aitken also argued that the county created the danger in Caspers Park by luring mountain lions into public areas with human-made watering troughs that attracted the lion's prey.

ENDANGERED FLORIDA PANTHERS

Everglades National Park, FL—The last two female Florida panthers known to exist in Everglades National Park were found dead. One of the panthers

Photo: Dave Maehr/Florida Game & Fresh Water Fish Commission

Researchers test an anesthetized Florida panther.

Q: *What percentage of plant species do scientists believe contain some compounds with ingredients that are active against cancer?*

was found in June with elevated levels of mercury in her blood and had died of apparent kidney failure. The other was extremely emaciated when found on July 22 and had an infection that apparently resulted from a puncture wound. Biologists at Everglades National Park believe that since there are no known breeding females left in the eastern portion of the Everglades, male panthers will leave the area to search for a mate. Biologists estimate only 30 to 50 Florida panthers now survive. Scientists have not yet determined what is putting dangerous levels of mercury into the wetlands of south Florida.

ROCKY FLATS

Boulder, CO—The plutonium recovery incinerator in Rocky Flats nuclear plant building 771 "shall not operate" until the US Department of Energy gets the proper federal permits, US District Judge Lewis Babcock ruled in August. Building 771 remains idle since the plant was shut down in 1989 because of health and environmental safety concerns. Officials say 771 may never be opened again, and it is possible that processes handled there could be consolidated and moved to other buildings at the plant.

Five new cases of chronic beryllium lung disease have been diagnosed in the last six months among past and present workers at Rocky Flats, bringing the total to 23. Beryllium is a non-radioactive metal used in the manufacture of plutonium triggers for nuclear weapons. The disease is thought to be contracted by 1 percent to 3 percent of those who inhale beryllium dust.

ANTARCTIC TREATY SIGNED

Washington, DC—Antarctic Treaty member nations agreed to ban exploration for oil and other minerals on the continent for at least 50 years. The signing of the landmark agreement in Madrid, Spain, was the result of two years of negotiations. The protocol protects Antarctica's flora and fauna and sets procedures to assess environmental effects of all human activities on the continent. It also regulates marine pollution and waste disposal.

Of the 26 treaty members with voting powers, 23 signed the accord; Japan, South Korea and India said they would sign it later. The consultative nations of the 40-member treaty formally committed themselves to sign by October 3, 1992. The ban will take effect when all 26 voting member nations ratify the document.

10 NEW YORK— Scientists at Stanford University sutured **tiny eyeglasses** to the heads of three 12- to 15-day-old owls to find new evidence that vision plays a crucial role in how animals learn the source of a sound. —*IHT (NYT)* 7/11

11 ALBANY, NY— Alcoa, a smelting and fabricating facility at Massena, New York, **pleaded guilty to state pollution charges** and agreed to pay $7.5 million in criminal and civil penalties. —*WP (AP)* 7/12

11 MAUNA KEA, HI—A **total eclipse of the sun** darkened a 150-mile-wide stretch across the Pacific Ocean and Central America. —*NYT* 7/12

15 WASHINGTON— KLM Royal Dutch Airlines, the largest transporter of wild birds to the US, and an Indonesian airline, Garuda Indonesia, agreed to **halt shipments of wild tropical birds**. —*NYT* 7/16

15 LONDON—Disappointed by US officials' apparent unwillingness to recognize a serious environmental issue, Britain sent a letter to the White House criticizing the **US position on global warming**. —*IHT (WP)* 7/15

16 NEW YORK—Nearly one-third of all **fish species have declined** in population in the last 15 years, researchers say. —*NYT* 7/16

A. **10 percent**
Source: *Natural Resources Defense Council*

16 CHICAGO—The Chicago Board of Trade voted to create a private market for **rights to emit sulfur dioxide.** The rights are to be issued to electric utilities by the EPA as part of a strategy to reduce acid rain. —*NYT 7/17*

17 BUCHAREST, Romania—Bucharest will import $285,000 worth of poison to rid itself of the more than **2.5 million rats** which have invaded Romania's capital. —*IHT (R) 7/17*

21 LA CROSSE, WI—Gateway Foods, an IGA store, in La Crosse, Wisconsin, **voluntarily recalled about 30,000 cans of tuna** after shoppers discovered a double labeling problem. One label, IGA Chunk Tuna in Water, indicated the tuna was intended for human consumption while a second label underneath indicated the tuna was produced as cat food. —*LAT 7/21*

21 NEW YORK—Shoreham Nuclear Power Station proponents lost a legal attempt to delay a license that permits the plant's owner to **begin dismantling** it. —*NYT 7/21*

22 PERTH, Australia—A burning Greek oil tanker off Australia's west coast broke apart, spilling an estimated **2.9 million gallons of light crude** oil into the Indian Ocean. —*IHT (AP) 7/22*

23 WASHINGTON—President Bush named 25 members, including top executives from

BIOSPHERE 2

Tucson, AZ—At sunrise on September 26, 1991, four men and four women entered Biosphere 2, a large, high-tech greenhouse located 20 miles north of Tucson, Arizona, in the Sonoran Desert. For two years the door will remained sealed and the crew will breathe recycled air, drink recycled water and grow all their own food. By learning more about the complex interactions within Biosphere 2, the researchers hope to learn how to improve stewardship of Biosphere 1—earth. They also hope to show how to

Reprinted by permission. Tribune Media Services.

build a self-sustaining community that could be used in a spaceship or on the surface of another planet.

At its tallest end, the Biosphere rises 85 feet above the ground, and its four-plus acres of glass enclose a volume of 7.2 million cubic feet. The five wilderness biomes, or ecosystems, within Biosphere 2—rainforest, ocean marsh, savanna and desert—fill the bulk of the structure. The wilderness areas do much of the work of Biosphere 2, removing pollutants from the air, soaking up carbon dioxide and releasing oxygen, purifying the water. They also provide a living laboratory where Biospherians inside the structure will be able to study the interactions of various species in detail. The Biospherians' ecosystem includes an intensive agriculture biome, a half-acre farm where they will grow their food. It consists of 18 garden plots ranging in size from 500 square feet to almost 950 square feet. Biospherian Jane Poynter hopes to fit three crops per year into each plot and achieve an efficiency about 11 times as great as that of a typical American farm. The Biospherians will also raise chickens, pygmy pigs, pygmy goats and tilapia, a fish species that will live in rice tanks. The animals will

Q: *What number of species are becoming extinct in the tropics each day?*

provide milk, eggs and occasionally meat. The crew of eight will spend approximately four hours per day working on the farm and maintaining the ecosystems and another four hours on scientific experiments.

The human habitat contains two-room apartments for each Biospherian, offices, workshops, laboratories, a medical clinic, a library, a gym and a communal kitchen. Massive refrigeration systems using outside cooling towers chill the air and water in Biosphere 2 to maintain maximum temperatures of about 85 degrees in summer and 65 degrees in winter. The fans also force the air through soil, where microorganisms and natural soil activity remove pollutants. Other equipment includes high-pressure apparatus for producing mist-clouds in the rainforest, pumps to circulate water around the structure, a wave-making machine and algae scrubbers for the ocean.

Shortly after the doors to Biosphere 2 were closed, Jane Poynter cut off the tip of her finger in a rice-hulling machine. Biospherian Roy Walford, M.D., sewed the tip back "within 15 to 20 minutes." On October 11, 1991, Jane Poynter left Biosphere 2 for four hours for further surgery on her finger. Since the second surgery, she has returned to Biosphere 2 and resumed her work.

ENDANGERED SPECIES ACT

Washington, DC—The Endangered Species Act of 1973, considered by some to be the most powerful environmental law in the world, is due for Congressional reauthorization in 1992. While still professing support of endangered species protection, some revisionists want to loosen its control.

The act's purpose is the full recovery of imperiled plants and animals. It requires the Department of Commerce, through the National Marine Fisheries Service, to develop and carry out plans to recover and aid marine species in danger of becoming extinct. It similarly requires the Department of the Interior, through the US Fish and Wildlife Service, to succor all other endangered plants and animals in the US and its territories.

The act has three provisions to secure compliance. First, the act prohibits any action funded, authorized or carried out by federal agencies from jeopardizing the existence of an endangered species. Second, the act prohibits anyone from "taking"—harming, killing

large industrial companies and leaders from prominent conservation groups, to a panel to advise him on **how to slow the destruction of the environment** without causing inordinate expense to business. — *NYT 7/24*

25 WASHINGTON—A team of astronomers from the University of Manchester at Jodrell Bank, England, believe they have **discovered a planet** 10 times the mass of Earth existing outside our solar system and orbiting a pulsar 30,000 light years away. —*WP 7/25*

30 NEAH BAY, WA—An **oil spill from a collision** between a Japanese fish-processing vessel and a Chinese freighter has polluted ocean beaches in Olympic National Park, home to a vast population of seabirds and marine mammals. —*NYT 7/31*

AUGUST

1 CEDAR POINT, AL— The recent discovery of **cholera in an oyster** collected off Cedar Point, Alabama, has forced federal and state officials to launch an intensified testing program in the Gulf of Mexico. —*LAT 8/1*

2 WASHINGTON— Some **32 solar panels in the White House**, installed by Jimmy Carter in 1979 and removed by the Reagan administration, will be used by Unity College in Maine as a source of renewable energy. —*WP 8/2*

A. *50 to 150*
  Source: Natural Resources Defense Council

3 LOS ANGELES—After nearly 10 years in protective custody, the **endangered California condor** will be returned to the wild in October. — *LAT 8/3*

3 WASHINGTON—Iraq is suffering a high incidence of child malnutrition and **facing famine** on a massive scale, according to a new report from the United Nations' Food and Agriculture Organization. —*WP 8/3*

8 BERLIN—Controversy has emerged in Germany over a mining operation that threatens a **former concentration camp,** sparking protests from activists who say that camps must be kept as a reminder of Nazi atrocities. —*IHT 8/8*

9 DES MOINES—People for the Ethical Treatment of Animals, an animal rights group, has taken out an advertisement **comparing meatpackers to accused mass killer** Jeffrey L. Dahmer. —*WP 8/9*

10 PORTSMOUTH, NH—Sandra and Lee Roseberry, a New Hampshire couple whose two daughters were **poisoned by lead paint** in a house they bought from the Department of Veterans Affairs, have accepted a settlement giving them $61,000 and requiring Veterans Affairs to take back the house. —*WP 8/10*

10 FORT LAUDERDALE, FL—The Department of Agriculture accused

or uprooting—an endangered species, regardless of who owns the land. Third, the act demands that decisions in every phase of the listing or delisting process be based solely on the rigors of biological science and not on data such as numbers of jobs lost, devalued

---

"Nobody's told me the difference between a red squirrel, a black one or a brown one.... Do we have to save every subspecies?"

Interior Secretary Manuel Lujan

---

land and other economic consequences exacerbated by the presence of an endangered species.

As is, environmentalists and government officials alike believe the act needs revision. One criticism is that the process of placing an animal on list for protection is slow, poorly designed and inefficient. At today's pace and level of funding, the Interior Department's Inspector General's investigators estimated that it could take anywhere from 38 to 48 years to simply list those species now thought to qualify for protection. In 1990, they reported that not only has the Fish and Wildlife Service failed to develop recovery plans for many of the listed plants and animals, but that it also has no uniform system for tracking recovery.

Some revisionists would like to see an amendment which allows for consideration of economic consequences of protecting an endangered species. Others feel that the growing influence of conservation biology and its litany of biological diversity has made significant inroads toward supporting an ecosystem approach—as opposed to the present species-by-species approach—to endangered species protection.

The Endangered Species Act has been amended four times over the past 18 years. In the past, Congress has consistently rejected measures that would loosen the act's control. However, recent cases like the northern Spotted Owl and the Mount Graham Red Squirrel may have negatively affected the fate of the act, due to the complicated economic aspects of those situations.

Q: *Disposable diapers take 500 years to degrade and occupy over what percentage of the land fill space?*

The Worst and Best Of 1991

Nineteen-ninety-one certainly had its share of environmental disasters, but all was not doom and gloom. The year offered many success stories. In an attempt to rate the 10 worst environmental disasters and the 10 best environmental advancements of the past 12 months, *Earth Journal* independently polled 19 environmental and special interest groups in the United States and asked their opinions.

These groups compose an informal society known within the environmental community as the "Green Group." Originally called the "Group of 10," this powerful network expanded this past spring to include organizations working in areas other than strictly environmental conservation, such as treatment of children, rights of indigenous people and population control. The "Green Group" feels this interconnected philosphy provides a more diverse and accurate lobby for common interests. In closed meetings, the CEOs of each group network and exchange information. Oddly, many staffers of these environmental groups are unaware of the tête-à-têtes, which occur roughly once a year.

Fifteen of the 19 groups responded to our questionnaire (the four that refused pleaded too busy to participate). They are listed below, first the original "Group of 10" and then new members. The results of the poll are rated by the average order of importance given by the respondents. After listing the top ten in each category, we have included additional listings in the order they were rated.

THE GREEN GROUP

Environmental Defense Fund
*The Wilderness Society
Sierra Club
National Audubon Society
National Parks and Conservation Association
National Resources Defense Council
Friends of the Earth, Environmental Policy Institute, Oceanic Society
National Wildlife Federation
*Izaak Walton League
Sierra Club Legal Defense Fund

Ocean World, a 3.5-acre Florida attraction, of **willfully violating the Federal Animal Welfare Act** on several accounts by keeping dolphins in an undersized petting pool and subjecting them to over-chlorinated water until their skin peeled off. —*NYT 8/11*

11 WASHINGTON—A highly infectious but still mysterious microbe is wiping out **black sea urchins,** the primary caretakers of the coral reefs in the Caribbean Sea and the Florida Keys. —*WP 8/11*

11 WASHINGTON—The EPA has issued regulations which will **close about half the nation's garbage dumps** and force those remaining to operate more safely. — *LAT 8/11*

12 TORONTO—The infestation of Lake Ontario by zebra mussels, small but prolific mollusks, has nearly shut down the municipal water supply of Lincoln, Ontario, because water-intake pipes have become **clogged with the mollusks.** —*WP 8/12*

12 TORONTO—Two groups of Canadian Native tribes have filed a lawsuit in Toronto seeking $1.3 billion (Canadian) in damages from Kimberly-Clark Corp. and The New York Times Company for **pollution of rivers** in their native territory in northern Ontario around James Bay. —*NYT 8/14*

13 OSWEGO, NY—An unexplained malfunction

A. *Over 5 percent*
Source: Earth First! Journal, August 1988 and The Activist, *June 1988*

in the control room alarm system triggered an **emergency shutdown of the Nine Mile Point** nuclear power plant. Officials say the problem caused no damage and power was restored to the plant two and a half hours later. —*IHT 8/14*

13 DAVIS, CA— Workers will begin a $1.2-million cleanup of **radioactive dog waste** produced from a University of California at Davis research experiment that killed more than 1,000 beagles. —*LAT 8/13*

14 SYDNEY, Australia—Australian scientists said that, in two years, they will begin producing the **world's first blue roses**, which will be sold at about $80 per bloom. —*LAT (R) 8/15*

14 WASHINGTON— Several top federal health authorities are reversing their previous position and are now say exposure to **the chemical compound dioxin**, once considered toxic enemy number one, is no more risky than spending a week sunbathing. —*NYT 8/15*

15 LOS ANGELES—The National Marine Fisheries Service is investigating whether a US cargo ship violated the Endangered Species Act when it **struck a 50-ton finback whale** that was later found dead outside the breakwater of Los Angeles harbor. —*LAT 8/15*

16 OTTAWA—The Canadian Supreme Court rejected a

Defenders of Wildlife
World Wildlife Fund
* Children's Defense Fund
National Toxics Campaign
Union of Concerned Scientists
* Native American Rights Fund
Planned Parenthood
Population Crisis Committee
Zero Population Growth

* did not repond to questionnaire

TEN WORST ENVIRONMENTAL DISASTERS OF 1991

1: Persian Gulf War—On January 25, 1991, just days after the Persian Gulf War began, millions of barrels of oil from Kuwaiti reserves began pouring into Gulf waters and its coastlines. Approximately 700 oil wells were set afire.

2: Bush's wetlands policy—President Bush's new policy redefines the term "wetland," relaxing the criteria for federal protection of certain marginal wetlands that are not as wet, or are not wet as often, as the more obvious swamps, bogs and marshes.

3: Global warming—On July 1, 1991, in Geneva, Switzerland, the United Nations meeting to discuss global warming and proposals to limit or cut carbon dioxide pollution ended in stalemate as the US, Soviet Union and Japan opposed changes in policy offered by many European nations.

4: Bush's energy policy—The legislation that was debated by the Senate Energy and Natural Resources Committee contained provisions that would continue reliance on coal, oil and nuclear power. The energy bill authorized oil and gas development in Alaska's pristine Arctic National Wildlife Refuge (ANWR) and contained no automobile gas mileage requirements. President Bush has vowed to veto any energy bill that does not contain provisions for drilling in ANWR.

5: Deforestation—World rainforests are being destroyed by cutting and burning for agricultural purposes, fuel or grazing lands at a rate of 42 million acres per year.

Q: *In order to absorb the excess CO_2 accumulating annually in the atmosphere, what size area of trees would need to be planted?*

6: Sacramento chemical spill—On July 14, 1991, a train tank car carrying a toxic pesticide jumped the tracks and fell from a bridge, beginning a spill which destroyed wildlife and vegetation along a 45-mile stretch of the Sacramento River in California.

7: GATT ruling on tuna—A panel of the General Agreement on Tariffs and Trade ruled that the US may not ban imports of tuna caught by Mexican boats, which use fishing methods that kill dolphins, because the ban violates GATT rules that prevent countries from dictating how other countries produce goods for export.

8: Ozone depletion—The ozone loss over the US is proceeding more than twice as fast as scientists had expected. The data show that ozone depletion extends farther south of the Arctic Circle than had been thought, reaching the southernmost parts of the US, and lasts longer, starting in late fall and extending into May.

9: Loss of biodiversity—The average rate of extinction is one species per day. It is predicted that within a decade, one species will be lost to extinction every hour.

10: ANWR considered to open for oil drilling—Alaskan citizens, state officials and major oil companies are taking part in a large lobbying campaign to persuade Congress to open the northern portion of the Arctic National Wildlife Refuge for oil and gas exploration.

11: Population increase
12: Mount Pinatubo eruption
13: Continued drought in California
14: Bush's veto of US funds for UN Population Fund
15: US' slow response to Kuwaiti fires and oil spill
16: Big Green ballot initiative failure
17: Explosion of Atlantic-Richfield plant in Houston
18: Bangladesh cyclone
19: US-Mexico Trade Agreement, granting Bush high authority
20: US Government report shows wildlife in danger from economic uses and poaching on refuges
21: Two chemical plant explosions where a total of

Teme-Augama Anishnabai tribe's land claim in northern Ontario and will permit **renewed mineral exploration** in the area. —*WSJ 8/16*

16 LOS ANGELES—The Nuclear Regulatory Commission has launched a nationwide search for Katia Steel Rolling Works-manufactured **steel fence parts** that were found to be radioactive when a truckload of them set off radiation monitors at a nuclear weapons plant in Washington state. —*LAT 8/16*

16 SAN DIEGO—A US Customs Service border official at San Ysidro, Mexico, confiscated a **white Siberian tiger cub**, an endangered species, valued at $45,000, from the back seat of a car headed for Mexico. Federal officials gave the cub to the San Diego Zoo. —*LAT 8/16*

24 WASHINGTON—The Taiwanese government, under threat of US trade sanctions, said it will comply with a United Nations' **ban on driftnet fishing** in the Pacific Ocean. —*LAT 8/24*

26 SYDNEY, Australia—Scientists have invented a **hormone that causes fleece to peel off sheep**, saving the animal from an unnerving experience of being shaved and cutting the amount of shearing labor by up to 25 percent. —*LAT (R) 8/26*

27 WASHINGTON—The Bush Administration says there **should be no**

A**.** *An area the size of Zaire*
Source: ZETA, March 1989

exceptions to a pending United Nations ban on driftnets because even when modified, driftnets still kill marine life indiscriminately. —NYT (AP) 8/28

29 MOSCOW—A decree issued by the President of Kazakhstan closed the nation's **nuclear weapons testing range at Semipalatinsk** and demanded unspecified compensation for health problems and birth defects attributed to fallout from testing. — NYT (AP) 8/30

29 MIAMI—Two teenagers who **fatally clubbed an endangered Key deer** were sentenced to maximum prison terms. Kevin Goodwin, who had a previous juvenile record, was sentenced to a year in federal prison; Tim Daniels received a 10-month prison sentence. —LAT 8/29

29 SYRACUSE, NY— A second-degree manslaughter charge was brought against Joseph R. Polvino, part owner of Polvino Construction Co. of Rochester, New York, who, prosecutors say, paid Carl R. Witherel Sr. to **illegally dump toxic chemical wastes**. Witherel was killed by chemical burns to his lungs from breathing fumes from the wastes. —LAT 8/29

30 LAS VEGAS, NV— Under a plan approved by county and federal officials, **desert tortoises** living on Las Vegas-area properties slated for construction will be removed

nine workers were killed (Carlston, SC and Sterlington, LA)

22: Puget Sound oil spill

23: Manuel Lujan, Secretary of the Interior

24: Bush Administration appeals Endangered Species Act overseas protection to Supreme Court

25: The paper and chemical industries' public relations campaign claiming that dioxin isn't dangerous

26: John Sununu, White House Chief of Staff

27: Resignation of Thurgood Marshall from the US Supreme Court

28: Scientific findings show over 15,000 dolphins still killed annually in Japanese driftnets

29: Congressional defeat of a proposed increase in grazing fees on public land

30: Discovery of high mercury levels in Great Lakes

31: US Department of Energy attempts to circumvent environmental regulations at nuclear weapons production facilities

32: Bush transportation policy did not represent a national strategy

33: Abandoning of military sites (toxic waste disposal)

34: Failure to reintroduce gray wolves to Yellowstone National Park

35: Continuing health hazards relating to lead poisoning in low income and disadvantaged communities

TEN BEST ENVIRONMENTAL SUCCESS STORIES OF 1991

1: Clean Air Act passage—The law, passed by Congress in 1990 to amend the 1970 Clean Air Act, is designed to clean up the nation's air, largely through controls on emissions by industry and automobiles.

2: Mineral mining ban in Antarctica—The US approved the far-reaching environmental protection provision to the Antarctic Treaty, which proposes a 50-year ban on mining on the continent.

3: Restore Grand Canyon's air quality by restricting Navajo power plant—Under an agreement between the power plant and environmentalists, owners of the Navajo Generating Station will install $430 million worth of air-pollution-control devices on its three giant smokestacks to clean the air and improve visibility at the Grand Canyon.

Q. *In India, 80 percent of the annual agricultural crop goes directly to human food. What is the percentage in the US?*

4. Everglades cleanup in Florida—In the settlement of a two-and-a-half year old federal lawsuit against the state of Florida, a new Everglades Park project has been established to reverse years of destruction due to population and industrial growth and recover the natural flow of the Everglade waters.

5: Dolphin-safe tuna—The public became aware that a side effect of tuna fishing was the death of more than 100,000 dolphins annually through the practices of purse seine and driftnet fishing. Bowing to public pressure to change these practices, the three main US tuna companies, Star-Kist, Chicken of the Sea and Bumble Bee, agreed to fish for tuna using methods which do not harm dolphins.

6: Spotted owl victories—The Department of the Interior officially declared the northern spotted owl a threatened species on June 26, 1990. In August 1991, the government proposed protecting 8.2 million acres of Northwest forest land to save the spotted owl from extinction. The proposal covers 3.8 million acres in Oregon, 2.7 million acres in Washington and 1.8 million acres in California.

7: UN driftnet ban—The Bush Administration says there should be no exceptions to the United Nations ban on driftnets because, even when modified, driftnets still kill marine life indiscriminately.

8: Black-footed ferrets reintroduced into Wyoming—Some 50 captive-bred black-footed ferrets were reintroduced into the wild just north of Medicine Bow, Wyoming. In 1985, the black-footed ferret was put on the endangered species list as only 18 known ferrets remained.

9: Global warming issue—In July 1991, a United Nations meeting was held to discuss global warming and proposals to limit or cut carbon dioxide pollution. Most United Nations members supported the proposals.

10: Passage of Oil Spill Liability Act—California legislation created an offshore oil-spill response fund to be used to prevent and respond to accidents. Days after the Sacramento River toxic pesticide spill, a bill was drafted that addresses inland spills of toxic materials.

to a Clark County animal care center. Those that are not adopted or relocated within five days will be killed by lethal injection. —*LAT 8/30*

31 LOS ANGELES—Scores of **wild mallards** have been found dead or dying along widely separated stretches of the Los Angeles River in Glendale and Long Beach, apparently victims of botulism aggravated by the drought, wildlife officials say. —*LAT 8/31*

SEPTEMBER

1 NEW YORK—Hundreds of dirty **hypodermic needles and empty medicine vials** and other medical waste washed ashore in New York City, closing Jacob Riis Park beach to swimmers. —*LAT 9/1*

3 BAGHDAD, Iraq—Iraq has begun destroying bombs and shells designed to carry **chemical weapons**, creating what one United Nations observer called a "chemical dustbin." —*IHT (R) 9/3*

3 HEGINS, PA—Some 85 people were arrested when an estimated 500 animal rights activists protested a 58-year-old Labor Day traditional **pigeon-shooting contest** in Hegins, Pennsylvania. —*LAT 9/3*

3 ROME—About 150 **dolphins** have reportedly washed up on the beaches of southern Italy since July, apparently victims of a virus that has spread from British seals in the North Sea to

A. *1 percent*
Source: World Monitor, May 1990

69

dolphins off the coast of Spain and further east into the Mediterranean. —NYT 9/4

6 CARLSBAD, NM— The US Fish and Wildlife Service proposed adding the **California gnatcatcher**, a small blue-gray bird, to the nation's endangered species list. —LAT 9/6

9 AUSTIN, TX—The Nature Conservancy, an environmental group, bought more than **10,000 acres of land** in the wooded hills surrounding Austin, Texas, from the Resolution Trust Corp. for $15.5 million. The land once belonged to six failed savings and loans. —WSJ 9/9

10 SAN FRANCISCO— Louisiana-Pacific Corp. and Simpson Paper Co. each agreed to pay the federal government $2.9 million in fines to settle a lawsuit stemming from **ocean contamination** by pulp mills in northern California. —WSJ 9/10

11 ANCHORAGE—A jury awarded 16 fishermen more than $2.5 million in damages and set a payout formula that could yield millions more to other plaintiffs who suffered damages as a result of the **Glacier Bay spill** in 1987. —WSJ 9/11

11 SACRAMENTO, CA—Republican California Governor Pete Wilson vetoed a bill that would have **banned use of animals in tests** for new cosmetics and household cleaning products. —WP 9/11

11: Two Forks Dam denial in Colorado

12: Fall of Communism leading to pollution cleanup and protection laws in eastern Europe

13: Court decisions protecting spotted owl/ancient forests in Pacific Northwest

14: Brazil's new President Collor de Mello reduces incentives for deforestation

15: Fast food chains waste-reduction—foam container phase out

16: Americans recycle more

17: International Whaling Commission continues ban on whaling

18: Plans to reintroduce the California Condor into the wild

19: James Bay Project delay

20: RU 486—the first new contraceptive technology to be introduced in a long time

21: Increased effort to improve status of women worldwide

22: Continued recovery of Chesapeake Bay

23: Environmental provisions included in the North American Free Trade Act

24: Partial ban on US offshore oil drilling

25: Alaskan judge throws out the Exxon settlement

26: The California Clean Air Act is signed

27: US bans wildlife trade from Thailand

28: Soviet coup fails

29: Greater environmental awareness of citizens

30: Indications that the Sahara Desert both retreats and expands

31: Arizona Biosphere 2 experiment

32: Debt-for-nature swaps

33: New Jersey bans importation and sale of wild-caught tropical birds

34: Los Angeles regulators vote to phase out use of hydrogen fluoride

35: More media coverage of environmental issues

36: Announcements of new fuel efficiency technologies for vehicles from Clemson University and Japanese automakers.

37: Use of alternatives to traditional economic measures to define national progress—like the United Nation's "Human Development Index"

38: New lower-polluting gasoline announced by major oil company in California

39: José Goldemberg selected as Minister of Education in Brazil

Q: *What percentage of farmers in the US farm organically?*

40: US availability of Norplant

41: Return of wolves to some western states

42: Basel, Switzerland agreement to limit transboundary export of hazardous waste

43: Bill introduced in Congress to immediately ban import and sale of wild tropical birds

44: Discovery of the cancer drug taxol, developed from the Pacific Yew tree of northwestern US

45: Farm Bill passage

46: Los Angeles opens a new light-rail transit line

49: Some species of salmon declared endangered

47: Congress protects 3.4 million acres of wilderness in Arizona, Illinois, Maine and Nevada

48: Designation of Niobrara River in Nebraska as wild and scenic

49: Release of Priority Statement on Population—endorsed by nearly 150 major environmental, scientific, family planning and population organizations

50: George Miller (Dem.-California) appointed head of House Interior Committee

51: Israeli court halts US Information Agency tower in major migratory bird corridor

52: Increased effort to make cities livable and sustainable

53: Japanese decision to ban sea turtle imports

54: GM promises to commercialize electric vehicles

55: Mono Lake, CA decision to protect the lake's water levels

56: New Jersey terminates ocean dumping

57: Green marketing

12 WASHINGTON—The Bush Administration announced new rules that will require municipal landfills to **monitor groundwater pollution** and impose firm federal standards on new disposal sites. —*LAT 9/12*

14 SACRAMENTO, CA—US Fish and Wildlife Service's Deputy Director Richard Smith has determined that **the Delta smelt should be listed** as a species "threatened" by extinction, rather than "endangered," because, he says, the smelt's population has been "relatively stable" for five years. —*LAT 9/14*

17 SACRAMENTO, CA—EPA has cited operators of 191 migrant labor camps in California for **providing contaminated drinking water** to farm workers and violating federal law by improperly testing water quality. —*LAT 9/17*

18 WASHINGTON—On a 60 to 38 vote, the Senate killed a measure that would have more than **doubled the grazing fees on federal range land** in 16 western states. —*WP (AP) 9/18*

20 LOS ANGELES—In an effort to restructure itself financially, Shell Oil Co. announced it will sell all of its oil and gas production properties in Alaska and **suspend drilling in the Chukchi Sea.** —*LAT 9/20*

THE POLITICALLY APPROPRIATE BRAIN

whales 10%
Rain Forests 10%
Apartheid 9%
GUILT 40%
COMFORTABLE SANDALS 30%

CALLAHAN

A. *. 1 percent*
Source: US Department of Agriculture

Eco-Forecasts For 1992

W*hat will be the hot environmental issues of a greening globe in 1992? Here's a look at the emerging trends that will make news and reviews and command action over the next year.*

The North/South divide: a crisis of multitudes

Overpopulation, impoverishment, childhood disease and death, famine and malnutrition—the Northern/Southern hemisphere division between wealth and underdevelopment has worsened. For 20 years, the South's repeated requests for environmentally benign technological assistance have met with little meaningful response from the Northern industrialized countries. The discussion will become louder in 1992 when the United Nations Conference on Environment and Development meets in Rio in June for the Earth Summit. Ironically, the next big issue—as the crisis of the multitudes explodes—is that in order to save the environment, we must *now* focus on development.

Pollution and poverty: whose backyard now?

People of color in a multicultural nation—those who have the least say and least probability of having their voices heard in the halls of decision-makers—have the most at stake. More grassroots groups are organizing, block by block, to keep the nation's wastes from being deposited in their backyards. Communities in 1992 will vociferously answer the question, "Whose backyard now?" with a new visibility, forcing an answer to the hazardous waste problem.

Who is who in the environmental movement?

The "New Environmentalist" is the new mainstream: One large membership group, representing some 36 million Americans over 50 years old, intends to put the environment on their national agenda for 1992. But that's just the beginning: In 1996, the first baby-boomers—those who have honed an environmental agenda since the 1960s—will turn 50, translating into 17 million more possible "Green Seniors." Environmental issues will become lifestyle issues—health, apparel and healthy food—with the new gray-green constituent.

Nuclear hot cakes: proliferation and cleanup

A two-fold nuclear threat awaits us in the post-Cold War era. First, the issue of nuclear arms proliferation has not been defused with the fall of Communism. The many nuclear arms of the Cold War are now in the hands of numerous republics anxious to display the weapons as a status symbol of their independence. Second, nuclear weapons manufacturing has created a new, secret weapon: Leaking waste around and below the weapons plants and storage sites. From inception to disposal, nuclear waste is being revealed as a more elusive and determined killer than the weapons that have sat unused. The nuclear proliferation of the superpowers' weapons, and the waste they left behind, will be a vital story of the 1990s.

Packaging: the source of problems for a new generation

Everybody's recycling. It's an achievement of a concerned, newly aware

Q: *In 1990, the US spent $303 billion to protect against military threats. How much did it spend on environmental threats?*

populace. But there's only so much recycling one person can do. The story of 1992 will be the source of the problem: packaging. If the product is overwrapped or offered in multilayers, it's easier not to buy it than to recycle all that stuff. The new consumer will be demanding simplified packaging to reduce the number of trips to the recycling bin. Will the market respond to the source problem?

Water: too little, too much, too dirty—a thirsty problem

Lack of water is the problem in some parts of the country. Competing uses and increasing demand will deplete the resources already overextended throughout the Western US. Drought may be cyclical but the lessons are not. Watch for more jockeying of uses to reprioritize water divisions. The other problem with water is there's too much of it with chlorine, lead and fluoride in it; accepted a generation ago as safe, these ingredients are now looked at with the same skepticism as are the ever-increasing traces of pesticides found in our drinking water. The quality of drinking water will be one of the biggest emerging issues of 1992.

Endangered Species Act

Look for the Endangered Species Act to face a God Squad of its own in 1992 when it comes up for reauthorization in Congress. This legislation has increasingly been used to stop development in the name of protecting species. With effort from the Bush Administration, the act is facing serious revision. Saving endangered jobs in lean economic times will become the new battle cry, rather than saving species from extinction.

The Environmental President

A national election that once again is strong on environmental rhetoric and slim on policy will disenfranchise the emerging environmental mainstream. If individuals are going out of their way to recycle, make a difference and, in some cases, sacrifice family income to spend more on environmentally-benign products, and if CEOs of America's big companies see the environment as a piece of a strategic business plan, government leaders, easy with platitudes and lean on decisive action, will face hostile voters.

Global warming hits home

The abstraction of global warming will hit home harder in 1992. Look for more revelations of species affected *now* by ozone holes and higher global climate temperatures. With global change taking place faster than global response, will action follow?

The expense of the environment

After the flower children united and became yuppies, they faced higher costs to raise their families. Buying a clean environment is more expensive than ever. In times of fiscal restraint, families will opt for cheaper rather than environmentally correct, especially when doing something simple doesn't seem to make any real difference in the big, bad environmental picture. Although the Earth can't afford the pollution humans create, humans seemingly can't afford the current solutions. The year 1992 will force a hard look at the bottom line. Environmental problems aren't going to disappear; they must be solved, no matter the cost.

—*Elizabeth Darby Junkin*

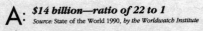

A. *$14 billion—ratio of 22 to 1*
Source: State of the World 1990, *by the Worldwatch Institute*

PART 2

EARTH PULSE

EARTHISSUES

Abstractions have a real effect; substances we cannot see, smell or feel are subtly rewriting the very future of our world. Here is the who, what, where and why of issues such as global warming, deforestation, endangered species, air pollution, etc., with discussions of what it will take to solve these problems and what you can do.

A World at Risk

- By Dr. James J. MacKenzie -

Our legacy to the new millennium is a host of unprecedented environmental threats—from regional problems such as smog, acid rain, degraded topsoils, contaminated waterways and deforestation to the global problems of climate change, ozone depletion and a species extinction rate unmatched in 65 million years.

At first glance, all these problems seem unrelated. And, unfortunately, they are being treated as such in public policy-making. Thus, according to common understanding, smog and acid rain arise from inadequate controls on motor vehicles and power plants and the solution to these problem—as prescribed by Congress in its latest revision of the Clean Air Act—lies Pin capping sulfur emissions from coal-fired power plants and tightening pollution standards for new cars and trucks. Climate change, on the other hand, is perceived largely as a problem of inefficient fossil fuel use. If only we drove smaller cars, used more efficient light bulbs, and perhaps built more nuclear power plants—none of which Americans seem prepared to do—we could reduce carbon dioxide emissions and thereby the threat of global warming.

But the world is more complicated than most policy-makers think. As a result, the incremental solutions they propose are unlikely to prove equal to the problems at hand.

Consider air pollution. Today's most serious problems are acid rain and tropospheric ozone (the principal ingredient of urban smog). Both arise naturally in amounts small enough to do no long-term damage to soils, vegetation and aquatic systems. But the prodigious amounts of sulfur and nitrogen compounds that fossil fuel use generates are overwhelming nature's restorative powers.

In the United States, for instance, we put out 10 to 20 times as much sulfur and nitrogen as is emitted through natural processes. Pollution persists despite past efforts to develop cleaner vehicle and power-plant designs, largely because such technological advances have been more than cancelled out by the growth in the number of vehicles, drivers and power plants. There is no reason to believe that—under current trends—the future will be any different: Unless we stabilize the number of pollution sources or fundamentally change our energy technologies, growth will eventually win out, and we will find ourselves no better off down the road than we are today.

Similar problems confront us in coping with climate change. Fossil fuels represent about 90 percent of global commercial energy use. Besides generating much of the world's air pollution, burning these fuels accounts for nearly half of the global warming threat. Despite widespread energy-efficiency improvements between 1977 and 1987, global energy consumption rose 20 percent. With no change in global per-capita energy use over this period, increased fuel burning can be attributed primarily to population growth. As a

> *At first glance, all these problems seem unrelated. Unfortunately, they are being treated as such in public policy-making.*

result, both global carbon dioxide emissions and regional air pollution increased.

There are other links between growth and environmental threats. For example, deforestation results at least partly from agricultural pressures, in turn related to growing populations. It is widely recognized that the disappearance of tropical forests results in a loss of biological diversity and in the emission of large amounts of carbon dioxide, the principal greenhouse gas. But deforestation results in the release of other air pollutants as well. Carbon monoxide, methane, nitrogen oxides and hydrocarbons are all emitted in the burning of the forests and contribute directly or indirectly not only to global warming but also to the formation of smog and acid rain. Moreover methane is released by termites from the remaining unburned wood.

These two important major threats —air pollution and climate change, linked together by deforestation and the burning of fossil fuels—illustrate the critical need to take a broader view in environmental policy-making. They also indicate how crucial policies affecting growth and technological change will be to the development of long-term solutions.

Our century's exponential growth trends—and their enormous momentum—show why there is such an urgent need for fundamental changes that affect growth and technology. Since 1900, world population has tripled while fossil fuel use has grown tenfold and the global economy twentyfold. It took all of history for the world economy to reach $600 billion in 1900, but now it grows by more than that sum every two years—and may, by the middle of the next century, be five times as large as it is today. It took some 400,000 years

for the human population to reach 2.5 billion by 1950, but only 37 years to double to well over 5 billion. Ten years ago, experts thought world population would level off at around 10 billion, but the latest United Nations, high-end projection sets the endpoint at a staggering 14 billion sometime in the next century. Taking today's road into that future will lead to a devastating crash, for we are already disrupting the planetary systems that support life.

Even if we managed to limit the numbers—of human beings and vehicles and power plants—we could not burn fossil fuels indefinitely. Like all finite resources, they would eventually be exhausted. Indeed, the oil and natural gas era will effectively come to an end during the first half of the next century. There will be plenty of coal left, but its climate impacts are far greater than those of oil and gas, severely limiting the amounts that can be burned. But, while we obviously cannot simply abolish the burning of fossil fuels, we also cannot guarantee our species' future unless we begin soon to take steps to replace them.

The long-term message conveyed by air pollution and global warming is clear: We must shift the world economy off fossil fuels long before we run out of them since exponential growth based on today's technologies puts us on a collision course with ecological disaster.

Since technological revolutions can take a generation or more, there's no time to waste in charting a path that will support economic development over the long term without jeopardizing the environment.

Dr. James J. MacKenzie has also written Energy Conservation. *Please see biography on page 101.*

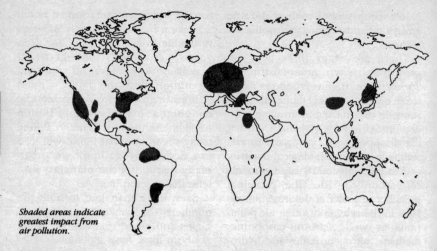

Shaded areas indicate greatest impact from air pollution.

WHAT YOU CAN DO:

ORGANIZE
• Organize "Ride to Work" days or weeks in your neighborhood. Emphasize bicycling as a viable mode of transportation. Work to get bicycle lanes established and bike racks installed at all public buildings.

• Organize car-pools with friends and neighbors or co-workers. Never drive alone.

YOU AND YOUR CAR
• The more gasoline your car uses, the worse it is for the earth. Example: For every gallon of gas a car uses, 20 pounds of carbon dioxide (the main greenhouse gas) enter the atmosphere.

• Cars are also responsible for 34 percent of US nitrogen oxides (which cause acid rain), and 27 percent of the smog-causing hydrocarbons.

Air Pollution

- By Paulette Bauer Middleton -

Truly "clean air" is composed of chemicals that have occurred naturally for thousands of years. Oxygen and nitrogen are the major chemicals that make up air. Clean air also is composed of varying amounts of water vapor and traces of gases such as helium and carbon dioxide. This air is referred to as clean because it does not contain harmful levels of chemicals that adversely affect human health and welfare.

In order to protect ourselves and our environment from harmful air, it is important to understand the causes and the effects of air pollution. Air pollution problems occur on three scales. Local problems are caused by chemicals that have an immediate effect on the nearby people and environments. On the regional scale (on the order of 5 to 600 miles around the sources of the pollution) damage results mainly from acids, oxidants and aerosols that were formed in the air through chemical reactions involving the emitted chemicals. On the global scale (the entire Earth), problems are associated with chemicals that do not have direct effects locally or regionally. Rather, these chemicals are transported up to the stratosphere where they can undergo chemical reactions that can change the incoming sunlight. These changes, in turn, can affect temperature and rainfall all over the earth.

Q. *How much more money is an Amazonian forest tract worth through selling fruit, cocoa or rubber than by turning it into cattle pasture?*

Sources of air pollution can be natural, such as volcanic eruptions, or human-caused, such as automobile exhaust. Until about 150 years ago, the levels of harmful chemicals in the air were quite low and the sources were mainly natural. As people began to build factories and automobiles, the levels of pollution increased. Most pollution caused by people is associated with the burning of fuels such as coal to run the factories and gasoline to operate the cars. The burning of such "fossil fuels" produces harmful gases such as sulfur oxides, nitrogen oxides and volatile organic compounds. The burning also produces small particulates such as soot and fly ash.

Whereas sulfur and nitrogen oxides are associated mainly with human activities, natural sources are a major contributor of volatile organic compounds (VOCs). Some of these VOCs, which most effectively interact with nitrogen oxides to form oxidants, come mainly from vegetation. In some areas where natural activities are the dominant source of VOCs, control of human activities leading to production of nitrogen oxides becomes even more important for reducing pollution.

Air quality has been an increasingly serious issue in many parts of the world for several decades. The greenhouse effect, acid rain and gray skies over large regions are familiar examples of adverse effects associated with airborne chemicals. Recognition of the harmful effects

• Keep your car tuned. A well-tuned car uses up to 9 percent less gasoline than a poorly-tuned car. That means 9 percent fewer toxic emissions, too.

GET THE LEAD OUT
• Leaded gas is an environmental hazard. It not only creates pollution, but ruins your car. Owners of pre-1979 cars often believe their vehicles must use leaded gas. The EPA says that's a myth—it's the octane reading and not the lead that's important. The only exceptions are cars carrying heavy loads or traveling at high speeds.

• The plastic hoods you see on many gas pump nozzles are actually designed to keep butane, a component of gas that creates smog when it evaporates, from escaping. The hood fits over the gas tank opening and sucks the fumes into an underground

Children in Mezibori, Czechoslovakia, wearing respirators to shield them from air pollution on their way to school.

A. *Twice the amount*
Source: Atlas of the Environment, by the World Wildlife Fund

storage tank. So if there's a vapor catcher, don't pull it back...and don't pull out the gas nozzle to top off the tank.

GREEN IT
• Plant a tree. If you don't know how to begin: Call or visit a local nursery, horticultural society, arboretum or botanical garden. Don't just stick it in the ground and ignore it. Like other plants, trees need care at first—water, vertical support and mulch. Tree planting is easier than you think and many people will not only be helpful, but enthusiastic.

RESOURCE
• *The Green Commuter,* by Joel Makower, will be published in 1992 by the National Press, Washington, DC.

DID YOU KNOW?
• In Mexico City, smog levels exceeded standards set by the World Health Organization on 312 out of 366 days in 1988. Schoolchildren were given a month off of school in 1989 due to severe air pollution.

• In China, people in urban areas are four to six times more likely to die of lung cancer than rural residents.

• In Hungary, between 35 percent and 40 percent of the people live with "inadmissable" air pollution.

of air pollution has resulted in increased public interest in understanding the social as well as the atmospheric environments leading to air pollution and in developing effective pollution solutions.

Expanding population and industrial growth have made it inevitable that foul air would move beyond city limits, cross national boundaries, create international tensions and present new difficulties for those attempting to control its harmful effects. Control of certain pollutants in the atmosphere, or finding the best pollution solutions, may be hard, but it is a goal that we can and must achieve.

One of the biggest problems now on the international agenda, climate change (that is, the greenhouse effect), demands that all countries of the world participate in solving the problem. There are so many chemicals and sources that could possibly cause climate change. The solutions to many of these global scale air pollution problems seem to require that poorer countries find a path toward prosperity that does not involve increased use of fossil fuels.

These paths include energy conservation, development of renewable energy options (e.g., solar, wind and biomass), and more effective use of more conventional energy sources. It is the responsibility of industrialized countries to help developing countries as well as themselves find the cleaner, more energy efficient paths to prosperity. Part of the solution also is education and communication among individuals worldwide. We must realize fundamentally that every living thing on the planet needs clean air and each of us does have an important role to play in the pollution solution.

Paulette Bauer Middleton has spent 18 years in policy-oriented atmospheric research and management in interdisciplinary groups within large research institutions. Bauer is currently a staff scientist at the National Center for Atmospheric Research in Boulder, Colorado. She has lectured extensively, including at the 1990 International Summer School on Science and World Affairs at Princeton University. She has also developed air pollution material for the American Meteorological Society. Recently published articles she has authored and co-authored include "Haze in the Grand Canyon, An Evaluation of the Winter Haze Intensive Tracer Experiment" and "Ozone Precursor Relationships in the Ambient Atmosphere."

Q. *In a lifetime, the average American will throw away how many times her or his adult weight in garbage?*

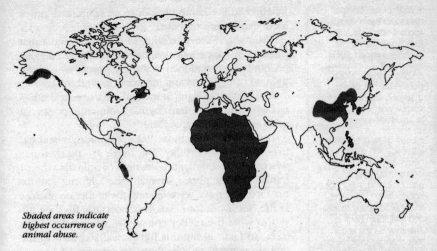

Shaded areas indicate highest occurrence of animal abuse.

Animal Rights

- By Cleveland Amory -

Contrary to what most people believe, the phrase "animal rights" is not a new one. It has a long and venerable history—indeed, I have a book in my office entitled *Animal Rights* by the great English humanitarian, Henry Salt. It was published in 1892.

Nonetheless I freely admit that both the Fund for Animals, which I head, and I myself bear a full measure of guilt in the phrase's more recent currency. It happened as follows: In the early days of the fund—in 1968—we were working on spaying and neutering problems on the island of Puerto Rico. By chance the Young and Rubicam advertising agency was having a convention there and, pleased with our work, Edward Ney suggested that one of the things the fund needed—at that time we needed almost everything—was a slogan. Accordingly, when we met the Young and Rubicam people in New York they suggested the slogan: "Animals have rights, too."

Almost immediately the phrase achieved wide popularity. Early on, however, I was asked what it meant and, frankly, I was not sure—it hadn't, after all, been my idea. Just the same, I attempted three short paragraphs, as follows:

The right to freedom from fear, pain and suffering—

WHAT YOU CAN DO:

EDUCATE
• Use bumperstickers with messages like "Fur is Dead," "Save the Squirrels," "Meat is Murder," and "Support Your Right to Arm Bears."

THE UGLY SIDE OF BEAUTY
• Do not be fooled by company claims that animal tests are required or that alternatives do not exist. No law requires companies to test on animals; they do it to limit their liability in case of a lawsuit.

• Many companies manufacture effective, safe and gentle products that are tested, not on animals, but through test tube studies (in vitro), with computer models and on human skin that has been cloned or attached to volunteers.

A. *600 times*
Source: The Recycler's Handbook, by the Earth • Works Group

• Write or call companies to let them know you will not purchase their products if they continue animal testing.

• Inform others. Most people are not aware that their "sierra sunset" lipstick was a product of animal suffering.

• Lead other companies into declaring a permanent ban on animal testing by circulating a petition in your neighborhood. Collect products that the company makes and mail them back in. This may be the action that changes their minds.

PET SHOP HORRORS
• Resist buying that "doggy in the window." If you want to share your home with a cat or dog, visit your local pound or shelter.

• Never buy animals as gifts. Tell others that are

whether in the name of science or sport, fashion or food, exhibition or service.

The right, if they are wild, to roam free, unharried by hunters, trappers or slaughterers. If they are domestic, not to be abandoned in the city streets, by a country road or in a cruel and inhumane pound.

And finally the right, at the end, to a decent death—not by a club, by a trap, by harpoon, cruel poison or mass extermination chamber.

Looking back on those lines, I think they still express what I feel today. But there are many times when the fund is fighting battles for animals when I frankly find the phrase "animal rights" difficult—as, for instance, when we were fighting the timber companies in the Northwest for killing bears because they ate the sap in what the timber companies regarded as their trees. In fact, during this fight I realized that, to the timber company people, the mere mention of "animal rights" conjured up bears marching down the main street toward the Capitol and then marching in to take seats and raising their paws to vote.

One thing is certain—if I have occasionally been unhappy about the phrase, our opponents have been far unhappier. Faced with the extraordinary advances of the animal movement—on the hunting front, the fur front and even the laboratory animal front—the

Photo: Dan McCoy/Black Star

This photo of pain research performed on monkeys has been widely distributed by animal rights organizations.

Q: *How much more energy does it take to make paper from wood pulp than to make recycled paper from waste paper?*

hunting fraternity, the furriers and the laboratory experimenters have joined together in a steady campaign of animal rights bashing.

This campaign against animal rights has undoubtedly had some effect. I maintain, however, that most of it is so exaggerated that it, too, will soon be faced with its own backlash. I remember vividly, for example, a moment at the March for the Animals in Washington, DC, when 30,000 people gathered, when Doris Dixon of Ann Arbor, Michigan—a gentle, motherly woman who was the first out-of-town correspondent for the Fund for Animals—stood up and with a winning smile declared, "I used to be a little old lady in tennis shoes. Now I'm a terrorist! Whee!" In contrast, at the unsportsmanlike Hegins, Pennsylvania, pigeon shoot last fall, many of the shotgunners shot pigeons—bred for the occasion and so disoriented they could hardly fly at all—at a distance of a few feet. Yet a large number of these shooters wore t-shirts saying either "Shoot Pigeons—Not Drugs" or "Save a Pigeon—Shoot a Protester."

The other side indeed acts as if every hunter faces injury from hunter harassment, that every fur-wearer is up against the danger of being spray-painted, and that every laboratory experimenter risks life and limb.

The plain facts are otherwise. Not a single animal abuser has ever been injured by any animal rightist. Indeed, when one comes to the laboratory experimenters, the chief injury has been to the American taxpayer. As Congressman John Dingell's House subcommittee on Oversight and Investigations has so amply proved, the universities are riding a gravy train of animal abuse for their own benefit. For every grant they get—for what they call "experimentation" and animal rightists call torture of animals—after adding every conceivable expense they can think of, including lab rentals, parking spaces and even cleaning fees, they then add on top of that what they call "overhead." At Harvard it's 88 percent; at Stanford 84 percent; at Yale 60 percent. At Harvard, $140,000 of the "overhead" went to refurbish the president's house. At Stanford the money went for the president's cedar-lined closets, his yacht, and even the enlargement of his bed.

Cleveland Amory is the founder and president of the New York-based Fund for Animals. His most recent books are The Cat Who Came For Christmas *and* The Cat And The Curmudgeon.

looking for an animal companion that there are wonderful pets at the shelter.

• Ask your local city or council members to pass an ordinance banning the importation and sale of exotic wildlife except for rehabilitation purposes.

RESOURCES
• *Save the Animals! 101 Easy Things You Can Do*, by Ingrid Newkirk, Warner Books, New York, 1990.

• *Kids Can Save the Animals! 101 Easy Things to Do*, by Ingrid Newkirk, Warner books, New York, 1991.

• *The Animal Welfare Institute Quarterly*, The Animal Welfare Institute, P.O. Box 3650, Washington, DC 20007.

• *PETA's Cruelty Free Shopping Guide.* Write to PETA, P.O. Box 42516, Washington, DC 20015, 1991.

• *Shopping for a Better World,* published annually by the Council on Economic Priorities, New York, 1990.

• *A Shopper's Guide to Cruelty-Free Products*, by Lori Cook, Friends of Animals, Bantam Books, New York, 1991.

A. *30 percent*
Source: The Recycler's Handbook, *by the Earth • Works Group*

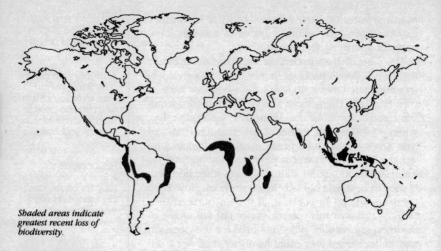

Shaded areas indicate greatest recent loss of biodiversity.

Biodiversity

- By Dr. Peter H. Raven -

Biodiversity is suddenly a potent word, but still a somewhat forbidding and technical one. What does it mean? The sum total of all the animals, plants, fungi and microorganisms that share this planet Earth with us—they constitute biodiversity.

Are there 10 million kinds of organisms on Earth, or 100 million? No one knows for sure. But what is certain is that we are destroying them rapidly, and forever. The explosive growth of a runaway human population that has more than doubled in the last 40 years; the unequal distribution of wealth, which leaves three-quarters of us making do with 10 percent to 15 percent of the world's goods while contributing tens of billions of dollars each year to the rich, industrialized nations; our greedy and seemingly tireless consumption of all that the world has to offer—these are some of the factors that are working together in our time, and will likely deny our children and grandchildren the pleasure of ever seeing, studying or using a fifth of the kinds of plants and vertebrate animals that exist now.

Some 50,000 kinds of plants may vanish during the next 30 years or so, out of a world total of about 250,000. Most of them will never have been examined in detail; the vast majority will be natives of largely

Q: Californians alone leak used motor oil into the ground each year in a quantity equaling how many Valdez oil spills?

tropical developing countries. If they are saved, some of them would doubtless turn out to be excellent timber trees, forage plants, sources of food or biomass—a means to capture solar energy. Others might contain substances that would cure cancer, deter the AIDS virus, form the basis for whole new industries to help alleviate the poverty of the regions where they grow. With such riches within our grasp, it seems all but unbelievable that we are not taking steps to secure them while they are still there. As many as 4,000 species of legumes, 2,000 species of grasses and 600 species of palm—to name only the three plant families that contribute the most to human welfare—may disappear forever during our lifetimes.

To solve this problem, we must accept the fact that the irreversible loss of the organisms on which we depend is the most serious global problem of all—more serious than the depletion of the stratospheric ozone layer, global warming or ocean pollution—because it is moving more rapidly and because it is completely irreversible. We must work to preserve biodiversity by setting aside and protecting selected natural areas in industrialized countries like the US.

We must also insist on effective foreign assistance programs that help other nations protect their biodiversity, to create a global network of parks and protected areas, seed banks, zoos and collections of cultures of microorganisms. Living lives that are

Commerce, 14th St. and Constitution Ave. NW, Washington, DC 20230.

• In the US, National Forests are divided into regions, the regions into forests, and the forests into ranger districts. You can direct your comments on a particular agency's lands or actions to the ranger of that district, to the supervisor of the national forest, or to the regional forester responsible for that area.

RESOURCE
• *Biodiversity,* edited by E.O. Wilson, National Academy Press, Washington, DC, 1988.

DID YOU KNOW?
• A single river in Brazil harbors more species of fish than all the rivers in the US.

• About 1.4 million living species have been named and described by scientists. Approximately

Photo: Jack Swenson/Tom Stack & Assoc.

A gladiator frog, one of countless species from a tropical rainforest in Venezuela.

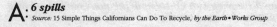

A. *6 spills*
Source: 15 Simple Things Californians Can Do To Recycle, *by the Earth • Works Group*

750,000 are insects, 41,000 are vertebrates and 265,000 are plants. The remainder includes invertebrates, fungi, algae and micro-organisms.

• Although rainforests make up only 7 percent of the earth's surface, over half the world's wild plant, animal and insect species live there. In a typical four-mile-square patch of tropical rainforest you would find over 750 species of trees, 1,500 kinds of flowering plants, 125 mammals and 400 kinds of birds. Only 1 percent of these species has ever been studied.

• The Rainforest Action Network estimates that four to 15 species each day become extinct in the world's rainforests.

• Organisms living on our coral reefs survive predators largely through undersea "chemical warfare." Science has used hundreds of these creatures to develop indispensable medical antidotes and treatments.

• Up to half of all prescription drugs are based on wild organisms. Worldwide, the annual commercial value of medication we would not have without wild or naturally indigenous species is more than $40 billion. The figure multiplies as we learn and adapt more of nature's secrets through genetic engineering.

ecologically sound, when we consume the Earth's bounty at 20 to 50 times the rate that is possible in most countries, could easily free up the $10 billion or so that might be required annually to begin to address this problem seriously.

In the industrialized countries, we can all contribute to the preservation of biodiversity by working to set aside protected areas in our regions, with representative samples of natural habitats, and striving to maintain the condition of those that are already protected. Groups such as The Nature Conservancy, the Audubon Society, the Sierra Club, the Center for Plant Conservation and many others deserve our support, and local chapters have up-to-date information on the kinds of efforts that are important locally.

A spirit of international cooperation is the best guarantee for the preservation of biodiversity in the future. Your elected representatives should hear from you about your interest in these matters and in effective programs of international legislation that exist for the preservation of species throughout the world.

Whether we choose to recognize it or not, we are, in effect, the proprietors of a kind of Noah's ark—we are choosing which kinds of plants and animals survive, and which die. We must choose whether we will be responsible proprietors or not and, if our decision is positive, take the appropriate steps. Only organisms, individually and in communities, make possible the sustainability on which we, and the proper functioning of the whole planet, depend. The kind of world that our descendants will inhabit a few decades from now will depend directly on the actions that we decide to take now.

Dr. Peter H. Raven is director of the Missouri Botanical Garden and Englemann Professor of Botany of Washington University. Dr. Raven is home secretary of the National Academy of Sciences, and chairman of the Report Review Committee of the National Research Council. He was appointed by President Bush as a member of the National Science Board in 1990. In 1990 he shared with E.O. Wilson the Prize of the Institut de la Vie in Paris. From 1985 to 1990 he was a John D. and Catherine T. MacArthur Foundation Fellow. He is the author or editor of 16 books, including textbooks in biology and botany, and more than 400 scientific papers.

Q: *How many days a year do women and children in the non-industrial world spend searching for fuel?*

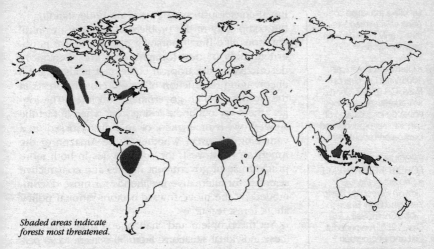

Shaded areas indicate forests most threatened.

Deforestation

- By Dr. Thomas Lovejoy -

The forests of the world are being destroyed at an unprecedented rate. World Resources Institute put the recent estimate at a rate of 40 million to 50 million acres annually or 80 acres per minute. With the destruction of forests, particularly tropical rainforests, go significant amounts of the world's variety of plant and animal life (about 0.2 percent per year according to a conservative estimate by Harvard scientist E.O. Wilson). As vast areas of the tropical forest are burned in the process of clearing, about 1 billion to 2 billion tons of carbon as carbon dioxide are added to the atmosphere every year—a significant contribution to the annual build up of greenhouse gas.

The world as a whole began to wake up to this problem in 1988. Satellite imagery conveyed the magnitude of the tropical deforestation problem. The hot summer made people focus on the greenhouse problem. And finally the assassination of Chico Mendes put a human face on what for many had previously seemed just an abstract concern. Brazil protested that its sovereignty was being infringed, and tropical countries felt they were being lectured by the industrial countries which could hardly be termed ecological white hats.

There has been an important transition from this

WHAT YOU CAN DO:

EDUCATE
• Learn about the unique ecosystem of forests and compare what you have learned to what the US Forest Service practices.

CONSCIOUSLY CONSUME
• *The Wood Users Guide*, by Pamela Wellner and Eugene Dickey, Rainforest Action Network, San Francisco, 1991. This guide, intended to be periodically updated, includes comprehensive information about tropical woods and alternatives.

• Earth Care Paper Company, P.O. Box 7070, Madison, WI 53707-7070, (608) 277-2900. Send for a catalog of their recycled paper products.

• Wild Birds Unlimited, 6425 N. Keystone Ave., Indianapolis, IN 46220. This environmentally

A. *100 to 300*
Source: Atlas of the Environment, *by the World Wildlife Fund*

sensitive franchise company sells birdfeeders made only from non-old-growth wood.

• Northwest Botanicals, 1305 Vista Dr., Grants Pass, OR 97527. Send a self-addressed, stamped envelope for a catalog of minor forest products and publications about them.

RESOURCES ABOUT FOREST ECOSYSTEMS
• *Secrets of the Old Growth Forest*, by David Kelly and Gary Braasch, Gibbs Smith, Salt Lake City, 1988. A wonderful text and photograph combination explaining the ecology of ancient forests.

• *Western Forests*, by Stephen Whitney, Audubon Society Nature Guides, Knopf Publishers, New York, 1985. How to identify and

initial consciousness to a growing understanding of the complexity of the problem. It is not just tropical countries like Brazil pursuing old destructive northern models of development that are even more destructive in the tropical context. It is also the US encouraging destruction of its old-growth forests in the Northwest with government subsidies. The loggers there cry out about losing jobs, when in fact the spotted owl is the symbol of an industry based on a vanishing resource. Whether in the Amazon or the American Northwest, the solution lies in both more prudent use of government monies and constructive searches for alternative livelihoods for those discommoded by the move toward a more rational policy about forest resources.

Yet the problem and challenge is larger than just these individual situations. From 50 percent to 90 percent of all biological diversity exists in and depends on forests. In many instances the long-term productive value of the land depends on using rather than destroying forests.

Clearly we need to move as rapidly as possible toward global management of forests and a global agreement on biological diversity. Both are under active discussion, but a forest convention is much easier

Photo: Gary Stewart/AP/Wide World Photos

Loggers fell an old-growth Douglas fir near Mount St. Helens in Washington.

Q: *Some 70 percent of America's 20,000 landfills were filled and closed between 1978 and 1988. By 1993, how many others are expected to close?*

to tackle and likely to come first. Yet while negotiating proceeds, the forests and their diversity continue to dwindle, so there is a need for action now. One of the greatest hurdles is lack of resources and strong institutions in tropical countries. This can be helped in a significant way, despite our own fiscal stringencies, by debt-for-nature swaps. These arrangements convert unpaid loans to indebted countries into funds for conservation activities in those countries. For the first time, government-to-government debt is being considered eligible and on a scale (billions of dollars) relevant to the extent of the problem.

It is essential for the forward progress on a world scale that the industrialized nations, including the US and Canada, improve their own performance. It makes sense on its own terms for the US to rapidly eliminate subsidies which encourage further destruction of old-growth forests of the Northwest, and create a rapid transition for the industries and employees involved. On a global scale it is even more important that the wealthiest nation on Earth take the exemplary course.

Plant and animal species are, in fact, the most sensitive indicators of environmental change. We have now taken pollution on the global scale, to the point of altering the basic physics and chemistry of the atmosphere. That and the current rate of species loss indicates society collectively is living beyond the environmental limits of the planet.

To halt this will certainly take tens if not hundreds of billions of dollars per year, but that is trivial compared to the value of those forests, that diversity and the benefit of a stable climate. Forests are a vital resource, an indicator of environmental stress and an important symbol. The time to act is very short.

Dr. Thomas Lovejoy is a tropical conservation biologist working as assistant secretary for External Affairs of the Smithsonian Institution since 1987. He has worked in the Amazon of Brazil since 1965. From 1973 to 1987 he was the program director of the World Wildlife Fund. He served as executive vice-president for his last two years at the fund, and was in charge of its scientific, western hemisphere and tropical forest orientation. He is also the founder of the public television series, "Nature," and a member of President Bush's Council of Advisors in Science.

understand what you see in the forest.

● *The Simple Act of Planting A Tree,* by Treepeople with Andy and Katie Lipkis, Jeremy P. Tarcher, Los Angeles, 1990. A hands-on manual based on Treepeople's extensive experience in Los Angeles.

● *Saving Our Ancient Forests,* by Seth Zuckerman and The Wilderness Society, Living Planet Press, Los Angeles, 1991.

RESOURCES ABOUT ALTERNATIVE FOREST MANAGEMENT
● *Last Stand: Logging, Journalism and the Case for Humanity,* by Richard Manning, Gibbs Smith, Salt Lake City, 1991.

● *The Forest and the Trees: A Guide to Excellent Forestry,* by Gordon Robinson, Island Press, Washington, DC, 1988. An experienced viewpoint on how forests should be sustainably managed.

● *Forest Watch,* monthly publication of Cascade Holistic Economic Consultants (founded by Randal O'Toole), with the most current thinking on forest issues. Includes *Reform!* a newsletter specifically devoted to restructuring the US Forest Service. Write to Cascade Holistic Economic Consultants, 14417 SE Laurie, Oak Grove, OR 97267.

● *Reforming the Forest Service,* by Randal O'Toole, Island Press, Washington, DC, 1988. A short analysis of the agency that manages more ancient forest than any other.

A. *2,000 landfills*
    Source: The Recycler's Handbook, *by the Earth ● Works Group*

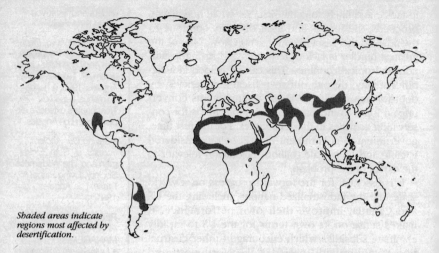

Shaded areas indicate regions most affected by desertification.

WHAT YOU CAN DO:

GET INVOLVED
• Become involved with the United Nations and agricultural programs that work on technique transfer to developing nations.

RESOURCES
• World Resources Institute, 1709 New York Ave. NW, Seventh Floor, Washington, DC 20006.

• United Nations Environment Program, 2 UN Plaza, Room 803, New York, NY 10017.

• World Hunger Year, 261 W. 35th St., #1402, New York, NY 10001-1906.

• Food and Agriculture Organization of the United Nations, Via delle Terme di Caracalla, Rome 00100, Italy.

• The Land Institute, 2440 E. Water Well Rd., Salina, KS 67401.

Desertification

- By Dr. Michael H. Glantz -

Desertification can be defined as the creation of desert-like conditions where none had existed in the recent past. Although the concept has become most closely associated with arid areas along desert fringes, it is now applied to high rainfall areas like the Amazon rainforest. Desertification is a mega-concept. It encompasses many processes such as wind and water erosion, soil salinization, overgrazing, water-logging and deforestation. It also has competing definitions, of which there are more than a hundred. This perspective sees desertification as a process of change, rather than just the end result of that change.

Desertification has a natural as well as a human component. In the ancient past its occurrence was dependent on land-climate interactions. In the past several thousand years the equation has been expanded to include humans. Today, desertification is dependent on land-climate-human interactions. Desertification in specific regions is occurring over decades and years instead of centuries and millennia. The difference is the human factor. We have not learned to live in harmony with our natural environment.

Many Americans believe desertification is a third world problem and not one we need be concerned about in North America. Yet aspects of desertification

Q. *How much of the rain which falls on the continents is received by the rainforests, which cover less than 7 percent of the earth's surface?*

are under way in our country: degraded rangelands, major dust storms, decreasing soil fertility. Do we have a federal office of desertification control? No. Do we have a bureau that deals with soil erosion? Yes. With grazing practices? Yes. While it appears that we are not doing much in North America to combat desertification (the mega-concept), we are quite active in combating those land-use problems that degrade our soil's productivity.

In North America desertification is an economic problem. It is a different situation, however, in the third world, where the inability to cope with aspects of desertification that encroach on agricultural fields, rangelands and on human settlements can mean the difference between life and death. Many people in sub-Saharan Africa live from one season to the next. They are on their own when it comes to survival, as their governments are either unwilling or unable to assist them. When the fertility of their soils declines, bringing down food production with it, they become malnourished, finding it even more difficult to work their fields. Ultimately they must abandon their land in search of land not yet degraded by human activities.

Decades ago when population densities were lower, farmers could migrate to new areas, leaving their farmland fallow. Over time, the fields would recover and in

DID YOU KNOW?

• The first use of the term "desertification" appeared in a 1949 government report by André Aubreville on climate and forests in tropical Africa. Today there are more than 100 definitions of the concept.

• In 1977, the first UN Conference was held to address the physical and societal aspects of desertification.

• There is no scientific agreement on the rates of desertification.

• Deforestation is considered by some scientists as the first step on the road to desertification.

• Each year, about 50 million acres provide no economic return because of the spread of desertification.

Photo: World Vision/Picture Group

Encroaching desert ruins land for farming or grazing in Mali.

A. *Over half*
   Source: Natural Resources Defense Council

• By the end of this century, one-half to three-quarters of all irrigated land will be destroyed by salt build-up in the soil.

• Throughout the world, an area the size of Kansas is impoverished by desertification and ruined for farming or grazing each year.

• The "fertile crescent" of Mesopotamia is now desert.

• Approximately 162 million acres south of the Sahara have turned to desert.

• In Ethiopia, about a billion tons of topsoil are washed away each year.

• In the last decade in China, a forest belt nearly 4,375 miles long and 250-1000 miles wide has been planted. Much cropland has been protected and annual grain harvests have increased by 13 percent.

• Desertification is caused by a variety of conditions:

deforestation
drought
firewood gathering
groundwater pollution
introduction of nonnative
    species
loss of biodiversity
overgrazing
pesticide poisoning
soil salinization
water erosion
wind erosion

a decade or two the farmers would rotate their farming back to the original site. With most of the arable land already in production, there is no possibility of letting the land lie fallow. Making a bad situation worse, animal manure is often collected in the fields to be used as fuel, eliminating a sorely needed source of fertilizer.

Poor countries do not have the funds to combat desertification. Industrialized countries apparently do not have the desire to address the sources of desertification in the third world in a major way. Lip service to combating desertification will not do the job. Training programs and technique transfer (as opposed to technology transfer) are necessary aspects of arresting desertification processes. It is far cheaper to train people to avert desertification than to reclaim land that has already been desertified.

Desertification is a long-term, low-grade, but cumulative environmental problem that, like air pollution, acid rain and global warming, keeps getting put on the back burner while governments address seemingly more pressing issues. Solutions, however, are often known but not applied for lack of appropriate funding. It will take lots of money to combat it. But those funds will have to be used more wisely in the future than they have been in the past. Education and training at the local level should be the highest priorities for agencies seeking to bring an end to desertification in those countries whose inhabitants are most threatened by the process.

Desertification deserves at least equal attention as other environmental changes that threaten "our plundered planet." Only time will tell if humans are smart enough to give it that attention.

Dr. Michael H. Glantz is a senior scientist with the National Center for Atmospheric Research (NCAR) and director of the Environmental and Societal Impacts Group, a program of NCAR. He is interested in how climate affects society and how society affects climate, especially how the interaction between climate anomalies and human activities can affect quality of life. He is a member of numerous national and international committees and advisory bodies related to issues of climate and society. In 1987 his article on drought in Africa (Scientific American) *was given an award by World Hunger Year. In March 1990 he received a "Global 500" award from the United Nations Environment Program.*

Q: **What causes 12 million acres of the Himalayan Mountains to be damaged annually in India by floods?**

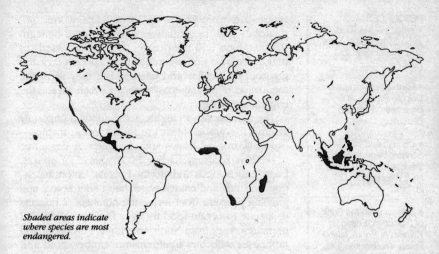

Shaded areas indicate where species are most endangered.

Endangered Species

- By Faith Thompson Campbell -

Endangered species are those poised on the brink of extinction. Every day, more species are pushed off the Earth forever. But if we act decisively, we can minimize the number of species lost and keep the Earth a more livable place for all of its inhabitants.

How many species are endangered? We can only estimate the numbers, because too little is known about those parts of the Earth where the largest numbers of species live—tropical forests, coral reefs and the bottoms of the oceans and bays. Best estimates are that there may be 30 million species on Earth, and that we are killing off as many as 17,000 each year.

The extinction crisis is caused by our own large and ever-growing population (we now number 5.4 billion and are expected to double by some time in the next century) and ever-increasing demand for natural resources. We and our livestock already use at least one quarter of the food, fiber and fuel produced by plants (the ultimate source of our products). If human populations grow as projected, and the poorest people raise their living standards a little, there will be *no* plant production left for wild animals.

Public attention has focused on big mammals and colorful birds such as the African elephant and California condor. But the greatest number of endangered

WHAT YOU CAN DO:

CONSCIOUSLY CONSUME
• Avoid buying live animals or plants or products made from their leather, fur, shells, wood, etc., when the species is overexploited in the wild.

• Minimize the numbers of your own children.

• Support financially and through political activism the efforts of conservation and family planning organizations working here and abroad.

• More than 6.5 million dolphins have been needlessly slaughtered by the tuna industry. Check to make sure the tuna you buy is labeled "dolphin safe"—or don't buy it. And write to Congress to support a bill that will require tuna to be labeled "dolphin-safe" or "dolphin-unsafe" so consumers can vote for protecting dolphins.

A. *Deforestation of the Himalayan Mountains*
Source: The Wilderness Society

RESOURCES
• World Wildlife Fund, 1250 24th St. NW, Suite 400, Washington, DC 20037.

• Earth Island Institute Dolphin Project, 300 Broadway, #28, San Francisco, CA 94133.

• US Fish and Wildlife Service, Department of the Interior, 1849 C St. NW, Washington, DC 20240.

• *Balancing on the Brink of Extinction*, Edited by Kathryn A. Kohm, Island Press, Washington, DC, 1991.

• *The Endangered Kingdom*, by Roger L. DiSilvestro, John Wiley and Sons, New York, 1991.

• *Dying Planet: The Extinction of Species*, by Jon Erickson, TAB Books, Blue Ridge Summit, PA, 1991.

DID YOU KNOW?
• Blue whales, along with many other kinds of whales, are becoming extinct because people kill them and sell their body parts for money. Whale meat is considered a delicacy in Japan and some other countries. The oil from whales has been used to make lipstick, shoe polish, margarine and transmission oil for cars and is sometimes used to lubricate weapons. It is now illegal to kill whales for food anywhere in the world. Japan and Norway still hunt whales, claiming the whales are hunted for research purposes.

species are invertebrates—insects, spiders, worms, soil microbes and their relatives living in mud beneath streams, bays and the oceans. Tens of thousands of plants are also endangered. These species lack the glamour of pandas and parrots, but they form the foundation of natural ecosystems on which *we* and the larger animals depend.

The number of species are not distributed uniformly around the world. Most are found in the tropics—especially tropical forests and coral reefs. A single tree in the Amazon may harbor 2,000 species of insects, frogs, lizards, birds and attached plants. Unfortunately, tropical lands and coastal waters are under severe and growing pressure from increasing numbers of humans desperate to obtain food for their families. Additional pressure comes from North Americans, Europeans and Japanese, who buy beef, shrimp, timber, gold and petroleum obtained from these biologically rich areas. Consequently, the largest numbers of endangered

Photo: Deborah Copaken/Gamma-Liaison

Rhinoceros are being hunted to the point of extinction for their horns.

Q. *If only 2 percent of crop production in the US is based on native species, where did most originate?*

species are found in certain tropical regions—eastern Brazil, Central America, West Africa, Madagascar, Malaysia, Indonesia and the Philippines.

Although the extinction threat is greatest in the tropics, the United States passed national legislation in 1973 to help stop the rising number of extinctions. The Endangered Species Act, which Congress will consider for reauthorization in 1992, has been widely acclaimed as the most powerful environmental law in the world. When invoked, the habitat is managed for the benefit of the troubled species and other uses must not further jeopardize it; the act has even been used to restrain economic development is favor of a species on the endangered or threatened list.

Since 1973, more that 550 species of animals and plants have been officially listed as being in imminent danger of extinction or threatened by extinction. Seven listed species in the United States have been declared extinct since 1973. More troubling is the backlog of more than 600 severely imperiled species, all stuck awaiting addition to the list of "endangered" species and the protection listing affords. Another 3,500 species are suspected of being threatened or endangered but not enough information has been complied to make the species candidates for listing.

With these overwhelming numbers, if current environmentally destructive trends continue, we will lose entire ecosystems and the already upset natural balance will be completely lost. Efforts must be focused immediately on ways to preserve the Earth's valuable biodiversity.

Faith Thompson Campbell has worked with the Natural Resources Defense Council since 1976, and was promoted to senior staff member in 1988. She has been a participant on the Plants Committee of the Convention on International Trade in Endangered Species of Wild Fauna and Flora since 1983. Her awards have included the Award of Achievement from the Natural Resources Council of America in 1980, the Golden Tortoise Award from the Desert Tortoise Preserve Committee in 1989, and the Certificate of Appreciation from the US Forest Service in 1989, in recognition of leadership in promoting the conservation of rare plants in the National Forests. She has published numerous articles in scholarly and popular journals on conservation of endangered species, especially plants.

• Millions of live animals are shipped around the world every year to supply the pet trade. Furs, leather and ivory are also traded in vast quantities.

• Between 60 percent and 80 percent of all live wild animals smuggled around the world die in transit. In 1990, customs officials at Madrid airport in Spain found 1,500 dead baby crocodiles in a shipment of crates containing 2,000.

• Typically a single year will see 50,000 live primates, tusk ivory from 70,000 African elephants, 4 million live birds, 10 million reptile skins, 15 million pelts, about 350 million tropical fish and about 1 million orchids bought and sold around the world.

• Daggers with handles fashioned from African rhino horn can fetch $12,000 each, and white Asian rhino horn sells at $13,000 a pound for medicines in the Far East. The Black rhino population has been reduced by 95 percent since 1970, mainly as a result of poaching, while the total population of the world's nine rhino species has fallen by 84 percent.

• A clouded leopard coat can be worth over $100,000 in Japan, while Vicuña coats sell for around $20,000 in the US.

A. *In the tropics*
Source: *Natural Resources Defense Council*

DELISTED ENDANGERED SPECIES

Finding a list of globally endangered species called for minor detective work. *The 1990 IUCN Red List of Threatened Animals* compiled by the World Conservation Monitoring Centre of England is the only global list available. It contains just over 5,000 species, comprised of 698 mammals, 1,047 birds, 191 reptiles, 63 amphibians, 762 fishes and 2,250 invertebrates.

The *1990 Endangered and Threatened Wildlife and Plants List,* compiled by the US Fish and Wildlife Service, lists threatened and endangered animals and plants in the US. Species listed are protected under the Endangered Species Act. Foriegn species included in the list are those that have been brought into the US. This resource cites only 1,167 animals and plants, 639 from the US and 528 foreign.

Only 16 species of animals and plants have ever been removed from the US Fish and Wildlife Service list. What follows are those species that have been delisted since 1966, including the reason for delisting.

Recovered (total: 5)

Common name:	historic range	former status	date delisted
dove, Palau	US, West Pacific	Endangered	9/12/85
fantail, Palau (Old World flycatcher)	US, West Pacific	Endangered	9/12/85
owl, Palau	US, West Pacific	Endangered	9/12/85
Milk-vetch, Rydberg (plant)	US	Threatened	9/14/89
cactus, purple-spined hedgehog	US	Endangered	11/27/89

Extinct (total: 7)

pupfish, Tecopa	US	Endangered	1/15/82
cisco, longjaw (trout)	US, Canada	Endangered	9/2/83
pike, blue	US, Canada	Endangered	9/2/83
sparrow, Santa Barbara song	US	Endangered	10/12/83
pearly mussel, Sampson's	US	Endangered	1/9/84
Gambusia, Amistad (fish)	US	Endangered	12/4/87
sparrow, dusky seaside	US	Endangered	12/12/90

Original error in data (Subsequent investigations show that the best data available at the time of the listing, or the interpretation of such data, were in error, i.e., more of the alleged "endangered" species were found, making their population stable.) **(total: 4)**

duck, Mexican	US to central Mexico	Endangered	7/25/78
tree frog, Pine Barrens	US	Endangered	11/22/83
turtle, Indian flap-shelled	India, Pakistan, Bangladesh	Endangered	4/29/84
butterfly, Bahama swallowtail	US, Bahamas	Threatened	8/31/84

SPECIES MOST ENDANGERED

Defenders of Wildlife, a Green Group member, responded to a request to make a list of which species they thought were the most endangered and in need of recovery. The expenditures are the actual amount spent on the species by state and federal agencies in 1991.

Alabama cavefish	$200	black-footed ferret	$1,126,700
black rhinoceros	$0	California condor	$892,700
Florida panther	$4,113,900	green pitcher plant	$42,300
Gulf of California harbor porpoise	$0	Kemp's Ridley sea turtle	$866,200
Mexican wolf	$0	Philippine eagle	$0

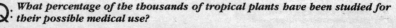

Q. *What percentage of the thousands of tropical plants have been studied for their possible medical use?*

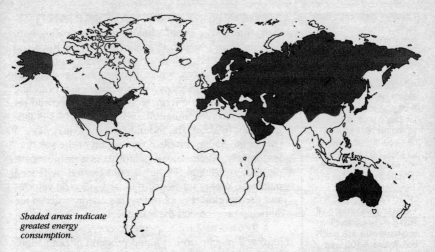

Shaded areas indicate greatest energy consumption.

Energy Conservation

- By Dr. James J. MacKenzie -

The "energy problem" is actually a complex of environmental and national security problems. Burning fossil fuels gives rise to environmental damage on many fronts, the most alarming of which is global climate change. But such "local" damage as oil spills, acid rain, wilderness destruction and soil and groundwater contamination also result from producing, transporting and using such fuels—especially oil and coal.

The latest Persian Gulf crisis illustrates once again the security and economic risks inherent in our dependence on imported oil. US oil production keeps declining while oil imports rise, with grave implications for the country's security and balance of trade. In 1989, the US imported about half its total oil supply at a cost of about $50 billion, almost half of the trade deficit. Since transportation consumes the bulk of US oil, the national security issue is very much a transportation issue. US dependence on foreign oil—and the attendant security and economic threats—will keep rising until measures are taken to curtail petroleum demand or substitute new energy sources for oil.

As a nation, we are a long way from adopting a rational response to energy-related problems. The US government, almost alone among the industrialized democracies, consistently downplays the need for

WHAT YOU CAN DO:

HOME HEATING
• According to Worldwatch, home heating is responsible for spewing 350 million tons of carbon into the atmosphere every year—which means over a billion tons of the most prevalent greenhouse gas, CO_2.

• Get a furnace tune up: Gas furnaces should be tuned every two years, oil furnaces annually. Call a heating technician; the whole job should cost around $40 to $60.

• If you have a forced-air system: Insulate ducts where they pass through unheated spaces.

• During the heating season, change your air filters once a month. Your heater uses more energy when the filters get full of dust.

• If you have electric resistance heating:

A. **Fewer than 1 percent**
  Source: Natural Resources Defense Council

Consider installing a heat pump, which uses thermal energy from outside air for both heating and cooling.

• If you have a hot water/steam system: Put a reflector behind your radiator (buy one or make it by taping aluminum foil on cardboard). This saves by throwing back heat you would normally lose through the wall.

LIGHTING
• One large incandescent bulb is more efficient than two small ones in a multi-bulb fixture. A 100-watt bulb, for example, puts out as much light as two 60s...and it saves energy.

• Try more efficient incandescents such as krypton-filled, tungsten-halogen or infrared-reflective coated. Or try compact fluorescents; they last longer and use

national energy policies that address the threat of global warming. The Bush Administration is dealing with the oil-import problem by deploying military force and promoting more exploration and development of domestic oil resources, while ignoring the need for improved energy efficiency. Meanwhile, federal funding for the renewable energy technologies that could reduce these environmental and security risks is languishing. In short, the federal government is more a part of the energy problem than a part of the solution. Fortunately, some states—California is a prime example—are moving to fill the vacuum created by federal paralysis. Energy efficiency standards, electric vehicles and the development of renewable energy sources are all being promoted at the state level.

A focused national response to energy-related problems will require an integrated program of both short-term and long-range initiatives. Over the next decade, we need measures to increase energy efficiency. Specifically, we should strengthen building codes; encourage higher new-vehicle fuel efficiency through fuel taxes, gas guzzler fees and annual registration fees based on efficiency; adopt programs to remove older (thus pollution-prone and inefficient) vehicles from our roads; and provide incentives to utilities to weatherize and retrofit existing buildings and to install and

Photo: Torin Boyd/Liaison International

Photovoltaic panels at a solar factory, a potential source of alternative energy.

Q: *How long will the known oil reserves in the world last at the rate we consume them?*

lease solar domestic hot water heaters. Longer-term efforts should focus on promoting widespread adoption of nonfossil energy technologies such as wind turbines, solar thermal power plants, photovoltaic cells and electric and hydrogen powered vehicles.

Historically, it has taken several generations to switch to new energy sources. Use of new fuels—coal in the 19th century, oil and gas in the 20th—generally grew by 6 percent to 7 percent per year, doubling every decade. If the past is prologue, it takes some 50 years or more for new energy sources to displace old ones.

But there is no fundamental reason why a transformation of energy technologies should take so long. During periods of national emergency such as the world wars of this century, factories were quickly converted to make entirely different products deemed critical to the national interest. If the US government—and the electorate—recognize the urgent need for new energy technologies, the transition to solar hot-water collectors, solar thermal power plants, wind turbines and other nonfossil technologies could be greatly accelerated, as could improvements in national energy efficiency.

The energy problem presents enormous challenges over the next few decades. Political leadership and foresight will be needed to change current practices—especially the inefficient burning of fossil fuels—and thereby mitigate the growing climate, pollution and security problems that loom over our future. Since the technological means of moving to an efficient, sustainable energy system are within our reach, the resolution of our long-term problem is not a matter of fate, but of choice.

Dr. James J. MacKenzie is a senior associate in the World Resources Institute's Climate, Energy and Pollution Program. Prior to joining World Resources Institute, MacKenzie was a senior staff scientist at the Union of Concerned Scientists where he authored numerous articles and papers on various aspects of the energy issue, including nuclear power safety, conservation, solar energy and global oil resources.

From 1977 to 1981, Dr. MacKenzie was a member of the Joint Scientific Staff of the Massachusetts and National Audubon Societies, where he wrote and lectured extensively on energy issues.

about one-fourth the energy of an incandescent bulb.

WATER HEATING
• Heating water is the second highest energy demand in the house, according to the Department of Energy.

• Use low-flow shower heads. They are relatively inexpensive and can reduce energy use for heating shower water by as much as 50 percent.

• Washing machines and electric dryers use as much as 25 percent of home electricity, and 90 percent of that goes to heating water. Try cold water wash and rinse cycles and cool water detergents. Also pay attention to the water level and set it to the size of the load.

• Make sure the lint-filter in your dryer is clean after each use and put heavy and light fabrics into separate loads. Try a clothesline.

INSULATION
• Caulk and weatherstrip your home. About 15 percent of home heating costs go to compensating for cold air that leaks in cracks.

• Temperatures in an attic can reach 150° F during warm summer months. Insulate and ventilate your attic to keep the rooms below cooler.

• Insulate your basement and crawl spaces, too. Nearly a third of your energy bill can be saved by preventing heat loss through the basement floor.

A. *35 more years*
  Source: The Next Step: 50 More Things You Can Do To Save The Earth, *by the Earth • Works Group*

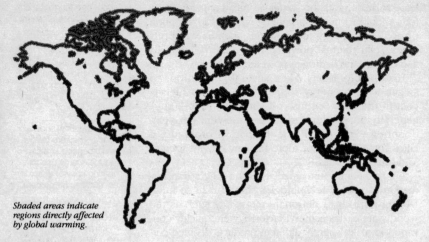

Shaded areas indicate regions directly affected by global warming.

WHAT YOU CAN DO:

HERE COMES THE SUN
• Burning fossil fuels is one of the main causes of the greenhouse effect. Switching to alternatives like solar energy will reduce global warming.

• Learn about it. Solar will never gain more acceptance if people do not know more about it.

• Check out demonstrations or exhibits of alternative energy. Science museums, nature centers or local utilities are likely places to find them.

USE LESS ENERGY
• Use hand tools instead of power tools, especially for small jobs. One kilowatt-hour of electricity saved will reduce carbon dioxide emissions at a coal-fired power plant by more than 2 pounds.

• Household energy use can contribute to global

Global Warming

- By Dr. Stephen H. Schneider -

Global warming has become, so to speak, the hottest topic in environmental conservation as the last decade of the 20th century begins.

Human industrial energy, produced largely by fossil fuels, inevitably produces carbon dioxide (CO_2) gas, and leads to a buildup of CO_2 in the atmosphere, adding to the natural greenhouse effect about 33 degrees Celsius (60 degrees Fahrenheit) of natural "greenhouse" warming. Since the industrial revolution, human activities (mostly fossil fuel burning, but perhaps 40 percent from deforestation) have led to a 25 percent increase in carbon dioxide, a 100 percent increase in methane and the introduction of human-made chemicals such as chlorofluorocarbons (CFCs). It is not controversial that these gases have trapped about two watts per square meter of extra radiative energy near the earth's surface since the industrial revolution, equivalent to the power of a small Christmas tree bulb in every square meter of earth.

What is controversial, however, is how to translate that extra two watts of heating into "x degrees" of temperature rise, since this involves yet unverifiable assumptions about how the heating will be distributed among temperature rise, evaporated water, melted ice, altered soil moisture, cloudiness, etc. These "feedback

Q: *If Americans would recycle one-tenth of their newspapers, how many million trees could be saved a year?*

processes" make our estimates of climatic warming from the buildup of greenhouse gases uncertain to about a factor of three. Most assessments, including the recent 200-scientist, UN-sponsored Intergovernmental Panel on Climate Change, have concluded that a warming of several degrees is quite likely by the middle of the next century and that a warming of four or more degrees Celsius is possible by the end of the next century. Human civilization, which developed over the past 10,000 years, has not experienced a planet more than one to two degrees warmer than present. A four-degree warming nearly equals the temperature difference between the end of the last ice age and the present interglacial epoch, a time that literally revamped the ecological face of the earth. Transitions in nature typically take 5,000 to 10,000 years; a climate change of several degrees in a century is at least 10 times, and perhaps 100 times, more rapid on a globally sustained basis than average natural change. This raises the specter of considerable disruption to natural ecological systems, human agriculture and water supplies, threatens to raise sea levels or intensify hurricanes, and could cause unknown alterations to human and animal health.

warming. Annual energy use for an average US household is between 7,000 and 10,000 kilowatt-hours (kwh) of electricity. You can keep about 1.5 pounds of CO_2 out of the atmosphere by conserving 1 kilowatt hour.

EDUCATE
• Slash-and-burn practices in the world's rainforests are adding untold amounts of CO_2 to the atmosphere. Take action to stop deforestation. Contact Rainforest Action Network, 301 Broadway, Ste. A, San Francisco, CA 94133, (415) 398-4404.

RESOURCES
• National Renewable Energy Laboratory, 1617 Cole Blvd., Golden, CO 80401-3393, (303) 231-1000.

Photo: Bob Pool/Tom Stack & Assoc.

Baked mud at the evaporating Warm Springs Reservoir in Stanfield, Oregon.

A. *25 million*
Source: The Recycler's Handbook, *by the Earth • Works Group*

• *Real Goods Source-book*, 966 Mazzoni St., Ukiah, CA 95482, (800) 762-7325. The bible of alternative energy products.

• National Appropriate Technology Assistance Service (NATAS), P.O. Box 2525, Butte, MT 59702-2525, (800) 428-2525. A public information phone line to help individuals and small businesses use renewable and other alternative energy sources.

• *The Greenhouse Trap*, by Francesca Lyman and the World Resources Institute, Beacon Press, Boston, 1990.

• *Global Warming*, by Stephen H. Schneider, Sierra Club Books, San Francisco, 1989.

DID YOU KNOW?
• Water waste adds CO_2 to the air. About 6 pounds of CO_2 are emitted with 1,000 gallons of water used, according to the Natural Resources Defense Council.

• Cars are a major contributor to global warming. Every gallon of gasoline burned adds 20 pounds of CO_2 to the air, and the average car uses 500 gallons a year.

• About 80 percent of the CO_2 released is caused by the burning of fossil fuels; the rest is caused mainly by deforestation. Some 24 billion metric tons of CO_2 are released each year, and that figure is steadily growing.

Estimates of societal and ecological disruptions have ranged from mildly beneficial to catastrophic. Currently, there is intense international debate among individuals, corporations, government officials and nations as to what, if anything, the world should do about this issue. Particular attention has focused on the creation of a framework convention to limit emissions of greenhouse gases.

The global warming environment/development debate has led to charges and countercharges about proposed actions or inactions that will condemn millions to poverty on the one hand or a planet to catastrophe on the other.

It is my belief that solutions can be found which do not require major unacceptable concessions from either side, at least for a period of a decade or so.

The magnitude of the investments needed to achieve environmentally sustainable development will probably take on the order of tens to hundreds of billions of dollars invested annually for decades. While this seems like a staggering sum on a global basis, the world currently spends some trillion dollars annually in armaments. The kinds of investments needed to deal with environmentally sustainable development are on the order of a tenth that amount.

If the world declared war on underdevelopment, overpopulation, over-affluence and environmental damage, it could cut back substantially its investment in armaments and divert perhaps half of those savings to environmentally sustainable development, allowing the rest to remain at home, satisfying demands for improved living conditions in all countries. Fundamentally, dealing with global warming is like dealing with many other global issues of environment, development and security. It involves a shift of priorities away from short-term national interests toward long-term global survival.

Dr. Stephen H. Schneider heads the Interdisciplinary Climate Systems Group at the National Center for Atmospheric Research. He is the author of over 100 papers and numerous books on climate, climatic change, the human impact on climate, the impact of climate on society, environmental policy, the effects of nuclear war on climate and the public understanding of science. He is co-author of The Coevolution of Climate and Life *and the author of* Global Warming.

Q. *How many tons of carbon dioxide can be absorbed annually by 800,000 square miles of young forest?*

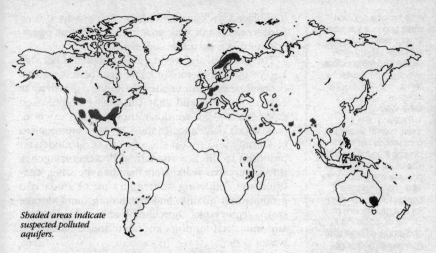

Shaded areas indicate suspected polluted aquifers.

Groundwater Pollution

- By Ann S. Maest and Lois Epstein -

Groundwater is the most mysterious part of our planet's hydrologic cycle. Many people imagine groundwater as pristine underground rivers that magically clean themselves of contaminants and supply us with an abundance of fresh, drinkable water. In the real world, underground rivers exist only infrequently in what are known as karst terrains (limestone areas carved by groundwaters). And groundwater, once contaminated, can remain so nearly indefinitely despite nature's magic and our best high-tech efforts to clean it.

Scientists and engineers once believed that "dilution was the solution to pollution," at least for surface waters. This naive axiom has proven to be ineffective for surface waters and even less appropriate for groundwater. The most common method for cleaning contaminated groundwater is to "pump and treat." This technique removes the tainted groundwater, chemically and physically treats it above ground to remove contaminants and then returns it to the aquifer (rock or soil that contains groundwater). Unfortunately, the aquifer material invariably holds some of the contamination and acts itself as a secondary source of contamination which will sully the cleaned water after

WHAT YOU CAN DO:

ECO-FLUSHING
• Each time you flush your toilet you use 5 to 7 gallons of water. But if you have a toilet tank, you can easily cut that amount by 15 percent to 40 percent. The cheapest and simplest way is to put a bottle in your toilet tank. Small juice bottles, dishwashing soap bottles or laundry soap bottles work well:

• Soak off the label, fill the bottle with water, put on the cap, and place it in the tank. To weight it you can put a few stones in the bottle.

• Be careful that the bottle doesn't interfere with the flushing mechanism.

• You may want to experiment with different bottle sizes. Different toilets need different amounts of water to maintain proper pressure for an effective flush.

A. **1 billion tons**
  Source: The Wilderness Society

• Or install a displacement bag or a toilet dam in your tank. These are available at hardware stores and are specifically designed for toilet tanks.

OILY WAY
• Throwing oil in the trash, even in an airtight container, is just like pouring it on the ground. The oil will leach out and contaminate groundwater when containers are crushed. Many mechanics and gas stations recycle the oil, so bring it in and drop it off or let them give you an oil change.

• Read *Recycling Used Oil,* EPA, Office of Solid Waste, 401 M St. SW, Washington, DC 20460. Tells you how to change and recycle your oil in ten easy steps.

GOODBYE OL' PAINT
• The easiest thing to do

it is placed back in the aquifer. This is why it is so hard to clean and why most pump and treat operations turn into perpetual care situations.

The health of the world's groundwaters is not well known in most cases. We know that there is massive contamination from unchecked industrial activity in eastern Europe and that this has contaminated groundwater—but we don't know to what extent or with which pollutants. In the US, states are required to identify and report the sources of groundwater pollution to the Environmental Protection Agency (EPA) every two years. More than half the states identified the following sources as major threats to groundwater quality: leaking underground storage tanks, septic tanks, agricultural activities, municipal and industrial landfills and abandoned hazardous wastes sites.

Other less-cited but equally insidious sources of contamination include: injection wells (deep wells used by industry to dispose of untreated hazardous and toxic wastes), land application of sewage and chemical sludges, road salting, salt water intrusion, salt and brine pits from oil extraction, mining activities, above-ground storage tanks, chemical spills and animal feedlots.

The deteriorated condition of much of the world's

Photo: Jorge Nuñez/Bettmann

Contaminated groundwater in Mexico City slums causes typhoid, dysentery and other serious health threats.

Q: *How many tons of carbon dioxide does the deforestation of virgin forests release each year?*

surface water, the difficulties and expense of cleaning groundwater and the fact that more than half of the population in the US alone (95 percent in rural areas) relies on groundwater for drinking, should compel us to use prevention as the real "solution to pollution."

But preventing groundwater pollution is difficult because there are millions of individual sources. For instance, there are approximately 5 million underground storage tanks (most store petroleum products), and 1 million of them are currently leaking. Most sources of groundwater contamination are "non-point" (they do not come out of a pipe), and these are more difficult to control than point sources of pollution.

Although many states have enacted their own groundwater protection legislation, no national groundwater protection legislation exists. A preventive groundwater program should identify and quantify all sources of pollution, protect all potentially potable water regardless of its current use, use standards below drinking water levels as "triggers" to warn of contamination before high levels are reached, and offer programs for reducing water and toxics use and for designing environmentally sound containments for pollution sources.

In the US and many other parts of the world, consumers do not pay the true price for drinking or irrigation water. The cost of cleaning already leaking underground storage tanks alone has been estimated at $70 billion. Higher water-use fees would be appropriate sources of money for these important projects.

Ann S. Maest is a hydrogeochemist specializing in water quality issues. While at Environmental Defense Fund (1989-1991), Dr. Maest developed approaches to promote pollution prevention and analyzed issues involving water quality, including groundwater protection and mining wastes. She is currently an environmental consultant in Boulder, Colorado, and specializes in water quality and hard rock mining waste issues.

Lois Epstein received her M.S. in civil engineering from Stanford University. She specializes in toxic chemicals issues, with particular expertise in groundwater. She has written two citizens' booklets on leaking underground storage tanks.

with old paint is to toss it in the garbage, but if you do that you will be contaminating soil and groundwater; 300 toxic substances have been found in commercial and latex paints. That gives you two alternatives: Use all your paint (couldn't it use a refresher coat?), or recycle it.

• To recycle, first separate oil-based paint from latex paint, and interior from exterior paint.

• If paint has been sitting around for years, check to see if it is still usable. The paint could be dried out or moldy, even if the lids have been on. If the paint is unusable, dispose of it at a hazardous waste facility.

• If your paint still looks fresh, and you have many cans of the same type, (i.e. latex or oil-based) try mixing them together. The blend makes a good primer—or a final coat, if you like the color.

• To recycle paint thinner: Put used thinner in a jar. Let it settle, then reuse the clean thinner on top, and let the sediment sink to the bottom. Eventually, you will accumulate enough sediment to necessitate disposal at a hazardous waste facility.

• Read *Paint Disposal...The Right Way*, National Paint and Coating Association, 1500 Rhode Island Ave. NW, Washington, DC 20005.

A. **About 1.4 billion tons**
   Source: Natural Resources Defense Council

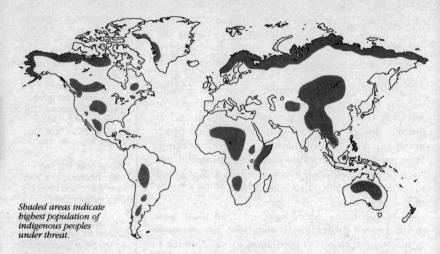

Shaded areas indicate highest population of indigenous peoples under threat.

WHAT YOU CAN DO:

• Look at *What You Can Do* under *Deforestation, Wilderness, Groundwater Pollution* and *Minorities and the Environment*—they all affect native peoples.

CONSCIOUSLY CONSUME
• Shop from catalogs that pay fair wages to indigenous people and support their culture by marketing their crafts.

• Contact Pueblo to People, P.O. Box 2545, Houston, TX 77252-2545, (800) 843-5257, for their catalog.

• The Body Shop Inc., 45 Horse Hill Rd., Hanover Tech Center, Cedar Knolls, NJ 07927, (201) 984-9200, makes shampoos and other cosmetics that are all-natural. They pay fair wages to the people who do their work in non-industrial countries.

Indigenous Peoples

- By Mary George Hardman -

There are an estimated 250 million tribal people in the world today, making up 4 percent of global population, living in over 70 countries. These people are often the victims of development for natural resources—minerals, oil, wood—and are treated as obstacles to "progress" of the so-called "developed" world. Their lands and lives are continually threatened by invasions of colonists and all too often ill-conceived development projects such as dam building, cattle ranching and highway construction.

Many of the world's tribal people live in tropical rainforests. By now, most people have heard the statistics: 50 million acres of rainforest are wiped out each year. That amounts to one and a half acres per second. But often these statistics ignore the human aspect of this environmental devastation.

Fewer than 6 percent of the tribal people survived the so-called "discovery" 500 years ago of the Amazon region in South America. Much of the destruction of these people stems from contempt for ways of living which developing countries do not understand. Underlying this contempt is racism, cultural arrogance, political and economic expediency and a total disregard for the human cost of environmental destruction.

Tribal people depend on land as no one else does.

Q: *What percentage of the tin on a can is saved when you recycle it?*

They get their food, medicines, building materials and spiritual meaning from their natural environment. Rather than being objects of study, exotic showpieces of tourism or potential converts to another religion, they are members of complex and viable societies with a sense of purpose, fulfillment and community that many in our "modern" societies might envy.

There is a difference between environmental rights and human rights problems, yet often they are one and the same. People do not exist outside of the environment, especially tribal people who live in rainforests. The traditional view of ecology is one of "destructive humans" versus "stable nature." When this view is applied to tribal people, the consequences are disastrous.

Whole tribes in Latin America have been annihilated because their land has been turned into national

Photo: Lionel Delevigne/Picture Group

A father and son from an endangered indigenous Amazon tribe at the Altamira Summit in Brazil in 1989.

WRITE
• Writing letters to governmental officials is one way any individual, anywhere in the world, can help tribal people. Letters have an impact on several levels. They let a government know that the outside world is watching, and they reinforce the voices of people within those governments and countries who are seeking to uphold tribal people's rights.

RESOURCES
• Contact Cultural Survival, 53A Church St., Cambridge, MA 01238, (617) 495-2562. They are working on a resource and guide book expected in spring 1992.

• Native Action, P.O. Box 316, Lame Deer, MT 59043, (406) 477-6390.

• Citizen Alert, 3680 Grant Ave., Suite J, Reno, NV 89509.

• Tonantzin Land Institute, P.O. Box 40182, Albuquerque, NM 87196-0182, (505) 256-0097.

• Native Resources Coalition, P.O. Box 93, Porcupine, SD 57772, (605) 867-5479.

• Good Road Coalition, 200 Legion Rd., Box 333, Rosebud, SD 57570, (605) 747-2874.

DID YOU KNOW?
• Loss of nature means loss of cultural diversity. Indigenous people have been living in balance with the land for thousands of years; it is

A. *80 percent*
  Source: The Recycler's Handbook, by the Earth•Works Group

inseparable from their culture, rituals and social fabric. As indigenous people are displaced by environmental destruction, their well-being and survival are threatened.

• There are more than 5,000 indigenous people's tribes in the world.

• If distinct African peoples are included, the figure above can double.

• In most countries, indigenous people are a minority:
—fewer than 0.1 percent in Brazil and Sweden
—fewer than 0.5 percent in the US

• In some countries they account for a large portion of the population:
—more than 90 percent in Greenland
—66 percent in Bolivia
—40 percent in Peru

• The greatest number of indigenous people are in Asia:
—86 million in China
—51 million in India, comprising 7 percent of the total population.

• Indigenous people are termed "fourth world peoples" because they believe that "the people belong to the land." This substantially differs from first, second and third world views, that "the land belongs to the people."

parks. People who have lived in remote natural habitats for thousands of years are suddenly denied land rights and forbidden to hunt in their traditional ways because developed countries decide to preserve animal species for our own study and pleasure. Yet it is not the tribal people who have brought the animals to the edge of extinction.

If tribal people are wiped out, we are going to lose much of the unique knowledge that they have on how to care for the environment. They've always been true conservationists. Unlike our fast, modern, "developed" society, tribal people developed ways to live in balance with their habitat—a balance that has not degraded their environment over millennia of use.

Tribal people understand the life-or-death struggle in which they are involved, and are becoming increasingly active in defense of their lives. They are forming their own organizations all around the world, communicating with each other and collectively demanding their rights.

Long-term solutions to the problems facing tribal people can only be found by changing worldwide public opinion. There is a great need for public education, a rewriting of history to let people know what really happened, that Columbus didn't "discover" America. Non-tribal people can get involved in this education, speak out, work in schools, try to provide alternative textbooks and other publications.

There is no way to put a price tag on what it would cost to save tribal people. The solution is not as simple as purchasing the land—tribal people should not have to buy their land. Even in cases where they are granted rights to land and continued use of the habitat, it's not the end of the story; they are continually threatened by colonists, or the discovery of gold or uranium. Indigenous people will never be secure. Not even in our dreams will their land be safe.

Mary George Hardman was executive director for four years of Survival International, USA, a worldwide movement established 20 years ago to support tribal people. She is now working as coordinator of the new Nashville Peace and Justice Center, headquarters for groups like Common Cause and Nashville SANE/FREEZE.

Q: *What renewable resource is the fourth largest export from the non-industrial countries?*

MAJOR INDIGENOUS PEOPLES UNDER THREAT

Africa

1. Western and Central Africa: Pygmy cultures threatened by tropical deforestation and encroachment of agriculture.

2. Mali and Niger: Tuareg nomads threatened by enforced settlement in refugee camps.

3. Central African Republic: Bororo peoples subjected to severe human rights abuse and expulsions.

4. Kenya: Masai under threat from land alienation. Degodia herders subjected to massacres; Somali herders subjected to massacre and human rights abuses.

5. Botswana and Namibia: San (Bushpeople) threatened by development and land alienation.

Asia

1. Bangladesh: Hill tribes of Chittagong threatened by resettlement programs.

2. Thailand: Karen peoples threatened by tribes displaced from the Indo-China war, and land exploitation for development.

3. Malaysia: Logging in Sabah and Sarawak threatens many indigenous peoples including the Penan. Kenyah and Kayan peoples threatened by a massive hydro-electric project.

4. Philippines: Manobo peoples threatened with land alienation by fruit and sugar cane plantations. Bangsa Moro peoples of southern Philippines threatened by various policies initiated by Marcos regime.

5. Indonesia: Oil exploration and government transmigration policy threaten indigenous peoples of Irian Jaya.

6. Micronesia: Indigenous peoples threatened by French and US weapons testing and military encroachment.

Central America

1. Guatemala: Guatamalan Maya Indians threatened by forced resettlement and military encroachment.

2. Nicaragua: Miskito Indians threatened as a result of civil war.

3. Costa Rica: Native reserves under threat from development and settlement.

4. Panama: 80,000 Guaymi threatened by private and state mining interests. East of the canal, Kuna under threat from tropical deforestation and developers.

South America

1. Columbia: Guambiano and Paez subject to land alienation.

2. Peru: Amuesha threatened by Pichis-Palcazu road project. Yagua threatened by mining interests.

3. Brazil: Grand Carajas hydro-electric scheme threatens many indigenous peoples. Yanomami threatened by mining interests. Txukarramae subjected to forcible land expulsion. Apinaye under threat from landless settlers.

4. Paraguay: Ache victims of genocide.

5. Chile: 1980s Government policy aimed at "liquidation of the Mapuche communities."

Arctic and Europe

1. Canada, USSR, Greenland, US: Inuit peoples face environmental degradation and pollution from mining projects, weapons testing and militarization in all five lands; also subjected to human rights violations.

2. Scandinavia: The Saami are subjected to environmental destruction due to governmental dam projects and pollution from western industry.

North America

1. Canada: Major groups include: Blackfoot, Iroquois, Oneida, Seneca, Cree, Innu, Meti, Micmac and Tuscarora. Deforestation and pollution due to governmental projects, especially the controversial James Bay Hydro-electric Dam, could destroy sacred lands of the James Bay Cree.

2. US: The Bureau of Indian Affairs recognizes 266 tribes and 216 Inuit and other peoples in Alaska. The most populous tribe suffering from environmental and cultural effects from mining projects are the Hopi. Iroquois and Lakota experienced severe cultural breakdown and environmental damage. Navajo are threatened by mining schemes and government mandated relocation of the most traditional Navajos at Big Mountain, Arizona. Shoshone are victims of weapons testing, militarization and serious human rights violations.

3. Mexico: Lacandon Maya Indians under threat from cattle ranchers and deforestation.

Sources: The Gaia Atlas of First Peoples, *by Julian Burger, Anchor Books, New York, 1990,* and Atlas of the Environment, *by the World Wildlife Fund, Prentice Hall Press, New York, 1990.*

A. *Natural rubber*
  Source: Natural Resources Defense Council

Shaded areas indicate presence of minorities involved in environmental activism.

WHAT YOU CAN DO:

• If there is already an industry in your neighborhood that you suspect is causing poor health among locals, you are faced with a monumental battle. You can push to ensure that safety standards are met and that emergency evacuation procedures are effective. In some cases, you can persuade the plant to shut down or move.

• If an industry is planning to move into your area, you may be an effective force in preventing it. It requires organization and, above all, persistence.

AWARENESS
• Go door to door, meet your neighbors, and ask them if they suffer from the same health conditions that you do. There is no substitute for going door to door. It is hard work, but essential.

Minorities and the Environment

- By Conger Beasley, Jr. -

In the old days it was different. A manufacturing company bought a big lot at a reduced rate along the bottomlands where a river curled through the old part of town. Immigrants lived in the bottomlands, foreign-speaking people from overseas who crowded into brick tenements with fresh laundry flapping from the windows and strange odors emanating through the walls. Children played in the garbage-strewn streets, vendors pushing two-wheeled carts hawked their wares, milk trucks drawn by spavined nags clattered along the cobblestones. Each morning a mass of pasty-faced men trudged down the street to the factory, where chimneys all day belched sooty fumes that settled over the tenements like a pall, soiling the laundry hung out to dry with a patina of grimy filth. Hard-working women drew water downstream from the factory, whose yawning pipes spilled forth the effluvium from the factory bowels, laced with trace minerals like mercury and lead. Even the most ignorant among the immigrants knew these conditions were deplorable, but to complain back then was to risk being stigmatized as an Anarchist or Socialist or (later) a Communist, which led to being blacklisted from a job which,

Q. *In 1990, what (above Antarctica) was the width of the US and the height of Mt. Everest?*

for the majority, was the only work they could find in the New World. So they toughed it out, breathing foul air, drinking the tainted water, polluting their lungs, corrupting their kidneys, dying of all sorts of liquid and protuberant diseases which the herbal and exorcistic formulas from the old countries were powerless to remedy. Meanwhile, the people who owned the factories and the agents who managed them lived high on the bluffs, upwind from the billowing stacks, where they enjoyed fresh water and varied their diets with vegetables and fruit.

With an inexhaustible pool of raw labor, with no legal process by which workers could agitate for better conditions, with markets opening up everywhere as new territories were converted into states, with the iron tracks of the railroad spanning land where buffalo once fed, it was easy to be bullish about this vast and expanding country. If a few immigrants contracted black lung or were seized by the bloody flux or developed tumors, well, that was the price an emerging superpower paid for the kind of rapid industrialization that was required to make it competitive with older industrial nations like Britain and France.

The children of the immigrants grew up, went to school, changed their names, married the sons and

Compile a database of your neighbors, including names, addresses, ailments and complaints.

MEET
• Hold public meetings. Contact your city council and invite them to a meeting of your neighbors and express your concerns.

RESEARCH
• Research other situations like yours. Find out if anyone in a nearby community has organized a similar committee. Research the company's history. Research the processes used at the plant in your neighborhood to understand what may be in the smoke that fills the sky.

REACH OUT
• Try reaching your local Environmental Protection Agency, television

Photo: Jimmy Dorantes/Gamma-Liaison

Many Hispanic farmworkers and other minority groups are exposed to unsafe agricultural pesticides.

A. *The ozone "hole"*
  Source: *Friends of the Earth*

station, newspaper, environmental groups, fish and wildlife service and your government environmental department, maybe a forester. If they can't help you they can direct you to someone who can.

CONTACT THE "ENEMY"
• After your research, if you have reason to believe your health effects were are caused by the industry, you must confront the company directly. Contact the public relations person at the plant and invite him or her to a meeting. At the meeting, present the information you gathered from your research and from your neighbors. Ask for information about the plant's processes and health records. If the company will not cooperate, use your leverage—through media, petitions and leaflets. Tell them you will be at the plant gates the next morning handing out pamphlets to workers and you will call the local television station.

RESOURCES
When you get discouraged:

Read:
• *Not In Our Backyards! Community Action For Health and the Environment*, by Nicholas Freudenberg, Monthly Review Press, New York, 1984.

• *Organizing: A Guide for Grassroots Leaders*, by Si Khan, McGraw-Hill, New York, 1981.

• *Of Pollution and Poverty*, by Conger Beasley,

daughters of the local gentry, invigorated their bloodlines, forced the system to expand and adapt, but remained capitalists to the core, firmly supportive of the American way of life. Meanwhile new waves of immigrants, mainly people of color—Latinos from south of the border, African Americans from the Mississippi Delta, Native Americans from the reservations, orientals from Southeast Asia—moved into the shabby brick tenements on the river bottoms and precipitated a whole new cycle of ferment and assimilation. But this time it wasn't the same. Unlike the Slavs and Italians and Irish who preceded them, these people were implacably different, with the customs and pigmentation to prove it. Assimilation for them would require a higher degree of personal sacrifice. Because of their non-European origins, some portion of their lives would always remain alien to the "mainstream" of American life.

Today it's not so easy for a company to move into a minority neighborhood and in return for a smattering of jobs send columns of smoke spiraling into the air and streams of toxic chemicals flooding into the watertable. The network of prospective laws administered by a ponderous bureaucracy has swelled unimaginably in the last hundred years; however, these laws traditionally have dealt with economic rather than environmental concerns, with wages and benefits rather than work-place conditions, with earning power rather than health issues.

Fortunately, in the last decade of the 20th century, new emphasis has been placed on the healthiness of the environment. Ultimately, there is no wage or benefit that can compensate for the ruination of the habitat in which one lives and works. Minorities and people of color are beginning to realize this and to take constructive steps to prevent it from happening. The number of grassroots organizations that have sprung up around the world during the past three decades is one of the most heartening developments in the gradual democratization of international politics. From India to Ecuador, from Zimbabwe to Lithuania, peasants and factory workers are saying "no" to economic ventures that threaten their health and well-being. According to Worldwatch Institute, in Indonesia alone there are 600 independent groups focusing on local environmental grievances. In Peru, the people in Lima's shantytowns are partially fed through as many as 1,500 community kitchens staffed

Q: *According to the USDA, using biological control to counter pest attacks brings how many dollars of benefit for every dollar invested?*

and operated by local women. In Sri Lanka, a "village awakening movement" to help lessen agricultural pollution has had a favorable impact upon nearly one-third of that island country's townships.

The real work has barely begun. With so many predators lurking in the wings (especially in the waste-disposal business in the US, as urban landfills top out to capacity), pressure on impoverished minority communities, such as those on Native American reservations, to yield to the lure of the buck has become enormous. Some communities in the USA have already suffered disastrously from unregulated industries. The deleterious health effects upon poor communities in Louisiana as a result of emissions from scores of petro-chemical refineries is incalculable. With no baseline health data and a manufacturer's lobby that insidiously subverts all efforts at clean-up, opportunities to rectify the situation are few.

It's time for minorities and people of color to take control of their destinies. The most effective point at which to stop an industry from polluting a region, neighborhood or reservation is *before* that industry has a chance to locate on the premises. And the way to do this is for people to become involved; in other words, *political*, which in the US has practically become a dirty word. But getting organized, standing up, voicing objections, offering alternatives, is the only way that disenfranchised people can protect themselves. The system ignores individuals on this matter; only organizations possess the necessary clout. It takes a bunch of fingers to make an effective fist. And a fist is what minorities must flourish if they want to be recognized. Today, all over the world, that lesson is being absorbed and translated into action by minorities and people of color who are determined to maintain their racial and cultural identities in the face of an economic Juggernaut that threatens to steamroll them into oblivion.

Conger Beasley, Jr., is a regular contributor to Buzzworm: The Environmental Journal. *He focuses on minority issues and was awarded the 1991 World Hunger Media Award for Journalism for his three-part* Buzzworm *series,* Of Pollution and Poverty. *His most recent article for* Buzzworm, Of Landfill Reservations, *examines the pros and cons of building a nine-square-mile landfill on the Rosebud Lakota reservation.*

Jr., three-part series in Buzzworm: The Environmental Journal, May/June 1990, July/August 1990, September/October 1990.

CONTACT OTHER GROUPS
• Southwest Organizing Project/Southwest Network for Environmental and Economic Justice, 211 10th St. SW, Albuquerque, NM 87102, (505) 247-8832.

• United Church of Christ Commission for Racial Justice, 475 Riverside Dr., Room 1948, New York, NY 10115, (212) 870-2077.

• Gulf Coast Tenants Association, P.O. Box 56101, New Orleans, LA 70156, (504) 949-4919.

• Community Environmental Health Center at Hunter College, 425 E. 25th St., Box 596, New York, NY 10010, (212) 481-4355.

• For a more complete list, see *Indigenous Peoples*, page 108.

• Invite a speaker to your community. Greenpeace and the Green party offer speakers for the price of a meal. Many other groups offer inspirational speakers.

A. *About $30*
Source: US Department of Agriculture

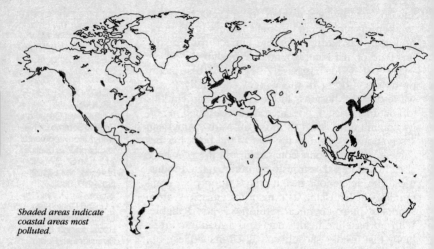

Shaded areas indicate coastal areas most polluted.

Ocean Pollution

- By Dr. Justin Lancaster -

The open ocean is healthy, because contaminants readily disperse in its vast volume. However, pollution from plastics, oil and nuclear wastes still present a concern. Floating plastic debris, often pieces of broken gill nets, kill fish and marine mammals. Oil in the ocean occurs naturally, but constant discharges and spills from ships contaminate the surface microlayer, an organic film which hosts floating larvae. Nuclear wastes were dumped into the ocean between the 1940s and mid-1980s. Although not a threat today, such dumping may be revisited as waste loads exhaust land options. Chernobyl's radioactive fallout has reached the Mediterranean and Black Seas through river runoff. Because nuclear wastes decay so slowly, any steady source to the ocean poses a long-term threat.

The coastal ocean, which includes seas, gulfs, bays, sounds, harbors and estuaries, is not healthy. Almost half the world's people now live near the coastal zone and the resulting stress is severe. Pollution from point sources (sewage outfalls, industrial plants) and from nonpoint sources (storm drains, agricultural runoff, atmospheric deposition and boats) presents risks to human health through contaminated seafood or direct human contact at beaches, endangers the health and survival of fishery resources and

Q. *Cortisone, a drug for skin irritations, and Diosgenin, the active ingredient in birth control pills, were originally derived from plants found where?*

degrades the aesthetic environment. The coastal habitats in jeopardy include mangrove swamps and coral reefs. These ecosystems hold value like the tropical rainforest—a billion-year old genetic heritage resides in a tremendous variety of species.

Sewage and other wastewater discharges carry toxins, pathogens and other contaminants into the coastal environment. Toxicants are absorbed on sludge particles and sludge is increasing along coastlines. Increased discharges are killing shellfish, both from pathogens in poorly treated water and from chlorine in over-treated water.

Our poisons have spread over all the oceans; DDT and PCBs have been found in Arctic seals and Antarctic penguins. Restricting pollution in the developed nations has led environmentally unfriendly industries to build new large industrial parks in developing nations where coastal protections hardly exist.

In the United States, marine protection legislation dates back more than a century. Modern enforcement

• Next time you go to the beach, bring a trash bag. Then spend a few minutes picking up trash.

RESULTS
• Join the National Beach Cleanup. Call the Center for Marine Conservation, 1725 DeSales St. NW, Suite 500, Washington, DC 20036, (202) 429-5609. Every year they sponsor a nationwide beach cleanup usually conducted in September during Coast Week. *Cleaning North America's Beaches: 1990 Beach Cleanup Results*, is based on 1990's cleanup. During a three hour period, some 109,000 volunteers participated, collecting

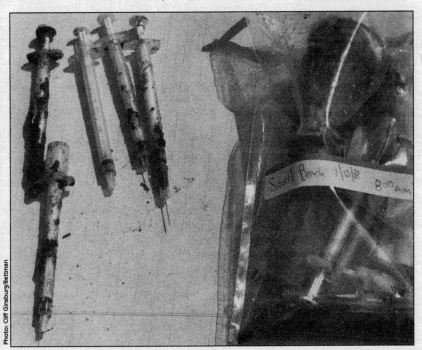

Photo: Cliff Ginsburg/Bettman

Medical and other waste from municipal sewage treatment plants has become a source of ocean pollution.

A. *In the Mexican and Guatemalan rainforests*
. Source: *Natural Resources Defense Council*

1,323 tons of trash from 3,656 miles of coastline. Volunteers collected 4,375,567 items of trash:

• Plastic debris was the most abundant item: 63.9 percent of all trash.

• Cigarette filters were the number one debris item: 531,828 collected.

• Number of wildlife specimens found during the cleanup either entangled in or having ingested trash: 142.

• Percentage of affected wildlife that was entangled in monofilament fishing line: 33.

• Number of plastic syringes collected: 3,738.

• Plastic tampon applicators: 17,125.

• Plastic beverage bottles: over 100,000.

• Plastic six-pack holders: 34,722.

• Balloons: 26,536.

• Number of kitchen sinks found during the cleanup: 10.

DID YOU KNOW?
• Today, the ports of Los Angeles, San Francisco and New York each host about 1,000 tanker visits a year. Some 4,000 oil platforms dot the new frontier, from the chilly waters of Alaska to the humid Gulf of Mexico. On this busiest marine frontier, some 25,000 kilometers of oil pipelines crisscross the seabed and coastal wetlands.

began to take shape with the Federal Water Pollution Control Act of 1956, and the legislation grew much stronger with the Clean Water Act amendments of 1977, which increased the authority of the EPA to regulate discharges into rivers, lakes and coastal waters. The Marine Protection, Research and Sanctuaries Act of 1972 (known as the Ocean Dumping Act) gave EPA and the National Oceanic and Atmospheric Administration (NOAA) important control over waste dumping.

There are many opportunities to step toward improved health of the coastal ocean. We must improve criteria for water quality, develop new health indicators for sewage and fund a reinvigorated mussel watch program. We should also study nontoxic waste disposal in the deep ocean, map coastal sludge deposits, and we must prohibit the use of plastic gill nets and require double-hulled tankers. Positive steps would include increasing US support of the United Nations Environment Program and improving our overall waste disposal strategy.

The improvement of public waste treatment in coastal cities, and the creation of cleaner industrial and agricultural practices, would cost more than a trillion dollars over the next 20 or 30 years. Yet less than 1 percent of the federal budget addresses environmental quality. The costs will not be as much for cleaning up the ocean as for curtailing the steady contamination from various sources. If the total cost is a trillion dollars, then global costs for improving the quality of the coastal ocean would exceed $30 billion per year, which is approximately 0.2 percent of the world's gross economic product.

It is encouraging that so much progress has been made over the past decade, yet the tremendous burden that a rapidly growing human population puts on the resources of the coastal zone, especially fisheries, mandates increased attention to the problem of coastal pollution. Although global in nature, solutions to oceanic pollution still can be applied locally and obtain rapid improvements.

Dr. Justin Lancaster is currently a research fellow at the Harvard School of Public Health. He is the executive director of the Environmental Science and Policy Institute. He was previously a post-doctoral researcher at the California Space Institute at Scripps Institution of Oceanography.

Q: *What causes four-fifths of all illness in non-industrial countries?*

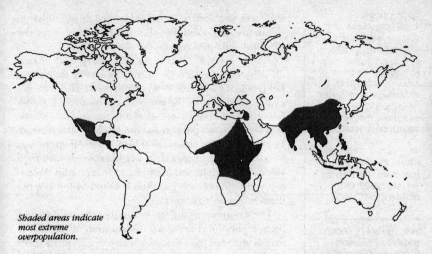

Shaded areas indicate
most extreme
overpopulation.

Overpopulation

- By Garrett Hardin -

The ecological view of population is based on the ideas of limits and interconnectedness. Business bookkeeping assumes limits: The books must balance. Science assumes limits: Equations must balance. In population theory the idea of limits leads to what has been called the "Eleventh Commandment": *Thou shalt not transgress the carrying capacity of the environment.*

In the 19th century technologists greatly increased the rate at which new stores of nature's riches were opened to humankind. Later, when radioactivity was discovered, it seemed for awhile as though there were no practical limits to energy. Ernest Rutherford said that the energy in one pound of radioactive material was as great as the energy in 100,000,000 pounds of coal. This appeared to make the limitedness of the Earth almost irrelevant.

Back in 1798, Malthus had thought that food would limit the size of the human population. But the per capita production of food is now greater than it was in Malthus's time. And given a bountiful supply of energy, we can always produce more food. So was Malthus completely wrong?

At this point the second great generalization of ecology is called for: *We can never do merely one thing.* As we utilize energy we cause unwanted changes. Particularly this is true with radioactive energy. Unwanted products are forms of pollution. The earthly "sinks"—air, water—

WHAT YOU CAN DO:

• The world's population grows annually by 95 million. Educate yourself about the complex issues surrounding overpopulation.

• If you are pro-choice, find out which politicians are pro-choice and support them. Write letters to politicians who are nonchoice and tell them why you do not support them. (See *How to Write Congress*, page 340)

• Whether you are pro-choice or opposed to all abortion, be constructive; organize in your community for birth control availability and better sex education in local schools.

• Join an advocacy group that promotes education, understanding and medical services for the world population to stabilize.

A. *Waterborne diseases*
Source: Atlas of the Environment, *by the World Wildlife Fund*

RESOURCES

• Zero Population Growth, 1400 16th St. NW, Suite 320, Washington, DC 20036, (202) 332-2200.

• Planned Parenthood of America, 810 Seventh Ave., New York, NY 10019, (212) 541-7800.

• Population Crisis Committee, 1120 19th St. NW, Suite 550, Washington, DC 20036, (202) 659-1833.

• *The Population Explosion*, by Paul R. Ehrlich and Anne H. Ehrlich, Simon and Schuster, New York, 1990.

DID YOU KNOW?

• More than 90 percent of the projected increase in population between now and 2025 will take place in developing nations in Africa, Asia and

that have to absorb pollution are limited. It seems that in the future, pollution, not shortage of food, will set the Malthusian limit to population.

A basic measure in ecological accounting is the "carrying capacity" of the environment. A humanly satisfactory life requires a lot more than merely food. The "cultural carrying capacity" of the environment includes its ability to be converted to homes, clothing, automobiles, television sets—the list goes on and on. Most of our wants can be expressed in energy units. The average American uses 100 times more energy than would be needed for food alone. The carrying capacity of a territory for an American-style life is much less than it would be for, say, the lifestyle of a poor African.

The existence of differences in lifestyles in different parts of the world brings up the question of "rights." Is there a universal right to food, which preempts other rights (e.g. private property and national sovereignty)? When people in rich countries hear of deaths by starvation in equatorial Africa, they naturally want to send food. The intention is admirable, but the results can be tragic.

Consider Ethiopia. The population has already grown beyond the mere "survival carrying capacity" of the land. The cattle are in wretched condition, and the over-exploited soil is washing down the rivers. In a sense, the

Photo: J-P Laffont/Sygma

Sunday on Nanjing Road in Shanghai, China, the country that houses one-quarter of the world's population.

Q: *On Earth Day, April 22, 1990, people celebrating in New York City left how many tons of litter in Central Park?*

too-numerous Ethiopians are "eating up" their land. Food sent to the country from outside will keep more Ethiopians alive, thus enabling them to eat up their land faster.

The ethicist Joseph Fletcher has given this rule for philanthropy: *Give if it helps, but not if it hurts.* In estimating the probable effect of a foreign intervention we should consider not only today, but tomorrow. And the day after tomorrow. Gifts of food that speed up the destruction of the carrying capacity are hard to justify.

Refusing to make gifts of food shifts the responsibility to the people who have produced the need. Those who produce pregnancies must accept the responsibility for keeping the product—babies, then people—alive.

To prevent ruination of the human environment, reproduction must be controlled. Both birth control and population control are needed. Birth control requires knowledge and materials, and individual decisions to use them. Birth control is a technological problem.

Population control, however, requires a community decision to promote (and perhaps enforce) birth control among individuals. Reaching the needed consensus is a political problem; outsiders cannot solve this problem. Each sovereign nation must find "acceptable" ways of persuading its citizens to use birth control often enough to achieve population control. If this political problem is not localized, and solved, the resources of the entire globe will be threatened.

When asked to indicate on a map where the worst population problems are generated, we are uncertain how to proceed. Places in the grip of poverty, deforestation and soil erosion, are shown on the accompanying map. But overpopulation *and overuse of resources* produce pollution of air and water that affect all regions—even Antarctica, where there are no permanent human settlements. To show truly the location and sources of all population-generated problems *all* regions of the world would have to be colored.

After earning his Ph.D. at Stanford, working on problems in the ecology of protozoa, Garrett Hardin taught general biology at the college level for more than twenty years. His textbook, Biology, Its Principles and Implications, *went through five editions. Becoming convinced that the principles of biology impinge on many areas of ethics, he published several books, including* The Limits of Altruism, Promethean Ethics, *and* New Ethics for Survival. *He has just finished writing a book entitled* The Population Maze.

Latin America; at present growth rates, these countries will double in population in 33 years.

• Nigeria, an African country twice the size of California, has one of the fastest growing populations in the world. Its population is expected to double in 22 years. At the present rate, the population of Nigeria will equal the entire population of the world today in 140 years.

• Countries with rapid population growth rank low on measures of the physical quality of life and high on measures of human suffering. Rapid growth is often accompanied by severe environmental degradation, including deforestation, desertification and soil erosion.

• The US is one of the fastest-growing industrialized countries. The current US population of 251 million grows by 2.3 million each year and is projected to reach at least 268 million by the year 2000, more than double the 1940 population of 132 million.

• To accommodate the growing population, nearly 3,500 acres of rural land are bulldozed in the US each day to create space for new buildings, highways and other development.

A. *Almost 160 tons*
Source: Department of Parks NYC

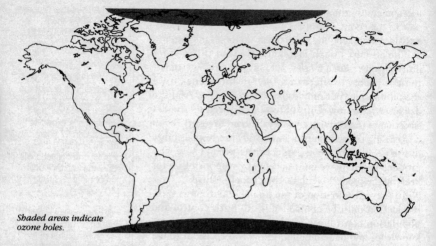

Shaded areas indicate ozone holes.

WHAT YOU CAN DO:

BE AN OZONE ACTIVIST
• Make a list of ozone-damaging products and take it shopping. Pick stores where you often shop. As a regular customer, your opinion carries weight. Grocery, hardware, auto supply and stereo stores all sell products that contain ozone depleting compounds.

• Share the list of ozone depleting products with the store manager. Suggest alternatives. For example: Aerosol dust removers that contain CFCs can be replaced with canned, compressed air. It works just as well for cleaning home stereo and photography equipment.

• Check the labels; get manufacturers' names and addresses. Let them know you will not buy

Ozone Depletion

- By Richard Elliot Benedick -

It is no exaggeration to state that life as it has evolved on Earth is dependent on the existence of a thin shield of molecules of a poisonous and unstable gas scattered throughout the upper atmosphere. This so-called ozone layer, six to 30 miles above the planet's surface, would, if compressed at ground level, amount to a veil as thin as gauze. And yet, the presence of an equilibrium level of ozone in the stratosphere, although individual molecules are continually being destroyed and recreated by natural chemical and radiative processes, serves to absorb lethal forms of ultraviolet radiation coming from the sun and thereby preventing them from reaching the planet's surface.

Even a slight depletion of the stratospheric ozone layer would allow an increased level of this radiation to reach earth, resulting, for humans, in millions of additional deaths from skin cancer, blindness from cataracts and injury to the immune system. It would also bring potentially catastrophic damage to marine life and agriculture. In addition, changes in the distribution of ozone at different altitudes could affect the world's climate in unpredictable ways.

In the early 1970s, some scientists warned that the ozone layer could be in jeopardy. They theorized that

Q: *What consumes one-fifth of the US's energy usage?*

certain human-made chemicals, called chlorofluoro-carbons (CFCs), had the capability of releasing chlorine atoms in the stratosphere which could unleash a complicated catalytic chain reaction resulting in the destruction of ozone.

These theories caused turmoil in the scientific community and were hotly debated for years. The powerful chemical industry and others mobilized their own efforts to deny vigorously that such useful chemicals, which were practically synonymous with modern standards of living, could be harmful. Indeed, CFCs and related compounds were being used in a growing range of industries and products, including refrigeration, air conditioning, aerosol sprays, insulation, health care, transportation, plastics, agriculture, fire fighting, telecommunications and electronics, to name but a few. Emissions of these chemicals into the atmosphere were rapidly approaching a million tons annually. Billions of dollars in investments and hundreds of thousands of jobs were at stake worldwide.

A process of negotiation was launched in 1982 that led to the first truly global environmental agreement. The 1985 Vienna Convention provided for international cooperation in research, monitoring and exchange of information. The even more significant 1987 Montreal Protocol on substances that deplete the ozone layer mandated far-reaching global controls over the suspect chemicals.

their products until they are "ozone friendly."

HOLD ON TO CFCS
• You may know that chlorofluorocarbons (CFCs) are destroying the ozone layer. But Methyl Chloroform (also called 1,1,1 trichloro-ethene), although weaker than CFCs, is used in larger quantities. It is in products like correction fluid, dry cleaning sprays, leather cleaners and aerosols—even some labelled "ozone friendly." Businesses use it mainly as a cleaning solvent in the fabrication of metal. It is also frequently used to fabricate adhesives and clean electronic parts.

• Have your refrigerators, freezer and automobile air conditioning checked. Pick a mechanic that uses a "vampire" (new machines that suck coolants out of appliances and trap them in bottles for recycling). Be sure your home air

A polystyrene recycling plant in Leominster, Massachusetts; an alternative to dumping ozone-depleting styrofoam in landfills.

Photo: Rob Crandall/Picture Group

A. *Lighting*
• Source: The Recycler's Handbook, *by the Earth • Works Group*

conditioner and refrigerator are serviced by a CFCs recycler, too. However, do not get unnecessary service on your air conditioner since this often releases CFCs.

• Buy only halon-free fire extinguishers. They say "Dry Chemical" or "Sodium Bicarbonate" on the label.

RESOURCES
• *Public Enemy 1,1,1*, The Natural Resources Defense Council, 40 W. 20th St., New York, NY 10011. A publication describing ozone-depleting products. The group also has information on ozone depletion and other environmental issues. NRDC also offers the Earth Action Guide *Saving the Ozone Layer.*

• Information and fact sheets on ozone-depleting products and compounds are available from Local Solutions to Global Pollution, 2121 Bonar St., Studio A, Berkeley, CA 94702.

• *Protecting the Ozone Layer: What You Can Do*, Environmental Defense Fund, 257 Park Ave. S., New York, NY 10010. A citizen's guide to reducing use of ozone-depleting chemicals.

These historic treaties represent the first time that the international community of nations could agree on taking costly short-term preventative actions to protect against future risks—before there was firm scientific evidence of damage.

In June 1990 in London, the protocol was significantly strengthened: More chemicals were brought under control and most were scheduled for complete phase-out within ten years. Additionally, 70 nations agreed to the first-ever global environmental fund to assist developing nations in acquiring new technology to permit them to bypass CFCs while not denying their citizens needed products to improve their living standards.

Nonetheless, challenges lie ahead. First, faced with impending phase-outs, industry has embarked on ambitious research programs to develop effective substitutes. While the costs of transition to safer substances will mount into billions of dollars, the new technologies will also create jobs and bring profits to innovative enterprises.

Second, to ensure that the treaty is not undermined, more developing countries must accept the protocol's obligations. This will depend on translating the good intentions of the London provisions into effective financial aid and technological transfer policies.

With these measures—and barring unexpected new scientific revelations—the international community has mounted a remarkable effort to protect the ozone layer from future damage. The Montreal Protocol, which many had once considered an impossible dream, is a genuine success story and one of the great international achievements.

Richard Elliot Benedick is a senior fellow of World Wildlife Fund, on detail from the State Department. He also serves as Special Advisor to the Secretary-General of the United Nations Conference on Environment and Development. He was chief US negotiator for the Montreal Protocol on protection of the ozone layer; his account of this landmark process, Ozone Diplomacy: New Directions in Safeguarding the Planet, *was published in 1991 by Harvard University Press. He has received the two highest presidential career public service honors, the 1988 Distinguished Service Award and the 1983 and 1990 Meritorious Service Awards.*

Q: *What percentage of Americans stated in a recent Gallup poll that they were willing to change their purchasing habits to buy items in recycled or recyclable containers?*

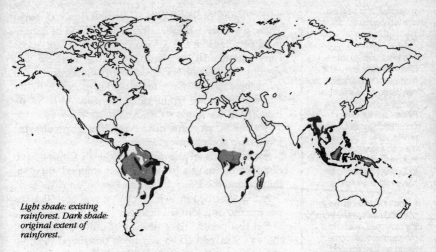

Light shade: existing rainforest. Dark shade: original extent of rainforest.

Rainforest Conservation

- By Randall Hayes -

Like most jail cells, this one was battleship gray, cold, and sterile. Staring down the hall into other cells I searched out any action that might break the terrible boredom. At least the thick steel bars provided something to grip and steady myself against the tedium. How ironic that my love for the rich green tropical rainforest should land me in such infertile environs.

My mind drifted back to my recent trip into the center of the Amazon. I could see the animal tracks in the mud as well as strange creatures under every leaf. I could hear countless sounds in the thick canopy above. As the sun set, fierce howler monkeys screeched. Blue iridescent mushrooms glowed in the darkness. The forest comes alive at night.

It was because of the rainforest, and its rapid disappearance, that I was in jail. Thirteen of us led a nonviolent protest against the World Bank and International Monetary Fund, blockading the limousine entrance to the annual meeting. The bank uses public money to fund development projects in countries like Brazil, Zaire and Indonesia. The World Bank has hijacked the public's generosity and kowtowed to the interests of multinational corporations, funding

WHAT YOU CAN DO:

• The greatest influence you may have is with people who provide financial support to countries with rainforests. Write letters expressing your concern. Write to your elected representatives.

• Promote "debt-for-nature" swaps. Here's how they work: Conservation groups buy part of a developing country's foreign debt, which most foreign commercial banks are glad to sell at a deep discount. The groups that buy the debt then sell it to the debtor country's central bank, which translates the debt into local currency and invests its face value in conservation.

CONSCIOUSLY CONSUME
• Support organizations involved in rainforest conservation. Indigenous people in the Amazon are trying to foster their own sustainable

A. **More than 50 percent**
Source: Pennsylvania Resources Council

rainforest-based economy; they need your support.

• Support new companies that are widening the market for sustainably harvested products from the rainforest. From the Rainforest, for example, donates 5 percent of their profits, as well as 5 percent on every pound of fruit and nuts purchased, to Cultural Survival, a non-profit organization.

• Don't buy things made of woods that come from the rainforest, such as mahogany, teak, rosewood and zebrawood. When buying furniture, ask the salespeople questions about what kind of wood you are buying and where it came from. Or try to buy secondhand wood items from thrift shops, yard sales or the "For Sale" section of the newspaper.

RESOURCES
• Rainforest Action

infrastructure projects such as dams and paved roads. These dams have flooded forest homelands of indigenous peoples like the Amazon's Kayapo. These roads carry commercial logging trucks, cattle ranchers, and agribusiness exporters of coffee, bananas and palm oil at the expense of the forest and its peoples.

The results are frightening. By now, most of us have heard the tragic statistics:

• over 50 percent of the world's tropical rainforests are gone forever.

• two-thirds of the Southeast Asian forests have disappeared, mostly for hardwoods shipped to Japan, Europe and the US.

• this destruction continues at a rate of 150 acres per minute or a football field per second.

But few people have heard that only 10 percent of the vast Amazon basin has been destroyed. Yes, 90 percent is still an ecological treasure. Fewer still know that in recent years an ever more powerful citizens' movement has shut down well over $1 billion of those bulldozing, bad investments.

With increasing success, heroic activists from Malaysia, Tokyo, The Netherlands, Brazil, Toronto, Atlanta, Boulder, Colorado, and even Washington, DC, have challenged the international economic order. People, lots of ordinary people, are doing extraordinary things. They have refused to cooperate in the face of such ecological injustice.

Photo: Altamiro Nunes/AP/Wide World Photos

An Amazon rainforest in Rondonia, Brazil, is burned to clear the land for cattle grazing or agriculture.

Q: *In France, how many representatives of the Green Party were elected to City Councils in 1989?*

Do you want to know how to plug into this movement? Those of us in the northern industrial countries bear a large part of the responsibility for the loss of the rainforest. The up side to this is that you have political leverage right here in the US that, if exercised, will help save large tracts of tropical rainforest. Rather than flooding forests, your foreign aid tax dollars can fund ecologically sound agriculture in areas surrounding intact forests. This can buffer the forests from the human tide. Our purchasing of rainforest beef for greasy hamburgers can be stopped. With public pressure, our importing of mahogany and cheap rainforest plywood can be banned.

I believe that in the short term there is more to be done in Japan, Europe and the US to save rainforests than in Brazil, Zaire or Malaysia. I also believe that politicians or professional planners won't save the forest for us. People-power got the US out of Vietnam. People-power provides the "leaders" with the guts to act. Politicians are typically followers and you, as citizen activists, are the true leaders.

Is it in your personal vision that rainforests will be saved? And if you choose to bring out the Martin Luther King, Jr., Rachel Carson and Gandhi in yourself, and act fast and ferociously on your convictions—then, in partnership with our friends in the rainforest countries, we will stop this ecological insanity, this march of false progress, and save the rainforest.

Yes, the forest comes alive in the nighttime. But in the daytime it is quiet and serene. I had to laugh again as my mind drifted back to my hands gripping the thick steel bars. Eight hours of Washington, DC, jail provided some much-needed rest and relaxation. For a few minutes it was soothing, almost refreshing. Jail time—perhaps it is not such a bad thing after all.

Randall Hayes is the founder and director of Rainforest Action Network. His training ground as an activist was documentary filmmaking. He produced the award-winning film, "The Four Corners, A National Sacrifice Area?" Now, as director of Rainforest Action, Randy is a leader in the effort to halt destruction of tropical rainforest and the fight for the rights of indigenous people. He works with organizers and regional networks in Africa, Australia, Latin America, Southeast Asia, Japan, North America and Europe in building a world rainforest movement.

Network, 301 Broadway, Suite A, San Francisco, CA 94133, (415) 398-4404. They have information on rainforests and what you can do to help.

• Rainforest Alliance, 270 Lafayette St., Suite 512, New York, NY 10012, (212) 941-1900.

• *The Rainforest Book,* by Scott Lewis with the Natural Resources Defense Council, Living Planet Press, Los Angeles, 1990.

DID YOU KNOW?
• One in four pharmaceuticals comes from a plant in a tropical rainforest. About 70 percent of plants identified by the National Cancer Institute as being useful in cancer treatment are found only in rainforests.

• The world's major cocoa-growing regions of West Africa would be out of business in a generation or so without the new genetic material from the forests of west Amazonia on which they depend.

• 80 percent of all Amazonian deforestation has taken place since 1980.

• The rainforests are being depleted because of agriculture and population resettlement, beef cattle ranching, logging and major power projects like hydroelectric plants and the roads that go with them.

• Consider alternatives to tropical hardwoods when buying furniture, lumber and plywood.

 A. *2,000*
Source: Can America Learn From the Greens? LA Weekly *July 14-20, 1989, by John Powers*

GOING

Countries with significant tropical forests: projected percentages of rainforest existing in 1989 that will still remain in the year 2000, at the current rates of deforestation.

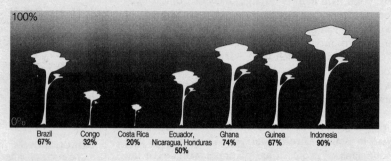

Brazil	Congo	Costa Rica	Ecuador, Nicaragua, Honduras	Ghana	Guinea	Indonesia
67%	32%	20%	50%	74%	67%	90%

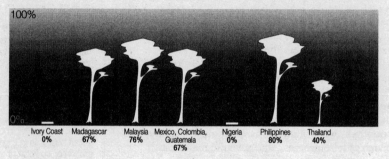

Ivory Coast	Madagascar	Malaysia	Mexico, Colombia, Guatemala	Nigeria	Philippines	Thailand
0%	67%	76%	67%	0%	80%	40%

GONE

The following countires have already destroyed large amounts of their rainforest: percentage of original rainforest remaining in 1989.

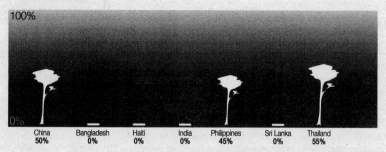

China	Bangladesh	Haiti	India	Philippines	Sri Lanka	Thailand
50%	0%	0%	0%	45%	0%	55%

Sources: The Earth Report, *edited by Edward Goldsmith and Nicholas Hildyard, Price Stern Sloan, Los Angeles, 1988, and* Atlas of the Environment, *by the World Wildlife Fund, Prentice Hall Press, New York, 1990.*

Q: *How many disposable razors do Americans throw out each year?*

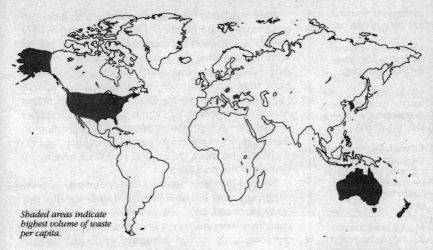

Shaded areas indicate highest volume of waste per capita.

Recycling

- By Jim Glenn -

Recycling is hardly recognizable these days. Long dismissed by many as a nicety, recycling is now touted as a vital component of the efforts in the "war on waste." These days environmentalists aren't the only proponents of recycling. Companies, particularly those that manufacture consumer goods, all want to show that their products or packaging are either recycled or recyclable, instead of hiding it. There probably isn't a solid waste hauler in the country that doesn't also consider itself a recycler.

There has always been a strong recycling industry in the US. But until recently it operated in the background. Scrap dealers concentrated on materials from the most economical sources—typically industries. Manufacturers used recycled feedstocks when they offered a competitive advantage.

Recycling has always been viable; now it is more visible. When the "garbage crisis" caused concern throughout the country, recycling began to be seen as an alternative to rapidly diminishing landfill space. This caused an explosion of state legislation both encouraging and mandating recycling efforts. States such as Oregon, New Jersey and Rhode Island led the way in the mid-1980s. Today, more than half the states have some form of recycling legislation in place.

WHAT YOU CAN DO:

COMPLETE THE CYCLE
• Check to see if your local recycling center will take: tin cans, office paper, brown bags, plastic containers or cardboard boxes.

• Call your local phone company to see if they have—or plan to have—a phone book recycling program. Phone books and other paper take up over half the space in every landfill.

• Start with basic sorting at home: Keep a box for glass, plastics and paper in a closet or in a container outside.

• Buy products made with "post-consumer" recycled materials. This will ensure the success of recycling programs.

• Precycle by thinking ahead and buying products which are

A. **2 billion**
Source: *The Recycler's Handbook, by the Earth • Works Group*

packaged in recyclable
and reusable materials.

• Buy in bulk whenever
possible to completely
eliminate packaging.

• If your municipality does
not have a curbside recy-
cling program, encourage
them to start one.

• If you have something
unusual (like ink or pho-
tographic chemicals) call
the specific trade asso-
ciation for recycling
ideas.

• Use your influence to
ask manufacturers and
retailers for recyclable
and recycled goods.

• Encourage your local
recycling center or pro-
gram to start accepting
plastics.

• Learn how you can re-
cycle your household

State legislation has been the precursor to a dramatic increase in the number of collection programs for
recyclables. A good indication of that increase can be
seen by examining the growth in the number of curbside recycling programs. At the end of 1988 there were
more than 1,050 curbside recycling programs operating in this country. By the end of 1990, that figure had
risen to more than 2,700, about ten times the number
in existence in 1981. Given the recycling legislation on
the books, it's not unreasonable to expect that by 1995
there will be more than 5,000 programs serving 50
percent of the population.

Beyond the sheer numbers, the complexity of recycling programs has also increased dramatically. Not
many years ago, only newspapers, aluminum and glass
containers were commonly collected. Today, it's not un-
common to also collect corrugated cardboard, tin cans
and several types of plastic bottles. And some programs
are also pushing the frontiers and including things like
mixed paper, household batteries and even film plastics.

For all the success recycling has enjoyed recently,
now is not the time to rest on laurels. There is still
much work to be done. For all of the progress, in 1990
only slightly more than 10 percent of our municipal
solid waste was recycled. While there is a substantial

Photo: Peter Morgan/Picture Group

Garden State paper recycling facility and paper mill in Garfield, New Jersey.

Q: *Scientists have examined only 10 percent of the data sent back to earth
from satellites in orbit. What percentage have they scientifically analyzed?*

base of state legislation for recycling, there are still more than 20 states that aren't covered. There is no firm federal legislation to support recycling. Even in states that have legislation, programs are often long on rhetoric and short on substance and funding.

In practical terms, states and municipalities that have put programs in place have tended to concentrate their collection efforts on highly visible curbside programs. Lagging behind have been ventures into extracting recyclables from apartment dwellers and the commercial sector.

Another shortcoming to date has been programs focusing on collection of materials at the expense of developing the infrastructure needed to manufacture and utilize products made with recycled materials. Without markets for recyclables it makes little sense to collect them. Unfortunately, there are far fewer states with market development legislation than there are with legislation that encourages collection of recyclables. And there are many more cities with curbside programs than with substantive procurement programs.

This concentration on supply side efforts, among other things, has led to a deterioration of markets for recyclables in many parts of the US. While the short term outlook is poor, over the long haul the market for most recyclables looks promising. Take, for instance, newspapers. Currently, there is an overabundance of newspaper from recycling programs on the market, which has depressed prices. There simply aren't enough plants in this country and Canada that can turn it into newsprint. However, because of pressure on newspaper publishers to use more recycled paper, numerous newsprint manufacturers have begun developing the needed capacity.

While all is not as it can be, or should be with recycling, it has come a long way in a very short time. The task at hand is to maintain the momentum that has built over the past three to four years and to continue to improve on what has been accomplished so far.

Jim Glenn has worked in the recycling field since 1980, first with the Pennsylvania Department of Environmental Resources and for the past four years as senior editor for BioCycle *Magazine. At* BioCycle, *he concentrates on recycling and yard waste composting policy and technology issues.*

goods, from clothing to motor oil to appliances.

RESOURCES
• *The Recycler's Handbook*, by the Earth•
Works Group, Berkeley, CA, 1990.

• *Why Waste A Second Chance: A Small Town Guide To Recycling*, National Association of Towns and Townships 1522 K St. NW, Suite 730, Washington, DC 20005, (202) 737-5200.

• Recycling Wheel, from Environmental Hazards Management Institute, 10 Newmarket Rd., Durham, NH 03824, (800) 446-5256. The fun way to get the basics on recycling.

DID YOU KNOW?
• 80 percent of garbage generated in the US is buried in landfills. But landfills are being closed permanently at a rate of two each day.

• Recycling one aluminum can saves enough energy to run a TV set for three hours.

• Americans throw away the equivalent of more than 30 million trees in newsprint each year.

A. 1 percent
Source: *World Resources Institute cited in* Eyes in the Sky, World•Watch *Magazine, September/October 1989*

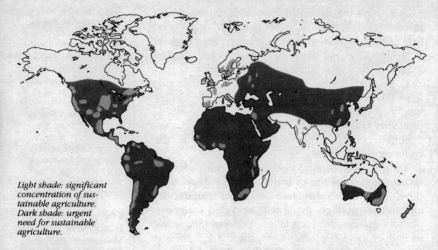

Light shade: significant concentration of sustainable agriculture. Dark shade: urgent need for sustainable agriculture.

WHAT YOU CAN DO:

ORGANIC MATTERS
• People were farming successfully without pesticides for thousands of years. Learn about alternatives (see *Gardening*, page 268).

• Don't use pesticides in your garden. Home pesticides are as lethal as agricultural ones. Over 100 active pesticide ingredients are suspected to cause birth defects, cancer and gene mutation. Children are especially susceptable.

• Buy organic: If you cannot find a local store that carries organically grown food, make a special request. You are not the only one who will be asking.

• In your garden, grow wildflowers and herbs. They will provide food for beneficial insects.

• Most foods you eat from the supermarket

Sustainable Agriculture

- By Terry Gips -

When it rains, it now pours DDT in the US, DDT that was blown in from Africa and Asia. After its use, the hazardous corn herbicide strazine volatilizes and rains back down on the Midwest and Europe. And Holland now has acid rain caused by its intensive animal feedlots.

These are just part of the widespread devastation caused by conventional agricultural practices. Not only have these methods contaminated our land, water, air and food with hazardous agrichemicals, but they have caused soil erosion, loss of precious genetic resources, and respiratory disease, hearing loss, cancer and physical injury to farmers and farmworkers.

There is an alternative—sustainable agriculture—food and agriculture systems that are ecologically sound, economically viable, socially just and humane. Sustainable agriculture is based on a holistic perspective that combines the latest scientific advances with traditional wisdom to create productive, safe food systems.

As defined by the International Alliance for Sustainable Agriculture and other groups (See *Breaking the Pesticide Habit*, by Terry Gips), sustainable

---

Q: *How many trees does the American Forestry Association want Americans to plant by the year 1992 through the association's "Global Releaf" program?*

agriculture has four essential components. First, it is ecologically sound. Farming systems must be re-designed to enhance the environment and health, while conserving energy and minimizing expensive, external inputs.

Second, it must be economically viable, giving farmers a fair return while accounting for all the hidden costs and subsidies, such as health and environmental impacts. Studies by the Dutch Government and the World Resources Institute indicate that organic food would cost *less* than conventional if such costs had to be paid, rather than passed on to future generations.

Third, sustainable agriculture must be socially just, assuring full participation by all people, from their access to land and resources to their ability to make decisions about their own destinies. Fourth, it must be humane, which means to embody our highest values. Most often, we think about our treatment of animals, but it applies as well to our treatment of human beings. Sustainable agriculture respects all life and preserves rural communities and culture.

In the past few years, sustainable agriculture has gained increasing acceptance by the agricultural establishment worldwide, although institutions often

have traveled over a thousand miles. Support locally grown organic food and save energy and the environment.

10 REASONS TO BUY ORGANIC
1. Our future generations' quality of life. Organically grown food provides a healthier legacy for all children.

2. Erosion of topsoil. Current farming practices erode topsoil at a rate of over 3 billion tons each year.

3. Preservation of water quality. The EPA estimates that pesticides have contaminated the groundwater in 38 states.

4. Organics save energy. Agriculture now consumes 12 percent of this country's total energy

"Mom and pop" operations are still the main force behind organic farming.

Photo: Terry Gips

. *100,000 trees*
. *Source: American Forestry Association*

supply, more than any other single industry.

5. Your personal safety—keep chemicals off your plate. Pesticides are poisons designed to kill living organisms.

6. Protects farm workers' health. California fieldhands currently suffer the highest rates of occupational illness.

7. Choosing organics supports smaller farms. With the USDA predicting that by year 2000 half of the US farm production will come from 1 percent of farms, organic farming may be one of the few survival tactics left for the small family farm.

8. It supports a "true" economy. If you add the real environmental and social costs of irrigation to a head of lettuce, its price can range between $2 and $3—not the 69¢ at the supermarket.

9. Organic farming eliminates mono-cropping. Supporting organics means supporting a system of farming that is in balance with nature, since a tenet of organic farming is plant diversity and crop rotation.

10. Organic food tastes better. From field to table we've lost many of the sensual pleasures of farm fresh produce.
　　　　—*Sylvia Tawse*

Reprinted by permission from *Alfalfa's Natural Foods Supermarket Newsletter*, September/October 1991.

PERMACULTURE
Permaculture is a design system for creating

ignore certain aspects of the definition. The top scientific body in the US, the National Research Council, concluded in *Alternative Agriculture* that successful alternative farmers can obtain equal yields at lower costs while reducing energy consumption and not harming the environment. Its recommendations that sustainable agriculture become a top policy and research priority were incorporated in the 1990 Farm Bill, although full funding has not yet been provided.

In 1991, the United Nations Food and Agriculture Organization conducted its first conference on sustainable agriculture, which called for "major changes to create the conditions of sustainability." Similar policy shifts have been backed by the World Bank, US AID and the US Department of Agriculture. Excellent programs are evolving at a number of land grant universities across the United States, particularly in response to the funding provided by the federal government through the Low-Input Sustainable Agriculture Program. Many states have established loan and grant programs for sustainable agriculture.

The billion dollar US organic foods industry has continued its rapid growth, with companies such as Earth's Best Baby Food experiencing a six-fold sales increase in just two years. Although organic sales are still only 1 percent of the market, a 1990 Harris Poll found that 84 percent of Americans would like to buy organic food and 44 percent would pay more for it.

Corporate America has responded by entering the organic market, either through buying smaller companies or by developing its own organic products. Such trends will be bolstered by the passage of National Organic Standards by Congress.

Even greater support for organic farming can be found in Europe, where Prince Phillip of England is converting the royal farm to organic, and countries such as Sweden, Germany and Holland have given farmers significant subsidies to go organic. These countries have developed excellent organic extension services and outstanding programs in organic agriculture at their universities.

The European Economic Community has backed organic standards and forbidden the use of growth hormones for livestock. Sweden has passed the world's strongest animal welfare law and achieved its goal of a 50 percent reduction in pesticide use in five years.

The meltdown of the Iron Curtain has encouraged

Q. *Some communities in the US pay more to get rid of their trash than to maintain what city department?*

the rapid blossoming of a sustainable agriculture movement throughout the Soviet Union and Eastern Europe. This has been fueled by both a recognition of widespread environmental devastation and Western Europe's rapidly increasing demand for organic food. The number of Hungarian organic farms has grown from only five in 1986 to 49 in 1990, covering 7,500 acres.

Organic farming has taken off in Israel, from just a handful of farms in 1980 to more than 200 providing $7 million in exports in 1990, with a ten-fold increase projected in five years. Sustainable agriculture has grown at an even greater pace in other industrialized countries, such as Canada, Australia, New Zealand and Japan, which has more than 20,000 organic farmers.

In the third world there is a great deal of interest in sustainable agriculture. In Latin America an excellent consortium of indigenous groups (CLADES) supports sustainable agriculture. The Philippines has a 60-organization network backing sustainable agriculture, while newer networks, groups and training programs are being formed across Africa and Asia.

More than 300 groups worldwide are working on pesticide reform through the Pesticide Action Network, which has succeeded in convincing many countries to ban the use of "the Dirty Dozen Pesticides."

But while these developments represent crucial breakthroughs, the increasing pace of worldwide destruction must be halted. Sustainable agriculture must become a top environmental priority. Consumers must support organic farmers by voting with their food dollars and their ballots.

Additional threats also must be checked, from the spread of genetic engineering and transnational corporate power to General Agreement on Trade and Tariffs and various free trade agreements that would weaken environmental safeguards, family farming and basic rights. To address them will require active citizen participation and a strong sustainable agriculture movement working closely with consumer, environmental and indigenous peoples' groups.

Terry Gips is co-founder and president of the International Alliance for Sustainable Agriculture, a nonprofit group based in Minneapolis that works with farmers, consumers, researchers and environmentalists worldwide.

sustainable human environments. The word itself is a contraction not only of *perman*ent agri*culture* but also of permanent culture, as cultures cannot survive for long without a sustainable agricultural base and landuse ethic. On one level, permaculture deals with plants, animals, buildings and infrastructures (water, energy, communications). However, permaculture is not about these elements alone, but rather about the relationships we create. For more information contact Permaculture Services International, 318 Ojo de La Vaca, Santa Fe, NM 87505, (505) 422-2229.

RESOURCES
• National Coalition Against the Misuse of Pesticides, 701 E St. SE, Suite 200, Washington, DC 20003. They produce a newsletter, numerous pamphlets and articles.

• *Breaking the Pesticide Habit—Alternatives to 12 Hazardous Pesticides*, by Terry Gips, International Alliance for Sustainable Agriculture, Minneapolis, MN, 1988.

• *Planting the Future—A Resource Guide to Sustainable Agriculture in the Third World*, edited by Dr. Meera Nanda, International Alliance for Sustainable Agriculture, Minneapolis, MN, 1990.

• International Alliance for Sustainable Agriculture, 1701 University Ave. SE, Room 202, Minneapolis, MN 55414.

A. *Police*
Source: The Recycler's Handbook, *by the Earth • Works Group*

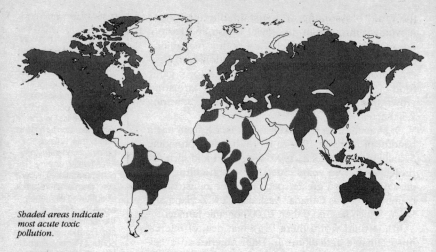

Shaded areas indicate most acute toxic pollution.

WHAT YOU CAN DO:

DON'T ASSUME
• Don't assume a product is toxic free just because no toxics are listed on the label. The government does not require manufacturers to list every ingredient if it does not violate "federal safety standards." Baby powder, for example, often contains asbestos. Pesticides have been found in shampoos, and nail polish is toxic in landfills.

• There are many toxic solvents and chemicals in the average home. Find out what toxics exist in your home, and replace them with safe, inexpensive, easy-to-use, natural alternatives.

• Find out whether your community has complied with the federal Community Right-To-Know Law, requiring that communities prepare local emergency response plans and that citizens be

Toxic Pollution

- By Dr. Joel S. Hirschhorn -

The problem with toxic chemicals and wastes is that there is too much being produced and too much in all the wrong places, like our air, soil and groundwater. In the US, well over 700 million tons of federally-defined hazardous wastes are being produced by industry annually.

Remarkable progress has been made in getting government, industry and the general public concerned about the very high use of toxic chemicals, the releases of enormous amounts of them into the environment and the continued generation of huge amounts of toxic waste. Government has developed a maze of regulations covering toxics, with laws like the Resource Conservation and Recovery Act concerning hazardous waste management, the Toxic Substances Control Act overseeing the production of toxic chemicals and, of course, Superfund regulating the cleanup of toxic waste sites. The requirement for industry to publicly reveal its releases of toxic chemicals into the environment yields the Federal Toxic Release Inventory.

But thousands of pages of government regulations and billions of dollars spent by industry on complying with those regulations have not produced enough change. What our fragile planet desperately needs is

Q: *Since 1986, Norway has increased its budget for environmental programs by what percentage?*

less use of toxic chemicals, less release of them into the environment and less generation of toxic waste.

Over the past 10 years there has been an increase in understanding of the benefits of pollution prevention, also called waste reduction, source reduction and toxics use reduction. The concept is both profoundly simple and elegant: Deal with the real origins of the problem in a preventive way. This means reduce and eliminate the use of toxic chemicals in manufacturing and in final products. Reduce and eliminate the production of all wastes and pollutants by making changes in industrial processes, materials and practices.

Pollution prevention is the front-end approach, whereas our current regulatory system is based on the back-end approach of using pollution control technology and waste management. Only a massive commitment to pollution prevention by every part of society can cope with rising population growth, rising consumerism and rising industrialization. The best thing that can be done in 1992 is to support individual state Pollution Prevention Initiatives like those in Massachusetts, Indiana and about eight other states.

Public and government attention to toxic chemical and waste issues seems to be declining as interest is focused on other critical environmental problems, allowed to participate in local emergency planning efforts. It also requires that companies respond to any official requests for information about chemical storage or use relevant to emergency planning.

CHARGE IT
• Use rechargeable batteries. Although they contain Cadmium, they last much longer than alkaline batteries and thus contribute less to our toxic waste problem.

• If it is possible in your area, recycle alkaline batteries. This technology to extract mercury and other metals from batteries does exist. Support it by recycling.

IMPORTANT DON'TS IN DISPOSAL
• Don't bury toxic items in your backyard.

Photo: Ed Reinke/AP/Wide World Photos

Cleanup of some 10,000 barrels filled with toxic chemicals at the Chem-Dyne hazardous waste site in Hamilton, Ohio.

A: *60 percent*
Source: Eco-2 Review, *Summer 1989; Newsletter of Resource Renewal Institute*

- Don't put liquid chemicals in the trash.

- Don't put used oil or batteries in the trash.

- Don't burn leftover chemicals.

- Don't mix chemical wastes together.

- Don't dump chemicals in a storm sewer—they will show up again, likely in a lake or stream in your neighborhood.

- Do contact your local waste hauler or EPA for advice on disposal.

RESOURCES
• *Home Ecology,* by Karen Christensen, Fulcrum Publishing, Golden, CO, 1990.

• *Guide to the Management of Hazardous Waste,* by J. William Haun, Fulcrum Publishing, Golden, CO, 1991.

COMPANIES REDUCING TOXICS
• Cleo Wrap, a producer of gift wrapping paper, switched from solvent-based inks to water-based inks to prevent the release of hazardous waste.

• The Minnesota Mining and Manufacturing Company (3M) replaced a metal alloy in a product and eliminated a waste stream containing toxic cadmium.

particularly ones that are global in nature, such as global warming and ozone layer depletion. But let us remember that we are vitally dependent on groundwater and that more and more groundwater is contaminated by toxic chemicals. For most chemicals, we really do not know their exact health effects. The thing to remember is that it is illogical and life-threatening to pit one legitimate environmental problem against another. We must effectively address all environmental problems, local as well as global ones.

Many studies have concluded that it is completely feasible, technically and economically, to make fundamental changes in industry processes and in products to greatly reduce the use of toxic chemicals and the production of toxic wastes. Many companies, like Polaroid and 3M, have already shown how practical it is to do waste reduction and make money at it because it improves the efficiency of their operations. More and more bans of chemicals will probably have to be made, but history has shown that necessity is indeed the mother of invention. Chemical bans and the pollution prevention movement stimulate technological innovation, force changes in consumer patterns and generally make society safer, more efficient and more sustainable. The key point about the pollution prevention movement is that it does not mean deindustrialization; rather it means restyling our industrial society to serve both long-term environmental and economic interests. In the coming decade, consumers will probably be the most effective force moving industry and government to increased practice of pollution prevention and toxics use reduction. Cleaning up all the contaminated land, water and buildings in the United States alone will probably cost between $500 million and $1 trillion over the next 50 years.

Dr. Joel S. Hirschhorn is president of EnviroSearch-East, an environmental consulting firm that provides environmental analyses for industry's problem solvers and planners. Previously he conceived and directed many influential studies at the Congressional Office of Technology Assessment (OTA) which in turn helped to define key environmental issues. During his 12 years at OTA, Dr. Hirschhorn examined at Congressional requests many Superfund sites, including Love Canal, Times Beach and the Rocky Mountain Arsenal.

Q: *Since the 1988 budget allotment, President Bush has cut the federal budget for wind energy research and development by what percentage?*

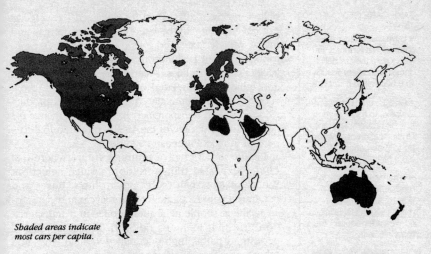

Shaded areas indicate most cars per capita.

Transportation

- By David G. Burwell -

Americans love automobiles. No doubt about it. What we *don't* love is the price we pay for our affection. We don't love 47,000 fatalities per year. We don't love pollution, noise, loss of open space, sprawl and global warming. We don't love wars to preserve energy security. We don't love 200 million discarded tires each year, plus 8.75 million junked cars, 138,000 tons of lead from old car batteries, millions of gallons of oil spilled on lands and in waterways, and more than 100,000 leaking underground gasoline storage tanks. We don't love traffic jams. And we certainly don't love what Lewis Mumford described as "the tomb of concrete roads and ramps covering the dead corpse of the city."

But that is the price of our love—and more. Our "love" of driving is gradually strangling our quality of life, particularly in urban and suburban communities, but all across America as well.

We are stuck in a traffic jam of our own making. As we stew, costs mount. Our highway-dependent transportation system is a primary reason the United States had a negative balance of trade in oil of $56 billion in 1990, accounting for more than half of our $100 billion total balance of trade deficit. We wasted more than 8 billion hours in traffic jams in 1990 adding at least $30

WHAT YOU CAN DO:

CAR CARE
• We all know cars have a serious impact on the environment—but because we depend on them in our daily lives, it's unrealistic to suggest that people stop driving altogether.

• Don't despair. Even if you drive every day, there are simple things you can do to help the Earth—from making sure your car is running efficiently, to recycling your old oil and antifreeze.

• Don't let your car idle unnecessarily. It takes less gas to start a car than it takes to let it idle. Idling becomes less efficient than restarting your car after about a minute.

• Keep fuel filters clean. Clean filters use less gas.

A. *90 percent*
  Source: American Wind Energy Association

TAKE CARE OF YOUR TIRES

• Save resources—your tires will last longer if you make sure they're balanced and (every 6,000 to 8,000 miles) rotated.

• Check your tires every 2 weeks to make sure they're properly inflated. Underinflation can waste up to 5 percent of a car's fuel.

• When you're ready to replace them: Radial tires really do improve gas mileage. Steel-belted tires are generally the most efficient.

DISPOSE OF MOTOR OIL AND ANTIFREEZE PROPERLY

• Both of these fluids can be recycled; oil can be re-refined, and antifreeze can be re-distilled.

• Before you have your car serviced, check to

billion in driver costs. Total "externalized" costs (costs not covered directly by users in the form of gas and motor vehicle taxes and tolls), including illnesses attributable to air pollution from motor vehicles, traffic accidents and fatalities, securing oil imports, oil spills and other environmental costs, are estimated to exceed $260 billion annually. At the same time, productivity growth in transportation has been an anemic 0.2 percent in the decade of the 1980s compared to 2 to 3 percent in most European countries.

Picture an alternative future. A future where real *choice* exists in transportation service selection. Where mass transit (subways, trolleys, buses and paratransit vans), commuter rail, bicycle and pedestrian facilities supplement automobiles in a transportation grid that includes rail corridors, bicycle and pedestrian paths, high occupancy vehicle lanes and other pathways as alternatives to single-occupancy vehicles. Where mixed land uses support communities that minimize the need and length of travel.

A future where *performance*—environmental quality, energy conservation, economic efficiency, quality of life—drives transportation investment decisions rather than the need to accommodate more and more automobiles and heavy trucks. Where we spend

Photo: Andrew Popper/Picture Group

Traffic during rush hour on the Long Island Expressway, New York.

Q: *On average, how much of all residential garbage is recyclable and compostable?*

more money on building transit facilities (presently about $5.8 billion at all levels of government) than we do on car *advertising* (currently about $6 billion). Where gas costs more than mineral water (it now costs about two-thirds that amount) because the environmental and social costs of driving are built into the pump price. Where nonpolluting fuels such as compressed natural gas, solar-powered vehicles, recyclable components, smart highways and other new technologies vastly reduce natural resource consumption in transportation. Where the efficient movement of *people* and *goods*, not motor vehicles, is the goal of transportation programs at all levels of government. Where transportation services consume less than a dime of your take-home dollar rather than twice that amount, as they do now.

This future can happen. It will not be easy. Forty years of federal transportation investments in new highway capacity, to the detriment of existing rail passenger and freight service, and the relative exclusion of new transit, has thrown our transportation grid out of whack. Add to that gas prices that have remained at 1947 levels in real (inflation-adjusted) dollars and little or no land use planning, and the result is urban-suburban gridlock of Gordian dimensions. Solutions include (1) development of performance-based criteria for transportation investments, (2) integration of land use, transportation and air quality planning, (3) pay-as-you-go pricing that rewards efforts to reduce consumption of transportation services and (4) more democracy in deciding which projects get built through involvement of regional and local governments—and the public—in project selection.

Federal surface transportation legislation is up for renewal in Congress now. Many of these proposed reforms will be debated in the spring of 1992 as the new legislation is implemented.

David G. Burwell is co-founder and president of the Rails-to-Trails Conservancy, a nonprofit membership organization devoted to the conversion of abandoned rail corridors to public trail use. He is also a member of the Executive Committee of the Surface Transportation Policy Project, the Transportation Law Committee and the Highway Research Review Committee of the Transportation Research Board.

make sure the shop recycles motor oil and antifreeze. Take your car to a shop that does.

• Try using alternative transportation like buses, trains, bicycles or walking, just one day a week. That may be tough—in most areas of the US, mass transit is woefully inadequate—but it is worth the effort.

• Support policies for local transit improvement and let your politicians know that you do not want more pavement but more and better quality mass transit.

RESOURCES
• Tire Industry Safety Council, P.O. Box 1801, Washington, DC 20013. Offers a "glove compartment tire safety and mileage kit." It includes an air pressure gauge, a tread depth gauge, four tire valve caps and a 12-page *Consumer Tire Guide*.

• For more information on how you can participate, write the Surface Transportation Policy Project, 1785 Massachusetts Ave. NW, Washington, DC 20036.

• *End of the Road: The World Car Crisis and How We Can Solve It,* by Wolfgang Zuckermann, Chelsea Green Publishing Co., Post Mills, VT, 1991.

DID YOU KNOW?
• It takes $100 million to build one mile of highway, and $15 million to build one mile of light rail mass transit, according to a Greenpeace study.

A. *50 percent and 25 percent respectively*
Source: State of Vermont Recycling Hotline (800) 932-7100

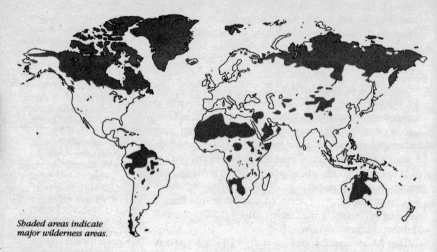

Shaded areas indicate major wilderness areas.

WHAT YOU CAN DO:

BUILD CAREFULLY
• Get the most out of your wood. North Americans use more lumber per person than any other region on earth.

• Use recycled lumber when possible. Recycle scrap wood.

BY ANY OTHER AGENCY
• Protected public lands in the United States total some 933 million acres. These lands receive different degrees of protection based on which agency manages the land, and the purpose of the land's designation as protected.

• The National Park Service is responsible for managing 358 separate units, totaling 80 million acres. These areas include National Parks, Monuments, Seashores, Recreation Areas, Battlefields, Rivers and many

Wilderness

- By T.H. Watkins -

In many different cultures spread over 4,000 years of human history, the concept of "wilderness" has taken on a complex variety of meanings. It has symbolized a fear of the unknown, and been welcomed as a place of refuge; it has been enshrined as holy ground, and condemned as the dwelling-place of Satan; it has inspired the love of poets and the greed of entrepreneurs, has been memorialized, celebrated, protected and destroyed. And, in the US, institutionalized as one of the spiritual and ecological treasures of the nation.

On September 3, 1964, President Lyndon B. Johnson signed one of the most revolutionary pieces of environmental legislation in American history: the Wilderness Act, which established a National Wilderness Preservation System in the US. More than 9 million acres of wilderness were immediately designated within that system, with stipulated rules and procedures for expansion of the system. "A wilderness," the act stated, "...is hereby recognized as an area where the earth and its community of life are untrammeled by man, where man himself is a visitor who does not remain...." Within these designated wilderness enclaves, no human structures were to be allowed, all vehicle access (except in specified emergencies) was to be prohibited, all commercial use (as

Q: *By 1992 the EPA wants Americans to be recycling what percentage of their garbage?*

in mining and logging) was to be forbidden, and human recreation, while encouraged, was to leave the land as it was found.

In the nearly 30 years since the act's passage, the National Wilderness Preservation System has grown to include 94.7 million acres of pristine mountains, meadows, river valleys, deserts, slickrock canyons, seashores and forests scattered from the White Mountains of New Hampshire and Maine to the sagebrush plains of the Sonoran Desert, from the "river of grass" of Florida's Everglades to the sharp-toothed mountains of Alaska's Arctic National Wildlife Refuge. These are not areas that have been magically *added* to the federal land base of more than 610 million acres, it should be noted. Wilderness designation under the terms of the Wilderness Act is an administrative classification imposed *upon* already existing federal lands—national parks, national forests, national wildlife refuges, and the lands of the Bureau of Land Management.

The present wilderness system is one of the American conservation movement's principal achievements—but it is by no means complete. Wilderness proponents estimate that as many as another 100

other sites. They are designated for multiple use: Hunting is generally prohibited; camping, fishing and fires depend on the individual parks rules. National Recreation Areas allow hunting, fishing, water sports and camping where specified.

LANDS PROTECTED BUT NOT MANAGED BY THE NATIONAL PARK SERVICE
• National Wildlife Refuges: There are approximately 470 refuges on 90 million acres nationwide. Administered by the US Fish and Wildlife Service under the Department of the Interior, wildlife refuges were established to protect wildlife habitat. Hunting, fishing and other uses (such as recreation) are permitted

View of Tuolumne Meadows from Lembert Dome in Yosemite National Park, California.

A. *25 percent*
Source: *Environmental Protection Agency*

if the activity is considered compatible with preservation of the habitat.

• National Forest Service: There are 155 forests managed by the US Forest Service encompassing 191 million acres. These are multiple use areas, including activities like outdoor recreation, range land, timber harvesting, watershed usage, hunting and fishing.

• Bureau of Land Management (BLM) Lands: Managed for multiple use, the BLM manages 272 million acres, public recreational uses and the production of resources. Over 300 million additional acres are sub-surface lands managed for mineral, oil and gas exploration. Hunting, fishing, logging and mining are allowed.

• Wilderness: There are over 94.9 million acres of wilderness protected within national forests, wildlife refuges, parks and BLM lands. There are 516 wilderness areas nationwide. Almost two-thirds of all wilderness acreage—56.5 million acres—is in Alaska. Wilderness areas are the most strictly protected—dams, logging roads, permanent structures, timber harvesting, operation of motorized vehicles and equipment are not permitted. Mining operations and livestock grazing are permitted. Since 1984, new mining claims and mining leases are not granted.

million acres of federal public lands qualify for wilderness designation in this country—places like the California Desert, Great Smoky Mountains National Park in Tennessee and North Carolina, or the unprotected forests of Idaho and Montana—and efforts continue to persuade Congress to add these acres to the nation's "bank" of pristine land.

Outside the US the wilderness question becomes more complicated. Recent studies by the Sierra Club suggest that as much as one-third of the Earth is still wilderness. Some 25 percent of this land is in Antarctica, and an international agreement to preserve most of the great continent as wilderness is currently being sought. In such wilderness-rich countries as the Soviet Union, Canada, China, Australia and Brazil, a combination of economic pressures and political expedience makes the preservation of wild land very difficult. Still, there are attempts being made. There is a nascent wilderness movement in Finland, for example, while Italy's own wilderness society is pushing for the designation of a portion of the country's Piedmont region as Europe's first wilderness area. Canada has enacted wilderness legislation similar to that of the US. Zimbabwe has established its first wilderness reserve, the Maruanda. And under the sponsorship of the International Wilderness Leadership Foundation, five international wilderness congresses have been held all over the world.

Proponents are encouraged by these and other developments, for only through wilderness preservation, they argue, is it possible to keep large natural areas from being exploited and degraded by human growth and development. To lose the wilderness that is left, they say, would be devastating, for wild country is nothing less than vital to the preservation of clean air, clean water, biological diversity, scenic beauty and open space—all those things that enhance and sustain the intricate web of life on Earth.

T.H. Watkins, a vice president of The Wilderness Society and editor of its quarterly magazine, Wilderness, *is the author of 19 books, among them* Vanishing Arctic: Alaska's National Wildlife Refuge, Time's Island: The California Desert, *and, most recently, a highly acclaimed biography of Franklin D. Roosevelt's Interior Secretary,* Righteous Pilgrim: The Life and Times of Harold L. Ickes, 1874-1952.

Q. *Schools buy more books than anyone else in the country. How many textbooks are printed on recycled paper?*

WILDERNESS OF THE WORLD

This list is a first-reconnaissance level inventory of wilderness areas of the world. Wilderness is defined as undeveloped land still primarily shaped by forces of nature. Most of this land has been lightly used and occupied by indigenous peoples who practice traditional subsistence ways of life. Only large blocks of wilderness more than 1 million acres were identified. The findings suggest one-third of the global land surface is still wilderness. However, 41 percent of that amount is in the Arctic or Antarctic and 20 percent in temperate regions. Most settled continents are between one-third and one-fourth wilderness. Two-thirds of the planet's land mass is now dominated by our species.

Top Twenty Countries with the Most Wilderness

Country	square miles	percent of total area	number of areas
Antarctica	5,283,593	100.0	2
Soviet Union	3,008,088	33.6	182
Canada	2,562,347	64.6	59
Australia	917,725	29.9	83
Greenland	869,600	99.9	1
China	843,104	22.0	47
Brazil	808,244	23.7	23
Algeria	561,697	59.0	42
Sudan	317,508	31.7	73
Mauritania	285,479	69.2	17
Saudi Arabia	271,554	28.3	17
Niger	262,532	55.3	15
Libya	261,987	37.2	32
Chad	245,017	47.7	24
Mali	235,255	47.4	17
United States	176,232	4.7	18
Egypt	170,161	42.5	17
Peru	146,640	28.5	9
Botswana	125,019	54.4	23
Venezuela	118,969	32.6	7

A. *Practically none*

Source: 50 Simple Things You Can Do To Save The Earth, *by the Earth•Works Group*

REGIONAL REPORTS

A region's environmental status is affected not only by climate and natural habitat but also by economics and politics. Regional Reports notes environmental threats and conservation initiatives in each region's ecology; using these reports, Earth Journal *assesses each region's greenness. Ratings range from "True Green," for regions dedicated to solving environmental problems, to "Pea Green," for regions where little if any conservation effort is being made.*

KEY TO GREEN STATISTICS

CONSERVATION ISSUES HAVE BECOME major popular and political concerns. National and international conservation organizations have been able to enroll support from governments, international development agencies, corporations and commercial organizations in the creation of international conservation treaties. *Earth Journal* used membership in these environmental conventions as a measure of a region's greenness.

CITES   Members of the Convention on International Trade in Endangered Species of Wild Fauna and Flora. (Declares species endangered internationally.)

RAMSAR   Contracting parties to the Convention on Wetlands of International Importance Especially as Waterfowl Habitat.

Bonn   Parties to the Convention on the Conservation of Migratory Species of Wild Animals.

ITTO   Members of the International Tropical Timber Organization.

Law of Sea   Signatories to the United Nations Convention on the Law of the Sea.

London   Contracting states to the London Dumping Convention.

Paris   Signatories to the Convention for the Prevention of Marine Pollution from Land-Based Sources.

MARPOL   Signatories to the Protocol on Substances that Deplete the Ozone Layer.

Montreal   Signatories to the Montreal Protocol on Substances that Deplete the Ozone Layer.

Basel   Signatories to the Basel Convention on the Control of Transboundary Movements of Hazardous Wastes and their Disposal.

30% Club   Signatories to the Convention on Long-Range Transboundary Air Pollution on the Reduction of Sulfur Emissions or their Transboundary Fluxes by at least 30 percent.

IUCN   Member states of the World Conservation Union.

WWF   Countries with World Wildlife Fund Affiliate or Associate National Organizations.

KEY TO GREEN RATINGS

True Green   Nations in the region are undertaking conservation initiatives of all types.

Spring Green   Nations in the region are beginning to undertake conservation initiatives of a wide variety, but need more encouragement and/or assistance to achieve their conservation goal.

Camouflage Green   Nations in the region may have joined international initiatives and followed up with active initiatives, but much more needs to be done to aid or improve conservation.

Pea Green   Environmental impacts are severe, but nations in the region are not actively responding with conservation initiatives.

Q: *How many pounds of carbon dioxide are produced by burning one gallon of gasoline?*

North Africa

DESERTIFICATION

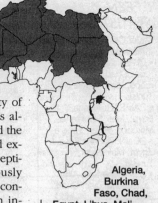

What's Happening: Fragile soils consisting of almost no organic matter make desertification a very serious threat to the area. The Sahara Desert, which already covers the majority of the region, is slowly creeping southward. It has already consumed over 270 square miles of Mali and the Sudan in the past 20 years. The harsh climate and extended periods of drought add to the region's susceptibility to desertification. Egypt has been seriously plagued with loss of arable land stemming from construction of the Aswan Dam. Food production increased initially, but the long-term effects are environmental disasters rather than economic boosts. Land that was once lush and arable has since become waterlogged and salinized. Some reactions to the water crisis in the region may advance desertification. Libya, for example, has proposed a $25 billion project to pump water from beneath the Sahara Desert to the country's more fertile coastal region to increase crop yield. With the agricultural and economic rewards from this project comes an immeasurable environmental price tag. The Saharan aquifers from which the water would be pumped are non-renewable and, while no one knows how much water the aquifers hold, their destruction could mean acceleration of the already rapid desertification in the area.

What's Being Done: In Burkina Faso, lines of stone have been placed in fields to trap soil that would otherwise be blown away by the wind. This practice has resulted in a 50 percent rise in crop yields. Other farmers in Burkina Faso are decreasing land erosion by using rocks to form inch-high dams to direct water into the ground rather than across it. This technique is being rapidly adopted by farmers since it has increased crop yields by as much as 90 percent.

WATER POLLUTION

What's Happening: This region has one of the world's worst sanitation sysytems, with raw sewage being dumped directly into streams and rivers. Considering the scarcity of fresh water, such pollution poses a number of serious health problems as well as

Algeria, Burkina Faso, Chad, Egypt, Libya, Mali, Mauritania, Morocco, Niger, Sudan, Tunisia, Western Sahara

REGIONAL STATISTICS

Population: 284,000,000

Land Area: 348,250 square miles

Geography: The Atlas Saharien Mountains in the north and the Sahara Desert in the south hem in the region with areas of plateau, savannah and steppe. Fertile land exists along the coastlines on the northern, eastern and western borders of the region as well as in the river valleys of Mauritania and the Sudan, but the majority of the area is barren and non-arable.

Climate: Hot, dry and arid throughout most of the region; moderate temperatures along the coast.

Resources: Crude oil, natural gas, iron ore, gypsum, uranium, manganese

A. *19 pounds*
Source: The Greenhouse Trap, *by Francesca Lyman*

GREEN STATISTICS

Major Conservation Initiatives:
• CITES: Algeria, Burkina Faso, Chad, Egypt, Morocco, Niger, Sudan, Tunisia
• RAMSAR: Algeria, Egypt, Mali, Mauritania, Morocco, Niger, Tunisia
• BONN: Burkina Faso, Egypt, Mali, Niger, Tunisia
• Law of the Sea: Algeria, Burkina Faso, Chad, Egypt, Mali, Mauritania, Morocco, Niger, Sudan, Tunisia
• London: Morocco, Tunisia
• MARPOL: Algeria, Egypt
• Montreal: Burkina Faso, Egypt, Morocco
• IUCN: Chad, Egypt, Mali, Mauritania, Morocco, Sudan
• ITTO, Paris, Basel, 30% Club, WWF: None

Protected Areas:
1.0–4.9%: Burkina Faso, Mauritania

Under 1%: Algeria, Chad, Egypt, Libya, Mali, Morocco, Niger, Sudan, Tunisia

GREEN RATING

Although some of the countries are members of important conservation initiatives, the desertification rates in the region is among the world's highest; water contamination is high due to poor sanitation; and the region is one of the biggest annual hunting and exportation of endangered animals. Lack of active effort within each country ranks this region **Camouflage Green.**

environmental problems. The Black Volta, White Volta and Komoé Rivers in Burkina Faso; the Niger River, the Oum er Rbia in Morocco; and the Nile which runs through Egypt and the Sudan are all highly polluted. Along with environmental destruction, waterborne diseases affect much of the population, especially in Mauritania, Morocco and Mali.

ENDANGERED SPECIES

What's Happening: Wildlife trade, while legal within CITES regulations, threatens a variety of species in the area. Live parrots and reptile skins are the most common wildlife exports from the region, with Mali and the Sudan reporting over 75,000 exported skins a year. This figure does not include illegal trade that, although immeasurable, is known to be extensive. More alarming is the hunting of endangered species such as the Edmi gazelle, the African elephant, the black rhino, the white rhino, the scimitar-horned oryx, the Abyssinian colobus monkey, the skylark and the turtle dove quail.

What's Being Done: Eight of the 12 countries in the region are members of CITES, but five of those are fulfilling less than 50 percent of their requirement to report imports and exports of CITES listed species. The majority of these countries seem to have opted for token membership rather than an active effort to protect wildlife.

HOT SPOT

The Sudd Swamps in the Sudan are being both helped and destroyed by the people in the area. Tribes such as the Nuer and Dinka have developed a migratory agricultural system that uses and revitalizes the wetlands. But the government's efforts to build the Jonglei Canal threaten to destroy seasonal farming as well as the fragile ecosystem. The canal is supposed to divert water to the Nile, but already it has been seen that, before it reaches its destination, the water evaporates as it crosses the Sudd.

Q. *Making a ton of recycled paper uses only what percentage of the energy needed to produce the same amount from virgin paper?*

Ivory Coast

TROPICAL FOREST DESTRUCTION

What's Happening: The Ivory Coast is one of the three major areas of rainforest in the world, yet in Nigeria and Côte d'Ivoire, it is estimated that by the year 2010, the rainforests simply will not exist. In Guinea, Ghana, Cameroon and Gabon, rainforests are also quickly being destroyed. This widespread destruction is primarily due to the tropical timber trade, small-scale and shifting agriculture and a fuel wood crisis.

What's Being Done: Cameroon has found a way to balance conservation and economic use of some rainforests. By creating a buffer zone around the most highly restricted areas of the Korup National Park, residents can engage in small-scale hunting, fish farming and forestry without harming the protected land and wildlife. In Gabon, where 85 percent of the rainforests are already destroyed from the timber trade, the government is advertising its remaining timber to foreign investors.

WILDLIFE LOSS

What's Happening: Throughout the region, species of animals and plants are disappearing at an alarming rate. Trade, farming and other economic endeavors all contribute to this threat of extinction. Côte d'Ivoire and Cameroon, two countries with vast biological diversity, have already lost 79 percent and 59 percent of their wildlife habitat respectively. Sierra Leone has lost close to 85 percent of its wildlife habitat. The wildlife trade is affecting the area with rapid decline of species, especially parrots and elephants. Senegal is one of the top exporters of live parrots, while Gabon is one of the top exporters of ivory.

TOXIC TRADE

What's Happening: Although the entire region has placed a ban on the importation of hazardous wastes as of 1989, Liberia continues to receive shipments from the United Kingdom, and the US is planning to send wastes to Senegal. And even though Guinea-Bissau, Guinea, Sierra Leone and Nigeria have rejected foreign

Benin, Cameroon, Côte d'Ivoire, Gabon, Gambia, Ghana, Guinea, Guinea-Bissau, Liberia, Nigeria, Senegal, Sierra Leone, Togo

REGIONAL STATISTICS

Population: 190,000,000

Land Area: 1,196,445 square miles

Geography: Forested plateaus, rainforests and mangrove swamps found along the coastal areas. Savanna-type areas cover the inland regions. Some semi-arid desert in the hilly northern interior. All countries have coasts on the Atlantic Ocean.

Climate: Ranges from sub-tropical and rainy to semi-arid desert. Winter brings dry weather and summer is considered the rainy season.

Resources: Timber, offshore oil, low-grade iron ore, bauxite, diamonds, rubber, petrol, tin, coal, marble.

GREEN STATISTICS

Major Conservation Initiatives:
• CITES: Benin,

A. *60 percent*
Source: The Recycler's Handbook, *by the* Earth • Works Group

Cameroon, Gabon,
Gambia, Ghana,
Guinea, Guinea-Bissau,
Liberia, Nigeria, Togo
• RAMSAR: Gabon,
Ghana, Senegal
• ITTO: Benin,
Cameroon, Ghana,
Nigeria, Senegal
• Law of the Sea: Benin,
Cameroon, Côte
d'Ivoire, Gabon, Gambia,
Ghana, Guinea, Guinea-
Bissau, Liberia, Nigeria,
Senegal, Sierra Leone,
Togo
• London: Côte d'Ivoire,
Gabon, Nigeria
• MARPOL: Côte
d'Ivoire, Gabon, Liberia,
Togo
• Montreal: Ghana,
Senegal, Togo
• IUCN: Benin,
Cameroon, Côte
d'Ivoire, Senegal
• WWF: Nigeria
• Paris, Basel, 30%
Club: None

Protected Areas:
10.0–19.9%: Senegal

5.0–9.9%: Côte d'Ivoire,
Togo, Benin, Gabon

1.0–4.9%: Gambia,
Guinea-Bissau, Guinea,
Equatorial Guinea

Under 1%: Sierra Leone,
Liberia, Ghana, Nigeria,
Cameroon

GREEN RATING

Deforestation is extreme-
ly high. Wildlife habitat
destruction is severe and
wildlife trade flourishes in
the region. This region
ranks **Pea Green**.

proposals for dumping, hazardous wastes received in the past may still remain.

What's Being Done: The step to ban all importation of hazardous wastes in 1989, though not a complete-ly successful one, shows a concerted joint govern-mental effort to stop importing toxins.

AIR POLLUTION

What's Happening: In Nigeria, the air pollution ex-ceeds international standards in several categories, posing serious health risks to the people in the cities.

What's Being Done: Two Nigerian cities, Lagos and Ibadan, have made the effort to test for air pollution and have gathered statistics about its high levels, but have not proposed any clean air initiatives.

PROMISING INITIATIVES

Nigeria: Natural farming techniques are gaining pop-ularity in Africa. Ogbuefi Mozie, head of the botany department at the University of Nigeria, discovered that the ashes of mango, African oil bean, cashew and gmelina trees could protect freshly cut yams and can be used to heal yams where sprouts were re-moved from tubers.

Cameroon: The Presbyterian Rural Training Centre has not only developed natural pesticides from plants such as castor bean and papaya trees, it has found a way to keep stored maize insect-free by mixing the grain with the ash from burned cow dung.

In addition, researchers in Gambia and Togo have achieved great results using fruits, leaves and seeds of the neem tree to make natural pesticides that repel insects from some vegetables and stored grains.

Q: *How much more radiation was released from the Chernobyl accident than from the atomic explosion at Hiroshima?*

Central and Southern Africa

WETLAND DESTRUCTION

What's Happening: In Botswana, the Okavango Swamp, created by the world's largest inland delta and some of the most extensive wetlands in the world, is threatened by proposed irrigation schemes and cattle ranching. And in an effort to combat the tse-tse fly, harmful pesticides are being used that are polluting the wetlands in Botswana. Despite all of Botswana's wetlands, the country is not a signatory of RAMSAR, the initiative to protect wetlands. The Bangweulu Basin wetlands in Zambia, like the Okavango Swamp, are threatened by hunting, irrigation schemes and by plans for hydro-electric projects.

What's Being Done: In a major conservation effort, the Department of Water Affairs in Botswana recently cancelled one project to divert water from the Okavango Delta to new areas for irrigation. Instead, farmers will begin using traditional methods of wetland agriculture called molapo farming that works the land safely without robbing it of nutrients. Water will continue to be diverted from the Boro River for diamond mining and ranching, activities that are causing the river to dry up in some places, jeopardizing fish and wildlife in the area.

TOXIC TRADE

What's Happening: Shipments of toxic waste are being received in Namibia from Germany, and in South Africa from the United States. Switzerland plans to ship hazardous wastes to Angola.

What's Being Done: Only Zambia and Zimbabwe have imposed a ban on the importation of toxic wastes.

TROPICAL FOREST DESTRUCTION

What's Happening: The C.A.R., Zaire, Zambia and Zimbabwe all export timber from their dense tropical rainforests. The rainforests in the Congo and Zaire are also threatened by the tropical timber trade. Zaire is one of the top timber exporters in the world. Sixty-eight percent of the Congo's rainforests are scheduled to be cut.

Angola, Botswana, Burundi, Central African Republic (C.A.R), Congo, Lesotho, Malawi, Mauritius, Namibia, Rwanda, South Africa, Swaziland, Uganda, Zaire, Zambia, Zimbabwe

REGIONAL STATISTICS

Population: 154,100,000

Land Area: 3,400,077 square miles

Geography: Countries of this region bordering the Atlantic Ocean are vast savanna and desert lands. The high interior elevation plateau stretches across the central part of the region creating rocky, arid conditions, notably the Kalahari Desert at 4,000 feet in altitude. One of the world's largest dams, the Kariba, is located in landlocked Zimbabwe, irrigating a vast high elevation veld of ranching and agriculture.

Climate: Dry and hot in the desert region and tropical rainy conditions

A. *90 times more*
Source: Two Minutes A Day For A Greener Planet, *by Marjorie Lamb*

in the scattered rain-forests. Cooler in the mountains and high plateaus, hotter in the lowlands.

Resources: Diamonds, gold, iron, oil, fish, copper, salt, gas, timber, uranium, limestone, zinc, platinum, asbestos, cobalt, silver, bauxite, coal, chrome, nickel, tin and potash

GREEN STATISTICS

Major Conservation Initiatives:
• CITES: Burundi, Botswana, C.A.R., Congo, Malawi, Mauritius, Rwanda, South Africa, Zambia, Zimbabwe
• RAMSAR: South Africa, Uganda
• Law of the Seas: Angola, Burundi, Botswana, C.A.R., Congo, Lesotho, Malawi, Mauritius, Namibia, Rwanda, South Africa, Swaziland, Uganda, Zaire, Zambia, Zimbabwe
• London: Zaire
• MARPOL: South Africa
• Montreal: Congo, Uganda
• IUCN: Mauritius, Zambia, Zimbabwe
• WWF: South Africa
• BONN, ITTO, Paris, Basel, 30% Club: None

Protected Areas:
10.0–19.9%: Botswana, Malawi

5.0–9.9%: C.A.R., Rwanda, Uganda, Zambia, Zimbabwe

1.0–4.9%: Angola, Congo, South Africa, Zaire, Swaziland, Mauritius

OVERPOPULATION

What's Happening: Malawi's overpopulation—its population density and population growth rank among the highest in Africa—has been cited as the cause of many of its environmental and health problems. Complicating Malawi's population problem is the influx of Mozambique civil war refugees.

LAND DEGRADATION

What's Happening: Overuse of Lesotho's land by unrestricted grazing, overcropping and poor farming methods has caused serious land erosion. Close to 2 percent of Lesotho's farming acreage is lost each year to erosion.

WATER POLLUTION

What's Happening: Along with land erosion, Lesotho is facing a serious water pollution problem. Human sewage dumped near reservoirs and expended industrial wastes flow into the Caledon River, creating diseased drinking water. Mauritius' water supply is being threatened by pesticide and fertilizer runoff and hazardous waste materials collected from industries sprung from rapid economic development. To date, Mauritius' solid waste collection methods have had little effect on keeping wastewater effluents from entering its drinking water supplies.

SPECIES LOSS

What's Happening: Mauritius' terrestrial ecosystems are being damaged by the increase of tourism, illegal logging and the introduction of exotic plants and animals. Also, Mauritius' marine ecosystems are being destroyed by coastal pollution and overfishing.

In Burundi, the high density of human and cattle populations has caused severe wildlife habitat loss and has endangered the existence of elephants and gorillas.

DESERTIFICATION

What's Happening: Overgrazing of sheep on the Karoo region in South Africa is destroying the grasslands, causing an ecosystem imbalance and encouraging desertification.

PROMISING INITIATIVES

Zambia: A year ago, Kafue Flats wetlands in Zambia was threatened by persistent poaching of antelopes

Q: *What percentage of all toilets in the US are leaking right now, (every year one leaky toilet can waste over 22,000 gallons of water)?*

and overgrazing of cattle. But with aid and guidance from the local government's Department of National Parks and Wildlife and the World Wildlife Fund, local people have begun to remedy the problems. Quotas were set for the number of antelope that could be killed. Tourists are now charged $500 (US) for each antelope killed. Already, the antelope population has increased significantly. Community pressure on ranchers has also helped lessen overgrazing by reducing the number of cattle in the area. Zambia and the World Wildlife Fund have entered into a debt-for-nature swap.

Zimbabwe: With elephant herds declining throughout Africa at an alarming rate, most countries have banned the ivory trade. One exception is Zimbabwe, yet the elephant population has actually increased in this country by one-third over the past five years. The rise has been attributed to the fact that local villagers own the elephants in their area, and are therefore highly protective of the herds. The neighboring country of Kenya has made the sale of ivory illegal. Still, elephant numbers have dropped from 65,000 to 19,000 in the past decade.

Namibia, South Africa, Swaziland and Zimbabwe: All four countries have started an education program called "We Care!" to teach students about the surrounding environment and the impact they have on it.

South Africa: Although the internal politics portend civil war, numerous national parks and wilderness areas have been set aside. Private and government-sponsored training programs are being initiated to increasingly involve the black majority in care and protection of the habitats and protected species.

Under 1%: Burundi, Lesotho

Almost all of the protected areas in Zambia are infested with the tse tse fly. But the flies have kept poachers out, and large game animals are thriving there.

Endangered Species Being Hunted:
Jackass penguin (Namibia), bontebok, black wildebeest (South Africa), African hunting dog (Botswana), African elephant (C.A.R., Rwanda,Uganda, Zaire), white rhino (C.A.R., Uganda), mountain gorilla (Zaire, Rwanda, Uganda), pygmy chimpanzee, (Zaire), black rhino (Rwanda)

GREEN RATING

Zaire is one of the world's largest exporters of timber. Conservation of lands is as much as 20 percent in some countries, with Zambia and the World Wildlife Fund negotiating debt-for-nature-swaps. Public awareness of environmental issues is growing through education programs. This area ranks **Spring Green**.

A. *20 percent*
Source: 50 Simple Things You Can Do To Save The Earth, *by the Earth • Works Group*

East Africa

Djibouti, Ethiopia, Kenya, Madagascar, Mozambique, Seychelles, Somalia, Tanzania

REGIONAL STATISTICS

Population: 26,500,000

Land Area: 1,846,889 square miles

Geography: Slashing the eastern side of Africa for 3,500 miles, the Great Rift furrows north from Mozambique to the Red Sea, forking into two branches. Deep lakes, such as Lake Tanganyika, the world's second deepest lake, trace the course of the western branch. The eastern branch is traced by shallow alkaline lakes and volcanoes such as Kilimanjaro, Africa's highest peak, located in Northern Tanzania.

Climate: Hot and humid in most regions, the highlands in Kenya and Ethiopia are cooler and moister than surrounding lowlands.

Resources: Gold, wildlife, limestone, minerals, salt, copper,

DESERTIFICATION

What's Happening: In Kenya, Tanzania and Somalia, desertification threatens all aspects of life with severe economic, health and environmental repercussions. The most severe case is Ethiopia, a once fertile region that is now wrought with starvation, drought and non-arable land. Since 1900, over 90 percent of the forests in the once rich and fertile highlands have been cut down, allowing over a billion tons of topsoil to wash away every year. This has resulted in 8,000 square miles of land becoming non-arable.

What's Being Done: In Kenya, women in many farming communities are planting trees around cropland to stop wind erosion. After years of famine, Ethiopia is only just beginning to organize grassroots programs that will begin the process of rebuilding the soil. The Inter-African Group, an organization of social scientists, agronomists and other specialists are beginning to look at ways to establish reforestation and sustainable agriculture projects.

TROPICAL FOREST DESTRUCTION

What's Happening: Only 32 percent of Madagascar's tropical forests remain. By 2010, it is estimated that its forests will be completely gone. Three of the top tropical timber exporters in the world are Kenya, Ethiopia and Tanzania.

What's Being Done: In Tanzania, the Chagga people of Mount Kilimanjaro are using a traditional form of agroforestry that greatly reduces the amount of land needed to farm. The system is based on a mixture of crop rotation and variation, and has been in practice in the region for thousands of years.

WILDLIFE TRADE

What's Happening: This region includes some of the top exporters of ivory, live parrots and live primates, three of the four major categories for wildlife trade. Somalia, Tanzania and Djibouti are three of the top ten exporters of ivory; Tanzania is one of the top exporters of live parrots; and Kenya and Ethiopia are two of the top exporters of live primates. Yet out of all

 Q: *Which state now has more vehicles than residents?*

of these countries, only Somalia fulfills 100 percent of CITES' regulations, which protects endangered species.

LAND DEGRADATION

What's Happening: Fires in the high grass of Swaziland, often started intentionally as part of slash-and-burn agriculture, have destroyed the forest of the Highveld. The fires have also emitted large amounts of such greenhouse gases as carbon dioxide and methane.

HOT SPOT

Tanzania, Kenya and Somalia banned the import of toxic wastes in 1989. Yet since that time, dumping by European countries is known to have occurred in Tanzania. Shipments of toxic waste to Kenya and Somalia are currently either planned or under consideration.

PROMISING INITIATIVES

Kenya: Near Isiolo, Kenya, 10,000 acres of land has been donated and privately funded to establish the Ngare Segoi Rhino Sanctuary that protects black and white rhinos. The sanctuary is small, protecting only about 17 rhinos, but the goal to protect and preserve has been established, and already six calves have been born there. Although the Kenyan government owns the rhinos, it provides no money for the preserve; but it has cooperated with the owners of the land in these conservation efforts.

Madagascar: Madagascar has engaged in a debt-for-nature agreement with Conservation International. Madagascar has also developed a National Conservation Strategy that encompasses its entire society—government, local people and conservationists—in a massive effort to protect its unique wildlife. Thirty-six national parks and reserves have been created along with reforestation and education programs.

platinum, chromium, graphite, semi-precious stones, uranium, diamonds.

GREEN STATISTICS

Major Conservation Initiatives:
- CITES: Ethiopia, Kenya, Madagascar, Mozambique, Seychelles, Somalia, Tanzania
- BONN: Somalia
- Law of the Seas: Djibouti, Ethiopia, Madagascar, Mozambique, Seychelles, Somalia, Tanzania
- London: Kenya,Seychelles
- MARPOL: Djibouti
- Montreal: Kenya
- IUCN: Ethiopia, Kenya, Madagascar, Seychelles
- RAMSAR, ITTO, Paris, Basel, 30% Club, WWF: None

Protected Areas:
5.0–9.9%: Kenya

1.0–4.9%: Ethiopia, Tanzania, Madagascar

Under 1.0%: Djibouti, Somalia, Mozambique

Tanzania's Ngorongoro Conservation Area was taken off the official list of Threatened Protected Areas of the World in 1989.

GREEN RATING:

Deforestation and desertification are severe. The region also has a high birth rate. Kenya, Tanzania and Somalia have banned all toxic importing. Individuals are increasingly returning to traditional farming methods and the area is increasing the value of wildlife. It ranks **Spring Green**.

A.*Florida*
Source: Two Minutes A Day For A Greener Planet, *by Marjorie Lamb*

North America

Canada, Mexico, United States

REGIONAL STATISTICS

Population: 366,600,000

Land Area: 8,154,348 square miles

Geography: Major mountain chains are the Appalachians in the east, the Sierra Nevada and the Cascades in the west and the Rocky Mountains in the western part of the US reaching up into Canada and including the Continental Divide. Much of the southwest and western US is arid or semi-arid, rocky terrain. Vast fertile farmlands and prairies extend to the north and south in central North America. Mexico is predominantly arid land with volcanic mountains in the southern exterior. Canada consists of vast central plains, and islands in the north that lie in the Arctic Ocean.

DEFORESTATION AND SOIL EROSION

What's Happening: North America boasts both temperate and tropical rainforests, both of which are being felled rapidly. These forests once ranged over 720,000 square miles, stretching from Alaska to northern California. Already, 60 percent of Canadian and 90 percent of US ancient forests have been cut. Presently, the most extensive damage is being done in Canada; less than one-twentieth of the original ancient forest is officially protected. Neither country's national parks are immune: One of Canada's biggest preserves, the Strathcoma Provincial Park on Vancouver Island, was recently opened for logging. Predictions range from two decades to an optimistic six decades before forests will be entirely cleared. While tropical forests are valuable partially for their abundant variety of species, the average plot of land in the Pacific Northwest coniferous forest contains more than twice as much plant matter as the most productive tropical rainforest, which is important to absorb carbon dioxide. It is the home of the oldest and largest trees on Earth. Destroying the forest will dry up rainfall, seriously endanger rare species and disrupt the world's richest salmon fisheries.

Rainforests in Mexico and on the island of Hawaii are also disappearing. Nearly a million acres of Mexico's forests are lost each year, and desertification is the nearly assured result. Bulldozers have begun razing the rainforest in Hawaii to make room for roads and drilling wells that will tap volcanic steam below 9,000 of the 27,000 acres of the Wao Kele O Puna forest.

What's Being Done: In early 1990, the US announced a plan to plant a billion trees per year during the next decade. If this project is successful, it will cover 16 million acres with trees (which is slightly over one-fifth of the area now covered by corn). However, logging in the nation's forests continues at a rate which exceeds the reforestation rate, which dwarfs any previous effort in reforestation. In response to the Hawaiian geothermal project, the

Q: *How many gallons of water do you waste if you leave the water running while you brush your teeth?*

Hawaii Rainforest Action Group staged protests to halt the project. Opponents of the project have also challenged it in federal court.

FERTILIZERS, PESTICIDES AND OTHER HAZARDOUS WASTES

What's Happening: The US alone generates roughly 240 million metric tons of hazardous and toxic waste per year, 70 percent of which comes from the chemical industry. In 1988, US farmers used almost 19 million tons of synthetic fertilizers and 255,000 tons of pesticides. The Environmental Protection Agency estimates that at least 66 of the roughly 300 pesticide ingredients commonly used by farmers are "probable carcinogens" and dozens are already known to cause birth defects and nervous system disorders. The nitrates from fertilizers are seeping into groundwater, polluting wells, rivers, lakes and oceans. A 1984 survey carried out by the US Environmental Protection Agency showed that out of the 124,000 wells sampled, 24,000 had elevated levels of nitrates and 8,000 were polluted above health limits. The US holds the record for abandoned hazardous waste dumps. The US Office for Technology Assessment estimates that there could be 10,000 sites needing immediate action and that 50 years and $100 billion would be needed to clean them up. In the late 1980s, the US was also shipping 143,000 tons of waste to Canada, 7,700 tons to Mexico, 33,000 to Brazil, 16,500 to Guinea, 7,600 to Zimbabwe and 5,000 to Haiti each year.

What's Being Done: The US and many other industrialized countries have prohibited the use of some pesticides as too dangerous to health or the environment, but they often continue to export these same pesticides to the third world. The US is one of the major exporters of fertilizers, providing 17 percent of the world fertilizer exports and 38 percent of the world pesticide exports; Canada provides an additional 17 percent of world fertilizers. These chemicals then reappear in the US as residue on the produce imported from those developing nations. Programs exist to help farmers end the pesticide and fertilizer cycle; Integrated Pest Management uses a variety of means to control pests including natural predators, crop rotation and the use of pest resistant strains.

Climate: Ranges are dramatic: from hot dry desert, to humid continental on the coasts to sub-arctic and tundra in the north.

Resources: Petroleum, timber, ores, silver, copper, gold, lead, zinc, hydro-power, minerals

GREEN STATISTICS

Major Conservation Initiatives:
- CITES: Canada, United States
- RAMSAR: Canada, Mexico. United States
- ITTO: Canada, United States
- Law of the Seas: Canada, Mexico
- London: Canada, Mexico, United States
- MARPOL: United States
- Montreal: Canada, Mexico, United States
- Basel: Canada, Mexico
- 30% Club: Canada, Mexico
- IUCN: Canada
- WWF: Canada, United States
- Paris: None

Protected Areas:

5.0–9.9%: United States

1.0–4.9%: Canada

Under 1.0%: Mexico

GREEN RATING

Only 1 percent of US' produce is grown organically. The US also is the world's leading consumer of goods, energy and water. Air pollution in Mexico City is so severe children are frequently advised to stay home. Almost all of the

A. *Five gallons*
Source: *50 Simple Things You Can Do To Save The Earth*, by the *Earth • Works Group*

ancient forests in Canada and the US have been cut down. Lively debate and opposition surround these issues, and initiatives are being taken or tried. This area ranks as **Camouflage Green**.

In the Slammer

Violators of environmental laws were given more time in jail in 1991 than ever before. The EPA said criminal environmental cases led to violators serving 550 months in jail in 1991, more than twice the amount served during 1990. The majority of crimes involved violations of federal hazardous waste laws. The increase in jail terms is seen as a sign that the agency is increasing its enforcement activities.

"The potential for erosion now is worse than in the 1930s. If it gets as dry as it was in the 1930s, we're in for some real trouble. You're in country now that man in his infinite wisdom did not improve upon."
—Bill Fryrear, head of US Department of Agriculture Research Service Station, Big Spring, Texas

"It's not an act of God. It's an act of greed. God doesn't have a plow."
—Texas rancher on dust storms caused by plowing rangeland

"A few of my neighbors share my belief that 'as you sow, so shall you reap,' and if you sow

Pesticides are used selectively with the goal of controlling, not eliminating, pests. The program has already proved extremely effective for growing cotton in Texas, apples in New York and almonds in California, but use is still not widespread. There is predictably much resistance from the agro-chemical industry. The US Office of Technology Assessment estimated that US pesticide use would drop by 25 percent if the program were adopted by all farmers. Consumers are putting pressure on the industry as well, opting more and more for organically grown produce.

The US military has begun an environmental cleanup program that may become one of the biggest engineering projects ever undertaken. The program is aimed at restoring the environment and reducing pollution at thousands of military and other government military-industrial installations in the US and abroad that have been contaminated with toxic substances.

Canada's Agriculture Department banned four insect repellents in August 1991 because of indications that the ingredient ethylhexanediol, made by Union Carbide Corporation, causes birth defects in laboratory animals.

WATER

What's Happening: Americans use more water than any other people on Earth, averaging 608,000 gallons per person per year. Canada uses water at a rate of about 400,000 gallons annually and Australia at a rate of 320,000. That translates into about 1,665 gallons of water use per day for the average American person (including agricultural and industrial use) and it is estimated that household water consumption will quadruple between the years 1967 and 2000, with industry increasing its demand five-fold.

What's Being Done: Between 1978 and 1983, US industry cut its water intake by a quarter through recycling, even though the number of factories increased, and further reductions are expected in the 1990s.

AIR POLLUTION

What's Happening: Mexico City is one of the largest cities in the world, and one of the most polluted. Mexico City's children have reportedly developed learning disabilities from the high level of gasoline in the air. A heavy concentration of industry plus a

 Q: *How many wars were being fought worldwide last year?*

motor vehicle fleet that has grown six times as fast as the population over the last 40 years has led to a smog level that exceeds World Health Organization standards on over 300 days out of each year. Areas in the US suffer from comparable levels of smog. In 1988, the air in Southern California exceeded health standards on 232 days, 75 of which were so bad that schoolchildren and the elderly were advised to stay indoors.

What's Being Done: The World Bank will loan Mexico over $300 million to fight pollution, more than two-thirds of which will be used to combat the smog produced by motor vehicle emissions, which produced 80 percent of the air pollution in Mexico City. This is the first transportation-related program for the World Bank.

In the US, Los Angeles has adopted stringent new regulations to cut pollution five-fold over the next 20 years. The Air Quality Management Plan includes 150 regulations that will cost almost $3 billion a year to implement. Like the Mexico City program, it focuses many of the new regulations on reducing auto emissions, forcing firms to reduce the number of car trips made by employees to work, with a possible penalty of $25,000 per day.

HOT SPOT

What's Happening: The Cree tribe of Quebec are struggling against the plans for the James Bay hydroelectric plant located on their ancestral lands. The development is planned in three phases: Phase one is already near completion. Phase one, called the La Grande project, would produce 14,791 megawatts of energy. The alterations to the environment would result in massive downstream erosion from five new reservoirs, widespread mercury poisoning of fish, wetlands loss and damage to caribou calving grounds. The final phases would designed to alter three river systems to produce power stations with combined capacities of 2,890 megawatts. Environmentalists fear approximately 2,000 square miles of wilderness would become flooded.

PROMISING INITIATIVES

The United States and Canada: On March 12, 1991, after extensive negotiations and delays, the US

pesticides you reap poison. I gave up chemicals in 1970, and if I had to go back to them I'd quit farming."
—Organic farmer, Illinois

"Like the constant dripping of water that in turn wears away the hardest stone, this birth-to-death contact with dangerous chemicals may in the end prove disastrous.... As matters now stand, we are in little better position than the guests of the Borgias."
—Rachel Carson, author of Silent Spring

"Why should the profits of chemical companies and convenience of farmers outweigh the importance of children's health?"
—Pamela Stephenson, Parents for Safe Food

"As far as I can tell, we're standing in the world's greatest Arctic ecosystem. We say, if they can drill here, where can't they drill? If we're going to develop this, we might as well go ahead and dam the Grand Canyon. You can make the same arguments for national energy needs."
—Tim Mahoney, Sierra Club, on plans to drill for oil in the Arctic National Wildlife Refuge

"Eighty percent of our pollution is caused by flowers and plants."
—Ronald Reagan, former US President and actor

"Smog over Los Angeles used to be a disaster, but now is normal, whereas a clear day on

A. *31, a decrease from 36 in 1986*
   Source: Atlas of the Environment by the World Wildlife Fund

which you can see the San Gabriel mountains is now a stroke of good fortune. Normality in Alaska is a series of toxic dumps, and soon Prince William Sound will become an 'ordinary' commercial channel like the Houston Ship Canal which periodically bursts into flame...'
—Alexander Cockburn, author and political commentator

"What I sometimes feel like doing, is enclosing a little packet of waste material with every one of the products we sell, just to remind people that they can't have one without the other."
—Chemical company waste disposal officer

"In the extreme, rather than build a new power station, one California utility just gave low energy light bulbs away."
—Dr. Bob Everett, Open University Energy and Environment Research Unit

and Canada signed an agreement to regulate emissions that cause acid rain. The two countries have agreed to set up clean air targets and monitoring programs, as well as an agency that will resolve air quality disputes.

The United States: Recent amendments to the US Clean Air Act set the goal of reducing both sulfur dioxide and nitrogen oxide emissions. Targets include a 10 million ton reduction of sulfur dioxide by the year 2000 and a 2 million ton reduction of nitrogen oxides by the year 1995.

Canada: Canada's newly adopted Green Plan provides $850 million (Canadian) to reduce solid waste and eliminate noxious chemicals from the air, land and water, $575 million to cut back on greenhouse gases and ozone depleting chemicals, $350 million to encourage ecologically conscious logging, fishing and farming, $175 million to purchase lands for national parks and protected areas and $500 million for environmental education and research, as well as for outreach programs to Native American and non-governmental organizations.

Canada's Parliament voted unanimously in June 1991 to protect 12 percent of Canada in its natural state. The 12 percent figure was cited as a desirable standard in the 1987 report for the United Nations, *Our Common Future*.

Mexico: Mexico's President Carlos Salinas de Gortari visited the Estuary de San Jose last year and pledged $500,000 in federal funds to preserve it as a sanctuary for 250 species of seabirds.

In 1991, President de Gortari announced a proposed constitutional amendment to reform the traditional ejido, or cooperative farms. The ejido is a legacy of the 1910-1917 uprisings in which farmworkers demanded their own land. He believes the 12-acre plots, traditionally awarded to peasants, are too small to be productive in the modern world. This proposal would allow peasants to sell or rend their 12 acres.

Q: *How many inches is the sea expected to rise by 2025 due to global warming?*

Central America

DEFORESTATION

What's Happening: As of the late 1980s, only 18 percent of Central America's original rainforest remained, and it is predicted that by 2010, only 5 percent will remain. Exports to the developed world are also doing their part to clear Central American rainforests: Barbados has replaced its forests with sugar cane to supply western nations. As a result of deforestation, 40 percent of the land on the Pacific side of the isthmus of Panama, where the majority of Panamanians live, is being eaten away by erosion. The Panama Canal is silting up with the soil stripped from local watersheds to the extent that ships may not be able to pass through it after another decade of silt build-up.

What's Being Done: Some of the most successful conservation efforts in Central America have been small scale and grassroots. Boscosa, for example, is a project working since 1988 to maintain the forest in the Golfo Dulce Forest Reserve in Costa Rica. Boscosa's staff—about a dozen geographers, foresters and social scientists—have been credited with raising the environmental consciousness among rural and village dwellers, called *campesinos,* on the peninsula and catalyzing the sustainable use of the forest reserve. The project, whose $25,000 annual budget is funded by the Conservation Foundation, the World Wildlife Fund and US AID, helped *campesinos* replant more than 200 acres of trees last year. It also helped put a larger area of forest under forest management, and aided in agroforestry efforts such as planting perennial cash crops between rows of rice and beans.

BARRIER REEF DESTRUCTION

What's Happening: In Belize, scientists suspect that fertilizers, pesticides and sediment, washed downstream as forest is cleared to plant banana and citrus crops, affects the 180-mile long barrier reef a few miles offshore. Overfishing and ever-increasing amounts of scuba divers and snorkelers present a

Bahamas, Belize, Costa Rica, Cuba, El Salvador, Guatemala, Honduras, Jamaica, Nicaragua, Panama

REGIONAL STATISTICS

Population: 42,300,000

Land Area: 253,048 square miles

Geography: Three countries in this region are islands: Cuba, Jamaica and Bahamas, which is made up of nearly 700 separate islands. Tropical forests average 30 percent of the total land coverage. Mountain chains tend to be volcanic in nature, creating fertile volcanic soil in the surrounding valleys and plateaus.

Climate: This region lies just north of the equator and is marked by heavy rains and tropical temperatures with an average temperature of 64° F. There is little change of seasons.

A. *Five to 15 inches*
Source: The Greenhouse Trap, *by Francesca Lyman*

Resources: Salt, fish, timber, aragonite, crude oil, nickel, gold, silver, lead, zinc, bauxite, gypsum, copper

GREEN STATISTICS

Major Conservation Initiatives:
• CITES: Bahamas, Belize, Costa Rica, Cuba, El Salvador, Guatemala, Honduras, Nicaragua, Panama
• RAMSAR: Guatemala, Panama
• Law of the Seas: Bahamas, Belize, Costa Rica, Cuba, El Salvador, Guatemala, Honduras, Jamaica, Nicaragua, Panama
• London: Costa Rica, Cuba, Guatemala, Honduras, Panama
• MARPOL: Bahamas, Panama
• Montreal: Panama
• Basel: Guatemala, Panama
• IUCN: Costa Rica, Nicaragua
• ITTO, Paris, 30% Club,
• WWF: None

Protected Areas:
10.0–19.9%: Panama

5.0–9.9%: Costa Rica

1.0–4.9%: Honduras, Cuba

Under 1.0%: Guatemala, Nicaragua, El Salvador, Jamaica

Insufficient data: Belize

GREEN RATING

Although torn by war and threatened by the poverty and development problems facing all of Latin America, this

more immediate threat to the reef's ecosystem. The barrier reef's crystalline waters harbor an astounding variety of life. One reserve alone is home to approximately 500 kinds of fish. Elkorn, brain and finger corals are also at risk with the destruction of the area.

What's Being Done: Biologist Janet Gibson is coordinating a Coastal Zone Management Project for the reef and outlying atolls which will designate a patchwork of commercial and recreational zones, marine preserves and wilderness areas. A management plan Gibson completed for an outlying atoll called Gover's Reef may be implemented by the end of 1991. It regulates fishing and closes off part of the reef to extractive use, except hand-line fishing practiced by some local subsistence fishermen.

HOT SPOT

The Pacuar River flows through the jungles of Costa Rica. Prized by whitewater paddlers the world over, it is also the center of a contentious face-off between conservation and development. The Costa Rican Electricity Institute (ICE) plans to start construction on a hydro-electric dam on the Pacuar within a decade. Opponents of the dam, united as the recently formed Costa Rican Association for the Protection of Rivers, charge that the government should initiate a comprehensive energy conservation and efficiency program before damming the Pacuar and two other rivers planned for hydro-projects. They note the 220-yard-high dam would flood valuable habitat, force the relocation of Cabecar indigenous people of the area and cut off a valuable and indefinite source of tourism revenue. ICE counters that Costa Ricans deserve the same level of development as enjoyed by the tourists who float down the river.

PROMISING INITIATIVES

Guatemala: Population increases are putting pressure on Central American forests. The people of the Petén province of Guatemala, for example, have sustainably logged, farmed, harvested and exported the fruits of the forest, primarily allspice and chicle, an ingredient in chewing gum, for generations. But the population of the Petén is growing at a pace that could spell doom for the region's forest. In three decades, the population has grown from 40,000

 Q: *Which state has the most landfills?*

people to 300,000. Conservation International, with help from US AID, has initiated a project to sustain the burgeoning population while maintaining the forest by increasing the profitability of products taken from it. The project aims to teach better management of trees and will also increase the amount of vegetation that produces marketable goods. Raw goods could be processed in the region, instead of exporting them, through the creation of manufacturing plants which would employ local people.

Honduras: Honduran farmers introduced the velvet bean plant to their fields to restore nitrogen in the soil, and the process increased maize yields threefold in only a little over three years. After testing the results of planting velvet beans, the farmers computed the gains and spread the word to other farmers, who are following suit.

Costa Rica: Biologists speculate that between 5 percent and 9 percent of the world's known species grow, creep, slither, crawl, jump, walk or fly in Costa Rica, which covers just 1/3,000th of the planet's land mass. A year-old project, called the National Biodiversity Institute, has undertaken the enormous task of collecting and cataloging all of Costa Rica's species. Intensive six-week training courses are already teaching park guards how to collect species in the field, moving their focus away from defending protected areas by force, toward educating local residents and visitors about the value of biodiversity.

region has taken conservation seriously and values its resources. It ranks **True Green**.

"Talamanca is a paradise, but we're going to lose this paradise unless the community gets organized. We are losing the beach, the reefs, the forests, our farms—and our culture." Two primary culprits are the uncontrolled expansion of the banana industry and the appearance of corporate-based tourism."
—Mauricio Salazar, president of Southeastern Costa Rica's Talamanca Association of Ecotourism and Conservation

Guatemala's Amigos del Bosque (Friends of the Forest) has hand-picked nearly a thousand community leaders from the countryside, which is mostly populated by people of Maya descent, to attend courses on how to prevent erosion and drought, how to start plant nurseries, purify water and build latrines.
—From BUZZWORM: The Environmental Journal, September/ October 1991

A**.** *Texas*
Source: The Recycler's Handbook, *by the Earth • Works Group*

South America

**Argentina,
Bolivia,
Brazil, Chile,
Colombia,
Ecuador, French
Guiana, Guyana,
Paraguay, Peru,
Suriname, Uruguay,
Venezuela**

REGIONAL STATISTICS

Population:
295,800,000

Land Area: 6,879,975
square miles

Geography: A continent connected to Central America by a tiny piece of Panamanian land, it touches the Atlantic Ocean in the east and the Pacific Ocean in the west. Dense Amazonian rainforests, snow-covered peaks of the Andes, Paraguayan lagoons and sandy, arid coastal strips typify this atypical region. A great diversity of extremes rules—from the fertile plains of the pampas in Argentina to the volcanic peaks of the Andes in Ecuador.

OIL DRILLING

What's Happening: American Texas Crude Oil Inc. has developed plans to drill for oil in Peru's largest Amazon nature reserve. The Pacaya-Samiria Reserve is a critical habitat for many rare species including grey and pink river dolphins, Amazonian manatees, giant South American river turtles and saddleback tamarins. The area is a unique flood zone where an oil spill would be devastating.

In Ecuador, the Energy Minister is expected to sign Amazonian exploration contracts with three foreign companies.

Bolivia signed a contract with an international consortium to drill for oil in a 5,700 square mile tract of Bolivian Amazon.

What's Being Done: North American environmental groups cooperating with South American environmental groups are forming an international coalition to put pressure on a Texas oil firm. Peruvians have been rallying to urge Peru's state company, Petroperu, not to sign the contract with Texas oil. In June 1991, a protest strike supported by the regional government shut down Iquitos, the largest city in Peru's Amazon, for one day.

DEFORESTATION

What's Happening: Colombia's Sierra Nevada Massif has lost over 75 percent of its rainforests in only 50 years. Much of this damage is the result of land being cleared to grow coca and marijuana.

Brazil contains 26.5 percent of the world's tropical rainforest. The Brazilian National Institute for Amazonian Research analyzed satellite photographs to decipher deforestation trends in the Brazilian Amazon. The analysis indicated that Brazil's deforestation is concentrated in areas where immigration and colonization are most intense and that rates increased exponentially between 1975 and 1980. Official government figures reveal that 60 percent of forest destruction between 1966 and 1975 was caused by large-scale cattle ranches. As of 1990, the Brazilian Forestry Department had set aside 200 million acres for timber development.

Q: How many tons of gasoline are burned by the average car in its lifetime?

What's Being Done: Begun as a personal effort by Juan Mayr, founder of the Fundación Pro-Sierra Nevada de Santa Marta, the Sierra Nevada Massif is being saved, through cooperatives, community monies and technical aid from the government's Ministry of Indian Affairs, Ministry of Agriculture, local peasants, indigenous tribes and national park authorities. Conservation efforts will be based on 1,500 year old Indian farming techniques, which will sustain the environment through farm terraces and store roads.

In June 1991, the Brazilian Government announced plans to create a $100 million (US) fund for the environment through debt-for-nature swaps, following an agreement between US President Bush and Brazilian President Fernando Collor de Mello. An environmental group or bank would buy the debt paper and sell it to the Brazilian government, cancelling a part of their $123 billion (US) debt. The money goes into a fund to save the forest. The debt paper is currently selling at 35 cents for each dollar of debt.

Brazilian President de Mello announced an end to subsidies for forest clearing and a commitment to enforce the permit required to burn forests. In June 1991, President de Mello unveiled a program permitting foreign financing of environmental projects in the region.

HYDRO-ELECTRIC PROJECTS

What's Happening: A proposed hydro-electric project on the Bío-Bío river in Chile would damage the wide range of plants and animals along the river and surrounding slopes and valleys. Endangered and rare species such as the guine wildcat, the Andean condor, araucaria tree and the cordillera cypress would suffer. Most sectors of this unique ecosystem have yet to be studied—a rich region between the dry central Chile and the lush rainforest of the south. The Bío-Bío region is also the ancestral land of the Pehuenche people, a group of Mapuche natives. The hydro-electric plant would flood their sacred lands, causing relocation of the Pehuenche.

What's Being Done: Although the Pehuenche people have lived relatively isolated in their mountain valleys, a public information group, the Chilean Coalition for the Bío-Bío, has been created to raise awareness of

Climate: The Atacama Desert in Chile has the honor of being the driest place on earth, with no measurable rainfall. Most of the region is tropical and humid, with cooler temperatures along the coast.

Resources: Timber, minerals, oil, copper, iron ore, tin, zinc, gold, silver, bauxite, fish, uranium, hydropower, antimony, bismuth, sulfur, tungsten

GREEN STATISTICS

Major Conservation Initiatives:
• CITES: Argentina, Bolivia, Brazil, Chile, Colombia, Ecuador, French Guiana, Paraguay, Peru, Suriname, Uruguay, Venezuela,
• RAMSAR: Bolivia, Chile, Suriname, Uruguay, Venezuela
• ITTO: Bolivia, Brazil, Peru
• Law of the Sea: Argentina, Bolivia, Brazil, Chile, Colombia, Guyana, Paraguay, Suriname, Uruguay
• London: Argentina, Brazil, Chile, Suriname
• MARPOL: Brazil, Colombia, Ecuador, Peru, Suriname, Uruguay
• Montreal: Argentina, Chile, Venezuela
• Basel: Argentina, Bolivia, Colombia, Ecuador, Venezuela
• IUCN: Argentina, Ecuador, Venezuela
• WWF: Argentina, Ecuador, Venezuela
• Paris, 30% Club: None

Protected Areas:
20.0% and over: Ecuador

A. *Three tons*
Source: Two Minutes A Day For A Greener Planet, *by Marjorie Lamb*

10.0–19.9%: Chile

5.0–9.9%: Venezuela

1.0–4.9%: Argentina, Colombia, Suriname, Brazil, Paraguay, Peru, Bolivia, Uruguay

Under 1.0%: Guyana

GREEN RATING

A large amount of deforestation is due to cattle ranching and planting of cash crops. Brazil has taken the lead in debt-for-nature-swaps and Ecuador, Chile and Venezuela all have high percentages of land set aside for conservation. This area is trying to balance conservation and development and ranks **Spring Green**.

the project's destructiveness throughout Chile.

ENDESA, Chile's electric company, is being required to carry out an environmental and social impact studies of its project. Although construction was started at the end of 1988, the environmental impact study of the dam is still underway.

TOURISM

What's Happening: The Galapagos Islands have experienced increasing numbers of tourists, which threatens unique varieties of wildlife and delicate ecosystems. Home to about 15,000 people, the Galapagos are visited by more than 50,000 tourists per year.

What's Being Done: Under pressure from environmental groups, The Charles Darwin Foundation and the Nature Foundation, the Ecuadorean government suspended in June 1991 a license to build a luxury resort. The state tourism agency drew sharp criticism after it granted private developers the right to build a 200-room hotel in the Galapagos capital, Puerto Baquirizo.

PROMISING INITIATIVES

Brazil: Facing criticism over its policies in the Amazon forest, the Parliament of the Federative Republic of Brazil redrafted the Brazilian Constitution in 1988 to include a chapter on the environment. Article 225 of Chapter IV, Environment, states:

> All have the right to an ecologically balanced environment, which is an asset of common use and essential to a healthy quality of life, and both the government and the community shall have the duty to defend and preserve it for present and future generations.

Q: *What companies routinely test new additives, which the FDA depends on to evaluate the additive's safety?*

Antarctica

POLLUTION

What's Happening: Antarctica's solid waste problem is reaching critical proportions. There are now 69 scientific research stations operating. In summer months the bases become small towns, while abandoned bases have been left as giant garbage heaps. The arrival of some 3,000 tourists each year adds to the waste being generated. Most food and all supplies to accommodate habitation on the frozen continent need to be flown or shipped in, and empty containers are simply left out in the open; biodegradation in Antarctica is speculated to be a hundred times slower than in temperate areas. The effect on wildlife is most visible: In order to reach a nearby breeding ground, penguins must walk over the broken glass and metal scraps of an Argentine landfill. In some areas the snow pack is already too polluted by air traffic to be used for research. Both onshore and offshore activities increase the pressure on Antarctica's few ice-free areas, which are in demand by birds, seals and other wildlife and increasingly by scientists and tourists.

What's Being Done: Much of the pressure on Antarctic Treaty nations to abide by an international convention agreement, which mandates removing wastes from the continent, has come from the environmental group Greenpeace, the first non-governmental organization to establish a base in Antarctica. By making public the offenses committed by each nation, Greenpeace specifically, but other environmental groups as well, have tried to humiliate treaty nations into following regulations.

ENDANGERED SPECIES

What's Happening: Whalers have killed an estimated 99 percent of the region's blue whales, 97 percent of its humpbacks and 80 percent of fin whales since early this century. They continue to hunt minke whales despite an international moratorium forbidding it.

What's Being Done: Australia, UK, US and the Netherlands are leading a campaign to stop nations

REGIONAL STATISTICS

Antarctic Treaty Nations with voting rights: Argentina, Australia, Belgium, Brazil, Chile, China, Finland, France, Germany, India, Italy, Japan, New Zealand, Norway, Peru, Poland, South Africa, South Korea, Spain, Sweden, United Kingdom, United States, USSR, Uruguay

Non-Consultative Parties: Austria, Bulgaria, Canada, Colombia, Cuba, Czechoslovakia, Denmark, Ecuador, Greece, Hungary, Netherlands, North Korea, Papua New Guinea, Romania

Land Area: 5.4 million square miles, expanding to some 8 million square miles, including ice pack, in winter.

Geography: While 70 to 75 percent of the world's fresh water is stored in the ice of Antarctica, it is considered a desert because the water, in its frozen state, is mostly unavailable as a life support. Precipitation averages only a little over one inch a year, similar to the Sahara.

A. *The company that wants to manufacture or use the additives*
   Source: Federal Food and Drug Administration

Only 2 percent of the continent's surface is free of ice, including about one-twentieth of the coast, the peaks of mountains and the dry valleys, where no rain has fallen for at least 2 million years. Over nine-tenths of the coastline is comprised of ice shelves or cliffs. The shelves stretch out over the sea and break off into often immense icebergs; one, sighted in 1956, was the size of Belgium. Another iceberg sighting in spring 1990 was the size of Rhode Island.

GREEN RATING

Antarctica's problems originate in industrial nations eagerly eyeing a continent of new resources. Yet international intiatives offer hope; this area ranks **Spring Green**.

such as Japan and the Soviet Union from increasing whaling quotas. The International Whaling Commission, which includes both offending nations, has recognized that commercial whaling is threatening the survival of some species.

TOURISM

What's Happening: Tourism in Antarctica is on the rise. At the present time, about 3,000 visitors arrive each year, in many cases for brief stays in modest hotel facilities. While harm is rarely intentional, the potential for damaging wildlife and fragile plant life, disturbing scientific research and polluting the environment increases with the number of tourists. Several tour companies have announced that they are expanding their capacity to transport visitors to Antarctica, and plans have been drafted to construct a substantial hotel there.

What's Being Done: Increasing control over tourism is on the Antarctic policy agenda, and several tour companies have voluntarily developed their own guidelines to avoid harm to research and the environment. Much difficulty remains in how to ensure that tour company ships registered in countries that are not party to Antarctic Treaty agreements will follow safety, waste disposal and pollution-control regulations.

PROMISING INITIATIVES

An international forum, sponsored by the US and consisting of legislators from 35 nations, met in May 1990 and resolved unanimously in favor of world park status for the continent. In the US, Congress passed two pieces of legislation in 1990 designed to protect Antarctica. The Gore/Owens Resolution calls for Antarctica to be protected as a global ecological commons. The Kerry/Conte bill makes it unlawful for US citizens to engage in commercial mineral activity there.

Q. *By what percent did energy use increase in the United States between 1973 and 1988?*

Arctic

INDIGENOUS PEOPLES

What's Happening: The Arctic's human population was decimated in the early 19th century by diseases from traders who also enslaved the native peoples. In the rush to exploit the Arctic peoples and land, traditional cultures were destroyed. Today, one in 10 deaths among native Arctic people is alcohol-related, and violent deaths among Canada's native peoples are three times the national average. Extensive commercial hunting by peoples of various border nations has had severe impact on the sustainable hunting practices of the native peoples.

What's Being Done: The Inuit Regional Conservation Strategy is an example of indigenous peoples organizing to champion their own interests. This group is being developed under the Inuit Circumpolar Conference (ICC), a non-governmental organization that represents the interests of the Inuit peoples of the US, USSR, Canada and Greenland. This project has won the active support of the UN Environment Program and has become an important vehicle for fostering international cooperation on environmental issues in the Arctic.

AIR POLLUTION

What's Happening: Prevailing winds blow sulfate compounds, sulfur dioxide, chlorofluorocarbons, carbon dioxide, soot and even radioactive particles from the midlatitudes into the far north. These pollutants accumulate in the Arctic atmosphere due to the relatively stationary air masses during most of the year and the cold temperatures that result in low rates of precipitation in the high latitudes. The result is Arctic haze over the fragile Arctic biome during the winter and spring months. The dense blanket of suspended particles over the Arctic rivals the smog of Los Angeles.

Arctic airmasses are particularly effective at trapping greenhouse gases, creating a greater depletion of ozone near the Arctic than in midlatitude areas. Because of the Arctic ozone hole, scientists predict the temperature increase over the Arctic to be two to three times as great as at mid-latitude.

REGIONAL STATISTICS

Geography: The Arctic is really an ocean, bordered by the northern tips of three continents: North America, Europe and Asia. The borders of the Arctic Circle are difficult to draw, and some scientists set the boundary at the point where the taiga (subarctic evergreen forests in Siberia, Eurasia and North America, also the Earth's largest forest) gives way to the sparse tundra.

Land temperature can reach –40° F, yet Arctic Ocean waters never go below 32° F.

The one-third of the Arctic Ocean that is underlaid by continental shelves is one of the world's most abundant fishing grounds, yielding a tenth of the annual global catch. During the spring, three-quarters of a million marine mammals summer in the rich waters of the north.

The land, rich in resources, ecologically sensitive and sparsely populated, is in a location that makes the Arctic of immense geopolitical importance.

A. *64 percent increase*
Source: The Greenhouse Trap, by Francesca Lyman

Unlike Antarctica, the sovereignty of Arctic-rim states over the land is never in question.

The US obtains over 20 percent of its oil from its land in the Arctic; the Soviet Union over 60 percent.

Although home to approximately 10 million indigenous peoples, the Arctic is regarded as a comparatively safe and convenient environment for the deployment and operation of strategic weapons systems.

GREEN STATISTICS

Major initiatives:
Grey Zone Arrangement: between Norway and the USSR covering the use of marine resources in the Barents Sea.

Marine Environmental Cooperation Agreement: between Canada and Greenland/Denmark dealing with the ecosystems of Davis Strait and the Baffin Bay.

Svalbard Regime (the regime for the conservation of northern fur seals and the regime for the conservation of polar bears) has 40 signatories and began in 1925.

GREEN RATING

The sustainable lifestyles of the indigenous peoples of the arctic are under threat both from other nations and the industrializing of this area. Because of the threats, the area ranks **Camouflage Green.**

What's Being Done: The consequences of the disruptive climate effects have yet to be truly understood. International protocols on greenhouse gases and climate change are being developed, but the hole is already far larger than expected.

HOT SPOT

In 1980, the US Congress declared 19 million acres of Alaska as permanent wilderness, including the Arctic National Wildlife Refuge, west of Prudhoe Bay near the Canadian border. However, 1.5 million acres of the refuge's coastal plain was reserved from wilderness protection pending study of the area's potential oil reserves. This coastal range represents the last undeveloped range along the northern slope of Alaska and is home to more than 160 animal species. Since 1987, developers, government, environmentalists and native peoples have been locked in a debate over whether it should be opened to oil exploration. With the Bush Administration's 1991 energy proposal to open the refuge to oil exploration, the prospect for continued protection of this piece of the Arctic coast appears jeopardized. Although the energy bill containing language to open the area to drilling did not make it out of committee, another energy proposal will be submitted in 1992. President Bush has stated he will veto any energy bill that does not allow drilling in the refuge. The potential oil exploration could result in major effects on the caribou population, musk oxen and snow geese, as well as decreasing habitat for the endangered and protected polar bears.

Q: *Most people overwater their lawns by twice as much. How much water does the average lawn need every week?*

East Asia

WILDLIFE TRADE

What's Happening: Taiwan offers passage for poached and smuggled elephant tusks and rhino horns from Africa and parrots and reptile skins from Latin America. The entire East Asian region is the world's top importer and exporter of ivory, reptile skins, live parrots, live primates and cat skins.

What's Being Done: The international community has been enraged by the Taiwanese wildlife trade. A new World Wildlife Fund report was published in November 1991 documenting the infractions of the trade. It was sent to high level authorities in China and Taiwan. While waiting for a response from authorities, the World Wildlife Fund has opened a Traffic office in Taiwan.

POLLUTION

What's Happening: Japan is facing a severe shortage of landfills, and dumps much of its trash into the Tokyo Bay. A top contributor to Japan's landfill waste is overpackaging. Japan has four deep-sea dump sites. Persistent coastal pollution exists in Japan, the Koreas and China, which also has a deep-sea dump site. Mount Everest, the world's tallest mountain, has become littered with trash by climbers.

What's Being Done: Japan has a growing green consumer movement. About one-fifth of all households belong to one of 665 consumer cooperatives, buying clubs that also manufacture products and operate markets. The coops lead the Japanese green movement by teaching consumers how to live ecologically.

Tezuka Kozan of Japan has developed a process whereby one ton of waste can be compressed into one cubic yard. This cube can then be coated with concrete and used as a building block.

Some international climbing groups have begun to lead cleanup climbs on Mount Everest.

Bhutan, China, Hong Kong, Japan, Mongolia, Nepal, North Korea, South Korea, Taiwan, Tibet

REGIONAL STATISTICS

Population: 1,355,800,000

Land Area: 4,610,900 square miles

Geography: This region is widely varied geographically. The Himalayas dominate Nepal, much of China and Bhutan, creating fertile valleys. Agricultural lands are found in northern Mongolia and parts of China, while the Gobi Desert dominates southern Mongolia. A series of mountain ranges run through North and South Korea, with many coastal harbors in South Korea. Japan is an archipelago extending 1,744 miles in the East China Sea.

Climate: Ranges from humid to semi-tropical, to montane to desert in southern Mongolia.

Resources: Timber, coal, natural gas, limestone, metals, marble, fish, copper, iron ore, copper ore, tungsten, graphite, gold, silver

A. *About an inch*
Source: 50 Simple Things You Can Do To Save The Earth, *by the Earth • Works Group*

GREEN STATISTICS

Major Conservation Initiatives:

- CITES: China, Japan, Nepal
- RAMSAR: Japan, Nepal
- ITTO: Japan, S. Korea
- Law of the Seas: Butan, China, Hong Kong, Japan, Mongolia, Nepal, N. Korea, S. Korea
- London: China, Japan
- MARPOL: China, Japan, N. Korea, S. Korea
- Montreal: Japan
- IUCN: N. Korea, Mongolia, Nepal
- WWF: Japan
- Paris, Basel, 30% Club: None

Protected areas:

10.0–19.9%: Bhutan

5.0–9.9%: S. Korea, Japan, Nepal,

Under 1.0%: China, Mongolia, N. Korea

GREEN RATING

Japan has one of the world's highest birth rates, is the leader in whale hunting and high sea driftnetting, although they have the technology and money to be a leader in the conservation world. Taiwan is a leader in the illegal trade of endangered wildlife. This area ranks **Pea Green**.

FISHERIES

What's Happening: Japan is a leading hunter of whales, and has resisted international pressures to stop whaling. Japan imports one-third of all shrimp worldwide, mainly from shrimp farms in Asia that contribute to the destruction of wetlands. China and South Korea are some of the world's largest fishing nations with catches increasing five times faster than the fish stock replenishes. Taiwan, North and South Korea and Japan continue to use driftnets in international waters.

What's Being Done: Japan requested an emergency quota of 50 minke whales under the humanitarian grounds provision to support small scale coastal whaling. The International Whaling Commission refused to grant permission.

PROMISING INITIATIVES

China: The Chinese delegation at the second preparatory meeting held in April 1991 for the UN Conference on Environment and Development proposed a "green fund" for forests and grasslands. The fund, which would be provided primarily by industrialized nations, would give third world countries the money they need for forestation programs.

Nepal: The snow leopard, a highly endangered and secretive cat, roams the Annapurna region of Nepal. The forests it inhabits offer over 100 varieties of orchids and the most extensive rhododendron forests in the world. Yet little is known about snow leopards because most of their habitat range is inaccessible. A new study is being conducted by the World Wildlife Fund to learn essentials about the animal including mapping of its prey (blue sheep), obtaining information on its population density and conducting interviews with local residents.

Q: *What kind of substance does the Food and Drug Administration normally allow in small amounts to be used in foods?*

Middle East

POPULATION

What's Happening: Iran has one of the highest population growth rates in the world with a 3.6 percent rate of natural increase annually and a total fertility rate of 6.3 births per woman. During the war with Iraq, Iran's officials viewed the high birth rate as a strategic plus, because it provided more soldiers. After the end of the war in 1988, however, Iran began to see the birth rate as an obstacle to economic reconstruction.

What's Being Done: The government of Iran has legalized female sterilization and will provide the surgery free of charge. There are conditions, however: The woman must already have three children, and she must have her husband's permission to be sterilized.

ENVIRONMENTAL EFFECTS OF WAR

Air Pollution: During the Persian Gulf War, in Kuwait, some 700 wells were set ablaze. In addition, 200 more wells, storage tanks and oil refineries were blown up in the fighting. Nearly 100 wells flowed uncontrollably into the desert, forming black lakes of oil. Independent estimates put the figure of oil flowing through the burning wells at 3 million barrels of oil a day. The last well was capped in November 1991.

The fluid that flows from an oil well in Kuwait consists of crude oil, gas (methane) and water. A burning rate of 3 million barrels of oil a day amounts to the daily combustion of 430,000 tons of crude oil. This injects 25,000 tons of smoke into the atmosphere each day, together with 285,600 tons of carbon dioxide, 42,840 tons of carbon monoxide, 10,200 tons of sulfur dioxide and 600 cubic feet of methane per barrel of oil.

The most serious climatic effect will be on regional food production. Scientists predict the possibility that the mass of smoke will be blown by the southern Gulf wind to the Indian sub-continent and interfere with the monsoon circulation system, influencing the duration of the monsoon season and possibly affecting the rice crops in Southeast Asia. This

Bahrain, Cyprus, Iran, Iraq, Israel, Jordan, Kuwait, Lebanon, North Yemen, Oman, Qatar, Saudi Arabia, South Yemen, Syria, Turkey, United Arab Emirate (UAE)

REGIONAL STATISTICS

Population: 187,200,000

Land Area: 2,427,414 square miles

Geography: This region is composed mainly of desert and semi-desert areas. The high Zagros Mountain Range is a natural border dividing Iran and Iraq. The Saudi Arabian desert is the world's largest sand desert. Natural meadows exist in the more humid areas of Israel.

Climate: Hot and dry throughout the region with more moderate temperatures in coastal and montane areas

Resources: Oil, fish, copper, asbestos, gypsum, clay, salt, building

A. *Cancer-causing*
Source: Federal Food and Drug Administration

stone, iron, natural gas, sulfur, potash, bromine, limestone, chrome, asphalt, magnesium, chromite, boron

GREEN STATISTICS

Major Conservation Initiatives:
• CITES: Bahrain, Cyprus, Iran, Israel, Jordan, UAE
• RAMSAR: Iran, Jordan
• Law of Sea: Bahrain, Cyprus, Iran, Iraq, Kuwait, Lebanon, Oman, Qatar, Saudi Arabia, UAE, North Yemen, South Yemen
• London: Jordan, Oman, UAE
• MARPOL: Cyprus, Israel, Lebanon, Oman, Syria
• Montreal: Israel
• Basel: Bahrain, Cyprus, Israel, Jordan, Kuwait, Lebanon, Saudi Arabia, Syria, Turkey, UAE
• IUCN: Bahrain, Iran, Iraq, Jordan, Oman, Saudi Arabia
• ITTO, 30% Club, Paris, WWF: None

Protected Areas:
1.0–4.9: percent Israel, Iran

Under 1.0 percent: All countries in the rest of the Middle East region

GREEN RATING

On average the population growth is high, with relative density of population above average. Damage due to war and the oil industry has been severe. This area ranks **Pea Green**.

would reduce food supplies for hundreds of millions of people.

Black rain has fallen in Pakistan, Afghanistan, Iran and deep into Turkey. Skiers in the Himalayas have come across fields of oily black snow.

Regional temperatures in Kuwait were between 10 to 27 degrees Fahrenheit lower than normal in the summer of 1991. Some 4 million tons of acid rain were predicted to fall in the region, where soil is less resilient to acidity than in Europe or North America. Crop yields will be seriously reduced and water supplies contaminated.

Water Contamination: Oil spillage into the Persian Gulf during the war may be the worst environmental result. The Gulf is small and shallow with very salty water and only one small outlet to the Indian Ocean. During the war, an estimated 3 million barrels of oil were intentionally and unintentionally spilt into Gulf waters.

Nuclear: On January 23, 1991, US bombers had destroyed two Iraqi nuclear reactors. The two small research reactors were mainly used to produce radioactive isotopes for medical purposes. It has not been reported whether any of the radioactivity from the bombed reactors leaked into the environment.

Other Long-Lasting Impacts of the War: So much attention was focused on the oil fires that other important environmental impacts were not widely reported. Great damage was done to the vegetation and surface of the desert by the massive coalition carpet-bombing, by maneuvers of large numbers of armored vehicles and by the enormous numbers of bulldozers that made trenches. Approximately 25 percent of Kuwait's landmass has been disrupted. The rate of sandstorms, it is estimated, will double, causing severe desertification. This desert destruction may have severe long-term repercussions.

Q: *How big was the hole in the ozone layer estimated to be in 1989?*

South Asia

WETLANDS

What's Happening: Wetlands loss in the South Continent has reached critical proportions. Pakistan, Bangladesh and northern India have lost half their wetlands in the last century. Specific wetlands under the most serious threat include the Sundarbans in India and Bangladesh, and the Keoladeo National Park, Laccadive Islands and Vedanthangal wetlands in India.

What's Being Done: India is a signatory of RAMSAR, the Convention on Wetlands of International Importance especially as Wildlife Habitat, but has set aside only one wetland, Chilka Lake, to meet the minimum requirement to be a RAMSAR signatory. Pakistan is also a signatory, but has not set aside any wetlands for protection.

FRESH WATER POLLUTION

What's Happening: India's rivers are practically open sewers. They carry untreated wastes from factories, and raw sewage from urban and rural areas out to the sea. Fewer than 10 percent of the industrial plants lining the Ganges River (considered holy) treat the effluents they are dumping into the river. About 70 percent of the country's surface waters are highly polluted, and the vast majority of towns and cities have absolutely no sewage treatment facilities. The problem is not limited to India—fewer than 25 percent of Afghans have access to safe drinking water, and fewer than 50 percent of those living in Pakistan and Bangladesh enjoy safe water.

What's Being Done: The Government of India has allocated $5 million for a cleanup program for the Ganges River.

WILDLIFE TRADE

What's Happening: Wildlife trading has reduced tiger populations in India from about 40,000 to less than 3,000. India is also a major exporter of live birds (mostly parrots) and a major ivory trader. Bangladesh is a major exporter of reptile skins.

Afghanistan, Bangladesh, India, Pakistan, Sri Lanka

REGIONAL STATISTICS

Population: 1,115,900,000

Land Area: 1,871,067 square miles

Geography: This region lies on the Arabian Sea just east of the Middle East. Afghanistan is mostly covered by the snow-capped mountains of the Hindu Kash and deep valleys. Pakistan, India and Sri Lanka have large regions of fertile plains intersected with various river systems. Bangladesh is mostly low-lying ravines frequented by tropical monsoons and floods. Most of eastern Pakistan is desert.

Climate: Ranges dramatically from hot arid deserts to wet humid valleys and cool mountain lands.

Resources: Natural gas, oil, coal, copper, sulfur, lead, zinc, iron ore, salt,

A. *26 million square kilometers*

Source: 1990-91 World Resources, *World Resources Institute*

EARTH JOURNAL

precious and semi-precious stones, limestone, manganese, bauxite, graphite

GREEN STATISTICS

Major Conservation Initiatives:
• CITES: Afghanistan, Bangladesh, India, Pakistan, Sri Lanka
• RAMSAR: India, Pakistan
• Bonn: India, Pakistan
• ITTO: India
• Law of the Sea: Afghanistan, Bangladesh, India, Pakistan, Sri Lanka
• London: Afghanistan
• MARPOL: India
• Basel: Afghanistan
• Paris, Montreal, 30% Club: None

Protected Areas
10.0–19.9%: Sri Lanka

5.0–9.9%: Pakistan

1.0–4.9%: India

Under 1%: Bangladesh, Afghanistan

GREEN RATING

Deforestation and wetland loss is occurring at one of the world's highest rates. Water contamination from sewage is widespread. India is beginning an attempt to clean up the Ganges. There is much potential for improvement if the long-term overpopulation problem can be controlled. This area ranks **Spring Green**.

What's Being Done: The Sundarbans, which stretches for nearly 2,400 square miles and is the world's biggest mangrove forest, has been set aside as a reserve for the Royal Bengal tiger. It also protects the coast of India and Bangladesh from the fierce cyclones that charge up the Bay of Bengal and offers protection for fish and shellfish spawning grounds.

DEFORESTATION

What's Happening: Much of South Asia's deforestation is a result of a fuel wood crisis. Urban demand puts more and more pressure on local firewood resources, and suppliers have to go further and further from the big cities to obtain the wood; firewood for Delhi comes from Madhya Pradesh, 420 miles away. India has one of the most rapidly increasing rates of deforestation in the world—368,000 acres of forest were being destroyed annually in 1980, and by 1990 the numbers had increased to 3.75 million acres annually. Bangladesh and Sri Lanka have also lost large areas of their rainforest. And the firewood scarcity crisis has become especially acute in northern Afghanistan.

What's Being Done: In Rajasthan, India, acacia trees imported from the Middle East were planted to stabilize 150,000 acres of sand dunes. Attempts are also being made to decrease the area's dependence on fuel wood. Solar ovens are being sold to the citizens of India with a 50 percent subsidy from the government. Over 80,000 ovens have already been bought.

HOT SPOT

Plans for Sardar Sarovar and Narmada Sagar dams in India, to be built with a $450 million World Bank loan, would force relocation of 70,000 people.

Q: *Is there evidence that biodegradable plastic bags safely degrade in landfills?*

Southeast Asia

TROPICAL FOREST DESTRUCTION

What's Happening: Tropical forest destruction in Southeast Asia threatens one of the world's important carbon sinks and an enormous amount of species endemic to the area. Yet the region remains one of the largest tropical timber exporters, supplying about three-quarters of world tropical timber exports. In the Philippine archipelago, the volcano Mount Makiliang has more species of woody plants than all of the US and has already lost 80 percent of its tropical forests, most of it to the tropical timber trade. A landless poor plus commercial logging combine to fuel the deforestation. A significant amount of the commercial trade is illegal, which allows exporters to sell more timber than is allowed by international regulations. This year, the Philippines reported exports four times less than what Japan reported receiving from them. In Malaysia, the forests are cut at the rate of 637,500 acres a year for new rubber and oil palm plantations, threatening the survival of 7,900 different species of flowering plants. Other countries in the region such as Thailand, Vietnam and Indonesia are rapidly losing their tropical forests to logging, fuel wood gathering, agricultural expansion and plantation development. Myanmar has increased forest felling six-fold in just ten years.

What's Being Done: Thailand and the Philippines recently moved to ban logging in their remaining rainforests. The Thai Cabinet abolished all timber concessions, which halted logging nationwide. Philippine President Corazon Aquino banned timber exports. The Indonesian government has begun to levy fines for violation of new environmental forest protection policies, and has already forced 70 timber companies to close because of violations. Lack of money, however, threatens to hamper conservation efforts in Indonesia. The country has proposed to reforest 50 million acres of devastated land, yet it can only afford to reforest about 740,000 acres. In Malaysia, public concern over logging in tropical forests has led to numerous protests against logging companies, sometimes ending in the arrest of protestors by the government.

Brunei, Cambodia, Indonesia, Laos, Malaysia, Myanmar (Burma), Philippines, Singapore, Thailand, Vietnam

REGIONAL STATISTICS

Population: 454,600,000

Land Area: 1,730,106 square miles

Geography: Tropical rainforests, as much as 75 percent in Brunei, cover much of this region. Several archipelagos of volcanic islands include Philippines, Indonesia and Singapore, all of which total more than 20,000 separate islands. Dense mangrove swamps cover Malaysia and fertile alluvial plains cover most of the Indochina Peninsula.

Climate: Tropical rainy and humid sub-tropical. No winter and annual rainfall exceeds annual rates of evaporation.

Resources: Timber, precious stones, petroleum, rubber, coal, natural gas, nickel, cobalt, copper, gold, tin, bauxite, tungsten, flourite

A. *At best, the bags break down into invisible, and likely toxic little chips*
  Source: The Recycler's Handbook, by the Earth•Works Group

GREEN STATISTICS

Major Conservation Initiatives
- CITES: Brunei, Indonesia, Malaysia, Philippines, Singapore, Thailand
- RAMSAR: Vietnam
- ITTO: Indonesia, Malaysia, Philippines
- Law of the Sea: Brunei, Myanmar, Cambodia, Indonesia, Laos, Malaysia, Philippines, Singapore, Thailand, Vietnam
- London: Philippines
- MARPOL: Brunei, Myanmar, Indonesia
- Montreal: Indonesia
- Basel: Philippines
- Bonn, Paris, 30% club: None

Protected Areas:

5.0–9.9%: Indonesia, Malaysia, Thailand

1.0–4.9%: Brunei, Philippines, Singapore

Under 1%: Myanmar, Cambodia, Laos, Vietnam

GREEN RATING

Deforestation is extreme, with over three-fourths of the world's timber exports coming from this region. The mangrove swamps are being destroyed at an alarming rate. Yet governmental efforts are being made, with Thailand and Philippines banning logging in the remaining rainforests. Vietnam has suffered massive environmental damage from the US bombings and defoliant spraying during the Vietnam War. This area is a

WETLAND DESTRUCTION

What's Happening: Myanmar and Malaysia have lost half of their wetlands in the past century. Indonesia, the Philippines and Singapore are also losing large portions of their wetlands to mining, logging, pollution and urban and agricultural development.

What's Being Done: Although Indonesia is not a signatory of RAMSAR, the country is taking some action to protect its wetlands, which are some of the most extensive and least disturbed wetlands in the region. The World Wildlife Fund, The World Conservation Union, and other groups are working with the Indonesian government to develop management plans.

WAR DAMAGE

What's Happening: During the Vietnam War, US herbicide teams dumped millions of gallons of herbicides (mainly Agent Orange) over half the forests in the country. In addition, over half of the coastal mangrove swamps in the south were destroyed by bombs, defoliants, napalm and bulldozers.

MANGROVE AND CORAL REEF DESTRUCTION

What's Happening: Mangrove forests supply important habitats for over 2,000 species of fish, invertebrates and plants and are at least as productive as good farmland. Southeast Asia has the largest mangrove ecosystem in the world. Over 800 square miles of Indonesia's existing mangrove forests are being felled by the woodchip industry for export to Japan and another 4,000 square miles have been converted into water ponds to cultivate prawns, shrimp and milkfish. Between 1920 and 1988 the mangrove area of the Philippine archipelago was reduced from 2,000 square miles to a mere 152 miles. Southeast Asia's coral reefs are also in danger, endangering in turn the food supply of the area—almost 90 percent of all fish caught by fisherpeople in Indonesia and 55 percent of the fish caught by the Filipinos depend on coral reefs. In Thailand and Malaysia, tourist resorts, overfishing and bucket dredging for tin are doing damage to the coral reefs. In the Philippines and Indonesia, blast fishing, coral mining, collection for the tourist

Q: *Of the six warmest years during the last century, how many occurred in the 1980s?*

trade and use of poisons are the biggest contributors to the destruction.

What's Being Done: Thailand actively cultivates mangroves to protect its coasts from erosion. Indonesia is rehabilitating damaged mangroves along the coastline of Java, as part of the United Nations Regional Mangrove Project for Asia.

PROMISING INITIATIVES

Indonesia: One woman's life-long campaign to reforest the Indonesian landscape, stripped bald by the logging of tropical timber, has led to legislative action by the country's government. Dr. Umi Hani'im Suseno has transformed the hilly land of Wana Gama from a barren wasteland back into its original lush forest habitat, a habitat designed to accommodate both the people of the area and the wildlife that has now returned. The Indonesian government has been so impressed with the project's success that it intends to establish versions of it throughout the country.

The Indonesian government has also decided that at least 10 percent of each of its 27 provinces will be included under parks protection, and a network of 52 Environmental Study Centers has been set up throughout the archipelago to help incorporate biodiversity considerations into the government's planning process.

Butterfly farming, already successful in Papua New Guinea, is spreading to Indonesia, and has given local people living near the Arfak Mountain Reserve in Irian Jaya a way to profit from protected areas without damaging them.

mix of **Camouflage Green** and **Spring Green**.

___

"Not even the sophisticated sonar of a dolphin can always detect the danger. So dolphins swim into the net. Whales, seals and sea turtles swim into it. Attracted by the trapped fish, seabirds dive into it and drown. Some victims of the nets may struggle through, only to die painfully, weeks or months later. Most marine creatures stay snared, writhing and dying. In the morning the net is lifted from the water and you can see the body count."
—Greenpeace report on Japanese driftnet fishing in the Pacific.

"Ocean fishing today is oceanic anarchy."
—Jacques Cousteau

A. *Six*
  Source: The Greenhouse Trap, *by Francesca Lyman*

Eastern Europe

POLLUTION

Albania,
Bulgaria,
Czechoslovakia,
Hungary, Poland,
Romania, Yugoslavia

REGIONAL STATISTICS

Population: 123,400,000

Land Area: 450,409 square miles

Geography: This region is on average 50 percent cultivated lands and the rest is rolling plains and forests. The Balkan Mountains run south and the Carpathian Mountains extend east-west; the fabled Transylvanian Alps in Romania extend east-west. Seas surround the countries with the Baltic Sea in the north, Adriatic to the southwest and the Black Sea to the southeast. Yugoslavia has over 2,000 miles of coast line.

Climate: This region has a cold winter and a warm summer season marked by few extremes of temperature.

Resources: Petroleum, minerals, timber, metals, coal, lignite, natural gas

What's Happening: Eastern Europe has the worst air quality in the industrialized world, water unfit even for industrial use, acid rain and forest death—all the result of thousands of inefficient, outdated factories pumping pollutants into the air and water.

In cities such as Bratislava, Czechoslovakia, and Miskolc, Hungary, residents are exposed to such high levels of pollution that their health is seriously endangered; recent studies have shown that one in 17 deaths and one in 24 disabilities in Hungary is due, directly or indirectly, to air pollution. In the Hungarian capital, Budapest, the state news agency reports that a one hour stroll through some of the city's most polluted streets is as damaging to the lungs as smoking 20 cigarettes, and between 35 percent and 40 percent of Hungary's 10.3 million people live with "inadmissible" air and water pollution. Residents of Katowice Province in Silesia, Poland, have a 15 percent higher incidence of circulatory illness, a 47 percent higher rate of respiratory illness and 30 percent more cases of cancer than the rest of the Polish population. Cracow, Poland, suffers under acidic smogs; the magnificent historic buildings of this world heritage site are disintegrating and weakening. Stone friezes and statues are flaking away.

Polish officials have admitted that the water of their largest river, the Vistula, is too polluted even for industrial use; it would corrode the machinery. In the Bohemian section of Czechoslovakia, power plants and chemical factories belch out so much sulfur dioxide that the region receives 127 tons of acid rain per square kilometer every year, in comparison to the national average of 25 tons. Men in the area have an average life expectancy of 52, which is ten years younger than the national average, and one in every ten babies is stillborn.

Acid rain and air pollution have taken their toll on Eastern Europe's forests as well. Polish scientists estimate that between 30 percent and 50 percent of Poland's forests will be damaged by 1995. Other countries particularly badly hit by forest death are Czechoslovakia, with 71 percent of its trees suffering

Q: *Worldwide, enough wheat, rice and other grains are produced to provide every human being with how many calories per day?*

from defoliation, and Bulgaria, with 43 percent.

Air pollution in Yugoslavia has damaged the forests across the country. Close to 25 percent of the trees in Slovenia are moderately to severely defoliated. The people of Yugoslavia are also suffering high mortality rates from respiratory diseases caused by air pollution.

In Bulgaria, approximately 115 square miles of land are polluted with heavy metals emitted from nearby metallurgical plants. Soil has been degraded by mining operations and waste dumped by industrial, domestic and agricultural sources. Bulgaria's rivers have been severely polluted by raw sewage, heavy metals, nitrates, oils and detergents. The sludge caught in these rivers then flows into the Black Sea.

Water quality is improving in Hungary, but currently only 20 percent of the country's waste water is correctly treated. Less than half of the population have and use adequate sewage facilities. Many areas in Hungary still do not have safe drinking water supplies because of high nitrate and arsenic pollution.

What's Being Done: The incredible cost of cleaning up Eastern Europe's factories and rivers is keeping the governments, which are already facing the immense costs of trying to privatize their economies, from taking drastic action. In Poland, official estimates of the cost of cleaning up the Vistula River have ranged from $100 million (US) up to $15 billion. The West German Institute for Economic Research estimates that $200 billion will be needed to clean up the industries of eastern Germany, Poland, Czechoslovakia, and the European part of the USSR.

Funding has started to arrive from Western Europe and the US. Newly unified Germany is spending millions of dollars on cleaning up its eastern industries. Sweden has given Poland $60 million to clean up the Vistula, which contributes about 40 percent of the total nitrogen run-off into the Baltic Sea. The European Community has committed $30.5 million to Hungary and $26.8 million to Poland for environmental aid and will contribute to the development of an environmental center for Eastern Europe in Budapest. The US is contributing as well, committing $40 million for environmental aid to Poland and Hungary through 1992.

HAZARDOUS WASTE

A. 3,600

Source: How to Make the World a Better Place, by Jeffrey Hollender, William Morrow and Company, New York, 1990.

GREEN STATISTICS

Major Conservation Initiatives:
- CITES: Hungary, Poland
- RAMSAR: Bulgaria, Hungary, Poland, Yugoslavia
- Law of Sea: Bulgaria, Czechoslovakia, Hungary, Poland, Romania, Yugoslavia
- London: Hungary, Poland, Yugoslavia
- MARPOL: Bulgaria, Czechoslovakia, Hungary, Poland, Yugoslavia
- Basel: Hungary
- 30% Club: Bulgaria, Czechoslovakia, Hungary
- ITTO, Paris, Montreal, IUCN, WWF: None

Protected Areas:
10.0-19.9%: Czechoslovakia

5.0-9.9%: Poland, Hungary

1.0-4.9%: Albania, Yugoslavia, Bulgaria

Under 1.0%: Romania

GREEN RATING

The environment has been poisoned and acid rain there is the most severe in the world. Life expectancy has decreased in the past 50 years. Now public awareness is growing and governmental concern is strong. We have hope for the area and rank it **Spring Green**.

"Levels of cancer, skin disease, respiratory problems, hypertension and premature births are all higher than average here. A man will come in with bronchitis but we have real difficulties diagnosing it because his problems are compounded by so many other diseases. One thing is certain—when these people retire at 50 they have been totally destroyed,"
— Dr. Ion Luca, physician, Copsa Mica industrial center, Romani

"Polluted first by Czechoslovakia, the Odra River is biologically comatose even before it crosses the border. And the Vistula, Poland's main artery, is so chemically active for 80 percent of its length that it is unfit even for industrial use; it corrodes the machinery. Around 10,000 factories sluice their effluent into it, unfiltered, and half of the 800 communities along its banks have no sewage treatment plants,"
—Peter Martin

"Radiation, heavy metals, chemical pollution, inadequate nutrition and psychological stress have caused essential changes in the health status of the Bylelorussian population," said Dr. Tamara V. Belookaya, a diagnostician at the Institute of Radiation Medicine in Aksakovshchina, USSR. "The medical and biological consequences of Chernobyl appear much more serious and

industries are also producing astounding amounts of hazardous waste. Groundwater contamination from overuse of agricultural chemicals poses a significant risk to public health and large amounts of hazardous waste shipped east by Western Europe add to the problem. Waste generators in Hungary reportedly dispose of over 500,000 tons of hazardous waste annually in illegal landfills. Prague's city planners cannot account for about 80 percent of the estimated 40,000 tons of hazardous waste produced in the city each year. The Danube River accumulates the industrial, agricultural and municipal waste of Germany, Czechoslovakia, Hungary, Yugoslavia, Romania and Bulgaria before emptying into the Black Sea, where it threatens Bulgaria's coastal resort trade.

What's Being Done: In Hungary, water pollution is a priority concern. Balaton Lake has undergone a major cleanup process, and progress was made in removing the phosphorus that contributed to the lake's decline. Poland and Czechoslovakia are reassessing the role of nuclear power in meeting their energy needs. Public concern was raised by the Chernobyl accident and widespread protests against the building of additional reactors have taken place.

ENDANGERED SPECIES

What's Happening: The widespread harvesting of trees and the heavy contamination of soil, water and air by industrial and agricultural pollutants have caused 40 percent of Bulgaria's bird species, 25 percent of its mammals, reptiles and amphibians and 20 percent of its plant species to be classified as endangered or rare, states the Bulgarian Academy of Sciences. Romania's Danube Delta is one of the largest reedbeds in the world and is home to more than 160 breeding species of birds. It also serves as a major stopping point for birds migrating between Europe, the Mediterranean, the Middle East and Africa. Government promotion of irrigated agriculture and construction of dikes to provide a shipping lane severely damaged the Delta.

What's Being Done: While little is yet being done to alter the activities that are leading to the endangerment of species, information on the problem is becoming more available.

 Q: *What type of plastic product is recycled in a closed loop?*

HOT SPOT

Just north of Cracow, Poland, the Nowa Huta steel mill development belches out 10,000 tons of noxious gases daily. And along with its annual 5.5 million ton steel production, it produces an annual dust emission containing 7 tons of cadmium, 170 tons of lead, 470 tons of zinc and 18,000 tons of iron. There are no sulfur filters in the energy plants, even though all are coal burning. All this has taken an immense toll on the population and on nearby Cracow. A mere 12 percent of Nowa Huta workers retire normally; an astounding 80 percent retire on disability pensions and 8 percent die while still working. Many economists agree that the only way that the industries will have sufficient profitability to pay for pollution control equipment is by scaling back unprofitable activities, which would force layoffs of thousands of workers. A 1980 government panel found that Poland loses between $3.5 billion and $6 billion annually to pollution; the figures include losses due to acid rain damage to timber and buildings as well as pollution-induced respiratory diseases and other health problems.

PROMISING INITIATIVES

Czechoslovakia: One of the first acts of the recently elected Civic Forum government was to create the Ministry of the Environment for the Czech Republic, an institution equivalent in both function and power to the US Environmental Protection Agency.

Hungary: Hungarian environmentalists succeeded in preventing the construction of a huge hydroelectric dam on the Danube that would have altered the course of 120 miles of the river, contaminated the drinking water of 2 million to 3 million people and endangered the lives of as many as 5,000 species of plant and animal life indigenous to the area.

Romania: Romanian environmentalists have won close to 5 percent of the seats in the Chamber of Deputies.

diverse than had been expected during the first years.

"The children born in 1988 [the Chernobyl disaster occurred in April 1986] to mothers who permanently lived in the region are weak, susceptible to infections, and have poorer development as compared with children of the same age from the so-called clean regions."

Romania under the rule of Nicolae Ceausescu was "equal parts dark Baltic fairytale and Orwellian prophecy— the labyrinth of secret tunnels under the capital city...the marble of the dictator's palace shining white amidst the soot and poverty of his people.

"Copsa Mica, Romania, seems a town of chimneysweeps. The coal-fired smoke from its Karbosin plant is appalling, yet soot is the least of the town's worries. A nearby metallurgical factory generates an invisible pollution—unfiltered bioxide and monoxide of sulfur—that is far more lethal.

"Copsa Mica's oil, milk and food are contaminated by lead and cadmium. The 6,000 townspeople suffer high rates of respiratory infection, anemia, premature birth, malnutrition, nervous disorders and retardation. Life expectancy is 55, and residents report that one in three babies is born dead."

—*One Earth*, Ellie McGrath, Collins, New York, NY, 1990

A. *Plastic bags are made into more plastic bags*
  Source: The Recycler's Handbook, *by the Earth • Works Group*

Western Europe

HAZARDOUS WASTE

What's Happening: The hazardous waste problem in Western Europe, and the cost of cleaning it up, has reached a critical level. Some 5,000 waste sites have been identified in the Netherlands alone, and at least 350 of them must be cleaned up immediately since they are posing serious threats to public health and the environment. The Dutch are already spending $80 million a year for the next 15 to 20 years to try to reduce the effects of many years of illegal and improper disposal. French authorities have identified 66 abandoned waste dumps that need immediate attention, and the Germans have several thousand to clean up. Nitrates from dumps are showing up in Europe's drinking water, which can cause blood poisoning in infants, gastric cancers in adults, and fetal malformations. The landfill crisis is especially acute, and most countries have turned to incineration, a high-cost means of waste treatment that produces air pollution and leaves a highly toxic residue which in turn needs disposal. Belgium, France, Germany and the UK burn some of their waste at sea on incineration ships, but this practice is coming under increased opposition in the international community, and is being phased out. Another "solution" to waste problems has been the extensive exporting of hazardous waste. There is a large flow of toxic waste between the various Western European nations, with Germany by far the largest exporter. And by 1989, nearly 2.2 million tons of hazardous industrial waste were being shipped from Western Europe to Eastern Europe and to the third world.

What's Being Done: The Basel Convention on the Control of Transboundary Movements of Hazardous Wastes and their Disposal, signed by 34 countries and the European Economic Community (EEC) in March 1989, requires party nations to produce as little hazardous waste as possible, to ensure safe disposal of the wastes produced, and to reduce exports and imports to a level "consistent with environmentally sound and efficient management."

Andorra, Austria, Belgium, Denmark, Finland, France, Germany, Greece, Greenland, Iceland, Ireland, Italy, Liechtenstein, Luxembourg, Netherlands, Norway, Portugal, Spain, Sweden, Switzerland, United Kingdom

REGIONAL STATISTICS

Population: 1,207,800,000

Land Area: 2,270,422 square miles

Geography: The Alps mountain range is renamed in each country it transverses: Austria, France, Germany, Switzerland, Liechtenstein and Italy. The central and southern part of the region is largely fertile plains and rolling hills intercepted by rivers and mountain ranges. The northern section, Greenland, Iceland, Sweden, Norway and Finland, are low plains regions with snow and

Q. *What year was ozone depletion over the Southern Hemisphere first observed?*

ACID RAIN AND FOREST DEATH

What's Happening: Acid rain and other airborne pollutants are eating away the marble of Athens' monuments; experts say that more architectural damage has been done to the city in the last 25 years than in the previous 2,400. More important ecologically is the damage acid rain is causing forests and lakes. In the southern half of Norway, 80 percent of the lakes and streams are either technically dead or on the critical list. Fish have been destroyed in lakes totalling an area of over 5,200 square miles. Every year, Norway is bombarded by rain as acidic as lemon juice (pH 3). Nearly a quarter of Sweden's 90,000 lakes are acidified to some extent, 4,000 of which are beyond the point of being able to sustain fish. About 54,000 miles of its rivers and streams are also affected. Acid rain is thought to be one of the main threats to Germany's and Switzerland's forests.

What's Being Done: The EEC countries have signed a convention to limit damaging emissions. Large fossil fuel plants will have to cut emissions of sulfur dioxide by about 40 percent by 1998 and about 60 percent by 2003. Nitrogen oxides will be cut by 30 percent by 1998 as well. And by 1993, all new cars sold in the EEC countries will have to be fitted with catalytic converters, which reduce emissions of nitrogen oxides and other pollutants. These figures are averages for the region—different reductions are allocated to different countries, based on the unique fuel supply, economical and geographical circumstances of each member state. Sweden is treating the symptoms of acid rain by adding lime to its lakes, which neutralizes the acidity. By 1984, it had added lime to 3,000 lakes at a cost of $25 million (US). Initiatives are coming from the private sector as well. BMW car manufacturer is spending one-third of its annual budget to meet the new clean up regulations, and Mercedes Benz is introducing a catalytic converter that will last 100,000 miles.

PROMISING INITIATIVES

Germany: Plastics are the least disposable of any garbage, and the proportion of plastics in solid waste is increasing dramatically. German scientists have now developed a strain of bacteria that can degrade plastic. For example, the bacteria can reduce the

ice-covered lands touching the Arctic Circle. Iceland is the most volcanic region on Earth. This area was entirely forested before human habitation and today is still 35 percent woodland.

Climate: A region of four distinct seasons, humid and warm in the summer and humid and cold in the winter. The mountainous regions and valleys have on average cooler temperatures. The southern-most countries have warmer, sunnier temperatures and lack seasonal diversity.

Resources: Mineral water, coal, iron, timber, brown coal, potash, marble (Italy), oil, salt, cryolite (Greenland), fish (Italy and Iceland), hydroelectric power; lead, barite, peat, silver, gypsum, dolomite, copper, mercury, petroleum, pyrites, tungsten

GREEN STATISTICS

Major Conservation Initiatives:
• CITES: All except Greece, Iceland and Ireland
• RAMSAR: All except Luxembourg
• ITTO: Belgium, Denmark, Finland, Germany, Greece, Italy, Luxembourg, Netherlands, Norway, Spain, Sweden, Switzerland, United Kingdom
• Law of Sea: All except Germany, Liechtenstein and United Kingdom
• London: All except Austria, Liechtenstein and Luxembourg
• Paris: Belgium,

A.**1985**
• *Source:*1990-91 World Resources, *World Resources Institute*

Denmark, France, Germany, Iceland, Ireland, Luxembourg, Netherlands, Norway, Portugal, Spain, Sweden, United Kingdom
• MARPOL: All except Ireland, Liechtenstein and Luxembourg
• Montreal: All except Iceland and Liechtenstein
• Basel: All except Austria, Iceland and Ireland
• 30% Club: All except Greece, Iceland, Ireland, Portugal, Spain, United Kingdom
• IUCN: All except Austria, Ireland, Italy, Liechtenstein
• WWF: All except Iceland, Ireland, Liechtenstein, Luxembourg, Portugal

Protected Areas:
20.0% and over: Luxembourg

10.0–19.9%: western Germany, Czechoslovakia

5.0–9.9%: France, United Kingdom, Austria

1.0–4.9%: Netherlands, Denmark, Switzerland, Italy, Spain, Portugal

Under 1.0%: Belgium, eastern Germany, Ireland

GREEN RATING

This region leads the world in hazardous waste sites (over 10,000). Water pollution and acid rain are extreme. Citizens are involved, laws and regulations are becoming more stringent, but until the region works out its hazardous waste problem without dumping it on Africa, the area ranks **Camouflage Green.**

plastic body of the German Trabant car to about 2 percent of its original weight.

Netherlands: Since previous attempts to stop dumping in the North Sea by bordering countries have been unsuccessful, Holland plans to declare a section of the North Sea a nature conservation area to allow the ecosystem to recover. If plans are followed, it will be the first time an entire sea area is officially protected against further environmental damage. The Parliament recently approved a project to build 2,000 new windmills, which will be the largest wind power endeavor since the 17th century. The windmills are expected to provide 10 percent of the nation's energy needs.

Sweden: While the concept of taxing polluters has often been criticized for allowing offenders to "buy" the right to pollute, Sweden has decided that economic incentives can be an effective temporary means of getting emissions down to a lower level. Taxes are to be levied on artificial fertilizers and pesticides, and on emissions of sulfur dioxide and carbon dioxide from combustion installations. A carbon dioxide tax on oil, coal, natural gas, paraffin (kerosene), liquified petroleum gas and petrol has been established. It is estimated that total emissions should fall by 5 million to 10 million tons (8 percent to 16 percent). And starting in 1992, emissions of nitrogen oxides from large combustion plants will be subject to tax as well, which is expected to further reduce emissions by 30 percent.

Q: *In tropical Latin America, 90 percent of the arable land is owned by 7 percent of the population, the poorest third owning only what percent of the land?*

Soviet Republics

DESERTIFICATION

What's Happening: When the USSR opened up marginal lands to farming by initiating heavy irrigation, more than 17.5 million acres were degraded to near desert. Irrigation with inadequate drainage caused severe salinization which sterilized the soils, rendering them unfit for further food production. As a result, across the central plain, salt and dust storms are large enough to be mapped, spanning thousands of miles. Some 910 million acres of good, arable land is eroding and 325 million acres of plowed land has lost up to 30 percent of humus while 128 million acres has lost over 40 percent. "In one rich area," according to a Soviet organic farmer, "some 1.25 million acres have blown away, the top soil turned to sand and lost." Soil and its degradation is the number one environmental problem facing the USSR, according to Goskompriroda.

WATER POLLUTION

What's Happening: Last year in Ufa, a city just west of the Urals, industrial chemicals were accidentally dumped into the town's water supply. For several weeks, until local authorities reported the incident, residents drank water with dioxin levels exceeding health standards by 147,000 times.

In Karalpakia, a town alongside the polluted Amu Dar'ya River, their home is referred to by residents as "the sewer of central Asia." Infant mortality is 60 deaths per 1,000 live births.

Groundwater in the grainbelt is poisoned by mineral fertilizers, pesticides and salinization from forced-land irrigation projects. Water must be boiled before drinking in St. Petersburg.

LAKE POLLUTION

What's Happening: A paper mill on Lake Baikal's southern shore is one of the largest mills in the USSR. The advanced pollution controls were never used and since the 1960s black effluents have spewed into the lake and smoke has damaged the surrounding forests. Over 23 square miles of the lake have been declared

Union of Soviet Socialist Republics

REGIONAL STATISTICS

Population: 289,000,000

Land Area: 8,649,489 square miles

Geography: Most of the Soviet Union is a vast plain stretching from Eastern Europe to the Pacific Ocean, separately called the North European Plain in the east, the West Siberian Plain in the center, the Steppes in the south and the Central Siberian Plain in the east. The north consists of frozen tundra, the central region contains a belt of temperate forests and grasslands and the south has steppes or prairies.

Climate: Ranges from cold, dry arctic conditions in the north to more temperate and humid conditions in the south.

Resources: Fossil fuels, hydropower, lead, zinc, timber, mercury, potash, phosphate, nickel

A. *1 percent*
   Source: Natural Resources Defense Council

GREEN STATISTICS

Major Conservation Initiatives:
- CITES: Yes
- RAMSAR: Yes
- ITTO: Yes
- Law of the Sea: Yes
- London: Yes
- Paris: No
- Marpol: yes
- Montreal: Yes
- Basel: No
- 30% Club: Yes
- IUCN: No
- WWF: No

Protected Areas:
Under 1.0% in total (no data available from recently independent states)

RAMSAR Convention Wetland Sites in USSR:

Volga Delta
Issyk-kul Lake
Lakes of Lower Turgay
    and Irgiz
Lake Khanka
Kourgal'dzhin and
    Tengiz Lakes
Kanadalaksha Bay
Krasnovodsk and North
    Cheleken Bays
Kirov Bays
Intertidal areas of
    Dounai, Yagorlits and
    Tendrov Bays
Matsalu Bay
Sivash Bay
Karkinitski Bay

GREEN RATING

Serious contamination of water, soil and air is due to the growth of agriculture, industry and urban areas without any environmental controls. Deforestation rates are equal with Brazil. Citizens are increasingly politicized. Money and technology from the West is being sought,

sterile. Because of geological dikes that divide the lake bottom into three sections that are hydrologically isolated, the pollution affects only the southern basin. However, the southern basin is where most of the fundamental biological activity takes place. Since 1989, there are more than 100 factories and plants on Baikal's shores. They all lack purification systems and, along with agriculture, pour millions of tons of wastewater, pesticides and fertilizers into the lake.

What's Being Done: Under pressure from new green organizations, the government has been considering alternatives, one of which is to convert the pulp mill into a furniture factory and use timber from outside Baikal's watershed. Yet in 1987, the plant was still operating and the government only agreed to a pipeline to carry the effluents farther away into the Irkut River. Environmental groups pointed out that the whole city's water supply is below the planned terminus of the pipeline. Demonstrations against the plan followed, causing the pipeline plan to be cancelled.

CHERNOBYL

What's Happening: The health impact of the Chernobyl nuclear disaster is proving more widespread and more serious than first thought. Thousands of people in Byelorussia are reportedly suffering from anemia, gastritis, tuberculosis and susceptibility to infections. Thyroid cancer among Byelorussian children jumped from 8 cases in 1989 to 42 cases in 1990. Studies from across the Soviet Union are substantiating claims that low-level radiation from the Chernobyl plant has entered the food chain. In addition to radiation exposure illnesses, a 15 percent rise in pulmonary tuberculosis is believed to be at least partly caused by heavy metal particles spewed from the reactor. Numerous other health problems that have increased in severity or frequency are being tied to the Chernobyl disaster.

What's Being Done: The World Health Organization has begun studying the health records of 227,000 cleanup workers and 300,000 residents of contaminated areas. In October 1991, Ukraine's Parliament voted to close the two remaining reactors at Chernobyl by 1993.

 Q: *The US consumes 6 billion barrels of oil annually. What is the amount of recoverable oil reserves in the US?*

AIR POLLUTION

What's Happening: The air in 103 cities across the USSR exceeds the Soviet health standards by ten-fold. In 1987, health cost due to pollution was estimated at about 11 percent of the GNP.

HOT SPOT

Many report the ecological catastrophe of the Aral Sea region to be "worse than Chernobyl." The Aral Sea is suffering from a depletion of its water sources. The sea has shrunk by 66 percent in volume and 40 percent in area since 1960. Water has been diverted to irrigate crops for larger agricultural output, causing severe soil salinization and acidification because of a lack of proper irrigation. Soviet media acknowledge that two-thirds of the people in the Aral Sea region suffer from typhoid, hepatitis or throat cancer from water-related pollutants. Infant mortality has skyrocketed and deformities are a common occurrence. Inhabitants call the Aral Sea the "salty sea of death."

PROMISING INITIATIVES

Launched in Spring 1988, the Green Party in Georgia now counts over 6,000 members in 18 regions and more than 100 local organizations of individuals from a variety of backgrounds. The Greens in Georgia carry out educational, economical, publishing and other activities.

One of the Georgian Greens' most recent successes was the struggle against the building of the Trans-caucasian Railway, which was mainly for military purposes and would have greatly endangered the river Aragui, the main drinking water source for Tbilisi City. Also the gigantic construction of the Khudoni hydro-electric power station was stopped on the Enquri River.

In March 1991, the first non-government organization conference on the environment ever held between the USSR and the US took place. Some 50 Americans representing environmental organizations came together with over 100 Soviet environmental groups. In the USSR, environmentalism is not just a quality of life issue as it often is in the west; environmentalism is a matter of survival.

but for the moment the area ranks **Pea Green**.

———————

"If only radiation were red," said one of the few doctors who stayed to work in the Zone, *"then these people would know what they are living in."*

"Chernobyl opened our eyes. For the first time we understand what sovereignty means, what democracy means, what freedom means. The Ukraine has been sacrificed. This nation, which possesses thousands of years of history, is now on its knees, its radioactive knees. This is not drama; this is tragedy. But the most important thing is the children. Without healthy children, we have no future. Please help the children of Chernobyl," said Soviet poet Ivan Drach.
—From "Children of Chernobyl," *Greenpeace Magazine*, January/ February 1991

A. **28 billion barrels**
. *Source: Rocky Mountain Institute*

South Pacific

Australia, New Guinea, New Zealand, Papua New Guinea, Solomon Islands, Fiji, Kiribati, Tonga, Tuvalu, Vanuatu, Western Samoa

REGIONAL STATISTICS

Population: 26,100,000

Land Area: 3,274,686 square miles

Geography: Consisting of over 585 islands with different geographic features, this region lies just south of the equator in the South Pacific Ocean.

Climate: Ranges from rainy tropical to dry desert to humid subtropical areas where seasons are more pronounced.

Resources: Iron ore, zinc, lead, tin, coal, oil, gas, copper, uranium, nickel, gold, timber, silver, fish, bauxite, copra

GREEN STATISTICS

Major Conservation Initiatives
• CITES: Australia, New Zealand, Papua New Guinea, Vanuatu
• RAMSAR: Australia, New Zealand
• ITTO: Australia, Papua

DEFORESTATION

What's Happening: Since European settlers came to Australia 150 years ago, 100 million acres of forests, half the original area, and 158 million acres of scrub and woodland, one-third of the original area, have been cleared. Australia now suffers from massive soil erosion at a rate of six tons of soil eroded for every one ton of produce grown.

What's Being Done: In 1990, Australia announced a national plan for the planting of 1 billion trees in the 1990s dubbed the "Billion Trees Program." If the program is successful it will restore two-thirds of the tree cover lost since European settlement.

CORAL REEF DESTRUCTION

What's Being Done: Responding to the designation of the Great Barrier Reef in Australia as a "Particularly Sensitive Area" by the UN International Maritime Organization in March 1991, Australia will soon introduce a reef protective regulation. The regulation will state that all ships exceeding 77 yards and all ships with cargo of oil, liquified gas or harmful chemicals will require extra assistance when using the inner route of the Great Barrier Reef.

HIGH SEAS DRIFTNETS

What's Happening: Driftnets are nicknamed "walls of death," because the large panel of plastic webbing, suspended vertically in the water by floats attached to the top and weights attached to the bottom, catches and kills all the creatures that swim into it. Japan, Taiwan and South Korea utilize driftnet fisheries in the South Pacific area.

What's Being Done: The South Pacific nations have opposed driftnetting with firm solidarity. As a result of this intense diplomatic pressure, Japan, Taiwan and South Korea agreed to reduce their driftnet fleets in the South Pacific. However, as of fall 1991, Japan had not reduced their fleets nor the number of deployments.

On December 22, 1989, the UN adopted a

Q: *How many miles does an airline passenger have to fly to generate 1 pound of carbon dioxide?*

resolution calling for an immediate ban on large-scale driftnetting in areas where it is not currently in practice and a halt to driftnetting in the South Pacific by June 1991, with a provisional moratorium in the rest of the world's oceans by July 1992.

On October 3, 1991, Japan declared publicly that it considers the ban on driftnetting, strongly supported by the US, as an emotional response with no scientific base.

HOT SPOT

Kalama Island or the Johnson Atoll, 700 miles west of Hawaii, is a tiny coral island home to more than a half million birds, 200 species of fish, monk seals, humpback whales and hawksbill turtles. It also is the burnsite for chemical weapons by the US Government. Driven by a Congressional mandate and a chemical arms treaty between Bush and Gorbachev, the US Army is rushing to incinerate the world's deadliest chemicals. Incineration began in June 1991 and will continue until August 1994.

What's Being Done: President Bush, in October 1991, pledged that no more chemical weapons would be sent to Johnson Island.

PROMISING INITIATIVES

Fiji: Fiji has joined the new and growing international ban on the export of Hawksbill turtle shells. The shell trade has endangered the Hawksbill turtle. The Solomon Islands will be the only remaining country allowing the export of shells once Japan adheres to its deadline.

Australia: A national strategy for minimizing and recycling waste was announced by the Minister of the Environment. The strategy includes a 50 percent cut in materials sent to landfills and a dramatic increase in recycling efforts by the year 2000.

The Australian government has increased funding for the "Save the Bush" projects. The grants aim at saving the remnant patches of Australian bush vital in maintaining biodiversity, protecting water catchments, controlling soil erosion and providing shade and shelter for livestock.

New Guinea
- Law of Sea: Australia, Fiji, Nauru, New Zealand, Papua New Guinea, Solomon Islands, Tuvalu, Vanuatu, Western Samoa
- London: Australia, Kiribati, Nauru, New Zealand, Papua New Guinea, Solomon Islands
- Marpol: Australia, Tuvalu, Vanuatu
- Montreal: Australia, New Zealand
- Basel: New Zealand
- IUCN: Australia, New Zealand, Western Samoa
- WWF: Australia, New Zealand
- Paris, 30% Club: None

Protected Areas:
10.0–19.9%: New Zealand

1.0–4.9%: Australia

under 1.0%: Papua New Guinea, Solomon Islands, Fiji

GREEN RATING

New Zealand and Australia suffer from salinization of their soil and heavy deforestation. The smaller islands are mostly victims of nuclear testing, driftnetting in their nearby seas and pesticides from the industrial world. The citizens are very opposed to these abuses, to no avail. Still, because of the hope that new initiatives will be effective, this area ranks **Spring Green**.

A. *Two miles*
  Source: The Greenhouse Trap, by Francesca Lyman

PART 3
ECOCULTURE

ARTS & ENTERTAINMENT

IV

Everything that combines the environment and culture, from new environmental books to green art to ecofashion, contributes to the emerging ecoculture of our world. Within Arts and Entertainment you will discover what "green" means to those personalities seen on the big and little screens. And at your fingertips are directories which will help you decide which films, television shows, books, recordings, magazines and computer software are worth your green money.

ECO-MAGS

The following is a list of environmental periodicals—ranging from newsletters of specific goal-oriented organizations to large circulation independent general audience magazines.

American Forests
Published bimonthly by American Forestry Association, 1516 P St. NW, Washington, DC 20005. *American Forests* is "the nation's most popular and influential magazine on environmental benefits of trees and forests. It presents the latest issues, lifestyles, how-to information, adventures and travels."

The Amicus Journal
Published quarterly by Natural Resources Defense Council, 40 W. 20th St., New York, NY 10011.
"*The Amicus Journal* is the quarterly, award-winning publication of the Natural Resources Defense Council. The journal covers national and international policy and has been called 'the leading journal of environmental thought and opinion.'"

Animals
Published bimonthly by the Massachusetts Society for the Prevention of Cruelty to Animals, 350 S. Huntington Ave., Boston, MA 02130. *Animals* appeals to a wide general audience with features on both pets and wildlife.

Animals' Agenda
Published monthly by the Animal Rights Network, Inc., 456 Monroe

Publishing for the Environment

With all the confusion about what's really happening to our environment, it's good to know that there are resources out there that help sort out all those facts, figures, opinions and predictions. Environmental periodicals arm the environmentalist with the most up-to-date information on a regular basis. Also, a large crop of environmental books sprang up in 1991, designed to add a green tint to any home library. And for the young environmentalist, the 1990s promise a flurry of kid-tested, adult-recommended fun and informative eco-books.

THE ENVIRONMENTAL MAGAZINE BUSINESS

- By Rodney Ho -

DEFYING LONG ODDS and a slumping advertising market, new environmental magazines are muscling their way onto newsstands and carving out a new publishing niche.

Meanwhile, such old standbys as *Audubon* and *Sierra* magazines are turning more consumer-oriented to attract readers and boost sales.

The new environmental magazines are few in number: No more than a half-dozen have solid national distribution, compared with more than 40 new sports magazines in the past year, according to Samir Husni, a researcher at the University of Mississippi's Department of Journalism who tracks new magazines. And many environmental start-ups in the past

Q: *In what environment are nine nuclear warheads and 50 nuclear reactors known to be lying, comprising the sixth largest "nuclear power" in the world?*

couple of years were stillborn or folded quickly for lack of seed money.

But those that have survived—such as *Garbage, E* and *Buzzworm*—are selling well at bookstores and newsstands. Between 50 percent to 60 percent of environmental magazine copies are sold, compared with 38 percent for the average magazines, Dr. Husni says. With enough magazines on the market, "they can be presented on the newsstand in such a way as to gain visibility and, hopefully, more subscribers," he adds.

Despite the ad-sales slump, these environmental offerings have been selling more space. Three-year-old *Buzzworm*, a magazine filled with high-quality photography and in-depth articles, saw ad pages for the first five issues in 1991 jump more than 40 percent to 170, compared with 120 during a comparable period in 1990. The nonprofit *E* magazine, which analyzes current issues such as toxic waste and the greening of cities, has seen gross ad sales increase 50 percent in the past year to $60,000 an issue and has built its circulation to 80,000.

Accelerating competition

"We've weathered the recession remarkably well considering we're a new magazine," says Patricia Poore, editor and publisher of *Garbage*, a two-year-old bimonthly with a focus on consumer-oriented news. Advertising has increased over 60 percent in a year, from 20 to 33 ad pages an issue.

Publishing veterans say the competition for advertisers and subscribers between the newcomers and oldtimers published by the Sierra Club and the National Audubon Society is accelerating. "They're all trying to hit the magic formula and steal readers," says Schellie Hagan, a former *Audubon* staffer.

Several old liners are exploiting their high name recognition to battle the upstarts for mainstream newsstand display. *Sierra* magazine began selling copies of its September 1991 issue in retail outlets for the first time. A bigger, bolder logo on the cover complements new features on health and home, says publisher Carole Pisarczyk.

"*Sierra* is a household name and that's important on the newsstand," Ms. Pisarczyk says. "We really need to appeal to the more broad-based consumer who isn't necessarily a member." So far, ad pages are up 23.7 percent over 1990.

Turnpike, Monroe, CT 06468.

"*Animals' Agenda* offers a broad range of materials and information about animals and environmental issues, and provides a forum for discussion of problems and ideas. It tries to reach people at all levels of consciousness and commitment to inspire a deep regard for, and greater activism on behalf of, animals and nature."

The Animals' Voice Magazine

Published bimonthly by the Compassion for Animals Foundation, Inc., 3960 Landmark St., Culver City, CA 90232.

"You won't find a more comprehensive source on animal defense issues than on the pages of *The Animals' Voice Magazine*."

Audubon

Published bimonthly by the National Audubon Society, 950 Third Ave., New York, NY 10022.

"*Audubon* reports on the state of the Earth. Coverage includes ecology, conservation, wildlife, policy, recreation and technology. It offers views of problems and proposed solutions, and it celebrates the natural beauty we must preserve."

Buzzworm

Published bimonthly by Buzzworm, Inc., P.O. Box 6853, Syracuse, NY 13217.

"As an independent magazine reporting on natonal and international environmental issues, *Buzzworm* strives to

A. *The ocean floor*
   Source: Greenpeace, July/August 1989

offer balanced and comprehensive coverage of the challenges facing the world so that the general reader may thoughtfully and actively respond."

The City Planet
Published monthly by The City Planet, 4988 Venice Blvd., Los Angeles, CA 90019.
"*The City Planet* will cover up-to-date information on ecological products and services, organic gardening,

GEOGRAPHIC SPARKS QUARANTINE

CANBERRA, Australia—Packets of American wildflower seeds used in a promotion by the *National Geographic* have prompted a quarantine alert in Australia.

The wildflower seeds sent with an issue of the magazine had not passed the country's quarantine checks.

"Some of the species ...may be host to seed-borne diseases which are not present in crop and native plants in Australia, [while] others pose a threat to the environment," Resources Minister Alan Griffiths said in a statement.

"To avert any possible environmental catastrophe Australian subscribers... who have received the... seeds should surrender them immediately," he said.
—The Washington Post, *August 15, 1991*

Sierra's most direct competitor, the traditionally independent and conservative *Audubon*, is also reshaping its marketing and content. In March, National Audubon Society president Peter A. A. Berle fired Les Line, *Audubon*'s editor for 25 years, and in July brought in Michael Robbins, a former editor of the now-defunct *Oceans* magazine, who dismissed almost the entire editorial staff. Former staffers accuse Mr. Berle of trying to "trivialize" the magazine's content in pursuit of more and younger readers.

Berle vehemently denies such accusations. "The magazine is evolving, but there will be no revolutionary change," Robbins says, noting that there will be more articles about the relationship between "humankind and the natural world" rather than mere nature-appreciation pieces. Marketing will include more copies on newsstands, he adds, but *Audubon* "isn't infatuated with numbers like people seem to think. Since we're dealing with important issues, we just want to reach the widest possible audience."

Recession's toll

Many of the older magazines such as *Audubon* and *Greenpeace* downplay the influence of the newer ones. "In a way, magazines like *E* and *Garbage* are fulfilling their internal mandate, but we still have a circulation that is four times their entire circulation combined," says Andre Carothers, editor of *Greenpeace*. Most of the magazine's readers belong to its parent organization, but it has sold about 8,000 copies per issue off the rack since its debut on newsstands in January 1991.

Such success, however, hasn't staunched the recent decline in donations and membership as the recession has taken its toll on many of the groups. Greenpeace recently reduced its bimonthly magazine to a quarterly to save money, and the Wilderness Society's *Wilderness* magazine dropped all advertising last winter, shrinking in size from 56 to 40 pages.

Among the competing environmental publications is *Mother Earth News*, which folded in 1990 and was then revived under the new management of Sussex Publishers Inc. New York-based Sussex pared *Mother Earth News*' circulation base from 550,000 to 350,000.

Another offering—two-year-old *Trilogy*—is trying to differentiate itself from the pack by touting its willingness to air both sides of the environmental debate, whether it's the National Rifle Association or radical

Q: *What percentage of Americans are actively contributing solutions to environmental problems?*

Earth First! With sections on recreation, industry and environment, *Trilogy* has emerged from the recession almost unscathed, going from quarterly to bimonthly in May and increasing its paid circulation to 77,000 for its latest issue from 5,000 five issues earlier. Though *Trilogy* is not yet profitable, Kevan Khanamirian, its founder and publisher, says he is aggressively promoting it, distributing free copies at airports and attracting advertising from companies like Chevron Corp. and Ashland Petroleum Co.

While increasing acceptance by mainstream advertisers and a widening subscriber base bode well for many of these publications, an economic recovery will mean more magazines and the inevitable shakeout, industry experts warn.

"I think the environmental/conservation market is already saturated," says Marlene Scott, general manager of Ingram Periodicals, a magazine distributor in Nashville, Tenn. "Everyone's heard about the rainforest and ozone. The survivors will need to go beyond that and show specifically how we can get involved to make substantial changes.... Becoming too generalized will be their demise."

Reprinted by permission from The Wall Street Journal, *"Environmental Magazines Defy Slump," by Rodney Ho, September 10, 1991.*

NEW ENVIRONMENTAL BOOKS OF 1991

These environmentally-relevant books were reviewed by Robert Merideth.

Biodiversity and Biological Conservation

African Silences, Peter Matthiessen, Random House, 1991, cloth $21.

By one of this country's best writers, author of the

socially responsible investments, vegetarianism, water and energy conservation" and more.

Common Sense on Energy and Our Environment

Published monthly by Common Sense on Energy and Our Environment, P.O. Box 215, Morrisville, PA 19067.

"*Common Sense* is the newsletter for independent thinkers who refuse to let their environmental agenda be set by others. It is the only newsletter that explores all aspects of the scientific, technical, economic, and political components of energy and environmental issues."

The Consumer's Guide to Planet Earth

Published biannually by Schultz Communications, 9412 Admiral Nimitz NE, Albuquerque, NM 87111.

The Consumer's Guide to Planet Earth is an information-packed resource book that lists sources for Earth-friendly products and services including adventure/eco-travel, organic foods, mail order catalogs, household and gardening products, personal care products, solar energy, natural pet products and much more."

Co-op America Quarterly

Published quarterly by Co-op America, 2100 M St. NW, Ste. 403, Washington, DC 20063.

"*Co-op America Quarterly* covers positive alternatives and practical

A. *22 percent*
Source: Roper Center for Public Research

strategies for creating a more just and sustainable society. Subjects recently covered include a sustainable energy policy, alternatives to the GNP, and community-supported agriculture. Each issue contains information on environmental investing, green consumers and the Boycott Action News."

Defenders
Published bimonthly by Defenders of Wildlife, 1244 19th St. NW, Washington, DC 20036. *Defenders* "provides provocative, in-depth coverage of major US and foreign wildlife conservation issues."

Design Spirit
Published three times per year by Design Spirit, 438 3rd St., Brooklyn, NY 11215.
Design Spirit supports "architecture that harmonizes with nature" and includes updates on nontoxic building materials, feng shui, earthquake-proof building, and traditional timber framing.

E: The Environmental Magazine
Published bimonthly by Earth Action Network, Inc., P.O. Box 5098, Westport, CT 06881.
E Magazine "is America's only not-for-profit independent magazine covering a wide range of environmental issues. Each issue contains feature articles on key issues and campaigns; industry and consumer product trends; interviews with leading advocates and thinkers; reviews of books, films and videos and tips on incorporating

classic *Wildlife In America*, this book presents a look at the imperiled state of wildlife and wilderness in Africa.

Behavior Guide to African Mammals, Richard Despard Estes, drawings by Daniel Otte, University of California, 1991, cloth $75.
An impressive compilation of information about the behavior of hoofed mammals, carnivores and primates of Africa, richly illustrated with line drawings. This could be an important resource for naturalists and travelers (however, a less expensive paperback version would be better).

Game Wars: The Undercover Pursuit of Wildlife Poachers, Marc Reisner, Viking, 1991, cloth $19.95.
By the author of *Cadillac Desert*, this book gives a behind-the-scenes look at the war against the poaching of wildlife in this country and shows the dedication, frustration, and successes of the men and women fighting this ongoing struggle.

Neotropical Wildlife Use and Conservation, John G. Robinson and Kent H. Redford, eds., University of Chicago, 1991, paper $28.
Nearly 50 experts in the emerging field of conservation biology discuss various ways to manage wildlife and maintain biological diversity in the Americas.

Trees of Life: Saving Tropical Forests and Their Biological Wealth, Kenton Miller and Laura Tangley, Beacon, 1991, paper $9.95.
One of the "Guides to the Environment" produced by the World Resources Institute in Washington, DC, this is a well-written overview of what is happening in the tropical forests, as well as the connections to life in the temperate zones.

Environmental History

Burning Bush: A Fire History of Australia, Stephen J. Pyne, Henry Holt, 1991, paper $14.95.
An intensively researched and well-written book, by a noted scholar on the cultural history of fire on earth.

Nature's Metropolis: Chicago and the Great West, William Cronon, W. W. Norton, 1991, cloth $27.50.

Q: *What vehicle transports more people in Asia alone than do all automobiles in the world combined?*

By analyzing the economic relationships between urban Chicago and the rural Midwest during the late 19th century, Cronon, an environmental historian and author of *Changes in the Land*, creates a framework with which to evaluate the significant environmental changes which occurred in the region.

Sierra Club: 100 Years of Protecting Nature, Tom Turner, Abrams, 1991, hard $49.95.

With text by the former editor of *Not Man Apart* and illustrated by noted photographers Galen Rowell, Philip Hyde and Eliot Porter, this book commemorates the centennial of the Sierra Club.

The Tourist in Yosemite, 1855-1985, Stanford E. Demars, University of Utah, 1991, paper $9.95, cloth $19.95.

A history of how Americans have viewed and used Yosemite National Park, an icon of the American wilderness. The author also shows how increased tourism in the area necessitated changes in park management.

Environmental Philosophy

Biosphere Politics, Jeremy Rifkin, Crown, 1991, cloth $20.

Rifkin offers yet another thought-provoking message to the human community; we need to adopt a new paradigm, a way of viewing the world, in which we see ourselves not as the center of everything, but rather as one of many components of the Earth.

Earth Prayers From Around the World, Elizabeth Roberts and Elias Amidon, eds., Harper, 1991, paper $12.95.

A valuable and useful collection of praises for the Earth, for all seasons and all occasions.

The Ideas of Wilderness: Prehistory to the Age of Ecology, Max Oelschlaeger, Yale University, 1991, cloth $29.95.

A comprehensive history of how human conceptions and philosophies of wilderness, including the way humans perceive their relationship to nature, has developed and changed from pre-historic hunter-gatherers to present day deep ecologists.

ecological principles into our daily lives."

Earth
Published bimonthly by Kalmbach Publishing Co., 21027 Crossroads Cir., Waukesha, WI 53187.
"Our primary job at *Earth* magazine is to present what we humans know about the planet we live on. We are dedicated to making that knowledge accessible and clear."

Earth Island Journal
Published quarterly by Earth Island Institute, 300 Broadway, Ste. 28, San Francisco, CA 94133-3312.
"*Earth Island Journal* delivers 'local news from around the world.' Eyewitness accounts from the environmental frontlines—from Malaysia to Moscow—with global eco-news and exposés you'll find nowhere else."

The Earthwise Consumer
Published eight times per year by *The Earthwise Consumer*, P.O. Box 279, Forest Knolls, CA 94933.
Edited and published by Debra Lynn Dadd, author of *Nontoxic, Natural & Earthwise*, *The Earthwise Consumer* "is a newsletter about the practicalities of living in a manner that fulfills our needs as individuals and at the same time is in harmony with the ways of the Earth."

The Ecologist
Published bimonthly by the MIT Press, 55 Hayward St., Camridge, MA 02142.

A. *Bicycles*
Source: World•Watch *July/August 1988*

"*The Ecologist* is one of the most relevant, influential and radical of the international green journals. For 20 years it has provided a forum for social and environmental activists who are seeking to change current development policies in both the 'developing' and the 'developed' worlds."

Environmental Action Magazine
Published bimonthly by Environmental Action, 1525 New Hampshire Ave. NW, Washington, DC 20036.
"*Environmental Action* was founded in 1970 by the organizers of the first Earth Day. Today, this bimonthly magazine still sets a standard for environmental reporting and service journalism. News, reviews and resources for activist and armchair readers alike."

Garbage: The Practical Journal for the Environment
Published bimonthly by Garbage, P.O. Box 56519, Boulder, CO 80322-6519.
"*Garbage* addresses environmental issues in order to help readers understand that concern and action in favor of the environment can start in their own home with products and services they use every day. Editorial content includes waste management, personal health and food issues, product reviews, alternatives to harmful products, gardening and conservation. The emphasis is on practical living with consciousness."

The River of the Mother of God and Other Essays by Aldo Leopold, Susan L. Flader and J. Baird Callicott, eds., University of Wisconsin, 1991, cloth $22.95.

A collection of the best of Leopold's remaining unpublished essays and manuscripts, compiled by two of the leading scholars of Leopold and his concept of "the land ethic."

Science, Technology and Society, Robert E. McGinn, Prentice Hall, 1991, paper $14.95.

As an introduction to the study of science and technology in society, this book provides the basis to analyze more competently and objectively a variety of environmental problems, including social and ethical considerations.

Environmental Politics and Economics

Blueprint 2: Greening the World Economy, David Pearce, ed., Earthscan, 1991, paper $16.95.

Written by a group of British environmental economists, this book provides creative ways of examining the economics of global environmental issues, such as climate change and deforestation.

Preserving the Global Environment: The Challenge of Shared Leadership, Jessica Tuchman Mathews, ed., W. W. Norton, 1991, paper $10.95, cloth $22.95.

This collection of papers, sponsored by the American Assembly and the World Resources Institute, looks at the potential threats to peace and security posed by declining environmental conditions around the world and stresses the role that governments should be playing to work toward solutions.

Thirst For Growth: Water Agencies as Hidden Government in California, Robert Gottlieb and Margaret Fitzsimmons, University of Arizona, 1991, cloth $35.00.

Written by two planning professors at UCLA, this book examines the political economy of the water industry of California and the American southwest.

Environmental Pollution

Chemical Deceptions: The Toxic Threat to Health, Marc Lappé, Sierra Club, 1991, cloth $24.95.

Lappé shows us how interdependent our lives are

Q: *What percentage of American churches were committed to environmental teaching in 1989?*

with the products and by-products of our industrial society, and the potential health problems that exist.

Healthy Homes, Healthy Kids: Protecting Your Children from Everyday Environmental Hazards, Joyce M. Schoemaker and Charity Y. Vitale, Island Press, 1991, paper $12.95, cloth $19.95.

A useful guide for parents on how to reduce or eliminate the exposure of children to environmental hazards around the home.

Ozone Diplomacy: New Directions in Safeguarding the Planet, Richard Elliot Benedick, Harvard University, 1991, paper $10.95.

A detailed history of the Montreal Protocol on Substances that Deplete the Ozone Layer ratified in 1987 and revised in 1990. Written by the US chief negotiator.

What Goes Up: The Global Assault on Our Atmosphere, John J. Nance, Morrow, 1991, cloth $20.

A close look at the interaction and conflict between the science and politics of regulating atmospheric pollutants.

Natural History

Learning to Listen to the Land, Bill Willers, ed., Island Press, 1991, paper $14.95, cloth $24.95.

A collection of literary writing which illuminates the relationship of people and the land. Includes important, but perhaps lesser known, works by such writers as Edward Abbey, Wendell Barry Commoner, David Ehrenfield, Anne and Paul Ehrlich, James Lovelock, Norman Myers, Wallace Stegner and E. O. Wilson.

Season at the Point: The Birds and Birders of Cape May, Jack Connor, Atlantic Monthly, 1991, cloth $21.95.

Connor describes the men and women who work at and enjoy Cape May, New Jersey, one of the most popular birding spots in North America. He characterizes the unique qualities of this area and their importance for numerous migrating bird species.

Reference

1991-1992 Green Index: A State-by-State Guide to the Nation's Environmental Health, Bob Hall and

---

ECO-BOOK PHENOMENON

If you own a copy of *50 Simple Things You Can Do To Save The Earth*, you're in good company! Over 3.5 million copies of this highly popular guide to personal environmental involvement have been sold. This brainchild of writer/entrepreneur John Javna has, in only two years, provided enough money and exposure to start a serious environmental publishing company called Earth•Works Group. In that short period Javna and his merry band of eco-wordsmiths have been churning out simple, short, yet highly substantial books on saving the Earth. The books are prepared and priced to hit middle America and they sell like hotcakes, in bookstores, on the back of cereal boxes and as premiums for utilities and large corporations. The ten titles currently in print have sold nearly 6 million copies!

The Earth•Works List
 50 Simple Things You Can Do To Save The Earth
 *50 Simple Things Kids Can Do To Save The Earth
 *The Next Step: 50 More Things You Can Do To Save The Earth
 The Recycler's Handbook
 50 Simple Things Your Business Can Do To Save The Earth
 50 Simple Things Kids Can Do To Recycle
 30 Simple Energy Things You Can Do To Save The Earth
 15 Simple Things Californians Can Do To Recycle
 Kid Heroes Of The Environment
 The Student Environmental Action Guide
 * Published by Andrews and McMeel

Coming this spring:
 Gardening For The Earth
 Vote For The Earth

Earth•Works Group, 1400 Shattuck Ave. #25, Berkeley, CA 94709

A**. 22 percent**
 Source: *North American Conference on Christianity and Ecology*

The Green Consumer Letter/The Green Business Letter

Published monthly by Tilden Press, 1526 Connecticut Ave. NW, Washington, DC 20036.

"*The Green Consumer Letter* is the authoritative, independent voice of environmentally safe shopping, written by Joel Makower, author of *The Green Consumer*. Full of investigations, product and company information, resources, trends, insight, inspiration, money- and Earth-saving tips." *The Green Business Letter* is the companion resource to *The Green Consumer Letter*. It is written for anyone involved in business who is concerned about the environment.

Green MarketAlert

Published monthly by MarketAlert Publications, 345 Wood Creek Rd., Bethlehem, CT 06751.

Green MarketAlert tracks the business impacts of green consumerism. Covers marketing/advertising, regulation, corporate strategies, green consumer surveys, products/packaging, international developments and more. Also provides resources for implementing green business strategies."

Greenpeace

Published bimonthly by Greenpeace, 1436 U St. NW, Washington, DC 20009.

Greenpeace magazine is a wide-ranging, feature-oriented publication which "offers investigative reporting on the most

Mary Lee Kerr, Island Press, 1991, cloth $29.95, paper $18.95.

Compiled by the Institute for Southern Studies in Durham, North Carolina, this guide uses a set of 256 indicators to measure and rank the environmental condition of each state.

The 1992 Information Please Environmental Almanac, World Resources Institute, Houghton Mifflin, 1991, paper $9.95.

An extensive collection of environmental facts on food, energy conservation, water, air pollution, nature and land conservation, recreation and eco-tourism. Includes names and addresses of the chief environmental executives in all 50 states and a "green" ranking of 50 major metropolitan areas.

Women and Nature

Sisters of the Earth: Women's Prose and Poetry About Nature, Lorraine Anderson, ed., Vintage Books, 1991, paper $13.

A collection of some 90 poems and essays that illustrates the diversity and strength of feminist voices and perceptions about nature.

Women and the Environment: A Reader, Sally Sontheimer, ed., Earthscan, 1991, paper $15.95.

This reader focuses on environment and economic development in the third world, particularly the role of women in balancing economic survival with sustainable uses of natural resources.

Women in the Field: America's Pioneering Women Naturalists, Marcia Myers Bonta, Texas A & M University Press, 1991, cloth $29.50.

From Jane Colden, colonial botanist, to Rachel Carson, pioneering ecologist, Bonta documents the lives and work of 25 women who made important contributions to the field of natural history.

Miscellaneous

Confessions of an Eco-Warrior, Dave Foreman, Harmony, 1991, cloth $20.00.

The collected thoughts of the cofounder of the radical environmental group Earth First! Foreman

Q: *What percentage of religious denominations were committed to environmental causes as of 1990?*

reflects on the role of monkeywrenching in the environmental movement, offers a blueprint for wilderness preservation and laments about the "professionalization" of environmental organizations.

Global Citizen, Donella Meadow, Island Press, 1991, cloth $24.94, paper $14.95.

This collection of essays drawn from Meadow's syndicated newspaper column highlighting people around the globe who are working for a sustainable society and environmental protection.

The Green Reader: Essays Toward a Sustainable Society, Andrew Dobson, ed., Mercury House, 1991, paper $11.95, cloth $24.95.

Some of the best writings on bioregionalism, ecofeminism, ecophilosophy, sustainable agriculture and development. Helps to define the "green" philosophy. A good complement to an earlier book (*Green Parties: An International Guide,* Sara Parkin, Heretic Books, 1989, paper $14.95), which describes the influence of many of these writings on the development of Green parties worldwide.

Save the Earth, Jonathan Porritt, ed., foreword by HRH the Prince of Wales, introduction by Robert Redford, Turner Publishing in association with Friends of the Earth International, 1991, cloth $29.95.

A companion to Turner's six-hour special program on the United Nations Earth Summit, to be held in Brazil next summer. The book contains contributions from many prominent environmentalists and is richly illustrated with color photographs.

Robert Merideth is staff writer/editor for the Groundwater Policy Education Project at Pennsylvania State University. He is author of The Environmentalist's Bookshelf: A Reader's Guide to the Best Books*, to be published in 1992 by G. K. Hall/Macmillan Reference, New York.*

pressing environmental issues and their political and economic ramifications. Its editorial mandate is to broaden public awareness about the state of the environment and to educate readers in asserting their right to a clean, safe habitat."

National Geographic
Published monthly by National Geographic Society, 17th and M Sts. NW, Washington, DC 20036.
"*National Geographic* is a source of information about the world and its people dealing with the changing universe and man's involvement in it, revealing the people and places of the world as well as the major technological advances that impact on our lives."

National Wildlife
Published bimonthly by the National Wildlife Federation, 8925 Leesburg Pike, Vienna, VA 22184.
National Wildlife magazine is published "to create and encourage an awareness among the people of the world of the need for wise use and proper management of those resources of the earth upon which our lives and welfare depend: the soil, the air, the water, the forests, the minerals, the planet life and the wildlife."

Orion
Published quarterly by The Myrin Institute, 136 E. 64th St., New York, NY 10021.
Orion "explores the reciprocal relationship between people and

A. **70 percent**
  Source: *North American Conference on Christianity and Ecology*

nature and features programs for positive environmental change. Through science, art and the humanities, *Orion* points to the connections between nature and human culture, social policy and environmental health—both local and global."

Preserve
Published bimonthly by Publisher's Service Corp., P.O. Box 557, Smyrna, DE 19977.
Preserve's "goal is to increase public awareness of environmental issues and support efforts to take positive action on these issues."

Safe Home Digest
Published monthly by Safe Home Digest, 24 East Ave., Ste. 1300, New Canaan, CT 06840.
'Safe Home Digest is dedicated to helping people improve their home environment. We research and report on the latest safe and healthful building products, interior design, in-home testing kits, alternative paints and finishes, low-toxic cleaning products, 'green' auto care and more."

Sierra
Published bimonthly by Sierra Club, 730 Polk St., San Francisco, CA 94109.
"*Sierra* is the award-winning magazine of the Sierra Club. Beautiful color photography and lively responsible editorials inform you about today's environmental issues. Reaffirm your commitment to protecting wilderness and

CHILDREN'S BOOKS

These children's books were reviewed by Kathleen Krull.

Bear, John Schoenherr, Pilomel, 1991, $14.95.
Caldecott Medalist Schoenherr tells a tension-filled survival story from the point of view of a young bear forced to start living on his own.

Cactus Hotel, Brenda Z. Guiberson, Henry Holt, 1991, cloth $15.95.
Cactus Hotel is a tale of the life and times (some 200 years) of the noble saguaro cactus of the Sonoran desert.

D Is for Dolphins, Cami Berg, Windom Books, 1991, cloth $18.95.
From A to Z, Cami Berg offers 26 noteworthy attributes of these perpetually smiling creatures, adding a glossary biased against keeping dolphins in captivity.

Elephant Book, Ian Redmond, Overlook Press, 1991, cloth $16.95.
This book offers excellent photographs in a magazine-style layout supplemented by a clear text relating everything one might conceivably want to know about wild elephants and their life cycle.

Kid Heroes of the Environment: Simple Things Real Kids Are Doing To Save the Earth, The Earth•Works Group, Catherine Dee, ed., Earth•Works Press, Berkeley, CA, 1991, paper $4.95.
Kid Heroes contains more than 25 stories about the things real kids are doing to protect our planet with details about how others can do them, too. This book

Q: *What federal agency produces twice as much hazardous waste as the top three industrial-waste producers?*

is an inspiring, easy-to-read guide from the authors of *50 Simple Things Kids Can Do To Save the Earth*.

My First Green Book, Angela Wilkes, Knopf, 1991, cloth $6.95.

Hands-on activities and projects accompany irresistible photography in the style of the much-admired "Eye-witness" books, in an oversize volume just right for its age group.

The Salamander Room, Anne Mazer, Knopf, 1991, cloth $13.95.

The economical text by Mazer, about the orange creature Brian finds in the woods, has the boy constructing an entire imaginary rainforest in his room.

Save the Earth: An Action Handbook for Kids, Betty Miles, Knopf, 1991, paper $6.95.

Each section—on water, energy, plants and animals, etc.—includes amazing facts, true stories of kids who've made a difference and, best of all, lucid explanations of problems and solutions.

Sierra, Diane Siebert and Wendell Minor, Harper-Collins, 1991, cloth $14.95.

Before well-known book-jacket illustrator Minor began these paintings, he hiked Yosemite's High Sierra Loop, while Siebert has camped and hiked throughout the Sierra Nevada. Their stately tribute makes a mountain both inspiration and narrator.

The Whales' Song, Dyan Sheldon, Dial, 1991, cloth $14.95.

Haunting oil paintings by Gary Blythe recreate the fantasies-come-true of Lilly, whose grandmother (much to her great uncle's practical-minded disdain) fills her head with tales of singing whales.

Window, Jeannie Baker, Greenwillow, 1991, cloth $13.95.

This book manages to encapsule 24 years of environmental destruction—without saying a word. Page after page shows the scene through a boy's window as he grows up and his neighborhood goes down, from flourishing-forest to ugly urban.

Kathleen Krull is author of It's My Earth, Too: How I Can Help the Earth Stay Alive.

parklands and capture the excitement of outdoor adventure."

Wild Earth
Published quarterly by Wild Earth, P.O. Box 492, Canton, NY 13617.
Dave Foreman, co-founder of Earth First!, is *Wild Earth*'s executive editor. *Wild Earth* is a "wilderness and biodiversity magazine."

Wildlife Art News
Published bimonthly by Pothole Publications, Inc., 3455 Dakota Ave. S, St. Louis Park, MN 55416-0246.
"The leading magazine of wildlife art explores the world of animals, birds and habitat with nearly 200 pages of full color '*National Geographic* quality' reproductions each issue."

Wildlife Conservation
Published bimonthly by New York Zoological Society, Bronx, NY 10460.
"Through its unique blend of exploration, adventure and scientific excellence, *Wildlife Conservation* inspires appreciation for, and understanding of wild creatures and wild habitats."

WorldWatch
Published bimonthly by Worldwatch Institute, 1776 Massachusetts Ave. NW, Washington, DC 20036.
"*WorldWatch* offers in-depth coverage of international environmental issues. We keep you fully informed of global problems and ways we can work toward a sustainable society."

A. **The Pentagon**
Source: US Department of Defense/US Environmental Protection Agency Citizen Action

ECO-FILMS

This list of award-winning and relevant environmental films was compiled by Richard Skorman, program director of the 1990 and 1991 US Environmental Film Festivals, and Nicolle Pressly.

ADAM'S WORLD, 20 min. 1989 Canada. Director: Donna Reed. Producers: Margaret Pettigrew, Rina Fraticelli and Kathleen Shannon. Distributor: National Film Board of Canada, (212) 586-5131.

This filmed lecture of theologian Elizabeth Dobson Grey provides a marvelous overview to feminist perspectives on ecology and women's place in history.

AGAINST THE CURRENT, 27 min. 1988 USSR. A film by Dmitri Delov. Produced by the Leningrad Science Film Studio. Distributor: The Video Project, (415) 655-9050.

This is a fascinating documentary about the residents of Kirishi, where an ecological crime takes place in the town where a major Soviet synthetic protein plant is located.

THE BAREFOOT ECONOMIST, 52 min. 1989 Australia. A film by Julian Russell and Tony Gailey. Produced by the "Visionaries Series" by 20/20 Productions. Distributor: Landmark Films, (703) 241-2030.

Turning his back on traditional economics, Chilean economist

Environmental Media

From vast landscape pan shots to stories centering around an environmental issue, the environment is being captured on film and television. To give visiblity and recognition to members of the creative community who have used their special talents to advance environmental themes within television programming, the Environmental Media Association created the Environmental Media Awards. Personalities and celebrities have begun to lend their hands as well as their names to the cause. Radio has begun to green its programming for the 1990s—environmental news spots are being broadcast from coast to coast.

ENVIRONMENTAL FILM

- By Richard Skorman -

ALTHOUGH THE MERE MENTION of the words "environmental film" may conjure up an image of the pedantic, "educational" documentaries that tormented most of us in junior high school biology class, environmental films come in every shape, size and cinemagraphic medium. It's no secret that we are a visual culture and that most of us receive our information through film and television. When a hundred million people see "Dances With Wolves," it alters our view of Native Americans. Reading about the thousands of elephants that are poached each year for their ivory will anger some. But if every American watched the segment of The Discovery Channel's "Ivory Wars" last year that shows a tearful elephant hovering over the remains of his murdered spouse, the message that we must never buy ivory would be permanently embedded into our consciousness. Reading about the dangers of pesticides in table grapes is certainly disconcerting to the environmentally aware. But if as many of us watched that portion of "The Wrath of Grapes" that shows the California clinic full of mentally and physically disabled farmworker children, as watched the 1991 Super Bowl, then César Chavez's plea to boycott grapes would finally be heard and acted upon.

All of the films described above are examples of

 Q: *According to the EPA, how many landfills in the US will eventually leak?*

powerful environmental films. There are feature-length fictional narratives, hard-hitting journalistic documentaries and television news reports, upbeat young people's programs, entertaining network television serials, lively music videos, outrageous animation, satires, black comedies, experimental films and interactive computer videos with environmental

Photo courtesy of First Run Features

Dairy Queen (with owner) stars in Mark Lewis's "Cane Toads—an Unnatural History."

themes. By definition, any film, video or television program that directly addresses an environmental issue is an environmental film. An "effective" environmental film achieves its desired goal of entertaining, informing, visualizing or shocking at the same time that it delves into an ecological problem or solution.

The reasons environmental films make such a big impression are simple: They bring to the screen, up close and in living color, critically important environmental problems and solutions, and they are made by people who care deeply about the issues they are addressing.

Manfred Max-Neef has developed a new theory of Barefoot Economics that tries to address the enormous problems of poverty in non-industrial countries. His vision is one of true social justice, environmental health and a sustainable future.

BREATH TAKEN, 36 min. 1990 US. A film by Bill Ravanesi. Distributor: Fanlight Productions, (617) 524-0980.

"Breath Taken" brings us face-to-face with those who have studied or are victims of asbestos-related diseases, forcing us to listen to the tragic impact corporate and government irresponsibility has had on thousands of lives.

BROKEN RAINBOW, 69 min. 1986 US. Producers: Maria Florio and Victoria Mudd. Directors: Victoria Mudd and Thom Tyson. Distributor: Direct Cinema, (800) 345-6748.

Recipient of the 1986 Best Documentary Oscar, this is a moving account of 12,000 Navajos relocated from their sacred lands to facilitate uranium development at Big Mountain, Arizona.

CANE TOADS, AN UN-NATURAL HISTORY, 46 min. 1988 Australia. A film by Mark Lewis. Produced by Film Australia. Distributor: First Run Features, (212) 243-0600.

Director Mark Lewis's ingenious use of the camera from the toad's perspective adds to the folly of this wildly entertaining film about the

A. *All of them*
  Source: The Environmental Protection Agency

importation of 102 cane toads into Australia.

CIRCLE OF PLENTY, 27 min. 1987 US. A film by Bette Jean Bullert and John de Graaf. Produced at KCTS, Seattle. Distributor: Bullfrog Films, (800) 543-FROG.

"Circle" examines biointensive agriculture, a technique developed by John Jeavons which combines deep digging and close planting to produce a maximum yield from minimum amounts of soil and fertilizer.

DEAFSMITH: A NUCLEAR FOLKTALE, 43 min. 1990 US. A film by Andrea Swift. Distributor: The Video Project, (415) 655-9050.

This important and timely film features a healthy dose of informed skepticism and grassroots activism by the residents of Deafsmith County, Texas, and Hanford, Washington, who are trying to defend the land they love from nuclear pollution.

DIRTY BUSINESS, 15 min. 1990 US/Mexico, Winner of Best Documentary Short at the 1991 US Environmental Film Festival. A film by Jon Silver. Distributor: Migrant Media Productions, (408) 728-8949.

A powerful exposé of the human and environmental tragedy caused by American agribusiness investment in Mexico, including child labor abuse and harsh conditions for Mexican workers.

Environmental filmmakers won't appear on the cover of *People* magazine or on talk shows. These films are made by people who often go into debt or take great personal risks to produce them.

Environmental films are made by people like Sam LaBudde, the marine biologist who posed as a cook on a Panamanian tuna boat to secretly film hundreds of dolphins as they were murdered in driftnets. LaBudde was luckier than most environmental filmmakers. His shocking footage was shown on nearly every television news show in the United States. Some think that LaBudde's daring pursuits resulted in our government's decision to ban driftnet fleets, and Star-Kist's and Heinz's decision to sell only "dolphin safe" tuna.

Environmental films are made by people like Vladimir Shevchenko, the director of "Chernobyl: Chronicle of Difficult Weeks"—a courageous man who tried to show the world the extent of the disaster immediately after it occurred. Shevchenko died from radiation exposure; his camera was so radioactive, it had to be entombed in cement. Yet, "Chronicle of Difficult Weeks" wasn't released until 1990 and has only been seen by a few thousand people since.

You might be saying to yourself, "Yeah, great, I can't wait to invite my friends over next Saturday night for pizza, beer and a film on Chernobyl or dolphin slaughter." But environmental films don't always have to be harrowing or depressing to be effective. There are dozens of entertaining feature films with environmental themes: for example, "On the Beach," "The China Syndrome," "Harlan County USA," "Blue Collar," "Silkwood," "The Emerald Forest," "Koyaanisqatsi," "The Atomic Cafe," "Silent Running," "Walkabout," "Blade Runner," "Local Hero," "A Flash of Green," "Wargames," "Star Trek IV" and "The Milagro Beanfield War" are all environmental films.

There are lively and upbeat children's films on the environment, from "Rainforest Rap" and Sesame Street's "The Rotten Truth," to the latest Teenage Mutant Ninja Turtle movie, "Secret of the Ooze." There is a popular, rough and tumble Saturday morning cartoon show (produced by TBS) called "Captain Planet and the Planeteers," where eco-avengers conquer villains like Hoggish Greedly, Verminous Scum, Looten Plunder and Duke Nukem.

Surprisingly, there are also a number of humorous

Q: *Recycled aluminum uses how much less energy than aluminum made from raw materials?*

films on the environment. Of course, some are inadvertently comical, like the film about "water pollution" that featured a naked man climbing in and out of a bathtub, or the filmed document of the sounds of rice growing. But there are also dozens of intentionally humorous films. Films like "Cane Toads: An Unnatural History"—an absurd Australian documentary about giant toads taking over Northern Australia, eating everything in their wake and ruining the lives of drug addicts who boil them down and roll their essence into highly hallucinogenic joints. Humor also arises in films such as Charles Haid's "The Last Supper"—a dark satire about a group of dinner guests who can never bring themselves to eat the delicacies on their plates because they keep talking about the ingredients in the food.

Of course, the majority of environmental films aren't humorous or upbeat. Most are hard-hitting films that document important problems and comprehensive practical solutions. The largest number of environmental films have been made on the rainforest and nuclear issues, with toxic waste, water pollution, global warming and garbage and recycling close behind. But there are also excellent environmental films made on almost every imaginable issue: ecofeminism, spiritual ecology, radical activism, animal rights, overpopulation, eco-racism, apartheid and the environment, corporate ethics and the environment, indoor pollution, sustainable agriculture, Native Peoples and the environmental cost of development in the third world.

Environmental films are being made in places as diverse as Iceland, Burkina Faso, the Seychelle Islands, Cameroon, Vietnam, Turkmania and the South Bronx.

Environmental film can trace its roots to the wilderness preservation films that David Brower made for the Sierra Club in the 1950s, and to wildlife television programs like Mutual of Omaha's "Wild Kingdom." During Lyndon Johnson's "Great Society" in the 1960s, film distributors couldn't stock enough "educational" environmental films to sell to schools and libraries. But at that time, non-scientific documentaries were dominated by issues like Vietnam, civil rights and the women's movement. The advent of hard-hitting, issue-oriented environmental films paralleled public interest in the 1970s and 1980s. There was a whole slew of hard-hitting environmental films released

DOWNWIND/DOWN-STREAM, 59 min. 1988 US. Producers: Robert Lewis and Christopher McLeod. Distributor: Bullfrog Films, (800) 543-FROG.

This is a detailed account about the serious threat to water quality, sub-alpine ecosystems and public health in the Colorado Rockies from mining operations, urbanization and acid rain.

HALTING THE FIRES, 52 min. 1990 UK/Brazil/Germany. Executive Producer: Nick Hart Williams. Director: Octavio Bezerra. Distributor: Filmmakers Library, (212) 808-4980.

This unique collaboration of three countries examines the economic, environmental and social consequences from the huge number of intentional fires set in the Amazon.

HBO'S EARTH TO KIDS: A GUIDE TO PRODUCTS FOR A HEALTHY PLANET, 28 min. 1990 US. A production of HBO and Consumer Reports Television. Executive Producer: Joyce Newman. Director: Hoite C. Caston. Distributor: Film Inc., (800) 323-4222.

This lively and informative program is designed to show kids that the choices they make about products can seriously affect the future of the planet for better or for worse.

KEEPERS OF THE FOREST, 28 min. 1988 US. Producer: Norman Lippman. Distributor: Umbrella Films, (617)

A. *95 percent*
  Source: The Recycler's Handbook, *by the Earth • Works Group*

277-6639. Distributor: (617) 277-6639.

A fascinating documentary on southern Mexico's Lacandon Maya tribe and their careful management of the fragile jungle ecosystem on which they depend.

LOVE, WOMEN AND FLOWERS, 56 min. 1988 UK/Colombia. Winner of the 1990 US Environmental Film Festival. Directors: Jorge Silva and Marta Rodriguez. Producers: Luis Crump, Antonella Ibba and Jonathan Curling. Distributor: Women Make Movies, (212) 925-0606.

This powerful documentary portrays the tragic lives of the 60,000 women who work in the Colombian flower industry, which uses highly toxic pesticides and fungicides banned in industrialized countries.

OLYMPIC, 30 min. 1990 US. Winner of the 1990 New York Film Festival, the Golden Eagle 1990 CINE Film Festival. Executive Producer: Thomas Hedges. Distributor: American Visions, (800) 553-8878.

A mood film of Olympic National Park blending still photography, film, original score and nature recording into an extraordinary multi-media portrait.

POWER TO SURVIVE, 29 min 1990 US, Winner of Best Young People's Program at the 1991 US Environmental Film Festival. Producer/Director: Shauna Garr. Distributor: New Day Films, (212) 645-8210.

around the first Earth Day in 1970. The mid-1970s brought films on the "energy crisis" and, in the early 1980s, nuclear threat films became popular as public fears escalated with Reagan's cold war rhetoric.

*   *   *

The problem with environmental film is not the effectiveness or quality of the films. The challenge lies in how they can be seen by a mass market. Although environmental films are widely available through independent distribution and production sources, few have a chance of making it to a movie theater or on television.

The American environmental film distribution market is dominated by two companies: Bullfrog Films and The Video Project. Bullfrog began with five films in 1973. Their library has now grown to 300 films. The Video Project began distributing films in 1983 with their own production, "The Last Epidemic." Their catalog has grown to include 150 titles.

There are other avenues for spreading environmental films and videos than independent and educational distribution. The Rockefeller Foundation and The Video Project have put together a "home" Green Video Collection of 30 videos that are distributed through The Seventh Generation catalog. Four years ago, The MacArthur Foundation distributed a Library Collection of environmental films to thousands of libraries across the country. The Media Project has published Green Gems and Safe Planet guides to environmental films that include hefty synopses and rental and purchase information. MCA/Universal's "Help Save Planet Earth" video with Ted Danson did quite well at video stores.

Perhaps one of the most interesting phenomena of the last five years is the advent of grassroots environmental filmmaking. Environmental groups like Greenpeace and Sea Shepherd have been nailing polluters and mammal killers with video cameras for a long time. But the affordability of video equipment has created a whole new army of environmentalists armed with camcorders. There have been literally hundreds of examples of local citizens bringing about significant change through grassroots environmental filmmaking.

More Americans receive their information from the television evening news than any other source. In the last five years, there have been significant strides in

Q: *What was the length of a single traffic jam in Tokyo in 1990?*

spreading the word about the environment through television news. Environmental reporters and special "earthwatch" programs are a staple of most network news shows.

Yet how concerned were TV journalists about the environment during the Persian Gulf war? And can TV journalists do justice to complex environmental issues in a 30-second to two-minute segment?

Network news magazines such as "60 Minutes," "20/20" and "48 Hours" have filled the gap with some excellent investigative journalism on the environment. "National Geographic Explorer," PBS's "Frontline," "Nova," "Conserving America" and "Infinite Voyage" have been tackling important environmental issues for years. Some prime-time programs such as "McGyver," "Cheers," "Harry and the Hendersons," "The Munsters Today," "Major Dad," "Northern Exposure" and "Murder She Wrote" increasingly have environmental messages peppered throughout their shows. But TBS's weekly environmental newsmagazine "Network Earth" (Sunday, 11:00pm EST) and the Saturday morning "Captain Planet" are the only weekly environmental programs on television. Paramount Television's eco-cop series "Earth Force" lasted on network television for less than two months because ratings were low. Cable and network television's push for environmental programming seemed to focus around 1990's Earth Day. Aside from local and national news, television's commitment to the environment hasn't been as deep or consistent as it could be.

Hollywood has joined in the environmental battle as well. Celebrities such as Chevy Chase, Ted Danson, Whoopi Goldberg, Robert Redford, Susan Sarandon and Meryl Streep regularly narrate PBS specials or appear in Public Service Announcements urging us to be more concerned about the environment. There have been numerous stories on Hollywood's new commitment to produce feature films and television programs with environmental themes. But how far has the "Greening of Hollywood" really gone?

Garrett De Bell, an environmentalist turned fulltime Environmental Consultant for MCA/Universal says that "there has been a lot of interest in putting environmental themes in television and feature film." Although to date, there have been very few feature productions with environmental themes, De

Against a backdrop of expert commentary on the energy crisis and pollution, four minority teenagers from Santa Monica and Venice, California, voice their common concerns about the environment amid crack, crime and poverty.

PROPHETS AND LOSS, 60 min. 1990 US. Producers/Directors: Nick Hart Williams and Gabrielle Kelly. Distributor: The Video Project, (415) 655-9050.

"Prophets And Loss" brings to the screen some of the world's most profound environmental thinkers to discuss climate change.

RIVER PEOPLE: BEHIND THE CASE OF DAVID SOHAPPY, 50 min. 1990 US. Producers/Directors: Michael Conford and Michelle Zaccheo. Distributors: Filmmakers Library, (212) 808-4980.

"River People" follows the story of David Sohappy, a Native American spiritual leader who served three years in prison for selling salmon out of season despite his ancestral and religious right to fish along the Columbia River. It is a document of the heated political controversy involving fishing rights and the right to religious freedom.

SADAKO AND THE THOUSAND PAPER CRANES, 29 min. 1990 US. Honorable Mention at the 1991 US Environmental Film Festival.

Set in 1955, Sadako is a wonderfully animated true story of a young

A. *84 miles*
   Source: Washington Report

Japanese girl who is stricken with leukemia as a result of the bombing of Hiroshima ten years earlier.

SOUTH AFRICA'S WASTED LAND, 52 min. 1990 UK. Director: Jamie Hartzell. Producer: Debonair Productions. Distributor: Film Maker's Library, (212) 808-4980.

This heart-rending film exposes the link between South Africa's apartheid policy and its rapidly eroding ecology.

SPACESHIP EARTH: OUR GLOBAL ENVIRONMENT, 25 min. 1990 US. Winner of 1990 US Environmental Film Festival. Produced by Kirk Bergstrom and World Link. Distributor: World Link, (213) 273-2636.

"Spaceship Earth" is a program designed to inform, inspire and motivate teens about deforestation, ozone depletion and global warming.

TO PROTECT MOTHER EARTH (BROKEN TREATY II), 60 min. 1989 US. Best Documentary Feature and Best of the 1991 US Environmental Film Festival. Producer/Director: Joel L. Freedman. Distributor: Cinnamon Productions, (212) 431-4899.

Narrated by Robert Redford, "To Protect Mother Earth" is a hard-hitting story of the Shoshone struggle to save their ancestral lands in Nevada from strip mining, nuclear tests and oil drilling.

Bell explains that "environmental concern really grew about a year and a half ago. If we want to insert an eco-theme into a television series, it takes a month. For feature films, the lead time is 18 months to three years." MCA/Universal, for example, is currently developing an action/adventure film on the Penan tribe of the Brazilian rainforest. "Species Unknown" screenwriter Jon Povill (one of the writers of "Total Recall") says he's "been trying to sell the studios on environmental themes for the last 15 years. It's not until recently that a company like Universal would take a chance on an environmentally themed project."

Others in Hollywood are taking the plunge as well. David Putnam is producing the Chico Mendes story and Oliver Stone, the Sam LaBudde story. Hector Babenco's ("Kiss of the Spider Woman") newest film, "At Play in the Fields of the Lord" delves into rainforest issues. Sean Connery stars as a biologist trying to save the rainforest in "The Last Days of Eden." Ted Danson is producing a feature on ocean life called "Whalesong." Sylvester Stallone is developing a futuristic thriller with toxic waste and air pollution as a backdrop. And 20th Century Fox is producing an animated feature entitled "Firn Gulley: The Last Rainforest."

Andy Spahn, the director of the Environmental Media Association, a Hollywood-based organization that actively urges studios and television production companies to insert more environmental themes, states emphatically that "we've seen great progress in television and features. For our Environmental Media Awards competition this year, we received 105 submissions, which is over double what we expected." These are certainly promising signs that Hollywood is becoming greener, but eco-features aren't yet glutting multiplexes and environmentally-themed programs aren't flooding prime-time television.

Spahn and De Bell allude to the fact that there's still a perception among many studio executives and television producers that the public doesn't want to be exposed to too much doom and gloom. Let's face it, although there are dozens of notable exceptions, those wacky environmentalists aren't out there making only screwball comedies on toxic waste and acid rain. Environmental documentaries and feature films

Q: *How many newspapers do Americans throw away each day?*

can be frightening and depressing because that's the reality of the crisis we are facing.

The problem doesn't lie with the lack of "good" material on the environment. Television and feature film development directors are overwhelmed with quality eco-themed projects. The problem is the perception that the American public wants to be insulated from the unpleasant situations they are facing in their everyday lives. But, Americans also want to learn more about environmental problems and solutions, or the 20th anniversary of Earth Day wouldn't have been the largest public event in our country's history. Americans want to learn more about the health of their children and their communities, or network news and news magazine shows wouldn't be full of environmental stories.

So what's the future of environmental film in the United States? The number of films produced seems to be directly related to the amount of money available for independent production and the nation's interest in the environment. If the economy gets worse, funding for independent film production will suffer. If there are more eco-catastrophes like Chernobyl, Valdez and the record heat of the summer of 1988 looming in the future, then more environmental films will be produced in response.

But can the industry sustain itself with catastrophe-driven films? The viewing public would quickly tire of films that address only doom and gloom. Besides, Hollywood and commercial television executives will probably not change their perception that viewers only want to be entertained. If environmental films are to have a solid future, then filmmakers will have to look for more entertaining ways to spread their message. They will also have to be more concise in presenting problems and commit to more time addressing solutions. Americans want to learn more about the environment through film and television if by doing so they can educate themselves on how to save it.

Richard Skorman was program director of the 1990 and 1991 US Environmental Film Festivals.

VOICES OF THE LAND, 20 min. 1991 US. A film by Christopher McLeod. An Earth Image Films Production in association with The Earth Island Institute. Distributor: Bullfrog Films, (800) 543-FROG.

By traveling to sacred places around the world, this film examines how the destruction of sacred land also means the destruction of the human spirit.

WHERE HAVE ALL THE DOLPHINS GONE?, 48 min. 1989 US. Winner of 1990 US Environmental Film Festival. A film by Sam LaBudde and Stan Minasian. A production of the Marine Mammal Fund and the American Society for the Prevention of Cruelty to Animals. Distributor: The Video Project, (415) 655-9050.

Narrator George C. Scott chronicles the history and failure of U.S. government laws protecting marine mammals.

THE WRATH OF GRAPES, 15 min. 1987 US. A film by Lorena Parlee. Distributor: United Farm Workers of America, AFL-CIO, (805) 822-5571.

Narrated by Mike Farrell, this shocking film documents the health dangers posed to farm workers in the US and the risk consumers take by eating table grapes heavily sprayed with these poisons.

For more information, contact: Environmental Film Resource Center, 324 N. Tejon St., Colorado Springs, CO 80903, (800) 7ENVFILM.

A. *32 million*
  Source: The Recycler's Handbook, by the Earth • Works Group

AND THE ENVELOPE PLEASE

The Environmental Media Association, a nonprofit group that works with Hollywood talent, selected its winners for the first annual Environmental Media Awards.

Listed below are the winners (designated in bold) and the runners up for the 1991 Environmental Media awards:

TELEVISION EPISODE DRAMA
"MacGyver" ("Bitter Harvest") ABC
"Shannon's Deal" ("Inside Man") NBC
"Highway to Heaven" ("Merry Christmas From Grandpa") NBC

TELEVISION EPISODE COMEDY
"The Simpsons" ("2 Cars In Every Garage, 3 Eyes On Every Fish") FBC
"Harry And The Hendersons" ("Harry Goes Home/Whose Forest Is It Anyway") Syn.
"Murphy Brown" ("Rootless People") CBS

TELEVISION SPECIAL
"A User's Guide To Planet Earth: The American Environment Test" ABC
"Ground Zero" VH-1
"Danger At The Beach" TBS

TELEFILM OF THE WEEK
"Chernobyl: The Final Warning" TNT
"The Last Elephant" TNT
"Incident At Dark River" TNT

Television & Radio

*B*efore television, it was radio that informed us of local and world events and provided the evening's entertainment. Since its invention, television has become the most powerful information tool available to the general audience. To aid the viewer and listener in turning the dial, Earth Journal *provides a list of television and radio programming with environmental concerns.*

EARTH MINUTE

EARTH MINUTE, produced by PlaNet Productions, is a nationally syndicated television news feature delivering positive news on environmental issues. Since November 1990, Earth Minute has provided viewers with their environmental news three times per week to local newscasts across the country from Syracuse, New York, to Fresno, California. News stations concerned about the environment find Earth Minute an important part of their news programming. Lili Shank, host of Earth Minute, lets individuals in on what they can do to help the environment. Shank provides information on where to recycle old paint, how to be environmentally aware consumers, how to compost, plus much more. Earth Minute viewers can also write the stations for free weekly tip sheets which provide additional information on segments shown that week.

NETWORK EARTH

THE TURNER BROADCASTING SYSTEM weekly environmental magazine series, Network Earth, has signed on human-rights advocate Kerry Kennedy Cuomo, environmental activist Sam LaBudde and environmental media specialist Barbara Y. E. Pyle. The three will collectively be known as the "E-Team" and will act as special contributors to the program. Each has expertise in fields relating to today's most important environmental issues and will host "some of the most controversial segments on Network Earth," says the program's spokesperson.

Network Earth is also collaborating with *Family Circle* magazine on a series of special print and video projects on environmental issues. Both the "E-Team" segments and the *Family Circle* series are being aired this 1991-1992 television season.

Q: *How do the environment and President Bush rank, among the most frequent topics of jokes on late-night network talk shows in 1990?*

GO PLANET

IN THE PAST YEAR, cartoon characters have taken on a serious real world issue—the environment. The young Saturday morning audience has been introduced to such eco-heroes as Captain Planet and the Planeteers and the Teenage Mutant Ninja Turtles.

These new "greentoons" seem to be teaching more than the usual mix of the 10 commandments and good guy/bad guy violence. The Planeteers are teens or younger and they, with the help of such wonders

Photo courtesy of TBS Prod., Inc. & DIC Ent., Inc.

Captain Planet and his five Planeteers

as magic rings and telepathic abilities, have the power to clean up this world. But the power is strongest when they join together: It takes all five of the racially-diverse ring holders to call on Captain Planet, the omnipotent, green-haired superhero who personifies the combined powers of earth, water, air, fire and heart, and always defeats the ecovillains.

CHILDREN'S PROGRAMMING/ ANIMATED
"Widget" ("Amazon Adventure") Syn.
"Tiny Toon Adventures" ("Whales Tales") Syn.
"Tale Spin" ("All's Whale That Ends Whale") Syn.

CHILDREN'S PROGRAMMING/ LIVE ACTION
"Earth To Kids: A Guide To Products For A Healthy Planet" HBO
"ABC Afterschool Special, 'A Town's Revenge'" ABC
"Reading Rainbow" ("Jack, The Seal, And The Sea") PBS

DAYTIME PROGRAMMING
"Days Of Our Lives" NBC
"Young And The Restless" CBS

FEATURE FILM
"Dances With Wolves" Orion
"The Rescuers Down Under" Disney
"Teenage Mutant Ninja Turtles 2: The Secret Of The Ooze" New Line

MUSIC VIDEO
"We Can Run" Grateful Dead
"Evergreen, Everblue" Raffi
"Yakety Yak, Take It Back" Take It Back Foundation (Assorted Artists)

ONGOING COMMITMENT (Tie)
"MacGyver" ABC and "Captain Planet and the Planeteers" TBS.

A. *1 and 2 respectively*
Source: Center for Media and Public Affairs

UPCOMING GREEN TELEVISION PROGRAMMING

TBS's 1992 Save the Earth programming

"Captain Planet and the Planeteers" special on February 23

"Save the Earth Original Special" on February 23

"National Geographic EXPLORER" on February 23

"Network Earth" special on February 23

"Cousteau" special on February 24

"World of Audubon" special on February 25

CNN

CNN's "Earth Matters" will cover stories on the Earth Summit (the United Nations Conference on Environment and Development) to take place June 1 through June 12 in Rio de Janeiro.

The Discovery Channel

In 1992, The Discovery Channel is launching "Earth Guide," a weekly series which explores practical actions individuals can take in their homes, offices and communities to help preserve the delicate balance of nature.

We may someday breathe a little easier knowing the next generation, armed with "Turtle Tips" and Captain Planet's "You have the power" motto, will treat the planet with more care than we have.

E-TOWN

E-TOWN is an issue-oriented live music radio program with an emphasis on the environment—great performances combined with the community spirit of a town meeting. Each week, E-TOWN, now broadcast nationally on National Public Radio, includes dynamic, informative speakers as well as entertaining segments of news and helpful tips. E-TOWN also features an array of roots-oriented musicians including David Wilcox, Lyle Lovett, Maura O'Connell, Edgar Meyer, the Subdudes, Michelle Shocked and more.

"Music will bring a large audience, and the information will follow," says E-TOWN Host and Executive Producer Nick Forster. "I'm not trying to be Reverend Billy Environment or to have E-TOWN be a big negative thing. E-TOWN is a way of getting the unadulterated information out, delivered by the people who, in some ways, are really America's cultural heroes—musicians, not politicians."

LIVING ON EARTH

In April 1991, National Public Radio (NPR) debuted "Living On Earth," a half-hour environmental newsmagazine. Hosted by veteran journalist Steve Curwood, the show aired on more than 100 NPR member stations nationwide. The newsmagazine, produced in Cambridge, Massachusetts, begins with a five-minute roundup of global and national environmental news and issues. The roundup is formatted to allow participating NPR member stations the option of inserting local environmental news. An indepth series of reports on a single issue follows the roundup.

Contributions from journalists around the world, interviews with news makers and commentaries from columnists and opinion leaders promote a thorough understanding of the changing environment. Occasionally, "Living On Earth" features a full-length documentary or debate special.

Q. *How many billions of dollars were spent by the US in 1988 on imported oil and other petroleum products?*

Green Stars

*I*n *the 1990s, public service spots have become both more star-studded and more frequent. In an attempt to find out if popularity is worth more than the cause,* Earth Journal *compiled a brief list of some of those celebrities who lend time, energy and money—not just their names—to further environmental causes. What we discovered was heartening: There are far too many seriously dedicated personalities aiding the environmental movement than we have room to list. What follows is a list of celebrity names and the organizations or causes to which they contribute.*

Kirstie Alley
Actress
On the Board of Directors of Earth Communications Office 1925 Century Park E., Ste. 2300, Los Angeles, CA 90067. Works with American Oceans Campaign, 725 Arizona Ave., Ste. 102, Santa Monica, CA 90401.

Cleveland Amory
Author
Animal rights activist
Founder of The Fund For Animals, 200 W. 57th St., New York, NY 10019.

Brigitte Bardot
Actress
Environmental activist
Member of People for Ethical Treatment of Animals, P.O. Box 42516, Washington, DC 20015.

Ed Begley Jr.
Actor
Founder and on the Board of Directors of Earth Communications Office, 1925 Century Park E., Suite 2300, Los Angeles, CA 90067.

Sandra Bernhard
Comedienne/Actress
Works with Conservation International, 1015 18th St. NW, Ste. 1000, Washington, DC 20036. Works with People for the Ethical Treatment of Animals, P.O. Box 42516, Washington, DC 20015.

Jimmy Buffett
Musician/Singer
Founder of the Save the Manatees Club, 500 N. Maitland Ave., Maitland, FL 32751.

Richard Chamberlain
Actor
Works with American Rivers 801 Pennsylvania Ave. SE, Ste. 303, Washington, DC 20003-2167.

Cher
Singer/Actress
Cofounder of Mothers and Others for the Environment 40 W. 20th St., New York, NY 10011.

Glenn Close
Actress
Environmental Activist
Hosted Earth Communications Office's 1991 Conference.

Ted Danson
Actor
Founder of American Oceans Campaign, 725 Arizona Ave., Ste. 102, Santa Monica, CA 90401. Participant in the National Audubon Society's Environmental Television Specials.

John Denver
Musician/Singer/Actor
Founder of Windstar Foundation, 2317 Snowmass Creek Rd., Snowmass, CO 81654. Cofounder of Aspen Institute on Global Change, 100 E. Francis, Aspen, CO 81611.

Dan Fogelberg
Musician/Singer
Environmental activist
Promotes Preservation of the Arctic National Wildlife Refuge.

Jane Fonda
Actress
Environmental activist

Whoopi Goldberg
Comedienne/Actress
Environmental activist
Works with Earth Communications Office, 1925 Century Park E., Ste. 2300, Los Angeles, CA 90067.

Goldie Hawn
Actress
Cofounder of Mothers and Others for the Environment 40 W. 20th St., New York, NY 10011.

Tom Hayden
Democratic Assemblyman
Environmental activist
Teaches an environmental college course at Santa Monica College in California.

Don Henley
Musician/Singer
Works with Defenders of Wildlife, 1244 19th St. NW, Washington, DC 20036.

Pee Wee Herman
Comic actor
Works with Greenpeace USA 1436 U St. NW, Washington, DC 20009.

Charlton Heston
Actor
World population activist

Billy Joel
Musician/Singer
Participant in a Long Island, New York, concert to raise money for The Nature Conservancy, 1815 N. Lynn St., Arlington, VA 22209.

Madonna
Singer/Actress
Works with Conservation International, 1015 18th St.

A. *$39 billion*
  Source: The Greenhouse Trap, *by Francesca Lyman*

EARTH COMMUNICA-TIONS OFFICE

ECO (Earth Communications Office) has been educating those in the media and in the entertainment business about environmental issues since its founding in January 1989 by Bonnie Reiss, an entertainment attorney.

ECO sponsors and hosts six educational forums and one conference per year, each focusing on a specific environmental issue. ECO rounds up scientists, experts in the field and leaders of environmental organizations and asks them to speak on a wide variety of environmental issues. ECO members and participants then take this information and integrate it into their art. Past forums and conferences have inspired such projects as environmentally-oriented episodes of a television series, automobile commercials showing passengers as well as a driver enjoying the car and movies with an environmental theme.

ECO is currently involved in an environmental public service announcement program shown in AMC (American Multi Cinema) theaters nationwide. Earth Communications Office, 1925 Century Park E., Suite 2300, Los Angeles, CA 90067, (213) 277-1665.

NW, Ste. 1000, Washington, DC 20036.

Bette Midler
Actress/Singer
Works with Mothers and Others for the Environment, 40 W. 20th St., New York, NY 10011. Member of Take It Back, a group of musicians/singers who produced the recycling song and video "Yakety Yak, Take It Back."

Olivia Newton-John
Singer/Actress
Honorary Ambassador for the United Nations Environmental Programme. On Board of Directors of Earth Communications Office, 1925 Century Park E, Ste. 2300, Los Angeles, CA 90067.

River Phoenix
Actor/Musician/Singer
On board of advisors for Youth for Environmental Sanity, 706 Frederick St., Santa Cruz, CA 95062. Member of People for Ethical Treatment of Animals, P.O. Box 42516, Washington, DC 20015.

Bonnie Raitt
Singer
Donated profits from her September 1, 1991, concert to environmental groups battling a proposed coal-burning power plant in upstate New York.

Robert Redford
Actor/Director
Enviornmental Activist. Founder of Center for Resource Management (formerly titled Institute for Resource Management), 1410 Grant St., Ste. C307, Denver, CO 80203.

Martin Sheen
Actor
Environmental activist
Anti-nuclear spokesman.

Parker Stevenson
Actor
On Board of Directors of Earth Communications Office 1925 Century Park E, Ste. 2300, Los Angeles, CA 90067.

Jimmy Stewart
Actor
Works with African Wildlife Foundation, 1717 Massachusetts Ave. NW, Washington, DC 20036.

Meryl Streep
Actress
Cofounder of Mothers and Others for the Environment 40 W. 20th St., New York, NY 10011.

Barbra Streisand
Singer/Actress/Director/Producer
Founder of the Streisand Foundation which has given grants to aid environmental causes.

Richard Thomas
Actor
Member of Morris Animal Foundation, 45 Inverness Dr. E, Englewood, CO 80112.

Cheryl Tiegs
Model
Works with The Wilderness Society, 900 17th St. NW, Washington, DC 20006-2596.

Dennis Weaver
Actor
Creator of the Earthship. Founder of Love is Feeding Everyone, 310 N. Fairfax Ave., Los Angeles, CA 90036.

Betty White
Actress
Member of Morris Animal Foundation, 45 Inverness Dr. E, Englewood, CO 80112.

Robin Williams
Actor/Comedian
Works with Mothers and Others for the Environment, 40 W. 20th St., New York, NY 10011.

 Q: *Every day, how many trees does America cut down?*

Fashion

Being ecofashionable means more than refusing to wear fur or using hair products that are cruelty-free. It also means looking seriously at how clothing is made and what products are used. This section takes a serious—and a not-so-serious—look at the ecofashion industry from concept to product.

THE FASHION INDUSTRY APPEARS TO THRIVE on waste and excess, with little correlation between wants and needs, and an emphasis on short product life cycles that maintain consumption. The comfort and pleasure of the person wearing clothes often appear to be neglected in favor of novelty and creating the right "look," with the result that too many clothes are not particularly human-friendly, let alone environment-friendly. With fashions changing so rapidly, designing long-lasting clothes might appear irrelevant—we should be aiming for flexibility and adaptability, so that clothes can be transformed to meet new themes. Reversible clothing could be one way of achieving flexibility and adaptability. Another approach is to design "classic" well-made clothes that will continue to appear stylish whatever the passing fashion may be. Many people have already decided to dress this way for economy as well as simplicity.

We also have to consider whether clothes always have to look brand new to be stylish. Many fabrics continue to look attractive when they have aged—even when they have been mended or altered. The attraction to the old and "interesting" is clearly seen in our fondness for antique rugs or curtains. Perhaps designers should consider how their products will age, and aim for materials which do not lose their color and shape after the first wash.

Second-hand clothes

The continual throwing-out of wardrobes does provide a form of recycling, although most people are very reluctant to discard clothes, even when there is no realistic prospect of their being worn. Second-hand clothes can be of high fashion interest—as seen by the desire for worn jeans—but in general there is still a reluctance to accept them as a logical part of the normal wardrobe. Some fashion designers are beginning to

CHOCOLATE MOOSE TO WEAR

Alaska's hottest souvenir item is an environmentalist's dream come true: It's 100 percent natural, biodegradable and exists in super-abundance.

And, if you get tired of wearing it, it also makes great fertilizer.

Capitalizing on last summer's rush of starry-eyed tourists, shrewd Alaskans are dashing around to scoop up piles of small brown moose nuggets that have been elevated from smelly nuisance to proud symbol. And thousands of "cheechakos" (Eskimo for greenhorns) are forking over $1.25 to $3 for their very own piece.

The nuggets, dried and shellacked, take many forms: earrings, necklaces, bolo-tie pieces, refrigerator magnets, swizzle sticks and Christmas tree ornaments. And entrepreneurs eager for a piece of the action are horning in with more innovative products, including a plastic-wrapped, untreated nugget containing seeds of Alaskan wildflowers, all ready for planting.

Reprinted by permission from The Wall Street Journal, *"They Make the Perfect Accessory To Go With Designer Dungarees," by Suein L. Hwang, August 16, 1991.*

A. *2 million*
  Source: The Recycler's Handbook, *by the Earth • Works Group*

Photo: Julius Vitali

GREEN HAIR

Just washed your hair and can't make a statement with it? So you thought. Terry Niedzialek of New York has an answer: environmental hair montage.

Niedzialek sculpts hair into smoke-belching factories or high seas carrying ships or giraffes caged in cinder block-like castle walls. She uses television sets, wire, clay, cement, tempera paint, styrofoam and many other found objects to create 3-D environments on top of people's heads. Formerly parting her time between hairdressing and environmental art, since 1983 she has created about 35 sculptures on both wigs and live models. Although the sculptures can be worn as everyday dos, they are more often shown in exhibits or created on commission.

These aren't just part of an environmental look, says Niedzialek. "Most of the hair montages reflect our relationship with nature and Earth. Hair turns into an environment and we become that."

consider recycled clothes as interesting materials, but so far there has been little serious attempt to design for recycled clothes.

Fur and leather

Demand for furs is falling as a result of successful campaigning by environmental and animal welfare groups, bringing to the public's attention the suffering endured by farmed as well as trapped animals. Some designers have moved from using real fur to fake fur. Some fake furs are obviously not intended to be realistic, but others aim to be indistinguishable from the real thing—an approach which will surely perpetuate the idea that furs are a suitable clothing material.

Designers can look for alternatives to leather products from both endangered and non-endangered species. A good example of this is fish leather, a by-product from food production which is an alternative to snakeskin.

Fashion trends

The fashion industry is predicting that "green" interests will be a strong influence on fashion themes during the 1990s: "eco-fashion," based on the colors of sea, sky and earth, with nature prints and shell jewelry, has been proposed. One of the first collections for the "pure" 1990s, however, from Rifat Ozbek, features an array of pure white clothes that are not only bleached, but require continual cleaning. It is not yet clear whether the fashion world will simply look upon the environment as another superficial styling gimmick, or whether there will be a real attempt to tackle some of the issues relating to the resource consumption and pollution created by textile manufacture and use. As in other areas of environmental product design, however, appearance not backed up by reality will cause confusion and attract criticism. The "natural look," which aims to convince consumers that it is environmentally conscious, but where none of the major issues relating to the production process have been considered, will have only a short-term appeal as consumer knowledge increases.

Reprinted by permission from Design for the Environment *by Dorothy Mackenzie, Rizzoli International Publications, Inc., New York, 1991.*

Q: *What percentage of Americans believe that a "major national effort" is required to improve the environment?*

Photo: Virginia Bing

ALL TIRED OUT

EVERY YEAR, AMERICAN'S TOSS OUT some 240 million tires, creating gridlock in the nation's landfills. At Used Rubber USA in San Francisco, Mandana MacPherson, 26, and Cameron Trotter, 30, are providing an environmentally fashionable afterlife for inner tubes of discarded car and truck tires.

MacPherson designs and Trotter markets rubber wares, which include purses, pouches, knapsacks, cycle saddlebags, belts and sandals, ranging in price from $10 to $180. "People know about the rainforests but not about piles of tires," says MacPherson. "[Our products] start out as inner tubes and end up as nice handbags. We're an example of what you can do with waste."

MacPherson and Trotter forage regularly for discards. Dumpsters, tire dealers, even shoulders of nearby freeways yield rich raw materials. MacPherson cuts the innertubes into strips, washes them and cuts them into patterns at the converted warehouse where she and Trotter live. Most in demand are bags with brand names like Firestone, Michelin and especially Pirelli, the Italian manufacturer. "They call it the Gucci of rubber," says Trotter. But unlike designer leather, Used Rubber's bags are waterproof, stainproof and come with a lifetime guarantee. So there's no need for spares. And should your bag get damaged, Trotter promises, "You can always bring it in for an overhaul." Contact Used Rubber USA, 597 Haight St., San Francisco, CA 94117, (415) 626-7855.

Reprinted by permission from People *magazine, August 12, 1991.*

I'VE BEEN PUMICED

With every action there is an equal and opposite reaction. Take stonewashed jeans as an example, the clothing often preferred by environmental activists when doing duty sitting in front of bulldozers or in trees. For the sake of fashion, forests are being strip-mined in order to reach pumice, the porous volcanic rock used to give stone- and acid-washed clothing their bleached look. The Jemez Mountain range in New Mexico is one of the areas being bulldozed for pumice. Local environmental organizations, such as the Jemez Action Group, are calling for a boycott of stone- and acid-washed clothing in order to lessen the demand.

Levi Strauss & Co., which holds the largest market share of stone- and acid-washed clothing, has recently reduced the use of pumice and has begun to replace it with chemicals—no better, but also no worse for the environment than bleach. Levi's aim, says David Samson, Manager of Communications, is to reduce the need for pumice to zero as soon as the chemicals alone prove satisfactory.

A. **78 percent**
Source: Roper Center for Public Research

Green Arts

*F*or centuries, a favorite subject of artists of all mediums has been Nature; its beauty and its strength. Today, a new twist on a timeless subject brings us environmental visual art, green theater productions and ecodance performances.

©1989 Robert Bateman. Courtesy of Mill Pond Press, Venice, FL.

THE ART OF NATURE

- By Ruth Rudner -

A PRISTINE, ANCIENT FOREST bathed in golden light covers the top fifth of the canvas. The painting depicts a perfect place. Eternal and inviting, it is a place of dreams. Below it, on the larger portion of canvas, a monochromatic jumble of wasted tree limbs and stumps, the dead refuse of a clearcut, fills the foreground. In the background, a logging road winds desolate, around a desolate mountain.

"Carmanah Contrast," by the Canadian painter Robert Bateman, is a powerful environmental statement. It is also powerful art. Bateman, an outspoken environmentalist, is not alone among artists who, taking the natural world as their subject, commit themselves to its preservation. The artist, reacting spontaneously to light, air, water and earth, to the vibrancy of animals and plants, connects to the environment in an intimate, instinctive way. The connection is not a new one.

When two landscapes were shown by the painter J. F. Cropsey in 1847, a reviewer (quoted by Barbara Novak in *Nature and Culture*) wrote: "The axe of civilization is busy with our old forests, and artisan

Q: *How many people in the world die from skin cancer each year?*

ingenuity is fast sweeping away the relics of our national infancy.... Yankee enterprise has little sympathy with the picturesque, and it behooves our artists to rescue from its grasp the little that is left, before it is too late."

For at least a century and a half, artists portraying the natural world have acted as partisans for the environment. That art has served the environment well is attested to by the very existence of Yellowstone National Park. Most 19th century exploratory or hunting expeditions included aritsts. Ferdinand Hayden's 1871 expedition to the Yellowstone region was no exception. Painter Thomas Moran and photographer William Henry Jackson were there sketching, painting and photographing everything in sight. Their work was prime in convincing Congress to set Yellowstone aside as the world's first national park.

Art is a powerful tool for conveying a message about the environment. Although Robert Bateman thinks art is less effective than television or film in this day and age, in some ways it may be more ideal than either, more ideal, even, than nature itself. The painting, the sculpture, the photograph stop a moment in time so that the particular moment can be entered over and over, revealing ever more about it. The painter, of course, can manipulate the moment, can idealize it. It was not unusual for 19th century painters to move details of a scene around, as Albert Bierstadt did in his flamboyant paintings of Yellowstone Falls, or as Moran did, in order to present an ultimate truth about the scene. The result is a viewer's enhanced ability to enter more aspects of the moment at once than is possible by standing on the spot where the painter stood. If the commitment to both art and nature is present, art about nature rings true to the viewer regardless of the rearrangement of details.

The technique is still viable. Bateman also moves details of his scene around, juxtaposing the living and destroyed forests. We do, indeed, get the point.

In her introduction to *Nature and Culture*, Novak writes, "The new significance of nature and the development of landscape painting coincided paradoxically with the relentless destruction of the wilderness in the early 19th century. The ravages of man on nature were a repeated concern in artists' writings, and the symbol of this attack was usually 'the axe,' cutting into nature's pristine...state." She quotes painter Thomas Cole's

CONNECTICUT

WILDLIFE GALLERY
172 Bedford St.
Stamford, CT 06901
(203) 324-6483
Gallery director: James Dugan, Founded: 1971, Type of art exhibited: Wildlife. Signed and numbered limited edition print.

DISTRICT OF COLUMBIA

KATHLEEN EWING GALLERY
1609 Connecticut Ave. NW
Washington, DC 20009
(202) 328-0955
Gallery director: Kathleen Ewing, Founded: 1976, Type of art exhibited: Fine art photography.

FLORIDA

AMERICAN WILDLIFE ART GALLERY
2516 Ponce de Leon Blvd.
Coral Gables, FL 33134
(305) 442-6717
Gallery director: Gordon Smith, Founded: 1984, Type of art exhibited: Specializing in wildlife, sporting, Western, marine and aviation. Originals, limited editions, bronzes, decoys.

ISLAND WILDLIFE GALLERY
2460 Palm Ridge Rd.
Sanibel Island, FL 33957
(813) 395-1100
Gallery director: Jerry Johnson, Founded: 1988, Type of art exhibited: The majority of the work recreates the unique sub-tropical environment of southwest Florida in woodcarvings, metal sculptures, oils, pastels, watercolors and porcelains.

A. *100,000*
  Source: The Greenhouse Trap, *by Francesca Lyman*

GEORGIA

CHUCKIE'S FRAMES, ETC.
2036-G Johnson Ferry
    Rd. NE
Atlanta, GA 30319
(404) 457-8669
Gallery director:
Katherine Towles,
Founded: 1985, **Type of art exhibited:** Wildlife, landscapes, seascapes, national park prints.

IDAHO

WILLOWTREE GALLERY
210 Cliff St.
Idaho Falls, ID 83402
(208) 524-4464
Gallery director: Kit Denier, **Founded:** 1987, **Type of art exhibited:** Western wildlife. Limited edition prints and originals.

1835 "Essay on American Scenery," "…with the improvements of cultivation the sublimity of the wilderness should pass away; for those scenes of solitude from which the hand of nature has never been lifted, affect the mind with a more deep toned emotion than aught which the hand of man has touched."

What the human hands have touched is precisely what British painter David Shepherd is trying to rectify with the conservation foundation he spearheads. Shepherd became a conservationist while painting in Africa in 1960 (making the first of the elephant paintings for which he is famous), when he came upon 255 dead zebra around a poisoned water hole. "When you see a sight like that," he said in an interview in the March 1990 issue of *US Art Magazine*, "You want to do something for wildlife. I'm a conservationist now in the sense that I don't just believe in saving rhinos or elephants…but it's the whole damn world we're messing up."

Art dealer and conservationist Mark Read calls Shepherd and Bateman "fabulous artists, without peer, who have given their guts and soul to conservation."

In the late 20th century, the artist's connection to

A HARVEST OF ART

Stan Herd is an environmental artist with dirt, not paint, under his fingernails. He uses tractors, plows and other traditional farm implements as brushes, and wheat, soybeans, clover, alfalfa, sunflowers, oats and other crops as paints. Herd plants giant images into 14- to 160-acre earth canvases outside Lawrence, Kansas. Because his "paintings" are temporary, the coloring and life of his work is left to Mother Nature. Herd, the son of a Kansas farmer, feels in touch with the personality of the land and the travails of farming. "I like to think that my earth pieces prove you can do something beautiful and in tune with our planet and yet leave no trace. To me, that is the art."

Herd's earth images spring from the land itself. His first works, portraits of Satanta, chief of the Kiowa tribe of the Plains, and of Will Rogers, depicted men who were tightly bound to their homelands. Herd's most recent work is a series of portraits of indigenous peoples. One of his eight earthworks was a piece he proposed for Absolut Vodka's advertising campaign.

Herd is not a farmer by trade. But his Kansas neighbors who do farm delight in his artistry, supply him with the necessary tools—including their acres—and often won't let him harvest the images, because, they believe, the aesthetic value frequently outweighs the monetary value.

ABSOLUT LANDMARK.

Q: *Each year, how many millions of pounds of paper do American paper companies import from Brazil?*

nature includes its protection. Sherry Sander, a Montana sculptor whose extraordinary work is based on her strong feelings for the animals she portrays, says, "I don't know how you could separate the work from a responsibility to the subject. You can't have a reverence for the animal without being concerned about its welfare. The more I work, the more worried about the animals I get."

Early artists' animal drawings on cave and rock walls were probably the purest images of the connection between artist and nature as have ever existed. Between that time and the 19th century, in a long detour in art away from nature, things became less simple. Where nature was acknowledged, it was apt to be as the Greeks acknowledged it—by including mountains, rivers and trees in art because they were essential parts of myth—the homes of gods, the sources of symbols. In medieval times, when earthly life was considered only a brief and difficult stop on the way to Paradise, nature was of little interest. In fact, because nature is experienced through the senses, it was seen as intrinsically sinful. For most of civilized (western) history, human beings have regarded wild places as the haunt of demons, brigands and similar dangers, and have focused their attention—and their art—on the progress of civilization.

This may have been one of the best things that ever happened to nature. So long as it remained infinite and terrifying, human beings instinctively stayed away from it. Superstition, fear, distrust of the unknown kept the environment safe. We could not destroy what we would not enter. Art, reflecting the civilization we invented, would not focus on nature.

A modern approach to landscape wasn't even possible until people were ready to look at nature with pleasure, with wonder and with awe. When the 14th century poet, Petrarch, climbed a mountain for the pleasure of the view, it was a revolutionary act. By responding to nature, Petrarch connected with a sentiment of the future. No one rushed to emulate him.

More than a century later, Albrecht Durer's watercolors of animals and plants documented his extraordinary sense of wonder. His desire to record the natural world around him was not different from that of modern painters like the Belgian, Carl Brenders, whose intricate, minutely detailed paintings of animals are so moving in their straightforwardness, or

INDIANA

HORIZON GALLERIES
2113 Southlake Mall
Merrillville, IN 46410
(219) 769-1122
Gallery director: Stan Salah, **Founded:** 1982, **Type of art exhibited:** Southwestern, landscape, Americana, wildlife. Limited edition prints and originals.

IOWA

DENNIS P. ROBERTS GALLERY
1111 73rd St.
Windsor Heights, IA 50311
(515) 277-4423
Gallery director: Connie Kelly, **Founded:** 1975, **Type of art exhibited:** Wildlife art. Originals and limited edition prints.

LOUISIANA

THE CRABNET
929 Decatur St.
New Orleans, LA 70116
(504) 522-3478
Gallery directors: Doug and Rita Lambert, **Founded:** 1981, **Type of art exhibited:** Wildlife art of Louisiana and the Gulf Coast in oils, watercolors, woodcarving and limited edition lithographs.

MARYLAND

SNOW GOOSE GALLERY
6831 Wisconsin Ave.
Chevy Chase, MD 20815
(301) 907-9240, (800) 875-SNOW
Gallery director: Shelby Purcell, **Founded:** 1980, **Type of art exhibited:** Americana, marine, Western and wildlife. Original works and limited edition prints and bronzes.

A. **800 million pounds**
Source: The Recycler's Handbook, by the Earth • Works Group

MICHIGAN

RIECKER'S OUTDOOR GALLERY
134 E. Front St.
Traverse City, MI 49684
(616) 946-0414
Gallery director: Steven and Nancy T. Riecker,
Founded: 1985, **Type of art exhibited:** Wildlife and landscape by award-winning local and national artists.

MISSOURI

CHRISMAN WILDLIFE ART
116 E. Stoddard
Dexter, MO 63841
(800) 325-8017
Gallery director: Joe Vinson, **Founded:** 1972,
Type of art exhibited: Wildlife art.

NEVADA

ALLEN AUGUSTINE GALLERY
5 Round Hill Mall
Zephyr Cove, NV 89448
(702) 588-3525
Gallery director: Christel Citko, **Founded:** 1987, **Type of art exhibited:** Outstanding works by local, national and internationally recognized artists. Original oils, acrylics, watercolors, bronze and stone sculpture, fine limited edition graphics, cast paper and works in fiber, clay and glass. Rotating exhibits.

NEW JERSEY

CARDINAL ART GALLERY
Rte. 94 and Vernon Crossing Rd.
Vernon, NJ 07462
(201) 764-5050
Gallery director: Tony Santarpia, **Founded:** 1984, **Type of art exhibited:** Specializing in

the marvelous Utah painter of animals and mountain men, Michael Coleman.

It was that sense of wonder that, at last, produced art about nature. Mark Read, whose Everard-Read Gallery in Johannesburg, South Africa, puts him close to the thick of African conservation, feels it is that same sense of wonder that makes the difference between good wildlife (or landscape) art and the commercial slickness of much of what is currently out there. Read was responsible for mounting an important exhibition of art about the natural world at the Fourth World Wilderness Congress in Denver in 1987. The exhibition was a personal vision of Read's, an uncompromising man when it comes to the quality of art. Merely because the painting or sculpture is about nature is not enough. "If one is looking at environmentally relevant painting or sculpture, one has to eliminate a good percentage of so-called wildlife artists," he says. "These paint for a market, and don't carry the weight of intellect necessary to convey the pulse of wilderness."

"The pulse of wilderness" sums it up—the life of art and the life of Earth. Wilderness is a living, breathing thing. Certainly its pulse beat insistently in the hearts of those 19th century American painters who filled their canvases with such glories of nature that to gaze on them today is still to transcend the line between Earth and self. So immense is the glow of light emanating from our wild country on those canvases that we are drawn forward into it and lose ourselves in light, in atmosphere, in incandescent wildness.

Some artists, working in and from and about nature, have had to wait awhile for an audience that thought only peasants worked outside. Yet, like the Impressionist Camille Pissarro, only happy painting out of doors, or like his contemporary, Paul Cezanne, obsessing as much over the facets of a rock as any climber ever did, they persisted in their vision. Inventing their art formed these painters, but it also had enormous influence on the public vision. Whether or not art collectors and audiences respond at once to a style or subject of art, the mood of art often seems to presage an era. It is as if artists, as creators, were privy to some special knowledge of the universe.

* * *

But most artists, regardless of the reason they choose their subjects, make art for art's sake. In the process of making the work, it is the work that matters.

Q. *How many papermills in the US make newsprint from 100 percent recycled paper?*

Raymond Harris-Ching, among the foremost contemporary painters of wildlife, acknowledges that drawing attention to the need for conservation may be part of his life, but his sole purpose in making a painting is an artistic one. He makes his meticulously observed, intensely alive wildlife pictures out of his interest in the process of painting.

So does Robert Bateman, activist that he is. Even his most controversial art—the paintings that are not pretty—"Carmanah Contrast"; a painting called "Wildlife Images" depicting an eagle shot through the wing, fur seal tangled in netting, oil spill, two dead sea birds and a plastic 6-pack holder; and a third called "Indian Images" that shows a fallen and rotting totem pole, an Indian elder, an abandoned Indian fishing boat and a logging truck—are made for the sake of the work. Bateman considers these pieces his best work. "I think I paint reality when I make beautiful paintings," he says, "But the other paintings are also a reality we can't close our eyes to."

It doesn't really matter what the painter's reason for the painting is; if the painting is honest, it will affect the viewer. The 19th century viewer of art was changed by that art. The land, wildness, began to enter the viewer's eye and mind and heart. A vision of the Earth that represented it in the honesty of the Earth's wild splendor and roughness was, perhaps, easier to accept for the art audience in America than it was in Europe. The European audience had been bred on a tradition of civilized beauties. In North America, nature was the only tradition we had.

Does art influence the contemporary viewer as it did the 19th century viewer? According to Mark Read, the buyer of wildlife art buys it almost as a souvenir of a safari or hunting or pack trip, rather than with any awareness of what it represents. The collector of contemporary painters, like John Alexander, is simply collecting the work of a hot painter, unaware of what Read calls a "tremendous feeling of wilderness that's completely amazing in Alexander's work. Conservationists should view him as being important. A lot of contemporary painters are involved in what's happening environmentally. It's not just in wildife art." Read believes the environmental consciousness of collectors is not expanded by viewing the art on their walls. Bateman believes the public he reaches is mainly a public already converted.

wildlife art, original paintings, limited edition prints, bronze and wood sculpture and duck and conservation stamp prints.

NEW MEXICO

FRAME DESIGN AND GALLERY
1605-G Juan Tabo
Albuquerque, NM 87112
(505) 275-3338
Gallery Director: Ed Simonson. **Founded:** 1986. **Type of art exhibited:** Posters and prints of work by Robert Bateman, animal wildlife and destruction of environment and wildlife.

NEW YORK

THE FUERTES ART COLLECTION AT THE CORNELL LABORATORY OF ORNITHOLOGY
159 Sapsucker Woods Rd.
Ithaca, NY 14850
(607) 254-BIRD
Founded: 1957, **Type of art exhibited:** Classical. An expansive gallery of original art and watercolors by Louis Agassiz Fuertes, acclaimed as one of America's greatest painters of birds.

G & R GALLERY OF WILDLIFE ART
2895 Seneca St.
Buffalo, NY 14224
(716) 822-0546
Gallery director: Ray Kegler, **Founded:** 1982, **Type of art exhibited:** Wildlife art. Limited edition prints and originals.

THE SHADOWBOX GALLERY
85 Hazel St.
Glen Cove, NY 11542
(516) 678-8044
Gallery director: Jack Appelman, **Founded:**

A.[2]
Source: 15 Simple Things Californians Can Do To Recycle, by the Earth•Works Group

1953, **Type of art exhibited:** Wildlife, Americana, Western, Civil War.

OHIO

GALLERY ONE
7003 Center St.
Mentor, OH 44060
(800) 621-1141
Gallery directors: Alan Brown, Norah Lynne and Jay Brown, **Founded:** 1974, **Type of art exhibited:** Prints, paintings and sculpture.

OKLAHOMA

FOX HOLLOW STUDIO
337 SE Fenway Pl.
Bartlesville, OK 74006
(918) 333-5593
Founded: 1978, **Type of art exhibited:** North American wildlife paintings and prints and wildlife photographs.

OREGON

FRAME ATTIC
220 W. Main St.
Sisters, OR 97759
(503) 549-9199
Gallery director: Paul Nichamoff, **Founded:** 1983, **Type of art exhibited:** Limited edition prints, posters and photography.

WASHINGTON

BLACK SWAN GALLERY
805 First Ave.
Seattle, WA 98104
(206) 624-8005, (800) 477-SWAN
Gallery directors: George Russell and Lewis Hall, **Founded:** 1985, **Type of art exhibited:** Wildlife, Western, equine, Americana. Prints and originals.

FARRENS GALLERY
2819 Wetmore Ave.

Maybe. But a consciousness that seems to change in relation to the environment with increasing fervor may well be open to the chance of art. Ellen Pederson, Planning and Development Manager at Mill Pond Press, publishers of some of today's top artists of the environment, says that after a talk by Robert Bateman, a number of CEOs in the audience came up to ask how they could get involved. (Bateman's answer is to support environmental organizations, to join as many as possible.)

Publishers like Mill Pond Press regularly make use of special projects—such as time-limited prints—to raise funds for conservation.

Many artists donate work to benefit environmental organizations. While they also benefit from having their names associated with conservation, there are probably few of them involved who do not feel the urgent necessity for action.

"Any of the artists we publish who are portraying the natural world," Ellen Pederson says, "are concerned about it. They were doing it before it became fashionable. It's not for show, it's for care."

Care is the key. The awe that comes from care, and the power to dare that comes from it, have consistently fueled the vision and energy of artists of the natural world. It is the same power that fuels the vision and energy of environmentalists. It is the same Earth that is being created over and over. Our reverence for nature, which, by now, means not the isolated waterfall or pristine lake or smoldering volcano of the 19th century painting, but the entire planet, mounts. It is a reverence clearly present in the work of contemporary artists: a Bateman grizzly veiled by the mist of roiling water as he surges forward, roaring into some unknown open space where, it would seem, he could stand unveiled, except that it is the point on which the human viewer stands; or a Michael Coleman polar bear, edging out from the tundra brush, glowing with the glow of snow and sky, alone, king, and at ease in the world that is his.

"Such intense reverence for nature came only with the realization that nature could be lost," Novak writes in *Nature and Culture*, about the 19th century landscape painters.

The story of artist and the environment is not new.

Ruth Rudner is the author of Greetings from Wisdom, Montana, *published by Fulcrum, Inc., Golden, CO, 1989.*

Q: *What is the projected average speed Californian automobiles will be capable of driving on the highway by the year 2010?*

ECODANCE

"Black Horn," Ann Patz (choreographer) in collaboration with Blane de St. Croix (design) and Richard O'Donnell (composer), performed at The Forum in St. Louis, Missouri, March 1991. This three-person dance performance pays homage to the black rhinoceros, protesting the killing of the rhino for its horn.

"Still Life," David Bintley (choreographer) and the Royal Ballet, performed at the Penguin Cafe, New York, 1991. "Still Life" is a dance performance commenting on acid rain, Aborigines, and the demise of the rainforest.

Forces of Nature dance company specializes in ecologically-themed dance performances. For information on the company's scheduled performances contact Abdel Salaam, Forces of Nature, 1047 Amsterdam Ave., New York, NY 10018, (212) 749-7720.

ECOTHEATER

"Endangered Species," Martha Clarke (choreographer) and her company, performed at the Brooklyn Academy of Music, New York, as part of the Next Wave festival, 1990. "Endangered Species" is a series of vignettes using actors, dancers, singers and animals to explore themes of domination and oppression. It was performed in a circus tent.

"Waste," The Living Theater, adapted by Hanon Reznikov and performed outdoors in New York, through August 25, 1991. "Waste" is a concoction of plays and operas covering 2,500 years and three continents to convey the issues of water and air pollution, vegtarianism, feminism, war, imprisonment, homelessness, wage slavery, nuclear contamination, the disappearance of species, garbage and the politics of all these.

"Columbus the New World Order," Bread and Puppet Theater, traveled to various cities worldwide in 1991. "Columbus the New World Order" puppet show takes on such Canadian topics as the James Bay project, indigenous peoples' rights to the land and the killing of the caribou. For information contact Bread and Puppet Theater, RD 2, Glover, VT 05839, (802) 525-3031.

Everett, WA 98201
(206) 259-0133
Gallery director: Darcy Farrens, **Founded:** 1978, **Type of art exhibited:** Western wildlife, landscape, floral, aviation, Southwest, contemporary. Limited edition prints and original paintings, bronze and wood sculpture.

HOWARD/MANDVILLE GALLERY
Harbor Square
120 W. Dayton, Suite D9
Edmonds, WA 98020
(800) 544-4763
Gallery directors: Dan and Pat Howard, **Founded:** 1972, **Type of art exhibited:** Wildlife, Western, Americana, fantasy, aviation. Limited edition prints and originals.

WISCONSIN

AMANN GALLERIES LTD.
2515 Wauwatosa Ave.
Milwaukee, WI 53213
(414) 476-9000
Gallery director: Ron Amann, **Founded:** 1979, **Type of art exhibited:** Specializing in wildlife, Western and landscapes.

VIRGINIA

FINE ART GALLERY
2156 Crystal Plaza
Arlington, VA 22202
(703) 415-0760
Gallery director: Conny L. Dempsey, **Founded:** 1984, **Type of art exhibited:** Wildlife. Limited edition prints and sculptures.

A. *11 miles per hour*
Source: California State Assembly

EARTH MUSIC

Following is a directory to environmental and indigenous music.

AMERICAN GRAMO-PHONE RECORDS
9130 Mormon Bridge Rd.
Omaha, NE 68152
(402) 457-4341
Example: Yellowstone: The Music of Nature.
Description: Recording of music played during benefit concert with Chip Davis and classical music selections with natural themes.

CANYON RECORDS
4143 N. 16th St.
Phoenix, AZ 85016
Example: Spirit Horses by Carlos Nakai. **Description:** Canyon specializes in all kinds of Native American music from traditional to rock.

CELESTIAL HARMONIES
P.O. Box 30122
Tucson, AZ 85751
(602) 326-4400
Example: Sacred Ceremonies: Ritual Music of Tibetan Buddhism. **Description:** This recording crosses the threshold of this ritual to explore the vibrant sounds of the monks' ancient musical meditations.

DAN GIBSON PRODUCTIONS
P.O. Box 1360
Minocua, WI 54548
Series: Solitude Series.
Description: A well recorded series of nature soundtracks, featuring a large variety of North American environments and wildlife species (includes 12 volumes).

Green Music

S ome argue that the origin of music comes from humankind's desire to imitate the sounds of nature. Or perhaps it was the only way humans could attempt to understand nature. Whatever its origin, music has become an important part of culture. Environmental music is not just recordings of whale talk—although it is that also. It is also not just a political song about saving a rainforest—although it is that also. It is the sound of everything wild and everything endangered.

- By Ed Ward -

IT WAS AT MIDEM IN 1990, the international music business convention in France, that I first heard the birds. Downstairs, Cannes' Palais des Festivals was jammed with hustlers and executives of every stripe, each with a licensing deal for a record you just wouldn't believe. There was tension and cigarette smoke in the air: MIDEM is not an inexpensive proposition, and a lot of these people had plenty on the line. I was representing Texas music and a conference I help run, and was observing all of this from the Texas exhibit. Across from Texas was Canada, where, I was pleased to see, Holger Petersen, the amiable president of a Canadian folk record label, had joined his countrymen in deal-making.

It was Petersen who took me to the birds. "I've found something you've got to check out," he said on the conference's third day. I told the Texans I was taking five, and Petersen and I walked toward the classical section of the trade show. "This guy only speaks French, but he's fascinating." And then we were there, at a booth like the others, but with a lot of people standing around smiling. We were surrounded by the sounds of a forest, and at a table, wearing a smile and a white goatee, sat the man responsible for all of this, Jean C. Roché, the eminent collector of European birdsongs. Like everybody else at MIDEM, he was looking for a deal: He'd put out several CDs of the sounds of forests and jungles, and wanted somebody in America to put them out. Through Petersen, I told him I'd do what I could, and he gave me a set of his recordings.

I passed his booth several times a day after that, and there were always people standing there, not

---

Q: *What item represents more than one-third of the waste produced in California, while less than 30 percent is recycled?*

necessarily talking to Roché, but standing with their eyes closed, smiling. There was music to be heard everywhere at MIDEM, but somehow, this seemed to be a place that drew people to it. I really wanted to figure out how this worked, and, as it turned out, I got my chance the next week in Berlin, where I'd gone to settle some difficult business. After a long night of intense discussion, and an unhappy resolution, I went back to my apartment and slept for hours. The next morning I reached into my suitcase and found one of Monsieur Roché's discs and put it on the player. A new day had started for me, all right, and it was as if the birds of the French forest were starting it with me, and I with them.

Until recently, I'd always thought of Jean Roché as something of a lovable eccentric; his "Birds Awakening," "American Forests and Lakes" and "African Forests and Savannas" discs seemed an amusing outgrowth of his serious scientific work of documenting the birdsong of every indigenous European species, work which is available on a multi-disc set. The avalanche of similar tapes and CDs I've received, though, proved that there was a wild world of sound out there about which I'd been completely ignorant.

Now, there are people who claim that the origin of music lies in humankind's attempt to imitate nature's sounds. I rather doubt it. True, hunting cultures tried to imitate the noises made by their prey to lure it to where they could kill it, but I think that instrumental music comes not so much from an imitation of nature, but from a desire to order it, to bend it to human will. Percussion instruments are hit at regular intervals to systematize body movement, and melodic instruments almost certainly have their origins in vocal music, reinforcing a vocal tone just as a percussion instrument reinforces a dance movement.

If this is so, though, then we're faced with an interesting proposition: Music exists to separate humankind from nature. After all, music, Edgard Varese, the pioneering 20th century composer once said, is organized sound. Over here, you have critters who make random sounds, and over here, you have ones who make organized sounds, usually with language attached. Just as, on the one hand, you have the animals who eat whatever they find lying around, and on the other, you have humans who plant food crops, and even go so far as to make them grow in

ELEKTRA NONESUCH
75 Rockefeller Plaza
New York, NY 10019
(212) 484-7200
Example: Ethnic Explorer Series. **Description:** Recordings of ethnic music including Mexican festival music, flute music from Japan, African ancient ceremonies and dances and Kenyan and Tanzanian witchcraft and ritual music.

EMERALD GREEN
P.O. Box 16144
Santa Fe, NM 87506
(505) 473-7383
Series: Sacred Sites Series. **Description:** This series from Rusty Crutcher includes Machu Picchu Impressions, Chaco Canyon and Amazon Song in a combination of state-of-the-art recordings of environmental sounds from locations that resonate spiritually, with musical compositions inspired by the land.

FOLKWAYS RECORDS
1 Camp St.
Cambridge, MA 02140
(617) 354-0700
Example: Bukhara: Musical Crossroads of Asia.
Description: Bukhara was made on location in mosques, synagogues and in the walled courtyards and intimate salons of Bukharan homes. Bukhara focuses on the spirited wedding songs, the Central Asian classical repertory known as shashmaqam and selections from the liturgical chant traditions of Moslems and Jews.

FOUR WINDS
P.O. Box 1887
Boulder, CO 80306
(800) 456-5444

A. *Paper*
Source: 15 Simple Things Californians Can Do To Recycle, by the Earth ● Works Group

Example: Kevin Locke Series. **Description:** Given the NEA award as a pure traditionalist for preservation of the songs of the Lakota, Locke plays the flute the way the Lakota have for generations, with titles such as Lakota Love Songs and Stories, Make Me A Hollow Reed and Seventh Direction.

GLOBAL PACIFIC RECORDS
270 Perkins St.
Sonoma, CA 95476
(707) 996-2748
Example: Global Voyage. **Description:** Recordings of sounds of Africa.

HARMONIA MUNDI USA
3364 S. Robertson Blvd.
Los Angeles, CA 90034
(503) 248-9062
No mail order available.
Catalog by request.
Series: Ethnic Music Scenes (on four separate labels). Ethnic Nadinedit, Le Chant Du Monde, Ocora, and Unesco. **Description:** Music from various areas such as Armenia, Africa, Vietnam, Cambodia and Brazil.

LIVING MUSIC
P.O. Box 72
Litchfield, CT 06759
(203) 567-8796
Examples: Songs of the Humpback Whale, Whales Alive, Callings. **Description:** Hauntingly exhilarating experiences of whale communication in an effort to raise people's awareness about the survival of each species.

LYRICHORD DISCS
141 Perry St.
New York, NY 10014

straight lines. And, needless to say, as human society got more complex, so did human music. Eventually, it even got to the point of pure abstraction, pure instrumental music completely detached from concerns of either text or dance. If there's anything that stands apart from nature, it's a Bach chorale prelude played on a great organ.

But of course, that's not entirely the case, either: That chorale prelude has its basis in a song that was written in an attempt to help people communicate with the deity they worshipped, something that could exist only in a situation where people felt they were out of touch with the forces that ran the natural world. The instrument itself is a technologically-enhanced lineal descendant of the panpipe, made of various reeds cut off at different lengths to produce different tones.

And, if we pay attention, even at the height of the Enlightenment we find music that attempts to imitate nature's sounds. In the early 17th-century collection of keyboard music, "The Fitzwilliam Virginal Book," there is a piece entitled "The Fall of the Leafe," as well as a representation of a storm. And Jean-Philippe Rameau's 1745 ballet buffoon "Platée" has a memorable moment where a chorus of frogs sings *"dis donc, pourquoi? Quoi? Quoi?"* in such a way that the "kwah kwah" is enough to shatter the artificiality of the rest of the music. All through the Baroque era, add-ons called *spielerei* were attached to organs to make them imitate birds of various sorts, and even though this was an era of strict abstraction, the day when the flute-trill-as-bird would be a cliché wasn't far off. Before long, we had Beethoven's "Pastorale" symphony, which opened the gates to all manner of attempts to imitate nature orchestrally, most of which—"Peer Gynt," "The Carnival of the Animals," "Calm Sea and Prosperous Voyage," "The Pines of Rome"—are deadly familiar from Music Appreciation.

And yet, as the contemporary era dawned, composers realized, as they paid more scientific attention to natural sounds, that they weren't coming close. Some, like Charles Ives, preferred, in pieces like "Three Places in New England," to present the spiritual qualities of places, while others, like French composer Olivier Messaien, spent considerable time observing the melodic and rhythmic complexities of birdsong, resulting in his compositions "Réveil des

Q: *How many Americans live in areas that exceed ozone pollution standards set by the Environmental Protection Agency?*

Oiseaux" and "Oiseaux Exotiques." In Messaien's case, natural sound proved to be a liberating influence, as he began to break loose from the restrictions of the Western scale and the concept of regular meter.

Science, of course, was several steps ahead of art in this respect, and once recording equipment became available, researchers began collecting natural sounds and analyzing them. What were birdsongs for, anyway? Why do lions roar? Do animals have language? An immense body of data began to accumulate, data that was used every way but aesthetically. But at least it was piling up.

Then came the whales.

The sudden discovery of ecology by the mass media in the late 1960s was a bizarre, scattershot sort of thing. After all, for most people, "ecology" meant not tossing your beer cans in the park. But it also came to mean a belated realization that thousands of species were endangered. Probably the most spectacular ones of all were whales. People had taken them for granted for so long, figuring that the plenty of the days of Moby Dick were still with us, that the news that they were on the way out was a shock. Even more shocking, along came Capitol Records, announcing that the whales had a record coming out. This had to be a joke, right? I mean, they had the Beatles, too, and they weren't insects. But no, Capitol had gotten hold of some recordings by Dr. Robert Payne of the Institute for Research in Animal Behavior and, in mid-1970, they gave mass distribution to the album Payne had pressed privately, "Songs of the Humpback Whale." The reaction was pretty much what you'd expect: People laughed. Sarcastic articles appeared. The rock press had tons of fun. The American composer Alan Hovanhess announced the premiere of a "concerto" for humpback whale songs and orchestra, "And God Created Great Whales."

In other words, whales, and the preservation thereof, were suddenly on the map big-time. And, as both Payne and Capitol had suspected, there were actually people out there who liked listening to the whales sing.

This development did not go unnoticed in the record biz: Before long, Atlantic Records announced that they'd signed a deal with some people who were putting out a series of records called "Environments," which were simply recordings of the surf

(212) 929-8234
Series: World Music (includes over 200 selections). **Description:** Traditional music from authentic native musicians recorded and compiled by renowned ethnomusicologist Colin Turnbull with selections such as Amazonia, Music of the Rainforest Pygmies and Songs of the Aborigine.

MUSIC OF THE WORLD
P.O. Box 3620
Chapel Hill, NC 27515-3620
Example: The Igede of Nigeria. **Description:** This is an exceptional recording of tribal musicians from Nigeria's Benue State. Ensembles from many different villages sing and play a variety of rhythmic drums and percussion instruments in accordance with sacred ceremonies and rites of passage.

NARADA PRODUCTIONS
1845 N. Farwell Ave.
Milwaukee, WI 53202
(414) 272-6700
Series: Narada Wilderness Collection. **Description:** The Artists of Narada (16 artists) have united to create a special recording as a collective paean to our wilderness lands.

THE NATURE COMPANY
2001 Western Ave.
Seattle, WA 98121
(206) 443-1608
Series: Environmental Sound Series. **Description:** Pure environmental sounds and synthesized sounds combined and created by Bernie

A. **80,000,000 people**
. *Source:* The Greenhouse Trap, *by Francesca Lyman*

Krause with themes such as Equator, Gentle Ocean and Meridian.

NATURE RECORDINGS
P.O. Box 2749
Friday Harbor, WA 98250
(800) 228-5711
Series: Nature Sounds.
Description: You can't get closer to 'world music' than natural Earth music and Nature Recordings' series of all organic, on location audiotapes is the next best thing to being there.

PETER ROBERTS PRODUCTIONS
121 Fifth Ave., Ste. 117
Edmonds, WA 98020
(800) 735-3298
Series: Earth Sounds.
Description: Natural voices of the Earth are presented with startling realism, using binaural microphones to capture the spatial depths of the wilderness settings. Gordon Hempton combines unaltered documents of Earth's living music.

RYKODISC
Pickering Wharf, Bldg. C
Salem, MA 01970
(508) 744-7678
Environment Series:
Atmosphere Collection by Ruth Happel. **Description:** A way of raising consciousness to the desperate survival of the rainforests; with natural recordings of sounds in the rainforest to make you feel as if you are actually there. Proceeds go directly to The Nature Conservancy in Brazil.
Indigenous Series:
Ryko World Series. **Example:** Voices of the Rainforest. **Description:** A soundscape of a day

gently hitting the beach, rain, brooks running through the woods or the Hawaiian jungle. They were advertised as stress-reducers, and one guy I read about even claimed one of them had cured his asthma.

Of course, it's hard to copyright the Pacific Ocean, and, as far as I know, no attempt was made to hook the humpbacks up with a music publisher, so, this being the dawning of the Age of the Synthesizer, people started trying to figure out if there were some

Photo: Michael K. Nichols/Magnum Photos

Bernie Krause recording the sounds of mountain gorillas in Rwanda.

way to do this natural sound, relaxation stuff in the studio. The pioneer was Bernie Krause, an engaging fellow who had started off in market research in Boston, and gave it up in 1963 to replace Pete Seeger in one of the late editions of the Weavers. Along with veteran soundtrack composer Paul Beaver, he helped to popularize the early synthesizers (a lesson on the Moog the two gave George Harrison found its way out of the studio and onto a record as "George Harrison: Electronic Sounds," an early Apple release), and his record, "The Nonesuch Guide to Electronic Music," was one of the first attempts to demystify this seemingly arcane technology. But all along, he was interested in natural "music," and in 1969, Beaver and Krause put out "In a Wild Sanctuary," an early mix of animal and synthesizer sounds, on Warner Bros.

There were more experiments along this line in the late 1960s and early 1970s: Douglas Leedy, a California composer, did a three-record "Entropical Paradise," which, the notes said, was intended not so much for listening as for ambiance-enhancing.

Q: *What are the chances that a piece of solar energy equipment manufactured in the US last year was exported?*

Without knowing it, Leedy had invented a type of music that, after a decade of experimentation, would become known as "New Age" music. Probably the most successful composition from natural sources was Charles Dodge's 1970 "Earth's Magnetic Field," in which the source material, the changes in the Kp index of the Earth's magnetic field caused by solar winds, was changed into sound by a computer program, resulting in a 29-minute piece that's still fascinating to listen to today.

The same can't be said of much of the synthesizer music from this era simply because the technology was, by today's standards, unbelievably primitive. The complexities of even the simplest bird-call were beyond the synthesizing capabilities of even such masters as Bernie Krause. Furthermore, the idea of using natural sound as musique concrète, manipulated tape sound, was hampered because field recording equipment was also quite primitive, although in France, composer Luc Ferrari continued to work in this style. The most successful environmental experiments of the 1970s were, once again, humanity imposing on the environment: Max Neuhaus with his sonic installations (pieces that make a sound and interact with their space, like the one he's installed in Times Square) and Brian Eno, whose "ambient music" concepts, derived in tandem with guitarist/mystic Robert Fripp, became extremely important not only in "New Music" circles in the early 1980s, but as another source of New Age music.

But the technology that made New Age music possible has also made not only Jean C. Roché's birds, but some very exciting advances in composition with natural sounds, possible. In particular, the advent of the portable DAT, or Digital Audio Tape recorder, has enabled us to hear our world on demand as never before. Furthermore, advances in research into human hearing capabilities have enabled digitally-equipped recordists to customize their recordings so they sound more "natural" than ever before.

Gordon Hempton is a purist. Unlike the other environmental sound workers, the recordings he releases under his Earth Sounds series contain "real time" sonic events: the sounds of nature just as they happened before his microphones. Equipped with a DAT and a weird rubber head with microphones in its ears which is, believe it or not, a state-of-the-art binaural

in the life of the Kaluli, the people of Papua New Guinea, produced by Mickey Hart and recorded on-site by Dr. Steven Feld.

SEQUOIA RECORDS
P.O. Box 280
Topanga, CA 90290
(818) 708-2672
Examples: Misty Forest Morning, Garden of Serenity. **Description:** The blending of music with natural sounds to reflect the beauty and healing properties of these serene environments.

SOUNDINGS OF THE PLANET
P.O. Box 43512
Tucson, AZ 85733
(800) 937-3223
Environment Example: Ocean Dreams, Desert Moon Song, Peaceful Pond. **Description:** A gentle blend of natural sounds and soothing music creating a peace-inspiring combination. **Indigenous Example:** Malkuri: Traditional Music of the Andes. **Description:** Very upbeat, joyous music performed by Otavalo group from the Andes of northern Ecuador; includes pan-pipes, guitar, mandolin, vocals and percussion.

SOUND OF AMERICA RECORDS (SOAR)
P.O. Box 8606
Albuquerque, NM 87198
(505) 268-6110
Example: Plight of the Red Man by XIT. **Description:** This album defines Native American issues through contemporary music using traditional and electronic instruments, as well as chants.

A. *1 in 2*
Source: Solar Energy Industries Association

SUKAY
3315 Sacramento St.,
Ste. 523
San Francisco, CA
94118
(415) 751-6090
Example: Cumbre. **Description:** One of the finest creative recordings of music from the Andes on the international market. Contemporary in style, inspired by the mountains and the natural relationship of the Bolivian people to the Earth.

TRIBAL MUSIC INTERNATIONAL
449 #1 Thomas Rd.
Tijeras, NM 87015
Example: 65th Intertribal Ceremonial, Music from the Hopi, Flute and Prayer Songs. **Description:** Recordings of endangered cultures in the purest traditional form of their music; over 200 titles available.

WILD SANCTUARY COMMUNICATIONS
124 9th Ave.
San Francisco, CA
94118
(800) 473-WILD
Environment Series: Habitat Series. **Description:** Designed to transport the listener into the dramatic ambient experiences of each unique ecosystem. Bernie Krause has recorded the nature and animal sounds with state of the art digital technology.
Indigenous Examples: Music of the Nez Perce, Nez Perce Stories. **Description:** These recordings feature the music of a group of Nez Perce drummers and singers who first gathered in the 1920s.

recording system, he's recorded eight "Authentic Audio Experiences of Wilderness Places," as his advertising puts it, so far.

"I'm like the second generation of photographers," Hempton told me, calling from a pay phone on the Olympic Peninsula, where he'd gone to collect sounds. "After the camera had been invented and everybody had taken pictures of things they wanted painted, like the Last Supper, photographers' attention turned to what was just there. I don't want to write a script for nature; whatever you hear is what actually happened." Recordings like "Dawn Chorus" are manipulated only in that the morning birdsongs heard on the disc progress from Atlantic habitats to Pacific ones over the course of the playing-time. It is likely that this intention of scrupulous documentary has won the Earth Sounds series the endorsement by the American Museum of Natural History.

Ruth Happel, too, started as a scientist, documenting animal sounds. "But that got tedious, so I switched to being more artistic," she said from her studio in Beverly, Massachusetts. "I wanted to be true to the animals, but to filter out some sounds. You're going to have to do that anyway, because there's nowhere on Earth you can be without being underneath a jet's flight pattern, or near a highway or road, no matter how little-used it is. Anyway, just by putting it on tape, you're changing it, taking it out of context."

Happel's ambitious project, "A Month in the Rainforest," a four-hour composition released by Rykodisc, is nothing short of brilliant, although many listeners might feel that the credit belongs more to the "musicians" of the jungle, the creatures whose incessant noise makes this series such compelling listening. But despite each of the four discs having a title like "Jungle Journey" or "Rain Forest," these are not, like the Earth Sounds recordings, undoctored sounds. At any given time, there can be as many as 15 tracks playing, although only one is in the foreground at any moment. Happel records digitally, then "dumps" it on a digital hard-drive recording system and mixes it all down with her computer. This enables such manually impossible tricks as a five-minute cross-fade of tracks to happen, something which, she feels, keeps the listener from getting too bored. Still, she insists that although the tracks are manipulated,

Q: *What is the miles per gallon of the most fuel efficient car developed?*

the sound is not artificially hyped or a misrepresentation of what the rainforest actually sounds like. If she's right—and I think she is—then what we've got here is some of the most amazing "minimalist" composition ever. "Animals are sort of natural composers," Happel agreed, "and I've been amazed at the rhythm and patterns they make. It's sort of like Philip Glass, in a way, but really, it's beyond musical composition." All I can say is, for all you may read about the destruction of the rainforests in Brazil, nothing can bring it to you more forcefully in the privacy of your home than listening to one of these discs. A thousand acres of rainforest is a blank statistic, but the biological diversity of that ecosystem is right here for you to hear. The thought that humanity is destroying something that sounds like this is enough to get me angry.

Making people aware of the sound of vanishing species is, of course, at the heart of these recordists'/composers'/naturalists' work, and yet there is also a need to shape the sounds in a way that will make them more than sonic wallpaper. With such a sonic challenge to meet, somehow it wasn't too surprising to encounter Bernie Krause's name popping up in the literature. Krause has had some odyssey since the Beaver and Krause "In a Wild Sanctuary" album in 1969, working in such fields as audio forensics, bioacoustic analysis and field recording of animals. In 1985, he hit the headlines in his home of San Francisco when a humpback whale, perhaps in search of royalties from Capitol Records, mistakenly entered the San Francisco Bay (Capitol is and always has been in Hollywood) and swam up the Sacramento Delta. Humphrey the Whale, as the media named him, was finally coaxed back into the Pacific by a boat headed out to sea, playing tapes of feeding humpback whales that had been specifically designed by Krause.

It was a media circus, sure, but it brought attention to Krause's serious work as designer of sound environments for museums, collector of such vanishing sounds as those produced by the mountain gorilla in Rwanda, and composer for his Wild Sanctuary label. The Wild Sanctuary compositions are very close in technique to Ruth Happel's mixes (and, in fact, Krause was a consultant on the Brazilian project). "I've taken the voices of habitats and creatures and

POP ECO-SONGS

What follows is a list of 1990 and 1991 environmentally-themed songs aired across the country. They are listed in order of artist, cut, album title, label and year.

Aleka's Attic
Across the Way
Tame Yourself, Rhino
    Records, 1991

The B-52's
Quiche Lorraine
Tame Yourself, Rhino
    Records, 1991

Adrian Belew
Men in Helicopters
Young Lions, Atlantic
    Records, 1990

Belinda Carlisle
Bless the Beasts and the
    Children
Tame Yourself, Rhino
    Records, 1991

Exene Cervenka
Do What I Have To Do
Tame Yourself, Rhino
    Records, 1991

Erasure and Lene Lovich
Rage
Tame Yourself, Rhino
    Records, 1991

Fetchin Bones
Slaves
Tame Yourself, Rhino
    Records, 1991

Julia Fordham
Genius
Porcelain, Virgin
    Records, 1990

Peter Gabriel
Red Rain, San Jacinto
Shaking the Tree, 16
    Golden Greats, Geffen Records, 1990

A. *121 miles per gallon*
   Source: Peace Resource Project

Nina Hagen and Lene Lovich
Don't Kill the Animals ('91 mix)
Tame Yourself, Rhino Records, 1991

Hot Rize
Where the Wild River Rolls
Take it Home, Sugar Hill Records, 1990

Human Radio
Another Planet
Human Radio, Columbia Records, 1990

Indigo Girls and Michael Stripe
I'll Give You My Skin
Tame Yourself, Rhino Records, 1991

Patty Larkin
Metal Drums
Live In the Square, Philo Records, 1991

Jeff Lynne
Save Me Now
Armchair Theatre, Reprise Records, 1990

Mutabaruka
Ecology Poem
Blakk wi Blak...K...K, Shanachie Records, 1991

The Pretenders
Born for a Purpose
Tame Yourself, Rhino Records, 1991

Strunz and Farah
Tierra Verde (Instrumental)
Primal Magic, Mesa Records, 1990

Toy Matinee
Last Plane Out
Toy Matinee, Reprise Records, 1990

scored with them," Krause explained. "I use samples that can be from 20 minutes to 15 milliseconds long."

Krause's interest in natural sound came from his work among the Nez Perce Native Americans in the late 1960s. One of the elders of the tribe told him, "You've never learned to shut up long enough to learn to hear the sounds of the earth," and dared him to be quiet for an hour and a half. Krause and the old man sat still, and the wind came up. "It sounded like a wind organ, and I was astonished. He took me over to a stand of reeds, and I saw that many of them were snapped off, so that they made that sound when the wind blew over them."

He was hooked, and began studying natural sounds. Almost immediately, he made an important discovery. "Many of these sounds are natural orchestrations. Certain insects inhabit part of the audio spectrum, and other animals occupy the niches around them. If you study a spectrogram, you notice that it's like radio stations, each broadcasting on a separate frequency so they don't step on each other's communication. Everything that lives makes sound: The metabolic rate generates sound, which is how some organisms find their food." Throughout the 1980s, Krause worked with the Nature Company on projects that mixed natural sounds and music, but eventually he decided that was a bad idea. "I never use the word nature to talk about this work," he said, "because that's a word that keeps us separated from the world we inhabit."

Krause, Hempton and Happel agree that the purpose of releasing the recordings commercially is to bring the listener into contact with the sounds as a means of relaxation or realization of the sounds around us that, as the Nez Perce man knew, we've stopped listening to. "Nature listening is an endangered species," Gordon Hempton said. "I'm on a mission to make people realize that there are very few quiet areas left in the world." But, thanks to him, and to Ruth Happel and Bernie Krause, we can still listen to what they've heard, and prepare ourselves to go out and hear it, perhaps, before it's all gone.

Ed Ward is a freelance writer based in Austin, Texas, and a regular contributor to National Public Radio's Fresh Air.

Q. *What most used type of plastic packaging has a consumption rate of almost 5 million tons annually?*

Software

Educational environmental software has proliferated over the last year, taking advantage of the format for up-to-date information and fun delivery of sometimes depressing material.

Marine Life Series (Macintosh)

Available from Chariot Software Group, 3659 India St., San Diego, CA 92103, (619) 298-0202.

Each program presents basic knowledge with lessons on topics in Marine Biology. All lessons are illustrated with detailed graphics. Various activities reinforce science vocabulary and help students identify anatomical structures and biological functions. The programs contain interactive quizzes.

TimeTable of Science and Innovation (Macintosh)

Available from Chariot Software Group, 3659 India St., San Diego, CA 92103, (619) 298-0202.

This interactive HyperCard stack is designed for K-12 and higher education. It includes over 6,000 stories covering science discoveries and technological innovations dating from the "Big Bang" to superconductors. Highly interactive, the stories are linked with graphic enhancements, animations and sound.

Decisions, Decisions: The Environment (Macintosh)

Available from Chariot Software Group, 3659 India St., San Diego, CA 92103, (619) 298-0202.

Students enroll as mayor of a town faced with the politics of cleaning up the environment. As they move through the simulation, students will learn about landfills, water pollution, recycling, the greenhouse effect and much more.

The Citizens' Environmental Laboratory Interactive Software (Macintosh)

Available from The National Toxics Campaign, 1168 Commonwealth Ave., Boston, MA 02134, (617) 232-0327.

The Citizens' Environmental Laboratory, a project of the National Toxics Campaign Fund and Design Engineering, an Apple developer and manufacturer of environmental monitoring systems for the Macintosh, have jointly developed a HyperCard stack which provides the user with information about the lab as well

COMPUTER GAMES

The following environmental games, both conventional and for computers, are informative, fun and intriguing.

Eco-Adventures in the Rainforest, Eco-Adventures in the Ocean (Macintosh and DOS)

Available from Chariot Software Group, 3659 India St., Ste. 100 San Diego, CA 92103, (619) 298-0202.

These two games require users to learn about the ecosystems of each habitat. Along the way, text, graphics and sound teach participants about the animals, plants, marine creatures and people they encounter.

Earthquest 2.0 (Macintosh)

Available from Earthquest Inc., 125 University Ave., Palo Alto, CA 94301, (415) 321-5838.

Earthquest 2.0 includes several new features that make the HyperCard-based application about the Earth, people and the environment more interactive. A new Starship Control Center was added as a way to access games, including two new games, Map Master and Searchcraft. The Workshop feature has been expanded to include animation and linking capabilities.

Eco-saurus (DOS)

Available from First Byte, Inc., 19840 Pioneer Ave., Torrance, CA 90503, (310) 793-6010.

A. **Low-density polyethylene (LDPE), the thin "filmy" substance**
   Source: The Recycler's Handbook, by the Earth ● Works Group

IF I HAD A PLANET . . .

Have you ever wanted to rule the world? Are you dissatisfied with the way things are going on our planet? Maybe if you could decide what kind of energy the planet uses, we wouldn't face resource depletion and the threat of nuclear accidents. Then again, maybe not.

"SimEarth, The Living Planet," is a computer game available for Macintosh or DOS by Maxis Company, makers of SimCity. In it, you create planets. You control everything: type of life forms, continental drift, placement and qualities of biomes, energy usage and civilization. You can work in geologic, evolution, civilized and technology time scales and survive through the Stone Age, the atomic age and the nanotech age. You monitor your planet's vital signs such as rainfall, disease, war, fossil fuels, pollution, temperature and gases. You control the quality of life on the planet. Your activities are regulated by energy usage; if you run out, you'll have to wait to fix the outbreak of war and plague. Having your own planet is not so easy, but it's worth it. Contact Maxis, 1042 Country Club Dr., Suite C, Moraga, CA 94556, (415) 254-9700.

"Designed for 4- to 9-year-olds, the game is an ecological lesson filled with charming characters, good graphics and great sound."

BOARD GAMES

Keep it Green
Available from Green Earth Games Company Inc., 314 E 26th St., N. Vancouver, British Columbia, V7N 1B1, Canada.

"An intellectual, fun game, Keep it Green shows what an individual can do in his or her everyday life to help the Earth stay 'green and living.' It also highlights what an individual might possibly do in his or her everyday life that makes the earth become 'dead and grey.'"

EarthAlert
Available from Earth-Alert, P.O. Box 20790, Seattle, WA 98102, (206) 324-2362.

"EarthAlert is an entertaining and provocative new board game for the 90s. Try to conserve oxygen while competing in four challenging categories: Q & A, roleplays, true/false, definitions. Participate in planet-saving activities."

as explicit directions for taking air samples for subsequent analysis by the lab.

Plant Identification (Macintosh)
Available from Chariot Software Group, 3659 India St., San Diego, CA 92103, (619) 298-0202.

These hyperstacks introduce the student to plant taxonomy, keying, biogeography, life zones and vocabulary. They are designed to teach the fundamentals of biological classification, use of the dichotomous key and identification of plants in California.

Conservation Biology (Macintosh)
Available from Chariot Software Group, 3659 India St., San Diego, CA 92103, (619) 298-0202.

Conservation Biology contains over 200 thought-provoking questions about the future of the Earth and conservation topics and crises. Collected in the context of a semester course in Conservation Biology at San Francisco State University.

Risk*Assistant (DOS)
Available from Thistle Publishing, P.O. Box 1327, Alexandria, VA 22313-1327, (703) 684-5203.

Risk*Assistant provides users of personal computers with an ability to rapidly evaluate exposures to, and human health risks from, chemicals in the environment, and to present the results in the form of detailed reports.

Electronic Cooperative Commentary on the Environment (ECCE!) (Macintosh)
Available from Students for Environmental Action at Stanford, Box 10909, Stanford, CA 94309.

"ECCE! is a Macintosh-based computer program

Q: *How many states in the US fund ride-sharing programs?*

which contains a large quantity of diverse and useful environmental resources, such as course listings from nine universities, and an environmental organizer's handbook."

Macrocosm USA Database (Macintosh)

Available from Macrocosm USA, Box 969, Cambria, CA 93428, (805) 927-8030.

"Macrocosm USA is primarily a solutions handbook with directories in progress, designed to provide concerned individuals in any field with tools for effective coalition-building, networking, journalism, research, education, career choice or coordinating events.

Save the Planet (DOS)

Available from Save the Planet Shareware, Box 45, Pitkin, CO 81241, (303) 641-5035.

Save the Planet keeps you up-to-date on the complexity and severity of global warming and ozone depletion. The program explores the topics of fossil fuel combustion, population increases, forest destruction and atmospheric chemistry. It also provides resources for further involvement.

ECONEWS RESOURCES

There are several news services to give you up-to-date environmental news. Here are a few:

EcoNet
3228 Sacramento St.
San Francisco, CA 94115
(415) 442-0220
An international, computer-based communication system committed to serving those working for environmental preservation.

Environmental News Service
3505 W. 15th Ave.
Vancouver, British Columbia
V6R 2Z3, Canada
(604) 732-4000
Daily environmental stories available via wire to media, environmental organizations, universities and individuals.

Earth Information System
Steve Jambeck
P.O. Box 311
Fort Tilden, NY 11695
(718) 318-7715
Commercial satellite network programming for local cable television devoted to news about the environment.

IMPACT Environmental Reports
News Travel Network
747 Front St.
San Francisco, CA 94111
(415) 397-2876
Provides on-location reports on worldwide environmental issues in 90-second news segments, seen on broadcast and cable television.

Earthword
Available from Earthword, Inc., Keyport, NJ 07735.

Earthword is a card game which provides the player with "the pleasure of learning more about our world and the environmental issues which are impacting on it daily."

Pollution Solution
Available from Aristoplay, Ltd., P.O. Box 7645, Ann Arbor, MI 48107.

"Gather your family or students around the township map. Each player owns a section of the township where pollution hits and spreads. To protect the environment players learn solutions as they battle pollution and stop its spread."

Trash is Cash
Available through The Benjamin Company, 38 Main St., Ste. 201, Northampton, MA 01060, (413) 586-7242.

"In playing the game, children assume the role of a trash hauler and set out on a maze of collections, learning about recycling along their way to make a million dollars." The game was developed by David Duseau as a way to help educate children about the importance of recycling.

A.*16*
Source: The Greenhouse Trap, *by Francesca Lyman*

ECOHOME

E cohome introduces and explores the concepts and details of living environmentally on the home front. Articles on home design, recycling, automobiles, gardening and urban ecology keep you current. Directories to recycling and resources for home improvements offer solutions to common concerns.

TEN TIPS FOR REDUCING HOUSEHOLD HAZARDS

The following ten tips for reducing household hazards are based on information from the EPA, the Federal Safety Commission, the National Cancer Institute and the Children and Environmental Regulations Project of the Center for Investigative Reporting in San Francisco.

1. Locate the source of pollution in your home. Complete information and advice on testing methods and much more is available from Renew America, 1400 16th St. NW, Suite 710, Washington, DC 20036, (202) 232-2252, and the Lawrence Berkeley Laboratory, 1 Cyclotron Rd., Berkeley, CA 94720, (510) 486-4000.

2. Increase ventilation everywhere you can, to reduce risk from radon, pesticides, cigarettes, smoke and gas. Open windows, particularly when laying new carpeting, painting or exterminating. Avoid smoking to reduce pollution. Exposed asbestos can be sealed with duct tape and should be removed only by a specialist.

3. New drapes, carpets, pressed wood coffee tables and kitchen cabinets often emit cancer-causing formaldehyde fumes. Chronic flu-like symptoms are a tip-off. Write or call the local health department and

Your Green Home

- By Debra Lynn Dadd -

Back in the late 1960s and early 1970s, when the current environmental movement first began, a handful of Americans started making changes in how they lived at home in order to benefit the Earth. They wore natural fiber clothing, grew their own vegetables, reduced their consumption, and recycled bottles, cans and newspapers. Some hand-built simply-fashioned solar water heaters and used soap instead of detergent. These were the pioneers, who began the search for a less environmentally-destructive way to live.

Now, with the 20-year anniversary of Earth Day passed, the concept of living at home in a way that is "environmentally-friendly" is a concern in every household. A survey released in July 1990, co-sponsored by a leading New York advertising agency and *Adweek's Marketing Week* publication, revealed that 96 percent of consumers say that environmental factors play a "very important" role in their purchase decisions. A poll taken later in the year by *Good Housekeeping* magazine confirmed that even with great concerns about an imminent recession and troops preparing for war in the Middle East, environmental issues remained a priority for the general public. In August 1991, a front page article in *The Wall Street Journal* reported that a new poll showed "concern and awareness of environmental problems are all but universal." Fifty-three percent of respondents said "it will take fundamental changes in lifestyle, rather than scientific advances, to bring about dramatic changes in the environment."

Clearly, the desire by the general public for environmentally-responsible living is no passing fad. Over the years, the fledgling ideas of the early environmental movement have grown to serve the mainstream. Health food stores now stock a natural version of almost every supermarket product and even supermarkets are now starting to carry the pesticide-free organically grown food that was difficult to find at all ten years ago. Community household hazardous waste collection has made us all aware of the toxic waste dumps under our kitchen and bathroom sinks. And recycling will soon become federal law as

Q: *What percentage of all toxic waste comes from chemicals used in photographic processes?*

our landfill space continues to diminish. There is a greater selection now of high quality goods of all kinds that also have high environmental integrity, and a greater scrutiny, regulation and certification of products that make environmental claims.

We are at the threshold of a new way of living that must become commonplace in order for our planet to survive. Some of the changes we need to make are easy—such as buying a natural cleaner or toilet paper made from recycled paper. Others—such as deciding to use solar panels for electricity instead of continuing to rely on more economically-priced but more environmentally-hazardous nuclear power from your utility company—require more information to make a decision, and need a substantial investment. But one by one we can make choices that will benefit both the planet and ourselves.

Here are some suggestions for making every room in your house part of your eco-home:

All around the house you can save natural resources by living simply. This doesn't mean depriving yourself; it means not buying in an excessive and wasteful way things that you don't really need or want. You may find that you enjoy having your home life be simple as a retreat from our complex world.

In every room you can save energy by turning out the lights, switching to energy-efficient compact fluorescent bulbs, or installing more windows or skylights to bring in natural light during the daylight hours. Reduce energy for heating and cooling with sweaters and hot herbal tea in the winter, and light cotton clothing and cool drinks in the summer.

In the kitchen, choose fresh, whole, organically grown foods to prepare instead of additive- and pesticide-laden packaged processed foods. You can save water by filling up pans for wash and rinse water instead of continually running the faucet while doing dishes, and save energy by eating healthful, raw foods, or making one-dish meals. Buy a few inexpensive cotton towels and napkins to use instead of the disposable paper variety. For a fun family project, build a solar oven from cardboard boxes, tinfoil and a piece of glass. Choose cleaning agents that are nontoxic and made from natural ingredients—many you can make yourself from baking soda, vinegar and natural soap. Recycle cans, bottles and newspapers, and start a compost pile for food wastes.

ask for advice. As an alternative kitchen countertop, use stone, stainless steel and solid plastic. If you use solid wood, use a nontoxic sealer. Have cabinets built from solid wood, metal or plywood made with phenol formaldehyde rather than urea formaldehyde, since the phenol form is much less of a health hazard.

4. Gas appliances pollute the air with petrochemicals and hydrocarbons, which increase the incidence of respiratory illnesses including colds, asthma, even mental depression, especially for allergy victims. Switch to electricity, if feasible, and get in touch with the American Academy of Environmental Medicine, P.O. Box 16-106, Denver, CO 80216, (303) 622-9755.

5. Keep accurate records of when, where and what pesticides and fumigants are used. Have all household appliances cleaned and professionally checked yearly or follow the manufacturer's recommendations.

6. Radon, a radioactive gas that is the nation's number two cause of lung cancer, says the National Council on Radiation Protection and Measurements, is more prevalent in newer well-insulated homes with poor ventilation or with stone foundations. Call your regional Environmental Protection Agency office for two pamphlets, "A Citizen's Guide to Radon"

A. *40 percent to 60 percent*
· Source: Sludge Newsletter, *8 November, 1989*

and "Radon Reduction Methods."

7. Scrape off peeling paint on walls, woodwork and outdoor surfaces that may contain toxic lead residue, and keep floors and windowsills damp-mopped to remove lead-bearing dust and dirt. Also wash children's hands frequently. A national study by University of Michigan researchers found that blood levels of lead as low as 20 milligrams are associated with increased blood pressure and lowered IQs. A child who consumes the same amount of lead as an adult absorbs nearly twice as much.

8. Educate yourself on the correct use of pesticides. Call the EPA's toll-free Pesticide Hotline, (800) 858-7378, for information. Find nontoxic alternatives to all pesticides, bombs and foggers and reduce your use of all chemical cleaning aids and all aerosol products. Write *The Earthwise Consumer*, P.O. Box 279, Forest Knolls, CA 94933, (415) 488-4614.

9. Tips on how to store, handle and dispose of poisons: Send a donation for *Everyone's Guide to Toxins in the Home* from Greenpeace, 1436 U St. NW, Washington, DC 20009, (202) 462-1177.

10. Read *The Healthy Home: An Attic-to-Basement Guide to Toxin-Free Living* by Linda Mason Hunter, Rodale Press, Emmaus,

In the bathroom, use nontoxic and natural cleaning products. Install low-flow showerheads and faucet aerators, and invest in a water-saving toilet. Replace your plastic shower curtain with a cotton one, and when your towels and bathmat need replacing, you can purchase bath linens made from unbleached, untreated cotton. Baking soda applied right after your shower makes a very effective deodorant. Go to your local natural food store for all-natural toiletries and cosmetics.

A natural-fiber mattress can be the centerpiece of your bedroom, covered with unbleached, untreated cotton sheets and natural-fiber pillows, blankets and comforters. Casual clothing can now be purchased made from organically grown, untreated cotton.

In the backyard, plant an organic garden and raise as much of your own food as you can. Even just an herb garden will bring you more in tune with the seasonal variations of nature. Try landscaping with beautiful vegetables, edible flowers, fruit- and nut-bearing trees, and endangered native species. Add garden wastes to the compost pile and spread nutrient-filled autumn leaves over your garden for a forest-like mulch. Feed the birds.

These are just a few ideas. As you become more aware of environmental issues and how you can help the Earth at home, you'll discover many things you can do that do make a difference. Just start doing them, one by one.

Debra Lynn Dadd is the author of the environmental consumer guidebook Nontoxic, Natural & Earthwise, *and* The Nontoxic Home & Office.

BAUBIOLOGIE

BAUBIOLOGIE IS THE BIOLOGY OF A BUILDING and how it contributes to people's health problems. According to the EPA, most people spend approximately 80 percent to 90 percent of their time indoors. Insufficient fresh air, faulty heating, ventilation and air conditioning, contaminated air filters and many other ailments of sick buildings often are the cause of health problems for the unsuspecting tenants. EPA researchers have also theorized that indoor pollution levels can be 100 times higher than outdoor levels and may account for over 11,000 deaths in the US each year.

Baubiologists consult, analyze and sanitize houses,

Q: *How thick is the ozone layer, if you could bring it down to the Earth's surface and measure it?*

apartments, worksites and buildings under construction or renovation. One specialty is the examination of homes and sleeping-rooms because the health risk from environmental stress factors are particularly high in these areas because of the amount of time spent in them.

A building-biology inspection includes analyzing the multiple fields, rays, gases and other corresponding environmental risks with sensitive and reliable physical instruments in a reproducible way, so that risks can be detected, described and excluded. So for a small fee, your home can be measured and charted, and while you can't necessarily control the environment outside, you can at least clean up your own home. For more information contact Environmental Testing and Technology, P.O. Box 369, Encinitas, CA 92024, (619) 436-5990; or Helmut Zeihe, International Institute for Baubiologie and Ecology, 708A N. Osceola, Clearwater, FL 34615, (813) 461-4371.

Photo: Justin Simpson

The Trujillo Earthship near Taos, New Mexico.

ALL ABOUT EARTHSHIPS

BUILDING A NEW HOUSE? After 20 years of experimental work toward the evolution of thermal-mass housing made from recycled materials, there emerges Earthships. They have met and exceeded the uniform building code, have been financed by conventional lending institutions, and have been scrutinized favorably by various engineers. The floor plan and structural section represent a highly economical and functional approach.

These buildings consistently run about 25 percent less in cost than an equivalent design built of conventional materials. Earthships have been built for

PA, 1989; and *The Secret House: 24-hours in the Strange and Unexpected World in Which We Spend Our Nights and Days*, by David Bodanis, Simon & Schuster, New York, NY, 1988.
—*Francis Sheridan Goulart*

EPA HOTLINES:

The Environmental Protection Agency offers these citizen hotlines:

• Asbestos Information Line and Toxic Substances Control Act Information Service: (800) 835-6700
• Radon test Information: (800) 767-7236
• Superfund Hotline: (800) 424-9346
• Safe Drinking Water Act Hotline: (800) 426-4791
• National Pesticides Telecommunications Network: (800) 858-7378. In Texas call (806) 743-3091

WATER IN THE HOME

How much water do you use?

1 toilet flush:
    5 to 7 gallons
1 bath: 25-30 gallons
1 ten-minute shower:
    50 to 70 gallons
1 washing machine load:
    25 to 40 gallons
1 dishwasher load:
    9.5 to 12 gallons

In a typical American household, each member uses about 80 gallons of water a day. Up to 75 percent of the water used in homes is consumed in the

A. *A quarter of a millimeter thick*
   Source: *Carl Sagan, quoted in* Earth Conference One, *by Anuradha Vittachi*

bathroom. Toilet flushing accounts for 50 percent of the water used in the bathroom.The toilet is flushed about 20 times per day by the average American family of four.

Pay close attention to your water bills and try to monitor the amount of water used for each activity in your house. You can reduce your usage by installing low flow showerheads and toilets. Install toilet dams. Make sure none of your faucets and toilets are leaking. Check to see that the toilet paper you use is made with recycled paper.

If you are trying to conserve water, but lose yourself in those long hot showers, you may want to get a Shower Timer to monitor your water consumption and possibly lower your water bills. The small digital device doubles as a clock and a timer and attaches with waterproof Velcro strips to your shower wall. When you start your shower, push a button to activate the timer, then push it again when you finish. By being aware of your shower length, you can pare it down to use less water.

If you've discovered you have lead in your water, increased water treatment, flushing standing water from household plumbing systems and replacing lead solder and pipes are the three known ways to solve the lead problem in drinking water.

as low as $20 per square foot and as high as $80 per square foot on a very deluxe model for the television star Dennis Weaver.

Earthships consists of three-foot thick bearing walls made by pounding earth into steel-belted automobile tire casings. This results in a rubber-encased adobe brick. Minor interior walls are made from aluminum cans laid in cement mortar. All interior walls are built out to a smooth, flat plane with a mud and sand formula that can be finished with a mud or conventional plaster. For more information consult *Earthship Volume 1* and *Volume 2*, available from Solar Survival Press, P.O. Box 1041, Taos, NM 87571, (505) 758-9870.

Another alternative to building your home from all new materials is to contact the companies that recycle used building materials. Contact Details, 783 Magellan Way, Napa, CA 94589, (707) 226-9443.

DESIGNING FOR CHILDREN

WHEN DESIGNING OR BUILDING A NURSERY or children's room, consider:

• Using nontoxic paints, safe from strong volatile organic compounds (VOCs) and heavy metals that will outgas for months and years.

• Inexpensive children's furniture is constructed of particle board which is held together with formaldehyde-based glues. Ideally, choose solid wood. When using particle board, edge all surfaces, tops, bottoms and sides.

• Almost all fabrics are treated with formaldehyde (guess what makes fabric "permanant press"). Laundering will eventually remove a good bit of these toxins. Choose washable fabrics with a minimum of surface finishes.

• The materials that are in children's mattresses, bumpers and pillows should be the most natural materials available.

• Carpet is a major contributor to indoor air pollution, so air out wall-to-wall carpeting extensively. There are presently a number of safer alternatives being developed by the carpet industry. Use nontoxic carpet adhesives.

Q: *A typical four-ounce hamburger made from rainforest beef involves the destruction of about how much tropical forest?*

- Consider flooring that is more environmentally safe, perhaps a rug made from natural fibers with a limited use of dyes. Or consider wood flooring finished with natural materials such as wax or low-toxic varnish.

- Psychologically, children need stimulus and the most natural quality light for growth and mental development. Use full spectrum lighting.

- Give children lots of exposure to nature.

- Also give them natural toys and art supplies. There are a number of nontoxic paints, crayons and glues for children. Remember that the colors yellow, bright red and orange may contain cadmium or lead.

Reprinted by permission from Interior Concerns Newsletter *May/June 1991*

GREEN ICE

CFCs AND REFRIGERATORS, dinosaurs and dumps, the most used appliance in your household may be waiting for some special attention to help bring it into the green decade. Refrigerators can account for as much as one-third of household energy expenditure and 2 percent to 4 percent of the refrigerator's energy is lost every day by hungry people standing with the door open, looking for culinary delights. But there's more to a green refrigerator than merely knowing how to read the energy efficiency chart attached to the new model you're drooling to buy.

Du Pont has invested $240 million to develop alternatives to CFCs, those nasty compounds that eat up the ozone layer when let loose into the atmosphere. The result of its work is a new family of 10 refrigerants you may find coming to a store near you in the not so distant future. At two commercial facilities for CFC alternatives, Du Pont is currently producing one refrigerant called "Suva" in commercial quantities.

How can you safely dispose of the old refrigerator? The answer a few years ago was leaving it in the garage until a safe way to dispose of the CFCs was found. Finally it has. Check around for appliance recycling programs, like Northeast Utilities' program in New England. The utility picks up spare operating refrigerators and freezers for free, to be dismantled in an environmentally safe way through Appliance Recycling Centers of America (ARCA), based in St. Paul,

GREEN STRIPPER

Have you been putting off refinishing that green and pink striped dresser you got at a yardsale, just because you don't like the goop you spread on it to remove the paint?

You don't like it with good reason—most strippers contain methylene chloride which produces toxic fumes, methanol, toluene and acetone, all of which are being reviewed by some state legislatures for their carcenogicity.

Creative Technologies Group offers Woodfinisher's Pride paint stripping gel and varnish stripping gel. The gels are nontoxic, nonflammable, biodegradable, nonirritating and they work. They clean up with soap and water, smell like citrus and come in "recyclable" containers. The strippers remove old paint and varnish in 30 minutes and regular stripping tools can be used.

The active ingredient in both gels is N-methyl-2-pyrrolidone (NMP), which has been in industrial use for about 20 years. Woodfinisher's Pride gels contain no water so they won't buckle your wood or loosen joints. It is recommended, however, that you wear gloves to avoid some very dry hands.

Woodfinisher's Pride was compared to 3M's Safest Stripper which makes similar claims about safety and nontoxicity. Safest Stripper is a water-based

A. *55 square feet*
   Source: Natural Resources Defense Council

product using dibasic ester (DBE) as an active ingredient. It does not harm your hands, but it was necessary to reapply the gel to fully remove the paint.

Either one of these alternative strippers is better than a toxic one, but Woodfinisher's Pride worked more effectively. Woodfinisher's Pride will recycle their containers and return $1.00 to customers if there are no recycling centers in local communities. Both strippers are available in hardware, do-it-yourself stores and paint stores.

For more information contact the Softness Group, 381 Park Ave. S, Fifth Floor, New York, NY 10016, (212) 674-7600; Consumer relations, 3M D14 Division, 3M Center, 515-3N-02, St. Paul, MN 55144, (612) 733-1110, Ext. 55.

Minnesota. ARCA's facility removes CFCs using a special evacuation system that prevents the contaminants from venting into the atmosphere. The recovered CFCs are prepared for reuse and the appliance cabinet is sent to a scrap metal dealer.

If you can't find a new refrigerator with "Suva" to your liking, consider insulating your old one to make it last longer and work more efficiently. David Goldbeck notes in his design guide, *The Smart Kitchen*, that an average of 10 percent savings can be attained by taping onto the sides and doors of the refrigerator just $20 or $25 worth of foil-faced rigid insulation—basically a payback of one year. Make sure the refrigerator is dry and that you wipe it down with a sanitizing solution before taping on the insulation.

Do one or all, but do something to make the most used appliance in your house a little greener.

ECOHEALTH RESOURCES

There are many resources to help you manage your environment and your health. Here are a few:

National Environmental Health Association
720 S. Colorado Blvd., Suite, #970
Denver, CO 80222, (303) 756-9090
Professional society of sanitarians.

The Well Adult Book, Mike and Nancy Samuels, Summit Books, New York, 1988.

Your Home, Your Health and Well Being, David Rousseau, et al, Ten Speed Press, Berkeley, 1988.

Well Body, Well Earth: The Sierra Club Environmental Health Sourcebook, Mike Samuels and Hal Zina Bennett, Sierra Club Books, San Francisco, 1983.

Medical Self-Care Magazine, P.O. Box 1000, Point Reyes, CA 94956.

Ecological Illness Report
P.O. Box 1796, Evanston, IL 60204

Occupational Safety and Health Administration, 200 Constitution Ave. NW, Washington, DC 20210, (800) 582-1708.

Office of Environment Safety and Health, 1000 Independence Ave. SW, Washington, DC 20585, (202) 586-6151.

National Center for Environmental Health Strategies, 1100 Rural Ave., Voorhees, NJ 08043, (609) 429-5358.

American Society for Testing and Materials, 1916 Race St., Philadelphia, PA 19103, (215) 299-5400.

 Q: *During 1989, US postal patrons received about how many catalogs?*

CLEANING YOUR HOME

Many cleaning products commonly used in our homes may be hazardous to our health. Luckily, with home products, we can choose to reduce our exposure to many hazards. Following is some guidance for reducing hazards in your cleaning practices.

Some common home toxics are:

aluminum cleaners
ammonia-based cleaners
toilet bowl cleaners • drain cleaners
tub and tile cleaners • disinfectants
window cleaners • floor cleaners/waxers
shoe polish • oven cleaner
furniture polish • metal polish with solvent
car wax with solvent • paint brush cleaner
wood preservative • varnish

Look for key words on labels like "poison," "danger," "warning" and "caution."

Making your own cleaners is the best and often cheapest alternative to hazardous cleaning products. Here is a list of some recipes for home cleaners that won't harm the earth. Alternatively, see *The Directory to Green Products*, page 314, for products you can buy.

All purpose cleaner:
• Use baking soda, borax, lemon juice, white vinegar or TSP (trisodium phosphate).
• Mix ½ cup borax, ½ teaspoon liquid soap and 2 teaspoons TSP into 2 gallons warm water.
• Mix 3 tablespoons washing soda in 1 quart warm water.

Laundry soap:
• Use 1 tablespoon TSP per washload of clothes.
• Mix ¼ cup soap flakes or grated bar soap, 1 cup water and ¼ cup borax in a saucepan and simmer until well blended.
• Use white vinegar, baking soda, borax or washing soda.

Bleach:
• strong chamomile tea.
• hang clothes in sun.

Dry cleaning:
• hand wash instead.
• nature's dryclean: hang clothes in cool night air.

Facial astringent:
• Use lemon juice in a little warm water.

Face packs:
• egg yolk (let dry on face).
• honey, unheated.
• mashed ripe banana and sunflower oil.

Afterwards, rub face with:
• olive or vegetable oil or mashed avocado for dry skin.
• lemon or fresh cut potato for oily skin.

Night Cream:
• 1 egg, ½ cup sunflower oil, 2 Tbsp lemon juice, ½ tsp kelp, mix in blender, refrigerate.

Silver polish:
• submerge silver in water containing aluminum (foil) and salt. Wait a few minutes, remove and wipe dry. Tarnish should be gone.

Copper and brass polish:
• rub with tomato juice.
• make a paste of lemon juice and cream of tartar. Apply, leave on for five minutes, then rinse.

Waterproofing shoes:
• olive oil, beeswax or candle wax.

Fleas:
• sprinkle 2 ounces of lavender oil extract over 2 or 3 quarts of rock salt. Let sit until oil is absorbed. Sprinkle salt under dressers, couches and rugs.
• feed your pet brewer's yeast, 25 mg. per 10 pounds of the animal's weight.

Closet fresheners:
• lavender, cedar chips or juniper.

Bathroom air fresheners:
• broken pine needles, fresh flowers, cut fruit, fresh mint or other herbs.

Lime deposits or bathtub rust:
• vinegar or lemon juice.

Dishsoap is a mild cleaner, can be used for: dishes, woolens, bathroom tub, tiles and toilet, windows, floors and your car.

Vinegar acts as an antiseptic: cleans mildew (add salt), toilet, windows, floors and kills ants.

Soda is a strong cleaner that can be used for the oven, greasy clothes, car engine and as a foot bath.

Olive oil can be used to polish leather, wood, floors and furniture (add vinegar for furniture).

For more recipes get *Clean and Green, 485 Ways to Clean, Polish, Disinfect, Deodorize, Launder, Remove Stains—Even Wax Your Car Without Harming Yourself or the Environment*, by Annie Berthold-Bond, published by Ceres Press, Woodstock, NY, 1990.

Nontoxic, Natural and Earthwise, by Debra Lynn Dadd, in collaboration with Steve Lett and Judy Collins, Jeremy P. Tarcher, Inc., Los Angeles, CA, 1990.

A. *12 billion catalogs*
   • Source: National Public Radio, 21 December, 1989

GUIDE TO RECYCLING

Everyone knows you can recycle glass, aluminum and newspapers. Most people also know you can recycle steel, office paper, computer paper and cardboard. But what about those phone books, glossy magazines, envelopes, paper grocery bags, motor oil and plastic? All of them are recyclable, but there are some restrictions.

Phone books: Phone books are made with the lowest quality of paper available, but can be made into ceiling tiles, record album covers and insulation. You can contact your phone company to ask if they recycle. The glue in phone books can clog paper-making machines, but some companies are now using different kinds of glue for easier recycling. Check with your local recycling center to see if they take them. You can probably rip the pages out of them and put them in a paper bin.

Magazines: Glossy paper is hard to recycle because it is coated with clay which turns into sludge in the recycling process. But because there is such a large quantity of glossy magazines available, recyclers are finding uses for them. Some recyclers add magazine scraps to their pulp to make newsprint brighter. The first thing to do is reuse glossy magazines by giving them to someone else to read. (Try the library.) Find a place to recycle them; ask your local recycling

Photo: Jed Wilcox/Picture Group

Recycling

What is recycling?

Collecting the materials that you know are reusable and taking them to someone who can make something new out of them. Many definitions of recycling are available depending on the context:

Official Definition: The EPA calls recycling "collecting, reprocessing, marketing and using materials once considered trash."

Classic Definition (from the dictionary): The same material is used over and over to make the same—or an equivalent—product. This cuts the amount of virgin materials required for manufacturing. Best examples: aluminum cans and glass bottles.

Plastics Definition: One-way recycling. A plastic container is used once, then the material is used in a new, different item. This keeps the material out of landfills temporarily, but doesn't cut down on resources used to keep making the original product.

Manufacturer's Definition: If a factory uses the same material twice, they feel they've recycled. The same goes if they use scraps (i.e. paper clippings leftover after envelopes are cut out).

Thrifty Definition: Reusing something.

Q: *By the next century, what percentage of the non-industrial world's people will lack a sustainable supply of firewood?*

Why recycle?
• America produces an average of over half a ton of garbage per person each year—about three and a half pounds a day. And the figure is still growing.
• In a lifetime, the average American will throw away 600 times his or her adult weight in garbage. If you add it up, this means that a 150-lb. adult will leave a legacy of 90,000 lbs. of trash for his or her children.

No more space
• 70 percent, or 14,000, of America's 20,000 landfills closed between 1978 and 1988. By 1993, another 2,000 are expected to close.

Safety first
• Most landfills were built before safety standards became a high priority. They're not equipped to stop toxic leachate from seeping into the groundwater.
• How many landfills might eventually leak? According to the EPA...all of them.

The burning issue
• According to Environmental Action, "Even with pollution controls, incinerators are the largest new source of air pollution in most communities. They spew out gases that contribute to acid rain, toxic heavy metals and dioxins. And incinerators produce millions of tons of toxic ash, which still have to go to landfills."

It's common sense
• Unlike landfills, which simply stockpile trash; or incineration, which leaves toxic ash to be disposed of, recycling removes waste completely, then turns it back into useful products.

It's quick
• According to Recycle Now, "A study done for the EPA showed that the total time used by a householder to recycle is only 73 minutes—a little more than an hour—per month. That's a little over two minutes per day."

It's economical
• Some communities pay more to get rid of their trash than they do to maintain their police departments.

RECYCLER'S TRADE NETWORK

The Recycler's Trade Network offers an on-line computer database of "Recycler's Information Pages," a database of 10,000 recycling resource companies, classified by materials handled, equipment available and services offered. Other services offered by the trade network include the "Materials Exchange" which provides sources and markets for raw materials and manufacturing waste materials. Materials are free to members of the network. For more information contact Recycler's Trade Network, 950 N. Grangeline, Suite E, Carmel, IN 46032, (317) 844-8764, (800) 786-1112.

center if they accept them. Don't mix magazines with other paper unless your recycling center says it's ok. Magazines can be processed into paperboard, the thin cardboard in which cookies and cereal are packaged.

Envelopes: Envelopes with lick-to-stick glue can be recycled. Envelopes with other types of adhesive or plastic windows cannot be recycled. The glue gums up machines. This includes "Post-it" notes and mailing address labels.

Paper grocery bags: These bags are made from kraft paper—the same material used to make corrugated

A. *Over half*
Source: Atlas of the Environment, *by the World Wildlife Fund*

cardboard. They can be recycled together.

Motor oil: Many communities have an oil recycling program. If yours doesn't, check with gas stations and oil-changing outlets. As a last resort, you can contact your local hazardous waste facility.

Plastic: There are currently six different resins—types of plastic—making up the majority of plastics found in America. These resins can be identified by recyclers because of a number coding system now mandated in 27 states. This coding system consists of a triangle with a number in the center containing any number from one through seven.

1: PET. This is short for polyethylene terephthalate. One in every four PET bottles are now recycled around the country. It is what soda bottles are made from.

2: HDPE. High Density Polyethylene is tough, lightweight and 62 percent of plastic bottles are made from it.This is recyclable, but it is rarely being recycled. Check with your local recycler before buying most milk jugs, butter tubs, detergent bottles and motor oil containers.

3: V. This is actually Polyvinyl Chloride, or PCV. It is used for water, shampoo and cooking oil bottles. It can be, but rarely is, recycled. About 5 percent of all plastic packaging is PCV. It is not easy to recycle yet. If PCV is mixed in with other plastics, it can ruin the batch. For more information about PCV recycling contact: The Vinyl

• Recycling saves towns and consumers money. When there's less garbage, we pay less to dump it.

• Individuals and businesses earn money by recycling. One family in Portland, Oregon, reportedly picked up enough aluminum cans along roadsides to pay for air fare to Hawaii. The Boeing Corporation has saved millions of dollars by recycling.

It can save natural resources

• We can make aluminum from aluminum cans...or from an ore called bauxite. At the rate we're using up bauxite, the Earth will be completely stripped of it in 200-300 years.

• We can use old newspaper to make new paper...or just keep harvesting trees for virgin pulp. Every day, America cuts down 2 million trees—but throws away about 42 million newspapers.

• We can re-refine old motor oil to make new motor oil...or keep using virgin oil to produce it. The known oil reserves in the world will only last an estimated 35 years at the rate we're using them.

It saves energy

• Every year we save enough energy recycling steel to supply Los Angeles with nearly a decade's worth of electricity.

• Making one ton of recycled paper uses only about 60 percent of the energy needed to make a ton of virgin paper.

• We save enough energy by recycling one aluminum can to run a TV set for three hours.

• Recycling glass lowers the melting temperature for new glass, saving up to 32 percent of the energy needed for production.

It helps save the rainforests

• According to *The Rainforest Book*, saving energy through recycling helps the rainforests by showing "the world that individual investments in energy efficiency can reduce the need to construct more dams and power plants for generating electricity. Dam construction in the rainforest accelerates deforesting."

• There's more: "Recycling your newspapers at home as well as white paper at the office will reduce the demand for both tropical and temperate timber."

Recycling can be done with curbside recycling,

Q: *What percentage of Soviet citizens say environmental problems should be addressed immediately?*

through recycling drives, at hazardous waste facilities, drop-off centers, buyback centers, 24-hour can-vending machines, and through composting.

CURBSIDE ENVY

RECYCLING IN AN APARTMENT BUILDING: Live in an apartment building? Are you and your neighbors suffering from "curbside envy?" Well, here's the cure: Start your own recycling program.

• Can apartments have curbside recycling?
Not the same type as houses. Generally, apartment buildings have limited space for storing recyclables, and with so many people involved, a lot of organizing is needed. Plus, apartment curbside recycling can be a problem for collectors, because they have to empty large dumpsters instead of small bins.

• Can our apartment have some other kind of recycling program, then?
Yes, if you can coordinate it with all the residents in the building, and find someone to pick up the materials.

• How many tenants have to participate?
The more people participating, the more materials you generate, and that's important. If there aren't enough materials, it won't be cost effective, and then you won't be able to attract a collector.

• How do we approach the building manager?
Mention that recycling can really save money because there will be less trash the building has to pay to have hauled away. Let him or her know that it might make money if enough materials are recycled.

• How do we find someone to pick it up?
If you know someone in another building that's already recycling, ask what company they're using. Otherwise, ask for suggestions from your trash collector, try your local recycling office, or look in the Yellow Pages under "Recycling."

Reprinted by permission from The Recycler's Handbook, *Published by* The Earth•Works Group, Berkeley, CA, 1990.

Institute, Wayne International Plaza II, 155 Rte. 46 W. Wayne, NJ 07470.

4. LDPE. Low Density Polyethylene is the stuff shrink wrap, sandwich bags and dry-cleaning bags are made of. Very little of it is recycled. Plastic bags and film wrappings account for 40 percent of our plastic garbage. Check with your local recycler and super market to see if they accept it. ("Cling" wrap is not made from LDPE; and cellophane is made from wood fiber.)

5: PP. Polypropylene is used to make things like plastic bottle caps, straws, carpet, rope and yogurt containers. It tops the EPA's list of "worst toxics." When it is incinerated, it gives off toxic nickel. About 1 percent of PP is recycled. It is technically recyclable, but rarely done.

6: PS. Polystyrene foam is the styrofoam cup your coffee is in, and the foam package your to-go food came in. It is recyclable, but rarely is. It never decomposes. It is made from benzene, a known carcinogen.

7: Other. This could mean that plastics have been blended with other plastics or other materials, or in some way are not pure or identifiable.

Some things cannot yet be recycled. Avoid them if at all possible: wax paper, butcher and bakery paper, juice cartons known as "brick packs," Federal Express or UPS envelopes, dogfood bags, fax paper, carbonless copy paper and blueprints.

A. **67 percent**
  Source: Alexi Yablokov, quoted in Surviving Together, *Fall/Winter 1989*

Directory to Recycling Resources

Aluminum Association
900 19th St. NW, Suite 300
Washington, DC 20006
(202) 862-5100
Manufacturers' organization.

Aluminum Company of America (ALCOA)
1501 Alcoa Bldg.
Pittsburgh, PA 15219
(412) 553-4545
Producer that promotes recycling of aluminum cans.

Aluminum Recycling Association
1000 16th St. NW, Suite 603
Washington, DC 20036
(202) 785-0951
Producers of aluminum alloys from scrap.

American Paper Institute
260 Madison Ave.
New York, NY 10016
(212) 340-0600

American Society for Testing and Materials
1916 Race St.
Philadelphia, PA 19103
(215) 299-5400

Browning-Ferris Industries
757 N. Eldridge St.
Houston, TX 77079
(713) 870-8100
Primary business is the disposal of solid and chemical waste.

California Waste Management Board
1020 Ninth St., Suite 300
Sacramento, CA 95814
(916) 322-3330

Center for Hazardous Materials Research
University of Pittsburgh Applied Research Center
320 William Pitt Way

Pittsburgh, PA 15238
(412) 826-5320
Seeks to develop practical solutions to the problems associated with hazardous waste management.

Center for Plastics Recycling Research
Rutgers University
Bldg. 3529, Busch Campus
Piscataway, NJ 08855
Publishes manuals on collecting and sorting disposed plastic products. Also operates a plastics recycling plant.

Central States Education Center
809 S. Fifth
Champaign, IL 61820
(217) 344-2371
Concerned with water policy and the recycling of solid, hazardous, and radioactive waste.

Clean Sites, Inc.
1199 N. Fairfax St., Suite 400
Alexandria, VA 22314
(703) 683-8522
Mediates between parties at cleanup sites and publishes *Making Superfund Work*.

Coalition for Responsible Waste Incineration
1330 Connecticut Ave. NW, Suite 300
Washington, DC 20036
(202) 659-0060
Promotes responsible handling and incineration of industrial waste.

Community Environmental Council
930 Miramonte Dr.
Santa Barbara, CA 93109
(805) 963-0583
Advises local governments

and businesses on recycling. Publishes *Gildea Review*.

Conservatree Paper Company
10 Lombard St., #250
San Francisco, CA 94111
(800) 522-9200
Sells recycled paper products and helps develop new markets for such products.

Council for Solid Waste Solutions
1275 K St. NW, Suite 400
Washington, DC 20005
(202) 371-5319
A plastics industry group interested in the waste and recycling of their products.

Dano Enterprises
75 Commercial St.
Plainview, NY 11803
(516) 349-7300
Produces Ecolobags, an alternative to plastic garbage bags.

Do Dream Music
P.O. Box 5623
Takoma Park, MD 20912
(301) 445-3845
Has created "Recyclemania," a cassette tape of songs by Billy B. to teach children to recycle.

Earth Care Paper Company
P.O. Box 14140
Madison, WI 53714-0140
(608) 277-2900
Manufactures recycled paper products.

Ecology Center
2530 San Pablo Ave.
Berkeley, CA 94702
(415) 548-2220
Specializes in public education on environmental alternatives, particularly recycling.

Q: *What percentage of Soviet citizens say environmental problems affect them personally?*

Free-Flow Packaging
1093 Charter St.
Redwood City, CA 94063
(415) 364-1145
Recycles polystyrene foam
packaging if you send it to
them (no CODs).

Geosafe
Battelle Pacific Northwest
Laboratories
4000 NE 41st St.
Seattle, WA 98105
(206) 525-3130
Has developed a hazardous
waste disposal process using
glassification.

Glass Packaging Institute
1801 K St. NW, Suite 1105L
Washington, DC 20006
(202) 887-4850
Promotes the manufacture,
use and recycling of glass
containers and closures.

**Governmental Refuse
Collection and Disposal
Association**
P.O. Box 7219
Silver Spring, MD 20907
(301) 585-2898
Public agency officials and pri-
vate corporate officials whose
goal is to improve solid waste
management services.

H.T. Berry Company
P.O. Box B
50 North St.
Canton, MA 02021
(617) 828-6000
Distributes a full line of recycled products, including toilet
tissue, paper towels and napkins.

**Hackensack Meadowlands
Development Commission**
Environment Center Museum
2 DeKorte Park Plaza
Lyndhurst, NJ 07071
(201) 460-8300
Has the Tunnel of Trash, a
simulated landfill, to help educate people on the reality of
waste issues.

**Hazardous Materials
Control Research Institute**
7237-A, Hanover Pkwy.
Greenboat, MD 20770-3602
(301) 982-9500
Disseminates technical information and promotes the use
of risk assessment methods
to achieve a balance between
industrial growth and the environment.

**Hazardous Waste
Federation**
c/o New Mexico Hazardous
Waste Management Society
Division 3314, P.O. Box 4439
Albuquerque, NM 87196
(505) 846-2655
Seeks to increase public
awareness and understand-
ing of the problems related to
hazardous waste manage-
ment and to ensure protection of the environment.

**Hazardous Waste
Treatment Council**
1440 New York Ave. NW
Suite 310
Washington, DC 20005
(202) 783-0870
Interested in using high technology to dispose of waste in
the interest of public health
and safety.

**Institute for Local Self-
Reliance**
2425 18th St. NW
Washington, DC 20009
(202) 232-4108
Published *The United States
Recycling Movement, 1968 to
1986*. Major projects include
urban waste management.

**Institute of Scrap Recycling
Industries**
1627 K St. NW
Washington, DC 20006
(202) 466-4050
Processors, brokers and consumers engaged in the recycling of metallic and non-
metallic scrap.

**Iowa Waste Reduction
Center**
University of Northern Iowa
Cedar Falls, IA 50614-0185
(319) 273-2079
Matches companies producing
waste in Iowa with others that
use waste as a raw material.

**Kaiser Aluminum and
Chemical**
300 Lakeside Dr.
Oakland, CA 94643
(415) 271-3300

Keep America Beautiful
9 West Broad St.
Stamford, CT 06902
(203) 323-8987
Encourages a behaviorally
based approach to recycling
and waste issues.

**National Association for
Plastic Container Recovery**
(NAPCOR)
4828 Parkway Plaza Blvd.
Suite 260
Charlotte, NC 28217
(704) 357-3250

**National Association of
Solvent Recyclers**
1875 Connecticut Ave. NW
Suite 1200
Washington, DC 20009
(202) 986-8150
Seeks responsible recycling
and reclamation of used industrial solvents.

**National Center for
Environmental Health
Strategies**
1100 Rural Ave.
Voorhees, NJ 08043
(609) 429-5358

**National Food &
Conservation Through Swine**
Box 397,.Fox Run Rd., RR 30
Sewell, NJ 08080
(609) 468-5447
Food waste collectors and
feeders of swine who claim to
be the oldest recycling industry in the US, since more than
6,000,000 tons of food are
recycled through swine.

A. *14 percent*
Source: Alexi Yablokov, quoted in Surviving Together, *Fall/Winter 1989*

National Recycling Coalition
1101 30th St. NW, Suite 305
Washington, DC 20007
(202) 625-6406
Encourages recycling in business.

National Resource Recovery Association
1620 I St. NW, Fourth Floor
Washington, DC 20006
(202) 293-7330
Encourages development of recycling programs and urban waste-to-energy systems.

National Solid Waste Management Association
1730 Rhode Island Ave NW, Suite 1000
Washington, DC 20036
(202) 659-4613
Publishes *Recycling: Treasure in Our Trash*. Maintains speakers' bureau, compiles statistics and conducts research programs.

Native Americans for a Clean Environment
P.O. Box 1671
Tahlequah, OK 74465
(918) 458-4322
Seeks to eliminate toxic and radioactive waste on Native American land.

Occupational Safety and Health Administration
200 Constitution Ave. NW
Washington, DC 20210
(800) 582-1708

Ocean Arks International
1 Locust St.
Falmouth, MA 02540
(508) 540-6801
Developing solar aquatic waste treatment plants.

Office of Environment Safety and Health
1000 Independence Ave. SW
Washington, DC 20585
(202) 586-6151

Paper Service, Ltd.
P.O. Box 45
Hinsdale, NH 03451
(603) 239-6344
Manufactures recycled napkins and toilet paper.

Pennsylvania Resources Council
P.O. Box 88
Media, PA 19063
(215) 565-9131
Experts in recycling, publishes the *Environmental Shopping Guide*.

Recoup
P.O. Box 577
Ogdensburg, NY 13669
(800) 267-0707
Lists 14,000 companies that purchase recyclable materials in *American Recycling Market* magazine.

Recycled Paper Company
185 Corey Rd.
Boston, MA 02146
(617) 277-9901
Offers a full line of copier paper, stationery, envelopes, computer paper and printing paper.

Recycled Paper Products, Inc.
3636 N. Broadway
Chicago, IL 60613
(312) 348-6410

Resource Recycling
P.O. Box 10540
Portland, OR 97210
Publishes *Resource Recycling: North America's Recycling Journal*.

Save A Tree
P.O. Box 862
Berkeley, CA 94701
(415) 526-9032
Sells washable canvas bags for shopping.

Society of the Plastics Industry
1275 K St. NW, Suite 400
Washington, DC 20005

(202) 371-5200
Publishes a list of companies that recycle plastic waste.

Steel Can Recycling Institute
Foster Plaza #10
680 Andersen Dr.
Pittsburgh, PA 15220
(800) 876-7274
Provides information and technical analyses to steel companies on methods of collection, preparation and transportation of steel metal scrap.

TOXNET
Specialized Information Services Division
National Library of Medicine
8600 Rockville Pike, Bldg, 38A
Bethesda, MD 20894
(301) 496-6531
A database system that leads callers step-by-step through the process of cleaning up toxic spills.

Waste Management, Inc.
3003 Butterfield
Oak Brook, IL 60521
(312) 242-4317
Major hazardous waste and refuse hauling company.

Waste Watch
Californians Against Waste
909 12th St., Suite 201
Sacramento, CA 95814
(916) 443-5422
Published *Waste Watcher*.

Wellman Inc.
1040 Broad St., #302
Shrewsbury, NJ 07702
(908) 542-7300
Largest plastics recycler in US.

Windstar Foundation
2317 Snowmass Creek Rd.
Snowmass, CO 81654
(303) 927-4777
Publishers of *Recycling: 101 Practical Tips for Home and Work* booklet.

Q: *Every year an area the size of West Virginia is rendered unusable due to what cause?*

Automobiles

Cars are proliferating worldwide. By 2030, some predict they will double to about 1 billion. Since the oil crisis in 1973, the US has greatly increased energy efficiency. Average gas mileage of new cars rose from 14 miles per gallon (mpg) in 1973 to 28 mpg in 1987, largely as a result of the CAFE standards (Corporate Average Fuel Economy) created by Congress in 1975. Congress is considering raising fuel economy standards from 28 mpg to 33 mpg by 1996.

While cars are more gas-frugal today than 15 years ago, the US transportation sector is now using 1 million more barrels of oil per day than in 1973, because:
•Individuals are driving more miles, with fewer people in their cars.
•More trips are being made in "light trucks," subject to lower gas mileage than "passenger cars."
•Urban driving has increased, as has urban congestion, both of which eat up gasoline.

Alternative fuels can work, but are they used? Here's what to expect:

Alcohol
You can run any gasoline-powered automobile on high-proof alcohol. The conversion requires three inexpensive changes. You can make the alcohol at home with a minimal investment. For more information, get *Forget the Gas Pumps—Make Your Own Fuel*, by Jim Wortham and Barbara Whitener, Marathon International Book Company, Louisville, KY, 1979.

Solar power
Solar powered cars get their power from vehicle-mounted solar cells, but, given the technology to date, they must be ultra lightweight and aerodynamic.

Electricity
Purely electric vehicles are great for very short trips. They are most often used currently as golf carts and people-mover carts in airports. Most electric cars now have a range of about 50 to 60 miles, but they serve nicely for local transportation. Electric vehicles require little maintenance, other than battery replacement every three to four years. Electric cars show about a

A. *Desertification*
Source: World•Watch, *May/June, 1989*

HOME OIL CHANGES

If you change your own car oil, you may owe the *Exxon Valdez* skipper an apology. According to the Department of Energy, people who change their own oil improperly dispose of some 200 million gallons of oil each year. That's almost 20 times as much as the *Exxon Valdez* spill.

The quick-lube chain Valvoline Instant Oil Change Inc. is out to help reduce that inky flow by aggressively soliciting used motor oil from do-it-yourselfers. The oil is collected, then picked up by waste haulers and recycled into industrial fuel or lubricants. Many recycling centers now handle used oil. Contact your local recycler for information, or contact the Communications Office, Valvoline Instant Oil Change, P.O. Box 14046, Lexington, KY 40512, (606) 264-7393.

98 percent reduction in carbon monoxide and hydrocarbons compared to standard gasoline powered cars.

Many different types of batteries are available for electric cars.

Lead-acid: This is a larger version of what's under your hood now. Cost: $1,500. Range: 120 miles; then it needs an eight-hour recharge. Lifetime: 25,000 miles.

Nickel-iron: Chrysler will put one in its TEVan. Cost: $6,000 to $10,000. Range: 120 miles before an overnight recharge. Lifetime: 100,000 miles.

Sodium-sulfur: This has more energy than the lead-acid battery. It is still experimental, but Ford hopes it will have a greater range than lead-acid types.

Nickel-cadmium: Still experimental, used by Tokyo Electric. Promises top speeds of 111 miles per hour and a range of 310 miles.

Solar electric

Solar electric cars blend the convenience of both solar-powered and electric cars and extend the range and performance of each. The solar panels recharge the electric batteries and increase the range of the cars.

Methanol

Methanol requires few engine modifications, may have lower NOx emissions than gasoline, is a good anti-knock fuel and is renewable if produced from biomass. Some disadvantages are that it requires more frequent refueling than gasoline, or larger tanks. It is more flammable than gas, and corrodes some metals. It produces formaldehyde, a suspected carcinogen.

Ethanol

This fuel has the same advantages as methanol. Its possible disadvantages are that it requires large volumes of corn, sugar cane or other feedstocks. Also, current distillation methods are energy intensive.

Compressed natural gas and liquid natural gas

These require few engine modifications, and global and US supplies are more plentiful than those of oil. Its use requires a cumbersome fuel tank and supplies are ultimately finite.

Source: Environmental Action, *July/August, 1989*

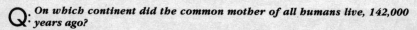

Q: *On which continent did the common mother of all humans live, 142,000 years ago?*

An electric car at the Detroit auto show.

STATE OF THE ART CARS

- By Joel Makower -

THE GOOD NEWS IS: Nearly every car maker is working to make environmental improvements in their products. The bad news is that most of these are several years away from mass production, and most cars won't sport more than a few improvements. Most of the technologies that would make cars drive cleaner are still in the experimental stage. And the feature that would make the biggest difference to the health of the planet—higher fuel-efficiency standards—is still being fought bitterly by the industry.

Consider catalytic converters. They represent one of the most successful anti-pollution devices ever, eliminating 96 percent to 98 percent of toxic tailpipe emissions. But car makers, spurred along by tough new laws in California, are being asked to do even better. General Motors is among the companies experimenting with techniques that will make the devices warm up faster so they'll do their job during the crucial first few miles when the car is running least efficiently.

Ozone-depleting chlorofluorocarbons (CFCs) are another area of intense research, thanks to laws phasing out their use. Several companies are vying for the honor of being the first to offer CFC-free air conditioners. In fact, Nissan, Saab and Mercedes are all claiming that distinction. The American car companies are trailing by a few lengths. Chrysler will put its first CFC-free

BEST & WORST

Here are the 10 cars with the highest mileage and the 10 with the lowest mileage in the annual fuel economy statistics announced by the Environmental Protection Agency.

Each auto model is listed followed by its mileage in city driving, then highway mileage.

Highest mileage:
Geo Metro XFi: 53, 58
Honda Civic HB VX (with shift indicator light): 48, 55
Suzuki Swift: 46, 50
Geo Metro: 46, 50
Geo Metro LSi: 46, 50
Honda Civic HB VX: 44, 51
Honda Civic (with shift indicator light): 42, 48
Geo Metro LSi Convertible: 42, 48
Honda Civic: 40, 47
Suzuki Swift (automatic): 39, 43

Lowest mileage:
Lamborghini DB132-Diablo: 9, 14
Rolls Royce Silver Spirit II: 10, 14
Rolls Royce Silver Spur: 10, 14
Rolls Royce Corniche IV: 10, 14
Rolls Royce Bentley Eight-Mulsanne S&S: 10, 14
Rolls Royce Bentley Continental: 10, 14
Aston Martin Virage Saloon: 11, 15
Ferrari Testarossa: 11, 16
Rolls Royce Bentley Turbo: 11, 16
Aston Martin Virage Saloon (manual): 12, 17
Ferrari F40: 12, 17
—*Reported from the Associated Press Wire Service*

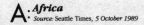

A. *Africa*
  • Source: Seattle Times, *5 October 1989*

TIRED TIRES

Some 300 million scrap tires are produced in the US every year. That's one tire per man, woman and child. They sit in mountains of unused waste. In 1989, over 13 percent of the tires discarded in the US were recycled into new products, converted into energy or reused for applications other than vehicle transportation.

More than 200 Kmart Auto Service Centers in the midwest are now turning in their used tires for recycling to the Environmental Management Corporation. The program's goal is to divert 70 percent of the used tires in participating states.

For more information about retreads, contact: Tire Retread Information Bureau, P.O. Box 374, Pebble Beach, CA 93953, (408) 372-1917

TIRE CONVERSION

Wolfgang Kutrieb, a German-born Wisconsinite, has invented and is manufacturing an environmentalist's dream-come-true called the Kutrieb Pyrolator. It converts tires into oil, gas or petroleum and separates fluids from solids. Nothing is wasted and the process works by applying heat in the absence of oxygen to a sealed reactor, causing molecular decomposition, so there is no discharge.

In addition to a gallon of oil, one tire can yield:
• Gas equal in heating value to 60 cubic feet of natural gas.

system on Jeeps early next year; GM's version won't hit the market until late 1993 and Ford hasn't yet announced its plans. But initial availability will be limited. Saab, for example, is introducing the new technology exclusively on its pricy 9000-series models.

Recyclability is another hot topic, with the Germans leading the way. BMW is said to be developing a fully recyclable car, with plans to disassemble and "process" 1,500 cars at a pilot plant near Munich. But full-scale recycling isn't envisioned until the year 2000.

The US car companies are looking into recycling, too, although there are no laws—or even proposals—to make this mandatory. Here, the focus is on plastics, which are claiming a growing share of cars' total mass, part of designers' efforts to make cars lighter and more fuel efficient. But not all automotive plastics are recyclable. Dashboards, for example, like squeezable ketchup bottles, are typically made of several different plastics, and it is impossible to separate them for recycling. And some of the most environmentally problematic parts of the car—batteries and tires come to mind—are still ending up in landfills in alarming numbers. Automotive glass, which contains plastic to enhance it with shatterproof qualities, is also difficult to recycle.

Alternative-fuel vehicles are another area of intense activity—once again, because of pressure by state regulators to produce no- and low-emissions vehicles. These offer some promise, but not for awhile. It will be necessary to make methanol, ethanol and natural gas nearly as accessible as gasoline before consumers will take these seriously.

And then there's the elusive electric car. After years of being derided as clunky toys, they are finally being considered viable by the industry. It appears GM will be first off the line with its curiously named Impact, probably sometime in 1993. Ford announced in April that it will build 100 test vehicles by 1993. Chrysler hasn't announced any plans.

So don't expect what's offered in your local auto showroom to change much for awhile.

Among the barriers to the availability of good, green cars is companies' uncertainty whether consumers will actually buy them. Despite the myriad polls stating Americans' desire to purchase products that are kinder and gentler to the planet, no one knows whether that desire extends to automobiles.

Q: *How much of Madagascar's forests still stand?*

Americans have always had a special relationship with cars, and industry analysts are skeptical about consumers' willingness to forgo power, performance and other ego-enhancing qualities in favor of the birds and the trees.

Joel Makower is editor of The Green Consumer Letter *and* The Green Business Letter. *His newest book,* The Green Commuter, *will be published in January 1992 by National Press, Washington, DC.*

AIR CONDITIONING

CHLOROFLUOROCARBONS (CFCs) are used to make many common products, such as foam cushions, insulation, cleaning agents and as a refrigerant for automobile air conditioners. These synthetic chemicals are commonly released into the air when car or truck air conditioners are serviced. When CFCs reach the stratosphere and react with ultraviolet radiation, the molecules break apart releasing chlorine, which attacks the ozone layer. Automobile air conditioners are the biggest source of CFC leakage in the US, responsible for 20 percent of all CFC emissions to the atmosphere, according to the EPA.

Ozone layer damage from air conditioners can be prevented if service shops recycle the refrigerant instead of releasing it into the air. Mechanics can use a machine to pull the refrigerant from the air conditioner into a holding tank and filter it. These CFCs can then be reused in automobile air conditioners.

Insist that your mechanic recycle CFCs!

WHO'S WHO IN CFC RECYCLING?

NATURAL RESOURCES DEFENSE COUNCIL surveyed major automobile companies about their CFC recycling policies. Here are their findings:

• Companies who said all or most dealerships already practice CFC recycling: Ford, General Motors, Honda, Nissan, Toyota

• Companies who said some dealerships already practice CFC recycling: BMW, Chrysler, Mitsubishi, Subaru, Volvo

• Service chain companies who said many outlets already recycle CFCs: Firestone, Goodyear, Sears

• Petroleum coke equal to over seven pounds of medium Btu coal.
• One pound of steel which may be sold as high grade scrap.
• Recoverable process heat which may be used to produce hot water, steam or electricity.

The Kutrieb Pyrolator accepts whole automobile and truck tires of any sort. Since no shredding equipment is required, the cost is only $300,000. For more information contact Kutrieb Corporation, 430 Philip St., Chetek, WI 54728, (715) 924-4871.
—*Mary Beth Scow*

NRDC TIPS

Natural Resources Defense Council offers these airconditioning tips:
• When your car air conditioner stops cooling, it probably has a CFC leak.
• Don't just refill your leaky air conditioner without getting the problem fixed. CFC refrigerant ("R-12", or Freon) is sold in refill cans at auto supply stores. But if you don't fix the leak, the CFCs you put in may be headed for the ozone layer tomorrow.
• Find a repair shop that recycles CFCs. Today most repair shops still let the refrigerant loose into the air and then refill the unit with new CFCs. Call and ask before you go.
• Don't have unnecessary service done on your car's air conditioner. If it's working, leave it alone.
• Just using your air conditioner does not cause CFCs to leak. Leaks can develop in the unit whether it is used or not.

A. *7 percent*
  Source: Natural Resources Defense Council

HOW TO COMPOST

Almost 18 percent of our garbage is made up of yard wastes and close to 8 percent is food. You can keep most of it out of our landfills by building a simple compost pile.

Composting is the process by which organic materials, such as vegetable and yard wastes, decompose naturally, creating nutrient rich soil.

HOW TO COMPOST

1. Lay down a six-inch layer of sticks, twigs and other coarse materials that will allow air to circulate beneath the heap. A base area of roughly four feet is preferable.

2. Add a layer of dry organic materials such as dry leaves, weeds or grass clippings.

3. Top that with a layer of green vegetation and kitchen waste. Cover each layer with a thin layer of leaves or soil. (Avoid composting meat, fat, cheese, bones or pesticide-laden plant debris.)

4. Continue layering kitchen waste, dry material and soil until the pile is at least three feet high.

5. At this point, start a new heap while the completed heap rots down.

6. After six to 12 months, with occasional turning, the compost should have rotted down to half its size. The compost is ready when it is

EcoGardening

Photo: Joseph E. Daniel

GARDENING FOR KIDS

- By Linda Slater -

FAMILY GARDENING CAN BE a peaceful, ecological activity, almost a meditation. Gardening with children can turn into a real-life, hands-on learning activity and can be a positive way for families to relate to one another. Through gardening, we can teach our children about self-sufficiency, eating healthy foods and respect for the land. The family can gradually improve the soil and each member learns a Zen patience as the compost slowly cooks and the corn ripens. The garden provides a way to teach children about birds, insects, color, scent and perseverance. One year the garden is hit by hail, and the next deluged with rain. An organic garden provides food and bouquets for the table, and a living laboratory for teaching and learning. Here are some tips for gardening with children.

1. Teach your children about organic gardening and the benefits of compost. Save all your pesticide-free grass clippings, kitchen wastes (except meats), garden leaves, and layer them with manure and soil to create a dark, crumbly, pleasant-smelling substance for your soil.

2. Teach your children about natural fertilizers such as manure, fish or bat fertilizer, granite dust and Greensand. Let your kids help you test your soil and

Q. *How many miles do you have to drive to send one ton of carbon dioxide into the air?*

order some earthworms which add valuable castings to your soil. Earthworms can be ordered from: Cape Cod Worm Farm, 30 Center Ave., Buzzards Bay, MA 02532. 1000 earthworms cost $9.95 postpaid.

3. Plant a fruit or shade tree with your children and talk about the greenhouse effect. Dwarf trees take up little room, bear within three years and are easy picking for short arms.

4. Consider allowing each child to plant his or her own small garden. It can be in a large pot on the patio or a small four-by-four foot square of soil. Small children enjoy planting large seeds like sunflowers, beans, peas and squash. They enjoy growing a "bean room," too. Simply put up four "walls" made of large tree branch clippings, wire or wooden stakes and plant pole beans all around the perimeter. The beans will form a private playhouse and can be harvested for the family in August.

5. An old garden rule is to "put in more than you take out." Kids can learn about soil replenishment by watching their parents sowing cover crops in the fall to be tilled in during the spring months. Good cover crops are winter wheat, rye, kale, soybeans or barley. The cover crop aerates heavy soil, prevents erosion and adds nutrients.

6. Learn to make your own "bug sprays" or shop for organic controls with the family. We can teach children, too, that "perfect" produce is not necessary. In his book *The Practical Gardener*, Roger Swain implores us to remember that "there is usually enough of the plant for both the two-legged and six-legged creatures." Children can learn about hand-picking of insects instead of the use of sprays. Beneficial insects such as ladybugs, green lacewings and praying mantises can be ordered from garden centers.

7. Try planting a "nectar garden" for the children and you. Bees and butterflies cross-pollinate vegetables and flowers and add to the beauty of your yard while hummingbirds roam the beds for nectar flowers. Plant these for nectar: honeysuckle, lilac, lavender, marigold, sweet william, coneflower, foxglove, liatris, daylily and borage. Butterfly caterpillars love dill, parsley, nasturtiums and violets and are attracted to bright colors and strong fragrance.

8. Attract birds to your yard and garden and watch your children begin to learn. Birds like: shade trees for cover, ornamentals and berries, birdbaths and

brown to black, has no unpleasant smell and contains no readily identifiable elements. It then can be used in the garden or elsewhere as a soil booster or fertilizer.

Some other ideas to help your compost pile:
• Sprinkle with ground limestone.
• Keep the pile moist.
• Turn the pile to aerate, every two to seven days.
• Add a layer of manure.

You can put your compost pile in a bin made from wood, or you can buy a composter at hardware and garden centers.

WHAT USE IS COMPOST?

The true worth of composting lies in the end product it yields. Compost can stimulate growth and suppresses diseases in plants, making it a valuable ingredient in potting soils and topsoils for crops. It can also be a valuable resource in landscaping and land reclamation. Compost can act as a soil erosion control and water retention enhancer.

The use of compost as a soil addition diminishes the need for chemical fertilizer and pesticides. Compost slowly releases plant nutrients over a period of years.

—*Solid Waste Composting Council*

Major compost markets
Residential:
• Food garden application
• Lawn and flower garden application

A. *4,000 miles*
Source: Huey D. Johnson, San Francisco Examiner, *4 October 1989*

Commercial:
- Greenhouses
- Nurseries
- Golf courses
- Landscape contractors
- Turfgrass farmers
- Industrial park grounds
- Cemeteries
- Agriculture
- Topsoil suppliers

Public Agencies:
- Public parks
- Playgrounds
- Roadside and median strips
- Military installations

Land reclamation:
- Landfill cover
- Stripmined lands
- Sand and gravel pits
- Derelict urban land.

Reprinted by permission from *Environmental Hazards Management Institute Re:Source™,* Summer 1991.

RESOURCES

Barclay Recycling
makers of Soilsaver®, recycling composter.
75 Ingram Dr.
Toronto, Ontario, M6M 2M2, Canada
(416) 240-8227

Eco Atlantic
Distributors of Green Cone
2200-C Broening Hwy.
Baltimore, MD 21224,
(301) 633-7500,
(800) 253-1119

Organic Gardening
magazine
Rodale Press
Dept 45186
33 E. Minor St.
Emmaus, PA 18098
(215) 967-5171

Gardens Alive!
5100 Schenley Pl.
Lawrenceburg, IN 47025
(812) 537-8650

Growing Naturally
P.O. Box 54
Pineville, PA 18946
(215) 598-7025

feeders and a steady supply of seed and water. Mountain ash produces a nice berry as do grapes, currants, elderberries, gooseberries and any other fruiting shrub or tree.

9. Think of the backyard and frontyard as two more rooms of the family house. Some folks plow up the entire yard and put in a series of mulched paths, raised beds and trees. A small city yard might become two large raised beds of buffalo grass and wildflowers bordered by edible fruit and brick paths, with wooden benches for children to read and dream on!

The next generation of gardeners is important. Gardening can be a source of wisdom, fun and rewards for every member of the family.

CHEMICALS AND YOUR LAWN

EVERY YEAR AMERICANS SOAK 67 MILLION POUNDS of chemical pesticides into their lawns and gardens. That's somewhere between five and 11 pounds per acre— and that's more than four times as many chemical pesticides per acre as commercial farmers use. Each year, Americans spend nearly $2.5 billion for chemical pesticides and fertilizers for lawns with another $1.5 billion going to lawn care service companies. But that may be changing. Sales of "green," naturally derived fertilizers and pest controls were expected to reach $600 million in 1991.

Buying chemicals for your lawn and garden couldn't be easier. Every nursery, garden center and hardware store has shelves crammed full of them. Even though many of the major manufacturers are introducing natural and organic products, finding the greener alternatives may still require some good detective work.

If you can't find organics at the local store, try ordering via mail order. The 136-page catalog from Harmony Farm Supply contains detailed information about using organic fertilizers and organic pest controls, installing drip irrigation and putting organic gardening practices to work. It includes a wide range of organic products, hand tools and more. Send $2.00 (refundable with purchase) for catalog to: Harmony Farm Supply, 3244 Gravenstein Hwy. N, Sebastopol, CA 95472.

A terrific all-natural, organic plant food that's safe and nontoxic is made by Maestro-Gro. A-Gro-Elite distributes Maestro-Gro products and sells its own

Q. *How much of the working population of the US lives within biking distance of work?*

Elite brand of products for clean and safe lawns, healthy gardens, purer groundwater supplies and safer playgrounds. For a brochure contact A-Gro-Elite Co., 265 S. Federal Hwy., Suite 308, Deerfield Beach, FL 33441, (800) 822-5882.

Why you should not use chemicals.
Artificial fertilizers and pesticides are a major source of land, water and air pollution. Pesticides are among the most deadly of chemicals, many developed out of nerve gas and other war related research. The US uses about 2 billion pounds of pesticides annually. Over 270 billion pounds of artificial fertilizers are used on the earth each year. The EPA continues its reassessment of the health risks of the 24,000 pesticides now available. So far, only two of the widely-used pesticides have been cleared. Consumer concern is apparently making a difference as large lawn care companies such as ChemLawn Services have begun test-marketing manure fertilizers and the non-use of pesticides.

YARD WASTES

YARD WASTES ACCOUNT FOR NEARLY ONE-FIFTH (over 31 million tons) of all garbage generated in the US each year, making yard wastes the second largest component (by weight) of the municipal solid waste stream.

Since these materials are relatively clean and biodegradable, disposal in landfills may be unnecessary and wastes space. Yard wastes also are generally unsuitable for combustion in incinerators due to their high moisture content, which can inhibit complete burning. Burning leaves and other yard wastes pollutes the air and can lead to uncontrolled fires. A number of states currently ban leaf burning, and some communities either ban leaf burning or restrict when it can take place.

The thing to do with your yard-waste is compost it.

MATCHBOX TOMATOES

WINDOW GARDENERS TAKE HEART. Researchers at the University of Florida's Institute of Food and Agricultural Sciences have developed the world's smallest tomato. The new variety stands no more than five to eight inches tall, yet it produces tasty bite-sized fruit about an inch in diameter. Researchers Jay Scott and Brent Harbaugh have named the plant Micro-Tom. "It

Green Pro
380 S. Franklin St.
Hempstead, NY 11550
(516) 538-6444
(800) 645-6464

Ringer
9959 Valley View Rd.
Eden Prairie, MN 55344
(612) 941-4180
(800) 423-7544

HOW TO MAKE YOUR OWN PESTICIDES

Chili Peppers
Boil a bowlful (half a kilogram) of thinly sliced ripe chili peppers in three litres of water for 15 to 20 minutes. Add 30 grams of soap and stir to make the solution soapy (so it will adhere to plants). Add three more litres of water. Let cool and strain. Use on vegetable gardens against caterpillars, aphids, flies, ants and other pests. Apply once a week if there is no rain, two to three times a week if it rains.

Neem Trees
Grind fresh leaves, dilute with water and strain. Is used on crops against a variety of pests. Particularly effective against caterpillars and weevils on soya beans.

Pyrethrum
Dry one half to one kilogram of young flowers until they are crumbly. Boil in four litres of water for 15 to 20 minutes. Add soap and stir. Add four litres of water. Strain before using in a sprayer. Use liquid as soon as it cools; apply in the same way as chili solution against the

A. *More than half*
Source: The Next Step: 50 More Things You Can Do To Save The Earth, *by the Earth • Works Group*

same pests. Best results if applied after sundown.

Powder of crushed flowers can be sprinkled around the house to kill fleas and on beds to kill bed bugs.

Mexican Marigolds

Place large quantities of freshly gathered flowers, leaves and stalks in a bucket of water. Let stand for five to seven days to decay. Stir often so material decays evenly. When decayed, dilute with equal amount of water and add soap. Acts as crop strengthener to help potatoes, beans, tomatoes and peas resist blight, mildew and other fungal diseases. Begin spraying before diseases start; continue regularly once a week. Effective if weather is not too damp. Also repels aphids, caterpillars and flies.

Wood Ash

Use fresh (but not hot) ash from cooking fires. Any sort of wood will do, although ash from eucalyptus or cyprus trees is most effective. Sprinkle handfuls of ash around seedlings as soon as they sprout to repel cut worms. Replace after every rain. Need only apply for first two to three weeks (until plants get too big for cutting). Also effective against root maggots, snails and slugs. Surrounding entire plot with 8- to 10-centimeter trench filled with ash has the same effect.

Reprinted by permission from *The African Farmer*, by Christian Spoor, published by The Hunger Project, New York, November, 1990.

establishes a whole new category for small tomato varieties. We call it a miniature dwarf tomato," Scott said. The average tomato plant is 20 times larger than Micro-Tom, which is bred for windowsill pots.

Reprinted by permission from East West Journal, *March 1990*

UNSEASONAL SEEDING

IT IS POSSIBLE TO SOW SEEDS FOR SOME PLANTS in the fall to save you time and produce excellent leafy vegetables. Some plants are not well suited to fall planting because they may not be tolerant of the cold. But some fall-sown crops that are well suited are: leaf lettuce, carrots, parsnips, parsley, spinach and onion. Fall seeding occurs just before the soil freezes. Seeding practices are the same for fall as they are for spring.

Reprinted by permission from Harrowsmith, *September/October 1987*

WHAT CAN YOU DO?

Buy organic:

Nearly 58 percent of Americans ate organic produce in 1989. Be willing to buy blemished produce, buy from local farmers and grow your own.

Why eat less meat?

•It takes between 22 and 44 times less fossil fuel to produce beans and grains rather than meat.

•It takes 16 pounds of feed and 2,500 gallons of water to produce one pound of beef.

•Half the world's grain harvest is fed to livestock.

•An estimated 85 percent of our topsoil erosion is associated with raising livestock.

•About half of the 25 million pounds of antibiotics produced in the United States annually is fed to livestock.

•Calorie for calorie, you can get an equivalent amount of protein from vegetables such as broccoli and cauliflower as you can from meat.

•In a study of 24,000 Seventh Day Adventists, meat eaters had a three times greater incidence of heart disease than did vegetarians.

 Q: *How many US nuclear bombs exploded on Japan?*

EcoFood

Eating green isn't just about eating greens. It's also about buying foods that are produced sustainably, without harming the environment. Choosing to eat green means pesticide-free, steroid-free and humane production practices. Eating green also means balancing nutritional and ecological needs. And it means being aware of the energy and materials expended when preparing a meal. With the introduction of eco-food, today's population is not only more informed but also healthier. And that leads to a healthier planet.

Although the debate over what "certified organic" means continues, "natural" and "organic" foods are becoming available to the mass market. America's corporate food giants are introducing organic product lines to their general market consumers: Gallo is converting its vineyards to organic; Cascadian Farm has been purchased by Welch's and is beginning to put its line of frozen organic fruits and vegetables on supermarket shelves; Ralston-Purina is promoting its new organic pet food. And the list is growing. Restaurants—vegetarian and carnivorous alike—now offer certified organic dishes. And organic food cookbooks are sprouting up in the chain bookstores.

Plantworks, Karen Shanberg and Stan Tekiela, Adventure Publications, Cambridge, MN, 1991.

Plantworks is a field guide, recipe book and activity resource all in one. This book, written for novices, naturalists, families and groups alike, provides a new appreciation for plants often thought of as weeds. Using a number of common wild edible plants, *Plantworks* provides the organic connoisseur with recipes for foods and drinks from quiche to coffee, yogurt to fettuccine. *Plantworks* also provides the botanist with illustrations, photographs and natural history information to successfully identify plants.

Thorsons Green Cookbook, Sarah Bounds, HarperCollins Publishers, Hammersmith, London, 1990.

Thorsons Green Cookbook provides the home cook with information on healthy cooking for the family and for the planet. This cookbook is packed with recipes to help change the way we eat. It explains in detail the importance of organic farming to help

---

LUCKY RED CLOVER FRITTERS

Ingredients:
2 cups red clover flowers
1 egg
1 cup flour
1 cup milk
1 tbsp. baking powder
¾ tsp. nutmeg
1 tbsp. sugar
vegetable oil

Optional: brown or powdered sugar

Directions:
Wash flower tops and shake off the extra water. Mix together the egg, milk, nutmeg and sugar. Mix flour and baking powder and stir in the liquid mixture until a medium-thick batter is made. Heat 1/4" oil in a large frying pan over medium heat. Dip flowers into batter and cook in hot oil until brown. Sprinkle with sugar and serve hot. *Serves 4*

Recipe by permission from Plantworks by Karen Shanberg and Stan Tekiela, Adventure Publications, Cambridge, MN,

---

A.[2] *Source: Kirkpatrick Sale, Resurgence No.137, November/December 1989*

sustain food production without harming the environment. It also shows how energy resources can be saved in the home to cut fuel bills and lessen the greenhouse effect.

The Wild Foods Forum, 4 Carlisle Way NE, Atlanta, GA 30308, one-year subscription $15.00.

As a result of her teaching and lecturing on wild foods, Deborah Duchon became convinced that foragers needed a network and source of up-to-date information on various wild foods. Duchon is now editor and publisher of *The Wild Foods Forum*, a monthly newsletter devoted to the use of wild plants, especially as food. *The Wild Foods Forum* is aimed at both veteran and beginning foragers and concentrates on wild foods events going on all around the country. Other articles report on usage, history, identification and recipes for various wild plants.

Organic Times

Published three times per year by New Hope Communications Inc., 1301 Spruce St., Boulder, CO 80302

Organic Times is dedicated to providing accurate, up-to-date information of interest to the organic products industry, including legislation, events, innovations in production, certification, distribution and marketing. It is also committed to facilitating communication within the trade and serving as a catalyst for the growth of the market.

ORGANIC RESTAURANT

Nora

On cool, quiet winter afternoons in Washington, DC, Nora Pouillon invites the farmers who grow food for her restaurants to come into town for a cup of hot tea. Together, they pour over seed catalogs, choosing vegetables and herbs that will become the gourmet selections on her menu.

Pouillon makes a special effort to find good farmers. Some grow exclusively for her. "It's unfortunate that these organic farmers are so rare, because I'm convinced food produced that way is unusually healthy, complete in nutrients, and has exceptional flavor and texture. 80 percent of the taste is how it's grown. Organic food tastes noticeably different."

Pouillon broadens the common ideas about organics to include meats, grain and processed foods. She

---

DANDELION CHOCOLATE COFFEE

Ingredients:
6-8 dandelion roots
kettle of water
tea ball
½ packet instant hot
chocolate mix (8 oz.)

Directions:
The roots are gathered at any time of the year they can be found. Cut off the root just below the crown, wash and scrub, and dry with a towel. Slowly roast the roots in a 200 degree oven with the door open for 30 minutes. Watch the roots carefully to avoid burning, which will foul the taste.

Use a blender or food processor to grind the roots, but take care not to grind them too finely, especially if you'll be using a tea ball. A percolating coffee maker with a filter works the best to brew this drink. Use 1 tsp. ground roots for each cup of hot water. After brewing, add 1/2 packet hot chocolate mix per cup.

Recipe by permission from Plantworks by Karen Shanberg and Stan Tekiela, Adventure Publications, Cambridge, MN, 1991.

Q: *How many US nuclear bombs exploded on Western Shoshone tribal territory?*

makes almost all items—even pasta and sausage—in-house, starting with organic ingredients.

She honors the growers by crediting their farms on her menus. And the menu selections are an enticing blend she calls "New American."

Reprinted by permission from Organically Grown, *Fall 1991, published by The Committee for Sustainable Agriculture, P.O. Box 1300, Colfax, CA 95713.*

THE SEXUAL POLITICS OF MEAT

- Myth from the Bushmen -

IN THE EARLY TIMES MEN AND WOMEN lived apart, the former hunting animals exclusively, the latter pursuing a gathering existence. Five of the men, who were out hunting, being careless creatures, let their fire go out. The women, who were careful and orderly, always kept their fire going. The men, having killed a springbok, became desperate for means to cook it, so one of their number set out to get fire, crossed the river and met one of the women gathering seeds. When he asked her for some fire, she invited him to the feminine camp. While he was there she said, "You are very hungry. Just wait until I pound up these seeds and I will boil them and give you some." She made him some porridge. After he had eaten it, he said, "Well, it's nice food so I shall just stay with you." The men who were left waited and wondered. They still had the springbok and they still had no fire. The second man set out, only to be tempted by female cooking, and to take up residence in the camp of the women. The same thing happened to the third man. The two men left were very frightened. They suspected something terrible had happened to their comrades. They cast the divining bones but the omens were favorable. The fourth man set out timidly, only to end by joining his comrades. The last man became very frightened indeed and besides, by now, the springbok had rotted. He took his bow and arrows and ran away.

Reprinted by permission from The Sexual Politics of Meat *by Carol J. Adams, The Continuum Publishing Company, New York, 1991.*

MOLLETES— MEXICAN SWEET ROLLS

1 cup milk
2 tablespoons shortening
1 large egg, slightly beaten
2 tablespoons warm water
1½ teaspoons anise seed
½ cup honey
1 cake yeast
4¼ cups unbleached flour

To milk in sauce pan add anise seed and bring just to the boiling point. Remove from heat, add shortening, honey and dash of salt. Mix well and let cool to lukewarm. Add egg and yeast. Mix well, making soft dough by adding flour. Cover with a damp cloth and let stand until double in size (1 hour). Turn onto floured board and divide dough into 24 equal pieces. Shape into balls and place 2 inches apart on a well greased baking sheet. Cover with a damp cloth. Allow to rise until double in bulk (1 hour). Brush with a little melted butter. Bake at 350 degrees for 20 minutes. Yields one dozen medium sized rolls.

Recipe by permission from The Ecology Cookbook: An Earth Mother's Advisory, *Nan Hosmer Pipestem and Judi Ohr, Celestial Arts, Berkeley, CA, 1991.*

A.**670**
Source: Kirkpatrick Sale, Resurgence No.137, *November/December 1989*

SOME
QUESTIONS TO
ASK ABOUT
YOUR CITY

How green is your city, not just in the physical sense, but in the political sense? Are you surrounded by trees? Do you have parks to enjoy? Do your political leaders look carefully at an industry's environmental record before encouraging it to move into its borders? Do they enforce environmental regulations of existing industry?

• Is your city maximizing the use of its resources? In other words, does it have a recycling program, a composting program, a source reduction program, a hazardous waste program? Does it mandate the purchase of recycled products?

• Does your city have an effective mass transit system that connects residential areas with its work areas? Is it promoting the use of alternative means of transportation such as bicycling? Better yet, is there a mix of businesses and homes within walking distance?

• What kind of air quality does your city have? Is it in violation of federal clean air standards? What about your water quality and method of treating sewage? Can you swim in your nearby lakes, rivers and streams?

• What kind of energy powers your city? Is it dirty coal, nuclear with

Urban Ecology

- By Andrea Trank -

The role of city government is changing; no longer is its sole mission to "protect the health and safety of its people and to promote prosperity within its borders," as many city charters read. Today, city officials are being called upon to lead the urban ecology movement. The stakes are certainly high enough: By the year 2005, 50 percent of the world's population may live in cities. Such a population shift is placing enormous strain on urban areas, but a growing number of city governments appear to be responding to the challenge—much more so than the federal government. According to Walter McGuire, Director of the Global Cities Project—an outgrowth of Earth Day 1990—more than 50 percent of the money being spent on environmental programs is at the local level.

While the idea of an "ecological city" may seem like an oxymoron to many, such a concept may offer the best hope for urban dwellers and their environment. The other choices are to move out of the city into suburbia, take over the rural areas, creating what has become known as "exurbia," or to start from scratch and build new cities. These attempted solutions are being tried, but at great expense—both economically and environmentally speaking. "It is really necessary for people to figure out how to make cities work, or the whole country will become suburbia. Then we will have to figure out how to make suburbs work," says Michael Leccese, senior editor of *Landscape Architecture* magazine. You can either transfer the problem, or correct it at its source, according to Leccese, who points out that most cities contain the raw elements to be ecologically-oriented. For instance, most cities were established before the advent of vehicles, so they are designed for people and public transportation, not cars. Most cities were built near rivers, have mature trees and established park systems. "There is great potential within those cities for restoration, which is an act of recycling," he concludes.

In an informal survey of "Eco-Cities," you may find the choices surprising and you may notice that several of them are in California. We picked these cities because they represent some of the most innovative

Q: *What is the percentage of energy in the US that comes from fossil fuels?*

ideas in urban ecology and they also have very successful public relations campaigns.

Newark, New Jersey!—An "Eco-City?" Incredible as it seems, yes. Of all the cities we surveyed, Newark knows a great deal about the underside of city life. For years, it has faced a declining industrial base. Without stable employment and with a growing drug and crime problem, Newark's neighborhoods seemed to epitomize the term "urban blight." In fact, five years ago, Newark was a city nearly in ruin. But led by Mayor Sharpe James, a new political leadership set out to reverse the slide and did so by stressing environmental themes. "Have you been to Newark lately?" asks Frank Sudol, Newark's Manager of Engineering, who oversees a myriad of the city's environmental programs. Today's Newark has 1,500 small-scale urban gardens producing $750,000 worth of fruits and vegetables. Compost from its city-wide yard waste program is feeding the gardens. Last year, the city planted 3,000 trees and hundreds more were planted by developers who were obeying a city law that says for every tree cut down, trees equal in diameter must be planted.

"We only do things we have public support for. What is the sense of planting trees if the community is not going to help nourish them?" asks Sudol. As the city took the lead in neighborhood improvements, he says, residents began to do things such as painting their houses. Even though few Newark residents are well-off financially, they have developed a new sense of pride in their community.

Newark has the largest recycling program on the East Coast, according to Sudol. The city has doubled the state-mandated goal of a 25 percent recycling rate by collecting more than just glass, aluminum and paper. Newark also recycles plastic, wood, oil, asphalt, anti-freeze, refrigerators and tires. All ozone-depleting compounds, including CFCs, are banned. Plastic containers made from polystyrene and polyvinylchloride are also banned. One by one, Newark's inefficient boiler plants, which emit large amounts of pollution, are being replaced with cogeneration units, which recover waste heat for a secondary source of electricity.

The price tag of Newark's renaissance is a whopping $4 billion, most of it from the private investment sector. "What we found is the more money you put

its highly radioactive waste, expensive electric or some newer forms of energy such as cogeneration, small scale hydropower, biomass, solar or wind power? Do city regulations favor energy conservation in industrial buildings and homes?

• Is your population remaining basically stable or growing beyond your city's capacity to service it? Are land use decisions being made with an eye for the preservation of farmland, wildlife and historical monuments?

• Most importantly, is your city actively seeking ways to improve the quality of life not just for your generation, but for future generations?

• Can any of the 3 billion people who today call the world's cities their home say yes to all these questions? Absolutely not! But at least the questions are being posed, and the greening spirit has taken hold in some cities.

—*Andrea Trank.*

A: *90 percent*
Source: The Greenhouse Trap, *by Francesca Lyman*

RATING THE RATINGS

There are numerous sources available that rate cities and states based on their sustainability and other factors. The problem is that variations in methodology quite often result in the same city receiving vastly different ratings.

• The *Places Rated Almanac*, the *Rating Guide to Life in American Small Cities*, The National Civic League's "All-America City Award," *East West Journal of Natural Health and Living*'s "Healthful Cities Study," Renew America's "States Ranked for Environmental Effort," the Zero Population Growth "Environmental Stress Index" and now, the Institute for Southern Studies' *Green Index* are just some of the efforts on the subject.

• *East West* put Minneapolis-St. Paul near the top, while Memphis, Tennessee, came in at the bottom. Half of the factors used in *East West*'s study related to the environment while the other half were more social in nature, such as crime, unemployment and divorce.

• The *Places Rated Almanac* has a chapter on the environment, but does not really incorporate the discussion into its rating scale.

• The *Rating Guide to Life in American Small Cities* puts San Luis Obispo, California, at the top because it scored well on 19 out of 20

into a cleaner city, the more investment you attract and the more jobs you create," says Sudol. While city officials feel proud about Newark's comeback, there are numerous environmental problems remaining— many of which relate to its close proximity to New York City and its location in New Jersey, the most densely populated state in the country. One example involves a waste-to-energy plant located within the city limits, but from which the city derives no use or benefit. The over-sized plant was expecting to use some of the garbage from Newark, but that material is being recycled. The plant then began importing garbage from other counties. In addition, the plant has been fined almost daily for exceeding airborne limits on nitrogen oxide, a greenhouse gas. Nevertheless, the city has shown what can be done to bring back an all-but-abandoned urban area.

The Newark example clearly shows that strong leadership is one critical factor in creating a "sustainable city." What also helps is having strong public commitment to environmental goals. Take San Jose, California, for instance. This city of 815,000 (larger than the city of San Francisco) lies in the heart of Silicon Valley, and has the unfortunate distinction of being part of a county that contains 27 superfund sites. But San Jose is not waiting for the federal government to make environmental decisions. The city has its own municipal Environmental Protection Agency, spurred on by an active community of grass roots organizations like the Silicon Valley Toxics Coalition.

When San Jose's version of the EPA—called the Office of Environmental Management (OEM)— opened in 1986, it had just three employees. Today it has 65 employees and an annual budget of $14.3 million. "The quality of life is very important to residents here. We are emphasizing environmental programs as a way of protecting that way of life," says Michele Yesney, OEM Director.

The city has invested heavily in energy conservation with an ambitious goal of reducing energy consumption by 10 percent by the year 2000. The only way to reach such a goal is to take a broader view of energy, says Yesney. To protect outlying areas from development, a 140-square-mile greenbelt has been proposed. By demonstrating the greenbelt would save millions in energy costs, OEM received the

Q: *Scientists believe there are between 5 million and 30 million plant and animal species on Earth. What number have been identified and given scientific names?*

support of the city's political leadership. According to Yesney, development pressure without greenbelt preservation could eventually lead to the construction of 13,000 housing units. By comparing that with an equal amount of development in downtown or along the existing transit corridor, OEM calculated the greenbelt development would require at least 200,000 miles of additional auto commuting every day and use 40 percent more energy for heating and cooling.

In the area of water conservation (crucial to drought-stricken California) the city is saving six million gallons a day in part by distributing low flow shower heads and toilet dams to 180,000 households. Recycling and composting are well-developed, and the city is considering food composting when its current contract expires in 1993. Yesney says San Jose is embracing the concept of a sustainable city across the board and in all of its city programs—from maintaining infrastructures like roads to synchronizing city traffic lights which also save energy and create less air pollution. "Sustainability is about closing the loop, about ensuring that our social and economic living patterns do not bankrupt the resources we depend upon," says Yesney. "It's about the increasing demands for resources managed effectively so economic growth can occur without the associated increasing demand on the environment."

Twenty miles east of Los Angeles in the San Gabriel Valley is Duarte, California, a city of 20,000. Duarte's motto is "city of health," a claim some might find hard to believe, since the city is located in an area with the worst air pollution in the US. But this fact is not lost on Duarte's civic leaders. Six years ago, Duarte realized its image as a health-promoting city was incompatible with an incinerator. The ensuing fight unified Duarte's residents who elected a local council with a strong environmental agenda. Soon after, city officials began implementing campaign promises like mandating the use of propane vehicles and switching to a four-day work week to try and improve air quality. Water pollution programs, recycling, composting and the acquisition of land to build a bike trail are some of Duarte's accomplishments. The city, which employs a few dozen people, has a part-time Environmental Counsel, an attorney who advises officials on the environmental impacts of all their decisions. "I am not so sure we have

environmental indicators. But William Seavey of The Greener Pastures Institute points out that the authors of the rating guide book ignore the fact that there is a nuclear power plant very close to the city.

• The National Civic League has been giving out a ten best cities award annually since 1950. Newark, New Jersey, made the 1991 list, scoring high based on the city's strong environmental record and its efforts to revitalize the inner city.

• Zero Population Growth's "Environmental Stress Index" looked at a total of 204 cities with populations over 100,000 and measured five environmental indicators—air, water, sewage, toxics and population change. Albany, New York, and Independence, Missouri, shared the top spot while El Paso, Texas, Reno, Nevada, Irvine, California, and four cities in Arizona were all ranked near the bottom. Zero Population Growth believes the most critical factor in determining environmental health is population stability, so it is no wonder that cities in the southwest and west did so poorly.

• Renew America used the concept of environmental activism in determining which states rank best and worst. Minnesota rated number one for putting out maximum effort to correct its ecological problems, while Alabama rated last.

A. *1,400,000*
Source: *Natural Resources Defense Council*

- Alabama also was last place in the most recent and comprehensive state ranking on the environment. *The Green Index*, published this past summer, looked at 256 indicators, including the environmental records of political leaders and the environmental condition of each state. Oregon, Maine, Vermont, California, Minnesota, Massachusetts, Rhode Island, New York, Washington and Wisconsin round out the top ten. The entire southeastern US with the exception of North Carolina, was at the bottom.

- The authors of the *Green Index* advise using the environmental ratings not as a guide to choosing your home town, but as a tool to encourage city and state officials to clean up their act. "It's not like we are identifying the best town to move to, but the criteria to use as you evaluate what is going on around you," says Bob Hall, Institute for Southern Studies director and co-author of the *Green Index.* "What we recommend is people enjoy and treasure their surroundings and fight like hell to safekeep it."

—*Andrea Trank*

made life substantially better, but we sure have avoided making life worse," says Terry Fitzgerald, Duarte's Environmental Counsel. "Except for the fact that we are right near LA, it is the perfect location to live," she adds.

Evaluating cities is fraught with uncertainty. Some of the most troubled urban areas are outpacing cities with far fewer pollution problems, with the curious result that cities with highly desirable reputations and lifestyles may fall short when compared to municipalities that have had no choice but to adopt environmentally beneficial policies. Nevertheless, don't pack your bags and head for Newark. Consider another approach: Help to turn your own city or town into an "Eco-City."

The Global Cities Project in San Francisco is providing a unique service to cities that want to become sustainable. They are producing how-to guides on a range of environmental issues from establishing a solid waste plan that stresses recycling and composting to setting up an energy conservation program. "We believe the city has a positive role to play in not just implementing federal and state law, but in taking a proactive position," says director Walter McGuire. McGuire believes a lack of resources and humanpower has hampered most cities' environmental efforts. "Small towns in many pristine areas have inadequate staff to think up new programs," he adds. Many times, city managers won't even look at environmental programs because they believe those programs won't add to the tax base or help the city prosper. McGuire and others in the global city movement are hoping to debunk that argument, pointing to real cities that have prospered through sustainability.

Andrea Trank runs "HomeWord Communications," an environmental writing and consulting firm in Charlottesville, Virginia.

Q: *Since 1989, what companies have increased their profits by 157 percent?*

HOME RESOURCES

BOOKS

Shopping for a Better World, 1991 edition, the quick and easy guide to shopping. The Council on Economic Priorities, 30 Irving Pl. New York, NY 10003 (212) 420-1133.

The Natural House Book
David Pearson, Simon and Schuster, Fireside Books, a Gaia Original, 1989.

Healthful Houses, How to Design and Build Your Own, Clint Good and Debra Lynn Dadd, Guaranty Press, Bethesda, MD, 1988.

Home Ecology
Karen Christensen, Fulcrum Inc., Golden, CO, 1990.

How to Get Water Smart, Products and Practices for Saving Water in the Nineties, Terra Firma Publishing, Santa Barbara, CA, 1991.

PERIODICALS

The Green Consumer Letter
Tilden Press
1526 Connecticut Ave. NW
Washington, DC 20036
(800) 955-GREEN

Interior Concerns Newsletter
P.O. Box 2386
Mill Valley, CA 94942

Environ
P.O. Box 2204
Ft. Collins, CO 80522
(303) 224-0083

Safe Home Digest
24 East Ave., Suite 1300
New Caanan, CT 06840

NONTOXIC PAINTS

AFM Enterprises Inc.
1140 Stacy Ct.
Riverside, CA 92507
(714) 781-6860

Auro Natural Paints
P.O. Box 857
Davis, CA 95617
(916) 753-3104

Livos Plantchemistry
1365 Rufina Cir.
Santa Fe, NM 87501
(505) 438-3448

Miller Paint
317 SE Grand Ave.
Portland, OR 97214
(503) 233-4491

Murco Wall Products
300 NE 21st St.
Ft. Worth, TX 76106
(817) 626-1987

CARPET AND FLOORING

Henderson Naturalik
8031 Mill Station Rd.
Sebastapol, CA 95472
(707) 829-3959

Collins and Aikman
P.O. Box 1447
Dalton, GA 30722-1447
(800) 826-3267

WATER

American Water Works Association
6666 W. Quincy Ave.
Denver, CO 80235
(303) 794-7711

ENVIRONMENTALLY CONCERNED HOME DESIGNERS

John Bower
7471 N. Shiloh Rd.
Unionville, IN 47468

Nicholas Geragi
P.O. Box 242, Rt. 5
Herkimer, NY 13350

Clint Good
P.O. Box 143
Lincoln, VA 22078

International Institute for Baubiologie and Ecology, Inc.
Box 387
Clearwater, FL 34615

Steve Janenka
28 Farley Dr.
Rensselaer, NY 12144

The Masters Corp.
P.O. Box 514
New Canaan, CT 06840

Stephen Robin Assoc.
P.O. Box 283
Woodstock, NY 12498

Carol Venolla
P.O. Box 694
39000 S. Hwy. 1
Gualala, CA 95445

GARDENING

Pesticide Alert
Lawrie Mott and Karen Snyder, Sierra Club, San Francisco, 1988.

For Our Kids' Sake
Anne Witte Garland
Sierra Club, San Francisco, 1990.

Environmental Fact Sheet About Yard Waste Composting
EPA Office of Solid Waste
401 M St. SW
Washington, DC 20460

Diet for a New America
John Robbins
Stillpoint, Dallas, TX, 1987.

Diet for a Small Planet
Frances Moore Lappé
Ballantine Books, New York, NY, 1971.

KIDS

Biobottoms Fresh Air Wear
P.O. Box 6009
Petaluma, CA 94953
(707) 778-7945
Pre-folded velour diapers.

Natural Baby Company
114 W. Franklin, Straube Ctr.
Pennigton, NJ 08534
(609) 737-2895
Manufactures cloth diapers.

Baby Bunz & Company
106 Petaluma Ave.
Sebastopol, CA 95473
(707) 829-5347
Pre-shaped cloth diapers.

National Association of Diaper Services
2017 Walnut St.
Philadelphia, PA 19103
(215) 569-3650

A. ***The 11 largest oil companies***
Source: First Boston Investment Broker

AMERICANS FAIL TEST ON ENVIRONMENT

In a test about environmental issues commissioned by S.C. Johnson & Son, conducted in July 1991 by the Roper Organization, Americans surveyed correctly answered only 33 percent of the questions. The test consisted of five multiple choice questions and five true-false questions about air, land and water issues. Even those people claiming to be environmentally active and educated scored a high of only 40 percent.

The question which posed the most trouble for the respondents was one regarding the disposal of motor oil. Only 10 percent of those surveyed knew that the following assertion is correct: Car owners dump more than 10 times the amount of motor oil into sewers as the 11 million gallons spilled off the coast of Alaska in the March 1989, *Exxon Valdez* disaster. Seventeen percent said that the amount dumped by motorists is twice the amount of the spill, 26 percent said it is half as much, another 17 percent said it is less than one-tenth, and 30 percent pleaded ignorance.

Other questions were met with equal confusion. When asked what is most affected by acid rain, only 25 percent correctly chose fish in New England streams. Thirty percent chose Central American

What You Said

*P*olls *are a sign of the times. They indicate which issues the public feels are important and what they are and are not willing to do. Many polls have been conducted about the environment in recent years, indicating that the environment has become an important enough issue for companies and poll conductors to be concerned about people's concerns. The following* American Demographics *article defines the very nature of environmentalism.*

THE EARTH'S BEST FRIENDS

- By Joe Schwartz and Thomas Miller -

Saving the environment is a high priority for most American citizens. But as consumers, most of us still are not willing to act on our beliefs. Over three-quarters (78 percent) of adults say that our nation must "make a major effort to improve the quality of our environment," according to a recent study commissioned by S.C. Johnson & Son and conducted by the Roper Organization. But at the same time, most say that individuals can do little, if anything, to help improve the environment.

Public concern about the environment is growing faster than concerns about any other issue monitored by Roper—at least before the Persian Gulf crisis and the softening of the economy. Businesses are tuning in to this trend by producing "green" products, services and advertising campaigns. But banking on environmental awareness can backfire, because the majority of Americans are already convinced that businesses are not environmentally responsible. Also, they are generally skeptical about the environmental claims being made in advertising and on labels.

If your company is launching "green" products or practices, you need to consider how these attitudes will affect every aspect of your marketing, advertising and public relations campaigns. The most environmentally active Americans are more affluent and better educated than those who take no actions. Green consumers are among the most influential Americans, but so far their influence has not swayed the bulk of the population. Different groups need to hear environmental information in different ways.

Q. *How much energy could the US save if it switched to the best available lighting technology?*

Americans tend to blame businesses for the environmental problems they see at global, national and local levels. More than eight in ten Americans say that industrial pollution is the main reason for our environmental problems, and nearly three-quarters of the public say that the products businesses use in manufacturing also harm the environment. Six in ten Americans blame businesses for not developing environmentally sound consumer products, and an equal share believes that some technological advancements made by businesses eventually produce unanticipated environmental problems.

Americans blame themselves, too. Seventy percent say that consumers are more interested in convenience than they are in environmentally sound products, and 53 percent admit that consumers are not willing to pay more for safer products.

In theory, almost every American is pro-environment. But the ardent environmental attitudes that come out in opinion polls cool down significantly when you look at consumer behavior. Perhaps badmouthing businesses is easier than making important lifestyle changes and accepting some of the blame.

Consumer behavior usually affects the environment at two points. First, consumers can either buy or reject environmentally unsound products. After the purchase, they affect the environment by either recycling products or sending them to the local landfill.

At the moment, recycling appears to be the most rapidly growing pro-environmental behavior. Between March 1989 and February 1990, the share of Americans who say they regularly recycle bottles and cans rose from 41 percent to 46 percent, and the share who regularly recycle newspapers rose from 20 percent to 26 percent. Those who sort their trash on a regular basis rose from 14 percent to 24 percent of all adults.

Altruism isn't the only force behind the recycling boom. Many states and municipalities have passed "bottle bills" and other mandatory recycling laws. People may be complying with the new rules and may even be doing more than is required. But in many cases, legislation stimulated their behavioral changes.

More than half of all adults (52 percent) never recycle newspapers. Only 16 percent say they avoid products that come from environmentally irresponsible companies, and just 7 percent regularly avoid restaurants that use foam containers. Only 8 percent of

rainforests, 6 percent answered Midwest school children and 2 percent selected black bears in the Smoky Mountains. A sizable 37 percent did not know.

In response to a question regarding the most widely recycled material in the US last year, just 15 percent knew that the correct answer was steel. Forty-six percent guessed paper, 18 percent plastics and 11 percent glass.

SURVEY SHOWS SHIFTING ENVIRONMENTAL VALUES

A report released in October 1991, commissioned by the Magazine Publishers of America and based on the annual Yankelovich Monitor survey, shows that America's concern for the environment is shifting. The number of respondents indicating an interest in the environment grew from 16 percent in 1986 to 29 percent in 1990. But in the last year that number has dropped to 24 percent, declining for the first time in five years.

Researchers attribute this drop to over-saturation in the media of environmental issues. Another factor may be the rise in environmental practices like recycling, which researchers say may make people feel the problems are becoming less urgent.

A. *25 percent*
Source: Peace Resource Project

OUTDOOR INDUSTRY AWARE OF ENVIRONMENT

Leaders in the outdoor industry are more aware of and feel more strongly about environmental issues than the general public, according to the second annual Polartec "An Inside Look at the Outdoors" survey, commissioned by Malden Mills. The survey was conducted in August 1991 at Outdoor Retailers annual Expo West.

The chart below shows the percentage of outdoor industry respondents compared to the general public who selected the classification "very serious" for these six categories:

Industry

General Public

Air Quality

42% versus 23%

Natural Areas

39% versus 24%

Water Quality

51% versus 19%

Endangered Animals

34% versus 12%

Public Areas Upkeep

30% versus 12%

Waste Disposal

50% versus 44%

Americans say they regularly cut down on their driving to protect the environment. More than three-quarters (76 percent) say they just motor on as usual, even though most acknowledge that emissions from private automobiles are a leading cause of air pollution.

The size of the gap between environmental attitudes and behavior varies widely. In its report, Roper used a clustering technique to divide Americans into five behavioral segments, based primarily on whether or not they engaged in a list of "environmentally friendly" practices.

True-Blue Greens account for 11 percent of the adult population. Members of this group are unique because their behavior reflects their very strong environmental concerns. They are the leaders of the green movement among the general population.

More than half (54 percent) of this group will not buy products from companies that they perceive as environmentally irresponsible, compared with just 16 percent of the general population. Moreover, 59 percent regularly recycle newspapers—more than twice the national average—and 55 percent avoid buying aerosol products.

True-Blue Green consumers tend to earn more and have more education than most Americans. Their median household income is $32,100, versus $27,100 for the national median reported by Roper's sample. Half have college educations, versus 41 percent of all adults. Twenty-five percent of this group are executives or professionals, versus 16 percent of the public. A majority (55 percent) live in the West or Northeast, and 51 percent live in large urban areas.

True-Blue Greens are far more likely than the general public to support car-pooling laws, to use biodegradable soaps and detergents, and to depend on environmental groups as a major information source. They are more likely than average to say that their political views are liberal. But they're not all fans of big government: True-Blue Greens also have the largest share of conservatives. They are the least likely to consider themselves "middle of the road" on political and social issues.

True-Blue Greens are proof that environmentalism is neither a conservative nor a liberal cause. It bridges the ideological gap.

Greenback Greens are as numerous as True-Blue Greens, at 11 percent of the adult population. They

Q: *What is the percentage of the oil used in industrialized countries that is consumed by American cars?*

are the group most willing to pay more money for environmentally safe products. Greenbacks will pay 20 percent more, compared with 7 percent for the general public.

Greenbacks will pay freely for environmental solutions, but they will not give up free time or their desire for convenience. They are willing to pay substantially more than others for less-polluting gasoline, for example, but they are no more likely to cut back on their use of automobiles. And they are less likely than True-Blue Greens to practice almost all of the pro-environmental activities that require individual effort.

The median household income of Greenback Greens ($31,600) is similar to that of the True-Blues. Also, 54 percent are college educated. A solid majority of this group (59 percent) say they are too busy to make changes in their lifestyle in order to help the environment. Perhaps this is because 43 percent have children under the age of 13, compared with 34 percent of the general public.

Sprouts are a key group. Compared with the first two groups, they hold ambivalent views about environmental regulations. They are also less certain about which side to take when confronted with the trade-off between protecting the environment and encouraging economic development. But they are more inclined to adjust their lifestyles than any other group except the True-Blues. And at 26 percent of adults, they can make a difference.

A large majority (75 percent) of Sprouts support regulations requiring that household products be sold in refillable containers, 42 percent regularly recycle newspapers, and 40 percent believe that individuals can do a lot about air pollution from automobile exhaust.

Like the two pro-environmental groups, the Sprouts are well-educated, have higher-than-average household incomes, and are more likely to be employed in executive or professional positions. They are the group most likely to be married. But Sprouts are no more likely than other groups to have young children at home.

GREEN PURCHASING BEHAVIOR VARIES

Eight in 10 Americans surveyed in a nationwide *Wall Street Journal*/NBC News poll in August 1991 regard themselves as environmentalists and, of those, half say they are "strong" environmentalists. But when it comes to making consumer decisions, cost and convenience still play a big role.

While 75 percent of those surveyed say a product's or manufacturer's environmental reputation is a crucial factor in their purchasing decisions, 46 percent claim they have bought a product in the last six months based on environmental reputation and 45 claim they haven't. In addition, 54 percent said they had bought a more expensive product over a cheaper one because of environmental concerns, but 53 percent said they avoided buying a product altogether because of the same concerns.

From *The Wall Street Journal*/NBC News poll, August 1991:
A) Overall, do you feel the environment has gotten better, gotten worse or stayed about the same over the last 20 years? B) In the past six months have you purchased any product specifically because the product or the manufacturer has a good reputation for protecting the environment? C) Would you choose a more expensive product over a cheaper one because of environmental concerns?

A   BETTER 20%   WORSE 66%   SAME 13%
B   YES 46%   NO 45%
C   BUY EXPENSIVE 54%   AVOID EXPENSIVE 55%

A. *13 percent*
Source: The Greenhouse Trap, *by Francesca Lyman*

GREEN MARKETING SURVEY SHOWS CONCERN

According to the first annual *Advertising Age*/Gallup Organization "green marketing" environmental study, Americans are looking for environmentally sensitive companies and would be willing to change their purchasing behavior accordingly. However, the majority of respondents admitted they couldn't name a marketer they feel is truly environmentally conscious. When asked which company came to mind as the most environmentally conscious overall, 66 percent said they didn't know. Of the remainder, 6 percent selected Procter & Gamble Co. and 4 percent selected McDonald's.

In general, consumers indicated they trust themselves more than product manufacturers or advertisers when choosing products. Seventy-five percent felt they knew how to select environmentally responsible products, 63 percent felt the product labelling provided accurate information, and 51 percent felt advertising provides accurate environmental information.

Finally, the US consumers surveyed showed considerable concern about the environment. Sixty-eight percent felt the American public was not worried enough, 73 percent and 76 percent felt the government and business/industry respectively were not worried enough.

Sprouts are a key segment because their political and social views closely reflect those of all Americans. They are the all-important "swing" group, both in debates over government regulation and environmental policy and in determining how far the green movement will spread into the marketplace.

Grousers are the fourth environmental consumer group identified by Roper. At 24 percent of adults, they are indifferent to the environment. However, they rationalize their indifference. They see consumer indifference as the mainstream attitude, and they see themselves as part of that mainstream. In 11 out of the 14 environmentally friendly practices, Grousers exhibit a lower level of commitment than the national average.

Grousers' median household income is below average ($24,900). Sixty-nine percent have a high school education or less, and 31 percent are blue-collar workers. A huge majority (88 percent) say that companies, not the public, should solve environmental problems; 84 percent say they are too busy to make lifestyle changes for the environment; and 77 percent say that other people aren't making sacrifices, so why should they. Only 17 percent regularly recycle newspapers, compared with 26 percent of the general public. They are willing to spend only 4 percent more for environmentally safe products, compared with the general public's 7 percent.

Basic Browns are the fifth, and largest, of the environmental consumer groups, at 28 percent of adults. They are characterized by a virtual absence of any pro-environmental activities. But unlike the Grousers, they do not rationalize their behavior or point to the alleged shortcomings of other people. Instead, their indifference stems from the belief that there is not much individuals can do about most environmental problems. They are also the group least likely to support government environmental regulations.

Basic Browns are the most socially and economically disadvantaged group of the five. They have the lowest household income ($21,200), and 69 percent have a high school education or less. (Three out of ten have not finished high school.) They have the largest proportion of workers in blue-collar occupations, the highest percentage of men (55 percent), and the highest percentage of people living in the South (48 percent) of all five segments.

People who regularly engage in pro-environmental

 Q: *How many tests are necessary to determine the safety of a chemical?*

consumer behavior are an elite group, with higher-than-average levels of educational attainment and household income. On the other hand, people who are least likely to be environmentally involved are among the least prosperous Americans.

In the study, the greenest consumers—the True-Blues and the Greenbacks—have a a median household income of almost $32,000, or 40 percent higher than the average household income of an environmentally "indifferent" person. Solid majorities of the most environmentally active Americans have been to college, while majorities of the least active groups have not.

A final demographic predictor is gender: Women are more environmentally active than men. This gender gap is particularly important because women still do most of the household shopping. Their dominance in supermarket aisles and at retail counters might make the positioning and eventual success of certain "green" products easier to achieve.

Although Grousers and Basic Browns make up the majority of US households, that doesn't mean that the environmental market is a myth. Vast majorities of Americans are worried about our environmental future. So far, only a minority have adopted more environmentally responsible lifestyles. But attitudinal changes generally precede behavioral ones.

The first stage—deep public concern about environmental problems—has certainly been reached. So far, voters have been largely unwilling to take the next step and approve sweeping changes. But the important attitudinal shifts of the 1980s should gradually change environmental behavior in the 1990s.

The stage, it seems, is finally set for the "greening of America."

Joe Schwartz is senior editor of American Demographics, *and Thomas Miller is senior vice president of the Roper Organization in New York City.*

Reprinted by permission from American Demographics, *February 1991.*

GREEN LIP SERVICE

According to a recent poll conducted by the Angus Reid Group of Toronto, 44 percent of 2,000 adults sampled are "doers." Most of the rest are "sayers." The poll ranked people in seven categories according to their commitment to the environment.

The seven groups include: Young activists, accounting for 15 percent of the national population, are willing to change their behavior for the environment; Community enthusiasts, 8 percent, actively volunteer, write letters and buy green products; Ambitious optimists, 21 percent, predict a better future and are politically conservative, financially successful and support environmental legislation; Mainstream followers, 21 percent, are "average" Americans who would make some sacrifices for the environment; Disillusioned survivors, 14 percent, are typically poorly educated, retired and fairly uninvolved with environmentalism; Hostile conservatives, 13 percent, are usually well educated, male and Republican, and they resist the green movement; Privileged bystanders, 8 percent, are usually well educated older females, who see environmental problems as serious but are unwilling to change their lifestyles.

A. *Over a thousand tests do not ensure safety*
  Source: Federal Food and Drug Administration

GREEN BUSINESS

The greening of business—from entrenched industry to the development of new businesses dedicated to the environment—has been a fast-growing trend in recent years. Ecopreneurs have creatively manufactured innovative and popular new green products. A lack of regulations has forced industrialists to hash it out among themselves; socially responsible investing has become chic; and consumers have opened a new world of products by demanding greener habits of business.

HOW TO SET UP A RECYCLING PROGRAM AT WORK

Your desk is piled high with paper again, and your waste basket is full. You can't fit one more "While You Were Out" message into it.

It's the same thing every day. You know you could be recycling all that paper, but you're not sure how.

Fortunately, recycling at work is so easy that you and your co-workers can do it without even putting in any overtime.

Focus on office paper

• Offices usually start recycling programs with "white paper"—white stationery, photocopy paper, computer paper, any forms on white paper and white scratch pads. It's clean and has long fibers, so it brings the highest price when it's sold. That makes it worth your company's effort to recycle it, and worth a waste paper dealer's effort to pick it up from you.

• You need to know how much paper your office generates. The rule of thumb is .5 pounds per day for each employee. That's 2.5 pounds a week per person.

Find a waste paper dealer to pick up your paper

• Ask your building manager for help. He or she may already be assisting other offices in your building with recycling programs.

• Check with city hall. Many large cities can

The Greening of Corporate America

- By Joel Makower -

For years, most discussions about business and the environment amounted to a zero-sum game: profits and productivity versus the birds and the trees. Protecting the earth meant reducing a company's ability to do business. Saving resources meant losing jobs. Conserving resources at home meant sending business abroad.

It is only recently that the infrastructure of these assumptions has begun to crack and crumble. As our understanding of the relationships between economics and ecology grows, "doing well" is increasingly being associated with "doing good" for the earth. Conservation is no longer seen as an inhibitor to growth, but as a stimulus for efficiency and profitability. Environmental responsibility is no longer just a corporate feel-good issue, but an obligation—to society, customers, investors, and others.

Not that there isn't a great deal of enlightened self-interest. In fact, the principal thrust to the greening of corporate America is that it makes good bottom-line sense to waste less and make the most of one's resources, whether they are raw materials, energy, supplies, facilities, inventory, capital or people. It doesn't take an MBA to understand that cutting waste, making better use of resources, and reusing, recycling or selling what used to be thrown away, can have a salutary effect on profits and productivity.

Take General Motors. In 1991 its Chevrolet-Pontiac-Canada Group implemented a WE CARE (Waste Elimination and Cost Awareness Rewards Everyone) program. Its ambitious goal: By January 1, 1994, its assembly plants will produce zero waste. The company already has laid down the law for its suppliers, banning polystyrene packaging, shrink-wrapped pallets, and other wasteful practices by suppliers. Company-wide, GM once discarded some 36,000 wooden shipping pallets a day—most after just one use. By switching to pallets made from recycled corrugated cardboard—which themselves can be recycled along with cardboard boxes—the company could save

Q. *Of the almost 3.2 billion pounds of plastic used for packaging in 1988, about what percentage was recycled?*

$100,000 in reduced disposal fees, and make an additional $40,000 by reselling the cardboard—every business day. And in the process, it will save untold mountains of trash a day from landfills.

In this case, what's good for General Motors really may be good for the country. Similar programs are beginning to catch on at a host of other large and small companies.

Which is not to suggest that GM and friends are no longer polluting, not by a long shot. In fact, some of the companies with the most innovative "greening" programs—3M and Dow Chemical, for example—are those that show up regularly on lists of the most polluting corporations. And there are thousands of companies in all sectors that haven't even considered integrating the environment into their operations. Even the most aggressive firms are forsaking quick fixes in favor of gradual, incremental change. Which is probably the kind that will last.

At whatever speed, change is evident and inevitable. The evolution of corporate environmentalism seems to be paralleling that of another hot business buzzword: Quality, specifically the pursuit of Total Quality Management (TQM) inspired by Edward Demming.

Consider the evolution of the quality movement. In the 1970s, companies mostly focused on customer compliance, a reactive stance. Their goal was simply to get done what was required; if there were a few mistakes or defects, that was just an inevitable part of doing business in a fast-growing economy. In the 1980s, the trend shifted to customer satisfaction, a more proactive stance, getting the bugs out and producing defect-free goods and services. In the 1990s, the move is toward customer success, with companies leading their customers toward innovation and increased efficiency and productivity. This is the reality of a fiercely competitive economy, where virtually nothing is certain, even for the most blue-chip of companies.

The trend toward greener businesses reflects this progression, albeit at a much faster pace. Up until relatively recently, most companies focused on environmental compliance, a reactive stance in which companies strove merely to earn a clean bill of health from regulators—or at least avoid government and public wrath for their products and processes. The majority of firms are still in this mode. With the

assist you in setting up a system and in finding someone to take your paper.

• If neither of those approaches works, look in the Yellow Pages under "Waste Paper" or "Recycling."

• Be sure to ask: What materials will they take? How much will they pay for each material (white paper, computer paper, newspaper, etc.)? Will they sign a long-term (i.e. one year) contract? How often will they make pick-ups? Can they supply references?

• Does your company destroy confidential documents? That's important to know because recyclers usually can't accept shredded paper; it doesn't mix well with the rest of the paper.

• Most dealers won't agree to pick up anything less than 500 to 1,000 pounds, so you need to know how much waste paper you plan to recycle before contacting them.

• If you don't generate enough paper, talk to businesses in your building (or nearby) and see if they want to recycle, too. By joining together, you make it worthwhile for a collector to make a pick up.

• If you still can't get a collector, you can always drop off the materials yourself at a recycling center.

Who's responsible?
• Recycling programs need attention to keep running smoothly, so it's a good idea to have a recycling committee—or a Green Team.

A. *2 percent*
Source: The Recycler's Handbook, *by the Earth • Works Group*

- Select one individual to act as a liaison among employees, management, janitorial staff and collectors who pick up your materials.
- Every division or floor (say, every 30 employees) should have a recycling coordinator. These people can answer questions and check to make sure people aren't putting trash in recycling bins.

The set-up
- The aim is simple: You want to direct paper that's been going into a trash can into a recycling container instead.
- Provide a small desktop container to each employee. This can be a simple cardboard box, or a more elaborate container with separate compartments for different kinds of paper.
- When the desktop box is filled: Each employee empties it into a larger central container. This can be a barrel, bin or box.
- Station a bin on each floor, in hallways or near a photocopy machine. (A lot of paper is discarded there.)
- Don't make employees walk more than 50 feet to empty desktop containers. If it takes too much effort, they won't do it.
- Keep it clean. The success of your program will depend on making sure you get only what you want in the recycling bins. If they're contaminated with other material, the paper dealer won't accept it. So make sure the recycling bin doesn't look like a trash

increased awareness of environmental issues spurred by Earth Day 1990, the trend is gradually shifting toward environmental satisfaction, a more proactive stance that involves molding one's corporate image, perhaps even one's policies, to reflect a concern for the planet's future. A very few cutting-edge companies are just beginning to focus on the ultimate goal: environmental success, in which companies affect a positive impact on the environment through significant shifts in management policy and style.

The links between quality and the environment don't end there. In striving for TQM, companies are finding it necessary to restructure their bureaucracies and their decision-making processes. Part of that process involves integrating some functions across departmental lines. In TQM, for example, companies must ensure that communication moves in all directions—up, down, and across, internally and externally. To do so often requires consolidating various duties and departments, all of which report to a Vice President for Quality.

So, too, with environmental quality. As companies address the new environmental paradigm, many are finding it necessary to restructure various parts of their organizations. The products of all this are interdepartmental alliances, new routes of communication, and a revamped decision-making structure—all of which is increasingly being headed by a Vice President for the Environment, or some similar senior executive.

Companies will have to work hard to improve their environmental images before the public. A 1991 survey by Decision Research in Lexington, Massachusetts, found that only 7 percent of Americans believe companies are taking appropriate steps to protect the environment. Fully 58 percent were unable to name a single company they consider "environmentally conscious." Another 1991 survey, by Arthur D. Little, found that Americans rank corporate environmental crimes as more serious than insider trading, antitrust violation, and worker health and safety abuses. Three-fourths of those surveyed said executives should be held personally liable for their companies' environmental offenses.

Part of the public's frustration stems from corporate image advertising and marketing campaigns, in which companies have painted their products—and themselves—with a bright green brush. If consumers

Q: *What percentage of the food on grocery store shelves did not exist ten years ago?*

were to believe the ads, they might be led to believe that some oil companies are in the primary business of saving bald eagles, that fast-food companies are among the world's eco-pioneers, and that using some spray deodorants will help to clean the air.

Such "greenwashing" campaigns, as they have come to be known, have been troublesome for both companies and consumers. The former have had to face the wrath of regulators and environmentalists for misleading claims; the latter have been stymied in their quest for environmentally sound products and companies. One ironic result is that while some companies continue to make small but significant improvements in their products, they are keeping relatively quiet about them, at least compared to the ad blitzes that appeared around Earth Day 1990. Example: Mobil Oil, maker of Hefty trash bags, was forced to remove the "degradable" claims from its products and ads after the Federal Trade Commission and several state Attorneys General objected. But packages of Hefty's newest line of Steel-Sak bags, which by using 30 percent less plastic offer some real environmental improvements, don't make any eco-claims.

One reason Mobil and others have become gunshy has to do with a morass of sometimes conflicting regulations governing companies' environmental claims. Consider what's going on in New York. In Suffolk County, outside New York City, laws state that food establishments cannot sell food unless it is "placed, wrapped, or packed in biodegradable packaging." But New York's state Attorney General is part of a national task force that believes "products that are currently disposed of primarily in landfills or through incineration—whether paper or plastic—should not be promoted as...'biodegradable'..." And the New York City consumer affairs commissioner is publicly taking to task—perhaps even to court—purveyors of so-called degradable products.

And we haven't even covered similarly confusing rules over such phrases as "made of recycled material," or simply "recyclable." Is it any surprise that so many consumers are confused about which kinds of products and packaging are kindest and gentlest to the Earth?

Green marketing is by no means the only arena in which there's a profusion of confusion. Automobile emissions offer another example of patchwork

can. Label the bin. If you want only white paper, make sure it says so clearly.

• When your bins are filled: They're taken to a central storage/pick-up area. Office recycling programs work best when they're integrated with the trash disposal system. So in many offices, maintenance people simply transfer materials in the central bins to a storage area in the basement or at the loading dock.

• Everyone needs to know about the recycling program. Post a memo before you begin. Then invite everyone to a meeting. Show how the system will work. Explain what can and can't be recycled. A handout helps. Note: Let people know if it's a success.

• Other materials. You should be able to find someone to pick up bottles, cans, newspapers or other materials if you have enough of them. Ask your paper collector if any other materials are accepted; if not, ask for a referral to a company that takes them.

The bottom line
• It's good business. Recycling programs can save thousands of dollars. The Boeing Corporation has actually saved millions.
• It saves trees. Since office paper is high quality, it gets used to make new paper...at the same time it saves money and landfill space. At Detroit Edison, all 1,800 office workers have desktop trays for collecting paper. Their program

A. **50 percent**
Source: Silvercat Publications

produces about eight tons of high-grade paper a week, and generates about $24,000 a year.

• It saves resources... and money. Chicago's 2,033-room Hyatt Regency hotel generates 7.2 million pounds of trash each month. To reduce this and its $200,000 annual disposal bill, the hotel started a recycling program in 1989. The equipment cost $25,000. In one month the hotel collects 25,000 pounds of cardboard, 20,000 pounds of glass, and 680 pounds of aluminum cans. The hotel's disposal bill dropped from $12,000 a month to $2,000.

For more information:
• *Your Office Paper Recycling Guide*, San Francisco Recycling Program, Room 271 City Hall, San Francisco, CA 94102. A wonderful booklet; $5. Make checks out to City and County of San Francisco.
• *Your Practical Guide to the Environmentally Responsible Office*. The Service Marketing Group, 8 S. Michigan Ave., Suite 2500, Chicago, IL 60603, (312) 332-0688. $7.95. Recycling guide.

Reprinted by permission from 50 Simple Things Your Business Can Do To Save The Earth, published by Earth•Works Press, Berkeley, CA, 1991.

lawmaking. Colorado, Texas and more than a dozen other states have enacted or are considering tough clean-air laws, like California's. That will leave car makers confronting a similar legal mish-mash.

At the bottom line, the world of green business seems to be in flux, to say the least. And it will take some time to sort things out. Will there be national standards that give companies—and consumers—a level playing field with which to make good, green choices? Will innovations by greener companies create sufficient reason to preempt some regulations altogether? Will companies truly opt for Total Environmental Quality? Will consumers continue to pressure companies to do so?

Stay tuned. There's a lot more to come.

Joel Makower is editor of The Green Business Letter *and* The Green Consumer Letter, *and author of more than a dozen books on business, consumer and environmental topics. For newsletter subscription information call 800-955-GREEN.*

HOW TO START A GREEN BUSINESS

THERE IS NO SUCH THING as a perfectly green company. Being in business is an inherently polluting activity, even for companies in "clean" industries.

True, not every organization is burdened with having to dispose of toxin-laden waste water, or with discharging black smoke into the sky. But everyone in every business does at least two things: consumes energy and other resources and creates wastes that must be disposed of. How your company does these two things can make a difference between being perceived as "green" or "ungreen." Increasingly, it can also make the difference between profitability and lack thereof.

Businesses are facing some of the same challenges—and confusion—consumers face in trying to "go green." The challenge is to be more environmentally responsible on a day-to-day basis, to reduce one's negative impact on the Earth as much as is practical.

The confusion begins with the overwhelming amount of seemingly conflicting information out there about the real problems and their would-be solutions. Added to that are issues of time and money: There never seems to be enough of either, never mind having to allocate additional resources to deal with environmental issues. And then there is the sheer scope of the

Q: *How much does it cost to build a mile of urban highway?*

subject matter: There are so many serious problems, it seems; how can one company make a difference?

Add to this mix the myriad of daily pressures faced by most businesses—from bosses, employees, customers, suppliers, stockholders, regulators, banks and all the rest—and it's easy to see how "saving the Earth" can take a back seat to simply saving the day.

The inevitable result: Organizational paralysis, at least as far as the environment is concerned.

This needn't be the case, not by a long shot. The fact is, making a few moves in the name of the environment can be as good for your bottom line as it is for the Earth's.

Let's take a look at what "going green" really means. At its essence, it boils down to two fundamental goals: reducing waste and maximizing resource use, whether those resources are your own (raw materials, supplies, facilities, inventory, capital, people), or everyone's (water, air, plants, animals, land). When you do these two things, whether you are running a business, heading a government agency, or shopping for groceries, you can't help but get a better return on your investment over the long run.

Becoming a greener company, then, is just good business sense. The rewards for your efforts can be considerable. Your company's investment in the environment can yield dividends far beyond the good it does for the Earth. Its actions can also send a loud and clear message to employees, customers, suppliers, competitors and the communities in which it does business. That makes your company, and everyone in it, a key player in our planet's future.

Reprinted by permission from The Green Business Letter, *by Joel Makower, June 1991, published by Tilden Press, Washington, DC.*

ECOPRENEURING

ECOPRENEURS, OR ENVIRONMENTAL ENTREPRENEURS, may be one of the best bets for restoring the air, water and earth on which all life depends. Of course, no single person or group of people can completely undo the damage that we've wrought on the planet since the Industrial Revolution. That will take a concerted and massive effort by legislators, heads of large corporations and government agencies. Nevertheless, the ecopreneur can lead the charge into a greener future while at the same time building a profitable enterprise.

WHAT SOME AMERICAN COMPANIES ARE DOING TO SAVE THE EARTH

Saving energy
• The management of the Pan-Am Building in New York installed solar film on all the building's windows, resulting in energy savings of $9,000 a month.

Saving water
• Polaroid Corporation devised a way to reuse wastewater, cutting water usage by 80 percent and saving at least $30,000 a year.

Recycling
• United Airlines recycles a ton of aluminum cans and eight tons of cardboard a week at O'Hare International Airport in Chicago. The scrap earns $28,800 a year and saves over $1,000 more in trash hauling fees.

Reducing air pollution
• Coca Cola's company fleet in Atlanta, Georgia, now uses natural gas, cutting emissions by 40 percent.

Minimizing toxics
• By switching to "greener cleaners," the Sheraton Grande Hotel in Los Angeles eliminated hazardous acid-based cleaners for their floors.

Reducing solid waste
• By developing a water-based ink to replace solvent-based ones used in

A. **$100 million**
  Source: Peace Resource Project

its wrapping papers, Cleo Wrap saves $35,000 a year in waste disposal costs.

Saving the ozone
• In 1991, General Motors began requiring its 10,000 dealers to recycle CFCs from car air conditioners. A dealer who services 35 air conditioners per week can recoup the cost of the recycling equipment in as little as 23 weeks by not having to buy new coolant.

Protecting wildlife
• Amoco Chemical Company's Cooper River Plant in South Carolina has planned a wildlife enhancement program on 6,000 acres of land adjacent to a national park. The preserve will provide habitats from several thousand species.

Conserving resources
• The Boeing Company has a surplus store from which nonprofit organizations can select items they need. In one case, Adopt-A-Stream selected $3,600 worth of surplus desks, chairs, computer stands and filing cabinets to set up an office.

The Ten Commandments of Ecopreneuring: How to Manage an Ecobusiness

1. Clarify your mission
Many entrepreneurs assume that they know exactly what their business does, when in fact they haven't formulated a clear mission. The mission statement of any company sets forth the core principle around which the entire enterprise revolves. It communicates a strong message to your customers, your employees and suppliers, and your competition. In a sense, a good mission statement serves as a flag around which all your "stakeholders" (everyone connected with your business) can rally.

2, Plan, plan, plan
Many people assume that entrepreneurship means flying by the seat of your pants on your creative instincts. As an ecopreneur, your enterprise must certainly spring from your creativity, but unfortunately, that's not enough. Boring as it may seem, the successful ecobusiness depends on meticulous planning. The more time you spend thinking of every detail affecting your business, from the price of gasoline to pending legislation, the better you'll be prepared to withstand the fickle winds of the marketplace.

3. Be ultrarealistic
The ability to cope with reality makes or breaks the ecopreneur. You should practice the art of multiplying and dividing expectations on the basis of your best- and worst-case scenarios. Doing so will help keep you in touch with reality.

4. Think total customer satisfaction
A business needs only one thing: happy customers. Strangely, many business people treat customers as the enemy, where time-honored slogans such as "The customer is number one," and "The customer is always right," mask hostile feelings about "those people who make our lives miserable with their demands and complaints."

5. Think total quality
This rule ties in closely with the preceding one— you'll never create total customer satisfaction unless

Q: *How much does it cost to build a mile of light rail mass transit?*

you deliver total quality. While quality can be as hard to define as "truth" or "beauty," it does not lie solely in the eye of the beholder. On one level, quality is simply the absence of flaws.

6. Study the competition

For some ecopreneurs, "competition" is a four-letter word. They assume no one could possibly vilify or attack them because, after all, protecting the environment is too important to permit cut-throat and calculating competition. Others believe that there's simply room for everybody to succeed. Actually, competition exists for every business, and it's healthy that it does. Competition forces businesses to be all they can be. As more and more eco-businesses begin dotting the landscape, only those with a competitive advantage will survive the inevitable shakeout.

7. Develop company strengths

Amazingly, many entrepreneurs do not fully comprehend or develop their personal and company strengths, usually because small business people are so busy doing what they do that they don't make time to step back and review their performance. They also tend to spend so much time putting out fires that they become preoccupied with fixing weaknesses rather than honing skills. Those who pay more attention to weaknesses than strengths usually lose their strength, while those who focus on strengths keep getting stronger.

8. Emphasize positive cash flow

You can boil business down to one very simple equation: Make more profit by spending less and selling more. That's what creates positive cash flow.

9. Manage your growth

You want to grow and grow and grow, right? Not necessarily. Ecopreneurs should carefully manage growth for two reasons. First, as a business develops in size, it expands exponentially in complexity. And the bigger the business, the harder it becomes to maintain your clear mission. No matter how steadfastly you inculcate your mission in your employees, customers and competitors, as your systems grow, they tend to take on a life of their own. And you

WHAT ECO-PRENEURS DO

Some ecopreneurs turn other people's trash into gold by starting companies that:

• Haul recyclable materials to manufacturers who can convert them into new products.

• Sell finished products made from recycled materials to individual consumers and business.

• Turn used motor oil that might formerly have been dumped on dirt roads into high-quality lubricant.

• Convert plastic milk containers into plastic "lumber" that never rots or needs maintenance.

• Use old newspapers to make inexpensive and bacteria resistant bedding for farm animals.

Other ecopreneurs take old proven ideas and give them a "green" twist by creating and/or selling:

• Foods free of pesticides and synthetic chemicals, and packaged in recyclable or biodegradable materials.

• Cleansers, polishes and other household items that contain no petroleum products or harmful chemicals.

• Paints, stains, glues, adhesives and other workshop items free of environmental and health hazards such as mercury or benzene.

A. *$15 million*
Source: Peace Resource Project

• Yard and garden supplies that do not contain organophosphates and other chemicals largely responsible for water pollution.

• Energy-efficient light bulbs, water-conserving toilets, and other simple household products.

Still others give old services a green spin:

• They package tours to environmentally sensitive areas to teach tourists the importance of ecology.

• They help companies assess their workplaces from the standpoint of environmental fitness.

• They offer carpet-cleaning and other services that use non-toxic chemicals.

• They sell advice on environmentally sound investments.

• They create games, books, and software packages designed to educate while entertaining.

Reprinted by permission from Ecopreneuring: The Complete Guide to Small Business Opportunities from the Environmental Revolution, by Steven J. Bennett, John Wiley & Sons, New York, 1991.

can't simply inject your values into a sprawling system. Suddenly, the quality of the products and services you offer suffers. People begin spending less time serving customers because they get so caught up in maintaining the system or complying with its bureaucratic needs.

10. Recession-proof your operation
During economic downturns, entrepreneurial businesses can flourish because they're more flexible than large, established companies. Whereas large companies typically react to negative changes in the economy by downsizing (a euphemism for massive layoffs), small entrepreneurial companies can react by finding new niches or by "right-sizing"—readjusting the work to match the existing work force.

Reprinted by permission from Ecopreneuring: The Complete Guide to Small Business Opportunities from the Environmental Revolution, *by Steven J. Bennett, John Wiley & Sons, New York, 1991*

CODE FOR ENVIRONMENTAL BUSINESS ETHICS
AFTER THE *EXXON VALDEZ* poured 11 million gallons of crude oil into Alaskan waters in March 1989, the Coalition for Environmentally Responsible Economies (CERES) dubbed their already planned code of environmental business ethics The Valdez Principles.

The principles are designed to "create a voluntary mechanism of corporate self-governance that will maintain business practices consistent with the goals of sustaining our fragile environment for future generations, within a culture that respects all life and honors its independence."

The CERES coalition began as a project of the Social Investment Forum, a Boston-based trade association for brokers, analysts, bankers and other social investors. Creation of the Valdez Principles was inspired by the Sullivan Principles, a code governing corporate conduct in South Africa. The purpose of the principles is to get companies to endorse the principles, to evaluate how well companies comply with the code's requirements, and to disseminate ratings to the public and encourage investors, consumers and others to act accordingly.

Q: *How much more water do Americans use during summer?*

The Valdez Principles

1. Protection of the biosphere

We will minimize and strive to eliminate the release of any pollutant that may cause environmental damage to the air, water, or earth or its inhabitants. We will safeguard habitats in rivers, lakes, wetlands, coastal zones and oceans and will minimize contributing to the greenhouse effect, depletion of the ozone layer, acid rain or smog.

2. Sustainable use of natural resources

We will make sustainable use of renewable natural resources, such as water, soils and forests. We will conserve nonrenewable natural resources through efficient use and careful planning. We will protect wildlife habitat, open spaces and wilderness, while preserving biodiversity.

3. Reduction and disposal of waste

We will minimize the creation of waste, especially hazardous waste, and wherever possible recycle materials. We will dispose of all wastes through safe and responsible methods.

4. Wise use of energy

We will make every effort to use environmentally safe and sustainable energy sources to meet our needs. We will invest in improved energy efficiency and conservation in our operations. We will maximize the energy efficiency of products we produce or sell.

5. Risk reduction

We will minimize the environmental, health and safety risks to our employees and the communities in which we operate by employing safe technologies and operating procedures and by being constantly prepared for emergencies.

6. Marketing of safe products and services

We will sell products or services that minimize adverse environmental impacts and that are safe as consumers commonly use them. We will inform consumers of the environmental impacts of our products or services.

VALDEZ PRINCIPLE COMPANIES

Twenty-seven leading-edge companies have endorsed the Valdez Principles as of August 1991:

Ally Capital Corp., Sausalito, CA
Atlantic Recycled Paper Co., Baltimore, MD
Aveda Corp., Minneapolis, MN
The Beamery, Inc., Heiskell, TN
Bellcomb Technologies, Inc., Minneapolis, MN
Calvert Social Investment Fund, Bethesda, MD
Clivus Multrum, Inc., Lawrence, MA
CO-OP America, Washington, DC
Crib Diaper Service, Crystal, MN
Domino's Pizza Distribution Corp., Ann Arbor, MI
Earth Care Paper Company, Inc., Madison, WI
Ecoprint, Silver Spring, MD
First Affirmative Financial Network, Colorado Springs, CO
Franklin Research and Development Corp., Boston, MA
Global Environmental Technologies, Philadelphia, PA
Harwood Lumber, Branscomb, CA
Intrigue Salon, Marietta, GA
LecTec Corp., Minnetonka, MN
Metropolitan Sewer District, Louisville, KY
Progressive Asset Management, Oakland, CA

A. *One-third more*
  Source: 50 Simple Things You Can Do To Save The Earth, *by the Earth • Works Group*

Service Litho-Print, Oshkosh, WI
Smith & Hawken, Mill Valley, CA
Stonyfield Farm Yogurt, Londonderry, NH
Sullivan & Worcester, Boston, New York, Washington
VanCity Investment Service Ltd., Vancouver, BC, Canada
Walnut Acres, Penns Creek, PA
Working Assets Funding Service, San Francisco, CA

CERES' efforts to persuade companies to endorse the Valdez Principles have led to dialogue with more than 500 companies. At least six Fortune 100 companies are close to signing. For more information contact CERES (Coalition for Environmentally Responsible Economies), 711 Atlantic Ave., Boston, MA 02111, (617) 451-0927, fax (617) 482-2028.

GREEN SPEAKERS

Environmental Speakers International (ESI) is a full service speaker's bureau that specializes in environmental topics. ESI represents high quality, professional speakers and trainers who are experts on environmental issues as they relate to business. Topics focus on issues that go beyond compliance such as product design, packaging, marketing, energy efficiency and changing corporate culture. Contact Jeanine Anderson at ESI, 8015 Holland Court, Suite C, Arvada, CO 80005, (303) 431-2468.

7. Damage compensation

We will take responsibility for any harm we cause to the environment by making every effort to fully restore the environment and to compensate those persons who are adversely affected.

8. Disclosure

We will disclose to our employees and to the public incidents relating to our operations that cause environmental harm or pose health or safety hazards. We will disclose potential environmental, health or safety hazards posed by our operations, and we will not take any action against employees who report any condition that creates a danger to the environment or poses health and safety hazards.

9. Environmental directors and managers

At least one member of the Board of Directors will be a person qualified to represent environmental interests. We will commit management resources to implement these Principles, including the funding of an office of Vice President for Environmental Affairs or an equivalent executive position, reporting directly to the CEO, to monitor and report upon our implementation efforts.

10. Assessment and annual audit

We will conduct and make public an annual self-evaluation of our progress in implementing these Principles and in complying with all applicable laws and regulations throughout our worldwide operations. We will work toward the timely creation of independent environmental audit procedures which we will complete annually and make available to the public.

Q: *Some papermills on the West Coast are starting to recycle what item, mixing it with newsprint during the manufacturing process?*

What Is Social Investing?

Socially responsible investing is the integration of both financial and social criteria when making investment decisions. The field might be broken into four parts:

1. Shareholder activism—using stock ownership as a lever to encourage corporations to behave in socially responsible ways.

2. Guideline portfolio investing—managing stock and bond portfolios within social constraints (using "negative screens" to eliminate companies active in nuclear power, for example, or "positive screens" to include companies with proactive policies like employee ownership).

3. Community development investing—meeting the needs of low-income communities through investments in intermediaries such as community loan funds, micro-business funds or housing funds.

4. Social venture capital—investing high-risk capital in young entrepreneurial companies that promise social benefit as well as financial return.

The socially responsible investing strategy asserts that investing is not value-neutral, and that there are significant ethical and social consequences in how we invest our money. It is a commitment, if you will, to achieving social good through investment.

Getting started

There is no "right" way to do social investing, just as there is no right way to make any investment decision. You can invest your entire portfolio using social criteria, or just a small piece of it. And just as you choose the financial criteria you deem important (steady income, for example, or high return), you can choose any social requirements you like, such as avoiding cigarette and alcohol companies, promoting local business development, or supporting environmental companies.

For some investors, a first step might be asking your financial advisor—whether or not he or she specializes in social investing—to put part of your money into a socially screened mutual fund. You might also choose to reserve a segment of your portfolio for a community development loan fund, or a low-income housing fund.

SOCIALLY RESPONSIBLE INVESTING GUIDELINES

Generally, exclude or avoid firms that:
• Have operations or are tied to South Africa
• Derive revenues from tobacco, alcohol or gambling
• Derive revenues from the sale of military weapons
• Own or operate nuclear power plants

Generally, favor firms that:
• Make a product or provide a service that is "responsible"
• Have good employee relations, strong equal opportunity employment programs and good employee benefits
• Take positive steps in environmental concerns or at least do not have bad environmental records
• Are in some way responsive to the communities in which they operate (through philanthropic activities, for example)
• Are owned or managed by women or minorities

SOCIAL INVESTMENT FUNDS

Calvert Social Investment Fund
4550 Montgomery Ave. Suite 1000 North Bethesda, MD 20814 (800) 368-2748; (301) 951-4800 in Maryland.

Calvert group offers the nation's first and largest family of socially and environmentally responsive mutual funds, including Calvert-Ariel Appreciation Fund, Calvert-Ariel Growth Fund and Calvert Social Investment Fund, made up of many market, bond, equity and managed growth "balanced" portfolios.

Domini Social Index Trust
6 St. James Ave.
Boston, MA 02116
(800) 762-6814

A passively managed fund that invests in an index of 400 companies that have passed broad social screens. It focuses on firms with positive records in providing useful products, employee relations, community activities and the environment. It excludes firms deriving revenue from weapons sales, tobacco, alcohol, gambling or nuclear power. The fund is new, with $2.5 million in assets; it is not currently in most newspaper listings.

Dreyfus Funds
200 Park Ave.
New York, NY 10166
(800) 782-6620, (800) 645-6561, (516) 296-6958 in New York.

A growth and income fund that invests in the stocks of companies with positive records in the areas of consumer protection, occupational safety and health, and environmental issues.

Freedom Environmental Fund
Freedom Capital Management
1 Beacon St.
Boston, MA 02108
(617) 725-2215.

This fund's prospectus states that it "will

Other options include purchasing certificates of deposit in a bank that supports its local community, or urging your company's board of directors to divest pension fund holdings in South African-related companies. You can start small and test the waters, or put your whole portfolio under management with social criteria.

Social investors' portfolios frequently hold stocks, bonds, money market accounts, and alternative investments. Some hold art, real estate, limited partnerships, venture capital or other less-traditional investments. As with any investment, it's up to you.

What does ethics have to do with investing?

Some advocate following the example of Alfred Nobel, who made millions on munitions and then was munificent to the masses. In this view, the professional investor cannot be sentimental. He or she should look only at financial results when making investment decisions.

This argument is naive. Most market participants use qualitative information when making investment decisions. It is interesting to note that the five companies with the highest scores on Fortune's Most Admired List in 1991—Merck, Rubbermaid, Procter & Gamble, Wal-Mart, and PepsiCo—are all included among the Domini Social Index stocks, which are screened for social criteria.

Warren Buffett, one of the most successful and respected American investors, says he routinely applies non-financial standards to his investments, particularly to his long-term holdings. "We do not wish to ally with managers who lack admirable qualities, no matter how attractive the prospects of their business," he says. "We have never succeeded in making a good deal with a bad person."

Doesn't narrowing the investment universe limit returns?

This is the oldest and most consistently used argument against socially responsible investing—the notion that if you narrow your investment universe, you will limit your return. In reality, anomalies in markets allow investors to achieve superior results by focusing on certain types of stocks at certain times. One of the most important anomalies is the size effect, which has been a subject of intense academic discussion for many years.

This issue is an important one for socially responsible investors, because they all accept some size risks;

Q. *How many garbage bags does the US Army estimate it will take per month to clean up war-devastated Kuwait?*

socially screened universes usually include a higher percentage of small capitalization stocks, which tend to be more volatile. The largest capitalization stocks, on the other hand, are more likely to be screened out by social criteria. (Large capitalization stocks are generally the Fortune 500, whereas small capitalization stocks are usually smaller and younger companies.)

While some studies show that over the long term—30 to 50 years—smaller companies have outperformed larger ones, commentators disagree on whether this offsets the transaction costs and higher risk associated with smaller stocks. Some argue that, all factors considered, smaller stocks have actually under-performed larger issues in the past 30 years.

But social investors can reduce their risk through substitution (replacing nuclear power companies with those in natural gas, for example). Short of applying less-stringent screens, however, they cannot reduce size risk. There is only one Exxon.

The practical effects of size risk in social portfolios have yet to be established. For example, WM Company, a consulting company in the United Kingdom, hires managers for portfolios of 126 charities with an aggregate market value of 3.7 billion pounds. Approximately 20 percent of these portfolios have social constraints. In its 1989 Annual Report, WM assessed its experience with ethical investing:

"Ethical constraints in their own right seem to have little impact on the performance of the constrained universe other than through the small company/large company effect. The performance of actual funds indicates that other factors, such as stock selection, can more than offset these constraints.

"At an extreme level of constraint, where a significant number of large companies are excluded, a very large fund may find difficulties with liquidity, but in practice this is unlikely to arise."

Critics of social investing also have argued that by limiting the investment universe, you reduce the opportunities for stock bargains. However, the main bias of social screens is against the largest companies. The largest capitalization companies are, under most market conditions, the most efficiently priced securities and, therefore, offer the fewest targets for bargain hunters. Most social screens eliminate a much lower percentage of smaller stocks—the universe where the most effective stockpickers tend to operate.

invest primarily in companies which the fund advisor believes contribute to a cleaner and healthier environment... the fund may invest in common stocks of companies that are engaged in the research, development, manufacture or distribution of products or services related to pollution control, waste management or pollution/waste remediation." Started August 1989.

Global Environment Fund
L.P., 1250 24th St., NW, Suite 300
Washington, DC 20037
(202) 466-0529

The partnership's primary objective is to realize long-term capital appreciation through investments that promote environmental improvement.

Kemper Environmental Services Fund
811 Main St.
Kansas City, MO 64105-2005
(800) 621-5027

This fund states in its prospectus that it "will invest at least 65 percent of its total assets in the equity securities of issuers engaged in environmentally related activities." Started March 1990.

New Alternatives Fund
295 Northern Blvd.
Great Neck, NY 11021
(516) 466-0808

"Invests in common stocks of companies in the solar and alternative energy industries.... Excluded are petroleum and atomic based energy sources and the processes utilized in connection with such

A. *1.5 million*
Source: US Army, Riyadh, Saudi Arabia

sources.... Nevertheless the Fund may invest in petroleum companies which are actively developing or producing such items as photovoltaic conversion of the sun's rays directly to electricity or producing other products related to the Fund."

Oppenheimer Global Environmental Fund
Individual investors.
P.O. Box 300
Denver, CO 80201-0300
(800) 525-7048

This fund invests "principally in companies offering products, services or processes which contribute to a cleaner and healthier environment...and will normally invest at least 65 percent of its total assets in common stocks of Environmental Companies located in the US and in at least three foreign countries." Started March 1990.

Parnassus Fund
244 California St.
San Francisco, CA
94111
(800) 999-3505; (415) 362-3505 in California

"The fund screens out...firms that generate electricity from nuclear power...and looks for companies with a good environmental protection policy."

Pax World Fund
224 State St.
Portsmouth, NH 03801
(800) 767-1729;
(603) 431-8022 in New Hampshire.

A balanced fund that invests in life-supportive goods and services such as healthcare, education, pollution control and renewable energy. It

Environmental mutual funds outperform the market

Competition among environmental mutual funds points out the holes in the argument that socially screened investments underperform others. In 1990, 11 new environmental funds faced off, eight of which did not eliminate major polluters from their portfolios. The three that defined themselves as being pro-environmental—excluding major polluters and investing in companies that are actually helping the environment—outperformed the other eight after the first year's results were tallied.

Indeed, they also outperformed all the major indices for the year: the Standard & Poor's 500, the Dow Jones Industrial Average and, perhaps most importantly, the Environmental Composite Index of environmental stocks.

The conclusion to be drawn is not that pro-environmental investing will always outperform investments that use no criteria of environmental responsibility. The 1990 comparisons are not scientific, and it is difficult to measure the role of chance and the role of temporary factors, such as the impact of the relatively small amounts of assets included in the pro-environmental funds. The victory does, however, disprove the notion that social funds underperform because they involve an opportunity cost inherent in a reduced investment universe.

Reprinted by permission from Business Ethics, *September/October 1991, reprinted from* The Social Investment Almanac 1992, *by Peter D. Kinder, Steven D. Lydenberg and Amy L. Domini, Henry Holt & Co, New York, 1991.*

Green Consumerism

- By Joel Makower -

Sometime around Earth Day 1990, a new realization seemed to strike the collective consciousness of the marketplace like a bolt from the polluted blue: There was a lot of money to be made catering to consumers' growing concern about the fate of the earth. This in itself was no revolutionary development. Manufacturers and retailers had long ago proven them-

 Q: *What type of disposable cups are completely non-biodegradable?*

selves ready, willing and able to jump on whatever societal bandwagon happened to be mobile at any given moment.

But this rush to greenness was different. For one thing, advertising and product label claims transcended traditional feel-good themes—looking good, feeling healthy, being popular, enjoying convenience and generally embracing life (and the sponsor and its product). This time, the ads and labels made a considerably more profound promise: Buy our product and you'll help save the Earth.

Who could blame these product purveyors for their ardor? When queried by market researchers, nearly nine out of ten Americans proudly professed their willingness to buy "biodegradable" trash bags and diapers, "ozone-friendly" deodorants, "recyclable" cereal boxes, "natural" cleaners, "recycled" toilet paper and a host of other products claiming to be kinder and gentler to the planet. When pressed further, many of these folks said they'd even be willing to pay extra for the privilege of doing so.

And so the parade of products began, neither a trickle nor a torrent, but a steady stream: air fresheners, batteries, coffee filters, detergents, eco-toys, furniture, games, hair products, insect repellents, juices and on down through the alphabet. Only one thing was missing: The truth.

Like so many other serious problems faced by our world, the problem of green shopping has turned out to be far more complex than anyone expected. First and foremost, there are no perfectly "green" products; everything is relative and there are few absolutes. There are green products packaged in ungreen ways. Ungreen products wrapped in green ways. Green products from ungreen companies. And green companies making ungreen products.

What's worse, trying to sort out what's what is akin to trying to throw a rock at a moving target. A couple of years ago, for example, "degradable" plastic trash bags seemed to be a reasonably green product—at least when compared with traditional "nondegradable" bags. As it turned out, the bags only degrade under laboratory conditions, not in the dark, airless conditions of landfills. Further, it seemed at least some of the makers of such bags knew this all along, but held to the claims anyway in the hopes of capitalizing on the growing environmental interest. The press, the

excludes firms that are engaged in or that contribute to military activities, as well as firms in the liquor, gambling or tobacco industries.

Prentiss Smith & Co. Inc., Portfolio Managment
103A Main St.
Brattleboro, VT 05301
(800) 223-7851
in Vermont: (802) 254-2913

Portfolio management firm that specializes in socially and environmentally responsible investing. The firm manages investment portfolios starting at $200,000 for individuals and institutions (including endowments, trusts and pension funds). Advises on community investments and charitable giving.

Working Assets Money Fund
230 California St., Suite 500
San Francisco, CA 94111
(800) 533-3863
(415) 989-3200 in California.

"We do not knowingly invest in companies that generate nuclear power or manufacture nuclear equipment or materials. We do not knowingly invest in corporations that consistently violate regulations of the Environmental Protection Agency or the Occupational Safety and Health Administrations."

A. *Polystyrene foam cups*
  Source: The Recycler's Handbook, *by the Earth•Works Group*

INVESTMENT RESOURCES

Social Investment Forum
430 First Ave. N, Suite 290
Minneapolis, MN 55401
(612) 333-8338.

Newsletter available.

Council on Economic Priorities
30 Irving Pl.
New York, NY 10003
(212) 420-1133

Conducts research on issues of corporate responsibility and economic concern.

Franklin Research and Development
711 Atlantic Ave., Fifth Floor
Boston, MA 02111
(617) 423-6655

Monthly newsletter available.

Investor Responsibility Center
1755 Massachusetts Ave. NW, Suite 600
Washington, DC 20036
(202) 234-7500

Monthly publication available.

Kinder, Lydenberg, Domini & Co., Inc.
7 Dana St.
Cambridge, MA 02138
(617) 547-7479

Developed the Domini Social Index for rating companies.

PUBLICATIONS

The Better World Investment Guide, by the Council on Economic Priorities, Prentice Hall Press, Old Tappan, NJ, 1991

regulators and the environmental community had a field day.

Trash bags haven't been the only case of "greenwashing." Not by a long shot. Aerosols claiming to be "ozone friendly" or "safe for the environment" have come under similar criticism, as have vague claims about a product's recyclability or recycled content. All of which has caught the attention of state Attorneys General, the federal government, and dozens of city and county legislators. The result has been a confusing patchwork of laws—some misguided at best—that seems to satisfy neither manufacturers, retailers, consumers, environmentalists or regulators. Will Uncle Sam step in and set uniform guidelines that will set a single uniform standard for eco-claims? Perhaps, although even they likely will be subject to endless controversy and debate.

Not that it's been all hype. The green consumer trend has inspired hundreds of companies to examine their products through a green lens, variously reformulating, repackaging, or simply repositioning them to accommodate the new green consciousness. Of course, there's more than a tad of enlightened self-interest involved. For example, when the makers of L'Eggs pantyhose announced plans to eliminate the hard-plastic egg-shaped packaging that had been its trademark for years, it hitched onto the eco-bandwagon in making its announcement, glossing over the fact that the new package would permit the company to shoehorn 25 percent more product onto the same shelf space. Still, the eggless version will cut out a lot of trash.

But do such actions really make a difference? Can L'Eggs new package really "save the Earth"? Of course not. For starters, there's some new evidence that the manufacture of nylon is significantly increasing emissions of nitrous oxide—both a greenhouse gas and ozone depleter—into the atmosphere. That fact didn't seem to make it into L'Eggs' environmental claims.

And then there's the whole paradox of green consumerism itself: Can we really shop our way to environmental health? Shopping, say some, is the principal problem; we simply should be buying less. Indeed, after the mindless marathon shopping of the 1980s, one can't help but wonder, "How much is enough?" Despite the phenomenal growth in income and consumption, public opinion polls consistently show that Americans are no more satisfied with their lives now than in the 1940s.

Q: *How many car manufacturers have built and tested autos that get more than 67 miles per gallon? And how many are currently on the market?*

Still, there's no question that the green consumer movement is having an impact. It took a relatively small segment of the consuming public to pressure McDonald's and the tuna industry to dramatically change their environmental ways. And some observers suggest that this sense of citizen empowerment evident in green shopping will grow, and perhaps even rekindle an era of citizen involvement.

After all, one's political vote doesn't seem worth much these days, at least compared with the considerable clout wielded by special business interests. Perhaps the small victories won in the green marketplace will inspire Americans with a sense that they can still influence change—in the check-out line, if not the voting booth.

Joel Makower is editor of The Green Consumer Letter *and* The Green Business Letter*, and author of more than a dozen books on business, consumer and environmental topics. For newsletter subscription information, call 800-955-GREEN.*

THE TROUBLE WITH GREEN PRODUCTS

- By Carl Frankel -

IF ANYONE COULD DO IT, you'd think it would be Mo Siegel. As a 21-year-old, Siegel founded Celestial Seasonings Teas, built it into a $30 million business, and sold it to Kraft General Foods in 1984, becoming an eight-figure millionaire in the process. After several years in the nonprofit world, the entrepreneurial itch struck Siegel again and he founded Earth Wise, Inc. As with Celestial Seasonings, he had a green objective—to make "deep-green" household cleaning and other products a legitimate alternative to traditional products in mainstream distribution channels.

It's been a struggle. In the year since its launch, Earth Wise has performed disappointingly; 1991 revenue projections, once in the $5 million range, have been sliced in half. A key problem, according to Siegel: "We've been having trouble getting our product into stores."

Siegel is not alone. The great majority of small, independent suppliers of "deep-green" products are having just as hard a time getting their products onto mass retailers' shelves. Their difficulties are reflected by share-of-market figures, which are miniscule. Only

The Environmental Factor, by Michael Silverstein, Dearborn Financial Publishing, Chicago, 1990

Ethical Investing: How to Make Profitable Investments Without Sacrificing Your Principles, by Amy L. Domini and Peter D. Kinder, Addison-Wesley Publishing Co., Reading, MA, 1986

Socially Responsible Investing: How to Invest with Your Conscience, by Alan J. Miller, New York Institute of Finance, New York, 1991

The Clean Yield, Box 1880, Greensboro Bend, VT 05842, (802) 533-7178.

Franklin's Insight: The Advisory Letter for Concerned Investors, 711 Atlantic Ave., Fourth Floor, Boston, MA 02111, (617) 423-6655.

Good money, P.O. Box 363, Calais Stage Rd., Worcester, VT 05682, (800) 535-3551.

Catalyst: Investing in Social Change, quarterly newsletter published by Catalyst Press, P.O. Box 364, Worcester, VT 05682, (802) 223-7943.

A. *7, 0 respectively*
Source: *International Institute for Energy Conservation*

HOW TO BE A GREEN CONSUMER

- Avoid needless shopping. Buy only what you need. This is the "greenest" thing you can do.

- Avoid vague environmental claims, such as "safe for the environment," which have no legal definitions. Whenever possible, seek out independent verification from accredited labeling programs such as Green Cross and Green Seal.

- Don't count on things to biodegrade in landfills or in the water supply. Few products truly do degrade; some break down so slowly they can still cause problems.

- Seek out products in minimal packaging. Avoid packages made from several layers of different materials, such as those used in squeezable ketchup containers or aseptic "juice boxes."

- Try to find packages that you can easily recycle in your community. And, of course, make sure they are recycled.

- Look for products in reusable containers, or for which concentrated refills are available.

- Don't confuse "green" with "healthy." Not everything packaged responsibly is necessarily good for you or the environment.

- Remember that there are few simple solutions or perfectly green products. There are almost always trade-offs.

- Whenever possible, try to look beyond products to the companies that

about 2 percent of sales of paper bath tissues and paper towels are of the "deep-green" variety—and they are a relative success story. For most "deep-green" product categories, the figure comes in at under 1 percent.

But this tells only one side of the story. The green products marketplace has two faces. There are "deep-green" products, and then there are "greened-up" products.

"Deep-green" offerings come from small suppliers and build their identities around their claimed environmental virtues—hence deep-green brand names like Earth Wise. These products by and large are having a hard time making their way onto retailers' shelves.

"Greened-up" products come from the industry giants, and are environmentally improved versions of established brands. They base their product identities on non-environmental attributes (but make green claims)—and are doing quite well, thank you.

The recent emergence of concentrates provides an excellent example of where the green success stories tend to be these days. Concentrates reduce the amount of product that is required to achieve a desired result—and as product requirements diminish, so does the need for packaging.

Procter & Gamble took its Downy fabric softener, re-formulated it as a concentrate, and offered it in a refillable carton, thereby reducing packaging by 75 percent. In national distribution for less than a year, the new Downy Refill now accounts for 40 percent of all Downy sales. "First, we're committed to source reduction," said Zeke Swift, Procter & Gamble manager of environmental marketing, "and second, we thought it was worth trying to reapply our European learning, to see if US consumers were willing to give up something of convenience for this environmental benefit. The answer, in fact, has been a resounding yes."

"Ultra" detergents provide another greened-up product success story. Although these super-concentrates, which carry names like "Tide Ultra" and "Cheer Ultra" and have been introduced by many of the leading consumer goods companies over the past year, are not primarily being marketed as green products, they do reduce packaging substantially, and they are rapidly attaining a leadership position in the detergent marketplace.

It should be noted that Ultra super-concentrates aren't the exclusive property of the majors. Earth Wise

 Q: *How many worms can you find in an area the size of a football field?*

also has an Ultra detergent. An Ultra can be a deep-green product when it isn't piggybacking on a pre-established brand name.

A complex set of reasons explains why the small, independent suppliers are having a difficult time.

Some deep-green products perform superbly; others, not so well. Says Bob Kulperger, president of New Canaan, Connecticut-based Natural Chemistry, a supplier of deep-green household cleaning products, "A green product that doesn't do the job only gets bought once."

In addition, deep-green products are often more expensive than their traditional counterparts. Although consumer polls indicate that environmentally conscious shoppers are more than willing to pay a modest premium for green products, retailers' experience is different. Says Mike Rourke, vice president of Communications and Corporate Affairs for Montvale, New Jersey-based A&P Stores, "Consumers will buy green products, but only if they don't cost more."

Retailers' caution further complicates the issue. Is a nontoxic, biodegradable household cleaner that comes in a non-recyclable plastic bottle "green"? What about biodegradable, compostable disposable diapers? No one is quite sure what makes a product "green."

The market is currently awash with environmental product claims, and no national mechanism is in place for determining if they are valid. "We have been arguing, in the industry and with the Federal Trade Commission, that we need uniform guidelines," said Proctor & Gamble's Swift. "And we need that because, for us and other large manufacturers like us, we operate nationally, not state by state. We are simply technically unable to tailor packages state by state. If we get into a situation where the state [regulations] are in conflict, our alternative is to take information off the package."

When it comes to evaluating green product claims, retailers (and consumers) are basically on their own. "None of us are experts on what is green," says Catherine Byrd, spokeswoman for the Birmingham, Alabama-based Bruno's supermarket chain. "We're hesitant to stock products which are premised on green claims."

This hesitancy is compounded by an extremely unsettled regulatory environment. Over the past year, several leading consumer goods companies have been charged with deceptive advertising. A number of states have developed environmental labeling laws, and the federal government is also considering regulating

make them. Avoid products from companies with bad environmental records.

• Bring your purchases home in a reusable cloth bag. There's no real difference between plastic and paper grocery bags. Neither is environmentally better. The best bag is the one you will reuse and ultimately recycle.

SEMIOTICS

Recycled logos, those three arrows in a circle, are appearing on many products these days. Originally, the logo was designed in 1973 by a Dutch paper group. Since then, it has become popular for use on many things besides paper, and with seemingly increasing confusion. The logo itself has a few variations. Here is an explanation to help businesses and consumers determine what they actually mean.

The arrows by themselves mean "recyclable." They can be either solid or an outline.

An arrow inside a circle means "made from recycled materials." This also can indicate something that is recyclable. The variations on this type of logo include a white outline of arrows within a black circle, white arrows within a black circle or outlines of both the circle and the arrows.

But these symbols, while they are useful, are vague. They do not, for example, define the percentage of recycled fibers or the ease of recycling. Perhaps the best solution is for manufacturers to write on their product the actual meaning for that product.

IS A "GREEN" PRODUCT REALLY "GREEN?"

Unfortunately for the consumer, in the wave of "green" products introduced daily, not all of the products are as green as they claim to be. Many questions about green products remain unanswered. "The problem is that terms like recyclable, degradable and environmentally friendly have no fixed meaning," Minnesota Attorney General Hubert Humphrey III told a conference of advertising executives in November 1989. So we're left guessing. However, a group of Attorneys General from six other states joined together to ask four companies to substantiate claims that their diapers or plastic bags are degradable. The group of Attorneys General now includes 11 states and has formed an ad hoc task force to study advertising trends, which they cover in *The Green Report*.

so-called "green marketing." Until the regulatory dust settles, many retailers will keep steering clear of potentially problematic products.

Their concern has a sound historical basis. In 1990, the 879-store Safeway supermarket chain started highlighting products it believed were environmentally friendly, only to get blasted by environmentalists who claimed the company had not done its homework about the products' environmental bona fides.

Retailers' caution is exacerbated by the fact that they are in an extremely low-margin business. With an average profit margin of about 2 percent, supermarkets are in no position to take fliers on green products—or on anything else, for that matter.

Another source of difficulty for small green product suppliers is slotting allowances. About five years ago, retailers began charging suppliers up-front fees for stocking their products. While the large, established companies have the financial wherewithal to wade through these so-called slotting allowances, that's not the case for the little guys.

Earth Wise's Mo Siegel is especially ardent in his condemnation of slotting allowances. "Our experience has been absolutely brutal. One retailer with an 18 percent share in a major city wanted us to pay $125,000. If the other supermarkets in that city had charged us comparably, it would have cost us $700,000 simply to get our product onto that city's supermarket shelves."

Siegel is also concerned about the long-term impact of slotting allowances on the consumer products industry. "Innovation has never been the password of the big companies. It's always come from the little guys. If slotting allowances make it impossible for them to market their products, it's going to make for a very unhealthy situation. What will happen if slotting allowances kill innovation?"

More difficulties arise when major players resist change. Established consumer products companies have generally opted not to develop new green product lines. "They're worried that their other product lines might be cannibalized," explains Bruce MacDonald, president of the Canadian Boyle-Midway Household Products division of Reckitt & Colman. "Nor do they need green products—they already have a substantial share of the market. There's also the danger of the slippery slope. Once they introduce a green line,

Q: *How many gallons of water do you waste if you leave the water running while washing dishes?*

there's a chance that people might start asking more questions about their other product lines."

Many independents are persuaded that the majors are also doing what they can to suppress the little guys' initiatives. In 1990, the Placentia, California-based American Enviro Products was charged by a task force of state Attorneys General with false advertising for language on its labeling which claimed that its Bunnies diapers were biodegradable. After an extended legal battle, a consent decree was reached under which American Enviro Products, while not admitting any wrongdoing, paid for the costs of the task force's inquiry. In return, the company was expressly authorized to include language on the labeling for its reformulated Bunnies describing precisely how its new diapers were biodegradable and compostable.

Robert Chickering, American Enviro Products' president, holds Procter & Gamble largely responsible for his extended battle. "P&G has paid lobbyists in five of the states which are task force members," says Chickering. "I think that says a great deal."

Kimberly Stewart, Procter & Gamble spokeswoman, rejects this notion. "The Task Force of Attorneys General is an independent body," she says. "It does what it wants to do. American Enviro Products' problem didn't arise because of anything we did, but because it claimed its products biodegrade in landfills when in fact nothing biodegrades in landfills."

Harry Colley, president of West Cornwall, Connecticut-based Cloverdale, Inc., a small supplier of green household cleaning products, summarizes the little guys' frustration succinctly. He refers to Procter & Gamble as "Procter & God."

Regardless of whether there is substance to the notion that the majors of the consumer goods industry are actively trying to undermine the small independents, it is clearly the big guys who are controlling how fast the US gets green.

Can mainstream business be relied on to drive the greening of America? For many, the answer is no. When surveys ask consumers if they think companies can be trusted to provide environmentally safe products, only 15 percent of respondents typically answer yes. For those who feel that the majors are not sincere in their environmental commitment, meaningful progress requires a fundamental shift in the balance of power. For these people, the inability of deep-green product

A coalition of consumer product manufacturers presented a set of national guidelines to the Federal Trade Commission. The proposal included regulations for claims that a product is made from recycled materials, that it can be composted, that it was manufactured in a way that wastes less material than similar products and that a package can be reused or refilled. This coalition is endorsed by 33 trade groups including the Council on Solid Waste Solutions, a plastics trade group, the American Paper Institute, the Council on Plastic Packaging and the Environment, the Flexible Packaging Institute and the Soap and Detergent Association. Unlike the Attorneys General group, the industry coalition did not consult with its environmental and consumer opponents.

The EPA and the US Office of Consumer Affairs invited the Federal Trade Commission to join them in developing voluntary national guidelines for the use of some environmental terms on product labels. The program will begin with definitions for the terms recycled and recyclable. The agencies will consult with states and organizations that have been active in labeling efforts. The first draft guidelines are expected to be proposed in 1992.

While more detailed governmental guidelines for what constitutes environmental soundness are awaited, a growing movement is afoot to take action independently.

A. *35 gallons*
Source: 50 Simple Things You Can Do To Save The Earth, by the Earth • Works Group

Environmentalists and consumer activists are looking at environmental labelling programs already established in some countries. The West German Blue Angel program, established in 1978, awards a seal of approval to products that are less harmful to the environment than others in their category. Canada's Environmental Choice or Environmentally Friendly Products Program, started in 1989, is modeled after the German program. In the beginning of 1990, Japan started its Eco-mark program, which is similar to both of the above programs, though its goals are slightly more wide-ranging. Countries such as Norway, Sweden, France and the Netherlands are establishing their own programs. The European Economic Community is considering a pan-European Environmental Quality Label as part of an "Ecological Products Scheme."

In the United States, there are two private companies, Green Cross Certification Company and the Green Seal, trying to regulate or at least make companies conscious that people are concerned. Green Cross is a nonprofit subsidiary of a food testing company that plans to measure the environmental effects of manufacturing, transporting, distributing and disposing of products. Green Seal, a nonprofit group funded by foundations and donations, plans to team up with the safety lab Underwriters Laboratories to perform

suppliers to penetrate mass distribution channels is grim news. Warns Dave Labovitz, a director of Ashdun Industries, an Englewood Cliffs, New Jersey-based supplier of environmentally-friendly paper products, "Without the widespread availability of truly green products, green consumerism could wither on the vine."

Other industry observers are more sanguine. "Green products are growing at just the right rate," says Walter Coddington, a principal at New York City's Persuasion Environmental Marketing. "Green products aren't a mass-market failure because they're not a mass-market product. They're a niche product, and a reasonably successful one at that. If green product sales grew any faster, they'd die."

"In this society, change occurs incrementally," notes A.J. Grant, president of Boulder, Colorado-based Environmental Communication Associates. "We're in a very healthy situation where the greening of products is concerned because that incremental change is occurring rapidly."

And how will this brisk rate of change be maintained? "Organically," says Grant. "There are more and more committed environmentalists inside large corporations. External pressure enables them to make that much more of a difference."

The small, independent suppliers, meanwhile, have an important role to play, for they are applying much of that pressure. The mere fact of their presence helps to define the character and direction of the green products marketplace. They are the tugboats who are steering the ships of big business into greener waters.

With the barriers to entry as high as they are, many of these tugboats are likely to sink. But that's par for the course: Capitalism has always favored those with capital. The way A.J. Grant sees it, the green products arena is no different from every hot new market area. Entrepreneurs flock in; most don't make it. She predicts, "The usual 2 percent will survive."

Mo Siegel is likely to be one of those survivors. He recently re-joined Celestial Seasonings as chief executive officer and brought Earth Wise with him. With big-company leverage behind him, Siegel seems likely to regain his Mo-mentum.

The prospects look promising for Chickering's American Enviro Products, too. Having come out of the "biodegradability wars" as the sole surviving vendor of biodegradable/compostable diapers, and with

Q: *Brazil, in effort to increase sustainable yields of rainforests, has established how many square miles of extractive reserves?*

projected 1991 sales in the $45 million range, the company seems to be well on its way.

Will the occasional entrepreneurial success be enough to keep the majors' noses to the environmental grindstone? The answer is probably yes. For one thing, the little guys aren't alone in applying the pressure. Regulators, the media, activist groups, a hard core of committed green consumers—all these players also have a role, and they are not going away.

In addition, the overall climate for green products is likely to improve. Not only will the entry of the federal government bring some much-needed order to green marketing, but comprehensive systems for certifying green products are being developed by Green Cross and Green Seal, two nonprofit product certification groups. Among other things, these changes should inspire retailers to support green products more actively—and retailers are the all-important gatekeepers who determine which products shall be granted right of passage into consumers' homes.

In the context of the overall market, the travails of the small suppliers are something of a red herring. The prospects for green consumerism are generally good. The next few years should bring a continuing integration of environmental issues into businesses' product development and marketing processes. It's also true, however, that the rate of change will not be particularly breathtaking. Green consumerism will dance to the stately rhythms of mainstream business rather than to the more upbeat tempo which many environmentalists would prefer.

In the final analysis, what is going on in the green products market is a matter of perspective. If you're a little guy, you're in a constant struggle for survival, and the big guys are the capital-E Enemy. If you're a big guy, the greening of products is rapidly becoming a central business issue, and the little guys are little more than a blip on the periphery of your consciousness.

From an eagle's-eye view, meanwhile, both the big guys and the little guys have essential roles to play—as organic, interactive participants in a green products "eco-system" which slowly but steadily is growing more green.

Carl Frankel is editor and publisher of the Bethlehem, Connecticut-based Green MarketAlert.

a selective examination. While there is some competition between the two American groups, they both plan, for a several thousand dollar fee, to examine manufacturing plants and test goods submitted by manufacturers, then affix logos to those that pass. Don't expect to see these seals all over your grocery aisles yet. They are still working out some bugs.

But companies like Procter & Gamble and Scott Paper company plan to ignore the Green Cross and the Green Seal. They are among 20 industry groups asking the Federal Trade Commission to set guidelines for product labeling.

**Green Cross
Certification Company**
1611 Telegraph Ave.
Suite 1111
Oakland, CA 94612-
 2113
(510) 832-1415

The Green Seal
P.O. Box 1694
Palo Alto, CA 94302
(415) 327-2200

A. *Over 8,000 square miles*
 Source: Natural Resources Defense Council

Directory to Green Products

*T**he green product industry is growing each year to meet the demand for environmentally sound alternative products that are truly organic, packaged minimally in recycled papers or are recycled or recyclable so they won't fill up landfills. Listed below is a sampling of 1991's newcomers. Our listing provides information to consumers about what to look for in products, where to find them and how the companies producing them practice what they preach. The letters "dnd" indicate that the company did not disclose the information.*

BIOZINE III AIR DEODORIZER
Description: An air deodorizer and surface disinfectant that's safe to use around children, pets and in the sick room. No artificial perfumes or harmful chemicals. **Green Qualifications:** Biodegradable, no CFCs, recyclable, minimal packaging. **Availability:** Drugstores nationwide; Jewel Food Stores; direct from the company. **Company:** Naace Industries, Inc., 5032 N. Royal Atlanta Dr., Tucker, GA 30084, (800) 438-1900. **Corporate Environmental Policy:** To freshen the immediate environment without using harmful chemicals or artificial perfumes.

CAN CYCLER
Description: Aluminum can and plastic container crusher. Rugged reinforced nylon, wall mount, all screws included. Also available: Big Foot (plastic crusher), natural wood, all screws included. **Green Qualifications:** Minimal packaging. **Availability:** Mail order catalogs and mail order direct. **Company:** Jo V Technologies, P.O. Box 4376, Sonora, CA 95370, (800) 869-6843. **Corporate Environmental Policy:** To support PETA. and Greenpeace and to teach people how to recycle.

CLOVERDALE CLEANSER
Description: Concentrated, fragrance-free, all-purpose cleanser/degreaser. **Green Qualifications:** Biodegradable, no phosphates, no CFCs, no animal testing, minimal packaging. **Availability:** Health food and grocery stores. **Company:** Cloverdale, Inc., P.O. Box 268, West Cornwall, CT 06796, (203) 672-0216. **Corporate Environmental Policy:** To sell only products that do not harm the environment.

EARTHRITE ALL-PURPOSE CLEANER
Description: Spray-on cleaner for every surface in home and garage. All natural, nontoxic, no synthetic dyes or perfumes, nonstreaking and nonabrasive. Contains no petroleum distillates or bleaches. **Green Qualifications:** Biodegradable, no phosphates, no CFCs, no animal testing, recyclable, minimal packaging. **Availability:** Grocery, hardware, health food and mass merchandise stores. **Company:** EarthRite, 23700 Mercantile Rd., Beachwood, OH 44122, (800) 328-4408. **Corporate Environmental Policy:** Donates 1% of profits to nonprofit organizations working to protect and preserve the environment. All stationery, shipping cartons and in-store displays are 100% recycled paper.

EARTHRITE TUB & TILE CLEANER
Description: Spray-on tub and tile cleaner safely removes mildew stain and soap scum. Nonabrasive, nontoxic, no chlorine, no fumes. Based on a nonpolluting, totally natural compound. **Green Qualifications:** Biodegradable, no phosphates, no CFCs, no animal testing, recyclable, minimal packaging. **Availability:** Grocery, hardware, health food and mass merchandise stores. **Company:** EarthRite, 23700 Mercantile Rd., Beachwood, OH 44122, (800) 328-4408. **Corporate Environmental Policy:** Donates 1% of profits to nonprofit organizations working to protect and preserve the environment. All stationery, shipping cartons and in-store displays are 100% recycled paper.

EARTHRITE COUNTERTOP CLEANER
Description: Sprays and wipes clean almost any surface used for or around food preparation. Colorless, odorless, removes grease and food stains. **Green Qualifications:** Biodegradable, no phosphates, no CFCs, no animal testing, recyclable, minimal packaging. **Availability:** Grocery, hardware, health food and mass merchandise stores. **Company:** EarthRite, 23700 Mercantile Rd., Beachwood, OH 44122, (800) 328-4408. **Corporate Environmental Policy:** Donates 1% of profits to nonprofit organizations working to protect and preserve the environment. All stationery, shipping cartons and in-store displays are 100% recycled paper.

EARTHRITE FURNITURE & PANELING CLEANER
Description: Cleans, renews luster and hides

Q. *How many rainforest tree species can yield some economic use other than timber?*

scuffs and scratches on furniture or paneling. Uses only natural elements—no synthetic oils, silicone or petroleum distillates. Leaves anti-static charge which prevents dust from resettling on just cleaned surface. **Green Qualifications:** Biodegradable, no phosphates, no CFCs, no animal testing, recyclable, minimal packaging. **Availability:** Grocery, hardware, health food and mass merchandise stores. **Company:** EarthRite, 23700 Mercantile Rd., Beachwood, OH 44122, (800) 328-4408. **Corporate Environmental Policy:** Donates 1% of profits to nonprofit organizations working to protect and preserve the environment. All stationery, shipping cartons and in-store displays are 100% recycled paper.

EARTHRITE ALL SURFACE FLOOR CLEANER

Description: Concentrated cleaner revitalizes wood, ceramic and vinyl floors. Makes 8 gallons, cold water activated, safely rinses down the drain. All natural—no waxes or phosphates. **Green Qualifications:** Biodegradable, no phosphates, no CFCs, no animal testing, recyclable, minimal packaging. **Availability:** Grocery, hardware, health food and mass merchandise stores. **Company:** EarthRite, 23700 Mercantile Rd., Beachwood, OH 44122, (800) 328-4408. **Corporate Environmental Policy:** Donates 1% of profits to nonprofit organizations working to protect and preserve the environment. All stationery, shipping cartons and in-store displays are 100% recycled paper.

EARTHRITE TOILET BOWL CLEANER

Description: Removes tough stains, odorless, no harmful fumes, noncorrosive. Has no polluting clays, plastics or silicas. Perfect for homes with septic tanks. **Green Qualifications:** Biodegradable, no phosphates, no CFCs, no animal testing, recyclable, minimal packaging. **Availability:** Grocery, hardware, health food and mass merchandise stores. **Company:** EarthRite, 23700 Mercantile Rd., Beachwood, OH 44122, (800) 328-4408. **Corporate Environmental Policy:** Donates 1% of profits to nonprofit organizations working to protect and preserve the environment. All stationery, shipping cartons and in-store displays are 100% recycled paper.

ECO-FORCE LIQUID LAUNDRY DETERGENT

Description: Biodegradable, concentrated liquid laundry detergent. No whitening agents. **Green Qualifications:** Bio-degradable, no phosphates, no animal testing, recyclable, minimal packaging. **Availability:** Health food stores. **Company:** Scandinavian Natural Health and Beauty Products, 13 N. Seventh St., Perkasie, PA 18944, (800) 288-2844. **Corporate Environmental Policy:** Donates ten cents for every case of Eco-Force sold. Donations go to environmental organizations.

ECOVER, INC.

Description: Fully biodegradable, non-chlorine, all-fabric, concentrated, 64 oz. bleach. **Green Qualifications:** Biodegradable, no petroleum-based surfactants, no phosphates, no polycarboxylates, no NTA or EDTA, no perborate, no chlorine bleaches, no optical brighteners, no enzymes, no synthetic perfumes, no colorings, no animal testing. **Availability:** Natural and health food stores, select supermarkets, mailorder but not directly through Ecover. **Company:** Ecover, Inc., 6-8 Knight St., Norwalk, CT 06851, (203) 853-4166. **Corporate Environmental Policy:** dnd.

ECOWORKS LIGHT BULBS

Description: Long-life, energy-saving, nuclear-free, incandescent light bulbs. 54-, 68- and 90-watt bulbs save energy over the higher wattage standard bulbs. Contains no mercury (unlike other fluorescents) and no radioactivity (unlike some compact fluorescent bulbs). **Availability:** Direct from company. **Company:** EcoWorks, Inc., Nuclear Free America, 325 E. 25th St., Baltimore, MD 21218, (301) 235-3575. **Corporate Environmental Policy:** 10% of profit goes to peace and justice organizations.

GOO GONE

Description: A citrus-based tough stain remover which uses orange oil. Quickly removes oil, grease, tar, crayon, wax, glue and other stains from both hard and soft surfaces and is nonabrasive. **Green Qualifications:** Biodegradable, no phosphates, no animal testing, recyclable, minimal packaging. **Availability:** Hardware stores and most grocery stores. **Company:** Magic American Corporation, 23700 Mercantile Rd., Beachwood, OH 44122, (800) 321-6330. **Corporate Environmental Policy:** Donates a percentage of profits to environmental groups.

GOOD SENSE TRASH BAGS

Description: Full line of indoor and outdoor garbage bags made from a minimum of 50% recycled plastic. **Green Qualifications:** Recycled, recyclable. **Availability:** Food stores

A. *Nearly one in six. Some examples are: perfume, shampoo and spice.*
   Source: Natural Resources Defense Council

nationwide. **Company:** Webster Industries, 58 Pulaski St., Peabody, MA 01960, (508) 532-2000. **Corporate Environmental Policy:** Environmentally responsible approach to products, programs and processes.

GOOD SENSE YARD COMPOSTING BAG

Description: Biodegradable lawn and leaf plastic bag. **Green Qualifications:** Biodegradable, recyclable. **Availability:** Food and hardware stores nationwide. **Company:** Webster Industries, 58 Pulaski St., Peabody, MA 01960, (508) 532-2000. **Corporate Environmental Policy:** Environmentally responsible approach to products, programs and processes.

GREEN FOREST TISSUE PRODUCTS

Description: Bath tissue, paper towels and napkins made with 100% recycled fibers. Green Forest recycles over one million tons of wastepaper each year to make their products. **Green Qualifications:** Biodegradable, recycled, recyclable, minimal packaging. **Availability:** Supermarkets and mass merchandise stores nationwide. **Company:** Fort Howard Corporation, P.O. Box 19130, Green Bay, WI 54307. **Corporate Environmental Policy:** Invests executive time in national efforts to promote recycling.

KLEAR SEAL

Description: Water-based emulsified acrylic clear sealer and top coat. Low toxic, no petrochemicals or heavy metal preservatives. **Green Qualifications:** Recyclable, no animal testing. **Availability:** Through AFM Enterprises distributors. **Company:** AFM Enterprises, Inc., 1140 Stacy Ct., Riverside, CA 92507, (714) 781-6860. **Corporate Environmental Policy:** To develop environmentally safe products.

LIFE TREE DISHWASHING LIQUID

Description: Liquid dishwashing detergent for dishwashing by hand. Made from renewable vegetable-derived surfactants, natural fragrance oils, super concentrated (means less packaging), packaged in recycled plastic containers. **Green Qualifications:** Biodegradable, no phosphates, no animal testing, recycled, recyclable, minimal packaging. **Availability:** Natural food stores nationwide or mail order (P.O. Box 1203, Sebastopol, CA 95472). **Company:** Sierra Dawn Products, P.O. Box 513, Graton, CA 95444, (707) 577-0324. **Corporate Environmental Policy:** Committed to producing environmentally sound products with no harmful by-products or wasteful practices.

LIFE TREE HOME-SOAP

Description: Natural all-purpose household cleaner, made from renewable vegetable-derived surfactants, natural fragrance oils, super concentrated (means less packaging), rapidly biodegradable, packaged in recycled plastic containers. **Green Qualifications:** Biodegradable, no phosphates, no animal testing, recycled, recyclable, minimal packaging. **Availability:** Natural food stores nationwide or mail order (P.O. Box 1203, Sebastopol, CA 95472). **Company:** Sierra Dawn Products, P.O. Box 513, Graton, CA 95444, (707) 577-0324. **Corporate Environmental Policy:** Committed to producing environmentally sound products with no harmful by-products or wasteful practices.

LIFE TREE LAUNDRY LIQUID

Description: Liquid laundry detergent made from renewable vegetable-derived surfactants, natural fragrance oils, super concentrated (means less packaging), rapidly biodegradable, packaged in recycled plastic containers. **Green Qualifications:** Biodegradable, no phosphates, no animal testing, recycled, recyclable, minimal packaging. **Availability:** Natural food stores nationwide or mail order (P.O. Box 1203, Sebastopol, CA 95472). **Company:** Sierra Dawn Products, P.O. Box 513, Graton, CA 95444, (707) 577-0324. **Corporate Environmental Policy:** Committed to producing environmentally sound products with no harmful by-products or wasteful practices.

NEAT-N-SWEET CAT LITTER

Description: Cat litter made of highly absorbent organic plant fiber that is rapidly biodegradable and "flushable"through any waste system. **Green Qualifications:** Biodegradable, certified organically grown, minimal packaging. **Availability:** Grocery/natural food stores east of the Mississippi. **Company:** Virginia Mills, 4012 Stuart Ave., Richmond, VA 23221. **Corporate Environmental Policy:** Focuses on environmentally friendly products and ingredients.

NOPE 100% COTTON SHOWER CURTAIN

Description: Shower curtain of 100% cotton duck. Washable, recyclable, long life. **Green Qualifications:** Biodegradable, recyclable, minimal packaging. **Availability:** Environmental stores or mail order. **Company:** nope (Non-Polluting Enterprises, Inc.), Dept. BW, P.O. Box 919, Old Chelsea Station, New York, NY 10011, (212) 989-4222. **Corporate Environmental Policy:** Offers low-impact substitutes to cut down on petrochemical products.

Q: *How many solar panels installed by President Carter on the White House roof are still there?*

OPTI FLUID
Description: OPTI Fluid is the first quick-drying, nontoxic correction fluid. Never requires a thinner. Works for all types of corrections; won't dry out in the bottle (which is biodegradable). **Green Qualifications:** No phosphates, no CFCs, no animal testing, minimal packaging. **Availability:** Office supply stores or mail order. **Company:** Citius USA, Inc., P.O. Box 6698, Marietta, GA 30065, (404) 953-3663. **Corporate Environmental Policy:** Offers nontoxic products with biodegradable packaging.

RECYCLED PLASTIC OFFICE SUPPLIES
Description: Rulers, push pins, pens, scissors and pencil sharpeners made of at least 75% post-consumer recycled plastic. Many new products are being developed. **Green Qualifications:** Recycled, recyclable, no animal testing, minimal packaging. **Availability:** Direct from manufacturer. **Company:** Pimby Co., P.O. Box 240, Purdys, NY 10578, (914) 277-8872. **Corporate Environmental Policy:** To sell products made from post-consumer recycled materials.

RENEW TRASH BAGS
Description: The first plastic trash bags to contain over 80% recycled plastics. Awarded Green Cross Certification due to state-of-the-art recycled plastic. Available in I3-, 26-, 30-, 33- or 39-gallon bags. **Green Qualifications:** Recycled. **Availability:** Food and hardware stores nationwide. **Company:** Webster Industries, 58 Pulaski St., Peabody, MA 01960, (800) 225-0796, ext. 125. **Corporate Environmental Policy:** Pioneers in photodegradable, biodegradable and recycled plastic technology.

RIGHTOUT CARPET CLEANER
Description: Industrial tested carpet cleaner. Removes stains, is nontoxic, nonflammable, biodegradable, pH neutral. **Green Qualifications:** Biodegradable, no phosphates, no CFCs, no animal testing, recycled, recyclable, minimal packaging. **Availability:** Food, drug, hardware and mass merchandise stores nationwide. **Company:** Outright Industries, Inc., 4041 W. Ogden Ave., Chicago, IL 60623, (312) 277-7100. **Corporate Environmental Policy:** Committed to producing environmentally safe consumer products.

RIGHTOUT LAUNDRY PRE-WASH
Description: Laundry pre-wash treatment for tough stains. Nontoxic, biodegradable, contains no known carcinogens, pH neutral. **Green Qualifications:** Biodegradable, no phosphates, no animal testing, recyclable, minimal packaging. **Availability:** Food, drug and hardware stores nationwide. **Company:** Outright Industries, Inc., 4041 W. Ogden Ave., Chicago, IL 60623, (312) 277-7100. **Corporate Environmental Policy:** Committed to producing environmentally safe consumer products.

RIGHTOUT SPOT REMOVER
Description: All-purpose spot remover removes stains such as coffee, tea, blood, food, make-up, wine, etc. Nontoxic, pH neutral, nonflammable. **Green Qualifications:** Biodegradable, no phosphates, no animal testing, recyclable, minimal packaging. **Availability:** Food, drug and hardware stores nationwide. **Company:** Outright Industries, Inc., 4041 W. Ogden Ave., Chicago, IL 60623, (312) 277-7100. **Corporate Environmental Policy:** Committed to producing environmentally safe consumer products.

SOAP FACTORY
Description: Full range of environmentally sensitive laundry and household cleaners, backed with thorough research. Spray cleaner, dishwashing liquid, delicate laundry detergent, baby laundry detergent. White 'n Bright Laundry Additive is an environmentally sensitive alternative to all other bleaches and whiteners. **Green Qualifications:** Biodegradable, no phosphates, no animal testing, recyclable, minimal packaging. **Availability:** Direct from manufacturer. **Company:** The Soap Factory, 14 Cushman Rd., St. Catharine's, Ontario L2M 6T2, Canada, (416) 682-1808. **Corporate Environmental Policy:** To meet ethical and social responsibilities; to make products to maintain the chemical, physical and biological integrity of the water supply.

VERMONT ORGANIC FERTILIZER
Description: All-purpose 5-3-4 organic fertilizer. Recycled and recyclable pail of fertilizer in 4-, 10- and 25-pound sizes. **Green Qualifications:** Biodegradable, certified organically grown, recycled. **Availability:** Garden centers, hardware and grocery stores nationwide, or mail order through Gardener's Supply Co., (802) 863-1700. **Company:** Vermont Organic Fertilizer Co., 26 State St., Montpelier, VT 05602, (802) 229-1440. **Corporate Environmental Policy:** To provide gardeners with a natural and organic plant food reflecting a deep commitment to the health and ecological balance of the environment.

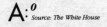
A: *o*
Source: The White House

YESTERDAY'S NEWS CAT LITTER
Description: Pelletized, premium cat litter made from recycled newspaper. **Green Qualifications:** Biodegradable, recycled, recyclable. **Availability:** Krogers, Wal-Mart. **Company:** Eco-Matrix, 124 Harvard St., Brookline, MA 02146, (617) 592-3373. **Corporate Environmental Policy:** Participates in recycling programs in various communities and uses that newspaper to make the cat litter.

BEEHIVE BOTANICALS
Description: Shampoo, conditioner and skin care products with no animal ingredients. **Green Qualifications:** Biodegradable, no phosphates, no animal testing, recycled, recyclable, minimal packaging. **Availability:** Health food stores or direct mail. **Company:** Beehive Botanicals, Inc., Rt. 8, Box 8257, Hayward, WI 54843, (800) 283-4274. **Corporate Environmental Policy:** No animal testing or animal products; recycled paper used for packaging.

BUMKINS ALL-IN-ONE CLOTH DIAPER
Description: Diaper has a waterproof outershell attached to soft 100% cotton flannel padding, elastic at legs and waist, velcro closures. **Green Qualifications:** Recyclable, minimal packaging. **Availability:** Juvenile, grocery and health food stores nationwide, or mail order catalogs: Seventh Generation (900) 456-1177; Walnut Acres (800) 433-3998; in Canada, Absolutely Diapers (800) 267-0008. **Company:** Bumkins Family Products, 1945 E. Watkins, Phoenix, AZ 85034, (602) 254-2626. **Corporate Environmental Policy:** Internal recycling, recyclable packaging and reuseable products.

CITRE SHINE HAIR CARE
Description: Hair care products formulated with natural citrus-based ingredients. Shampoo, conditioner, shaping gel, holding spritz, glossing treatment, nonaerosol/nonpropellant glossing spray. **Green Qualifications:** Biodegradable, no phosphates, no animal testing, recyclable, minimal packaging. **Availability:** Food, drug, beauty supply and discount stores nationwide. **Company:** Advanced Research Laboratories, 16580 Harbor Blvd., Ste. O, Fountain Valley, CA 92708, (714) 839-1940. **Corporate Environmental Policy:** Committed to introducing only environmentally friendly products.

ECOLOGNE
Description: Ecologne is a unisex cologne and aftershave. Nontoxic, nonallergenic, made from essential oils and absolutes extracted from vegetables, flowers, herbs and trees. 100% botanically derived aromatics blended in grain alcohol. No animal ingredients. Recycled paper box, recyclable glass bottle. **Green Qualifications:** Bio-degradable, no animal testing, recycled, recyclable, minimal packaging. **Availability:** Natural Choice Catalog, 1365 Rufina Circle, Santa Fe, NM 87501. **Company:** ECO Design Co., 1365 Rufina Cir., Santa Fe, NM 87501, (505) 438-3448. **Corporate Environmental Policy:** To offer environmentally sane products of the highest quality.

FAMILY CLUBHOUSE DIAPERS
Description: Reuseable Terrytails contoured cloth diapers; Dovetails paper, disposable, biodegradable diapers; Pelican Pouches water-repellent duffel bags; Nikky Diaper Lovers. **Green Qualifications:** Biodegradable, no animal testing, recycled, recyclable, minimal packaging. **Availability:** Health food stores, children's stores, or call for catalog. **Company:** Family Clubhouse, Inc., 6 Chiles Ave., Asheville, NC 28803, (800) 876-1574. **Corporate Environmental Policy:** To produce environmentally safe products.

HEALTHY KLEANER
Description: Heavy-duty skin cleanser for oil, grease, adhesives, tree sap, permanent markers and oil base inks, tar (including beach tar), crayon, gum, etc. **Green Qualifications:** Biodegradable, no animal testing, recycled, recyclable, minimum packaging. **Availability:** Health food stores or direct phone order. **Company:** Healthy Kleaner, P.O. Box 4656, Boulder, CO 80306, (800) EARTH29. **Corporate Environmental Policy:** Donations to Greenpeace, Sierra Club, Rocky Flats Coalition, Friends of the Sea Lion, etc.

ONLY NATURAL SOAPS
Description: All natural soaps packaged in 100% recycled paper boxes. Aloe vera, chamomile, cucumber, oatmeal and Baby Cakes (goats' milk and honey). **Green Qualifications:** Biodegradable, no phosphates, recycled, minimal packaging. **Availability:** Seventh Generation (800) 456-1177; Pure Earth Products (800) 926-1239; The Natural Choice (800) 621-2591; Internatural (800) 633-3313. **Company:** Only Natural, Inc., 14 Buchanan Rd., Salem, MA 01970, (508) 745-9766. **Corporate Environmental Policy:** Has been making environmentally safe soaps for 12 years.

SAFE BRANDS HAIR & SKIN CARE
Description: Biodegradable shampoos,

Q: What is the highest grade of paper and the easiest to recycle?

conditioners and lotions. No artificial dyes, no animal products, no mineral oil. **Green Qualifications:** Biodegradable, no phosphates, no animal testing, recyclable, minimum packaging. **Availability:** Food, drug and mass merchandise stores, including Safeway and Wal-Mart. **Company:** Safe Brands, Inc., 431 Crown Point Cir., Grass Valley, CA 95946, (916) 272-3130. **Corporate Environmental Policy:** Donates 1% of gross sales to environmental causes.

UN-PETROLEUM JELLY
Description: The petroleum-free alternative to Vaseline. Emollient skin conditioner. **Green Qualifications:** Biodegradable, no phosphates, no animal testing, recyclable, minimal packaging. **Availability:** Natural food stores everywhere. **Company:** Autumn Harp, 28 Rockydale Rd., Bristol, VT 05443, (802) 453-4807. **Corporate Environmental Policy:** Donates 1% of sales for environmental work—publishing, research, education, seminars.

ECOFOOD

CELESTIAL SEASONINGS TEA
Description: Organically grown black tea, naturally decaffeinated black tea, herb teas and blends of imported teas packaged in 100% oxygen bleached tea bag paper. **Green Qualifications:** Biodegradable, certified organically grown, no animal testing, recyclable, minimal packaging. **Availability:** National distribution in grocery and natural foods stores, or through mail order. **Company:** Celestial Seasonings, Inc., 4600 Sleepytime Dr., Boulder, CO 80301-3292. **Corporate Environmental Policy:** Donations to local and national Earth Day projects and the 1990 Greens Gathering.

LEROUX CREEK FRUITS
Description: Organic dehydrated fruits, fruit bars, apple butter, chunky applesauce. **Green Qualifications:** Certified organically grown, recycled, recyclable and minimal packaging. **Availability:** Natural food stores nationwide. **Company:** Leroux Creek Food Corporation, 970-3100 Rd., Hotchkiss, CO 81419, (303) 872-2256. **Corporate Environmental Policy:** All paper products are made from recycled paper.

LITTLE BEAR CHILI
Description: Vegetarian chili, regular or spicy, no salt added. Organically grown pinto beans, slow cooked with a special blend of whole corn and other select vegetables and spices. **Green Qualifications:** Certified organically grown, recycled, recyclable and minimal packaging. **Availability:** Natural food stores nationwide and some grocery stores. **Company:** Little Bear Organic Foods, 860 Via de la Paz, Suite B2, Pacific Palisades, CA 90272, (213) 454-4542. **Corporate Environmental Policy:** Supports a wide range of environmental causes.

LORIVA SUPREME OILS
Description: Fresh-flavored basil oil and garlic oil, rice bran oil and canolive oil (a mixture of canola oil and Italian extra virgin olive oil). **Green Qualifications:** Biodegradable, certified organically grown, recycled, recyclable, minimal packaging. **Availability:** Natural food, grocery and specialty stores. **Company:** Loriva Supreme Foods, 40-10 Oser Ave., Hauppage, NY 11788, (516) 231-7940. **Corporate Environmental Policy:** Packaged in recyclable glass.

LOW FAT BODY MUESLI
Description: Blueberry and strawberry banana breakfast cereal made with all natural fruits, nuts, grains. Packaged and mixed by disabled people. **Green Qualifications:** Biodegradable, no CFCs, no animal testing, recyclable, minimal packaging. **Availability:** Southern California health food stores. **Company:** Faber Foods and Aeronautics, 419 N. Larchmont Blvd., #269, Los Angeles, CA 90004, (213) 381-7635. **Corporate Environmental Policy:** Investing in a Save the Rainforest Campaign.

TOFURELLA
Description: TofuRella is a cholesterol-free cheese alternative, low in calories and saturated fat. **Green Qualifications:** Certified organically grown, minimal packaging. **Availability:** Natural food stores in United States; natural food and grocery stores in Canada; mail order. **Company:** Sharon's Finest, P.O. Box 5020, Santa Rosa, CA 95402-5020, (707) 576-7050. **Corporate Environmental Policy:** Donates 5% of profits to groups protecting the rainforests.

SOURCES

ECO SOURCE
Description: A catalog of environmentally friendly products for home and office, including recycled paper goods, water and air purifiers, energy-efficient lighting and biodegradable household and health supplies. Products for a safer, cleaner world. **Company:** EcoSource, 9051 Mill Station Rd., Sebastopol, CA 95472, (800) 688-8345.

 . *White computer paper*
Source: 50 Simple Things Your Business Can Do To Save The Earth, *by the Earth • Works Group*

ECOLOGICAL PRODUCTS DISTRIBUTION
Description: Ecological products catalog containing unique products from Hawaii including eco-art notecards printed on recycled paper with soybean inks in four colors. **Company:** Environmental Products Distribution, 250 Alamaha St., N-8, #146, Kahului, HI 96732, (800) 955-4558.

NATURAL RESOURCES NETWORK/ ALLERGY RESOURCES
Description: Over 300 ecologically safe products, including cotton pillows, bed covers, air and water purifiers. **Company:** Natural Resources Network/Allergy Resources, P.O. Box 888, Palmer Lake, CO 80133, (800) USE-FLAX.

ORJENE NATURAL COSMETICS
Description: A catalog of natural shower gels, shampoos, lotions, bath oils, creams. The products are not tested on animals, are made with no animal ingredients and packaged in recyclable containers. **Company:** Orjene Natural Cosmetics, 5-43 48th Ave., Long Island City, NY 11101, (718) 937-2666.

WE CARE
Description: An earth-friendly and user-friendly mail order catalog offering environmentally responsible products for the home and office. We Care gives its customers a chance to select which one of four environmental groups they would like to see benefit most from a 10% donation of their pre-tax profit. **Company:** We Care, 77-725 Enfield Ln., Suite 120, Palm Desert, CA 92260, (800) 356-4430.

ECONET
Description: An international computer-based communications system serving organizations and individuals working for environmental preservation and sustainability. It is accessible by any kind of computer with a modem, usually through a local phone call anywhere in the world. One of the more than 170 electronic conferences on EcoNet is the Green Store Conference which contains substantial information about a wide range of environmentally sensitive products. **Company:** EcoNet, 3228 Sacramento St., San Francisco, CA 94115, (415) 442-0220.

MESSAGE!CHECK PERSONAL CHECKS
Description: Socially conscious personal checks which carry messages of national organizations. Checks are printed on partially recycled paper. 20% of net profits is donated to environmental groups. **Company:** Message!Check Corp., P.O. Box 3206, Seattle, WA 98114, (206) 324-7792.

THE GREEN CONSUMER LETTER/THE GREEN BUSINESS LETTER
Description: Two eight-page monthly newsletters—one filled with the latest news and product information; the other with the most current information and insight into the greening of business. They both offer news about companies, products, tips and resources that can help you make smart business and consumer decisions. **Company:** Tilden Press, 1526 Connecticut Ave. NW, Washington, DC 20036, (800) 955-GREEN.

EARTHWORD ENVIRONMENTAL GAME
Description: A new recreational and educational game which encourages adults and teens to become more aware of environmental issues. 800 multiple-choice questions plus an easy-to-set-up and play game-card format allows play almost anywhere. Printed on recycled materials. **Company:** Earthword, Inc., 104 Church Street, Keyport, NJ 07735, (201) 264-3012.

THE GREEN BUILDING NEWS
Description: The global newsletter for ecological building practices, a forum that pulls both sick buildings and energy conservation together in one place. Healthy materials, energy, events, lawsuits, experts, hands-on are just some of the topics. Sample copy: send $3 to: The Green Building News, 21 1/2 Dudley Ave., Venice, CA 90291, (213) 399-9318.

Q: *What is the average life span of a tree in New York City watered with 22,000 gallons of dog urine a year?*

GREEN BUSINESS RESOURCES

PERIODICALS AND BOOKS

The Green Business Letter
Tilden Press
1526 Connecticut Ave. NW
Washington, DC

50 Simple Things Your Business Can Do to Save the Earth
Earth•Works Group
Berkeley, CA, 1991

Ecopreneuring
Steven J. Bennett,
John Wiley & Sons, Inc., New York, 1991

MARKETERS AND ADVERTISERS

Burke Marketing Research
800 Broadway
Cincinnati, OH 45202
(513) 852-8585

Gaia Communications
P.O. Box 69193
W. Hollywood, CA 90069
(213) 274-1456

Stephen Garey & Associates
2436 Third St.
Santa Monica, CA 90405
(213) 396-8675

GSD&M
One Cielo Center
1250 Capital of Texas Hwy.,
Suite 400
Austin, TX 78746
(512) 327-8810

The Hartman Group
1280 Bison, Suite B-9550
Newport Beach, CA 92660
(714) 644-2540

Johans+Son Advertising
8800 Venice Blvd.
Los Angeles, CA 90034
(213) 559-1041

J. Ottman Consulting
315 E. 69 St.
New York, NY 10021
(212) 255-3800

Schultz Communications
9412 Admiral Nimitz NE
Albuquerque, NM 87111
(505) 822-8222

ENVIRONMENTAL CONSULTANTS

City Spirit
Jerome Rubin
590 Pacific St.
Brooklyn, NY 11217
(718) 857-1545

Corporate Conservation
4 Brattle St., Suite 306
Cambridge, MA 02138
(617) 868-6864

CT Donovan Associates
P.O. Box 5665
22 Church St.
Burlington, VT 05402
(802) 658-9385

Environmental Communication Associates
1881 9th St., Suite 200
Boulder, CO 80302
(303) 444-1428

Gil Friend and Associates
2118 7th St.
Berkeley, CA 94710
(510) 548-7904

NRH Associates
P.O. Box 1537
Burlington, VT 05402
(802) 372-5443

Out-Of-The-Dumps
P.O. Box 70
Mt. Rainer, MD 20712
(301) 270-0833

The Recycling Group
1155 Camino Del Mar
Del Mar, CA 92014
(619) 259-4939

PRODUCTS FOR YOUR OFFICE

Acme United Corp
75 Kings Hwy. Cutoff
Fairfield, CT 06430
(413) 736-7211

Accutone
2800 NW 55th Court
Ft. Lauderdale, FL 33309
(800) 562-TONE

GREEN PACKAGING

Deltapaper
2925 State Rd.
Croydon, PA 19021
(215) 788-1800

EcoPak Industries
7859 S. 180th
Kent, WA 98032
(206) 768-9600

Silver Bay Packers
215 N. Oberlin Ave.
Lakewood, NJ 08701
(908) 367-0559

RECYCLED FAX PAPER

Paper Systems
185 Pioneer Blvd.
P.O. Box 150
Springboro, OH 45066
(800) 950-8590.

The Recycled Paper Company
185 Corey Rd.
Boston, MA 02146
(617) 277-9901

RECYCLED TONER CARTRIDGES

Alfa Cartridge Recyclers
20 E. 30th St.
New York, NY 10016
(800) 366-0303

Laser Tech
2230 Floral Dr.
Boulder, CO 80304
(303) 449-5794

American Laser
9300 Georgia Ave. Third Floor
Silver Spring, MD 20910
(800) 345-0315

LASER 1
1901 N. Moore St., Suite LL50
Arlington, VA 22209
(703) 532-6620

PM Co.
24 Triangle Park Dr.
Cincinnati, OH 45246
(513) 772-5057

A. **7 years**
Source: Smithsonian, *April 1990*

ECOTRAVEL

Taking care of your home ground is all good and well, but you must also tread softly on Mother Earth when you travel. As travelers become more ecologically concerned, biologically-rich countries are taking steps to safeguard their treasures to continue attracting foreign currency. Tourism, which in many places has been the bane of conservation, is emerging as a powerful force for environmental protection.

CODE OF ETHICS FOR TOURISTS

1. Travel in a spirit of humility and with a genuine desire to learn more about the people of your host country. Be sensitively aware of the feelings of other people, thus preventing what might be offensive behavior on your part. This applies very much to photography.

2. Cultivate the habit of listening and observing, rather than merely hearing and seeing.

3. Realize that often the people in the country you visit have time concepts and thought patterns different from your own. This does not make them inferior, only different.

4. Instead of looking for the "beach paradise," discover the enrichment of seeing a different way of life, through other eyes.

5. Acquaint yourself with local customs. What is courteous in one country may be quite the reverse in another—people will be happy to help you.

6. Instead of the Western practice of "knowing all the answers," cultivate the habit of asking questions.

7. Remember that you are only one of thousands of tourists visiting this country and do not expect special privileges.

Photo: Ned Gillette/Adventure Photo

Traveling by camel in the Sahara Desert in Morrocco.

EcoTravel

- By Lisa Jones -

We carpool to our offices; we recycle in our homes. It only makes sense, then, that when we go on vacation, Acapulco is no longer enough. Tourists are putting down their tutti-frutti cocktails and picking up binoculars. They are abandoning their beach towels and walking into the jungle. More and more travelers are seeing their vacation time not as a time of inactivity, but of intense activity, both physical and mental.

Visitors can count nesting sea turtles on Caribbean beaches. They can inspect the canopy of the rainforest from a suspended metal cage in the Central American jungle. They can canoe through the Everglades or inspect Anasazi ruins with a Navajo guide in Arizona.

The World Tourism Organization (an affiliate of the United Nations) reports that adventure travel (which includes ecotourism) accounted for about 10 percent of the tourist market in 1989, and was growing by 30 percent each year. Tourism is the second largest industry in the world, and is on the way to being the largest, the World Tourism Organization reports.

The developing world receives some $55 billion in tourism receipts, reports Tensie Whelan, editor of *Nature Tourism.* Kenya, the world leader in ecotourism, earns about $350 million annually from its visitors,

Q: *Installing a new fluorescent bulb to replace a 70-watt incandescent bulb saves the consumer $15 and prevents how many pounds of coal from burning?*

almost all of it due to wildlife tourism. One estimate contends that a single Kenyan elephant generates $14,375 per year, or $900,000 in its lifetime, in tourist expenditures. In Costa Rica, where 60 percent of visitors are interested in visiting the internationally-lauded national parks system, some $138 million was earned in 1986. Ecuador's Galapagos Islands brought $180 million in foreign exchange in 1986, mostly from ecotourism.

Kenya and Costa Rica join Nepal, Tanzania, China and Mexico as the most popular ecotourism destinations, where visitors trek, bird watch, take photos, camp, climb, fish, raft and do botanical studies.

The rising tide of ecotourism has brought with it a flood of challenges. Central to these challenges are a pair of intertwining questions: How can nature buffs be prevented from loving to death the places they visit? How can local residents be invited to profit from ecotourism, thereby ensuring that they will take part in protecting the land they live in?

There is ample proof that nature lovers can harm the places they visit: Curious visitors have badly disturbed wildlife in Kenya's Amboseli and Masai Mara national parks. The World Conservation Union said in 1990 that of 109 countries with coral reefs, 90 are being damaged by sewage from hotels, anchors from cruise ships, and tourists breaking off chunks of the reefs. In Nepal, 120,000 trekkers a year accelerate deforestation by seeking baths and meals warmed with wood.

In Ecuador's Galapagos Islands, visitors have increased from around 10,000 to 45,000 per year over the last decade and the resident population has gone from 4,700 to 10,000, prompting speculation that the wildly diverse islands could go the way of Hawaii, which has lost the majority of its native plants and animals.

Forestalling such a fate will take planning and monitoring—words which have rarely been spoken in the same breath as tourism. But through the efforts of some concerned governments and ecotourism operators, common sense and planning are being put into action. The Ecuadorian government commission and groups like the US-based Ecotourism Society are working to develop a tourism plan on the Galapagos, and Ecuadorian President Rodrigo Borga Cevallos has put a temporary freeze on new tourism permits.

In Kenya, park guards have become better trained

8. If you really want your experience to be a "home away from home," it is foolish to waste money on traveling.

9. When you are shopping, remember that the "bargain" you obtained was possible only because of the low wages paid to the maker.

10. Do not make promises to people in your host country unless you can follow through.

11. Spend time reflecting on your daily experience in an attempt to deepen your understanding. It has been said that "what enriches you may rob and violate others."

—Issued by the Ecumenical Coalition on Third World Tourism.

GREEN WINGS?

As you fly to your jungle safari lodge in Timbuktu, Africa, adjust the seat to recline and await a cool orange juice, do you ever wonder what happens to the plastic cup after you—much too desperately—guzzle the juice?

Airlines used to be notorious polluters. Each flight filled up landfills with tons of cups, trays and those miniature liquor bottles that we thought were so great when we were ten. The project of repainting the fleets every few years produced highly toxic chemicals that stripped the paint as it poisoned the ground. Air quality

A. *400 pounds*
  Source: Rocky Mountain Institute Newsletter, *August 1988*

was poor, especially for people who suffer from sensitivities or allergies, because no physical barrier prevented the cigarette smoke from traveling up through the aisles.

Today airlines are taking steps, however tentative, to improve their ecological track record. Smoking is not allowed in any six-hour-or-under domestic flight.

"People anticipated the extension of the law from 2 to 6 hours to be a problem, but it was actually very easy," comments Mike Mitchell, public relations representative at America West. "People were demanding clean air quality on flights."

Almost every domestic carrier has some type of recycling program. American Airlines relies on employee intiative to begin recycling efforts.

America West says they have the most extensive environmental plan. Being the newest airline in the skies, they

and financed over the past few years. A portion of funds collected from the parks have gone to nearby landowners, who often find themselves the unwilling hosts to herds of wildlife on their land.

In Belize, a zoning scheme patterned after one utilized for Australia's Great Barrier Reef is being formulated to regulate use of its reef, the longest in the hemisphere and the focus of the Caribbean nation's fishing and tourism industries.

In ecotourism hot spots like the Galapagos and Monteverde cloud forest reserve in Costa Rica, visitors frequent only a tiny fraction of the area, leaving the rest undisturbed for wildlife. And the part that is open to tourists amounts to a persuasive piece of advocacy for rainforest protection.

"What's a better way to get people to want to save tropical forests than to have a good experience there?" postulates George Powell, a National Audubon Society biologist working to create more small-scale ecotourism operations at Monteverde.

Work like Powell's—including as many local people as possible in ecotourism—is key to the industry's success, especially in poor regions. Often, local people have subsisted by cutting the forest, fishing the reef, or otherwise extracting the natural resources. For them, whether or not they protect the forest boils down to a simple choice: If they can make a better livelihood protecting resources rather than extracting them, that's what they'll do.

"If people can't make a living from the forest,

BURN-OUT

Don't you hate it when you look forward to gazing up at desolate peaks on your trip and instead your view is blocked by hundreds of Winnebagos and clothes lines? We interviewed various members of the ecotourism field and asked them what areas they feel are overcrowded, and what the next best alternative is.

Burn-out Spot	Alternative
• Yosemite Valley (in the summer)	• Bighorn Canyon National Recreation Area
• Kenya	• Tanzania
• Galapagos	• Marshall Islands
• Belize	• Guatemala
• Costa Rica	• Venezuela
• Nepal	• Indonesia
• Brazil	• India

 Q: What percentage of the world's water is freshwater?

they'll start slashing and burning to plant crops," points out Bob Heinzman, who manages a Conservation International-US AID program aiming to sustain the forest of Guatemala's remote Peten province. Heinzman plans to set up a system of small loans to local people to help them launch small-scale ecotourism operations such as bed and breakfasts.

"The key point is that the dollars are really being captured for improving the welfare of the local people," Heinzman says. "They're the ones that are swinging the machetes."

This can work. A group of farmers near the village of Bermudian Landing, Belize, agreed six years ago to protect the trees that are habitat for the endangered black howler monkey. These landowners now split the profits from the entrance fee to the Community Baboon Sanctuary, which is also home to Belize's first natural history museum.

Rara Avis, a private nature reserve in the rainforest of northern Costa Rica, has also achieved some success. The reserve, which is home to sustainable extraction of rainforest products such as wicker and plants as well as tourism and scientific research, employs numerous local employees. And residents of the African nation of Rwanda are becoming increasingly protective of mountain gorillas as they realize the tourist revenues the animals generate.

Meanwhile, some ecotourism outfitters donate a portion of their profits to conservation projects in the countries they frequent. International Expeditions of Helena, Alabama, has gone a step farther: It has formed a nonprofit foundation to fund biological research, conservation and education in Peru's Amazon Biosphere Reserve. The foundation not only uses money from International Expeditions' clients, but from outside private sources.

"I think ecotourism is one of the important sustainable development tools," says Megan Epler Wood, executive director of the Ecotourism Society. "It also allows for human development; it can be really positive—if it's well-planned."

Lisa Jones is editor of BUZZWORM: The Environmental Journal *'s EcoTravel section.*

Sources: The Christian Science Monitor *and* Nature Tourism, *by Tensie Whelan.*

have the most fuel efficient planes, making their company less vulnerable to energy price fluctuations. They have been recycling aluminum since 1983 and paper since 1990.

Most airlines have taken steps to clean up their dangerous toxic paint methods. America West uses a dry stripping method of beads to bypass the toxic chemical solvents. Continental uses lower volatile organic compounds paints and TWA recycles the solvents.

Almost all the airlines use recyclable food trays. Yet the packaging of food, from the peanut bags to the sugar packets to the plastic-covered barbecue beef, could be planned to reduce waste. They might begin with reusable plastic cups and a handful of peanuts from the flight attendant.

So, rest your head back on the complimentary pillow. Look out at the tops of clouds and drift off to sleep.... What do they do with the mystery-fabric pillow sheath after you leave the plane? They are thrown away after every flight.

Improvements are needed. Make friendly suggestions to your flight attendant or airline personnel. They listen to customer suggestions.

—*Nicolle Pressly*

A. *3 percent*
Source: The Real World, *edited by Bruce Marshall*

EXOTIC BIRD BAN

As of November 1991, some 41 airlines have stopped transporting wild-caught birds. You may want to consult this list before you book your air travel.

This information was obtained from the Environmental Investigation Agency, 1506 19th St., #4 NW, Washington, DC 20036, (202) 483-6621.

Aerolineas Argentinas
Air France
Air New Zealand
Air UK
Alitalia
ALM Antillean Airlines
American Airlines
Arrow Air
Austrian Airlines
British Airways
BWIA Int'l Airways Corp.
Challenge Air Cargo, Inc.
Continental Airlines
CSA Czechoslovak Air
Dan-Air Services Ltd.
Danzas Corporation
Delta Airlines, Inc.
DHL
Elal Isreal Airlines
Ethiopian Airlines, Inc.
Federal Express Corporation
Garuda Indonesia
Iceland Air
KLM Royal Dutch Airlines
Lan-Chile
Lauda Air
LOT Polish Airlines
Lufthansa German Airlines
Marinair Holland N.V.
Northwest Airlines
Quantas Airlines
Royal Jordanian
Sabena World Airlines
Singapore Airlines
South African Airlines
Swissair
Trans World Airlines
Turkish Airlines

Photo: Lenny Johnson/ Mountain Stock

Trekking at 17,000 feet in front of Ama Dablam in the Kuurbu region of Nepal.

ECOTOURISM REVISITED

- By Kurt Kutay -

Green entrepreneurship has come of age in special interest travel. The burgeoning demand for adventure travel and the call for environmentally and socially responsible tourism has spurred a new ethic and style of travel dubbed "ecotourism." Hundreds of US tour operators have become overnight self-acclaimed ecotourist companies.

Ever more governments are promoting the attractions of wildlife, national parks and traditional culture as much as fun-in-the-sun tourism destinations. More tour operators are selling the same fragile destinations. Hoteliers are building more lodges near natural areas and small communities already pressed to their capacity. As burgeoning hordes of ecotourists tromp over the once unbeaten path, tour operators are pressed to open new destinations and host countries are ill-prepared to properly manage their land and resources.

Is ecotourism really green? Whose responsibility is it to guarantee responsible tourism? And what can be done to avoid the pitfalls and achieve the touted potentials of ecotourism?

Although the term ecotourism has no concise meaning, a recent conference representing tour operators, guides, governmental officials, non-governmental conservation and development

Q: *What renewable resource provides the power to operate emergency telephones on some California freeways?*

agencies, travel agents, travel writers, educators and environmentalists, were able to reach a common ground as to what ecotourism is all about. It was suggested the term ecotourism be dropped for a more neutral and distinguished one: ecotravel.

One definition proposed by Dr. Richard Ryel, president of International Expeditions, states ecotravel is "purposeful travel to natural areas to create an understanding of the cultural and natural history pertaining to the environment, emphasizing care not to alter the integrity of the ecosystem, while producing economic benefits that encourage the preservation of the inherent resources of the environment." In these broad terms, many companies qualify as green tour operators. Any successful nature tour at least brings attention to natural areas. It educates and enlists the traveler as a new recruit to help protect the environment.

At the very least any company operating a trip to a fragile area should take care to minimize its impact. The National Audubon Society, which sponsors a worldwide tour program, has prepared a comprehensive "Travel Ethic for Environmentally Responsible Travel" which it requires all operators conducting Audubon tours to sign. "Unfortunately, there is not much information for operators to avoid impacts taking tourists into natural areas," notes Ray Ashton, former tour manager and current director of International Ecotourism Services for the Water, Air and Research Company. He suggests a merger between researchers and operators to come up with more practical knowledge about ecotourism impacts in fragile areas.

Ashton points out that even though conscientious operators minimize their group size to reduce their individual impact, many operators sending small groups to the same location create a collective impact which can be enormous. "Because everybody uses the same basic locations for ecotourism worldwide," Ashton asserts, "very soon you end up with use on a larger and heavier scale than most people realize. Even with ecotravel we must plan for high density, high impact tourism to protect biodiversity."

Ashton believes it's important for conservationists, biologists and others who are not in the industry to understand the realities of the travel business. Tour operators exist to make a profit, he notes, but it is very competitive and the profit margins are

United Airlines
US Air
Virgin Atlantic Airways

Meanwhile some 25 airlines continue to participate in wild bird trade:

Aero Peru
Alberto Sacio, Pres.
Avenue Jose Pardo
601 13th fl.
Lima 27, Peru

Aeroflot
Mr. Novoselov
1604 K St. NW
Washington, DC
20006

Aeronica
Orlando Chavez,
Manager
7270 NW 12th St., #640
Miami, FL 33126

Aerovias Venezolanas
S.A.
Mr. Henry Lord
Boulton
Torre El Chorro
Avda. Universidad
Caracas, Venezuela

Air Afrique
Yve-Roland Billrecart
P.D.G.
Boite Postale 1575
Abidjan 01
Ivory Coast

Caribbean Air Cargo
Peter Look Hong
Grantley Adams Airport
Christ Church, Barbados

China Airlines
Peter Yap, Director
131. Section 3.
Nanking E. Rd.
Taipei 104, Taiwan
Republic of China

Cubana Airlines
Ing. Rolando Teutelo,
Director-General
Edisiciso LA Rampa

A. *Solar panels*
    Source: 15 Simple Things Californians Can Do To Recycle, *by the Earth • Works Group*

23 y P Vedado
Havannah, Cuba

Egypt Air
Mr. Abdel Moneim
Osman, General
Manager
720 5th Ave.
New York, NY 10019

Guyana Airways Corp.
Guy Spence, Chairman
32 Main St.
Georgetown, Demerara
Guyana

Iberia Airlines
Miguel Aguilo, Pres.
Valasquez 30
Madrid, Spain

Japan Airlines
Matsuo Toshimitsu
2-7-3 Marunouchi
Chiyo-Daku
Tokyo 100, Japan

Kenya Airways
Mr Phillip Ndegwa
Secretary-Chairman
Box 19002
Nairobi, Kenya

Korean Air
C. K. Cho
41-3 Seosomun-Pong
Chung Gu
South Korea

Ladeco Airlines
Jose Lusi Ibanez
Ala Meda 107
Santiago, Chile

Linea Aereas Costarri-
censes
Armando Junes,
Manager
Box 1531
San Jose, Costa Rica
1000

Linea Aeropostal Vene-
zolana
Piso 48, Torre Este
Parque Central
Caracas, Venezuela
Malaysia Airlines

very small. Therefore, they must have a certain level of volume to make it worthwhile to pay for all the marketing and overhead, let alone making a profit. "I'm really worried," observes Ashton. "I see a lot of people out there saying, for example, 'We'll get the Mayans to put people in their houses and they will make all this money.' And I see this happening for a little while as a fad and then it's all going to fall apart. Because most tour operators who are concerned about the environment are not going to be able to support that kind of program unless it's done in a certain manner so they can sustain a certain number of people there, one group after another, over a period of time so they can actually make a profit."

But this threatens the very experience most eco-travelers seek. "The best experiences are when a very small group of travelers has been privy to a spontaneous experience of natural history or a cultural event even as simple as a meal in a local home," Dr. Will Weber, director of Journeys International of Ann Arbor, Michigan, notes. "These are the kinds of things that quickly disappear if you try to package them, sell admission or present them to a large number of people on a regular basis. I don't think we have solved the dilemma of destroying the experience we seek," he concludes. Most experts agree it's not primarily a matter of limiting volume, but rather better on-site planning and management.

But many green tour companies have developed very specific and direct ways to make a positive contribution through travel. Mountain Travel/Sobek Expeditions, from El Cerrito, California, designates certain trips as "Environmental Adventures" in which up to 10 percent of the land cost is contributed to a conservation organization working to preserve areas visited on the tour.

But truly committed and responsible ecotravel is more than giving donations and creating special experiences for clients. In the opinion of Victor Emmanuel, president of his own nature tour company and a recognized leader in ecotravel, "An ecotour is defined by the way the tour is run, by the [host country] operators selected, by the procedures used to run the tour, the type of guides that are used and the relationship to the local country. How is the consumer going to know which companies have really done something?"

Q: *The US consumes about what percentage of the world's production of oil every year, 60 percent of which is used for transportation?*

"Just because a company advertises in *Audubon* Magazine doesn't make it ecologically oriented or even reputable," notes Ashton. Many travelers sign up with an organization involved in the environment such as a zoo, museum or conservation club assuming this guarantees quality and ecological sensitivity. But these organizations usually act more as a marketing front, sub-contracting the trip operation to a tour operator. The US tour operator contracts with a local in-bound operator to handle ground services in the host country which in turn hires the local guides. There are no guarantees unless all levels of tour management share the same ethics and commitment to environmentally sound tour management.

So just how does an individual consumer pick a tour company? Ashton outlines several criteria in a chapter from *Ecologue*, a new environmental consumers' guide. First, know where you want to go and identify which companies specialize in that destination. You cannot count on your average travel agent for advice in adventure travel, although more agents are beginning to specialize in special interest travel and may have valuable inside industry information. Compare several companies. Check their reputations. Ask for references. Inquire about their local ground operators.

Carefully evaluate the itinerary, especially what is not in the printed literature. How much time is spent in the field versus the city or traveling in a vehicle? What is the means of transport? Do they use large air-conditioned buses or a less conspicuous, locally-owned vehicle? Do they recommend using the national airline of the host country? If not, a substantial portion of the trip costs never reach the host nation. What kind of accommodations are used? Do they reflect the high standards of a foreign traveler or the local social, economic and environmental realities of the area visited? Are hotels owned by foreigners, expatriates living in the country or residents indigenous to the region visited?

Another important aspect of a genuine ecotour is that local people are involved in organizing and leading the tour. Otherwise ecotravelers are simply observing a new culture through the eyes of an American guide. "The people themselves are the experience," states Weber. "And it's not guides who have been trained to provide experiences through a

Mr. Ahmad Fuaad
5933 W. Century Blvd.
Los Angeles, CA 90045

Mexicana Air
Ing. Guillermo Martinez
PO Box 12-813
AV Xola 535
Mexicana Bldg.
Mexico City, DF Mexico

Pan American World Airways
Russ Ray, CEO
Pan Am Building
200 Park Ave.
New York, NY 10166

Scandinavian Airlines
Froesundaviks Alle 1
Solna S-161
87 Stockholm, Sweden

Suriname Airways
Mr. M. Mungre, Pres.
P.O. Box 2029
Coppenamestraat 136
Pramaribo, Suriname

TACA International Airlines
Gloria Granillo, DC Dir.
1010 16th St. NW, 4th fl.
Washington, DC 20036

Varig Brazilian Airlines SA
Mr. Rubel Thomas, Pres.
Av. Silvio Va Noronha 365
Aeroporto Santos Dumont
Rio de Janeiro 20021
Brazil

Venezolana Internacional de Aviacion S.A.
Eduardo Quintero, Pres.
Torre Viasa
Calle Sur 25 con Plaza Morelos, Los Caobos
Caracas, Venezuela

A. *40 percent*
Source: World Watch Paper 84

RESOURCES

Buzzworm: The Environmental Journal, bimonthly (6 issues per year, $21). For more information: Buzzworm, P.O. 6853, Syracuse, NY 13217, (800) 825-0061.

Directory of Environmental Travel & Volunteer Activities, by Dianne Brause, One World Travel Family, Lost Valley Center, 81868 Lost Valley Lane, Dexter, OR 97431.

Eco Vacations: Enjoy Yourself and Save the Earth, by Evelyn Kaye, Blue Penguin Publications, Leonia, NJ, 1991.

Environmental Vacations: Volunteer Projects to Save the Planet, by Stephanie Ocko, John Muir, 1990.

Great Expeditions magazine, a journal of adventure and off-the-beaten-path-travel, 5 issues per year, $18. For more information: *Great Expeditions,* P.O. Box 8000-411, Sumas, WA 98295, (604) 852-6170.

Lonely Planet Publications offers a wide variety of shoestring travel guides with an "ecotravel" theme covering virtually all of the third world. For more information: Lonely Planet Publications, Embarcadero West, 112 Linden St., Oakland, CA 94607, (415) 893-8555.

Nature Tourism: Managing for the Environment, edited by Tensie Whelan, Island Press, Washington, DC, 1991.

Western standard, but who are living their lives according to their own culture, and on those terms, who are providing assistance and interpretation."

As the special interest travel industry continues to diversify, standard adventure travel and natural history tours may still be the best choice for most travelers. The success or failure of genuine ecotravel depends on the character of the ecotourist. Traveling responsibly requires self-imposed limits—staying on the designated trail, not using recorders to attract birds when not permitted, not giving big tips to encourage safari drivers off designated roads for better photographs, etc. It means understanding, and accepting, that life is not the same as it is at home, even if it means losing valuable vacation time waiting, sleeping in a hard bed or other discomforts and annoyances.

Ecotourists should be aware (and informed by their travel company) about the cultures they are visiting so they don't have false expectations and can appreciate the culture on its own terms. When a contrived, staged setting is presented as the real culture, an ecotraveler should demand to see the authentic culture and environment. (When in Hawaii, ask: Where are the native Hawaiians?) It may mean being willing to pay more or go to greater lengths in order to have that authenticity as part of the experience.

"Every company is going to say I am an ecotourist company," Emmanuel notes. "We're all for the environment. But let's get down to actual specifics by asking what each ecotravel company specifically has done for the environment. These kinds of questions are going to put moral and ethical and marketplace pressures on people to do better."

For more information about conferences and other ecotravel developments contact the Ecotourism Society, 801 Devon Pl., Alexandria, VA 22314, (703) 549-8979.

Kurt Kutay is a tourguide who frequently writes and lectures about ecotravel.

 Q: *What percentage of the US energy needs could be supplied by wind power?*

Photo: Timm Delaney/Adventure Photo

Ecotourists viewing rhinos in the Ngorongoro crater region of Tanzania.

THE ECOTOURIST AS ACTIVIST

- By Tensie Whelan -

The ecotourist will be a key player in the success or failure of ecotourism. In Monteverde, Costa Rica, the nesting of quetzals occasionally is disrupted by tourists who rap on the nests and then stand poised with a video camera to capture the quetzals' flight. In Yellowstone, visitors feed the bears, encouraging them to accost people for food and making them extremely dangerous. In the Caribbean, tourists buy jewelry made from black coral and other rare reef marine life. In Botswana, tourists treat natives with a rude curiosity, not asking for permission to enter their villages and take photographs. Trekkers in Nepal and elsewhere leave behind litter from food and other items they have carried in.

Ecotour operators must instill a conservation ethic for environmentally sensitive travel in their clients if they are to continue bringing visitors to fragile sites. The National Audubon Society, which conducts ecotours in many countries, has developed a travel ethic that must be adhered to by all its tour operators. The basic guidelines are as follows:

1. Wildlife and their habitats must not be disturbed.
2. Audubon tourism to natural areas will be sustainable.

New World of Travel, by Arthur Frommer Prentice Hall Press, New York, 1988.

Outside Magazine, a magazine for outdoor enthusiasts, published monthly at $18 per year. For more information: *Outside Magazine,* Box 54729, Boulder, CO 80322-4729, (800) 678-1131.

Travel and Learn, by Evelyn Kaye, Blue Penguin Publications, Leonia, NJ, 1991.

*Travel Link,*Co-op America, 2100 M St. NW, #403 Washington, DC 20063.

Wildlife Tourism Impact Project, 524 San Anselmo Ave., Suite 103, San Anselmo, CA 94960.

A. *100 percent*
Source: *Department of Energy, Pacific North West Laboratory*

3. Waste disposal must have neither environmental nor aesthetic impacts.

4. The experience a tourist gains in traveling with Audubon must enrich his or her appreciation of nature, conservation, and the environment.

5. Audubon tours must strengthen the conservation effort and enhance the natural integrity of places visited.

6. Traffic in products that threaten wildlife and plant populations must not occur.

7. The sensibilities of other cultures must be respected.

Audubon tour operators are required to sign a contract stating that they agree to abide by these strictures. Audubon passengers receive a copy of the guidelines and are asked by questionnaire at the end of the trip if the tour operator followed the ethic. So far, Audubon has not received negative feedback.

The ecotourist can do more than learn from the experience. He or she can get involved. Some tour operators run tours to areas that have suffered from overuse; clients help clean up the mess left behind by previous visitors and work to restore endangered habitats. Some organizations such as Earthwatch involve tourists in "citizen scientist" activities: counting turtle eggs on the beaches of Costa Rica, for example. On returning home, quite a few tourists become involved with such issues as tropical deforestation and illegal traffic in endangered species.

Ecotour operators and conservation organizations both in the destination country and in the home country need to work harder to get the ecotourist actively involved in sustainable development. Ecotourists represent a potential army of recruits with free time and money to spend on sustainable development efforts.

Reprinted by permission from Nature Tourism: Managing for the Environment, *edited by Tensie Whelan, Island Press, Washington, DC, 1991.*

NEW ECOTOURISM FILM

A new documentary has been completed by Ecotourism Society Executive Director and Producer Megan Epler Wood, entitled "Ecotourism: Conservation and Tourism in the Wild." Filmed on location in Belize, Kenya and Montana, the program investigates the origins of ecotourism, its use as a conservation tool and its misuse. This hour-length program is hosted by Sam Waterston as a National Audubon Society Special. It will appear on national television (date to be announced) in 1992. The program is available now for non-commercial use. Contact Megan Epler Wood at Eco-Tourism Society, 801 Devon Pl., Alexandria, VA 22314, (703) 549-8979; or Delores Simmons at National Audubon Society, 666 Pennsylvania Ave. SE, Suite 301, Washington, DC 20003, (202) 547-9009.

Q: *What contaminated US town had 225 families apply to purchase houses this year?*

Companies Offering EcoTravel Adventures

AAI, Adventure Associates Inc.
P.O. Box 16304
Seattle, WA 98116
(800) 553-7466
East Africa, Pacific Northwest, Costa Rica, Mexico, Morocco, Thailand

Above the Clouds Trekking, Inc.
P.O. Box 398
Worchester, MA 01602
(508) 799-4499
Himalayas, South America, Africa, Bhutan, Europe, Nepal, Madagascar

Adventure Center
1311 63rd St., Ste.200
Emeryville, CA 94608
(800) 227-8747
Africa, Asia, South America, South Pacific, Europe, Middle East

Adventures in Paradise
155 W. 68th St., Ste. 525
New York, NY 10023
(800) 736-8187
Southeast Asia

Alaska Discovery
369 S. Franklin
Juneau, AK 99801
(907) 586-1911
Alaska, Siberia and more

American Museum of History
Discovery Tours & Cruises
Central Park West at 79th
New York, NY 10024
(800) 462-8687
Alaska, Africa, Antarctica, South America, Asia, Hawaii, Galapagos

American Wilderness Experience, Inc.
P.O. Box 1486
Boulder, CO 80306

(800) 444-0099
(303) 494-2992
US, Australia, New Zealand, Belize

Arizona Raft Adventures
4050 E. Huntington Dr.
Flagstaff, AZ 86004
(602) 526-8200
(800) 786-RAFT
Grand Canyon and San Juan, Costa Rica, Idaho

Asia Pacific Adventures
826 S. Sierra Bonita Ave.
Los Angeles, CA 90036
(800) 825-1680
Asia including the Himalayas, Pakistan and China

Baja Expeditions
2625 Garnet Ave.
San Diego, CA 92109
(800) 843-6967
Baja California, Sea of Cortez, Costa Rica

Big Five Expeditions, LTD
110 Route 110 S
Huntington, NY 11746
(800) 541-2790
South America, North America, Pacific, Africa, Asia

Biological Adventures
2838 Garrison St.
San Diego, CA 92106
(619) 726-2228
Baja California, Sea of Cortez

Biological Journeys
1696 Ocean Dr.
McKinleyville, CA 95521
(800) 548-7555
The Pacific—from the San Juan Islands to the Great Barrier Reef

Bolder Adventures
P.O. Box 1279
Boulder, CO 80306
(800) 397-5917

Thailand, Southeast Asia

Borton Overseas
5516 Lyndale Ave. S
Minneapolis, MN 55419
(800) 843-0602
Africa, Scandinavia, Lapland, Greenland, Spitsbergen

Breakaway Adventure Travel
1171 E. Putnam Ave.
Riverside, CT 06878
(800) 955-5635
USA and worldwide

Cheeseman's Ecology Safaris
20800 Kittredge Rd.
Saratoga, CA 95070
(408) 741-5330
Call for destinations

Creative Adventure Club
3007 Royce Lane
Costa Mesa, CA 92626
(800) 544-5088
Southeast Asia, Pacific Asia, Russia, Indochina, Africa, South America, Jamaica

Crow Canyon Archaeological Center
23390 County Rd. K
Cortez, CO 81321
(800) 422-8975
Southwestern Colorado, Four Corners Area, Utah, New Mexico, Arizona

Ecosummer Expeditions
1516 Duranleau St.
Vancouver, British Columbia, V6H 3S4 Canada
(604) 669-7741
Worldwide expeditions

Ecotourism International
Forum Travel International, Inc.
Gregory Lane, Suite 21
Pleasant Hill, CA 94523
(415) 671-2900

A. *Love Canal*
Source: The Love Canal Revitalization Agency

Latin America, Africa, Asia, Europe, Australia/Pacific, North America, Antarctica

Effie Fletcher's Himalayan High Treks
241 Dolores St.
San Francisco, CA 94103
(415) 861-2391
Nepal and Indian Himalaya, Tibetan Plateau

Escalante Canyon Outfitters
P.O. Box 1325
Boulder, UT 84716
(801) 335-7311
Canyons of southern Utah

Geo Expeditions
P.O. Box 3656
Sonora, CA 95370
(800) 351-5041
Africa, Latin America, Asia and the Pacific

Goldeneye Nature Tours
P.O. Box 30416
Flagstaff, AZ 86003
(800) 624-6606
California, Arizona, Idaho, Texas and New Brunswick, Canada

Great Expeditions
5915 West Blvd.
Vancouver, British Columbia, Canada V6M 3X1
(604) 263-1476
Yukon, British Columbia

High Desert Adventures
5500 Amelia Earhart Dr.
Salt Lake City, UT 84116
(800) 345-7238
Southwest US

Holbrook Travel
3540 NW 13th St.
Gainesville, FL 32609
(800) 451-7111
Americas, Asia, Europe, South Pacific

Inca Floats
1311 63rd St.
Emeryville, CA 94608
(415) 420-1550
Galapagos, Peru, Ecuador

Innerasia Expeditions
2627 Lombard St.
San Francisco, CA 94123
(415) 922-0448
Tibet, Nepal, Bhutan, Hunza, Patagonia, Japan, Soviet Union, Indonesia, Turkey, Alaska, North and South Poles

International Expeditions, Inc.
One Environs Park
Helena, AL 35080
(800) 633-4734
Americas, Africa, Asia, South Pacific

Journeys International
4011 Jackson Rd.
Ann Arbor, MI 48103
(800) 255-8735
Americas, Africa, Asia

Lone Wolf Tours
P.O. Box 40092
Tucson, AZ 85717
(602) 881-0234
China, Mexico, Copper Canyon

Massachusetts Audubon Society Natural History Travel
South Great Rd.
Lincoln, MA 01773
(800) 289-9504
National and International trips

Morris Overseas Tours
418 Fourth Ave.
Melbourne Beach, FL 32951
(800) 777-6853
Costa Rica, Panama

MOT McHugh Ornithology Tours
101 W. Upland Rd.
Ithaca, NY 14850-1415
(607) 257-1616
Americas, Europe, Asia, South Pacific

Mountain Madness
4218 SW Alaska, Ste. 206
Seattle, WA 98116
(206) 937-8389

North America, South America, Africa, Asia, USSR

Mountain Travel/Sobek
6420 Fairmont Ave.
El Cerrito, CA 94550
(800) 227-2384
Worldwide adventures

National Audubon Society Travel
950 Third Ave.
New York, NY 10022
(212) 546-9140
Specializes in cruises, call for destinations

Natural Habitat
One Sussex Station
Sussex, NJ 07461
(800) 543-8917
Harp Seals—Gulf of St. Lawrence, Canada

Navigations And Expeditions
10650 Irma Dr., Ste. 21
Denver, CO 80233
(800) 336-9007
Amazon River Area

O.A.R.S.
P.O. Box 67
Angels Camp, CA 95222
(209) 736-4677
Tuolumne River in California and Grand Canyon

Oceanic Society Expeditions
Ft. Mason Center, Bldg. E
San Francisco, CA 94123
(415) 441-1106
Americas, Africa, South Pacific

Overseas Adventure Travel
349 Broadway
Cambridge, MA 02139
(800) 221-0814
USSR, Ecuador, Africa, Mexico

Questers Worldwide Nature Tours
257 Park Ave. S
New York, NY 10010-7369
(800) 468-8668

 What continent has the highest birthrate in the world?

Americas, Europe, Asia, Africa, South Pacific

Safaricentre
3201 N. Sepulveda Blvd.
Manhattan Beach, CA 90266
(800) 223-6046
Worldwide expeditions

Scripps Aquarium
A-007
LaJolla, CA 92093
(619) 543-4578
Baja California, Sea of Cortez, Santa Catalina Island and Fiji Island

Silvercloud Expeditions
P.O. Box 1006
Salmon, ID 83467
(208) 756-6215
Wilderness areas of the Salmon River

Southern Cross Expeditions
63 Walnut St.
Southhampton, NY 11968
(800) 359-0193
Brazil, Argentina, Peru, Ecuador

Southwind Adventures, Inc.
1861 Camino Lumbre
Santa Fe, NM 87505
(505) 438-7120
Peru, Ecuador, Bolivia, Patagonia

Special Expeditions, Inc.
720 Fifth Ave., Suite 605
New York, NY 10019
(212) 765-7740
Alaska, Africa, American southwest, Caribbean, Belize, Costa Rica, Galapagos, Arctic Norway, Greenland, Canada, Australia, Papua New Guinea

SUMMITS Adventure Travel
P.O. Box 214
Ashford, WA 98304
(206) 569-2992
Worldwide mountain expeditions

Victor Emmanuel Nature Tours
P.O. Box 33008
Austin, TX 78764
(800) 328-8368
Americas, Europe, Asia, Africa, South Pacific

Voyagers, International
P.O. Box 915
Ithaca, NY 14851
(607) 257-3091
Americas, Asia, South Pacific, Africa and Ireland

Wilderness Southeast
711 Sandtown Rd.
Savannah, GA 31410
(912) 897-5108
Everglades, Great Smoky Mountains, Costa Rica, Belize, Amazon, Bahamas, Florida Springs

Wilderness Travel
801 Allston Way
Berkeley, CA 94710
(800) 247-6700
91 different itineraries, call for destinations

Wildland Adventures
3516 NE 155th
Seattle, WA 98155
(800) 345-4453
Andes, Amazon, Himalayas, Africa, Costa Rica

Woodstar Tours
908 S. Massachusetts Ave.
Deland, FL 32724
(904) 736-0327
Costa Rica, South Africa, Thailand, Venezuela, Yucatan

Yeti Tours
C/o Alan Gardner
P.O.Box 140
Ohakune, New Zealand
(0658) 58-197
Wanganui River and other great New Zealand rivers

ECO-RESORTS

Las Ventanas de Osa Wildlife Refuge
Box 1089
Lake Helen, FL 32744-1089
(904) 228-3356

Little St. Simons Island
P.O. Box 1078
St. Simons, GA 31522
(912) 638-7472

Maho Bay Camps
17A East 73rd St.
New York, NY 10021
(800) 392-9004

ORGANIZATIONS PROMOTING ECOTRAVEL

Co-op America
2100 M St. NW #403
Washington, DC 20063
(202) 223-1881

Cultural Survival, Inc.
53A Church St.
Cambridge, MA 02138
(617) 495-2562

Center for Responsible Tourism
2 Kensington Rd.
San Anselmo, CA 94960
(415) 843-5506

The Ecotourism Society
801 Devon Pl.
Alexandria, VA 22314
(703) 549-8979

The Earth Preservation Fund
3516 NE 155th
Seattle, WA 98155
(206) 365-0686

Ecumenical Coalition on Third World Tourism
P.O. Box 9-25
Bangkhen, Bangkok 0900, Thailand

A. *Africa*
  Source: Zero Population Growth

Action and involvement are needed in order to begin to heal Earth's woes. EcoConnections shows the individual how and where to get involved, from writing Congress to volunteering with small and large environmental organizations. Directories to environmental organizations, environmental education programs and ecology-minded religious organizations are also included. And to honor those already contributing and to inspire others to achieve recognition, Earth Journal provides a list of environmental awards and the most recent award winners.

HOW TO WRITE CONGRESS

Writing elected officials is an easy and effective way to continue to cast votes even after election day. With the number of environmental issues being voted on today, expressing your concerns is more important than ever. Here are a few reminders when writing:

1. Write letters about timely issues only. Information or suggestions about a certain issue are useless unless there is still time for an elected official to act. Call environmental hotlines such as Audubon Actionline, (202) 547-9017, for updated reports on which issues need the most immediate support.

2. Be specific in your letter about which bill or issue you are addressing. Use the popular titles (i.e. "the Big Green," "the Endangered Species Act") and, when possible, use the bill's number.

3. Try to limit your letter to one issue, and keep it brief. Short and to-the-point is the best approach when writing to members of Congress who receive hundreds of pieces of mail per day.

4. Back your emotions or opinion with solid reasoning. Tell your elected official about specific scenarios he or she may not be familiar with. Share the knowledge you have about a particular issue.

5. Even if you don't feel like an expert, write your

Volunteer!

Listed here are national and international opportunities to volunteer for the environment. Volunteering can be fun, rewarding and good for the earth. Interested persons should contact the organizations to find out details about the activities, such as where the opportunities are available, whether housing is provided, skills desired, type of commitment expected and whether other opportunities exist.

MONARCHISTS

Volunteers are needed to participate in the monarch monitoring project of the CALIFORNIA MONARCH STUDIES program. Field surveyors record roosting habitats and tag butterflies at monarch overwintering sites along the California coast. Site location and training provided. Contact Walt Sakai, CALIFORNIA MONARCH STUDIES, Santa Monica College, 1900 Pico Blvd., Santa Monica, CA 90405-1628, (213) 450-5150, ext. 9713.

WATER PICS

CEDAM INTERNATIONAL needs volunteers to document marine species, map underwater topography, participate in cleanup dives and take underwater photographs. Land projects are also offered. Members can participate for share-of-cost donation. Contact CEDAM INTERNATIONAL, Fox Rd., Croton-on-Hudson, NY 10520, (914) 271-5365.

BRUSH UP

VOLUNTEERS FOR OUTDOOR WASHINGTON work in national forests and parks in western Washington, Seattle and surrounding areas, the San Juan Islands and other public lands. Trail crews are needed for maintenance, brush clearing, tread construction and foot bridge building. Urban park cleanup crews are needed for maintenance, litter control and painting. Contact VOLUNTEERS FOR OUTDOOR WASHINGTON, 4516 University Way, NE, Seattle, WA 98105, (206) 545-4868.

RADIO, TV & YOU

EDUCATIONAL COMMUNICATIONS needs volunteers nationwide to work on air and water quality, resources, population, area preservation, energy, land

---

Q: *How much of Brazil's Atlantic coast forests have been destroyed?*

use and planning, parks, wildlife, pollution, waste and education. Volunteers are needed to produce radio and television programs, report on environmental issues, organize projects and participate in continuing conservation efforts. Contact EDUCATIONAL COMMUNICATIONS, P.O. Box 35473, Los Angeles, CA 90035, (213) 559-9160.

EARTH WORKS

EARTHWATCH needs volunteers to participate in worldwide research projects. On Maria Island National Park in Tasmania, volunteers watch Tasmanian hens and record behaviors such as feeding, copulating, sexual and aggressive displays and paternal care. In southeastern Poland, volunteers are needed to observe and census deer and wolf populations in the Bieszczady Mountains. Volunteers may also record bear behavior in northern Minnesota, and research bottle nosed dolphins in Costa Rica. Many other opportunities offered. All projects require fees. Contact EARTHWATCH, 680 Mount Auburn St., P.O. Box 403N, Watertown, MA 02272, (617) 926-8200.

WILD LOBBYING

The 51 affiliated offices of the NATIONAL WILDLIFE FEDERATION seek volunteers to work on various environmental projects conducted by each group. Projects may include lobbying, coordinating events, maintaining correspondence, working on youth camps and grassroots mobilization. Contact in writing, Affiliate and Regional Programs, NATIONAL WILDLIFE FEDERATION, 1400 16th St. NW, Washington, DC 20036.

AMAZON

INTERNATIONAL RESEARCH EXPEDITIONS offers opportunities to conduct international research. Volunteers may go to Australia to radio collar animals and collect plant specimens, to the Bahamas to document bird populations, or work in the Amazon observing, interviewing and photographing residents of remote Peruvian villages. Projects are available in archeology, zoology, ornithology, marine biology, ecology and primatology. Activities are available for a fee. Contact INTERNATIONAL RESEARCH EXPEDITIONS, 140 University Dr., Menlo Park, CA 94025, (415) 323-4228.

own views. They will help to balance or reinforce what major lobbying groups are saying.

6. Try to show awareness of how one issue can affect not only the environment, but your community's citizens and their jobs. Be encouraging and offer solutions or alternatives.

7. Ask for specific action, or a form letter is sure to follow. Suggest that the politician cosponsor a bill or support a certain amendment.

8. Don't hesitate to ask questions and request a response. Be sure to include a complete return address to facilitate a reply.

9. Focus on the elected officials from your own delegation.

10. Address your letter properly. It's simple: The Honorable (fill in name), US Senate, Washington, DC 20510.

Remember, your letters really have an impact!

VOTE FOR THE EARTH

"Election Day *is* Earth Day" is the theme of a new book by the Earth•Works Group. Authored by the League of Conservation voters, *Vote For the Earth* addresses environmental issues at a local, state and national level and provides an "environmental scorecard" on US Senators and Representatives. Available in 1992, Earth•Works Group, Berkeley, CA.

A. *99 percent*
   Source: Natural Resources Defense Council

ECO-AWARDS

As the decade of the environment began in 1990, so did ways to encourage ecologically minded acts of organizations, individuals and businesses to insure that the trend of taking care of the planet would continue. The following is a list of environmental awards given to those whose commitment has meant a healthier earth.

BUSINESS

BUSINESS CONSERVATION LEADERSHIP AWARD
National Association of Conservation Districts, 509 Capitol Ct. NE, Washington, DC 20002.

Established in the 1960s by the National Association of Conservation Districts to recognize outstanding examples of cooperation between businesses and conservation districts. Winners are chosen from a pool of businesses nominated by conservation districts.
1991 recipient: The AMAX Coal Company.

NATIONAL ENVIRONMENTAL DEVELOPMENT ASSOCIATION'S HONOR ROLL AWARD
National Environmental Development Association, 1440 New York Ave. NW, Suite 300, Washington, DC 20005.

Established by the National Environmental Development Association, an association of corporations, labor unions and other sector members, to annually recognize outstanding US companies and organizations for their commitment to

DUNE

ASSATEAGUE ISLAND NATIONAL SEASHORE consists of dunelands, pine forests and marshland, surrounded by ocean and saltwater bays. The island uses volunteer biological technicians to assist with research and labor-intensive resource management activities. Interpretive internships are also available for part of the year. Housing, uniform and small subsistence provided. Contact Chief of Interpretation, ASSATEAGUE ISLAND NATIONAL SEASHORE, Rte. 2, Box 294, Berlin, MD 21811.

UTAH AND YOU

UTAH STATE PARKS AND RECREATION offers statewide volunteer opportunities. Volunteers may choose a park to work in. Activities may include interpretation, guiding visitors, research, maintenance and more. Contact Mary L. Tullins, Division of Parks and Recreation, 1636 W. North Temple, Salt Lake City, UT 84116, (801) 538-7220.

WILDER BUILDER

WILLAMETTE NATIONAL FOREST needs volunteers in wilderness administration and rehabilitation positions. Small crews work for five to ten days informing and educating the public. Site cleanup and rehabilitation volunteers work with trail crews on specific projects and fire suppression. Exposure to harsh weather conditions likely. Volunteers must be in good shape and have map and compass reading skills. Contact John Bowman, WILLAMETTE NATIONAL FOREST, P.O. Box 10607, Eugene, OR 97440, (503) 465-6421.

NATIONAL CITY PARK

ROCK CREEK PARK, in the city of Washington, DC, seeks volunteers to assist with historical and natural interpretation, resource management and office work. The nearly 1,800-acre park has 28 miles of trails and numerous other recreational activities. Training.opportunities are available. Must be 18 years old and have a current driver's license. Own transportation helpful. Contact Volunteer Coordinator, ROCK CREEK PARK, 5000 Glover Rd. NW, Washington, DC 20015, (202) 426-6832.

CEDAR MESA PATROLS

NATURAL BRIDGES NATIONAL MONUMENT needs campground hosts to conduct patrols of campground,

Q: *What percentage of the 45,000 pesticides that have been introduced since 1948 have been tested for possible health effects?*

provide general information to campers, clean facilities and perform minor maintenance. Some expenses reimbursed, minimum stay of two weeks required. Contact NATURAL BRIDGES NATIONAL MONUMENT, Box 1, Lake Powell, UT 84533.

CAMP HOST

YOSEMITE NATIONAL PARK uses volunteers as campground hosts, for campground maintenance, interpretation, wildlife management and backcountry monitoring. Contact VIP Coordinator, P.O. Box 577, Yosemite National Park, CA 95389, (209) 372-0264.

GET A JOB

STUDENT CONSERVATION ASSOCIATION organizes groups of volunteers to work in cooperation with public management agencies and in other programs. Participants have the opportunity to do a large variety of tasks, such as interpretation and visitor services, resource management, recreation planning, forestry, range and wildlife management, trail construction and maintenance, backcountry and river patrols and research in archeology, geology and hydrology. Projects are available around the country. Contact STUDENT CONSERVATION ASSOCIATION, P.O. Box 550, Charlestown, NH 03603, (603) 826-4301.

DEVELOP A GOOD HABITAT

ARANSAS NATIONAL WILDLIFE REFUGE is the wintering home of the highly endangered whooping crane. Habitat management projects, environmental education and scientific research studies are conducted regularly. Volunteers are sought who have interest in carpentry, computers, painting, bird identification, guided tours, exhibit development and environmental education. Contact Ellen Michaels, ARANSAS NATIONAL WILDLIFE REFUGE, P.O. Box 100, Austwell, TX 77950, (512) 286-3559.

WATERFOWL SURVEYS

CHEQUAMEGON NATIONAL FOREST seeks volunteer forestry and wildlife assistants. Duties include wildlife/waterfowl surveys, forest inventories for red pine and spruce stands, tree planting and map drawing. Volunteers must be able to identify water birds such as loons and ducks, have skills in map reading, tree species identification in the Great Lakes area and

improve the environment through educational programs or environmental enhancement. Nominations of organizations and companies will be reviewed and judged by a panel of leading environmental experts. Winners are announced in June.

Some 1991 recipients: Linde Division of Union Carbide Industrial Gases Inc., AT & T, Anheuser-Busch Companies, Monsanto Chemical, Consolidated Coal Company, Ashland Oil Inc. and Heinz USA.

COMMITMENT AND ACHIEVEMENT

MACARTHUR FOUNDATION AWARDS GRANTS MacArthur Foundation, 5520 N. Magnolia Ave., Chicago, IL 60640-1307.

Established in 1978 to emphasize an interdisciplinary, collaborative approach to the human dimensions of environmental change. For 1991, the grants total $3.9 million. The grant recipients are chosen by an advisory board.

Some 1991 recipients: Harvard University's John F. Kennedy School of Government to study the management of global environmental risks such as climate change and ozone depletion; National Center for Food and Agricultural Policy's Resources for the Future to examine the effects of the regulation of agriculture in developed countries on the rural environment of less developed countries; University of California

A. *10 percent*
Source: Omni *Magazine, September 1989*

Center for Chinese Studies to compare approaches to rural transformation, the role of markets and environmental change in the USSR, China, Hungary, Cuba and Ethiopia.

NATIONAL ENVIRONMENTAL ACHIEVEMENT AWARDS
Renew America, 1400 16th St. NW, Suite 710, Washington, DC 20036.

Established in 1990 by Renew America to honor successes in correcting or preventing harm to the environment. The public is invited to submit entries.

Some 1991 recipients: Natural Resources Defense Council for its work to protect the stratospheric ozone layer; Littleton, Massachusetts' Groundwater Protection and Monitoring Program for its program which integrates land-use planning, environmental audits and groundwater monitoring in an aggressive and comprehensive aquifer and watershed protection program; League of Women Voters of New Castle, New York, who offer educational supermarket tours.

PEW SCHOLARS PROGRAM IN CONSERVATION AND THE ENVIRONMENT
Pew Scholars Program in Conservation and the Environment, University of Michigan, 2042 Dana Bldg., 430 E. University, Ann Arbor, MI 48109-1115.

Established in 1988 by the Pew Charitable

forestry skills. Contact Dave Nelson, Hayward Ranger District, Rte. 10, Box 508, Hayward, WI 54843, (715) 634-4821.

PARK FLORIDA
FLORIDA PARK SERVICE has over 100 state parks. They include springs, woodland and coastal environments. Campground hosts are needed year-round at the 42 parks which feature camping. Volunteers are also needed to assist with maintenance, visitor centers, tours, research and interpretation. Duties vary per park. Contact Brenda Garland, FLORIDA PARK SERVICE, 1843 S. Tamiami Trail, Osprey, FL 34229, (813) 966-2256.

MARSHLANDS
TINICUM NATIONAL ENVIRONMENTAL CENTER, which cares for the largest remaining freshwater tidal marsh in Pennsylvania, is home to a variety of plants and animals typical of a wetland environment. Nature guides are wanted to lead walks on weekends. Some knowledge of plant or animal identification and natural history is needed. Contact TINICUM NATIONAL ENVIRONMENTAL CENTER, Suite 104, Scott Plaza 2, Philadelphia, PA 19113, (215) 365-3118.

LAND WORKS
BUREAU OF LAND MANAGEMENT wants volunteer participants to work with wildlife biologists, range conservationists, botanists, geologists, realty specialists and range technicians on a variety of projects. Activities may include campground construction and maintenance, fencing, spring development, habitat development, mineral compliance, plant community surveys and public land boundary identification. Contact Gene Wehmeyer, BUREAU OF LAND MANAGEMENT, 1133 N. Western Ave., Wenatchee, WA 98801, (509) 662-4223.

LOGGERHEADS
SEA TURTLE RESTORATION PROJECT needs help to support the first wildlife refuge proposed for an endangered species. The establishment of the Archie Carr Refuge would protect some of Florida's east coast beaches from development and create a sanctuary for the world's second largest loggerhead sea turtle population and for 40 percent of all green

Q. *Eighty percent of the chemicals sprayed on crops are sprayed for what purpose?*

turtles that nest in Florida. Contact SEA TURTLE RESTORATION PROJECT, Earth Island Institute, 300 Broadway, Suite 28, San Francisco, CA 94133.

TALK LAKE MEAD

LAKE MEAD NATIONAL RECREATION AREA needs interpretive assistants to contact visitors, assist in programs and lead walks. Maintenance helpers do light cleaning, irrigation, pruning and minor repair. Boat operators are needed to patrol the lake. Free camping provided. Contact VIP Coordinator, LAKE MEAD NATIONAL RECREATION AREA, 601 Nevada Hwy., Boulder City, NV 89005, (702) 293-8918.

PACIFIC FORESTS

The US FOREST SERVICE in the Pacific northwest needs volunteers in 19 national forests with 102 ranger districts. Opportunities are available in many areas, from management to recreation, from wildlife to research. Activities vary according to the interests or skills of the volunteers. Contact Drinda Lombardi, Volunteer Coordinator, U.S FOREST SERVICE, Pacific Northwest Region, P.O. Box 3623, Portland, OR 97208, (503) 326-3816.

ALL HANDS ON DECK

SEA SHEPHERD CONSERVATION seeks volunteers to work on one of their two ships stationed in California. Volunteers will help with the maintenance and running of the ships while participating in civil disobedience in matters of illegal or harmful shipping activities. Fee may be required depending on time spent on the ship. Contact SEA SHEPHERD CONSERVATION, P.O. Box 7000-S, Redondo Beach, CA 90277, (213) 373-6979.

ARSENAL

Volunteer opportunities are available at the ROCKY MOUNTAIN ARSENAL. Volunteers will help with a variety of activities, including guiding tours, planning events and coordinating programs at the Visitor Center and the Eagle Watch. Contact the US Fish and Wildlife Service, ROCKY MOUNTAIN ARSENAL, Bldg. 111, Commerce City, CO 80022-2180, (303) 289-0232.

Trusts, a national philanthropy based in Philadelphia. The Pew Scholars Program awards grants of $150,000 each to US environmental scientists, lawyers, advocates, academics, public policy or business leaders with demonstrated excellence in their fields. Pew scholars are chosen annually from a pool of 60 candidates nominated by the chief executive officers of their institutions or by one of the program's independent nominators.

Some 1991 recipients: Donella H. Meadows, adjunct professor of environmental and policy studies at Dartmouth College, for her work with sustainable resource management; Kamaljit Bawa, University of Massachusetts at Boston, for his work with conservation and management of tropical forest genetic research; Georgia Mace, Zoological Society of London, for her work with genetics, small population biology and extinction processes.

THE PRESIDENT'S ENVIRONMENTAL AND CONSERVATION CHALLENGE AWARDS
President's Environmental and Conservation Challenge Awards Program, The White House Council on Environmental Quality, 722 Jackson Pl. NW, Washington, DC 20503.

Established in 1991 by President Bush's Council on Environmental Quality "to honor a select group of individuals and organizations who best exemplify the cooperative,

A. *Beautification*
Source: Omni Magazine, September 1989

innovative spirit which I believe offers our greatest hope for permanent environmental progress," says President Bush of the awards. The awards, presented each fall, are given in four areas: Partnership, Quality Environmental Management, Innovation and Education and Communication. Up to three awards are given in each category. The awards competition is open to all US residents, businesses, nonprofit organizations, professional and trade associations, communities and state and local governments. Application deadline is July.

Some 1991 recipients: The Virginia Coast Reserve: The Nature Conservancy and partners, Washington, DC, for fostering cooperative approaches to environmental needs; Pacific Gas and Electric Company: Environmental Policy and Programs, San Francisco, California, for demonstrating that environmental values can be integrated into sound management decisions and practices; and Project Wild, Boulder, Colorado, for developing informational programs that inspire respect for the environment and raise the public's environmental awareness.

SIERRA CLUB HONORS AND AWARDS

Honors and Awards Committee, Elden Hughes, 14045 Honeysuckle Ln., Whittier, CA 90604.

Established to recognize Sierra Club members, individuals and organizations for

DOLPHIN DAZE

OCEANIC SOCIETY EXPEDITIONS offers volunteer opportunities with their Bahama dolphin project. Under the guidance of researchers, participants will collect data on dolphin family and social structure, behavior and habitat requirements and communication. Travel and accommodations will be aboard the *Jennifer Marie*, a 70-foot schooner designed for comfort. Trip members must know how to swim. Fee required. Contact OCEANIC SOCIETY EXPEDITIONS, Ft. Mason Ctr., Bldg. E, San Francisco, CA 94123, (800) 326-7491.

DAM

The COLORADO ENVIRONMENTAL COALITION invites volunteers to work on a variety of issues including public lands, rivers, water quality, timber and environmental health. The coalition has been working to stop large dam construction on various rivers throughout Colorado and is working to control the impact of oil and gas drilling. The coalition's environmental health committee needs volunteers to assist with an ongoing energy conservation project. Contact Dorothy Cohen, COLORADO ENVIRONMENTAL COALITION, 777 Grant St., Suite 606, Denver, CO 80203, (303) 837-8701.

WILD ISLANDS

CHINCOTEAGUE NATIONAL WILDLIFE REFUGE, located on Assateague Island, a barrier beach island off Virginia, seeks volunteer biological assistants, public-use interpreters and maintenance workers. Biological assistants are needed to monitor wildlife populations and collect information on threatened and endangered species found in the refuge. Contact Volunteer Coordinator, CHINCOTEAGUE NATIONAL WILDLIFE REFUGE, P.O. Box 62, Chincoteague, VA 23336, (804) 336-6122.

HAWK COUNT

HAWKWATCH INTERNATIONAL has volunteer field positions available. Field participants are needed to assist with migration counts, capture and banding programs and nest surveys of hawks and other birds of prey in several western states. Experienced applicants are preferred. Volunteers are expected to participate for four to 15 weeks. Send letter of application, resumé and three references to Stephen W. Hoffman,

Q: *For the world's first power plant of its kind, what plentiful resource was used in California, and is generating power for 20,000 homes?*

HAWKWATCH INTERNATIONAL, P.O. Box 35706, Albuquerque, NM 87176-5706, (505) 255-7622.

MARINE BIOLOGY

FOUNDATION FOR FIELD RESEARCH offers volunteer research positions worldwide in many fields. Areas of study include marine biology and mammalogy, archeology, botany and more. Volunteer positions are available in Grenada, Mexico, Africa, Ireland and elsewhere. Fee required. Contact FOUNDATION FOR FIELD RESEARCH, P.O. Box 2010, Alpine, CA 91903, (619) 445-9264.

WHALE TRACKS

PACIFIC WHALE FOUNDATION seeks volunteers for field studies in Hawaii or Australia. Volunteers are needed to photograph, track and document behaviors of whales and dolphins in the wild from January to April and June to October. Volunteers are also needed to work on a tropical reef during July, August and October. The two-week program requires a fee. Contact PACIFIC WHALE FOUNDATION, Kealia Beach Plaza, Suite 25, 101 North Kihei Rd., Kihei, Maui, HI 96753, (808) 879-8811, (800) 942-5311.

WILD WOLF

The WILD CANID SURVIVAL AND RESEARCH CENTER AND WOLF SANCTUARY offers volunteer positions ranging from fundraisers to naturalists. The Center also offers an Adopt-a-Wolf program. Contact WILD CANID SURVIVAL AND RESEARCH CENTER, P.O. Box 760, Eureka, MO 63025, (314) 938-5900.

NORTHERN NATURALISTS

ALASKA STATE PARKS is recruiting volunteers for a variety of positions including campground host, ranger assistant, trail crew member, planner and naturalist. Opportunities are available May through September. Training, uniforms, housing and a food stipend may be offered. Participants are asked to make a minimum four-week commitment. Contact Volunteer Coordinator—BW, ALASKA STATE PARKS, P.O. Box 107001, Anchorage, AK 99510-7001, (907) 762-2655.

strong and consistent commitment to environmental issues. Deadline for public nominations is February.

Some 1991 recipients: Celia Hunter and Jenny Wood for decades of distinguished conservation service in the protection of the wild lands of Alaska (John Muir Award), Barbara Y. E. Pyle, Vice President of Environmental Policy for Turner Broadcasting System, Inc., for expanding environmental coverage and production of outstanding issue-oriented television documentaries (David Brower Award) and Representative Henry Waxman of California in recognition of his leading role in the passage of the Clean Air Act of 1990 (Edgar Wayburn Award).

EDUCATION
LINDBERGH GRANTS
The Charles A. Lindbergh Fund, 708 S. Third St., Suite 110, Minneapolis, MN 55415.

Established in 1978 by The Charles A. Lindbergh Fund, Inc., to fund "research and educational projects which will contribute to a technology/ nature balance." Grant monies in 1991 were up to $10,580. Deadline to apply is June.

Some 1991 recipients: Carol B. Brandt for her project "Sustaining Traditional Crops of the Zuni Pueblo Indians of West-Central New Mexico: A Harvest for Local and Global Agricultural Communities"; Dr. Donald E. Hagen for his project "Environmental Impact of

A. *Cow manure*
Source: The Philadelphia Enquirer, *cited by* Arizona Light, *September 1989*

New High Speed Civilian Aircraft"; and Dr. Lee R. Lynd for the project "Cellulose Ethanol: A Technology Promoting Better Balance Between Transportation Fuel Demands and Environmental Quality."

NATIONAL HUMANE EDUCATION TEACHER OF THE YEAR

The National Association for Humane and Environmental Education, 67 Salem Rd., East Haddam, CT 06423-0362.

Established as an annual award by The National Association for Humane and Environmental Education to recognize a classroom teacher who routinely teaches about humane and environmental issues. The winner is selected from publicly nominated entries by a selection committee.

1991 recipient: Karen Smith, special education teacher at Cottonwood Elementary School in Cottonwood, Arizona.

GOVERNMENT

PTI TECHNOLOGY ACHIEVEMENT AWARDS

Public Technology, Inc., 1301 Pennsylvania Ave. NW, Washington, DC 20004.

Established in 1982 by Public Technology Inc. to identify innovative solutions to local government problems and have those solutions transferred to other jurisdictions. Winners are chosen from publicly nominated entries. Deadline for entry is December.

Some 1990 recipients:

TALK TO THE ANIMALS

LINCOLN PARK ZOO seeks volunteers to lead tours, give talks, conduct animal observations and perform a variety of responsibilities. Limited handling of small animals is involved. Zoo volunteers are required to make a one-year commitment of four to six hours per week. Training is provided. Contact THE LINCOLN PARK ZOOLOGICAL SOCIETY, 2200 N. Cannon Dr., Chicago, IL 60614, (312) 294-4676.

KIDDIE ZOO

SAN FRANCISCO ZOOLOGICAL SOCIETY needs volunteers to work in research and education, the Children's Zoo, the Insect Zoo, the Animal Resource Center, the Avian Conservation Program, the Adopt-An-Animal program, fundraising, administrative projects and special events. Research to determine whether or not the Hawaiian humpback whales are being displaced, will be conducted off the coast of Maui for a two week period in February and March. This program requires a fee. Contact the Volunteer Coordinator, SAN FRANCISCO ZOOLOGICAL SOCIETY, One Zoo Rd., San Francisco, CA 94132, (415) 753-7068.

EGG HUNT

The MASSACHUSETTS AUDUBON SOCIETY needs volunteers to support work with endangered green sea turtles in July and August when the turtles nest in Costa Rica. Participants will live and work with scientists on the beach. A fee is required and volunteers must commit to a 10- or 17-day stay. Contact Natural History Travel, MASSACHUSETTS AUDUBON SOCIETY, S. Great Rd., Lincoln, MA 01773, (800) 289-9504, (617) 259-9500, ext. 7411.

A WHALE OF A TALE

The ALASKA WILDLIFE ALLIANCE seeks volunteers to observe endangered humpback whales and other types of wildlife in Glacier Bay National Park. Volunteers monitor whale behavior, whale numbers and vessel traffic impacts on whales within the bay. Participants should have kayaking and wilderness camping experience and be willing to staff an observation post for two weeks. Contact ALASKA WILDLIFE ALLIANCE, P.O. Box 202022, Anchorage, AK 99520, (907) 277-0897.

Q: *How many trees has President Bush proposed to cut from the Forest Service's tree-planting programs since April 1991?*

STREAM ENHANCEMENT

The ADOPT-A-STREAM FOUNDATION seeks volunteers to join its network of Stream Keepers who are involved in monitoring, enhancing and watchdogging the streams of Washington state. The foundation will conduct 12 free training workshops in Washington state through August 1992. Send a self-addressed stamped envelope to Environmental Education Coordinator, ADOPT-A-STREAM FOUNDATION, Box 5558, Everett, WA 98206.

BEAR VIEWING

The Tongass National Forest ADMIRALTY NATIONAL MONUMENT is seeking a wilderness ranger volunteer to work from mid May through early September. The applicant will monitor visitor use, help in light trail maintenance and provide information at the bear viewing area. Benefits include food, bunkhouse, stipend and round-trip travel from Seattle upon completion of the field season. Contact John Neary, ADMIRALTY NATIONAL MONUMENT, 8461 Old Dairy Rd., Juneau, AK 99801, (907) 586-8790

VIP

The NATIONAL PARK SERVICE volunteers work at a variety of jobs ranging from working at an information desk to designing visitor brochures to assisting resource managers and researchers by making wildlife counts. Volunteers may work a few hours a week or month, seasonally or full time. Participants should be in reasonably good health and a medical examination may be required for some jobs. Contact the Volunteer in Parks coordinator at the desired national park to request an application.

MAMMAL PATROL

The MARINE MAMMAL CENTER offers volunteer opportunities in all areas of operation, including animal care, administration, grounds-keeping, information interpreter and more. Contact Ann Forsell, The MARINE MAMMAL CENTER, Marin Headlands, Golden Gate National Recreation Area, Sausalito, CA 94965, (415) 331-SEAL.

LOONY BEHAVIOR OBSERVED

The LOON PRESERVATION COMMITTEE seeks volunteers in the New Hampshire area to help observe

the City of San Diego, California; Montgomery County, Maryland; the City of Sarasota, Florida; and the City of San Jose, California.

HUMAN RIGHTS AND THE ENVIRONMENT

READSBORO AWARD FOR COMMUNITY SOLIDARITY IN SUPPORT OF HUMAN RIGHTS AND THE ENVIRONMENT

Arctic to Amazonia Alliance, P.O. Box 73, Stafford, VT 05072.

Established in 1991 by Arctic to Amazonia to commend community efforts in situations in which human rights and environmental protection are supported. Persons interested in nominating communities for future awards can contact Arctic to Amazonia Alliance.

1991 recipient: Readsboro, Vermont, "in recognition of the residents of Readsboro's unanimous vote of March 4, 1991, rejecting the town utility's purchase of power from the culturally and environmentally destructive James Bay II hydroelectric project in northern Quebec."

INDIVIDUAL CONTRIBUTIONS

GOLDMAN ENVIRONMENTAL PRIZE

The Goldman Environmental Foundation, 1160 Battery St., Suite 400, San Francisco, CA 94111.

Established in 1990 by the Goldman Environmental Foundation to honor "men and women of vision and courage

A. *32 million*
Source: US Forest Service

who take great risks for the environment." Awards of $60,000 are given annually to six representatives from six continents for their grassroots efforts to preserve and enhance the environment. Nominations are accepted May 1 through September 1 each year.

1991 recipients: North America representative Sam LaBudde for his role in publicizing tuna fishing practices that kill dolphins; South/Central America representative Evaristo Nugkuag for organizing indigenous peoples and forming creative alliances; European representative Roland Tiensuu, a 12-year-old who founded *Barnens Regnskog* (Swedish for "Children's Rainforest"). He shares the Goldman with Eha Kern, his teacher who taught him about rainforests; Australian At Large representative Catherine Wallace for her activism in a broad scope of conservation issues; Asian representative Yoichi Kuroda for coordinating the Japan Tropical Forest Action Network's campaign to expose and reform Japan's role in tropical deforestation; Africa representative Wangari Muta Maathai for launching the now internationally acclaimed Green Belt Movement, a grassroots tree planting project composed mainly of women.

THE GREAT OUTDOORS AWARD
American Recreation Coalition, 1331 Pennsylvania Ave. NW, Suite 726, Washington, DC 20004.

loon behavior, patrol nesting areas and protect nests. Contact LOON PRESERVATION COMMITTEE, Audubon Society of New Hampshire, High St., Humiston Bldg., RR #4, Box 240-E, Meredith, NH 03253, (603) 279-5000.

ADOPT-A-MANATEE

The SAVE THE MANATEE CLUB offers an Adopt-a-Manatee program. More than 20 manatees that regularly migrate to Blue Spring State Park near Orange City, Florida, have been chosen as "adoptees." Each of the animals has a known history and some have been tracked by radio telemetry by US Fish and Wildlife Service researchers. The fee will help protect and preserve the manatee and its habitat. Contact SAVE THE MANATEE CLUB, Adopt-a-Manatee, 500 N. Maitland Ave., Maitland, FL 32751, (800) 432-JOIN.

MOUNTAIN MENDERS

The US FOREST SERVICE in the intermountain States is comprised of nine regions and several research stations, all of which have a variety of volunteer opportunities. Intermountain Region volunteers help manage and maintain national forest lands in Idaho, Nevada, Utah and western Wyoming. The Intermountain Research Station's volunteers help by providing scientific knowledge to aid resource managers. Transportation, housing, uniforms and allowance are available depending on the nature of the project. Contact USDA Forest Service, Regional Volunteer Coordinator, 324 25th St., Ogden, UT 84401, (801) 625-5175.

YOUNG ENVIRONMENTALISTS

YOUTH SERVICE INTERNATIONAL needs 17- to 25-year-old volunteers to participate in worldwide project expeditions which focus on environmental conservation and human service. Applicants must speak English and be able to swim 500 yards. Fee required. Contact YOUTH SERVICE INTERNATIONAL, 301 N. Blount St., Raleigh, NC 27601, (919) 733-9366.

GONE FISHING

The US FISH AND WILDLIFE SERVICE needs volunteers at fish hatcheries around the country. Activities vary according to the area, and may include habitat modification such as constructing and maintaining fresh water impoundments, fish culture and trout

Q. *How many trees did President Bush pledge to plant in the US during the next five years?*

spawning. Volunteers are also needed at research stations, offices and wildlife refuges. Contact US FISH AND WILDLIFE SERVICE, 18th and C Sts. NW, Washington, DC 20240 for the office nearest you.

CRY WOLF

The TIMBER WOLF INFORMATION NETWORK needs volunteers to join their Adopt-A-Wolf Pack Program. The program educates teachers, student groups, citizen groups and families about the recovery of the wolves in Wisconsin and Michigan's Upper Peninsula. The $75 annual fee pays for educational materials and the continuing study and recovery of the wolf population. Contact TIMBER WOLF INFORMATION NETWORK, E110 Emmons Creek Rd., Waupaca, WI 54981, (715) 258-7247.

UNDER THE BOARDWALK

THE NATURE CONSERVANCY has volunteer opportunities at many of its 1,600 preserves across the country. Volunteer activities range from building boardwalks at a wetlands preserve to maintaining and clearing trails, planting trees or assisting in prescribed burnings in prairie states. Contact Robert Byrne, THE NATURE CONSERVANCY, 1815 N. Lynn St., Suite 400, Arlington, VA 22209, (703) 841-4832.

BUILD A BRIDGE

The AMERICAN HIKING SOCIETY needs volunteers to help preserve America's parks and forests. Volunteers spend 10 days on a variety of projects ranging from trail maintenance in Texas to bridge building in Wyoming. Most of the work sites are in remote and primitive areas. Volunteers must be at least 16 years old, experienced hikers and physically fit. Registration fee required. Winter, spring and fall projects also available. For free information about the program, send a stamped, self-addressed envelope to AMERICAN HIKING SOCIETY, Volunteer Vacations, P.O. Box 86, Dept. AHS/VV, North Scituate, MA 02060, (617) 545-7019.

INTERNATIONAL COOPERATION

Summer volunteers are needed to join the UNIVERSITY RESEARCH EXPEDITIONS PROGRAM on projects ranging from a survey of plants in the tropical forests of Ecuador to a study of how white pelicans are

Created by the Board of Directors of the American Recreation Coalition in 1989 to commemorate and to continue work inspired by Sheldon Coleman, the "lantern man," by honoring special Americans whose personal efforts have enhanced opportunities for others to enjoy the outdoors. Nominations are solicited and received from public and private sector conservation and recreation organizations and from individuals. Awards are given annually in June.

Some past recipients: F. Dale Robertson, Chief of the US Forest Service, and George H. W. Bush, President of the US.

HUGH HAMMOND BENNETT

Soil and Water Conservation Society, 7515 NE Ankeny Rd., Ankeny, IA 50021-9764.

Established in 1973 by the Soil and Water Conservation Society to honor an individual for superior and distinguished service in recognition of national and international accomplishments in the conservation of natural resources. Deadline for public application is December 31 of each year.

1991 recipient: Ted Sheng for his work with international conservation and watershed projects, especially his Taiwan watershed program.

NATIONAL OUTDOOR LEADERSHIP SCHOOL ALUMNI AWARD

The National Outdoor Leadership School, P.O. Box AA, Lander, WY 82520.

A. *5 billion*
    Source: The White House

Established in 1991 to recognize a graduate of the National Outdoor Leadership School who has drawn on his or her experience to help make a difference, especially in the areas of outdoor education or wilderness. The award is given in September of each year.

1991 recipient: Liz Nichol, cofounder of the Everest Environmental Expedition, for her work to remove garbage which had accumulated on Mount Everest.

OUTSIDER OF THE YEAR
Outside, Mariah Publications Corporation, 1165 N. Clark St., Chicago, IL 60610.

Established by *Outside* magazine to salute significant environmental achievements. Selected and awarded by editors of *Outside* magazine.

1990 recipient: Bruno Manser for his work in Borneo and with the Penan tribal people.

THE RENE DUBOS ENVIRONMENTAL AWARDS
Rene Dubos Center for Human Environments, Inc., 100 E. 85th St., New York, NY 10028.

Established in 1984 and given by the Rene Dubos Center for Human Environments, Inc., a nonprofit education and research organization, to highlight the creative aspects of human interventions in nature and the improvement of the quality of humanized environments. The awards are presented annually in May to individuals who

endangered by pesticide runoffs in California's Klamath Basin. Opportunities to participate in archaeology projects, marine studies, animal behavior observations and art programs are also offered. No previous experience is necessary. Tax-deductible contribution to cover expenses is requested. For an application contact UNIVERSITY RESEARCH EXPEDITIONS PROGRAM, Desk H11, University of California, Berkeley, CA 94720, (510) 642-6586.

CAVING

TIMPANOGOS CAVE NATIONAL MONUMENT needs volunteers to participate in park operations such as maintenance, visitor information services and presenting interpretive programs. Benefits include training and job experience. Housing is available in nearby communities. Contact Mike Tranel, TIMPANOGOS CAVE NATIONAL MONUMENT, R.R. 3, Box 200, American Fork, UT 84003, (801) 756-5239.

NO-TRACE CAMPING

TARGHEE NATIONAL FOREST offers wildlife aide, range aide and wilderness ranger positions. Aides assist in wildlife inventories, range-grazing monitoring and bald eagle observation. Rangers help educate visitors about no-trace camping. Contact Ellen Spickerman, Volunteer Coordinator, TARGHEE NATIONAL FOREST, 3659 E. Ririe Hwy., Idaho Falls, ID 83401, (208) 523-1412.

CONSERVATION EDUCATION

The ATLANTIC CENTER FOR THE ENVIRONMENT seeks volunteers to help in a variety of areas including conservation education, research, natural history, program administration, publications and community service. Opportunities are offered in northern New England, eastern Canada, Scotland, and the Caribbean and the UK. Interns will receive a small stipend. Contact Julie Early, Director of Program Operations, ATLANTIC CENTER FOR THE ENVIRONMENT, 39 S. Main St., Ipswich, MA 01938, (508) 356-0038

VARIED VOLUNTEERS

The SIERRA CLUB is looking for volunteers in all 57 chapters. Opportunities include leading outings, environmental education programs, lobbying, leadership

Q. *Since 1960, how much more garbage has been generated due to the increase in packaging?*

training, public speaking and newsletter publication. Contact your local chapter or SIERRA CLUB, 730 Polk St., San Francisco, CA 94109, (415) 776-2211.

FOREIGN ECOLOGY

The SCHOOL FOR FIELD STUDIES offers many volunteer opportunities for environmental work worldwide. Activities include study of plant communities and ecosystem ecology, wildlife ecology, marine biology, animal behavior and sustainable development. The 1992 summer program sites include Alaska, Mexico, Australia, Ecuador, Costa Rica, Kenya, the Caribbean and elsewhere. Stipend offered. Air fare not included. Contact Volunteer Coordinator, the SCHOOL FOR FIELD STUDIES, 16 Broadway, Beverly, MA 01915-2096, (508) 927-7777.

PARK AND RECREATE

NEW HAMPSHIRE DIVISION OF PARKS AND RECREATION offers statewide volunteer opportunities at lakes, mountains and seacoast areas. Volunteers are needed to assist park managers, coordinate education programs, work as campground hosts, staff visitor centers and serve as interpreters and information officers. Specific interests of the volunteer may be accommodated. Contact Mary Goodyear, P.O. Box 856, Concord, NH 03302, (603) 271-3254.

TURTLE TALK

The CARIBBEAN CONSERVATION CORPORATION needs volunteers to join their Turtles of Tortuguero research program in Costa Rica. Volunteers will assist with collection of biophysical data and monitor the nesting beach. Additional opportunities exist to simultaneously assist a team of scientists with other studies in the Tortuguero Lagoon and Beach. Programs last from seven to ten days and require a fee. Opportunities exist for room and board at the Green Turtle Research Station. Contact CARIBBEAN CONSERVATION CORPORATION, P.O. Box 2866, Gainesville, FL 32602, (904) 373-6441.

RAPTOR RAP

ROCKY MOUNTAIN RAPTOR PROGRAM seeks volunteers to help with a wide range of opportunities including feeding, cage cleaning, administering antibiotics, performing physical therapy and general

have distinguished themselves by developing significant strategies for dealing with environmental problems.

Some 1991 recipients: Charles W. Powers, founding partner of the Boston firm Resources for Responsible Management for his leadership in management ethics and in improving public-private sector collaboration on environmental health and safety issues; Harry E. Teasley, Jr., President and CEO of Coca-Cola Foods for his leadership in recycling; Lee M. Thomas for his work as administrator of the EPA from 1985 to 1989.

SOL FEINSTONE ENVIRONMENTAL AWARDS
State University of New York, College of Environmental Science and Forestry, 122 Bray Hall, 1 Forestry Dr., Syracuse, NY 13210-2778.

Established by State University of New York, College of Environmental Science and Forestry, to recognize significant individual contribution to improving the environment through outstanding voluntary action. The Sol Feinstone awards consist of five $1,000 prizes. Nominations are accepted through December each year.

Some 1991 recipients: Eddie C. Bridges, Greensboro, North Carolina; David L. Harrison, Boulder, Colorado; R. Michael Leonard, Winston-Salem, North Carolina; Charles Russell, Arvada, Colorado; and

A. *More than 200 percent*
  Source: The Washington Spectator, *May 1990*

Clinton B. Townsend, Canaan, Maine.

WINDSTAR AWARD

The Windstar Foundation, 2317 Snowmass Creek Rd., Snowmass, CO 81654.

Established by the Windstar Foundation and given annually to a global citizen who actively contributes to the creation of a healthy and peaceful future. The Windstar Foundation jury selects the nominee and awards the $10,000 prize in September.

1991 recipient: Lester R. Brown, president and founder of the World-Watch Institute and co-author of the State of the World reports.

WRITING

PACT AWARDS

Conservation Technology Information Center, 1220 Potter Dr., Rm. 170, Purdue Research Park, West Lafayette, IN 47906-1334.

Established in 1990 by the Conservation Technology Information Center "to honor superior writing and broadcasting by North American journalists on the environmental and economic aspects of conservation technology." Awards are open to North American journalists and broadcasters generating original material for an agricultural or general news publication or program. The winning entry in each category receives a $2,000 cash prize. Entries must be received by May.

Some 1991 recipients: Craig Cramer, author of "'Grass Farming' Bests Corn!" published in The

care for injured birds of prey. Volunteers have the opportunity to help raptors by increasing public awareness. A four-step training program teaches everything from general care procedures to therapy and treatment techniques. Contact ROCKY MOUNTAIN RAPTOR PROGRAM, Colorado State University, Veterinary Teaching Hospital, 300 W. Drake, Fort Collins, CO 80523, (303) 491-0398.

JOHNNY ELMSEED

The ELM RESEARCH INSTITUTE is seeking volunteers to assist in the "Johnny Elmseed Project." Volunteers will help to initiate the Johnny Elmseed Project and plant the new, disease-resistant American Liberty elm in areas across the nation. Volunteers may also help with organizing the Conscientious Injectors Program. Participants of this program inject mature American elms to protect them from Dutch elm disease. Contact John P. Hansel, Executive Director, ELM RESEARCH INSTITUTE, Main St., Harrisville, NH 03450, (603) 827-3048, (800) FOR-ELMS.

ADOPT-A-TEACHER

The NATIONAL ASSOCIATION FOR HUMANE AND ENVIRONMENTAL EDUCATION offers an Adopt-A-Teacher Partnership Program. Each adopted teacher receives free monthly issues of KIND (Kids in Nature's Defense) News, a student newspaper arriving in bundles of 32 copies, complete with a three-page teaching guide. Teachers also receive a KIND poster, 32 student ID cards and the 80-page teaching magazine titled KIND Teacher. The cost of adopting a teacher is $18 per year. Adoptions can be made by humane societies, businesses, clubs or individuals. Contact NATIONAL ASSOCIATION FOR HUMANE AND ENVIRONMENTAL EDUCATION, 67 Salem Rd., East Haddam, CT 06423-1736, (203) 434-8666.

PAWS A MOMENT

PROGRESSIVE ANIMAL WELFARE SOCIETY (PAWS) seeks volunteers to help in a variety of areas including animal care, animal rights, wildlife rehabilitation, education programs, building maintenance and general office assistance. Orientation meetings for new volunteers are held regularly. Contact PROGRESSIVE ANIMAL WELFARE SOCIETY/ PAWS, P.O. Box 1037, Lynnwood, WA 98046, (206) 743-1884.

Q: *Insects make up what ratio of all species?*

ROAD WORK AHEAD

The ALLIANCE FOR A PAVING MORATORIUM needs volunteers nationwide to send in newspaper and magazine clippings, highway department plans, names, addresses and phone numbers of citizen groups fighting roads, and any scientific or economic background on the impact of roads. The alliance also needs volunteers to circulate petitions against the building of roads. Contact ALLIANCE FOR A PAVING MORATORIUM, c/o Fossil Fuels Policy Action Institute, Federal Square-E, P.O. Box 8558, Fredericksburg, VA 22404, (703) 371-0222.

GARDENS GALORE

The AMERICAN HORTICULTURAL SOCIETY needs volunteers to assist with horticultural and non-horticultural activities. Volunteers will help maintain and enhance the gardens and grounds, staff the Gardeners' Information Service and help with the National Backyard Compost Demonstration Park. Participants also assist with public relations and a variety of other activities. Contact Maureen Heffernan, AMERICAN HORTICULTURAL SOCIETY, 7931 E. Boulevard Dr., Alexandria, VA 22308, (703) 768-5700.

TALL TRAILS

APPALACHIAN MOUNTAIN CLUB Trails Program volunteers maintain over 1,400 miles of trail in the Northeast, including major sections of the Appalachian Trail. Many volunteer trail activities are available from Maine to Washington, DC. Contact APPALACHIAN MOUNTAIN CLUB Trails Program, P.O. Box 298, Gorham, NH 03581, (603) 466-2721.

TRUE GRIT

The AMERICAN HORSE PROTECTION ASSOCIATION, INC. needs volunteers who are interested in becoming state representatives. Volunteers will assist in a variety of duties including sending clippings about horse-related issues, educating interested groups about the plight of America's wild horses and monitoring for abuses at auctions and competitions. Contact the AMERICAN HORSE PROTECTION ASSOCIATION, INC., 1000 29th St. NW, Suite T-100, Washington, DC 20007, (202) 965-0500.

New Farm; Eric Sorensen, Grayden Jones, Kevin Taylor and Lonnie Rosewald, authors of "Seeds of Change," which appeared in *The Spokesman-Review Spokane Chronicle;* and Lyndon Anderson, author of "Let's See More Field Cover," from *Farm and Ranch Guide*.

EDWARD ABBEY ECOFICTION AWARD
Buzzworm magazine, 2305 Canyon Blvd., Suite 206, Boulder, CO 80302.

Established in 1990 by *Buzzworm* magazine and Patagonia, Inc. to recognize outstanding literary achievement in the spirit of Edward Abbey as well as to encourage and support original novel-length works of fiction that address environmental conservation and the willingness to speak out and act in defense of our natural world. Recently published novels and novels scheduled for publication are eligible for consideration. Deadline for submission is April 1.

1991 recipient: Barbara Kingsolver for *Animal Dreams*.

MARKETING
DIRECT MARKETING ASSOCIATION ROBERT RODALE ENVIRONMENTAL ACHIEVEMENT AWARD
Direct Marketing Association, Inc., 11 W. 42nd St., New York, NY 10036-8096.

Established in 1991 to recognize and honor

A. *Three-fourths*
Source: *Natural Resources Defense Council*

environmental achievements in the direct marketing field. The award is a $10,000 contribution in the winning company's name to an organization, chosen by the winner, that is dedicated to encouraging or developing solutions to environmental concerns. Only Direct Marketing Association members can enter the competition.

NATURAL RESOURCE PROTECTION

CHEVRON CONSERVATION AWARDS
Chevron Conservation Awards, P.O. Box 7753, San Francisco, CA 94120.

Sponsored by Chevron since 1986 and established in 1954 by Ed Zern, a nationally known sportsman and outdoor writer for *Field and Stream* magazine, to honor the environmental accomplishments of citizen volunteers, professionals, organizations and public agencies for their efforts in protecting and enhancing natural resources. Each of the 25 winners receives a $1,000 cash award. Public nominations are submitted for the annual award in these categories: professional, citizen volunteer and nonprofit organization/ public agency.

Some 1991 recipients: Martine Colette, a former Hollywood fashion designer who founded the 160-acre wildlife waystation which provides food, shelter and medical care to injured and homeless wild and exotic animals; Michael J.

PLANT CARE

The MISSOURI BOTANICAL GARDEN seeks volunteers to work on ongoing Center for Plant Conservation projects. Volunteers will cultivate and tend to live plants, germinate seeds, repot, conduct library research, organize files and help maintain records on rare plants. Contact Jeanne McGilligan, Manager of Volunteer Programs, MISSOURI BOTANICAL GARDEN, P.O. Box 299, St. Louis, MO 63166-0299.

NETWORKING

RAINFOREST ACTION NETWORK seeks volunteers in the San Francisco region to help with clerical work, special campaign work and information tabulating. Mostly daytime work offered, with some evening and weekend work available. Contact Sally Kauffman, RAINFOREST ACTION NETWORK, 301 Broadway, Suite A, San Francisco, CA 94133, (415) 398-4404.

MARINE ENTANGLEMENT

CENTER FOR MARINE CONSERVATION offers volunteer programs in marine habitat protection, sea turtle, marine mammal and seabird conservation, marine debris and entanglement, fisheries management and conservation. Volunteers are also needed to help with mailings and office work. Applicants should send a resume and two- to five-page writing sample to Volunteer Coordinator, CENTER FOR MARINE CONSERVATION, 1725 DeSales St. NW, Suite 500, Washington, DC 20036, (202) 429-5609.

SUPERIOR POSITIONS

The SUPERIOR NATIONAL FOREST seeks volunteers to spend part of their summer in or near the Boundary Waters Canoe Area Wilderness working in a variety of fields including trail maintenance, campsite rehabilitation, wilderness ranger positions, campground hosts, naturalists, cultural resource, recreation, wildlife or fisheries aides. No experience necessary. Applicant must be at least 18 years old. Housing or free camping, cooking facilities and daily compensation for living expenses provided. Contact Volunteer Coordinator, SUPERIOR NATIONAL FOREST, P.O. Box 338, Duluth, MN 55801, (218) 720-5324.

Q: *The US could eliminate all Mideast oil exports without opening more land to drilling by improving automobile efficiency by only how many miles per gallon?*

SPECIES INVENTORY

Volunteer wildlife aides are needed on BUFFALO GAP NATIONAL GRASSLANDS to assist with fish and waterfowl potential site inventory and with threatened and endangered species inventories. Range and recreational aides are also needed for grazing and motorcycle area management. Contact USDA Forest Service, BUFFALO GAP NATIONAL GRASSLANDS, 209 N. River, Hot Springs, SD 57747, (605) 745-4107.

FISH EYES

TROUT UNLIMITED needs volunteers to help local chapters with Embrace-A-Stream projects. Volunteers may assist in a variety of duties including monitoring coldwater habitats to document damage, restoring deteriorated lakes, improving salmonid habitats and educating the public through workshops and seminars. Contact TROUT UNLIMITED, 800 Follin Ln. SE, Suite 250, Vienna, VA 22180-4906, (703) 281-1100.

TIMBER!

BALDWIN RANGER DISTRICT offers year-round volunteer opportunities in recreation, trail management, wildlife habitat management, archeology and minerals and timber management. Applicants with experience working with hand tools, wood-working talents and an interest in botany are preferred. Contact Paul Forrest, Volunteer Coordinator, BALDWIN RANGER DISTRICT, P.O. Drawer D, Baldwin, MI 49304, (616) 745-4631.

HAWAIIAN HELP

The HAWAII VOLCANOS NATIONAL PARK seeks volunteers to provide visitor information, lead talks and tours, help with library and custodial projects and assist in park photography and artwork. Volunteer resource managers are also needed to help control non-native plants and animals in the region. Housing may be available and some expenses may be reimbursed. Three-month commitment required. Contact Richard Rasp, HAWAII VOLCANOS NATIONAL PARK, P.O. Box 52, Hawaii National Park, HI 96718, (808) 967-7311.

DOLPHIN RESEARCH

The WILD DOLPHIN PROJECT seeks volunteers to help with a variety of jobs including office work,

Caire, MD, who has been instrumental in the protection of the endangered Louisiana black bear; The Vermont Institute of Natural Science, which developed the Environmental Learning for the Future Project, providing interactive field trips for more than 7,000 school children and 20,000 adults to help them understand and protect nature.

NATIONAL CONSERVATION ACHIEVEMENT AWARDS
National Wildlife Federation, 1400 16th St. NW, Washington, DC 20036.

Established in 1965 by the National Wildlife Federation to honor individuals and organizations whose achievements in natural resource conservation deserve national recognition. Winners are selected by the awards committee from publicly nominated entries. Deadline for nomination is July.

Some past recipients: Edmund S. Muskie (Jay N. "Ding" Darling Medal Conservationalist of the Year), The Los Angeles Times (Communications), Patagonia, Inc. (Corporate), Madeleine Kunin (Government), Southeast Alaska Conservation Council (Organization) and 1988/1989 Fourth Grade Class, Vandenboom Elementary School, Marquette, Michigan (Special Achievements).

TAKE PRIDE IN AMERICA NATIONAL AWARDS
Take Pride in America

A. *3 miles per gallon*
 Source: Amory Lovins, Calypso Log, *October 1989*

National Awards Program, 1849 C St. NW, Rm. 5123, Washington, DC 20240.

Established in 1985 to increase awareness of the need for wise use of our nation's natural and cultural resources, to encourage an attitude of stewardship and responsibility toward public resources and to promote volunteerism. Activities nominated by the public must have occurred during the current or previous year. The awards are given in July. In 1990, 119 winners were chosen.

Some 1990 recipients: WJBK-TV of Michigan, the Montana Council of Boy Scouts, the Academy of Model Aeronautics and the National Forest Recreation Association.

SCIENCE AND TECHNOLOGY

THE CRAFOORD PRIZE

The Royal Swedish Academy of Sciences Information Department, Box 50005, S-104 05, Stockholm, Sweden.

Established by the Royal Swedish Academy of Sciences to stimulate national and international scientific cooperation. The award is a $1.5 million cash prize and the winner is chosen by the academy.

1991 recipient: Dr. Allan R. Sandage from the Observatories of the Carnegie Institution of Washington in Pasadena, California, for fundamental contributions to Extragalactic Astronomy including Observational Cosmology.

project research, education and boat support provisioning. Volunteers interested in helping with dolphin research must have a working knowledge of Macintosh computers, audio/video equipment and a biology or psychology background. Applicants wishing to work as an education aide should have a strong background in teaching and public relations. Volunteers must be local or commit to a minimum of two months and will have the opportunity to work one week in the field participation program. Contact WILD DOLPHIN PROJECT, 21 Hepburn Ave., Ste 20, Jupiter, FL 33458, (407) 575-5660.

CALL OF THE LOON

LONG POINT BIRD OBSERVATORY seeks volunteers to survey lakes in the summer and record information about the breeding of loons. Volunteer surveyors watch for pairs of loons and nesting behavior, observe the appearance of newly hatched chicks and record how many chicks have survived the summer. Volunteers will receive a survey kit with instructions and a report form to be returned at the end of the season. Contact Canadian Lakes Loon Survey, LONG POINT BIRD OBSERVATORY, P.O. Box 160, Port Rowan, Ontario N0E 1M0, Canada, (519) 586-3531.

KENTUCKY CAMPOUT

LAND BETWEEN THE LAKES needs volunteers to work as campground hosts and help with trail maintenance. Trail maintenance work includes public contact with campers and hikers, trail reconstruction, campsite inventory, restoration and trash pickup. Must be 18 years or older. Contact LAND BETWEEN THE LAKES, 100 Van Morgan Dr., Golden Pond, KY 42211-9001, (502) 924-5602.

CHILD'S ZOO

The ZOOLOGICAL SOCIETY OF PHILADELPHIA has volunteer positions available to help with the Children's Zoo. Volunteers will assist staff members by performing duties such as enriching animal enclosures, giving pony rides to children, distributing animal food and assisting with animal programs. Participants must be 14 to 17 years old. Contact Volunteer Coordinator, the ZOOLOGICAL SOCIETY OF PHILADELPHIA, 3400 Girard Ave., Philadelphia, PA 19104, (215) 243-1100.

 Q: *How many people still live on land contaminated by the Chernobyl accident?*

DANCING WITH WOLVES

The MEXICAN WOLF COALITION needs volunteers to help with an activist network to promote wolf recovery in Arizona, New Mexico and Texas. Participants will work as part of a grassroots educational program to inform the public of the conditions facing the Mexican wolf. Volunteers will write letters to agencies and Congress, participate in fundraisers and provide educational talks to schools and community groups. Contact Bobbie Holaday, Preserve Arizona's Wolves, 1413 E. Dobbins Rd., Phoenix, AZ 85040, (602) 268-1089, or Susan Larson, MEXICAN WOLF COALITION, 207 San Pedro NE, Albuquerque, NM 87108, (505) 265-5506.

CARING FOR COLORADO

VOLUNTEERS FOR OUTDOOR COLORADO seeks caretakers for Colorado. Volunteers may take part in activities such as constructing hiking trails, planting trees, constructing handicapped access facilities and working on other projects. Contact Shelley Gile, VOLUNTEERS FOR OUTDOOR COLORADO, 1410 Grant St., B105, Denver, CO 80203, (303) 830-7792.

WIND CAVE

WIND CAVE NATIONAL PARK seeks volunteers to assist with visitor services, guided tours, resource management, maintenance and campground hosts. Activities include vegetation plot studies, fire monitoring, elk roundup, wildlife census counts and information assistance at the visitor center desk and on the campgrounds. Positions of various lengths are available. Contact Kathy Steichen, WIND CAVE NATIONAL PARK, Rt. 1, Box 190-WCNP, Hot Springs, SD 57747, (605) 745-4600.

SUSTAINABLE LIFESTYLE

The FELLOWSHIP FOR ECOLOGY AND THE ARTS seeks volunteer staff at its wilderness ranch in southwestern New Mexico. Positions include cook, maintenance person, administrative assistant, organic gardener and wrangler. Volunteers will assists in the following FEA programs: Sanctuary Retreat, Artists in Residence, Wilderness Horse Trips, Apprenticeships and Llama Treks. Lodging and food provided. Contact FELLOWSHIP FOR ECOLOGY AND THE ARTS, Rt. 11, Box 70, Silver City, NM 88061, (505) 536-2879.

GOOD EARTH FAMILY AWARDS PROGRAM

Good Earth Family Awards Program, 321 D St. NE, Washington, DC 20002.

Established in 1983 by National Endowment for Soil and Water Conservation to highlight individual contributions of environmental improvements in farming and ranching. National winners receive a $1,000 cash award. Deadline to apply is June.

Some 1990 recipients: Larry and Norma DeVilbiss of Alaska; Walter and Paula Auclair of New York; and George and Anne Beals of Virginia.

R & D 100 AWARDS

R & D Magazine, 1350 E. Touhy Ave., Des Plaines, IL 60018.

Established in 1962 by R & D Magazine to recognize the 100 most significant technological advances of the year. Deadline for public application is March 1 each year.

A 1991 recipient was: Alcan Aluminum Limited for its plasma dross treatment process.

WASTE HANDLING AND RECYCLING

AMERICAN SOCIETY OF MECHANICAL ENGINEERS' SOLID WASTE PROCESSING DIVISION SCHOLARSHIP PROGRAM

American Society of Mechanical Engineers Solid Waste Processing Division Scholarship Chairman, 38 Sunset Rd., Demarest, NJ 07627.

Established in 1992 to encourage engineering

A. *2.2 million*
  Source: *Byelorussian Soviet Socialist Republic Mission to the UN*

students to enter careers in solid waste management. The division sponsors five scholarships with awards totaling $14,000. All undergraduate engineering students and graduate students currently enrolled in a solid waste management program at an accredited North American university are eligible to apply. Applications are accepted through February 1.

BEST PAPER RECYCLING STORY CONTEST

Robert Marston Marketing Communications, Inc., 485 Madison Ave., 4th Fl., New York, NY 10022.

Established in 1989 by the Paper Recycling Committee of the American Paper Institute to recognize the activities of dedicated paper recyclers who are actively involved in expanding the collection system for recovered paper. A total of $6,000 in prizes is awarded annually. The contest is open to all involved with paper recycling. Application deadline is April.

Some 1991 recipients: Sally Kobulnicky of Carlsbad, California, who raised the environmental awareness of her school by organizing a paper recycling drive; Professor Stanley Shetka of St. Paul, Minnesota, who recently patented a process for recycling used paper into bricks; Yosemite National Park/Curry Company for its 16-year-old recycling campaign.

HEINZ NATIONAL RECYCLING AWARDS PROGRAM

Heinz National Recycling

TWO TURTLE DOVES

The NATIONAL AUDUBON SOCIETY requests birdwatchers to participate in the Audubon Christmas Bird Count to be held each December to January. Participants form groups which count birds seen within a 15-mile designated area in a 24-hour calendar day. The Christmas Bird Count Editor at American Birds magazine then counts and tabulates the number of species seen. The count totals are published in a special issue of the magazine. Contact the NATIONAL AUDUBON SOCIETY, 950 Third Ave., New York, NY 10022, (212) 832-3200.

H_2O

The AMERICAN LITTORAL SOCIETY seeks volunteers for its Baykeeper program. Volunteers will monitor waterway usage in the New York/New Jersey Harbor, watch for incidents of pollution and record measurements of salinity, temperature and water clarity. Both land-based and boat-borne volunteers are needed. Contact Beverly DeAngelis, AMERICAN LITTORAL SOCIETY, Sandy Hook, Highlands, NJ 07732, (908) 291-0055.

OPEN SPACE

MIDPENINSULA REGIONAL OPEN SPACE volunteer program offers a variety of restoration, construction, resource enhancement and trail maintenance projects. Crew leadership training courses are offered as well as group service projects on 28 separate open space preserves. Other volunteer options include working in the district office or in the field on an individual basis. The open space region encompasses close to 35,000 acres. Contact Volunteer Coordinator, MIDPENINSULA REGIONAL OPEN SPACE, 201 San Antonio Cir., Bldg. C, Suite 135, Mountain View, CA 94040, (415) 949-5500.

THINK GLOBALLY

WILDLANDS STUDIES offers a worldwide field studies program to help protect wildlife and preserve wilderness environments. Summer activities include a first-hand search for the existence of endangered timber wolves in the Northern Cascades, on-site investigation of whale behavior in Canada, examination of threatened Rocky Mountain wilderness land, and studies of Hawaii's environments and cultures.

Q: *What was the budget for solar energy research at the high point of the Carter Administration?*

Opportunities for field studies in Nepal, New Zealand, Thailand and Alaska are offered as well. Participants can earn three to 14 university credits. Contact Crandall Bay, Director, WILDLANDS STUDIES, 3 Mosswood Cir., Box B, Cazadero, CA 95421, (707) 632-5665.

GREETINGS FROM YELLOWSTONE

The GREATER YELLOWSTONE COALITION seeks volunteer assistance with activities involving Yellowstone wildlife and habitat protection, public education, community organizing, lobbying and legislative work and direct action on public agency activities. Duties include writing letters and making phone calls to public officials on critical issues, attending meetings, conducting research and inventories and assisting with general office activities. Contact Gwen Arnesen, GREATER YELLOWSTONE COALITION, P.O. Box 1874, Bozeman, MT 59771, (406) 586-1593.

ECO-RETAIL

RECREATIONAL EQUIPMENT, INC. offers volunteer opportunities through its annual service projects in communities served by its 30 retail stores. The company's service projects operate in 17 States and focus on enhancing outdoor recreation opportunities through trail building and maintenance, campground rehabilitation and enhancement, shoreline cleanups and other community projects. For information regarding service projects in your area contact RECREATIONAL EQUIPMENT, INC., Public Affairs, Service Projects, P.O. Box 88126, Seattle, WA 98138-2126, (206) 395-5957.

PROJECT RESTORE

RESTORING THE EARTH seeks volunteers for Project Restore. Volunteers will help with promotion of restoration projects in unique native habitats in the San Francisco Bay area, educate the public about environmental restoration and mobilize concerned individuals to take a leadership role in repairing damaged public lands. Training provided. Contact RESTORING THE EARTH, 1713 C Martin Luther King Jr. Way, Berkeley, CA 94709, (510) 843-2645.

TURTLE TIME

The NEW YORK TURTLE AND TORTOISE SOCIETY

Awards Program, The United States Conference of Mayors, 1620 Eye St. NW, Washington, DC 20006.

Sponsored by the H. J. Heinz Company Foundation and the United States Conference of Mayors to recognize outstanding waste reduction and resource recovery initiatives in America's metropolitan areas. Winning cities, selected from nominees by the cities' US Conference of Mayors' chief elected official, receive a $20,000 prize.

1991 recipients: Minneapolis, Minnesota, and Olympia, Washington (Grand Award winners).

KEEP AMERICAN BEAUTIFUL, INC. NATIONAL AWARDS
Keep America Beautiful, Inc., 9 W. Broad St., Stamford, CT 06902.

Established to honor ongoing community programs that motivate individual responsibility and promote change in individual and community waste handling practices. Community entries are judged by a panel and the winner is selected in October.

Some 1991 recipients: Keep Texas Beautiful; Gastonia Junior Women's Club of North Carolina; Albany-Dougherty Clean Community Committee of Georgia; Keep Mobile Beautiful of Alabama; and Fairview Middle School of Nashville, Tennessee.

RECYCLER OF THE YEAR AWARD
California Resource Recovery Association, Box

A: **$600 million**
Source: Seattle Times 17 January, 1991

1-300, 13223 Black Mountain Rd., San Diego, CA 92129.

Established in 1976 by the California Resource Recovery Association to honor community recycling organizations' public and private solid waste managers and secondary materials industries.

1991 recipient: Margaret Gainer, founder and principal consultant of Gainer & Associates, for her valuable contributions to the development of California's growing recycling industry.

YOUTH

WINDSTAR YOUTH AWARD
The Windstar Foundation, 2317 Snowmass Creek Rd., Snowmass, CO 81654.

Established in 1991 by the Windstar Foundation, this $2,500 scholarship award is given annually to an individual between the ages of six and 15 who has demonstrated extraordinary commitment to and leadership on an environmental issue. The Windstar Foundation jury selects the winner from individuals nominated by the public and awards the prize in September.

1991 recipient: 12-year-old Kortney (Kory) Johnson, founder and president of Children for a Safe Environment.

needs volunteers to help with turtle care and rehabilitation. Volunteers will be trained in turtle handling and will work to find temporary homes for the turtles until they are released back into the wild. Participants will also act as watchdogs to report any violations of legislation that protects turtles and tortoises. Contact Lori Cramer, NEW YORK TURTLE AND TORTOISE SOCIETY, 163 Amsterdam Ave., Suite 365, New York, NY 10023, (212) 459-4803.

ELK CONSERVATION
ROCKY MOUNTAIN ELK FOUNDATION needs volunteers to assist in evaluating conservation project ideas, promoting elk habitat preservation and enhancement, and in organizing fundraising banquets to benefit the elk and other wildlife. Contact ROCKY MOUNTAIN ELK FOUNDATION, Attn. Field Operations, P.O. Box 8249, Missoula, MT 59807, (800) CALL-ELK.

BOG PATROL
VOYAGEURS NATIONAL PARK, an area of many lakes, hundreds of islands, dense forests and impenetrable bogs, needs many volunteers. Aquatic research aides are wanted to assist with sampling fish in park lakes and recording and compiling data. Volunteer naturalists are needed to help staff the visitor center and assist in naturalist-guided activities such as canoe trips and nature walks. Wildlife research assistants are wanted to assist with research on large mammals. Housing is available. Contact Ron Meer, VOYAGEURS NATIONAL PARK, HCR 9, Box 600, International Falls, MN 56649, (218) 283-9821.

HABITAT REHAB
The PRIEST LAKE RANGER DISTRICT in Idaho needs volunteers to assist with wildlife and natural resource management. Volunteers are needed to help with threatened and endangered species habitat evaluation and improvement projects. Housing and subsistence will be provided. Contact Randy Edgar, PRIEST LAKE RANGER DISTRICT, Rte. 5, Box 207, Priest River, ID 83856, (208) 443-2512.

 What was the budget for solar energy research at the low point under the Reagan Administration?

Religion and the Environment

Where the environmental movement is concerned, heaven and earth, are closely linked. Pope John Paul II recently spoke about the interconnectedness of religion and the environment. And the Presbyterians declared that trashing the planet is a sin. Native American groups have always believed that the spirit world and the Earth world are one. Many people have designated areas across the land as sacred ground, visited by spirit powers. Eastern religions also revere nature and the divine as interconnected, using nature's cycle as a guide to human life and attitude. A directory of ecology-minded religious groups follows.

CENTER FOR RESPECT OF LIFE AND ENVIRONMENT

2100 L St. NW
Washington, DC 20037
(202) 778-6133

Affiliate of the Humane Society of the US that promotes coordination of ecological and theological issues, including a curriculum for seminaries.

ECO-JUSTICE WORKING GROUP, NATIONAL COUNCIL OF CHURCHES

475 Riverside Dr., Room 572
New York, NY 10115
(212) 870-2483

Ecumenical coalition that works on issues of environmental and economic justice.

ECUMENICAL TASK FORCE OF THE NIAGARA FRONTIER

259 Fourth St.
Niagara Falls, NY 14303
(716) 284-7789

An interfaith group of members of Jewish, Protestant and Catholic faiths that was formed after the first Love Canal evacuations. The task force is now one of the leading parties in a lawsuit filed against the Love Canal Revitalization Agency by the state of New York.

IMPACT

100 Maryland Ave. NE
Washington, DC 20002
(202) 544-8636

Legislative information network sponsored by national agencies of 17 religious groups.

INTERFAITH COALITION ON ENERGY

P.O. Box 26577
Philadelphia, PA 19141
(215) 635-1122

Provides weatherization and energy conservation information for religious groups in the Philadelphia area.

INTERNATIONAL COORDINATING COMMITTEE ON RELIGION AND THE EARTH

c/o Wainwright House
260 Stuyvesant Ave.
Rye, NY 10580
(914) 967-6080

Organizes interfaith conferences on religion and ecology.

LOUISIANA COASTAL WETLANDS INTERFAITH STEWARDSHIP PLAN

c/o First United Methodist Church
P.O. Box 2039
Lafayette, LA 70502

Works to educate the public about wetlands loss, to organize a network of interested people and to provide technical information and advice.

NORTH AMERICAN COALITION ON RELIGION AND ECOLOGY

5 Thomas Cir. NW
Washington, DC 20005
(202) 462-2591

Works to promote education and networking of religious and environmental organizations. Published a viewer's guide to the PBS series "Race to Save the Planet."

NORTH AMERICAN CONFERENCE ON CHRISTIANITY AND ECOLOGY

444 Waller St.
San Francisco, CA 94117

Coordinates conferences on Christianity and the environment. Publishes quarterly newsletter, *The Firmament*.

UNITED NATIONS ENVIRONMENT PROGRAMME

2 United Nations Plaza
Room DC2-803
United Nations, NY 10017
(212) 963-8139

Organizes an environmental sabbath program for North American congregations each June and publishes the *Sabbath Newsletter*.

WEST COUNTY TOXICS COALITION

1019 McDonald Ave.
Richmond, CA 94804
(415) 232-3427

Works to pressure Chevron, Richmond's major industry, to reduce and responsibly report toxic releases from its petrochemical and agricultural chemical plants.

WORLD WILDLIFE FUND NETWORK ON CONSERVATION AND RELIGION

10 rue des Fosses
CH-1110 Morges,
Switzerland

International link between religion and ecology. Publishes newsletter called *The New Road*.

Reprinted by permission from Environmental Action, January/February 1991 issue.

A. **$70 million**
Source: Seattle Times *17 January, 1991*

Directory to Environmental Groups

*T*he Earth Journal *Directory to Enviromental Organizations will introduce you to organizations who work to save and preserve our natural world. This directory provides you with a diverse list of organizations with small to large memberships, local to worldwide opportunities, specific biospheres to varied plant and wildlife population research programs. Each organization was asked to provide information about their purpose, current emphasis, membership, funding and expenditures. The letters "dnd" next to a heading signifiy that an organization did not disclose that particular information.*

THE ACID RAIN FOUNDATION, INC.

1410 Varsity Dr.
Raleigh, NC 27606
(919) 828-9443

Purpose: To foster greater understanding of global atmospheric issues by raising the level of public awareness, supplying educational resources and supporting research. **Current Emphasis:** Acid rain, global atmosphere, recycling and forest ecosystems. **Members:** dnd. **Fees:** $35. **Funding:** Membership, 2.5%; Corporation, 0%; Other: Direct Public Support, 53.5%; Programs, 44%. **Annual Revenue:** $100,000. **Usage:** Administration, 24%; Fundraising, 9%; Programs, 67%. **Volunteer Programs:** Education, development, library and marketing.

AFRICAN WILDLIFE FOUNDATION

1717 Massachusetts Ave. NW
Washington, DC 20036
(202) 265-8394

Purpose: Working directly with Africans at all government and private levels in over 25 countries since 1961, AWF's staff promotes, establishes and supports grassroots and institutional programs in conservation education, wildlife management training and management of threatened conservation areas. **Current Emphasis:** Public awareness campaign to encourage ivory boycotts and support of Mountain Gorilla Project in Rwanda. **Members:** 100,000. **Fees:** No minimum for membership; $15 to receive newsletter. **Funding:** Membership, 60%; Corporation, 15%; Foundations/Donor, 25%. **Annual Revenue:** $4,676,000. **Usage:** Administration, 7%; Fundraising, 10%; Programs, 83%. **Volunteer Programs:** "How You Can Help" letter lists ways in which interested people can help curtail the demand for ivory.

ALLIANCE FOR ENVIRONMENTAL EDUCATION

10751 Ambassador Dr., Suite 201
Manassas, VA 22110
(703) 335-1025

Purpose: To serve as an advocate for a quality environment through education and advanced communication, cooperation and exchange among organizations. **Current Emphasis:** In partnership with the US Environmental Protection Agency, the Alliance is estabishing a network of interactive environmental education centers based at colleges, universities and institutions across America. **Members:** 175 organizations, millions of individuals. **Fees:** $100-$250. **Funding:** Membership, 10%; Corporation, 20%; Other, 70%. **Annual Revenue:** $500,000. **Usage:** Administration, 20%; Fundraising, 10%; Programs, 70%. **Volunteer Programs:** Board membership, task forces, special committees, regional advisory councils and internships.

AMERICAN ASSOCIATION OF ZOOLOGICAL PARKS AND AQUARIUMS

7970-D Old Georgetown Rd.
Bethesda, MD 20814
(301) 907-7777

Purpose: A professional organization representing 156 accredited zoos and aquariums in North America. The primary goal is to further wildlife conservation and education and to enforce a code of ethics for all individual members and zoological institutions. **Current Emphasis:** Wildlife conservation through captive propagation. **Members:** 5,600. **Fees:** $30 for associates. **Funding:** Membership, 60%; Foundation/Donor, 9%. **Usage:** Conservation, 33%; Membership, 38%; Administration, 7%. **Volunteer Programs:** None.

Q. *What was the budget for solar energy research under the Bush Administration in 1990?*

AMERICAN FORESTRY ASSOCIATION

P.O. Box 2000
Washington, DC 20013
(202) 667-3300

Purpose: To maintain and improve the health and value of trees and forests, to attract and cultivate the interests of citizens, industry and government in tree and forest resources through action-oriented programs, information and communication. **Current Emphasis:** Global Releaf, an international campaign to encourage and assist people, businesses and governments to plant and care for trees to improve the environment and help curb the effects of global warming. Primary organizers of the Fifth National Urban Forest Conference, November 12-17, 1991, Los Angeles. **Members:** 112,000. **Fees:** From $24. **Funding:** Membership, 30%; Grants, 32%; Other, 38%. **Annual Revenue:** $3,355,729. **Usage:** Administration/Fundraising, 7%; Education, 62%; Projects, 15%.

AMERICAN GEOGRAPHICAL SOCIETY

156 Fifth Ave., Suite 600
New York, NY 10010-7002
(212) 242-0214

Purpose: To expand and disseminate geographical knowledge through publications, awards, travel programs, lectures and consulting, with a strong emphasis on ecology and environmental issues abroad and in the US. **Current Emphasis:** Publication of *The Geographical Review* and *Focus* magazine, educational travel program, provision of lecturers to educational and business audiences and award program to encourage research. **Members:** 1,500. **Fees:** $22. **Funding:** Membership, 8%; Corporation, 15%; Foundation, 7%; Other: Subscriptions, travel program, investments. **Annual Revenue:** $540,000. **Usage:** Administration, 28%; Programs, 72%. **Volunteer Programs:** Volunteer positions available.

AMERICAN HIKING SOCIETY

P.O. Box 20160
Washington, DC 20041-2160
(703) 385-3252

Purpose: Dedicated to protecting the interests of hikers and preserving America's footpaths. Over 70 club affiliates provide for information exchange within the trails community. **Current Emphasis:** Maintaining a public information service to provide hikers and other trail users with facts regarding facilities, organizations, and best use of trails to protect the environment. **Members:** 5000. **Fees:** $25. **Funding:** Membership, 36%; Corporation, 5.5%; Other:

Publications and programs. **Annual Revenue:** $250,000. **Usage:** Administration, 22%; Fundraising, 3.5%; Publications, 41%. "Volunteer Vacations," 10%; Events, 9.3%; Legislative, 1.6%. **Volunteer Programs:** Encourages volunteers in trail building and maintenance through work trips called "Volunteer Vacations" and by publishing a directory of volunteer opportunities on public lands.

AMERICAN HORSE PROTECTION ASSOCIATION, INC.

1000 29th St. NW, Suite T-100
Washington, DC 20007
(202) 965-0500

Purpose: Dedicated entirely to the welfare of equines, wild and domestic, by fighting for the humane treatment of horses through litigation, investigation and public awareness of proper and humane horse care. **Current Emphasis:** Preserving and protecting horses and burros; preventing abuse of horses in competition; solving problems of neglect and mistreatment of horses; promoting safe and humane equine transportation. **Members:** 8,000. **Fees:** $15. **Annual Revenue:** $260,000. **Volunteer Programs:** State Representative program.

AMERICAN HUMANE ASSOCIATION

P.O. Box 1266
Denver, CO 80201
(303) 792-9900

Purpose: To prevent the neglect, abuse, cruelty and exploitation of children and animals and to assure that their interests and wellbeing are fully, effectively and humanely guaranteed by an aware and caring society. **Members:** 30,000. **Fees:** $15-$50. **Funding:** dnd. **Annual Revenue:** $3,000,000. **Usage:** Administration/Fundraising, 20%; Programs, 80%. **Volunteer Programs:** None.

AMERICAN PEDESTRIAN ASSOCIATION

P.O. Box 624
Forest Hills, NY 11375

Purpose: Works to preserve, protect, support and defend the pedestrian environment against vehicular encroachments of all types. Relates environmental costs to vehicular traffic. **Current Emphasis:** Supporting Urban Environmental Trust Fund as counter to vehicular Highway Trust Fund. **Members:** 150-200. **Fees:** $5, domestic; $8, foreign. **Funding:** Membership, 100%. **Annual Revenue:** $500-$600. **Usage:** Administration, 10%; Programs, 90%. **Volunteer Programs:** Occasionally.

A. *$110 million*
 Source: Seattle Times *17 January, 1991*

AMERICAN RIVERS

801 Pennsylvania Ave. SE, Suite 400
Washington, DC 20003
(202) 547-6900
Fax (202) 543-6142

Purpose: Nonprofit conservation organization leading the effort to protect and restore the nation's outstanding rivers and their environments. The organization has effectively preserved over 10,000 river miles for clean water, threatened fish and wildlife, recreation and scenic beauty. Concerns include dams, diversions, channelizations and adverse development. **Current Emphasis:** Federal, state river conservation efforts; wild and scenic river system; river threats—dams, developments, mining, etc.; hydropower relicensing; greenways; how to protect rivers. **Members:** 15,000. **Fees:** Begin at $20. **Funding:** Membership, 33%; Corporation, 33%; Foundation/Donor, 33%. **Annual Revenue:** $1,800,000. **Usage:** Administration, 10%; Fundraising, 12.3%; Programs, 77.7%. **Programs:** Federal river protection program; state river protection program; National Center for Hydropower Policy; rivers on public lands program; public education. **Volunteer Programs:** River activist network; office assistance. Special skills welcome. Occasional opportunities for interns; write for details.

ANIMAL PROTECTION INSTITUTE OF AMERICA

2831 Fruitridge Rd.
Sacramento, CA 95822
(916) 731-5521

Purpose: To eliminate fear, pain and suffering inflicted on animals and to preserve threatened species. **Current Emphasis:** Publications, animal welfare issues, education and legislative issues. **Members:** 120,000+. **Annual Revenue:** dnd. **Volunteer Programs:** Teachers are encouraged to participate in educating students using API "Know a Teacher" literature.

THE ASSOCIATION OF FOAM PACKAGING RECYCLERS

1025 Connecticut Ave. NW, Suite 515
Washington, DC 20036
(800) 944-8448

Purpose: With more than 45 plant locations nationwide to serve as central collection points, AFPR brings the recycling of foam packaging to every major metropolitan area. This establishes the basis to produce protective foam packaging made with recycled content. **Current Emphasis:** Encouraging the re-use of loose fill foam packaging, and the recycling and reprocessing of molded foam packaging. **Funding:** Corporation, 100%. **Annual Revenue:** dnd. **Usage:** dnd. **Volunteer Programs:** None.

CENTER FOR ENVIRONMENTAL INFORMATION

46 Prince St.
Rochester, NY 14607
(716) 271-3550

Purpose: Established to provide timely, accurate and comprehensive information on environmental issues. CEI has developed a multi-faceted program of publications, education programs and information services. **Current Emphasis:** Environmental education, ethics, laws, communication and global environmental change. **Members:** 700. **Fees:** $25. **Funding:** Membership, 50%; Corporation, 50%. **Annual Revenue:** $500,000. **Usage:** Administration, 5%; Fundraising, 10%; Programs, 85%. **Volunteer Programs:** Library services, conferences and program coordination and publications.

CENTER FOR HOLISTIC RESOURCE MANAGEMENT

5820 4th St. NW
Albuquerque, NM 87107
(505) 344-3445
Fax (505) 344-9079

Purpose: Community development based on a proven process of goal setting and decision making that helps communities restore their well-being and the natural resources on which they depend. **Current Emphasis:** Expanding the numbers of individuals capable of offering training in holistic resource management. **Members:** 1,500. **Fees:** $35. **Funding:** Membership, 4%; Corporation, 11%; Foundation/Donor, 22%; Programs, 63%. **Annual Revenue:** $900,000. **Usage:** Administration, 16%; Fundraising, 6%; Programs, 78%. **Programs:** Regular and special courses on holistic resource management, community development. **Volunteer Programs:** Currently looking for volunteers interested in becoming trainers in holistic resource management.

CENTER FOR MARINE CONSERVATION

1725 DeSales St. NW, Suite 500
Washington, DC 20036
(202) 429-5609
Fax (202) 872-0619

Purpose: Center for Marine Conservation is the leading nonprofit organization dedicated solely to the conservation of marine wildlife and their habitats. Focusing on five major

Q: How many species become extinct every second?

goals: conserving marine habitats; preventing marine pollution; fisheries conservation; protecting endangered species; and promoting and educating about marine biodiversity. **Members:** 110,000+. **Fees:** $20. **Funding:** Membership, 54%; Corporation, 15%; Foundation/Donor, 31%. **Annual Revenue:** $3,600,000. **Usage:** Administration, 10%; Fundraising, 13.5%; Programs, 54%. **Volunteer Programs:** National Beach Cleanup in September. Some internships at national and regional offices.

CENTER FOR PLANT CONSERVATION
P.O. Box 299
St. Louis, MO 63166
(314) 577-9450
Fax (314) 664-0465

Purpose: To conserve rare and endangered native plants through research, cultivation and education at botanical gardens and arboreta in the US. Through 20 affiliated gardens and arboreta, the Center establishes off-site germplasm collections in the National Collection of Endangered Plants. **Current Emphasis:** Five priority regions: Hawaii, Florida, California, Texas and Puerto Rico. **Funding:** Donations. **Annual Revenue:** $865,000. **Usage:** Administration, 17%; Fundraising, 13%; Programs, 70%. **Volunteer Programs:** None.

CENTER FOR SCIENCE INFORMATION
4252 20th St.
San Francisco, CA 94114
(415) 553-8178
Fax (415) 861-4908

Purpose: To educate decision makers and journalists about the environmental applications of biotechnology. **Funding:** Corporation, 5%; Foundation/Donor, 95%. **Annual Revenue:** $150,000. **Usage:** Administration, 10%; Fundraising, 5%; Programs, 85%. **Programs:** Publishing and distributing briefbooks and briefsheets. **Volunteer Programs:** None.

CITIZEN'S CLEARINGHOUSE FOR HAZARDOUS WASTE (CENTER FOR ENVIRONMENTAL JUSTICE)
Rowell Ct.
P.O. Box 6806
Falls Church, VA. 22040
(703) 237-2249

Purpose: To create an organizing effort working with individuals and communities to clean up waste dumps through legal action. **Current Emphasis:** Contaminated sites campaign. Convicting the EPA for child abuse for not cleaning up these sites. **Members:** 20,000. **Fees:** $25. **Funding:** Membership, 31%; Foundation/Donor, 51%; Mini grants, 10%; Churches, 8%. **Annual Revenue:** $680,000. **Usage:** Administration, 12%; Programs, 88%. **Volunteer Programs:** Volunteer positions and paid field internships are available.

CLEAN WATER ACTION
1320 18th St. NW
Washington, DC 20036
(202) 457-1286
Fax (202) 457-0287

Purpose: National citizens' organization working for clean and safe water at an affordable cost; control of toxic chemicals; protection and conservation of wetlands, groundwater and coastal waters; safe solid waste management; public health; and environmental safety of all citizens. **Current Emphasis:** Citizen organizing and education to effect environmental change and safety. **Members:** 600,000. **Fees:** $24. **Funding:** Membership, 98%; Foundation/Donor, 2%. **Annual Revenue:** $9,000,000. **Usage:** Administration, 7%; Fundraising, 27%; Programs, 66%. **Volunteer Programs:** Consumer education programs, community organizing.

CONSERVATION INTERNATIONAL
1015 18th St. NW, Suite 1000
Washington, DC 20036
(202) 429-5660
Fax (202) 887-5188

Purpose: To conserve ecosystems and biological diversity, and the ecological processes that support life on earth. **Current Emphasis:** Works with partner organizations and local people in tropical and temperate countries, particularly the "megadiversity" countries containing over half of all species, to develop and implement ecosystem conservation projects. **Members:** 50,000. **Fees:** $15. **Funding:** Members, 15.2%; Corporation, 6%; Foundation/Donor, 78.8%. **Annual Revenue:** $8,288,216. **Usage:** Administration, 7.9%; Fundraising, 6.6%; Programs, 85.5%. **Programs:** 21 country programs, science, communications, membership development and services, public education. **Volunteer Programs:** dnd.

THE COUSTEAU SOCIETY, INC.
930 W. 21st St.
Norfolk, VA 23517
(804) 627-1144

Purpose: Dedicated to the protection and improvement of the quality of life. Founded in

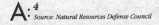

A·⁴
Source: Natural Resources Defense Council

1973 by Captain Jacques Cousteau and Jean-Michel Cousteau in the belief that an informed and alerted public can best make the choices to insure a healthy and productive world, the Society produces television films, books, membership publications, articles and offers lectures and a summer field study program. **Current Emphasis:** In the current "Rediscovery of the World" expedition, teams aboard the Society's research vessels *Calypso* and *Alcyone* are circumnavigating the Earth to take a fresh look at the global ecosystem. **Members:** 350,000. **Fees:** Individual, $20; Family, $28. **Funding:** Nonprofit, membership-supported. **Annual Revenue:** $14,576,328. **Usage:** Program services, 67%; Management and General, 10%; Fundraising, 23%. **Volunteer Programs:** Norfolk headquarters only.

DEFENDERS OF WILDLIFE
1244 19th St. NW
Washington, DC 20036
(202) 659-9510

Purpose: A national nonprofit organization whose goal is to preserve, enhance and protect the national abundance and diversity of wildlife and preserve the integrity of natural ecosystems. Defenders recognizes the intrinsic value of wildlife, the importance of its humane treatment and the many benefits of wildlife to society. **Current Emphasis:** Protecting and restoring habitats and wildlife communities, reducing environmental hazards to wildlife and promoting wildlife appreciation and education. Specific projects include: restoring the gray wolf to its former range in Yellowstone National Park; preventing entanglement of marine mammals in plastic debris and discarded fish nets; working with Congress to develop a bill to strengthen our National Wildlife Refuge System, and combating the trade of wild caught birds. **Members:** 73,000. **Fees:** Individual, $20; Students/Seniors, $15. **Funding:** dnd. **Annual Revenue:** $4,345,902. **Usage:** Administration, 13%; Membership, 10%; Programs, 64%. **Volunteer Programs:** Defenders has an activist network consisting of more than 6,000 individuals. Volunteers are also welcome to assist staff at national headquarters or at any one of the four regional offices.

DUCKS UNLIMITED, INC.
One Waterfowl Way
Long Grove, IL 60047
(708) 438-4300
Fax (708) 438-9236

Purpose: To conserve and enhance wetland ecosystems throughout North America.

Members: 550,000. **Fees:** $20. **Annual Revenue:** $67,000,000. **Usage:** Administration, 3.8%; Fundraising, 17.9%; Programs, 76.3%. **Volunteer Programs:** Wetland habitat conservation and enhancement projects.

EARTH ISLAND INSTITUTE
300 Broadway, Suite 28
San Francisco, CA 94133
(415) 788-3666
Fax (415) 788-7324

Purpose: To develop innovative projects for the conservation, preservation and restoration of the global environment. **Current Emphasis:** *Earth Island Journal*, the International Marine Mammal Project, the Sea Turtle Restoration Project, Baikal Watch, Urban Habitat Program, and International Green Circle, among others. **Members:** 35,000. **Fees:** Individual, $25; student, $15. **Funding:** Members, 55%; Foundation/Donor, 35%. **Annual Revenue:** $1,300,000. **Volunteer Programs:** Volunteer programs and internships available in most projects.

EARTHWATCH
P.O. Box 403
680 Mt. Auburn St.
Watertown, MA 02172
(617) 926-8200

Purpose: Sending volunteers to work with scientists around the world who are working to save rainforests and endangered species, preserve archeological finds and study pollution effects. **Current Emphasis:** Working to research and create management plans to help alleviate crucial environmental problems. **Members:** 70,000. **Fees:** $25. **Funding:** Membership, 80%; Corporation, 10%; Foundation, 10%. **Annual Revenue:** dnd. **Usage:** Administration, 16%; Fundraising, 4%; Programs, 80%. **Volunteer Programs:** Work in 46 countries with scientists from around the world on projects ranging from two to three weeks.

ENVIRONMENTAL ACTION & ENVIRONMENTAL ACTION FOUNDATION
6930 Carroll Ave., Suite 600
Takoma Park, MD 20912
(301) 891-1100
Fax (301) 891-2218

Purpose: To protect our resources for present and future generations by encouraging pollution prevention and conservation of natural resources. Environmental Action believes an unpolluted environment is a fundamental human right. **Current Emphasis:** Includes solid

 Q: *What nation has the world's lowest fertility rate? (1.3 children per woman)*

waste disposal, toxic waste disposal, community right to know, lobbying, and energy issues. **Members:** 20,000. **Fees:** $25/year. **Funding:** Membership, 40%; Foundation, 60%. **Annual Revenue:** $1.3 milllion. **Usage:** Administration, 3%; Fundraising, 17%; Programs, 80%; **Volunteer Programs:** Yes, in some areas.

ENVIRONMENTAL DATA RESEARCH INSTITUTE
797 Elmwood Ave.
Rochester, NY 14620
(716) 473-3090
Fax (716) 473-0968

Purpose: Established in 1989 to provide the environmental community with information on organizations, publications, and funding. EDRI has developed a comprehensive database of environmental grants, which provides detailed custom reports on who's giving money, who's getting it, where it goes, and for what purpose. **Current Emphasis:** Analysis of funding by topic (biodiversity, energy, toxics, etc.), activity (research, advocacy, etc.), geographic region and scope. **Funding:** Foundation/Donor, 100%. **Volunteer Programs:** Some internships are available.

ENVIRONMENTAL DEFENSE FUND
257 Park Avenue S
New York, NY 10010
(212) 505-2100

Purpose: To link science, economics and law to create innovative, economically viable solutions to today's environmental problems. **Current Emphasis:** Solid waste management, global climate change, tropical rainforest deforestation and toxin control. **Members:** 200,000. **Fees:** $20. **Funding:** Membership, 53%; Corporation, 1%; Other, 46%. **Annual Revenue:** $16,900,000. **Usage:** Administration, 3%; Fundraising, 13%; Programs, 82%. **Volunteer Programs:** Summer internships are available in various departments in all seven offices.

THE ENVIRONMENTAL EXCHANGE
1930 18th St. NW, Suite 24
Washington, DC 20009
(202) 387-2182

Purpose: To facilitate grass roots environmental projects through the exchange of information from organizations to the public about working environmental projects. **Current Emphasis:** Currently working on solid waste reduction, recycling, energy alternatives, and toxic waste disposal. **Annual Revenue:** $300,000. **Usage:** dnd. **Volunteer Programs:**

Internships available for college or graduate students helping primary researchers seek out information.

ENVIRONMENTAL SUPPORT CENTER, INC.
1731 Connecticut Ave. NW, Suite 200
Washington, DC 20009
(202) 328-7813
Fax (202) 265-0492

Purpose: The center operates programs to strengthen regional, state, local and grassroots organizations working on environmental issues. ESC pays for most of the cost of contracting with professionals to provide training and technical assistance to those groups in fundraising, organizational development, and strategic planning. ESC obtains equipment and services for groups. **Current Emphasis:** In addition to the programs listed above, the center also helps groups make use of workplace solicitation as a fundraising tool. **Membership:** dnd. **Funding:** Foundation/Donor, 100%. **Annual Revenue:** $500,000. **Usage:** dnd. **Volunteer Programs:** None.

FISH AND WILDLIFE REFERENCE SERVICE
5430 Grosvenor Ln., Suite 110
Bethesda, MD 20814
(301) 492-6403

Purpose: A computerized information retrieval system and clearinghouse providing fish and wildlife management research reports. **Current Emphasis:** Fish and wildlife management and protection of endangered species. **Members:** 9,000. **Fees:** Some user fees. **Annual Revenue:** $10,000. **Volunteer Programs:** Up to five nonpaid interns.

FRIENDS OF THE EARTH
218 D St. SE
Washington, DC 20003
(202) 544-2600

Purpose: Global environmental advocates dedicated to the conservation, protection and rational use of the Earth. Engaged in lobbying in Washington, DC, and various state capitals and disseminating public information on a wide variety of environmental issues. FOE publishes an award-winning magazine, *Friends of the Earth*, and is affiliated with 42 other Friends of the Earth groups around the world. **Current Emphasis:** Ozone depletion, agricultural biotechnology, toxic chemical safety, groundwater protection, nuclear weapons production wastes, oceans and coasts, coal strip-mining abuses, tropical deforestation and various international projects. **Members:** 50,000. **Fees:**

A. *The home of the Roman Catholic Church: Italy*
Source: *Population Reference Bureau*

Individuals, $25; Student/low-income/senior, $15. **Funding:** dnd. **Annual Revenue:** dnd. **Usage:** dnd. **Volunteer Programs:** Internships available.

THE FUND FOR ANIMALS
200 W. 57th St.
New York, NY 10019
(212) 246-2096
Fax (212) 246-2633

Purpose: To oppose cruelty to animals—whether wild or domestic—wherever and whenever it occurs and to preserve biodiversity. **Current Emphasis:** To oppose all sport hunting, to limit the breeding of domestic animals, and to preserve rare species and systems. **Members:** 200,000. **Fees:** $20. **Funding:** Membership, 98%; Foundation/ Donor, 2%. **Annual Revenue:** $1,800,000. **Usage:** Administration, 20%; Fundraising, 10%; Programs, 70%. **Volunteer Programs:** Washington, DC, office internships.

GRAND CANYON TRUST
1400 16th St. NW, #300
Washington, DC 20036
(202) 797-5429

Purpose: To advocate the preservation and wise management of the natural resources of the Colorado Plateau and the Grand Canyon. **Current Emphasis:** Glen Canyon Dam operations, air pollution in the canyon and Utah Wilderness designation. **Members:** 3,600. **Fees:** $25. **Funding:** Membership, 65%; Foundation, 35%. **Annual Revenue:** dnd. **Usage:** Administration, 7%; Fundraising, 20%; Programs, 73%. **Volunteer Programs:** Washington DC and Flagstaff, AR offices use volunteers.

GREAT OLD BROADS FOR WILDERNESS
P.O. BOX 368
Cedar City, UT 84721
(801) 586-1671

Purpose: A nationwide group of women aged 45 and over who enjoy the wilderness and want to take an active part in preserving and protecting it; dedicated specifically to the growth and protection of the National Wilderness Preservation System. **Current Emphasis:** Supporting wilderness bills currently before Congress and on the way to Congress. **Members:** 800. **Fees:** $15. **Funding:** Membership, 100%. **Annual Revenue:** dnd. **Usage:** Programs, 100%.

GREATER YELLOWSTONE COALITION
P.O. Box 1874
Bozeman, MT 59771
(406) 586-1593

Purpose: To ensure the preservation and protection of the Greater Yellowstone ecosystem, one of the largest essentially intact ecosystems in the temperate zones of the earth. **Current Emphasis:** Concerned with inappropriate oil and gas development on national forest lands, logging, mining, grazing and excess development. **Members:** 4,000+ individuals, 90 organizations. **Fees:** Basic, $25; Patron, $500. **Funding:** Membership, 45%; Corporation, 5%; Foundation, 50%. **Annual Revenue:** $600,000. **Usage:** Administration, 25%; Fundraising, 13%; Programs, 62%. **Volunteer Programs:** Internships available.

GREENPEACE USA
1436 U St. NW
Washington, DC 20009
(202) 462-1177

Purpose: A direct action organization with offices in 24 countries, dedicated to protecting and conserving the environment and the life it supports. **Current Emphasis:** Greenpeace campaigns to stop global warming, ozone depletion, tropical deforestation, international waste trade, nuclear weapons production and the needless slaughter of marine mammals and endangered animals. Greenpeace also works to reduce toxic and nuclear waste, convert to clean, efficient energy sources, and protect the ocean ecology and Antarctica. The award-winning *Greenpeace* magazine is published on a bimonthly basis. **Members:** 2.3 million. **Fees:** $15. **Funding:** Supporters, 98%; Corporations, less than 1%; Foundations/ Donors, less than 1%. **Annual Revenue:** $50,000,000. **Usage:** Administration, 4%; Fundraising, 21%; Programs, 75%. **Programs:** Direct Action, education, grassroots organizing and research. Lobbying conducted by sister organization Greenpeace Action. **Volunteer Programs:** Interns and volunteers accepted in most offices.

HAWKWATCH INTERNATIONAL, INC.
P.O. Box 35706
1420 Carlisle NE, Suite 100
Albuquerque, NM 87176-5706
(505) 255-7622

Purpose: The conservation of birds of prey and their habitats in western US through research and public education. Supports six field projects to monitor trends and migration patterns of migratory raptors in the Rocky

Q. *What is the change, since 1988, in the fuel efficiency of new cars sold in the US?*

Mountain West. **Current Emphasis:** Standardized counts of migrating raptors at strategic observation points and large-scale capture and banding program. **Members:** 2,200. **Fees:** Individual, $20. Family, $30. **Funding:** Membership, 50%; Corporation, 10%; Government contracts, 40%. **Annual Revenue:** $190,000. **Usage:** Administration, 10%; Fundraising, 10%; Programs, 80%. **Volunteer Programs:** Spring and fall research and education internships. Volunteer banders also needed.

HEARTWOOD

Route 3, Box 402
Paoli, IN 47454
(812) 723-2430

Purpose: Heartwood is a new association of groups and individuals formed in December 1990 dedicated to the health and well-being of the native forests of the central hardwood region as well as its plant and animal inhabitants, including the humans. Heartwood believes that the principal role of public land is the conservation of functioning ecological systems and the wealth of genetic information they contain. Various other uses of the land should be permitted only if they are compatible with that essential purpose. **Current Emphasis:** Education and outreach through grassroots organization and individuals concerned about forest protection. **Members:** Not yet known. **Annual Revenue:** $5,000 startup. **Usage:** Programs, 100%. **Volunteer Programs:** Volunteer work available and appreciated.

THE HUMANE SOCIETY OF THE UNITED STATES

2100 L St. NW
Washington, DC 20037
(202) 452-1100

Purpose: Working to prevent cruelty to all living creatures. Mindful that humans have been uniquely endowed with a sense of moral values, the HSUS believes we are responsible for the welfare of those animals that we have domesticated and those upon whose natural environment we encroach. **Current Emphasis:** The Shame of Fur campaign; Be a PAL—Prevent a Litter campaign; marine mammal protection, laboratory animal welfare, The Beautiful Choice campaign. **Members:** 1,187,162. **Annual Revenue:** $15,142,844. **Volunteer Programs:** Contact your local organization for area activities.

INFORM

381 Park Ave. S
New York, NY 10016
(212) 689-4040

Purpose: Environmental research and education organization that identifies and reports on practical actions for the preservation and conservation of natural resources and public health. Current research focuses on such critical environmental issues as hazardous waste reduction, garbage management, urban air quality and land and water conservation. Approximately six reports published per year. **Current Emphasis:** Chemical hazards prevention, business recycling and municipal solid waste incineration. **Members:** 1,000. **Fees:** From $25. **Funding:** Membership, 22%; Corporation, 18%; Other, 60%. **Annual Revenue:** $1.5 million. **Usage:** Research and education. **Volunteer Programs:** Occasional availability in clerical and communications.

INSTITUTE FOR CONSERVATION LEADERSHIP

2000 P St. NW, Suite 413
Washington, DC 20036
(202) 466-3330
Fax (202) 659-3897

Purpose: To serve the entire conservation/environmental community with leadership training and organizational development programs. To help build volunteer involvement, increase organizational leadership, help establish state networks and improve individual leadership skills and abilities. The goal is to increase the number and effectiveness of volunteer organizations and leaders in the entire community. **Current Emphasis:** Week-long, individual training sessions, state networking conferences, board-of-directors training and long-range planning facilitation. **Members:** 1324. **Fees:** None. **Funding:** Foundation/Donor, 90%; other, 10%. **Annual Revenue:** $270,000. **Usage:** Administration, 30%; Fundraising, 10%; Programs, 60%. **Volunteer Programs:** None.

INSTITUTE FOR EARTH EDUCATION

P.O. Box 288
Warrenville, IL 60555
(509) 395-2299

Purpose: IEE develops and disseminates educational programs that help people build an understanding of, appreciation for, and harmony with the earth and its life. Through its worldwide network of branches, the Institute conducts workshops, provides a seasonal journal, hosts international and regional

A: **–0.5 miles per gallon**
Source: *Environmental Protection Agency*

conferences, supports local groups, distributes an annual catalog and publishes books and program materials. **Current Emphasis:** Earth Education program development and support for teachers and leaders. **Members:** 2,000+. **Fees:** Personal, $20; Professional, $35; Affiliate, $50; Sponsor, $100. **Annual Revenue:** $300,000+. **Programs:** Program development. **Volunteer Programs:** Available through international sharing centers.

INTERNATIONAL ALLIANCE FOR SUSTAINABLE AGRICULTURE
1701 University Ave. SE
Minneapolis, MN 55414
(612) 331-1099
Fax (612) 379-1527

Purpose: IASA works for the worldwide realization of sustainable agriculture—food systems that are ecologically sound, economically viable, socially just and humane. The Alliance focuses on three goals: 1) building a strong sustainable agriculture industry and movement; 2) widespread understanding of and participation in sustainable agriculture; and 3) universal adoption of policies that implement sustainable agriculture. **Current Emphasis:** Passage of Circle of Poison Legislation, federal funding for the Organic Standards Board, publication of a national directory on humane sustainable agriculture and a Minnesota directory on sustainable agriculture, food and the environment. **Members:** 800. **Fees:** $10–$1,000. **Funding:** Membership, 6%; Corporation, 23%; Foundation/Donor, 71%. **Annual Revenue:** $187,000. **Usage:** Administration, 13%; Fundraising, 2%; Programs, 85%. **Volunteer Programs:** Opportunities are available in every area of current emphasis described above and through formal committee and volunteer structure. Call for more information.

INTERNATIONAL FUND FOR ANIMAL WELFARE
411 Main St.
Yarmouth Port, MA 02675
(508) 362-4944

Purpose: An international animal welfare organization dedicated to protecting wild and domestic animals from cruelty. **Current Emphasis:** Preservation of harp and hood seals in Canada, dog and cat abuse in the Philippines and South Korea, elephants in Africa, the use of animals in laboratory testing for the cosmetics industry and whales and other marine mammals around the world. **Members:** 650,000. **Fees:** dnd. **Funding:** Donors. **Annual Revenue:** $4,916,491. **Usage:** Expenses equal 108% of donations. Administration, 18%; Fundraising, 17%; Programs, 73%. **Volunteer Programs:** Pilot whale stranding network on Cape Cod for residents of Massachusetts.

INTERNATIONAL PRIMATE PROTECTION LEAGUE
P.O. Box 766
Summerville, SC 29484
(803) 871-7988

Purpose: Dedicated to the conservation and protection of apes, monkeys and prosimians, maintenance of a gibbon sanctuary and support of overseas projects. Includes a quarterly newsletter, *The IPPL Newsletter*. **Current Emphasis:** Uncovering illegal trafficking in primates and support of primate sanctuaries overseas. **Members:** 11,500. **Fees:** $20. **Funding:** Membership, 75%; Corporation, 1%; Other, 24%. **Annual Revenue:** $250,000. **Usage:** Administration, 20%; Fundraising, 10%; Programs, 70%. **Volunteer Programs:** None.

THE JANE GOODALL INSTITUTE
P.O. Box 41720
Tucson, AZ 85717
(602) 325-1211
Membership line, (800) 999-CHIMP

Purpose: Ongoing support and expansion of field research on wild chimpanzees and studies of chimpanzees in captive environments. The Institute is dedicated to publicizing the unique status and needs of chimpanzees to insure their preservation in the wild and their physical and psychological well-being in captivity. **Current Emphasis:** Field research activities at Gombe Stream Research Centre in Tanzania; the ChimpanZoo study of active chimpanzees in zoos or other captive colonies in the US and conservation activities targeting wild and captive chimpanzees, including those in biomedical research laboratories. **Members:** 2,314. **Fees:** From $25. **Funding:** Membership, 20%; Corporation, 2%; Lecture Tour, 39%; Other, 39%. **Annual Revenue:** $599,800. **Usage:** Administration, 15%; Fundraising, 15%; Programs, 70%. **Volunteer Programs:** University of Southern California Goodall Fellowship.

THE LAND AND WATER FUND OF THE ROCKIES
1405 Arapahoe, Suite 200
Boulder, CO 80302
(303) 444-1188
Idaho office:
P.O. Box 1612

Q. *Each year, what type of environmental pollution is responsible for 50,000 to 200,000 human deaths?*

Boise, ID 83701
(208) 342-7024

Purpose: "Legal Aid for the Environment," to provide free legal aid to grassroots environmental groups in Arizona, Colorado, Idaho, Montana, New Mexico, Utah and Wyoming. LAW Fund staff attorneys and a regional network of local volunteer attorneys supply advice and counsel, and will litigate for client groups. Founded 1990. **Current Emphasis:** Public lands, water and toxics, energy efficiency. **Members:** 250. **Fees:** Regular, $25; Student/senior/limited-income, $15; Organization, $100; Special, $50-$1,000. **Funding:** Membership, 3%; Other, 1%; Foundation, 96%. **Annual Revenue:** $450,000. **Usage:** Administration, 25%; Fundraising, 1%; Programs, 74%. **Volunteer Programs:** Pro Bono Attorney Program, "Adopt-A-Forest," opportunities for technical experts.

THE LAND TRUST ALLIANCE
900 17th St. NW, Suite 410
Washington, DC 20006-2596
(202) 785-1410

Purpose: A national organization of local and regional land conservation groups that provides programs and services to help land trusts reach their full potential, fosters public policies supportive of land conservation and builds public awareness of land trusts and their goals. **Current Emphasis:** Providing educational materials and technical assistance for land trusts and other land conservation professionals. **Members:** 700. **Fees:** From $30. **Funding:** dnd. **Annual Revenue:** $800,000. **Usage:** Administration, 19%; Fundraising, 10%; Programs, 80%. **Volunteer Programs:** An internship program is available and volunteers are needed by land trusts across the country.

LEAGUE TO SAVE LAKE TAHOE
989 Keys Blvd., Suite 6
S. Lake Tahoe, CA 96150
(916) 541-5388

Purpose: Dedicated to preserving the environmental balance, scenic beauty and recreational opportunities of the Lake Tahoe Basin. Subsidiary organizations include League to Save Lake Tahoe Charitable Trust and Lake Tahoe Land Trust. **Current Emphasis:** Reversing the water and air quality decline at Lake Tahoe. **Members:** 3,700. **Fees:** $35. **Funding:** dnd. **Annual Revenue:** $250,000. **Usage:** Administration, 54%; Programs, 46%. **Volunteer Programs:** None.

LIGHTHAWK
P.O. Box 8163
Santa Fe, NM 87504
(505) 982-9656

Purpose: To use and encourage the advantages of flight to shed light on and correct environmental mismanagement and empower others to do the same. The goal is to greatly enhance humankind's capacity to sustain biological diversity, intact ecosystems and ecological processes that support life on earth. **Current Emphasis:** Working to protect America's national forest system, particularly the last vestiges of our once vast Pacific Northwest rainforests. **Members:** 3,000. **Fees:** $35, $100 and up. **Funding:** dnd. **Annual Revenue:** $800,000. **Usage:** Administration, 10%; Fundraising, 2%; Programs, 88%. **Volunteer Programs:** Volunteer aircraft owner/pilots with at least 1,000 hours flight time in their own aircraft needed.

MANOMET BIRD OBSERVATORY
P.O. Box 1770
Manomet, MA 02345
(508) 224-6521

Purpose: A center for long-term environmental research and education. MBO's scientific studies improve understanding of wildlife populations and natural systems and foster conservation action throughout the Americas. The education programs provide training in field biology for college students and offer programs and support for science educators in schools. **Current Emphasis:** Ecology and conservation of neotropical migrant land birds, migration ecology and conservation of shorebirds, field techniques workshops for Latin American biologists, conservation and management of North American fisheries and studies of the effects of oil pollution on wading bird populations. **Members:** 2,500. **Fees:** Regular, $25; Student, $15. **Funding:** dnd. **Annual Revenue:** $1,500,000. **Usage:** Research/education programs. **Volunteer Programs:** Field biology training program and international shorebird survey, among others.

NATIONAL ARBOR DAY FOUNDATION
211 N. 12th St., Suite 501
Lincoln, NE 68508
(402) 474-5655
Fax (402) 474-0820

Purpose: An education organization dedicated to tree planting and conservation. **Current Emphasis:** Programs such as Trees for America, Tree City USA, Conservation Trees, Celebrate Arbor Day and the National Arbor Day

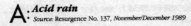

A: *Acid rain*
Source: Resurgence No. 137, *November/December 1989*

Center. **Members:** 1,000,000. **Fees:** $10. **Funding:** Membership, 61%; Other, 39%. **Annual Revenue:** $14,700,000. **Usage:** Administration, 1%; Fundraising, 10%; Programs, 89%. **Volunteer Programs:** dnd.

NATIONAL ASSOCIATION OF BIOLOGY TEACHERS

11250 Roger Bacon Dr., #19
Reston, VA 22090
(703) 471-1134

Purpose: Dedicated exclusively to the concerns of biology teachers. Publishes *The American Biology Teacher*, a nationally recognized journal which highlights research findings, innovative teaching strategies, laboratory exercises and reviews of publications, computer programs and videos. **Current Emphasis:** Projects underway include middle school teacher training, biotechnology labs and equipment loan programs, alternative use of animals in the classroom and elementary education environmental curriculum. **Members:** 7,000. **Fees:** $38. **Funding:** Membership, 40%; Other, 60%. **Annual Revenue:** $700,000. **Usage:** Administration, 33%; Fundraising, 1%; Programs, 66%. **Volunteer Programs:** None.

NATIONAL ASSOCIATION OF INTERPRETATION

P.O. Box 1892
Fort Collins, CO 80522
(303) 491-6434

Purpose: A professional organization serving the needs and interests of interpreters employed by agencies and organizations concerned with natural and cultural resources, conservation and management. **Current Emphasis:** Representing all those whose job it is to convey the meanings and relationships between people and their natural, cultural and recreational world. **Members:** 2,300. **Fees:** Student, $25, individual, $40. **Funding:** Membership, 90%; Corporation, 10%. **Annual Revenue:** $132,000. **Usage:** Administration, 38%; Programs, 62%. **Volunteer Programs:** None.

NATIONAL AUDUBON SOCIETY

950 Third Ave.
New York, NY 10022
(212) 832-3200
Fax (212) 593-6254

Purpose: Audubon is a grassroots environmental organization dedicated to protecting wildlife and its habitats. Audubon's 600,000 members and staff of scientists, lobbyists, lawyers, policy analysts, and educators work through field and policy research, lobbying, litigation, and citizen action to protect and restore various habitats throughout the Americas. **Current Emphasis:** Activism; high-priority campaigns: Ancient Forests, Arctic National Wildlife Refuge, wetlands, Platte River. **Members:** 600,000. **Fees:** $20. **Funding:** Membership, 30%; Bequests/Contributors, 32%; Other, 38%. **Annual Revenue:** $37,000,000. **Usage:** Administration, 9%; Fundraising, 8%; Programs, 73%. **Programs:** Wildlife preservation, science and field research, environmental education, membership and publishing, chapter activities. **Volunteer Programs:** Annual Christmas Bird Count and Breeding Bird Census; Audubon Activist Network and involvement through local chapters, and state and regional offices.

NATIONAL AUDUBON SOCIETY EXPEDITION INSTITUTE

P.O. Box 170
Readfield, ME 04355
(207) 685-3111
Fax (207) 685-4333

Purpose: Graduate, undergraduate and high school education program which offers year-long and semester expeditions providing an alternative to traditional education emphasizing environmental education. Exciting list of courses offered. **Members:** 80-100 per year. **Fees:** Semester, $6,100; year, $10,400. **Funding:** Membership, 90%; Foundation/Donor, 10%. **Annual Revenue:** dnd.

NATIONAL COALITION AGAINST THE MISUSE OF PESTICIDES

701 E St. SW, Suite 200
Washington, DC 20003
(202) 543-5450

Purpose: To serve as a national network committed to pesticide safety and the adoption of alternative pest management strategies which reduce or eliminate dependency on toxic chemicals. **Current Emphasis:** To affect change through local action, assisting individuals and community-based organizations in this endeavor. **Members:** dnd. **Fees:** $20. **Funding:** Membership, 33%; Grants, 67%. **Annual Revenue:** dnd. **Usage:** dnd. **Volunteer Programs:** Internships available.

NATIONAL WILDFLOWER RESEARCH CENTER

2600 FM 973 N.
Austin, TX 78725-4201
(512) 929-3600

Purpose: To study North American wildflowers and other native plants with the aim of

Q: *What is the estimated percentage of the oil spilled from the* **Exxon Valdez** *that has been cleaned from the environment?*

reestablishing native plants in landscapes, thereby aiding in the repair and beautification of the environment. **Current Emphasis:** Research on wildflowers and native plants, education of the public about their importance in the environment, and promotion of their use in planned landscapes and their conservation. **Members:** 17,000. **Fees:** From $25. **Funding:** dnd. **Annual Revenue:** dnd. **Usage:** dnd. **Volunteer Programs:** Active volunteer program and public relations internship through University of Texas.

NATIONAL WILDLIFE FEDERATION
1400 16th St. NW
Washington, DC 20036
(202) 797-6800
Fax (202) 797-6646

Purpose: To be the most responsible and effective conservation education association promoting the wise use of natural resources and protection of the global environment. The Federation distributes periodicals and education materials, sponsors outdoor education programs in conservation and litigates environmental disputes in an effort to conserve natural resources and wildlife. **Current Emphasis:** Forests, energy, toxic pollution, environmental quality, biotechnical fisheries and wildlife, wetlands, water resources and public lands. **Members:** 5,600,000. **Fees:** $15-$20. **Funding:** Membership, 47%; Educational Materials, 39%; Foundation/Donor, 14%. **Annual Revenue:** $90,000,000. **Usage:** Administration/ Fundraising, 11%; Membership/Development, 21%; Programs, 68%. **Volunteer Programs:** The National Wildlife Federation oversees 51 state and territorial affiliate organizations.

NATURAL RESOURCES DEFENSE COUNCIL
40 W. 20th St.
New York, NY 10011
(212) 727-2700

Purpose: To protect America's natural resources and improve the quality of the human environment. NRDC combines legal action, scientific research and citizen education in an environmental protection program. **Current Emphasis:** Major accomplishments have been in the area of energy policy and nuclear safety, air and water pollution, urban transportation issues, pesticides and toxic substances, forest protection, global warming and the international environment. **Members:** 170,000. **Fees:** $10. **Funding:** Membership, 50%; Foundation/Grants, 50%. **Annual Revenue:** $16,000,000. **Usage:** Administration, 10%;

Fundraising, 16%; Programs, 74%. **Volunteer Programs:** Legal internships as well as internships for graduate and undergraduate college students in several offices.

THE NATURE CONSERVANCY
1815 N. Lynn St.
Arlington, VA 22209
(703) 841-5300

Purpose: International organization committed to preserving biological diversity by protecting lands and the plants and animals that live on them. Manages a system of over 1,100 nature sanctuaries. **Current Emphasis:** Land protection in 50 states in US and 12 countries in Latin America. **Members:** 550,000. **Fees:** $15. **Funding:** Membership, 70%; Corporation, 9.6%; Foundation, 20.4%. **Annual Revenue:** $168,554,000. **Usage:** Administration, 7.9%; Fundraising, 8%; Programs, 80.3%; Other, 3.8%. **Volunteer Programs:** Positions available. Call (800) 628-6860 for information.

NORTH AMERICAN NATIVE FISHES ASSOCIATION
123 W. Mt. Airy Ave.
Philadelphia, PA 19119
(215) 247-0384

Purpose: To bring together people interested in fishes native to this continent for scientific purposes or aquarium study; to encourage increased scientific appreciation and conservation of native fishes through observation, study and research; to assemble and distribute information about native fishes. **Current Emphasis:** dnd. **Members:** 400. **Fees:** $11-$15. **Funding:** dnd. **Annual Revenue:** dnd. **Volunteer Programs:** None.

NORTHERN ALASKA ENVIRONMENTAL CENTER
218 Driveway
Fairbanks, AK 99701
(907) 452-5021

Purpose: Dedicated to the protection of the quality of the Alaskan environment through action and education. NAEC covers areas north of the Alaska Range and works closely with government agencies on land-use issues such as the Arctic National Wildlife Refuge, implementation of the Alaska Lands Act, oil and gas leasing, and placer goldmining. **Current Emphasis:** Wilderness designation for the coastal plan of ANWR and arctic development issues. **Members:** 750. **Fees:** Individual, $25; Family, $35. **Funding:** Membership, 55%; Grants, 30%; Events, 15%. **Annual Revenue:** $90,000. **Usage:** Administration, 17%;

A. *8 percent*
Source: US Congressional Office of Technical Assessment

Fundraising, 11%; Programs, 72%. **Volunteer Programs:** Opportunities for research internships and a wide variety of volunteer programs.

NUCLEAR INFORMATION AND RESOURCE SERVICE

1424 16th St. NW, Suite 601
Washington, DC 20036
(202) 328-0002

Purpose: To serve as a networking and information clearinghouse for environmental activists concerned with nuclear power and waste issues; to provide citizens with the information and tools necessary to challenge nuclear facilities and policies; to work for increased energy efficiency and toward a sustainable, renewable energy future. **Current Emphasis:** Stopping deregulation of radioactive waste, publishing an energy audit manual for towns and universities and working to prevent a new generation of nuclear reactors. **Members:** 1,200. **Fees:** $20. **Funding:** Membership, 20%; Foundation/Donor, 80%. **Annual Revenue:** $275,000. **Usage:** Administration, 12%; Fundraising, 5%; Programs, 83%. **Volunteer Programs:** Intern applications accepted year-round and $100/week stipend offered.

PACIFIC WHALE FOUNDATION

101 N. Kihei Rd., Suite 25
Kihei, HI 96753
(808) 879-8860 or (800) WHALE-11

Purpose: The scientific study of the ocean and its marine mammal inhabitants; the application of research findings to the preservation of the marine environment; education and conservation programs to enhance ecological awareness. **Current Emphasis:** Conducting field research worldwide and assisting government and nongovernment agencies in developing conservation policies and plans for endangered marine life. **Members:** 5,000. **Fees:** Student, $15; Individual, $20; Family, $25; Foreign, $30; Institution, $50; Contributing, $100; Patron, $500. **Funding:** Membership, 50%; Programs, 50%. **Annual Revenue:** $700,000. **Usage:** Administration/Fundraising, 25%; Programs, 75%. **Volunteer Programs:** Ocean Outreach Docents and marine debris cleanup fundraising.

POPULATION CRISIS COMMITTEE

1120 19th St. NW, #550
Washington, DC 20036
(202) 659-1833
Fax (202) 293-1795

Purpose: To stimulate public awareness, understanding and action toward reducing population growth rates. Advocates universal and voluntary access to family planning services to achieve world population stabilization. **Current Emphasis:** Relationship between population growth and environmental degradation, contraceptive availability. **Annual Revenue:** $4,000,000. **Usage:** Administration, 9%; Fundraising, 5%; Programs, 86%. **Programs:** Publications and public information, research and analysis, project support.

POPULATION-ENVIRONMENT BALANCE

1325 G St. NW, Suite 1003
Washington, DC 20005-3104
(202) 879-3000
Fax (202) 879-3019

Purpose: A national, nonprofit membership organization dedicated to education and advocacy of measures which would encourage population stabilization in the US, in order to safeguard our environment. **Current Emphasis:** Environmental protection, birth control availability/research, local growth control and immigration policy. **Members:** 5,000. **Fees:** $25. **Funding:** Membership, 35%; Foundation/Donor, 65%. **Annual Revenue:** $650,000. **Usage:** Administration, 25%; Fundraising, 10%; Programs 65%. **Programs:** Public education and outreach. **Volunteer Programs:** Volunteer positions regularly available.

PROTECT OUR WOODS

P.O. Box 352
Paoli, IN 47454
(812) 678-4303

Purpose: Protect Our Woods is comprised of groups of landowners and concerned individuals working toward preserving and protecting the forests of Indiana and the wild and rural areas of the state. **Current Emphasis:** Improving forest management on both public and private lands. **Members:** 800. **Fees:** $10-individual, $20-family /household. **Funding:** Membership, 100%. **Annual Revenue:** $10,000. **Usage:** Administration, 5-10%, Programs, 90-95%. **Volunteer Programs:** Volunteer positions are available.

RAILS-TO-TRAILS CONSERVANCY

1400 16th St. NW, Suite 300
Washington, DC 20036
(202) 797-5400

Purpose: Converting thousands of miles of abandoned railroad corridors to public trails for walking, bicycling, horseback riding, cross-country skiing, wildlife habitat and nature ap-

Q: *How many gallons of drinking water does the average American use to flush 130 gallons of bodily waste yearly?*

preciation. **Current Emphasis:** Linking major metropolitan areas via rail-trails and established greenways. **Members:** 50,000. **Fees:** $18. **Funding:** Membership, 44.4%; Grants, 47.6%; Other, 8%. **Annual Revenue:** $1,544,293. **Usage:** Administration, 1.3%; Fundraising, 9.8%; Programs, 75.5%; Membership Services, 13.4%. **Volunteer Programs:** Six-month paid internships are available at the national office in Washington, DC and volunteers can serve at chapter offices and on specific projects.

RAINFOREST ACTION NETWORK

301 Broadway, Suite A
San Francisco, CA 94133
(415) 398-4404

Purpose: Nonprofit activist organization working to save the world's rainforests. Works internationally in cooperation with other environmental and human rights organizations on major campaigns to protect rainforests. **Current Emphasis:** Protecting rainforests in Hawaii, Amazonia and Southeast Asia. **Members:** 31,000. **Fees:** $15 minimum. **Funding:** Membership, 70%; Corporation, 20%; Foundation/Donor, 10%. **Annual Revenue:** dnd. **Usage:** Administration, 15%; Fundraising, 10%; Programs, 75%. **Volunteer Programs:** Internship program is available and volunteers are needed in all locations.

RAINFOREST ALLIANCE

270 Lafayette St, #512
New York, NY 10012
(212) 941-1900
Fax (212) 941-4986

Purpose: Dedicated to the conservation of the world's tropical forests, the Rainforest Alliance's primary mission is to develop and promote sound alternatives to the activities that cause tropical deforestation—opportunities for people to utilize tropical forests without destroying them. We are also involved in public education and building new constituencies for conservation. **Current Emphasis:** Timber project (including "Smart Wood" certification); Periwinkle Project (medicinal plant information); Tropical Conservation Newsbureau; Kleinhaus Fellowship for Tropical Agroforestry; Edelstein Fellowship for Medicinal Plant Research in Brazil; Committee for Conservation and Higher Education. **Members:** 15,000. **Fees:** $20. **Funding:** Membership, 20%; Corporation, 15%; Foundation/Donor, 65%. **Annual Revenue:** $900,000. **Usage:** Administration, 9%; Fundraising, 11%; Programs, 80%. **Volunteer Programs:** Variety of programs.

RARE CENTER FOR TROPICAL BIRD CONSERVATION

1529 Walnut St., 3rd Floor
Philadelphia, PA 19102
(215) 568-0420
Fax (215) 568-0561

Purpose: RARE Center is a small organization doing innovative work to preserve threatened habitats and ecosystems in Latin America and the Caribbean. RARE focuses on endangered birds because of their value as environmental indicators and rallying points for conservation initiatives. **Current Emphasis:** Conservation education and applied research. **Members:** 1,000. **Fees:** $30. **Funding:** Membership, 40%; Foundation/Donor, 60%. **Annual Revenue:** $300,000. **Usage:** Administration, 20%, Fundraising, 15%; Programs, 65%. **Volunteer Programs:** Occasionally.

THE RENE DUBOS CENTER FOR HUMAN ENVIRONMENTS, INC.

100 E. 85th St.
New York, NY 10028
(212) 249-7745

Purpose: An independent, education and research organization founded by the eminent scientist/humanist Rene Dubos to focus on the humanistic and social aspects of environmental problems. The center's mission is to develop creative policies for the resolution of environmental conflicts and to help decision-makers and the general public formulate new environmental values. **Current Emphasis:** Forums and related activities on integrating waste management; education programs for teacher trainers and business/industry on environmental quality and responsibility for "The Decade of Environmental Literacy."

RENEW AMERICA

1400 16th St. NW, #710
Washington, DC 20036
(202) 232-2252

Purpose: Dedicated to the development of a safe and sustainable environment, Renew America provides information and recommendations to policy makers, media and other environmental organizations. **Current Emphasis:** "Searching for Success" is an identification, verification and awards program honoring those working to solve environmental problems. Renew America catalogs and promotes environmental success stories to be used as models throughout the country. **Members:** 7,000. **Fees:** $25. **Funding:** Membership/Corporation, 22%; Foundation/Donor, 73%; Publication, 5%. **Annual Revenue:** $1,000,000.

A. *9,000 gallons*
   Source: Garbage *Magazine, January/February 1990*

Usage: Administration, 23%; Membership, 22%; Programs, 44%; Reports, 11%. **Volunteer Programs:** Internship positions available.

RHINO RESCUE USA, INC.

1150 17th St. NW, Suite 400
Washington, DC 20036
(202) 293-5305

Purpose: To save the rhinoceros from extinction by funding rhino sanctuaries and research, organizing Congressional hearings and working with the US State Department and international experts to try to end the illegal trade in rhino horn. **Current Emphasis:** Funding rhinoceros sanctuaries and the research needed to effectively manage and increase remaining rhino populations. **Funding:** Individual donors and foundations. **Annual Revenue:** $22,000. **Usage:** Administration/Fundraising, 15%; Programs, 85%. **Volunteer Programs:** Contact the above address if interested in fundraising in your local area.

ROCKY MOUNTAIN RECYCLERS ASSOCIATION

P.O. Box 224
Denver, CO 80214-1896
(303) 441-9445

Purpose: To improve economic conditions for the Colorado recycling industry. To organize this industry to achieve economic policy reform; and to assist groups and individuals with recycling concerns. **Current Emphasis:** All of the above. **Members:** 10. **Fees:** $18-$500. **Funding:** Membership, 25%; Corporation, 25%; Foundation/Donor, 50%. **Annual Revenue:** $70,000. **Usage:** dnd. **Volunteer Programs:** Volunteer positions are available.

THE RUFFED GROUSE SOCIETY

451 McCormick Rd.
Coraopolis, PA 15108
(412) 262-4044

Purpose: Dedicated to improving the environment for ruffed grouse, American woodcock and other forest wildlife. **Current Emphasis:** Direct assistance in cooperation with land managers in creating and improving young-forest habitat on public lands. **Members:** 25,000. **Fees:** $20. **Funding:** Membership, 42%; Banquet, 52%. **Annual Revenue:** $1,500,000. **Usage:** Administration/Fundraising, 20%; Programs, 80%. **Volunteer Programs:** Assisting with local banquets and chapters.

THE SACRED EARTH NETWORK

426 Sixth Ave.
Brooklyn, NY 11215
(718) 768-8569

Purpose: The Sacred Earth Network seeks to re-acquaint people with their fundamental connection with the natural world through any nonviolent means neccessary. To enhance ties with Soviet environmentalists through the establishment of an electronic mail network, translating "cutting edge" solutions to environmental problems from English to Russian and Russian to English. **Current Emphasis:** To continue more translations, workshops, and seminars in deep ecology. Protecting and preserving the forests of the Siberian Wilderness. **Members:** 1,100. **Fees:** $25. **Funding:** Memebership, 50%; Foundation/Donor, 50%. **Annual Revenue:** $31,000. **Usage:** Administration, 15%; Programs, 85%. **Volunteer Programs:** No volunteer programs have been established yet.

SAVE THE DUNES COUNCIL, INC.

444 Barker Rd.
Michigan City, IN 46360
(219) 879-3937

Purpose: Preservation and protection of the Indiana Dunes for public use and enjoyment by working for the control of air, water and waste pollution affecting the National Lakeshore and Northwest Indiana area. Involved in shoreline erosion and shoreline, policy issues affecting the Indiana Lake Michigan shoreline, wetlands preservation and groundwater protection. **Current Emphasis:** Water and air pollution, wetlands, shoreline management, parkland purchase and planning and development issues affecting the Indiana Dunes National Lakeshore. **Members:** 1,800. **Fees:** Senior, $10; Couple, $30; Life, $500. **Funding:** Membership, 80%; Other, 20%. **Annual Revenue:** $25,000. **Usage:** Fundraising, 1%; Programs, 99%. **Volunteer Programs:** Volunteers operate the Dunes Shop, whose revenue supports the Council.

SAVE-THE-REDWOODS LEAGUE

114 Sansome St., Room 605
San Francisco, CA 94104
(415) 362-2352
Fax (415) 362-7017

Purpose: To purchase Redwood groves and watershed lands for protection in public parks; to support reforestation, research and educational programs. **Members:** 50,000. **Fees:** $10. **Funding:** Membership, 100%. **Annual Revenue:** $2,000,000. **Usage:** Programs, 100%. **Volunteer Programs:** None.

Q: *What percentage less federal funding for solar energy research and development is there today than in 1980?*

SAVE THE WHALES, INC.

P.O. Box 2397
Venice, CA 90291
(213) 392-6226

Purpose: To educate children and adults about marine mammals, their environment and their preservation. Save the Whales is beginning educational programs via a mobile unit (Whales on Wheels) which will bring lectures and hands-on materials to schoolchildren. **Current Emphasis:** Education through our newsletters (four times per year), lectures, and letter-writing campaigns. **Members:** 800. **Fees:** Adults, $15; Children, $10; Classroom, $30.

SCENIC AMERICA

216 7th St. SE
Washington, DC 20003
(202) 546-1100

Purpose: To protect America's scenic landscapes and clean up visual pollution. Provides information and technical assistance on billboard and sign control, scenic areas preservation, growth management and all forms of aesthetic regulation. **Current Emphasis:** Visual pollution, scenic highways and billboard control. **Members:** 5,000. **Fees:** dnd. **Funding:** Membership, 20%; Corporation, 20%; Other, 60%. **Annual Revenue:** $300,000. **Usage:** Administration, 10%; Fundraising, 10%; Programs, 80%. **Volunteer Programs:** Internships in environmental journalism, political organizing and land-use regulation.

SEA SHEPHERD CONSERVATION

1314 Second St.
Santa Monica, CA 90401
(310) 394-3198

Purpose: To protect marine animals and marine habitats. **Current Emphasis:** Prevention of killing of dolphins by the tuna industry in the tropic Pacific; protecting pilot whales in the Faroe Islands; enforcing a moratorium on whaling, rescue of whales and marine mammals in distress and opposing the capture of dolphins in the Gulf of Mississippi. **Members:** 20,000. **Fees:** Donations. **Funding:** Membership, 100%. **Annual Revenue:** $500,000. **Usage:** Programs, 100%. **Volunteer Programs:** Sea Shepherd is entirely a volunteer organization.

SIERRA CLUB

730 Polk St.
San Francisco, CA 94109
(415) 776-2211

Purpose: To promote conservation of the natural environment by influencing public policy decisions—legislative, administrative, legal, and electoral. To practice and promote the responsible use of the Earth's ecosystems and resources and to educate and enlist humanity to protect and restore the quality of the natural and human environment. **Current Emphasis:** Old-growth forest protection; global warming/auto fuel efficiency/energy policy; Arctic National Wildlife Refuge protection; Bureau of Land Management wilderness/desert/national parks protection; toxic waste regulations; International Development lending; tropical forest preservation. **Members:** 648,000. **Fees:** Individual, $35; Student/Senior, $15. **Funding:** Membership, 35%; Contributions, 32%; Other, 33%. **Annual Revenue:** $40,659,100. **Usage:** Fundraising, 8%; Membership, 12%; Chapter Allocations, 6%; Programs, 74%. **Volunteer Programs:** Extensive opportunities available throughout the country.

SIERRA CLUB LEGAL DEFENSE FUND

180 Montgomery St., 14th Floor
San Francisco, CA 94104
(415) 627-6700

Purpose: To provide legal representation to environmental organizations on matters involving land use, public lands, pollution, endangered species and wildlife habitats. **Current Emphasis:** Currently involved in many endangered species cases which involve the use of public lands. New offices have opened in Louisiana and Florida and are currently involved in pollution liability and groundwater rights cases respectively. Also attempting to protect native Ecuadorians and rainforest lands from oil exploration. **Members:** 150,000. **Fees:** $10. **Funding:** Membership, 75%; Foundation/Donor, 20%; Court Awarded Attorney Fees, 5%. **Annual Revenue:** $9 million. **Usage:** Administration and Fundraising, 25%; Programs, 75%. **Volunteer Programs:** Law internships available in most offices.

SINAPU

1900 Allison St.
Lakewood, CO 80215
(303) 237-6280

Purpose: SINAPU is a new organization which supports the reintroduction and protection of wolves in the state of Colorado. **Current Emphasis:** Increase visibility and membership. **Members:** 50. **Fees:** $15-$35. **Funding:** Membership, 100%. **Annual Revenue:** dnd. **Usage:** Programs, 100%. **Volunteer Programs:** SINAPU functions totally on volunteer labor.

A. **90 percent**
Source: US Congressional Research Service

SOIL AND WATER CONSERVATION SOCIETY

7515 NE Ankeny Rd.
Ankeny, IA 50021-9764
(515) 289-2331

Purpose: The mission of the Soil and Water Conservation Society is to advocate the conservation of soil, water and related natural resources. **Members:** 12,000. **Fees:** First-time, $30; Regular, $44. **Funding:** Membership, 32%; Corporation, 1%; Foundation/Donor, 20%. **Volunteer Programs:** Journalism intern, public affairs specialist intern, Soil Conservation Service - Earth Team.

STUDENT CONSERVATION ASSOCIATION INC.

P.O. Box 550
Charlestown, NH 03603
(603) 826-4301
Fax (603) 826-7755

Purpose: Since 1957 SCA has provided educational opportunities for student and adult volunteers to assist with the stewardship of our public lands and natural resources while gaining experience that enhances career directions or personal goals. Volunteers serve in national parks, national forests, wildlife refuges and other public or private conservation areas nationwide. **Current Emphasis:** Volunteer assistance for ecological restoration; strengthening support for SCA volunteers and other youth (especially minorities) interested in conservation careers; publishing *Earth Work*, a magazine for and about current and future conservation professionals. **Members:** 12,000. **Fees:** $15 and up. **Funding:** Membership, 20%; Corporation, 4%; Foundation/Donor, 12%. **Annual Revenue:** $3.8 million. **Usage:** Administration, 19%; Fundraising, 14%; Programs, 65%. **Volunteer Programs:** The heart of SCA's activity is two volunteer programs: Resource Assistant Program (year-round) for college students/other adults, and the High School Program (summer) for students 16-18. No fee; most expenses paid; 1,500 openings per year. Listings and applications available.

THORNE ECOLOGICAL INSTITUTE

5398 Manhattan Cir.
Boulder, CO 80303
(303) 499-3647
Fax (303) 499-8340

Purpose: TEI is committed to educating individuals about the wise use of the environment. **Current Emphasis:** Educational programs for adults, children and community. **Members:** 400. **Fees:** $25-$1000. **Funding:** Membership, 10%; Corporation, 70%; Foundation/ Donor, 20%. **Annual Revenue:** $225,000. **Usage:** dnd. **Volunteer Programs:** Both internships and volunteer opportunities are available.

UNION OF CONCERNED SCIENTISTS

26 Church St.
Cambridge, MA 02238
(617) 547-5552
Fax (617) 864-9405

Purpose: The Union of Concerned Scientists is an independent nonprofit organization of scientists and other citizens concerned about the impact of advanced technology on society. UCS's programs run on two tracks—energy and arms. **Current Emphasis:** The energy program focuses on global warming, national energy policy, renewable energy, transportation, and nuclear power/safety. **Members:** 90,000. **Funding:** Membership, 80%; Foundation, 20%. **Annual Revenue:** $3,300,000. **Usage:** Administration, 3%; Fundraising and Sponsor communications, 23%. Programs: Energy and environmental programs, 41%; Nuclear Arms Program, 22%; Legislative Program, 11%. **Volunteer Programs:** Three- to five-month paid internships are available in both the Cambridge and Washington, DC, offices. Many volunteer opportunities are available as part of the Scientists Action Network.

UNITED NATIONS ENVIRONMENT PROGRAMME

2 United Nations Plaza, Room DC2-303
New York, NY 10017
(212) 963-8193
Fax (212) 963-7341

Purpose: Created in 1972 as a result of the Stockholm Conference on the Human Environment, The United Nations Environment Programme (UNEP) is the environmental conscience of the United Nations whose primary function is to motivate and inspire, and to raise the level of environmental action and awareness at all levels of society worldwide. **Current Emphasis:** The promotion of environmentally sound development activities. **Members:** dnd. **Funding:** Governments, 100%. **Annual Revenue:** dnd. **Usage:** dnd. **Volunteer Programs:** Does not conduct a formal internship program but accommodates students whose academic concentrations meet the requirements of internal projects.

Q: *Before pesticide use, farmers would lose 33 percent of their crops to pests. With the use of pesticides today, what percentage of the crops are lost to pests?*

UNIVERSITY RESEARCH EXPEDITIONS PROGRAM

University of California
Berkeley, CA 94720
(510) 642-6586
Fax (510) 643-8683

Purpose: To promote public involvement in on-going worldwide scientific research and educational activities in the environmental, natural and social sciences. **Current Emphasis:** Projects in cooperation with scientists from developing nations, focused on preserving the earth's resources and improving people's lives. **Members:** 400 participants per year. **Fees:** Participants make a tax-deductible donation to the university to support the research and cover their expenses. **Programs:** Field research projects in the natural and social sciences; teacher development; student scholarships. **Volunteer Programs:** Volunteer participants needed from all walks of life to serve 2 to 3 weeks as field assistants on research teams.

WILD CANID SURVIVAL AND RESEARCH CENTER/WOLF SANCTUARY

P.O. Box 760
Eureka, MO 63025
(314) 938-5900

Purpose: Environmental education. Captive breeding of the endangered red and Mexican wolves for the purpose of reintroduction into the wild. **Current Emphasis:** Providing as much breeding space as possible for the rare Mexican gray wolf. **Members:** 2,800. **Fees:** From $25 up. **Funding:** Membership, 80%; Corporation, 10%; Foundation/Donor, 10%. **Annual Revenue:** $98,000. **Volunteer Programs:** Volunteers assist with fundraising, educational programs and administration.

THE WILDERNESS SOCIETY

900 17th St. NW
Washington, DC 20006
(202) 833-2300

Purpose: Protecting wildlands and wildlife; safeguarding the integrity of our federal public lands, national forests, wildlife refuges, national seashores, recreation areas and public domain lands. **Current Emphasis:** Arctic wildlife refuge, national forest policy, national parks and ecosystem management and the economics of public land use. **Members:** 400,000. **Fees:** New, $15; Renewal, $30. **Funding:** Membership, 50%; Grants, 16%; Foundation, 16%; Other, 18%. **Annual Revenue:** $10,932,448. **Usage:** Administration, 10%; Fundraising, 6%; Programs, 72%; Recruiting, 12%. **Volunteer Programs:** None.

WILDLIFE CONSERVATION INTERNATIONAL

Bronx Zoo
Bronx, NY 10460
(212) 220-6891
Fax (212) 364-7963

Purpose: To help preserve the earth's biological diversity and valuable ecosystems. With 122 projects in 46 countries, WCI addresses conflicts between humans and wildlife and explores locally sustainable solutions. **Current Emphasis:** Tropical rainforests; African elephant and rhino; Tibetan plateau and conservation training. **Members:** 60,000. **Fees:** $25. **Funding:** Membership, 60%; Corporation, 10%; Foundation/Donor, 30%. **Annual Revenue:** $4,500,000. **Usage:** Administration, 5%; Programs, 95%. **Volunteer Programs:** Grants for graduate students and professionals in wildlife sciences upon proposal submission.

WILDLIFE DAMAGE REVIEW

P.O. Box 2541
Tucson, AZ 85702-2541
(602) 882-4218

Purpose: Founded to bring public scrutiny to the government agency, Animal Damage Control (ADC) which controls predators, often by lethal means, which inhibit the livestock industry. WDR wants to enlighten the public about ADC's goal and method with the hope of eventually eliminating the agency. **Current Emphasis:** Encouraging public action against ADC. **Funding:** Corporation, 100%. **Annual Revenue:** $9,000. **Usage:** Programs, 100%. **Volunteer Programs:** Volunteer positions available, and WDR is willing to set up internships on an individual basis.

THE WILDLIFE SOCIETY

5410 Grosvenor Ln.
Bethesda, MD 20814
(301) 897-9770
Fax (301) 530-2471

Purpose: The Wildlife Society is a nonprofit, scientific and educational organization dedicated to conserving and sustaining wildlife productivity and diversity through resource management and to enhancing the scientific and technical capability and performance of wildlife professionals. **Current Emphasis:** Providing current scientific and management information on wildlife resources and enhancing the professionalism of wildlife managers. **Members:** 8,900. **Fees:** From $33; Students from $17. **Funding:** Membership, 37%; Publications, 42%; Contributions, 4%; Other, 17%.

A. *33 percent*
  Source: 50 Simple Things You Can Do To Save The Earth, *by the Earth • Works Group*

Annual Revenue: $900,000. **Usage:** Administration, 8%; Fundraising, 1%; Member Services, 24%; Programs, 67%. **Programs:** Publishing scientific journals and books, providing certification and professional development programs, sponsoring meetings and workshops, enhancing wildlife curricula at colleges and universities, providing policy makers with scientific information on wildlife conservation issues, and promoting international wildlife conservation. **Volunteer Programs:** A 3- to 6-month wildlife policy internship program with stipend is available.

WORLD RESOURCES INSTITUTE

1709 New York Ave. NW, Suite 700
Seventh Floor
Washington, DC 20006
(202) 638-6300
Fax (202) 638-0036

Purpose: A research and policy institute helping governments, the private sector, environmental and development organizations and others address a fundamental question: How can societies meet human needs and nurture economic growth while preserving the natural resources and environmental integrity on which life and economic vitality ultimately depend? **Current Emphasis:** Forests, biodiversity, economics, technology, institutions, climate, energy, pollution, resource and environmental information, governance. **Members:** Not a membership organization. **Funding:** Private foundations, governmental and intergovernmental institutions. **Volunteer Programs:** none

WORLD SOCIETY FOR THE PROTECTION OF ANIMALS

P.O. Box 190
Boston, MA 02130
(617) 522-7000
Fax (617) 522-7077

Purpose: International animal protection/wildlife conservation organization working primarily in less-developed countries where animal protection societies are nonexistent or ineffective to prevent animal suffering worldwide. WSPA is the only international animal protection organization with consultative status with the UN. **Current Emphasis:** To enact animal protection legislation; humane education programs; anti-fur activities; animal spectacles; humane transport and slaughter of livestock; Disaster Relief Program to aid animal victims of natural and human-caused disaster anywhere in the world. **Members:** 10,000/US. **Fees:** $20. **Funding:** Individual, 50%; Foundation/corporation, 6%; Bequests, 28%. **Annual**

Revenue: $630,000. **Usage:** Administration, 39.8%; Fundraising, 5.5%; Programs, 54.7%. **Volunteer Programs:** Occasional.

WORLD WILDLIFE FUND

1250 24th St. NW, Suite 400
Washington, DC 20037
(202) 293-4800.

Purpose: Working worldwide to preserve endangered wildlife and wildlands by encouraging sustainable development and the preservation of biodiversity, particularly in the tropical forests of Latin America, Africa and Asia. **Current Emphasis:** Conservation of tropical rainforests, preserving biological diversity. **Members:** 1,000,000. **Fees:** $15. **Funding:** Membership, 62%; Corporations, 2%; Other, 36%. **Annual Revenue:** dnd. **Usage:** Administration/Fundraising, 15%; Programs, 85%. **Volunteer Programs:** Call for information.

XERCES SOCIETY

10 SW Ash St.
Portland, OR 97204
(503) 222-2788
Fax (503) 222-2763

Purpose: Working globally to prevent human-caused extinctions of rare invertebrate populations and their habitats. The society is committed to protecting invertebrates as the major component of biological diversity. Because invertebrates sustain biological systems, invertebrate conservation means preserving ecosystems and ecological functions as well as individual species. **Current Emphasis:** Conservation science for reserve design in Madagascar and Jamaica; in-country conservation training and public education; public policy initiatives protecting invertebrates; protecting Pacific Northwest old-growth forests. **Members:** 2,400. **Fees:** $25 to $40. **Funding:** Membership, 37%; Corporation, 7%; Foundation/Donor, 56%. **Annual Revenue:** $200,000. **Volunteer Programs:** Internships in conservation science, conservation techniques and fundraising for foreign nationals only.

ZERO POPULATION GROWTH

1400 16th St. NW, Suite 320
Washington, DC 20036
(202) 332-2200

Purpose: To achieve a sustainable balance between the earth's population, its environment and its resources. Primary activities include publishing newsletters and research reports, developing in-school population education programs and coordinating local and national citizen action efforts. **Current**

Q: *Only 26 countries had an environmental protection agency in 1972. Today, how many countries do?*

Emphasis: Urbanization and local growth issues, global warming, sustainability, transportation, family planning and other key population concerns. **Members:** 40,000. **Fees:** Student/senior, $10; Individual, $20. **Funding:** Membership, 80%; Foundation/Grants, 20%. **Annual Revenue:** $1,300,000. **Usage:** Administration, 11.6%; Fundraising, 5.7%; Programs, 82.7%; **Volunteer Programs:** Action Alert Network, Roving Reporter, Growthbusters.

For more information on environmental groups, consult the following:

The Environmental Address Book: How to Reach the Environment's Greatest Champions and Worst Offenders, Michael Levine, The Putnam Publishing Group, New York, 1991.

National Wildlife Federation 1991 Conservation Directory, 36th edition, National Wildlife Federation, Washington, DC, 1991.

The Nature Directory, Susan Lanier-Graham, Walker Publishing Company, New York, 1991.

Your Resource Guide to Environmental Organizations, edited by John Seredich, Smiling Dolphins Press, Irvine, CA, 1991.

Directory to Environmental Education Programs

M*any consider education the key to making the environmental movement more accessible and more effective for more people.* Earth Journal*'s Directory to Enviromental Education Programs contains a diverse sampling of educational programs for all ages—from outdoor skills workshops to classroom curricula to degree programs at the undergraduate and graduate level.*

EDUCATION PROGRAMS

ACID RAIN FOUNDATION, INC.
1410 Varsity Dr.
Raleigh, NC 27606
(919) 828-9443
Emphasis: Acid rain, air quality, global change, air pollutants and forests. **Programs:** Information, education services, curriculum. **Type:** Outdoor education, natural resources. **Cost:** N/A. **Age Emphasis:** All ages. **Application Deadline:** N/A.

ADIRONDACK OUTDOOR EDUCATION CENTER
Pilot Knob, NY 12844
(518) 656-9462
Emphasis: Outdoor recreation on Lake George. **Programs:** High Ropes, Team Building, Lake & Wetland Study, Map & Compass, Expedition Leading & Outfitting. **Type:** Outdoor education, expedition/experiential, natural science/history, residential. **Cost:** $20 per person per day, 1-5 days. **Age Emphasis:** All ages. **Application Deadline:** March 15.

APPALACHIAN MOUNTAIN CLUB
Pinkham Notch Camp, P.O. Box 298
Gorham, NH 03581
(603) 466-2721

Emphasis: Wide variety of environmental/outdoor and conservation education programs. A new residential school program promotes environmental awareness and land stewardship. **Programs:** Guided hikes, field seminars (college credit available), workshops, residential school programs, mountain leadership school, program for inner city youth. **Type:** Outdoor education, natural science/history, residential. **Cost:** Varies, from free to $350/week. **Age Emphasis:** All ages. **Application Deadline:** N/A.

AUDUBON NATURALIST SOCIETY OF THE CENTRAL ATLANTIC STATES
8940 Jones Mill Rd.
Chevy Chase, MD 20815
(301) 652-5964
Emphasis: Environmental education classes and programs, family activities, field trips. **Programs:** Natural History Field Studies adult education program, children's programs, adult programs. **Type:** Expedition/experiential, natural science/history. **Cost:** Varies. **Age Emphasis:** All ages. **Application Deadline:** N/A.

BEAR MOUNTAIN OUTDOOR SCHOOL, INC.
Rt. 250
Hightown, VA 24444
(703) 468-2700
Programs: Mountain ecology, outdoor educa-

tion for teachers, outdoor classroom for public and private schools. **Type:** Outdoor education, natural science/history, natural resources, residential. **Cost:** Varies. Teacher workshop, $150. **Age Emphasis:** All ages. **Application Deadline:** Contact Bear Mountain for schedule.

B.O.C.E.S./OUTDOOR ENVIRONMENTAL EDUCATION
P.O. Box 604
Smithtown, NY 11787
(516) 360-3652

Emphasis: In-service teacher training for integrating environmental education into traditional curricula; residential service for teachers and their classes; in-depth specialized topics and publications. Focuses on hands-on, experiential learning. **Programs:** Day use, residential and special services. **Cost:** Varies. **Age Emphasis:** All ages. **Application Deadline:** Service contracts are due by April 15.

BOK TOWER GARDENS
P.O. Box 3810
Lake Wales, FL 33859
(813) 676-1408

Emphasis: Horticulture, Florida history, natural history, art and/or music. **Programs:** Adult Education Program; adult day and overnight trips to unique places; lectures; workshops; "A Garden Classroom" for fourth-graders. **Cost:** Fourth-graders, free; adult costs vary. **Age Emphasis:** All ages. **Application Deadline:** N/A.

CAL WOOD ENVIRONMENTAL EDUCATION RESOURCE CENTER
P.O. Box 347
Jamestown, CO 80455
(303) 449-0603

Emphasis: Conservation education, focus on natural resource management; team building and individual development; international leadership development (Mexico). **Programs:** Tailored to meet needs of individual groups. Center contracts with schools, organizations, etc. (no openings for individuals). **Type:** Outdoor education, expedition/experiential, natural science/history, natural resources, residential. **Cost:** Base fee $25/per student/ per day. **Age Emphasis:** All ages. **Application Deadline:** 3 to 6 months in advance; one year in advance for large programs.

CAPE OUTDOOR DISCOVERY
47 Old County Rd.
East Sandwich, MA 02537
(508) 888-4741

Emphasis: To increase environmental awareness by providing students with positive experiences in a natural environment. Emphasis on marine environments and ecological lifestyles. **Programs:** Group Challenges, whale watching, local history, residential programs, day programs, Cape Cod Environmental Data (publication). **Type:** Outdoor education, natural science/history, natural resources, residential. **Cost:** Varies, from $65 to $135 per student, depending on length of stay (school group rates). **Age Emphasis:** Youth. **Application Deadline:** None.

CARRIE MURRAY OUTDOOR EDUCATION CAMPUS
1901 Ridgetop Rd.
Baltimore, MD 21207
(301) 396-0808

Emphasis: Year-round outdoor education program for children and adults; raptor rehabilitation and education program; adventure education trips and workshops; summer nature camps. **Type:** Outdoor education, expedition/experiential, natural science/history. **Cost:** $1-$5 for classes and workshops; $15-$800 for trips. **Age Emphasis:** All ages. **Application Deadline:** N/A.

CITY OF AURORA, UTILITIES DEPT.
1470 S. Havanna, Suite 400
Aurora, CO 80012
(303) 695-7381

Emphasis: Water conservation via xeriscape, or indoors with retrofit or renovation; water awareness video for grades K-12; copublished "Landscaping for Water Conservation: Xeriscape!" **Programs:** Audio visual resources. **Type:** School education, residential. **Cost:** Varies. **Age Emphasis:** All ages. **Application Deadline:** N/A

CITY OF BOULDER ADVENTURE PROGRAM
P.O. Box 791
Boulder, CO 80306
(303) 443-5173

Emphasis: Instruction and trips in rock climbing, kayaking, mountain biking, canoeing, skiing and general mountaineering with a focus on minimum impact camping and experiential education. **Programs:** Rock climbing, canoeing, mountain biking and kayaking trips in Colorado and Canyonlands. **Type:** Outdoor education, expedition/experiential, natural science/ history. **Cost:** Varies, $30-$300 depending on course. **Age Emphasis:** All ages.

Q: *Which country's forests are being cut down at the same rate as Brazil's?*

Application Deadline: Courses run year-round.

COALITION FOR EDUCATION IN THE OUTDOORS
Box 2000, SUNY College at Cortland
Cortland, NY 13045
(607) 753-4971
Emphasis: The Coalition is a network of affiliated businesses, professional organizations, institutions, centers and groups in support of outdoor/environmental education. **Programs:** Conferences, symposia, quarterly newsletter. **Type:** Outdoor education, expedition/ experiential. **Cost:** Graduated scale based on membership category. **Age Emphasis:** N/A. **Application Deadline:** N/A.

COLORADO MOUNTAIN COLLEGE
P.O. Box 10001BW
Glenwood Springs, CO 81602
(303) 945-8691.
Emphasis: Transfer-level outdoor studies and recreation courses; weekend and summer programs; outdoor semester in the Rockies. **Programs:** Recreation management, outdoor leadership, avalanche awareness, rock climbing, nordic and alpine skiing. Mountain, desert, snow and canyon orientation. **Type:** Outdoor education, degree program, expedition/experiential, natural science/history, residential. **Cost:** $50/credit hour in-state; out of state, $150/credit hour. **Age Emphasis:** Adults. **Application Deadline:** August 31.

COLORADO OUTWARD BOUND SCHOOL
945 Pennsylvania
Denver, CO 80203
(303) 837-0880
Emphasis: Wilderness expeditions teaching mountaineering, white water rafting and kayaking, horse trailing, desert and canyon exploration. Special heath services programs. **Type:** Outdoor education, Expediton/Experiential, Natural Science/History, Residential. **Cost:** $500-$6,200. Scholarships available. Length: 5-83 days. **Age Emphasis:** 14 and up. **Application Deadline:** Ongoing.

CREATIVE MEDIA/ENVIRONMENTAL EDUCATION/NORTHWEST TRAVEL & STUDY
9730 Manitou Pl.
Bainbridge Island, WA 98110
(206) 456-1854
Emphasis: Environmental education program planning; workshops for educators. Consultation. **Programs:** Environmental education, wetlands, recycling, water quality education. **Type:** Outdoor education, natural science /history, natural resources. **Cost:** N/A. **Age Emphasis:** All ages. **Application Deadline:** N/A.

CUSTOMIZED GUIDED EXCURSIONS
P.O. Box 964
Hershey, PA 17033-0964
(717) 944-2724
Emphasis: Individual and small group programs to discover the natural world, including local and national geology, natural resources, appreciation and respect for the environment. **Programs:** Customized guided excursions. **Type:** Outdoor education, expedition/experiential, natural science/history, natural resources. **Cost:** Varies. **Age Emphasis:** All ages. **Application Deadline:** Open.

DEFENDERS OF WILDLIFE
1244 19th St. NW
Washington, DC 20036
(202) 659-9510
Emphasis: Provides fact sheets and information on wildlife to students and educators upon request. *Defenders* magazine available with membership (six issues per year). **Type:** Natural science/history. **Cost:** Membership is $20/year; students $15/year. **Age Emphasis:** All ages. **Application Deadline:** N/A.

ECOLOGIC
P.O. Box 1514
Antigonish, Nova Scotia, B2G 2L8, Canada
(902) 863-5983
Emphasis: Designs and facilitates environmental education programs for teachers, industry, community groups, government. Specializes in participatory workshops with emphasis on global issues. **Programs:** Global issues, noncredit university extension programs. **Type:** Expedition/experiential, natural science/history. **Cost:** Varies. **Age Emphasis:** All ages. **Application Deadline:** N/A.

EDUDEX ASSOCIATES, KETTLE MORAINE DIVISION
604 2nd Ave.
West Bend, WI 53095
(414) 334-4978
Emphasis: Natural and human resources organization designs, delivers and evaluates outdoor, conservation and environmental experiential programs on an international level. Assists individuals, groups, classes, etc. **Programs:** Programs prepared by foresters, soil scientists, wildlife biologists, education staff.

A. *The Soviet Union's Zhores Medvedev*
 Source: The Ecologist, *January/February 1990*

Type: Outdoor education, expedition/experiential, natural science/ history, natural resources. **Cost:** Based on ability and need. **Age Emphasis:** All ages. **Application Deadline:** None.

EDWARDS CAMP AND CONFERENCE CENTER

1275 Army Lake Rd.
P.O. Box 16
East Troy, WI 53120
(414) 642-7466

Emphasis: Environmental education for 15 days in YMCA resident camp setting. Stresses diversity of ecosystems, lesson plans and curriculum, recreation opportunities. **Programs:** Wildlife, aquatic, forest/ prairie, environmental awareness, weather, astronomy, recreation and sports. **Type:** Outdoor education. **Cost:** Two nights, seven meals: $49.50, cabins; $56.10, lodges. **Age Emphasis:** Youth. **Application Deadline:** Arrange with camp prior to stay.

ENVIRONMENTAL MEDIA

P.O. Box 1016
Chapel Hill, NC 27514
(919) 933-3003

Emphasis: Environmental Media manages the design, production and distribution of media to support environmental education. We produce principally instructional television programs and guides. "Oceans Alive!" is a series of single-concept science progams using marine plants and animals to illustrate science targeted at middle schools; "Seahorse," concepts in science for preschools; "Full Circle," a 30-minute program targeted at high schools on the topic of recycling in schools and homes. **Type:** Educational media. **Age Emphasis:** Youth. Application deadline: N/A.

EXECUTIVE EXPEDITIONS

131 Village Parkway, Suite 4
Marietta, GA 30067
(404) 951-2173

Emphasis: All programs are contract and custom designed. **Programs:** Leadership, team building, empowerment, management issues. Experience-based learning environments for executive and management groups, using the outdoors as a learning vehicle to breathe new life into management concepts, feedback, work sessions. **Type:** Expedition/experiential. **Cost:** $1,300/per person for 3 days; food, lodging, professional facilitation included. **Application Deadline:** None.

FOUR CORNERS SCHOOL OF OUTDOOR EDUCATION

East Route
Monticello, UT 84535
(801) 587-2859

Emphasis: Educational field programs in the southwest. Focus on archeology, geology, cultural studies, as well as photo and writing workshops, backpacking, river rafting, and base camp experiences on the Colorado Plateau. **Programs:** Rock Art, Geography of the San Juan River, Kaiparowits Plateau Survey, Dig the Past; etc. **Type:** Degree program, outdoor education, expedition/ experiential, natural science/ history, natural resources, residential. **Cost:** Most programs, $375-$875. **Age Emphasis:** All ages. **Application Deadline:** Varies.

GLEN HELEN OUTDOOR EDUCATION CENTER

1075 Route 343,
Yellow Springs, OH 45387
(513) 767-7648

Emphasis: Two simultaneous programs, a residential environmental education experience for (mostly) sixth graders, and a training program for naturalists/interns. Interns get stipend, room, board, and graduate or undergraduate credits. **Type:** Outdoor education, expedition/experiential, raptor rehabilitation, natural science/history, natural resources, residential. **Cost:** None. **Age Emphasis:** All ages. **Application Deadline:** None.

GREAT SMOKY MOUNTAINS INSTITUTE AT TREMONT

Rt. 1, Box 81
Townsend, TN 37882
(615) 448-6709

Emphasis: Wide variety of programs emphasizing cultural and natural resources of Great Smoky Mountains National Park. **Programs:** School programs, adult workshops, teacher training, camps, elder hostel. **Type:** Outdoor education, natural science/history, natural resources, residential. **Cost:** Varies, $20-$30/per day. **Age Emphasis:** All ages. **Application Deadline:** N/A.

GUIDED DISCOVERIES, INC.

P.O. Box 1360
Claremont, CA 91711
(714) 949-0687

Emphasis: Marine biology, island ecology, physical science, astronomy. **Programs:** Catalina Island Marine Institute at Toyon Bay and Cherry Cove, and Astrocamp. **Type:**

Q: *How many tons of trash were retrieved from Mount Everest since April 1991.*

Outdoor education. **Cost:** Toyon: 3 days/ $120, 5 days/$215. Cherry: 3 days/ $118, 5 days/ $213. Astro: 3 days $95/5 days $190. **Age Emphasis:** Youth. **Application Deadline:** N/A.

HOUSEHOLD HAZARDOUS WASTE PROJECT

1031 E. Battlefield, Suite 214
Springfield, MO 65807
(417) 889-5000

Emphasis: Award-winning community education program to identify and minimize household hazardous products. Emphasis on safety, storage, disposal, promotion of safer alternatives. **Programs:** Training workshops, learning materials, audio-visual programs, "Guide to Hazardous Products Around the Home" (personal action manual). Telephone information request line. **Cost:** Training and course materials are $42.50. **Age Emphasis:** All ages. **Application Deadline:** Training course offered in fall and spring.

HOUSTON INDEPENDENT SCHOOL DISTRICT'S OUTDOOR EDUCATION CENTER

Rt. 3, Box 135D1
Trinity, TX 75862
(409) 594-2274

Emphasis: Designed to serve the children of Houston as an extension of the classroom, to promote concern for the environment, and to provide interaction among children of different economic, racial and cultural backgrounds. **Programs:** 4-day programs, September-May. **Type:** Outdoor education, residential. **Cost:** No cost to students. **Age Emphasis:** Youth. **Application Deadline:** N/A.

HUNTSMAN MARINE SCIENCE CENTRE

Brandy Cove Rd.
St. Andrews, New Brunswick E0G 2XO, Canada
(506) 529-8895

Emphasis: Marine science education for students, teachers and the public. Experience-based programs that access the Bay of Fundy ecosystem (one of the most productive on the planet) and the facilities of the Science Centre. **Programs:** Intro to Marine Biology and Intro to Marine Vertebrates (high school), Sea Trek (adults). **Type:** Outdoor education, expedition/experiential. **Cost:** Varies, $450-$550 Canadian. **Age Emphasis:** Youth and adult. **Application Deadline:** May 31.

ISAAC W. BERNHEIM FOUNDATION

Bernheim Forest Arboretum
Clermont, KY 40110
(502) 543-2451

Emphasis: Environmental education, arboretum, art classes. **Programs:** Research Institute for Education and the Environment. **Type:** Outdoor education. **Cost:** N/A. **Age Emphasis:** All ages. **Application Deadline:** N/A.

JOY OUTDOOR EDUCATION CENTER

Box 157
Clarksville, OH 45113
(513) 289-2031

Emphasis: Outdoor, environmental education for elementary and high schools, summer camp for disadvantaged children, corporate teambuilding program. **Programs:** Camp Joy; Venture Out! **Type:** Outdoor education, residential. **Cost:** $45-$55 for 2-day youth program; $90-$165 for adults. **Age Emphasis:** All ages. **Application Deadline:** N/A.

KEEWADEN ENVIRONMENTAL EDUCATION CENTER

Lake Dunmore
Salisbury, VT 05766
(802) 352-4247

Emphasis: Natural communities and human impact and responsibility. Local history, including Native Americans, early settlers, early industries. **Programs:** Spring and fall at Lake Dunmore; winter at Seyon Ranch in Groton, VT. **Type:** Outdoor education, natural science/history, natural resources, residential. **Cost:** $30-$90, depends on length of stay. **Age Emphasis:** Youth. **Application Deadline:** Ongoing.

KORTRIGHT CENTER

Shoreham Dr.
Downsview, Ontario M3N 1S4, Canada
(416) 832-2289

Emphasis: Field study programs on the environment and natural history. Topics include water, wildlife, energy conservation, and forestry. **Type:** Experiential, Natural Science/ History, Natural Resources. **Cost:** $2-$45. **Age Emphasis:** All Ages. **Application Deadline:** On-going.

LEGACY INTERNATIONAL

Route 4, Box 265
Bedford, VA 24523
(703) 297-5982

Emphasis: Youth leadership training. YES provides in-depth environmental training based on field trips to different environmentally significant locations. Provides leadership training and

A. *2 tons*
Source: *Mount Everest International Peace Climb*

project planning skills for the students' return home. **Programs:** Youth Environmental Services, Dialogue, Global Issues, and Summer Youth Leadership Training. **Type:** Experiential, Natural Resources, Residential. **Cost:** $3,500. Length: 6 weeks. **Age Emphasis:** 15-18. **Application Deadline:** Ongoing, apply early.

MAINE CONSERVATION SCHOOL
P.O. Box 188
Bryant Pond, ME 04219
(207) 665-2068
Emphasis: Nature study and conservation education through a residential program of issues-oriented topics. **Programs:** School programs, teacher workshop, adult programs. **Type:** Outdoor education, natural science/history, natural resources, residential. **Cost:** $25 per day. **Age Emphasis:** All ages. **Application Deadline:** Ongoing.

MINNESOTA VALLEY NATIONAL WILDLIFE REFUGE
3815 E. 80th St.
Bloomington, MN 55425
(612) 854-5900
Emphasis: Environmental education and interpretive programming, training for teachers, activities/events to create environmentally literate citizens motivated to take action. **Programs:** Volunteer Wildlife Interpreter course; teacher training workshops; Wildways course; environmental education for school groups; seasonal interpretive programs and events. **Type:** Natural resources, environmental education. **Cost:** No fee. **Age Emphasis:** All ages. **Application Deadline:** N/A.

MOHICAN SCHOOL IN THE OUT-OF-DOORS, INC.
21882 Shadley Valley Rd.
Danville, OH 43014
(614) 599-9753
Emphasis: Curriculum enrichment emphasizes resident outdoor/environmental education. **Programs:** Resident programs and field trips for grades 4-7. Adult workshops. **Type:** Outdoor education, natural science/history, natural resources, residential. **Cost:** $105/5 days. **Age Emphasis:** All ages. **Application Deadline:** N/A.

NATIONAL AUDUBON EXPEDITION INSTITUTE
P.O. Box 170
Readfield, ME 04355
(207) 685-3111
Emphasis: A nonprofit traveling education

program which offers year-long and semester expeditions providing students an alternative to traditional education and an understanding of nature's spiritual dimension. Requires the desire to be challenged academically and an open attitude toward global environmental issues. **Programs:** High school, B.S. and M.S. in Environmental Education. **Cost:** $6,100/semester or $10,400/year. **Age Emphasis:** Youth, college student. **Application Deadline:** N/A.

NATIONAL ENVIRONMENTAL EDUCATION DEVELOPMENT (N.E.E.D.)
P.O. Box 896
Truro, MA 02666
(508) 349-3475
Emphasis: Natural and human history of Cape Cod. Facility is an old Coast Guard station overlooking ocean, dunes, woodlands and the Pamet River Valley. Field trips on national seashore. **Programs:** Pond study, dune ecology, saltmarsh exploration, astronomy. **Type:** Outdoor education, natural science/history, residential. **Cost:** $3000 (up to 25 students). **Age Emphasis:** 4th, 5th, 6th grades. **Application Deadline:** N/A.

NATIONAL WILDLIFE FEDERATION— EDUCATOR'S SUMMIT
1400 16th St. NW
Washington, DC 20036-2266
(800) 432-6564
Emphasis: The Educators' Summit provides teachers and other professional educators with advanced training in environmental education and prepares them to develop creative lessons on environmental issues and ecological concepts. Hands-on activities, field trips, teaching strategies and techniques. **Programs:** Educators' Summit, Silver Bay, New York, on Lake George. **Type:** One week residential environmental education for educators (college credit available). **Cost:** $200 program fee, plus housing. **Age Emphasis:** Adult or college students. **Application Deadline:** Usually filled by March or April.

NATIONAL WILDLIFE FEDERATION— NATUREQUEST
1400 16th St. NW
Washington, DC 20036-2266
(800) 432-6564
Emphasis: NatureQuest is the National Wildlife Federation's certified training program for camp directors, nature and science counselors, naturalists and outdoor educators. Three-day workshops expose participants to the "Quest" model, then participants design

 Q: *30 percent of North America is wildernes. How much of Africa is?*

sites and needs. **Programs:** NatureQuest. **Type:** Outdoor education training. **Cost:** $175 program fee, plus housing. **Age Emphasis:** Adult. **Application Deadline:** One month prior to session; sessions are in March and April.

A NATURALIST'S WORLD
P.O. Box 8005, Suite 357
Boulder, CO 80306-8005
(303) 440-0902

Emphasis: Field research with in-depth examination of the natural history and ecology of specific subjects or locations. **Programs:** Greenland, Great Bears of North America. **Type:** Experiential, Natural Science/History, Residential. **Cost:** $2000-$3000. **Length:** 2 days to 2 weeks. **Age Emphasis:** Adult. **Application Deadline:** N/A.

NEWFOUND HARBOR MARINE INSTITUTE AT SEACAMP
Rt 3, Box 170,
Big Pine Key, FL 33043
(305) 872-2331

Emphasis: Combines direct, hands-on experience with conceptual learning. Offers marine environmental education courses to increase understanding of the ocean and natural ecosystems in a diverse tropical community. **Programs:** Coral reef ecology, shallow bay ecology, mangrove ecology, coastal ecology, ichthyology, tropical island botany, ornithology. **Type:** Outdoor education, expedition/experiential, residential, marine science. **Cost:** Average cost, $90/day inclusive. **Age Emphasis:** All ages. **Application Deadline:** Ongoing.

NIZHONI INSTITUTE/ ACADEMY FOR ECOLOGY AND ENERGY
1304 Old Pecos Trail
Santa Fe, NM 87501
(505) 982-8293

Emphasis: International boarding school with 3 1-month environmental trips. 1-week programs for adults "Sense of Earth" in Santa Fe County. Focusing on individual abilities to make a significant difference spirituality. **Programs:** "Sense of Earth." **Type:** Degree program, outdoor education, expedition/experiential, residential. **Cost:** $15,000 for boarding school, $2,300 for "Sense of Earth." **Age Emphasis:** All ages.

NORTH CASCADES INSTITUTE
2105 Highway 20
Sedro-Woolley, WA 98284
(206) 856-5700

Emphasis: Natural and cultural history of the Pacific Northwest. Most seminars cover natural history, but art, photography and writing workshops are also offered. Seminars are experiential and field-based. **Programs:** Varied; everything from wildflowers and mushrooms to North Coast Native American carving. **Type:** Outdoor education, natural science/history, natural resources. **Cost:** Varies, $35-$300. **Age Emphasis:** All ages. **Application Deadline:** First come, first served.

OUTDOOR LEADERSHIP TRAINING SEMINARS/ BREAKING THROUGH ADVENTURES
P.O. Box 200281
Denver, CO 80220
(303) 333-7831 or (303) 320-0372

Emphasis: Trains outdoor leaders in outdoor skills, transformational leadership approaches. Workshops emphasize deep ecology, personal transformation, nature ritual, inner learning. **Programs:** Outdoor Growth Leadership Seminar; Breaking Through Adventures; Centered Ski Touring Seminars. **Type:** Degree program, outdoor education, expedition/experiential. **Cost:** Varies; $100/per weekend; $500-$800/per week; $3900/8-month training. **Age Emphasis:** All ages. **Application Deadline:** Nonrestrictive.

PARADIGM VENTURES
29 Azul Loop
Santa Fe, NM 87505
(505) 988-1813

Emphasis: Personal and professional development. Customized programs utilizing southwest wilderness areas. Ropes course programs. **Programs:** Customized to client needs and abilities. **Type:** Expedition/experiential. **Cost:** Varies. **Age Emphasis:** All ages. **Application Deadline:** N/A.

ROCKY MOUNTAIN SEMINARS
Rocky Mountain National Park
Estes Park, CO 80517
(303) 586-2371, ext. 294

Emphasis: Uses natural resources of Rocky Mountain National Park as an education tool. **Programs:** Wide variety of topics, from photography to geology and ecology of the park. **Type:** Outdoor education, expedition/experiential, natural science/history. **Cost:** $150/week-long seminars, $80/weekend, $40/one day. **Age Emphasis:** All ages. **Application Deadline:** None; classes are open until they fill.

A. *About the same*
. Source: The Sierra Club

ROGER TORY PETERSON INSTITUTE
110 Marvin Pkwy.
Jamestown, NY 14701
(716) 665-2473
Emphasis: Nature in education programs for teachers and nature education professionals. **Programs:** Nature Journals (workshop for middle school teachers to facilitate integration of nature and whole language curriculum); conferences for teachers and nature educators. **Type:** Natural science/history. **Cost:** Varies. **Age Emphasis:** Adults who work with youth. **Application Deadline:** N/A.

SAFARI CLUB INTERNATIONAL
4800 W. Gates Pass Rd.
Tucson, AZ 85745
(602) 620-1220
Emphasis: Each ten-day workshop provides challenging experiences in wildlife ecology, management and conservation, together with instruction in fire-arm safety, fly tying, wilderness survival, archery, outdoor interpretive techniques, Project WILD and outdoor ethics. **Programs:** American Wilderness Leadership School. **Type:** Degree program, outdoor education, natural science/history, natural resources, residential. **Cost:** $600. **Age Emphasis:** Adult. **Application Deadline:** April 30.

SAN DIEGO COUNTY OUTDOOR EDUCATION
6401 Linda Vista Rd.
San Diego, CA 92111-7399
(619) 292-3696
Emphasis: Outdoor education, natural science, social skills, earth sciences. 5-day, 4-night residential program. **Programs:** Conservation, geology, astronomy, animal/-plant study, ecology, folk dancing, environmental games, weather study, social skills. **Type:** Outdoor education, natural science/history, natural resources, residential. **Cost:** $141. **Age Emphasis:** 6th graders. **Application Deadline:** San Diego schools only; one year in advance.

SCHOOL FOR INTERNATIONAL TRAINING/EXPERIMENT IN INTERNATIONAL LIVING
P.O. BOX 676
Brattleboro, VT 05302-0676
(802) 257-7751/ (800) 451-4465
Emphasis: Programs give students a first-hand experience of the environment in different parts of the world and point out how it is being jeopardized. **Programs:** Australia; Natural & Human Environment, Kenya; Coastal Studies, Tanzania; Wildlife Ecology & Conservationism, Ecuador; Comparative Ecology. **Type:** Expedition/Experiential, Natural Resources, Residential. **Cost:** $8,300-$10,300. Length: 15 weeks. **Age Emphasis:** College Student. **Application Deadline:** October 15, May 15.

SOLO
Rt. 1, Box 163
Conway, NH 03818
(603) 447-6711
Emphasis: Wilderness and emergency medical programs. **Programs:** Backcountry Medicine, Wilderness First Responder, Wilderness EMT. **Type:** Outdoor education, expedition/experiential, residential. **Cost:** Varies, $75-$1100. **Age Emphasis:** All ages. **Application Deadline:** Open.

THAMES SCIENCE CENTER
Gallows Lane
New London, CT 06320
(203) 442-0391
Emphasis: Environmental science curriculum focuses on local watersheds. Teachers and students conduct lab and field experiments. **Programs:** Watershed Worlds, Global Views/ Regional Perspectives. **Type:** Outdoor education, expedition/experiential, natural science/ history, natural resources, residential. **Cost:** Open to classroom teachers, stipend provided. **Age Emphasis:** Adults. **Application Deadline:** N/A.

THORNE ECOLOGICAL INSTITUTE
5398 Manhattan Cir.
Boulder, CO 80303
(303) 499-3647
Emphasis: TEI is committed to educating individuals about the wise use of the environment. **Programs:** Boulder and Denver Natural Science Schools, Annual Symposium: Issues and Technology in the Management of Impacted Wildlife, Viewpoints, Environmental Stewardship 2000. **Type:** Natural Science/History, Natural Resources. **Cost:** free-$120. Length: 1 day to 2 weeks. **Age Emphasis:** All ages. Application Deadlines: Ongoing.

TREES FOR TOMORROW
611 Sheridan St.
P.O. Box 609
Eagle River, WI 54521
(715) 479-6456
Emphasis: Stresses proper management and wise use of all natural resources for long-term good of everyone. **Programs:** Natural resources education. **Type:** Natural resources.

Q: *How long would the quantity of oil believed to be under the Arctic National Wildlife Refuge supply US oil needs?*

Cost: $75/3-day program (school rate). **Age Emphasis:** All ages. **Application Deadline:** None.

UNITED STATES BOTANIC GARDEN
245 First St. SW
Washington, DC 20024
(202) 226-4082

Emphasis: Displays of plants from around the world, including many rare and endangered plants. **Programs:** Horticultural classes. **Type:** Natural science. **Cost:** Free. **Age Emphasis:** All ages. **Application Deadline:** N/A.

URBAN OPTIONS
135 Linden St.,
East Lansing, MI 48823
(517) 337-0422

Emphasis: Nonprofit community service provides educational programs and services on energy and the environment. **Programs:** Demonstration house; environmental information service; weatherization programs; tool lending; library; newsletter; classes. **Cost:** Varies from free to $200. **Age Emphasis:** All ages. **Application Deadline:** N/A.

WESLEY WOODS UNITED METHODIST OUTDOOR MINISTRIES, INC.
329 Wesley Woods Rd.
Townsend, TN 37882
(615) 448-2246

Emphasis: Outdoor experiential and environmental education. **Programs:** Outdoor/Environmental Education, Residential Summer Camp, Youth Trips & Adventure Programs, Elder Hostel. **Type:** Outdoor Education, Expedition/ Experiential, Natural Science/History, Natural Resources, Residential. **Cost:** Varies according to program and length. **Age Emphasis:** All ages. **Application Deadline:** Ongoing.

WILD BASIN WILDERNESS PRESERVE
P.O. Box 13455
Austin, TX 78711
(512) 327-7622

Emphasis: Preservation of 227-acre nature preserve located near urban area; education in all aspects of the environment for adults and children. **Programs:** Wild Basin Environmental Education (for schoolchildren); Moonlighting, Stargazing, etc. (for adults). **Type:** Outdoor education, natural science/ history, natural resources. **Cost:** Most programs are free. **Age Emphasis:** All ages. **Application Deadline:** N/A.

WILDERNESS SOUTHEAST
711 Sandtown Rd.
Savannah, GA 31410
(912) 897-5108

Emphasis: Nonprofit school of the outdoors. Small groups camp in diverse wilderness areas for a close-up look at remarkable ecosystems. Leisurely pace and flexible itineraries. Relax and unwind, stretch both mind and muscles. **Programs:** Natural history. **Type:** Outdoor education, expedition/experiential, natural science/history. **Cost:** $235 to $2985, 3-4 days. **Age Emphasis:** All ages. **Application Deadline:** N/A.

WILDERNESS TRANSITIONS, INC.
70 Rodeo Ave.
Sausalito, CA 94965
(415) 331-5380 or (415) 332-9558

Emphasis: Wilderness vision quest trips. Small groups share two days in base camp, then live alone three days to rediscover one's self and one's connectedness to the earth and all living beings. **Programs:** Vision Quest (includes instruction in nature lore and wilderness living). **Type:** Outdoor education, expedition/experiential. **Cost:** $460/week. **Age Emphasis:** All ages over 15. **Application Deadline:** Varies.

WOODSWOMEN, INC.
25 W. Diamond Lake Rd.
Minneapolis, MN 55419
(612) 822-3809

Emphasis: Supportive and challenging learning opportunities in the context of safe, enjoyable outdoor and wilderness travel experiences and leadership development. Courses provide healthy living, options, skills development, new perspectives on natural history. **Programs:** Adventure travel for women. **Type:** Outdoor education, expedition/experiential, natural science/history. **Cost:** $18-$100/day. **Age Emphasis:** Adult women/ college women. **Application Deadline:** Ongoing.

THE YELLOWSTONE INSTITUTE
Box 117
Yellowstone National Park, WY 82190
(307) 344-7381

Emphasis: Enhancement of people's appreciation of the park through the presentation of various natural and human history topics. **Type:** Expedition/Experiential, Natural Science/History, Natural Resources, Residential. **Cost:** $35-$100/day. **Length:** 2-6 days. **Age Emphasis:** All ages. **Application Deadline:** N/A.

A. *1 month to 2 years*
Source: The Global Citizen, *by Donella Meadow*

YMCA OF GREATER NEW YORK, GREENKILL OUTDOOR ENVIRONMENTAL EDUCATION CENTER

YMCA Greenkill
Huguenot, NY 12746
(914) 856-4382

Emphasis: Environmental education resident experience for elementary through high school students, focusing on environmental science, outdoor skills and history. Stresses interrelationship and cooperation. **Programs:** Environmental Science, Outdoor Skills, History, Challenge Education. **Type:** Outdoor education, natural science/history, residential. **Cost:** $85-$130/per person. **Age Emphasis:** Youth. **Application Deadline:** N/A.

YMCA OF THE ROCKIES—ESTES PARK CENTER

Tunnel Rd.
Estes Park, CO 80511
(303) 586-3341, ext. 1106

Emphasis: Curriculum instruction, hands-on experiences, and exploration of the natural world provided through discovery and linked to interdisciplinary approach. **Programs:** Barney Beaver, Kinship, Star Challenger, Nocturnal Enchantment, Adventurer (ropes), Pathfinder (orienteering), Hug-a-tree (wilderness survival), Earthwalker, Nature Graphics, Writer's Camp. **Type:** Outdoor education. **Cost:** $18/lodging and food. **Age Emphasis:** All ages. **Application Deadline:** N/A.

YOSEMITE ASSOCIATION

P.O. Box 230
El Portal, CA 95318
(209) 379-2646

Emphasis: Outdoor natural history seminars. College credit, family trips, backpacking trips for beginners through advanced. **Programs:** History, botany, geology, Native American studies, art, photography. **Type:** Outdoor education, natural science/history. **Cost:** $45-$350 (some include meals and lodging). **Age Emphasis:** All ages, plus families. **Application Deadline:** Write for free brochure.

YOSEMITE NATIONAL INSTITUTE

Golden Gate National Recreation Area,
Bldg. 1033
Sausalito, CA 94965
(415) 332-5771.

Emphasis: Environmental learning experiences for teachers, students and the general public. Three campuses: Yosemite National Park, Olympic National Park and Golden Gate National Park. **Programs:** Residential environmental education. **Type:** Outdoor education, expedition/experiential, natural science/history, natural resources, residential. **Cost:** Varies, $150-$200 per week, including all meals, lodging, instruction. **Age Emphasis:** All ages. **Application Deadline:** N/A.

YUKON CONSERVATION SOCIETY

P.O. Box 4163
Whitehorse, Yukon YIA 3T3, Canada
(403) 668-5678

Emphasis: Advocacy, education and research on conservation issues in the Yukon territory. **Programs:** Nature appreciation, travel guides, green consumer guide. **Type:** Natural Science/History, Natural Resources. **Cost:** N/A. **Age Emphasis:** All Ages. **Appliication Deadline:** N/A.

NATURE CENTERS

ANDORRA NATURAL AREA

Northwestern Ave.
Philadelphia, PA 19118
(215) 685-9285

Emphasis: Interpretive programs centering on natural and woodland stream areas of Fairmount Park, one of the world's largest urban parks. **Programs:** Bird walks, campfires, interpretive hikes, maple sugaring program. **Type:** Outdoor education. **Cost:** Most programs are free. **Age Emphasis:** All ages. **Application Deadline:** N/A.

ANITA PURVES NATURE CENTER

1505 N. Broadway
Urbana, IL 61801
(217) 384-4062

Emphasis: Nature Center and adjacent Busey Woods provide a natural resource for individuals, families and school groups. Center exhibits highlight animals, birds and natural phenomena. **Programs;** Vary seasonally. **Type:** Expedition/experiential, natural science/history, natural resources. **Cost:** Free or varied fees; most under $20. **Age Emphasis:** All ages. **Application Deadline:** Generally open, but depends on program.

BANDELIER NATIONAL MONUMENT

HCR 1, Box 1, Suite 15
Los Alamos, NM 87544
(505) 672-3861

Emphasis: Bandelier National Monument was established to preserve Native American ruins in a beautiful, wild setting. **Programs:** Native American culture, past and present; plants; wildlife; geology; wilderness; etc. **Type:** Natural science/history, natural resources. **Cost:** Free.

Q. *What percentage of the cargo shipped from the Port of New York is wastepaper?*

Age Emphasis: All ages. **Application Deadline:** Programs available on request as time permits.

CABLE NATURAL HISTORY MUSEUM
P.O. Box 416
Cable, WI 54821
(715) 798-3890
Emphasis: Natural history of the northern Great Lakes region. **Programs:** Workshops, lectures, field trips, etc. **Type:** Outdoor education, expedition/experiential, natural science/history, natural resources. **Cost:** Varies, from $1 to $600. **Age Emphasis:** All ages. **Application Deadline:** N/A.

CABRILLO MARINE MUSEUM
3720 Stephen White Dr.
San Pedro, CA 90731
(213) 548-7563
Emphasis: 1-day workshops focusing on southern California marine life. Field study at adjacent tidepools, mudflats and sandy beaches. Involvement in shorebased research projects. Also summer youth day camps. **Programs:** Science at the Seashore, lab/field program. **Type:** Outdoor education, natural science/history. **Cost:** From $1 tidepool walks/discovery centers to $70 week-long morning day camps. **Age Emphasis:** All ages. **Application Deadline:** Offered quarterly.

CALLAWAY GARDENS
Pine Mt., GA 31822
(404) 663-5154
Emphasis: Wide variety of natural history and gardening programs. **Programs:** Summer Recreation Program, Summer Internships. **Type:** Outdoor education, natural science/history. **Cost:** Varies. **Age Emphasis:** Adults; internships available for college students. **Application Deadline:** March 1.

CAMP ALLEN
Rt. 1, Box 426
Navasota, TX 77868
(409) 825-7175
Emphasis: To provide educational experiences that encourage students to actively participate in solving and preventing the problems facing their generation and future operations. **Programs:** The Discovery Program. **Type:** Outdoor education. **Cost:** Varies/ $25-$40 per day. **Age Emphasis:** All ages. **Application Deadline:** None.

CAPE COD MUSEUM OF NATURAL HISTORY
P.O. Box 1710, Rt. 6A
Brewster, MA 02631
(508) 896-3867
Emphasis: Nonprofit, education and research science center focused on the natural environment of Cape Cod. To promote better understanding and appreciation of the environment and the means to sustain it. **Programs:** Environmental education. **Type:** Marine labs, outdoor education, teacher education, kids ecology club, natural science/history, natural resources, nature camp. **Cost:** From $5 per year to $66 per class. **Age Emphasis:** All ages. **Application Deadline:** Ongoing enrollment.

CENTER FOR ALASKAN COASTAL STUDIES
P.O. Box 2225
Homer, AK 99603
(907) 235-6667
Emphasis: Intertidal studies and forest ecology, Northwest Coast rainforest. **Type:** Outdoor education, expedition/experiential, natural science/history, natural resources, residential. **Cost:** $50 per day, unsubsidized (plus transportation). **Age Emphasis:** All ages. **Application Deadline:** None.

CINCINNATI ZOO AND BOTANICAL GARDEN
3400 Vine St.
Cincinnati, OH 45220
(513) 381-4701
Emphasis: Extensive captive breeding and research, emphasis on local solutions to global environmental problems. One of the largest captive collections of endangered species. **Programs:** College internships; college courses; high school vocational program; accelerated nature study for gifted students; members' programs; multimedia environmental materials. **Type:** Outdoor education, expedition/experiential, natural science/history, natural resources. **Cost:** Varies. **Age Emphasis:** All ages. **Application Deadline:** N/A.

CLAY PIT PONDS STATE PARK PRESERVE
83 Nielsen Ave.
Staten Island, NY 10309
(718) 967-1976
Emphasis: 250-acre natural area on Staten Island. Once the site of a clay mining operation, the Park contains a mixture of unique habitats such as wetlands, sandy barrens, fields, etc. Managed to retain unique ecology and to provide educational programs.

A. *45 percent*
· *Source: Port Authority of New York-New Jersey*

Programs: Year-round nature programs. **Type:** Outdoor education, natural science/history, natural resources. **Cost:** Free. **Age Emphasis:** All ages. **Application Deadline:** None.

COLORADO OUTDOOR EDUCATION CENTER, SANBORN WESTERN CAMPS
2000 Old Stage Rd.
Florissant, CO 80816
(719) 748-3341 or (719) 748-3475
Emphasis: Exciting 35-day residential programs in the outdoors for school groups, 5-week summer camp programs for boys and for girls; individually planned adult programs for natural history groups, businesses, agencies and organizations. **Programs:** High Trails Outdoor Education, The Nature Place, Sanborn Western Camps. **Type:** Outdoor education, expedition/experiential, natural science/history, residential. **Cost:** Depends on session. **Age Emphasis:** All ages. **Application Deadline:** Depends on program.

DALLAS MUSEUM OF NATURAL HISTORY
3535 Grand Ave.
Fairpark, Dallas, TX 75226
(214) 670-8458
Emphasis: Regional museum focusing on the natural history of Texas. Collects, preserves and interprets the record of the natural world, of humans and their environment. Also, research and teaching. **Programs:** Weekend discovery centers and Saturday science minicourses. Also, summer classes and week-long day camps, outreach programs, teacher courses (accredited). **Type:** Natural science/history, natural resources. **Cost:** Some programs are free; others range from $4-$30. **Age Emphasis:** All ages. **Application Deadline:** Varies, but registration is required for all courses.

EAGLE'S NEST CAMP
633 Summit St.
Winston Salem, NC 27101
(919) 761-1040 (winter);
(704) 877-4349 (summer)
Emphasis: Wilderness experience, natural history, art, music, community life, cultural exchange. **Programs:** Summer camp, Hante mountaineering, whitewater, Paleo man experiment, Longhouse journey. **Type:** Outdoor education, expedition/experiential, natural science/history, natural resources, residential. **Cost:** $356/week. **Age Emphasis:** Youth. **Application Deadline:** Spring.

ELGIN PUBLIC MUSEUM
225 Grand Blvd.
Elgin, IL 60120
(708) 741-6655
Emphasis: Museum of Natural History, including anthropology, botany, geology, paleontology, zoology. Emphasis on North America, specifically the Midwest. Discovery Room. **Programs:** Preschool through high school environmental education and natural history. Adult lectures. **Type:** Outdoor education, natural science/history. **Cost:** Admission fee, $1/adults, 25¢/children and seniors. Group fee charged for group programs. **Age Emphasis:** Youth. **Application Deadline:** N/A.

GREENBURGH NATURE CENTER
Dromore Rd. off Central Ave.
Scarsdale, NY 10583
(914) 723-3470
Emphasis: Natural history exhibits, live animal museum, programs for all ages, college and high school internships, special events, environmental education, cultural programs. **Programs:** Plant and Animal Adaptation; To Build or Not To Build; etc. **Type:** Outdoor education, natural science/history, natural resources. **Cost:** Varies. **Age Emphasis:** All ages. **Application Deadline:** N/A.

THE HAWAII NATURE CENTER
2131 Makiki Heights Dr.
Honolulu, HI 96822
(808) 973-0100
Emphasis: Discovery of nature through one-of-a-kind, hands-on experiences for children. Outdoor field trips for kindergarten through fifth grades. Family nature adventures. Guided interpretative hikes. **Programs:** Numerous school and community programs. **Type:** Outdoor education, expedition/experiential, natural science/history. **Cost:** Varies. **Age Emphasis:** All ages. **Application Deadline:** None.

THE HIGH DESERT MUSEUM
59800 S. Hwy. 97
Bend, OR 97702
(503) 382-4754
Emphasis: Natural and cultural history of the Intermountain West. **Programs:** Field excursions; fall/spring/summer classes; speaker series. **Type:** Outdoor education, expedition/experiential, natural science/history, natural resources, wildlife art, landscape photography. **Cost:** Varies. **Age Emphasis:** All ages. **Application Deadline:** N/A.

Q. *It would take 83 million acres of solar panels to fulfill all human energy needs. This represents what percentage of the earth's landmass?*

HOUSTON MUSEUM OF NATURAL SCIENCE

1 Hermann Circle Dr.
Houston, TX 77030
(713) 639-4686

Emphasis: Resource center for the public and teachers. Ecological principles behind environmental issues. **Programs:** Teacher workshops, lectures, inservice programs, children's classes. **Type:** Natural science/history, natural resources. **Cost:** N/A. **Age Emphasis:** All ages. **Application Deadline:** N/A.

HULBERT OUTDOOR CENTER

RR 1, Box 91A
Fairlee, VT 05045
(802) 333-9840

Emphasis: Year-round residential and wilderness trip programs in teambuilding, natural history, photography, outdoor skill development. **Programs:** Youth groups, adult groups, schools, corporations, elder hostels. **Type:** Outdoor education, expedition/experiential, natural science/history, residential. **Cost:** Varies from $30 to $250 per person, per day. **Age Emphasis:** All ages. **Application Deadline:** Open.

ISLAND INSTITUTE

4004 58th Pl. SW
Seattle, WA 98116
(206) 938-0345

Emphasis: Marine science immersion experiences; sea kayaking, snorkel/SCUBA, whale watching, island explorations in the San Juan Islands. **Programs:** Whale Camp, Boat Camp. **Type:** Degree program, expedition/experiential, natural science/history, natural resources, residential. **Cost:** $695/per week. **Age Emphasis:** All ages. **Application Deadline:** Register by May 15.

KEYSTONE SCIENCE SCHOOL

P.O. Box 8606
Keystone, CO 80435-7998
(303) 468-5824

Emphasis: Field science focuses on ecosystems of the Central Rockies; Montana; subalpine and alpine ecology; forest ecology; aquatic ecology; winter ecology; snow physics; geology, mining/cultural history; wildlife biology. **Programs:** School groups, teacher workshops, elder hostels, summer discovery camp. **Type:** Outdoor education, natural science/history, residential. **Cost:** $45/day. **Age Emphasis:** All ages. **Application Deadline:** Usually filled 9-12 months in advance.

KOKEE NATURAL HISTORY MUSEUM

P.O. Box 100
Kekaha, HI 96752
(808) 335-9975

Emphasis: Natural history of Kauai and Hawaiian archipelago. Museum is open 365 days per year/free admission. **Programs:** Forest-Wise Earth Education Camp, Earth-Wise Symposium and Festival. **Type:** Outdoor education, expedition/experiential, natural science/history, residential. **Cost:** Varies, from free to $250/week. **Age Emphasis:** All ages. **Application Deadline:** N/A.

LAC LAWRANN CONSERVANCY

724 Elm St.
West Bend, WI 53095
(414) 335-5080

Emphasis: Natural sciences, environmental education programs for the general public on an appointment basis, regularly scheduled public education programs during most weekends, and scheduled youth, adult and school programs during the fall and spring. **Programs:** Project Wild, Living Lightly in the City, NatureScope, Dream Chasers, or other national programs. **Type:** Outdoor education, expedition/experiential. **Cost:** Free on site, at cost off site. **Age Emphasis:** All ages. **Application Deadline:** N/A.

LAKE ERIE NATURE AND SCIENCE CENTER

28728 Wolf Rd.
Bay Village, OH 44140
(216) 871-2900

Emphasis: Provides nature experiences and stimulates environmental action through education. **Programs:** 25 physical and natural science classes (K-8) plus various preschool and adult programs. **Type:** Expedition/experiential, natural science/history. **Cost:** $2/per child. **Age Emphasis:** Youth. **Application Deadline:** N/A.

MARINE MAMMAL STRANDING CENTER

P.O. Box 773
Brigantine, NJ 08203-773
(609) 266-0538

Emphasis: Responsible for rescuing, rehabilitating and releasing marine mammals and turtles in New Jersey. The Center has worked with over 650 animals since 1978, and these animals are the basis for the educational program. **Programs:** Bringing the Ocean Alive, Ocean's Barometer, etc. **Type:** Natural science/history, natural resources. **Cost:** $1 per person, on site; fees vary by mileage away from site from one hour to full day. **Age Emphasis:** All ages. **Application Deadline:** Throughout the year.

NATIONAL MARINE SANCTUARY PROGRAM

1825 Connecticut Ave. NW, Suite 714
Washington, DC 20235
(202) 673-5126

Emphasis: Long-term resource protection, research and education. **Programs:** Various resource and educational opportunities. **Type:** Outdoor education, expedition/experiential, natural science/history, natural resources. **Cost:** Varies. **Age Emphasis:** All ages. **Application Deadline:** Ongoing programs.

NORTH PARK VILLAGE NATURE CENTER

5801 N. Pulask
Chicago, IL 60646
(312) 744-5472

Emphasis: Nature Discovery school fieldtrip program; maple syrup education program and festival; Arbor Day activities; public programs for natural history education, bird walks, wildflower identification, etc.; teacher workshops. **Type:** Outdoor education, expedition/experiential, natural science/history, natural resources. **Cost:** Most programs are free. **Age Emphasis:** All ages. **Application Deadline:** N/A.

OGLEBAY INSTITUTE NATURE EDUCATION DEPARTMENT

Ogelbay Park
Wheeling, WV 26003
(304) 242-6855

Emphasis: Daily concentrated nature study in the field at a rustic site on Lake Terra Alta in West Virginia's Appalachian Plateau. Fieldtrips to such diverse habitats as a boreal bog, virgin forest and geologically-unique high valley. **Type:** Outdoor education, expedition/experiential, natural science/history, residential. **Cost:** $300 includes instruction, meals and lodging, with a limited number of single-week registrations available at $155. **Age Emphasis:** Adults and college students. **Application Deadline:** April 15.

POINT BONITA YMCA OUTDOOR EDUCATION CONFERENCE CENTER

Bldg. 981
Fort Barry, Sausalito, CA 94965
(415) 331-9622

Emphasis: Hands-on learning experiences about coastal ecology, environments and habitats. Lighthouse and military history resources nearby. **Type:** Outdoor education, expedition/experiential, natural science/history, natural resources, residential. **Cost:** $34 lodging, 3 meals, day and evening program. 15 days. **Age Emphasis:** Youth. **Application Deadline:** None.

POTOMAC OVERLOOK REGIONAL PARK & NATURE CENTER

2845 Marcey Rd.
Arlington, VA 22207
(703) 528-5406

Emphasis: Interrelationships between people and the rest of nature. **Programs:** Examples: The Human and Natural Heritage of Potomac Overlook Regional Park; Canoe the Marsh. **Type:** Outdoor education, expedition/experiential, natural science/history, natural resources. **Cost:** Most are free; $5 per person charge for group canoe trips. **Age Emphasis:** All ages. **Application Deadline:** Usually 2 weeks.

ROCKY MOUNTAIN NATURE ASSOCIATION

Rocky Mountain National Park
Estes Park, CO 80517
(303) 586-2371

Emphasis: Field seminars on the geology, ecology, and natural history of Rocky Mountain National Park. **Type:** Experiential, Natural Science/History, Natural Resources, Residential. **Cost:** $40-$600. **Length:** 1-7 days. **Age Emphasis:** All ages. **Application Deadline:** N/A.

SAN FRANCISCO BAY BIRD OBSERVATORY

P.O. Box 247
Aliso, CA 95002
(408) 946-6548

Emphasis: Research and education focuses on marshes, sloughs and salt ponds of the South San Francisco Bay. Volunteers run research and education programs. **Programs:** Varied. **Type:** Outdoor education, expedition/experiential, natural science/history. **Cost:** Varies, $30-$100. Tours (camping) range from $35-$500. **Age Emphasis:** All ages. **Application Deadline:** Ongoing.

SEACAMP

Rt 3, Box 170
Big Pine Key, FL 33043
(305) 872-2331

Emphasis: The marine science program is the heart of Seacamp. Activities include SCUBA, windsurfing, sailing, arts and crafts, snorkeling, fishing and photography. **Type:** Outdoor education, expedition/experiential, natural science/history, natural resources, residential, marine science. **Cost:** $1,700. **Age Emphasis:** 12-17. **Application Deadline:** First come, first served; usually booked by March.

Q.: *What percentage change was proposed by President Bush in federal funding for energy conservation?*

SLIDE RANCH

2025 Shoreline Hwy.
Muir Beach, CA 94965
(415) 381-6155

Emphasis: Programs focus on human dependence upon the earth's resources to provide food, clothing, shelter and energy. The wildlands, ocean shore and farmstead provide an outdoor classroom for exploring life, water and energy cycles. **Programs:** School and family programs, intern program (interns live and work at Slide Ranch gaining practical experience leading programs for children, seniors, disabled, family groups). **Type:** Outdoor education, expedition/experiential, natural science/history, natural resources, residential, farm. **Cost:** Volunteers must commit for six months; room and board provided. School and Family sessions, $10 per person per day. **Age Emphasis:** All ages. **Application Deadline:** N/A.

SOMERSET COUNTY PARK COMMISSION'S ENVIRONMENTAL EDUCATION CENTER

190 Lord Stirling Rd.
Basking Ridge, NJ 07920
(908) 766-2489

Emphasis: Environmental education programs for schools and the general public. **Type:** Outdoor education, expedition/experiential, natural science/history, natural resources. **Cost:** Varies. **Age Emphasis:** All ages. **Application Deadline:** N/A.

SONORAN ARTHROPOD STUDIES, INC.

P.O. Box 5624
Tucson, AZ 85703
(602) 883-3945

Emphasis: Environmental and science education focusing on insects and other arthropods with an emphasis on interrelationships and biodiversity. Conservation is high priority, especially reduction of pesticide use through increased knowledge. **Programs:** Large variety, from lectures to expeditions. **Type:** Outdoor education, expedition/experiential, natural science/history. **Cost:** Varies, $10-$75 for workshops and day trips, $5-$1,500 for expeditions. **Age Emphasis:** All ages. **Application Deadline:** Continuous through year. Members notified through publications; public through media.

TREE HILL, JACKSONVILLE NATURE CENTER

7152 Lone Star Rd.
Jacksonville, FL 32211
(904) 724-4646

Emphasis: Tree Hill is a nature preserve featuring two nature trails, garden parcourse, two science laboratories and a natural history museum. Field experience in a "nature classroom" focuses on forest ecology. **Programs:** Environmental education for elementary grades in Duval County; forest ecology for Scouts; senior citizen programs; Science Day Camp. **Cost:** Contracts with agencies; some programs fee-based. **Age Emphasis:** All ages. **Application Deadline:** N/A.

WYOMING GAME AND FISH DEPARTMENT

5400 Bishop Blvd.
Cheyenne, WY 82006
(307) 777-4543

Emphasis: Wildlife Conservation Education/interpretive education; wildlife and wildland viewing experiences in Wyoming under the "Wyoming Wildlife—Worth the Watching" program. **Programs:** Visitor centers, Viewing areas, Nature areas tour guide. **Type:** Outdoor education. **Cost:** No charge at visitor centers and other facilities. **Age Emphasis:** All ages. **Application Deadline:** N/A.

YOUTH

3-2-1 CONTACT EXTRAS (PRODUCED BY CHILDREN'S TELEVISION WORKSHOP)

VCA Teletronics, 50 Leyland Dr.
Leonia, NJ 17605
(800) 822-1105 operator #12

Emphasis: 3-2-1 Contact has produced the following programs: "The Rotten Truth," a 30-minute program about garbage; "You Can't Grow Home Again," a 60-minute program about rainforests; "Down the Drain," a 30-minute program about water. **Cost:** 30-minute videos $14.95, 60-minute $19.95 plus S/H. **Age Emphasis:** 8-12 and their families.

BETSY-JEFF PENN 4-H EDUCATIONAL CENTER

Rt. 9, Box 249X
Reidsville, NC 27320
(919) 349-9445

Emphasis: Interdisciplinary approach to exploring the environment. Environmental education program for grades 2-8; global awareness seminars (high school); teaching in a living

A. *–36 percent*
Source: OMB Watch

classroom (for teachers). **Programs:** Pond ecology, forest communities, wildlife adaptations. **Type:** Outdoor education. **Cost:** Varies, $65/3 days, $120/5 days. **Age Emphasis:** Youth. **Application Deadline:** Year-round.

CHEWONKI FOUNDATION, INC.
Rt. 2, Box 1200
Wiscasset, ME 04578
(207) 882-7323

Emphasis: Residential and day environmental education programs for school groups; summer camp; wilderness expeditions for youth, families and adults. **Programs:** Summer camp for boys, ages 8-14; coed wilderness experience in inland Maine, coastal Maine and Quebec, ages 14-18; The Maine Coast Semester (personal and academic challenge for 11th graders interested in environmental issues and natural science); family and adult wilderness expeditions. **Type:** Outdoor education, expedition/experiential, natural science/history, residential/day, academic semester. **Cost:** Varies, from $12/day to $8,250/semester. **Age Emphasis:** All ages. **Application Deadline:** Depends on program.

CLEARING MAGAZINE—ENVIRONMENTAL EDUCATION PROJECT
19600 S. Molalla Ave.
Oregon City, OR 97045
(503) 656-0155

Emphasis: Provides high-quality resource materials, teaching ideas, and information for parents and teachers (K12) interested in providing environmental education. **Programs:** *Clearing* Magazine (subtitle: Environmental Education in the Pacific Northwest). **Type:** Magazine. **Cost:** $15/year (5 issues). **Age Emphasis:** All ages. **Application Deadline:** Subscriptions accepted any time.

CORNELL WASTE MANAGEMENT INSTITUTE
468 Hollister Hall
Ithaca, NY 14853-3501
(607) 255-8444

Emphasis: Solid waste, recycling and composting education for K-12. **Programs:** Audio visual resources, games, workbooks, posters, videos, computer disks. **Type:** Natural resources. **Cost:** N/A. **Age Emphasis:** Youth. **Application Deadline:** N/A.

EBERSOLE ENVIRONMENTAL EDUCATION AND CONFERENCE CENTER
3400 Second St.
Wayland, MI 49348
(616) 792-6294

Emphasis: Environmental education programs for school-age children. Site includes fen, lake, climax hardwood forest, prairie. **Programs:** Varied; discovery-oriented curriculum; offsite wilderness canoe trip; 2-week summer camp; 10 days in Canadian wilderness. **Type:** Outdoor education, natural science/ history, natural resources, residential. **Age Emphasis:** Youth. **Cost:** Varies, $50-$120. **Application Deadline:** None.

ECHO HILL OUTDOOR SCHOOL
Worton, MD 21678
(301) 348-5880

Emphasis: Helping children learn about the environment and themselves in residential programs designed to heighten awareness and appreciation of the natural world. **Programs:** Outdoor School, Explore, Quicksilver Project. **Type:** Outdoor Education, Experiential, Natural Science/History, Natural Resources, Residential. **Cost:** N/A. **Length:** 3-5 days. **Age Emphasis:** Youth. **Application Deadlines:** Ongoing.

EDUCATIONAL DEVELOPMENT SPECIALISTS
5505 E. Carson St., Suite 250
Lakewood, CA, 90713
(213) 420-6814

Emphasis: Natural resource and energy source education programs for grades K-12. **Programs:** "Think Earth" for grades K-6; "Energy Source" for K-12. Program is private; local government or business sponsors exist in some areas. **Type:** Natural resources. **Cost:** Varies. **Age Emphasis:** Youth. **Application Deadline:** N/A.

EXPEDITION YELLOWSTONE!
National Park Service
P.O. Box 168
Yellowstone National Park, WY 82190
(307) 344-7381, ext. 2338.

Emphasis: Curriculum and story book about Yellowstone Park, targeted to grades 4-6. Expeditions to the park in spring and fall. Learning activities cover geology, history, wildlife; suitable for classroom or outdoors. **Type:** Outdoor education. **Cost:** Write for information. **Age Emphasis:** Youth. **Application Deadline:** Write for information.

GEOTHERMAL EDUCATION OFFICE
664 Hilary Dr.
Tiburon, CA 94920
(800) 866-4GEO

Emphasis: K-12 and adult education about

Q: *What percentage of US oil use could be replaced by the natural gas emitted from garbage dumps and rotting vegetation?*

geothermal energy and renewables, with environmental orientation. **Programs:** Materials only; no programs. User-friendly lay information. **Type:** Natural resources. **Cost:** Single sets of information, $3. Minimal cost for classroom sets. **Age Emphasis:** All ages. **Application Deadline:** N/A.

THE GREEN SCENE
University of Arizona School for Renewable Natural Resources
Tucson, AZ 85721
Emphasis: Joint effort of the Wilderness Society, University of Arizona, and USDA Forest Service. **Program:** The Green Scene. **Type:** Curriculum for middle schools (grades 4-8) on forest ecology and wilderness. **Cost:** $5. **Age Emphasis:** Youth. **Application Deadline:** N/A.

HIDDEN VILLA ENVIRONMENTAL EDUCATION PROGRAM
26870 Moody Rd.
Los Altos Hills, CA 94022
(415) 948-4690
Emphasis: Providing children with first-hand experiences with nature, emphasizing the interrelatedness of all living things. **Programs:** Farm Tours, Farm and Wilderness Exploration. **Type:** Experiential, Natural Science/History. **Cost:** $6-$12/person. **Age Emphasis:** Youth. **Application Deadline:** Ongoing.

K.E.E.P.—KERN ENVIRONMENTAL EDUCATION PROGRAM
Star Rt. 1, Box 311
Posey, CA 93260
(805) 536-8403
Emphasis: Provides environmental education to Kern County 6th grade students. Emphasis is placed on wildlife, plants, water, and human impacts on the environment. **Type:** Experiential, Natural Science/History, Natural Resources, Residential. **Cost:** $120-$150/child. Length: 5 days. **Age Emphasis:** 11-13. **Application Deadline:** N/A.

KEYSTONE SCIENCE SCHOOL
Box 606
Keystone, CO 80435
(303) 468-5824
Emphasis: Promotes a scientific understanding of nature and our relationship to the natural environment. **Programs:** Elder Hostel, Discovery Camp, Project Wild 2. **Type:** Outdoor Education, Experiential, Natural Science/History, Natural Resources, Residential. **Cost:** $45/day. Length: 2-14 days. **Age Emphasis:** K-12. **Application Deadline:** Ongoing.

KIWANIS CAMP WYMAN
600 Kiwanis Dr.
Eureka, MO 63025
(314) 938-5245
Emphasis: Environmental education, adventure education, outdoor education. Summer camp, day camp, retreat facilities. **Programs:** Earthkeepers, Sunship Earth, customized programs. **Type:** Outdoor education, expedition/experiential, natural science/history, natural resources, residential. **Cost:** $6-$60/day. **Age Emphasis:** All ages. **Application Deadline:** N/A.

LEARNING FORUM
1725 S. Hill St.
Oceanside, CA 92054
(619) 722-0072
Emphasis: Accelerated learning programs for self confidence, personal growth, self esteem and motivation. **Programs:** Super Camp and College Forum. **Type:** Residential. **Cost:** $14-$45. **Age Emphasis:** All ages. **Application Deadline:** Applications accepted until program is full.

THE NATIONAL ASSOCIATION FOR HUMANE AND ENVIRONMENTAL EDUCATION; YOUTH EDUCATION DIVISION OF THE HUMANE SOCIETY OF THE US
67 Salem Rd.
East Haddam, CT 06423-1736
(203) 434-8666
Emphasis: Humane and environmental education, focus on teaching tools, reading, health, math, art, social studies and career education. Also contains science lessons and writing assignments. **Programs:** NAHEE'S Adopt-A-Teacher, KIND (Kids in Nature's Defense) NEWS. **Type:** Elementary Education, Residential. **Cost:** N/A. Length: 9 month school year. **Age Emphasis:** Youth. **Application Deadline:** September 30.

NATIONAL WILDLIFE FEDERATION
1400 16th St. NW
Washington, DC, 20036-2266
(800) 432-6564
Emphasis: Environmental/ Natural history magazines for children. *Your Big Backyard* (ages 3-5), *Ranger Rick* (ages 6-12). **Cost:** Yearly subscriptions $12.00 (*Your Big Backyard*), $15.00 (*Ranger Rick*). **Age Emphasis:** Youth.

A. *100 percent*
    Source: Seattle Post, *Intelligencer, 3 October, 1990*

NATIONAL WILDLIFE FEDERATION— CLASS PROJECT

1400 16th St. NW
Washington, DC 20036-2266
(703) 790-4504

Emphasis: Curriculum supplement for middle school educators, encourages students to initiate conservation projects in their communities. Program: The CLASS Project. Curriculum investigates energy use, habitat management, hazardous substances, etc. **Type:** Environmental education, natural science/history, natural resources. **Cost:** $8 plus shipping/handling. **Age Emphasis:** Middle school educators. **Application Deadline:** N/A.

NATIONAL WILDLIFE FEDERATION— LEADERSHIP TRAINING

1400 16th St. NW
Washington, DC 20036-2266
(800) 432-6564

Emphasis: Leadership Training Program teaches leadership skills to teens ages 14-17 who aspire to lead and teach younger children in an outdoor setting. Participants assist counselors at the National Wildlife Federation's Wildlife Camp. **Programs:** Trainees assist with crafts, recreation activities, evening programs, daily camp activities. **Type:** Outdoor environmental education, residential camp. **Cost:** $550. **Age Emphasis:** Youth, ages 14-17. **Application Deadline:** Sessions usually fill by March or April.

NATIONAL WILDLIFE FEDERATION— NATURE SCOPE GUIDES

1400 16th St. NW
Washington, DC 20036-2266
(703) 790-4504

Emphasis: Education activity guide series for K-8 educators. 18-issue series; each focuses on a different topic, such as pollution, tropical rainforests, oceans, endangered species, etc. Program NatureScope Activity Guides. **Type:** Environmental education, natural science/history, natural resources. **Cost:** $7.95 per issue; $99 for all 18 issues, plus shipping/handling. Discount prices for bulk orders. **Age Emphasis:** Educators, grades K-8. **Application Deadline:** N/A.

NATIONAL WILDLIFE FEDERATION— NATURE SCOPE WORKSHOPS

1400 16th St. NW
Washington, DC 20036-2266
(703) 790-4359

Emphasis: Hands-on participatory workshops using NatureScope series. Educators learn to integrate environmental education into the curriculum. **Programs:** NatureScope Environmental Education workshop program. **Type:** Outdoor education, natural science/history, natural resources. **Cost:** Varies. **Age Emphasis:** Educators of grades K-8. **Application Deadline:** N/A.

NATIONAL WILDLIFE FEDERATION— TEEN ADVENTURE

1400 16th St. NW
Washington, DC 20036-2266
(800) 432-6564

Emphasis: Teen Adventure is for ages 14-17. Teens discover nature by being active members of the natural world in wilderness areas seldom disturbed by human activity. While hiking and backpacking, participants navigate trails with maps and' compass, set up overnight campsites using minimum impact techniques, and study wildlife biology, ecosystems, land management, geology and Native American culture. **Programs:** Eastern Teen Adventure, Black Mountain, NC; Western Teen Adventure, Estes Park, CO. **Type:** Outdoor environmental education, residential camp. **Cost:** $550. **Age Emphasis:** Youth, ages 14-17. **Application Deadline:** Sessions usually filled by March or April.

NATIONAL WILDLIFE FEDERATION— WILDLIFE CAMP

1400 16th St. NW
Washington, DC 20036-2266
(800) 432-6564

Emphasis: Wildlife Camp is for children ages 9-13 to develop an understanding of the natural world and foster an attitude of environmental citizenship. Campers participate in Quests and MiniQuests which cover areas such as plant ecology, lakes and streams, birds, wilderness survival, Earth Savers, and outdoor challenges. **Programs:** Eastern Wildlife Camp in Asheville, NC; Western Wildlife Camp in Boulder, CO. **Type:** Outdoor environmental education, residential camp. **Cost:** $572-$630. **Age Emphasis:** Youth, ages 9-13. **Application Deadline:** Sessions usually filled by March or April.

NATURE SCIENCE CENTER

Museum Dr.
Winston Salem, NC 27105
(919) 767-6730

Emphasis: Programs for school groups and adults; addresses issues of environmental awareness and protection. **Programs:** Living Links, Endangered Species, Recycling. **Type:** Outdoor education, natural science/history.

Q: *What percentage of Americans live in cities where the air does not meet the standards of the 1970 Clean Air Act?*

Cost: $1.50/per person. **Age Emphasis:** All ages. **Application Deadline:** N/A.

ORANGE COUNTY OUTDOOR SCIENCE SCHOOL
1829 Mentone Blvd.
Mentone, CA 92359
(714) 794-1988
Emphasis: Natural science program for grades 5-6. **Program:** 5 day residential program. **Type:** Natural science. **Cost:** $160/week/per student. **Age Emphasis:** Grades 5-6. **Application Deadline:** Ongoing.

PROJECT WILD
National Office
P.O. Box 18060
Boulder, CO 80308-8060
(303) 444-2390
Emphasis: Project WILD is an interdisciplinary, supplementary, environmental and conservation program emphasizing wildlife, for teachers of K-12. Available in all 50 states. Contact the National Office for information on local programs. **Programs:** Project WILD workshops for teachers of K-12. **Type:** Outdoor education, natural science/history, natural resources. **Cost:** Free. **Age Emphasis:**Teachers. **Application Deadline:** Varies.

RIVERBEND ENVIRONMENTAL EDUCATION CENTER
P.O. Box 2
Gladwyne, PA 19035
(215) 527-5234.
Emphasis: Hands-on environmental education for children of all ages, school teachers, group leaders. **Programs:** 14 programs focusing on aspects of the environment. **Type:** Outdoor education, natural science/history, natural resources. **Cost:** $3/per child. **Age Emphasis:** All ages. **Application Deadline:** N/A.

RIVERBEND ENVIRONMENTAL EDUCATION CENTER—CAMP GREEN HERON
P.O. Box 2
Gladwyne, PA 19035
(215) 527-5234
Emphasis: Summer day camp focusing on environmental themes. **Programs:** Games, songs, crafts, explorations. **Type:** Outdoor education, natural science/history. **Cost:** $45-$90/week. **Age Emphasis:** Ages 2-11. **Application Deadline:** N/A.

SOUTH SLOUGH NATIONAL ESTUARINE RESERVE
P.O. Box 5417
Charleston, OR 97420
(503) 888-5558
Emphasis: Education about estuaries, ecologically oriented program. **Programs:** Treasures of the South Slough, Secret of the Medallion, Estuary: An Ecosystem and a Resource, Love of the South Slough. **Type:** Outdoor Education, Experiential, Natural Science/History, Natural Resources. **Cost:** free. **Age Emphasis:** Youth. **Application Deadline:** Ongoing.

TRAILSIDE DISCOVERY PROGRAMS
519 W. 8th, Suite 201
Anchorage, AK 99501
(907) 274-5437
Emphasis: Nature camps and outdoor education programs for young people ages 4-18. Located in the amazing wild lands of south-central Alaska. **Programs:** Marine science, ornithology, alpine ecology, spirit keepers, Alaskan Quest trips. **Type:** Outdoor education, expedition/experiential, natural science/history, natural resources, residential. **Cost:** $65-$300, depending on program. **Age Emphasis:** Youth. **Application Deadline:** Ongoing programs.

UNIVERSITY OF GEORGIA ENVIRONMENTAL EDUCATION PROGRAM
350 Rock Eagle Rd. NE
Rock Eagle 4-H Ctr.,
Eatonton, GA 31024
(404) 485-2831
Emphasis: Residential environmental education for grades 3-8. **Programs:** Outdoor education at Jekyll Island, Tybee Island, Rock Eagle and Wahsega 4-H Centers. **Type:** Outdoor education, natural science/history, expedition/experiential, natural resources, residential. **Cost:** $50/per person. **Age Emphasis:** Youth. College students can apply for internships. **Application Deadline:** Ongoing.

WATER POLLUTION CONTROL FEDERATION
601 Wythe St.
Alexandria, VA 22314-1994
(800) 666-0206
Emphasis: Protects water resources and maintains water quality through Water Environment Curriculum Series. **Programs:** Surface water video, Waste Water Treatment, The Groundwater Video Adventure, Saving Water/The Conservation Unit. **Type:** Natural resources. **Cost:** $49 per program includes

A. *58 percent*
Source: Natural Resources Defense Council, Clean Air Coalition

teacher guide and 20 student guides. **Age Emphasis:** Youth. **Application Deadline:** N/A. Send SASE for information and brochure.

Y.O. ADVENTURE CAMP, INC.
HC 01, P.O. Box 555
Mountain Home, TX 78058-9705
(512) 640-3220

Emphasis: Outdoor skills, environmental education activities, challenge/adventure activities. **Programs:** Outdoor Awareness Program. **Type:** Outdoor Education. **Cost:** $55/day. **Age Emphasis:** Youth. **Application Deadlines:** Apply 6 months in advance, for summer programs 2-3 months in advance.

ZERO POPULATION GROWTH, INC.
1400 16th St. NW, Suite 320
Washington, DC 20036
(202) 332-2200.

Emphasis: Teacher training workshops for hands-on activities in population education for K-12; development of teaching materials for population education. **Programs:** ZPG teacher training workshops. **Type:** Hands-on workshop. **Cost:** Varies. **Age Emphasis:** Teachers. **Application Deadline:** N/A.

UNIVERSITY PROGRAMS

ANTIOCH NEW ENGLAND GRADUATE SCHOOL
103 Roxbury St.
Keene, NH 03431
(603) 357-3122

Emphasis: Graduate professional training programs for the environmental field. Includes resource management, environmental administration, environmental communications, environmental education and teacher certification in biology, general science and elementary science. **Programs:** Master of Science in Environmental Studies, Master of Science in Resource Management and Administration. **Type:** Degree program, outdoor education, expedition/experiential, natural science/history, natural resources. **Cost:** 50 Credit, Resource Management MS: $13,150. 40 Credit, Environmental Studies MS: $10,500. **Age Emphasis:** Adults. **Application Deadline:** Entry points are September, January, June.

BARD COLLEGE—GRADUATE SCHOOL OF ENVIRONMENTAL STUDIES
Annandale Rd.
Annandale, NY 12504
(914) 758-7483

Emphasis: Education, business, government

and public planning are some of the areas in a broad-based, cross-disciplinary expertise in environmental studies and the solutions it can offer. **Programs:** Master of Science in Environmental Studies. **Type:** Degree program, outdoor education, expedition/experiential, natural science/history, natural resources, residential. **Cost:** Tuition $4,700; some financial aid available. **Age Emphasis:** Adults. **Application Deadline:** May 1.

BASTYR COLLEGE
144 NE 54th
Seattle, WA 98105
(206) 523-9585

Emphasis: Extensive clinical training of practitioners of natural therapeutics. **Programs:** Naturopathic medicine, acupuncture, nutrition. **Type:** Degree program, residential. **Cost:** 4-year, $9,000/yr; 3-year, $5,000/yr; 2-year, $4,500/yr. **Age Emphasis:** Adults. **Application Deadline:** April 1 and June 1.

BAYLOR UNIVERSITY—INSTITUTE OF ENVIRONMENTAL STUDIES
P.O. Box 97266
Waco, TX 76798-7266
(817) 755-3405

Emphasis: Renewable energies; hazardous waste management; air and water pollution; sustainable agriculture; permitting and regulations; environmental ethics. **Programs:** Bachelor of Science; Bachelor of Arts; Master of Science; Master of Environmental Studies. **Type:** Degree program, natural sciences/ history, natural resources. **Cost:** $12,000/year for B.A./B.S. program; $7,250/ year for M.S. (negotiated with Director for full support). **Application Deadline:** 90 days before semester begins.

BELOIT COLLEGE, DEPT. OF BIOLOGY
700 College Ave.
Beloit, WI 53511
(608) 363-2287

Emphasis: An ecologic approach to concepts and issues, rooted in a liberal arts tradition with strong emphasis on practical experience, individualized programs, management and research. **Programs:** Environmental biology. **Type:** Private residential degree program. **Cost:** $14,000 per year less financial aid. Length of program: 4 years. **Age Emphasis:** Adult, college student. **Application Deadline:** no fixed date.

BRADFORD WOODS
5040 State Rd. 67N
Martinsville, IN 46151
(317) 342-2915

 Q: *What percentage of Americans consider themselves environmentalists?*

Emphasis: Outdoor education, challenge education, summer camp, leadership development, internships. **Type:** Degree program, outdoor education, expedition/experiential, residential. **Cost:** Varies. **Age Emphasis:** All ages. **Application Deadline:** N/A.

CALIFORNIA STATE UNIVERSITY AT HAYWARD

Dept. of Teacher Education
Hayward, CA 94542
(415) 881-3016

Emphasis: Leadership training and environmental education. **Programs:** Undergraduate environmental studies in Geography Department; M.S. curriculum option in Environmental Education. **Type:** Degree program, outdoor education, natural science/history, natural resources (undergraduate), residential. **Cost:** Approximately $900 in-state tuition; $1,050 non-resident tuition. **Age Emphasis:** Adults. **Application Deadline:** Quarterly acceptance.

THE CITY COLLEGE OF C.U.N.Y., SCHOOL OF EDUCATION

138 St. and Convent Ave., R5/208
New York, NY 10031
(212) 650-7953

Emphasis: Science and social studies. **Program:** An interdisciplinary graduate program leading to an M.A. degree and New York state teacher certification. **Type:** Degree program. **Cost:** $82/credit; 30 credit program. **Age Emphasis:** Adults. **Application Deadline:** For fall matriculation, March 1; for spring, October 1.

CORNELL LABORATORY OF ORNITHOLOGY

159 Sapsucker Woods Rd.
Ithaca, NY 14850
(607) 254-BIRD

Emphasis: International center for study, appreciation and conservation of birds. Develops, applies and shares tools for understanding birds and protecting bird populations. **Programs:** Home study course in bird biology, field courses in bird study and bird song recording, educational birding tours. **Type:** Expedition/experiential, natural science/history. **Cost:** Home study course, $135; field courses, $100 and up; tours, $1,500 and up. **Age Emphasis:** All ages. **Application Deadline:** Write for information.

CUEST (CENTER FOR UNDERSTANDING ENVIRONMENTS, SCIENCE AND TECHNOLOGY)

Box 740
Northern State University
Aberdeen, SD 57401
(605) 622-2627

Emphasis: CUEST is an environmental education resource center for teachers that offers environmental education workshops, pre-service and in-service teacher training, provides audio visual and printed matter on environmental issues, and activities and speakers for community outreach. **Type:** Degree program (undergraduate and continuing education), natural resources. **Cost:** $64/undergraduate credit hour, $76/graduate credit hour. **Age Emphasis:** All ages. **Application Deadline:** N/A

DAHLEM ENVIRONMENTAL EDUCATION CENTER

Jackson Community College
2111 Emmons Rd.
Jackson, MI 49201
(517) 782-3453

Emphasis: Comprehensive field study curriculum for P-6th graders; special events, workshops, weekend programs for teachers, adults and families; summer ecology day camp (P-12); "Biking for Independence" (ages 7-12); county-wide "Bring Back the Bluebirds Project;" hosts Celebrate Wildlife/Bluebird Festival each March. **Programs:** Internships for college students and recent graduates (interpretation, wildlife biology, research). **Type:** Natural science/history, natural resources. **Cost:** Varies. **Age Emphasis:** All ages. **Application Deadline:** Intern applications accepted seasonally.

DE ANZA COLLEGE—ENVIRONMENTAL STUDIES/BIOLOGY

1250 Stevens Creek Blvd.
Cupertino, CA 95014
(408) 864-8525

Emphasis: Promotes environmental education, environmental biology careers and environmental awareness. **Type:** Outdoor education, expedition/experiential, natural science/ history, natural resources, residential. **Cost:** Varies. **Age Emphasis:** All ages. **Application Deadline:** N/A.

EASTERN KENTUCKY UNIVERSITY— DEPT. OF ENVIRONMENTAL HEALTH SCIENCE

219 Dizney Bldg.
Richmond, KY 40475-3135
(606) 622-1939

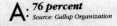

A. **76 percent**
Source: Gallup Organization

Emphasis: Environmental health. **Programs:** B.S. in Environmental Health Science. **Type:** Degree program. **Cost:** Tuition plus fees. **Age Emphasis:** Adults. **Application Deadline:** N/A.

GARRETT COMMUNITY COLLEGE
Mosser Rd.
McHenry, MD 21541
(800) 695-4221or (301) 387-6666

Emphasis: Prepares students for careers in wildlife management, soil and water conservation, fisheries management, water quality monitoring and other natural resources areas. **Programs:** Natural Resources and Wildlife Technology. **Type:** Degree program, outdoor education, expedition/experiential, natural science/history, natural resources. **Cost:** $1200/resident tuition, $3600/out-of-state tuition. **Age Emphasis:** Adult. **Application Deadline:** Must register before classes begin in September.

ILLINOIS STATE UNIVERSITY—DEPT. OF HEALTH SCIENCES
103 Moulton Hall
Normal, IL 61761
(309) 438-8329

Emphasis: Majors available in Environmental Health or Health Education. Combinations of the two degrees are available as a major and minor. **Programs:** Bachelor of Science in Health Science. **Type:** Degree program. **Cost:** Tuition, fees and books are approximately $1300 per semester. **Age Emphasis:** Adults. **Application Deadline:** Submit as early as possible.

IOWA STATE UNIVERSITY—ENVIRONMENTAL STUDIES PROGRAM
201 Bessey Hall
Ames, IA 50011
(515) 294-4787 or (515) 294-4911

Emphasis: Comprehensive program of departmental and multidisciplinary environmental courses in the natural and social sciences and humanities, leading to the minor or second major. **Type:** Degree program. **Cost:** N/A. **Age Emphasis:** Adults. **Application Deadline:** N/A.

JORDAN COLLEGE ENERGY INSTITUTE
155 Seven Mile Rd. NW
Comstock Park, MI 49321
(616) 784-7595

Emphasis: Degree programs in renewable energies, applied environmental technology, energy management, energy efficient construction and design, solar retrofit technology and business courses available. Degree program

offered. **Cost:** $120 per credit hour maximum, financial aid available. Length of program: 1-year certificates, 2-year associates degrees, 4-year bachelors. **Age Emphasis:** Adult College student. **Application Deadline:** N/A.

MCNEESE STATE UNIVERSITY—DEPT. OF BIOLOGICAL AND ENVIRONMENTAL SCIENCES
P.O. Box 92000-0655
Lake Charles, LA 70609-2000
(318) 475-5674

Emphasis: Studies in biology, microbiology, chemistry and mathematics to aid students in finding creative solutions to the complex problems of our environment. Graduate students specialize in air and water quality studies. **Programs:** B.S. and M.S. in Environmental Science. **Type:** Degree program. **Cost:** Tuition varies. **Age Emphasis:** Adults. **Application Deadline:** Fall registration, Aug. 15., Spring registration, Dec. 15.

MURRAY STATE UNIVERSITY—DEPT. OF ELEMENTARY AND SECONDARY EDUCATION
Murray, KY 42071
(502) 762-2747

Emphasis: Teacher training, pre-service, in-service, community and public school outreach, curriculum development and dissemination, research, resource room. **Programs:** Environmental Van, Center for Environmental Education Resource Room, Western Kentucky Environmental Consortium. **Cost:** N/A. **Age Emphasis:** All ages. **Application Deadline:** N/A.

NEW YORK UNIVERSITY
737 East Bldg., 239 Greene St., NYU
Washington Square
New York, NY 10003
(212) 998-5637 or (212) 998-5495

Emphasis: Non-science interdisciplinary M.A. program based on core courses in social, philosophical and organizational aspects of the environment with half the credits in electives. Internship required. **Programs:** M.A. in Environmental Conservation Education. **Type:** Degree program, interdisciplinary. **Cost:** $418/credit; 37 credits. **Age Emphasis:** Adults. **Application Deadline:** Rolling admissions.

NEW YORK UNIVERSITY—SCHOOL OF CONTINUING EDUCATION
50 W. Fourth St.
New York, NY 10003
(212) 998-7080

Emphasis: Business and the environment.

Q: *About how many automobiles have been discarded in the US since 1946?*

Programs: Business & the Environment: Managing for the Future, Environmental Law, Marketing in the **Age** of Environmental Consumerism. **Type:** Continuing Education. **Cost:** $250-$300. **Length:** 8-12 weeks. **Age Emphasis:** Adult. **Application Deadline:** N/A.

NORTHLAND COLLEGE
   Ashland, WI 54806
   (715) 682-1699
Emphasis: Environmental education, field experience, internships. **Type:** Degree program, Outdoor Education, Expedition/Experiential, Natural Science/History, Natural Resources, Residential. **Cost:** $11,000 per academic year. Financial Aid available. **Age Emphasis:** College Student. **Application Deadline:** N/A.

OBERLIN COLLEGE—ENVIRONMENTAL STUDIES PROGRAM
   Rice Hall
   Oberlin, OH 44074
   (216) 775-8409
Emphasis: Interdisciplinary program of study (natural science, social science, humanities) leading to A.B. degree. **Programs:** Environmental Studies Major. **Type:** Degree program. **Cost:** N/A. **Age Emphasis:** Adult. **Application Deadline:** N/A.

OHIO SEA GRANT EDUCATION PROGRAM
   Ohio State University
   29 W. Woodruff Ave.
   Columbus, OH 43210-1085
   (614) 292-1078
Emphasis: Curriculum development and teacher education in Great Lakes education. **Programs:** Great Lakes Education Workshop. **Type:** Natural science/history, natural resources. **Cost:** $30 materials fee, plus University tuition. **Age Emphasis:** Teachers. **Application Deadline:** N/A.

OPPORTUNITIES IN SCIENCE, INC.
   P.O. Box 1176
   Bemidji, MN 56601
   (218) 751-1110
Emphasis: Correspondence course for adults focuses on Environmental Education. **Programs:** WILDWAYS: Understanding Wildlife Conservation. **Type:** Degree program. **Cost:** $450 for text and computer disks. **Age Emphasis:** Adult. **Application Deadline:** None.

PRESCOTT COLLEGE
   220 Grove Ave.
   Prescott, AZ 86301
   (602) 778-2090
Emphasis: 4-year liberal arts college with an environmental mission. Curriculum is interdisciplinary, emphasizing field work throughout the southwest. **Programs:** Environmental Studies, Human Development, Humanities, Outdoor Leadership, and Cultural and Regional Studies. **Type:** Degree program, outdoor education, expedition/experiential, natural science/history, natural resources. **Cost:** $7,200/year. **Age Emphasis:** Adult. **Application Deadline:** Fall, June 15., Spring, Nov. 15.

PURDUE UNIVERSITY—ENVIRONMENTAL ENGINEERING DEPT.
   1284 Civil Engineering
   W. Lafayette, IN 47907-1284
   (317) 494-2194
Emphasis: Industrial Wastewater Treatment, Drinking Water, Air Toxics/Noise, Municipal/Hazardous Waste, Physical/Chemical Treatment, Environmental Chemistry, Groundwater Remediation, Water Quality Management. **Programs:** Master of Science, MSCE, Ph.D. **Type:** Degree programs. **Cost:** N/A. **Age Emphasis:** Adults. **Application Deadline:** N/A.

RAMAPO COLLEGE OF NEW JERSEY
   505 Ramapo Valley Road,
   Mahwah, NJ 07430-1680
   (201) 529-7743
Emphasis: To train individuals to address environmental problems by balancing scientific knowledge and activity to communicate across social, political and economic boundaries. Degree programs in environmental science and environmental studies offered. **Cost:** $900 per semester, $3300 total. Length of program: 4 years. **Age Emphasis:** College student. **Application Deadline:** N/A.

SHAVER'S CREEK ENVIRONMENTAL CENTER—PENN STATE UNIVERSITY
   Dept. of Leisure Studies
   203 Henderson Bldg.
   University Park, PA 16802
   (814) 863-2000
Emphasis: On- and off-site natural history programs for schools, scouts, general public, raptor rehabilitation, teacher workshops, cooperation course, high ropes source, extensive intern program and Penn State student training courses. Residential Outdoor School for 5th and 6th graders. **Programs:** Season

A. *300 million*
  • *Source: R.L. Polk and Co.*

Discovery Walks, Traveling Road Shows, Group Initiatives, Outdoor School, Maple Sugaring, Summer Day Camps. **Type:** Outdoor education, natural science/history, residential. **Cost:** Varies. **Age Emphasis:** All ages. **Application Deadline:** N/A.

SONOMA STATE UNIVERSITY—DEPT. OF ENVIRONMENTAL STUDIES AND PLANNING

1801 E. Cotati Ave.
Rohnert Park, CA 94928
(707) 664-2306

Emphasis: Bachelor degree programs in environmental education; energy management and design; hazardous materials management; natural resources and park; water quality; and city and regional planning. **Programs:** Bachelor's degree in Environmental Studies and Planning. **Type:** Degree program, outdoor education, natural science/history, natural resources, residential. **Cost:** $450/semester. **Age Emphasis:** Adults. **Application Deadline:** Fall admission, Dec. 1., Spring admission, June 1.

SOUTHERN VERMONT COLLEGE

Monument Ave.
Bennington, VT 05201
(802) 442-5427

Emphasis: Environmental studies. **Programs:** 2-year Associate and 4-year Bachelor programs in environmental studies. **Cost:** Tuition, room and board $10,600 per year. **Application Deadline:** N/A.

STATE UNIVERSITY OF NEW YORK AT CORTLAND

P.O. Box 2000, Park Ctr.
Cortland, NY 13045
(607) 753-4941

Emphasis: The College at Cortland offers undergraduate and graduate courses and degree options in outdoor education, environmental education and interpretation, and outdoor pursuits. The college maintains three field campuses, including historic "great camp" in the Adirondacks. Cortland is also headquarters for NYS Outdoor Education Association and the Coalition for Education in the Outdoors. **Type:** Degree program, outdoor education, expedition/experiential, natural science/history, natural resources, residential. **Cost:** $45/hour in-state undergraduates, $90 graduate students. **Age Emphasis:** Adults. **Application Deadline:** N/A.

TETON SCIENCE SCHOOL

Box 68
Kelly, WY 83011
(307) 733-4765

Emphasis: Experiential natural science education programs in the greater Yellowstone ecosystem for people of all ages. Natural science education using research as a tool. School group programs, adult seminars, 4 accredited college courses, high school field ecology. **Programs:** Ecology, Field Ornithology, Environmental Ethics, Winter Ecology. **Type:** Degree Program, Experiential, Natural History/Science, Natural Resources, Residential. **Cost:** $40-$50/day. **Length:** 1 day to 6 weeks. **Age Emphasis:** All Ages. **Application Deadline:** N/A.

THIEL COLLEGE

75 College Ave.
Greenville, PA 16125
(412) 589-2068

Emphasis: B.A. in environmental science with emphasis in land analysis, includes introduction to GIS and land-use planning. **Programs:** B.A. **Type:** Degree program. **Cost:** $12,400/year, including room and board (tuition: $8,400). **Age Emphasis:** Adults. **Application Deadline:** The spring prior to fall semester.

UNIVERSITY OF ARIZONA—NATURAL RESOURCES CONSERVATION WORKSHOPS

RNR/BSE 325
Tucson, AZ 85704
(602) 621-7269

Emphasis: For educators, camp directors, interpretive naturalists and school teachers (K-12). Basic natural resource conservation. **Programs:** Natural resources conservation workshop for educators. **Type:** Degree program, outdoor education, natural science/history, natural resources. **Cost:** $175 plus tuition for university credit. **Age Emphasis:** Adults. **Application Deadline:** May 15, 1991.

UNIVERSITY OF TAMPA—DIVISION OF SCIENCE AND MATH

401 W. Kennedy Blvd.
Tampa, FL 33606
(813) 253-3333

Emphasis: Bachelor's degree in biology with a specialized Environmental Science track. **Programs:** Degree program includes several ecologically-oriented biology and chemistry courses, and recommends work in scientific writing, economics, statistics, political science,

Q: *An item of food travels on average how many miles in the US before it is eaten?*

and interdisciplinary studies. **Type:** Degree program. **Cost:** University tuition. **Age Emphasis:** Adults. **Application Deadline:** N/A.

UNIVERSITY OF UTAH—RED BUTTE GARDENS AND ARBORETUM

Bldg. 436
Salt Lake City, UT 84112
(801) 581-8936

Emphasis: Environmental education (K-12), general horticulture and gardening techniques, native plants and ecosystems, nature programs. **Programs:** Examples—Walks in the Wasatch, Green Horizons, Paper Making, etc. **Type:** Outdoor education, expedition/experiential, natural science/history, residential. **Cost:** Varies from free workshops to $90/quarter university credit. **Age Emphasis:** All ages. Application deadlines: Ask for quarterly program announcement.

UNIVERSITY OF VERMONT—DEPT. OF BOTANY

Marsh Life Science Bldg.
Burlington, VT 05405-0006
(802) 656-2930

Emphasis: Integrative field science, environmental problem solving, strong communication skills. **Programs:** Field Naturalist Program. **Type:** Degree Program. **Cost:** Fellowship. Length: 2 years. **Age Emphasis:** College Student. Application deadline: March 1.

WAYNE STATE UNIVERSITY—DEPT. OF CHEMICAL ENGINEERING

5050 Anthony Wayne Dr.
Detroit, MI 48202
(313) 577-3800

Emphasis: Graduate certificate in hazardous waste management, Master of Science in hazardous waste management. **Type:** Degree program. **Cost:** $111.75/credit, resident; $242.50/credit, nonresident. **Age Emphasis:** Adult. **Application Deadline:** Fall, July 1; Winter, Nov. 1; Spring and Summer, March 15.

WILLIAMS COLLEGE—CENTER FOR ENVIRONMENTAL STUDIES

Kellogg House, P.O. Box 632,
Williamstown, MA 01267
(413) 597-2346

Emphasis: Environmental policy, planning, ethics, science. **Programs:** Undergraduate degree with concentration in Environment Studies. **Type:** Degree program. **Cost:** $20,000/year for tuition, room and board at residential liberal arts college. **Age Emphasis:** Adults. **Application Deadline:** N/A.

YUKON COLLEGE

Box 2799
Whitehorse, Yukon Y1A 5K4, Canada
(403) 668-8778

Emphasis: Explore the Yukon's magnificent heritage while reflecting upon the environment, society, role of education. **Programs:** Two week program in July—Environmental Studies and Education. **Type:** Expedition/experiential, philosophical, natural science/history. **Cost:** $215 Canadian for tuition and field activity fee. **Age Emphasis:** Adults. **Application Deadline:** June 1.

A. *1,200 miles*
  Source: Worldwatch Institute

PART 4

ECOVOICE

EARTH DIGEST

A selection of recent essays and commentary from the best of the environmental scribes. These words of eco-insight will enlighten and inspire you into better understanding the challenges and actions needed to counteract our global environmental crisis.

Too Confused To Care?

- By Melinda Worth Popham -

Once, years ago, knowing better but doing it anyway, I spent an afternoon trying to save a dying tree in the Arizona desert. What has reminded me of my endeavor is a recent survey by *Time* magazine which found that a whopping 80 percent of Americans feel so confused about environmental issues that they don't know what to do. I may have been an environmental ignoramus, but I wasn't confused about what I wanted to do to lend a helping hand.

The tree was a paloverde; it was dying from mistletoe. We'd been camped by it for several days. Obliged, like the coyotes, lizards and jackrabbits we glimpsed, to seek shade during the day, I had chosen this tree for its gnarled roots, flash-flood watermarks and amazing bark—and, too, because its scanty flowers meant fewer bees. A paloverde in full bloom is an ethereal swath of yellow and a Mecca for bees.

Whiling away hours in its shade, I grew fond of this old-timer. The patchy islands and knobby peninsulas of bark it had grown in its old age endeared it to me. Paloverdes aren't supposed to have bark; it's an extravagance their smooth, leaf-green skin can't afford. Bark on a paloverde is a badge of hard-earned longevity, a mark of venerability. It was the damn-the-cost bark this tree had grown that compelled me to do something about the dark, devouring cloud of mistletoe choking first its flowers and soon the life out of this magnificent tree. Forget about stolen kisses under Christmas sprigs. For trees infested with it, mistletoe is the kiss of death.

Wearing White Mule work gloves, I set about yanking out fistfuls of the leathery-leafed, parasitic enemy invader. When I'd cleared the pendent clumps festooning the lower branches I positioned our old CJ-7 Jeep so I could stand on it—bumper, then hood—and snag some of the higher clumps with a rib from a dead saguaro. For a period of time nothing else mattered to me except how much mistletoe I could pull off that tree. Watching it pile up on the ground filled me with hand-rubbing glee. When I set fire to the pile, it burned with greasy ease, its foul smoke routing my downwind husband who, to his credit, did not ask me what good I thought I was doing. Not that I felt any confusion about it. I was saving a tree's life. Well, *extending* it anyway. At any rate, I definitely felt saintly.

But had my good-hearted deed done any good? Nah. It was sheer folly, my taking on Mother Nature like that. The out-of-reach mistletoe in "my" paloverde would soon spread its dominion, and mistletoe from nearby paloverdes would breeze over to speed up the process. This much I had gotten right though: Square one *is* caring. Of course there's caring and then there's *effective* caring; but having your heart in the right place paves the way for getting your head on straight.

Trying to sort out the environmental issues tugging at your sleeve, wallet and heartstrings and getting them to have some sort of narrative coherence is like coming in late to a movie and having to figure out who's who, what's happening and why everybody's laughing. The environmentally bewildered want to know: "Where can I begin? How do I find a starting place?"

Q: *How many children die worldwide of starvation every minute?*

Finding one's own personal "it" is it. What matters is that something matters to each of us. In his poem "Requiem for Sonora," Richard Shelton gets to the crux of what this means when he says, "...oh my desert, yours is the only death I cannot bear." Ask yourself what you feel that way about. What place makes your spirit well up within you? What creature do you feel a resonance with? What natural wonder startles tears into your eyes?

For me, it's the Sonora desert of Arizona with its signature creature the coyote. Having always wanted to know some chunk of nature well and truly, it wasn't until I saw the Sonora desert that I felt inspired to take a crack at it. I know why, too. It wasn't the razzle-dazzle of its sunsets nor my stunned admiration for the survival skills of its inhabitants that inflamed me with resolve to learn the names and ways of everything I came across in it. It was that here was a piece of Nature so streamlined and finite, so elegantly economical, so pared down to bare minimums that even I, a kindergartner in the natural world, could grasp it. As Wendell Berry says, "Our wish to preserve the planet must somehow be reduced to the scale of our competence. Only love can do it."

Enamored with the clear-cut, bone-clean beauty of the desert, my mind and senses were invigorated by a can-do spirit. On alpine or coastal turf I always had to fight off a pessimistic lethargy of will when it came to tackling the identities of the seemingly teeming hordes of winged, rooted and four-legged denizens. The one-at-a-time way each thing in the desert caught my eye—a solo ocotillo; one lone, lean coyote—energized me to learn about them, get to know them and, eventually, through my writing,

put in a good word for them.

Small wonder, when you think of it, this nationwide mass confusion over environmental issues. Accustomed to having high-tech, computer-generated, satellite-bouncing gizmos provide us with instant results, quick fixes and best and worst case scenarios, we don't like being asked to take "maybe" for an answer, and we have lost all patience with the pensive, tortoise pace of gathering wisdom, informing our spirits. The aesthetic and recreational forays we make into Nature give us a backslapping relationship with it and serve to remind us that Nature isn't just real estate in the form of "raw" land or an ocean "vu." Our experience of Nature needs to simmer, stew and steep in us, gaining in strength and color, richness and depth over time before it begins to produce wisdom, concern and, above all, reverence for it at the highest and purest ethical level.

Once you have whooped "Eureka!" over your own personal "it," in your subsequent eagerness to know it inside out, to do right by it and to become intermingled-unto-blurred with it (à la John Muir's "We are now in the mountains, and they are now in us"), you may become discouraged by the slowness of this brewing process. If so, take heart:

I have an acquaintance who sought inner self-education by backpacking alone in the Sierra Nevadas. He trudged for days and with gathering dismay discovered that his thoughts were utterly mundane and trivial and that he could not mentally transcend the immediate discomforts from temperature swings and the fiery blister on his heel. After going several days without seeing another soul, he came upon a hiker who hadn't seen a human for three weeks. My acquaintance, already feeling like a

A.²⁷

Source: Earth Facts, by Earthbooks, Inc.

philosophical flop and a lousy outdoorsman, was humbled to think of the inner stamina, blazing insights, soul-searched answers and lofty whatevers this man must have found in himself in the course of those solitary weeks.

"My God!" he burst out. "What have you thought about all that time?"

Looking down at the ground, the man said fervently, "Milkshakes, *chocolate* milkshakes."

Melinda Worth Popham is the author of Skywater, *winner of the 1990 Edward Abbey Award for EcoFiction.*

A Dying Crusader, Witness to Chernobyl's Horrors

- By Peter Matthiessen -

Sagaponack, New York—One morning last month in Morelia, Mexico, while swimming in a hotel pool, I observed a gaunt man in a dark suit whom I recognized as a fellow participant in an environmental conference sponsored by Mexico's Group of 100. This conclave of scientists, environmentalists and writers was seeking to avert global catastrophe.

Dr. Vladimir Chernousenko stood alone on a terrace smoking a cigarette and was still smoking when my wife and I joined him for breakfast.

According to his translator, Mr. Chernousenko, who ate little and paid small attention to his health, is not expected to live more than two years. Yet in public his words and manner are unfailingly so spirited and cheerful that by the time he had finished his public presentation he was the hero of the conference.

Mr. Chernousenko, 50, a nuclear physicist, was the scientific supervisor of the emergency team sent into Chernobyl a few days after a meltdown in nuclear reactor No. 4 caused a fatal explosion on April 26, 1986.

Mr. Chernousenko arrived there five days later. He was also director of the Scientific Exclusion Zone, the so-called Dead Zone, which extends in all directions for about 30 kilometers (19 miles) from the black hulk of No. 4, known as "the sarcophagus."

Before his arrival the other reactors had been shut down and the zone's villages belatedly evacuated.

Mr. Chernousenko's orders were to "liquidate the consequences" of the accident—he enunciates this bureaucratic euphemism with irony and despair, because the consequences will remain unliquidated for millennia—and to reactivate the other reactors as soon as possible, at any cost.

In an accident at Chernobyl in 1982, Mr. Chernousenko said, the wind carried radioactive particles toward Siberia, where the fallout passed almost undetected except by the unfortunates in its path. But in 1986 the winds were blowing westward and the radioactivity was detected by scientists in Sweden ten days later.

This time the disaster was revealed by the authorities, who received international credit for their candor; as the world has since discovered, this "candor" was disingenuous at best.

In 1986 the radiation from the ruined reactor represented 80 percent of

Q: *How many million acres of lawns are there in the US?*

its full charge of uranium, not the 3 percent the government reported; even today the region remains a hundred times more contaminated than is thought safe for humans.

From the start it was known that the amount of energy produced by the restarted reactors would be insignificant, that there was no valid reason to send people back into Chernobyl and every reason to evacuate the region.

Mr. Chernousenko and his team personally warned Mikhail Gorbachev that a premature cleanup would drastically increase the human damage. Even so, the government decided that the cleanup should not await the arrival of modern technology and machines but should start at once with manpower and shovels.

At the conference, Mr. Chernousenko called this decision "a criminal and needless sacrifice of human life."

Local coal miners, the first to volunteer, collapsed from radiation poisoning within an hour.

The officials then turned to untrained and unprotected army reservists and conscripts, some of whom, says Mr. Chernousenko, fainted upon realizing what was being asked of them. Even when radiation suits arrived from the United States, they proved all but useless.

No one was permitted to remain more than one minute on the roof, from which graphite debris was shoveled down into "the sarcophagus" before it was sealed.

Mr. Chernousenko presented a terrifying documentary film that showed bulky figures running out on the roof. There was only time for two small frantic scoops with narrow, old-fashioned shovels before they fled—"10th century technology being used to fight 20th century catastrophe," Mr.

Chernousenko said.

Clutching official certificates of honor, these young men were immediately removed from the dead zone.

Even so, without exception, those sent out on the roof are dead.

Mr. Chernousenko said that all of his approximately 100 associates and friends at Chernobyl are already gone.

The official figure of 31 mortalities represents those who died in the original explosion. The actual toll of those who perished as a result of the "cleanup" is 5,000 to 7,000, and many thousands more throughout southern Russia will die of radiation poisoning or related cancers, especially in Byelorussia, which received even more fallout than the Ukraine.

Mr. Chernousenko believes that at least 35 million people have been damaged. Eight million to 10 million live in heavily contaminated regions, including a number who have returned to their villages, persuaded by propaganda that Chernobyl has been modified and is now safe.

"We are faced with an apocalypse," Mr. Chernousenko said in an intense, quiet voice of warning. "This is an international disaster."

Yet, he said, the international nuclear agencies discount many serious accidents with vague phrases, unchecked data and false conclusions to assuage the public's increasing uneasiness about the safety and practicality of nuclear power.

Mr. Chernousenko believes the Chernobyl catastrophe eliminated the last hope of practical use of nuclear power. It is impossible, he said, to build a "safe" reactor, and even if one managed such a feat, the technology would be too expensive. Nuclear energy cannot compete economically with other energies in the open market.

A. *20 million*
Source: 50 Simple Things You Can Do To Save The Earth, *by the Earth • Works Group*

Five years after the explosion the government has yet to release his dire report on the emergency operation at Chernobyl. Mr. Chernousenko is devoting the remainder of his life to presenting his evidence because, he said, "events that cause so many human deaths should not be hidden."

Mr. Chernousenko left the Soviet Union for France last year for medical treatment, then went to Germany and is now in Britain.

This April, while writing a book about Chernobyl, he was dismissed from the Institute for Theoretical Physics in Kiev, because his opinions are unwelcome to his government.

At the conference in Mexico, all who listened to this eloquent and quiet man came away disturbed and stirred, not only by his talk but by the exhilarating spectacle of a brave man set free by his passionate commitment to the truth, even while penniless and dying.

The conference participants have urged the leaders who will attend the Earth Summit in June 1992 to commit themselves to ending ecocide. They proposed the creation of an International Court of the Environment.

These words should be heeded.

Peter Matthiessen is a writer and environmentalist. His most recent book is African Silences.

Reprinted by permission from The New York Times, *October 14, 1991.*

An Opportunity For Justice

- By Kofi Awoonor -

The Group of 77 is deeply involved in the United Nations Conference on Environment and Development not only because the Earth Summit promises to provide a clear vision of what needs to be done to promote environmental protection and enhancement programs at the national and international levels, but because this forum is seriously exploring the underlying causes of environmental degradation, particularly in developing countries. It could be an opportunity for all of us, developing and industrialized countries alike, to meet around a common table where our collective destiny as a species on this planet can be discussed as equals.

The simple fact remains that the alarming environmental deterioration in many developing countries is the direct result of poverty, and the principal cause of this poverty is the global economic imbalance that characterizes North-South relations. It is also clear to us that the developing countries are not poor or underdeveloped because we do not work hard, but because of our historical role in an increasingly exploitive international economic system.

We cannot afford to sustain the current arrangement in which the industrialized countries in effect confiscate our products by paying prices nowhere near parity to the products they sell to us. We are, in the present international economic order, subsidizing standards of living in the North with our underpriced products. What is worse, these standards reflect patterns of overconsumption that no one can seriously argue are sustainable, much less extendable to the rest of the developing world.

The over-exploitation of our resources for export in the desperate scramble to earn foreign currency and maintain debt payment schedules is

Q. *To water America's lawns, how many gallons of water do we need every single week?*

taking a terrible ecological toll on our forests, our oceans, our lands and our rivers. Our precious biodiversity is being devastated further each day.

It cannot be expected that, because of the present perverse economic order, those who earn $200 *per capita* in the great democratic, free marketplace are the ones to make sacrifices so that those who, by dint of the massive advantages of technology and an exploitive international economic structure, can breathe cleaner air or escape the torments that global warming may bring in its wake.

Yet the industrialized countries have resolutely opposed reversing this untenable situation. The development assistance they provide us arrives with humiliating conditions and paternalistic lectures regarding the virtues that surround wealth and development. Basic development technology arrives with price tags that not only deepen our poverty but extend our condition of peonage to our so-called benefactors.

Until this situation is redressed by a serious and equitable global economic program, we must insist on a number of interim measures, some of which can be integrated into the post-Earth Summit mechanisms that are currently being negotiated in the Preparatory Committee process.

The developing countries will require compensatory financial outlays from the industrialized countries if we are to implement environmental protection measures. These should not be construed as charity but necessary and just transfers for what is due for years of continuous labor.

Consideration should also be given to the diversion of the peace dividend that will accrue from disarmament toward the cost of development and rehabilitating the environment. This can be done not merely by preserving forests or organizing safer chemical waste disposal, but by guaranteeing investment for development in the poor countries where the environment is the first victim of acute poverty, urban overcrowding and the loss of arable land to overexploitation.

It is unacceptable that the vast savings that result from peace and detente go to support the consumption habits of the rich and further expand the misery of the poor through sheer denial of access. If this happens, we shall be nowhere near the new world order that will guarantee our collective survival.

The rich North, we hope, will weigh our views as legitimate pleas for understanding. And if we are collectively to leave a sound Earth to the coming generations, then let us end poverty, let us eradicate communicable diseases, let us guarantee food, shelter and water for all peoples of the planet.

Our will as developing countries to undertake the tasks required to protect and enhance our environment remains strong. But our efforts and concerns for economic development are thwarted, at every turn, and undermined by a hostile economic environment.

The global partnership needed so sorely to reverse environmental degradation cannot work if we in the developing world are persistently ignored. Unless these attitudes and tendencies change, we cannot, and we will not, be able to join the industrialized countries in this vital task to make the Earth safe for all of us and to save our planet for the future.

Kofi Awoonor is president of the Group of 77, representing developing countries in the General Assembly, and is the permanent representative of Ghana to the United Nations.

Reprinted by permission from Development Forum, *September/October 1991.*

A. *540 billion gallons*
Source: 50 Simple Things You Can Do To Save The Earth, *by the Earth • Works Group*

A Silence of Meadowlarks

- By James Eggert -

If I were a CEO or the head of a government agency, I doubt whether I would hire a contemporary economist. This may seem an odd comment from someone who has spent his past 22 years teaching college Econ classes. Indeed, on countless occasions, I've defended my discipline's importance to my students and others.

What is economics' special contribution? Economists' stock in trade includes: recognizing scarcity, helping to make choices, identifying trade-offs and making (sometimes hidden) connections between the larger economy and one's own individual economic world. So what's the problem? It's this: We economists lack an understanding of ecology and ecological values.

"Ecology." The words economics and ecology derive from the same root, "eco," literally "household." Thus the original definition of economics implied an understanding, a caring for and management of human households, whereas ecology implied an understanding and appreciation of the interrelationships within nature's "household." I believe these two households are becoming more interdependent, their futures more and more intimately linked. When we fail to calculate ecological values or to see the connections, it eases the way for unintended, unwanted losses. One example (on a small scale, to be sure) is now occurring in our area, a dairy farming region in the upper Midwest. We are losing our meadowlarks!

The people who walk our rural roads enjoy the few meadowlarks that are left. Their song is pleasing, their color and swoop-of-flight enchanting. The complete disappearance of meadowlarks would, plain and simple, be wrong ethically and also would diminish the quality of our lives.

Why are we losing meadowlarks? Most likely because of a modern haying method—haylage. Farmers now cut hay "green" (with minimal drying) two or three weeks sooner in the spring than once was traditional, and blow it right into the silo. A decade ago, most farmers let hay grow two to three weeks longer before cutting it, to be dried, raked into windrows and baled. This gave field nesting birds such as meadowlarks and bobolinks time to establish a brood and fledge their young before the mower arrived.

Haylage improves farm "efficiency"—substituting machinery for labor, minimizing time and costly rain delays that plagued the old method. Agricultural economists and other experts blessed such changes. But who was valuing the meadowlarks?

Despite their sweet song, these birds have no voice economically or politically. They represent a zero within our conventional economic accounting system (we don't even buy birdseed or build birdhouses for meadowlarks). Their disappearance would not create even the tiniest ripple in Commerce Department spreadsheets that supposedly measure our standard of living.

Of course, the demise of the meadowlark is not the only example. In truth, "Meadowlark Values" are everywhere. They are found in estuaries and sand dunes, wetlands and woodlands, native prairies and Panama

Q. *How long will it take to make enough plastic film to shrink-wrap the state of Texas?*

rainforests. It is quite probable that the quality of your own life is to some degree dependent on these values. Just look about and you will find them (like our meadowlarks) on your road, or next door, or even in your own backyard.

Meadowlark Values were underrepresented when President Bush's economists advised him to open up the Arctic National Wilderness Refuge for oil and gas exploration. Meadowlark Values were shortchanged when economists pointed out (quite correctly) that Exxon's oil spill actually *increased* our gross national product (GNP) with billions in cleanup dollars fattening paychecks as well as state and national income.

Perhaps it is time we economists began to rethink our strict adherence to dollar and GNP values. We should not discard our valuable skills: of recognizing scarcity, making efficient choices and pointing out trade-offs. But it's time to broaden our approach, to incorporate ecological thinking and ecological values *with* market thinking and values—call it, if you wish, "Meadowlark Economics."

I'm ashamed to admit I took my first ecology class only after teaching economics for more than two decades. I have a ways to go. I am beginning to read (and appreciate) some of the latter day economists who represent this new thinking: Ken Boulding, Hazel Henderson, Leopold Kohr, Herman Daly and Lester Brown, to name a few.

In addition, I hope that more and more prominent economists, the Friedmans, the Boskins, Bradys and Greenspans of today—and the future—will learn to value the integrity of the environment along with the "bottom line;" promote development, but also protect the standard of living of the other organisms with whom we share the planet.

Along with environmental impact statements (EIS), perhaps future economists can devise what might be called GIS or "grandchild impact statements," making sure our kids and their kids will have sustainable quantities of biological as well as other resources and helping preserve our soils and waters, fisheries and forests, whales and bluebirds—even the tiny toads and butterflies—so that these entities too will have their voices represented.

So, all you National Association of Business Economists, government advisers (and us teachers too) let's dedicate ourselves to a new standard of—what?—Meadowlark Economics, if you will, of protecting and sustaining, for the future, a larger and more comprehensive set of durable values.

James Eggert teaches economics at the University of Wisconsin-Stout. His latest book is Invitation to Economics, *published by Bristlecone/Mayfield in 1991.*

Reprinted by permission from The Washington Post, *August 4, 1991.*

A. *1 year*
   Source: The Recycler's Handbook, *by the Earth•Works Group*

Keep It Simple
- By John Nichols -

Once I led a pretty modern life. I could juggle many different preoccupations at once: family, garden, children, friendships, chores, grandiose ideas, political activism, fishing, hiking, drinking, novel writing, script writing, nature photography and so forth. In a single year I could travel to Europe, San Francisco, Seattle, Los Angeles, Austin, Boston, Chicago and New York without blinking an eye. While talking on the phone I could at the same time cook supper, scan the newspaper, make love and write notes to myself. I had a 20-track mind. I was seething with manic energy.

Then one day I got sick. My heart started fibrillating. I experienced searing pains in my neck and burst out in cold sweats. The pain traveled upwards, popping in both ears. Tachycardia hit, I went dizzy, nearly sank to my knees, almost blacked out. I thought: Dammit, I'm going to die.

Don't ask how, but I made it to a doctor. He put me through a battery of tests: echograms, dopplers, thalium treadmills. He concluded maybe I'd already had a heart attack. It was decided to catheterize my heart, shoot it full of dye, check out the arteries. I entered the hospital, they did their thing, and announced, "Nope, the arteries look great."

Then they put me on digitalis for the rest of my life.

When I asked what's wrong with me, the doctors shrugged and said I was probably so stressed out I couldn't see straight.

Then one of them said, "Why don't you kick back and mellow out a little?"

Another advised, "Take the time to stop and smell the flowers."

A third hoped that I would "...learn how to keep it simple."

Fair enough: I set about making my life simple. I quit answering the telephone and, just to make certain, I petitioned for a new unlisted number. When people somehow got through and asked me to do things, I told any old baldface lie to weasle out of the commitment. I taught myself not to feel guilty for doing this. I ceased driving my old Dodge truck and started riding a bicycle. My sense of time slowed down. Things became less urgent. I stopped drinking coffee and eating salt and gobbling cookies.

Nevertheless, I soon realized that even if I quit killing myself, everybody else on earth was still eager to do me in. The air was so full of carcinogens, my asthma was being triggered regularly. Rays of sunshine galloped through vast holes in the ozone, eager to forge melanomas in me. Big time agribusinessmen continued painting my tomatoes with pesticides. Lee Iacocca was still manufacturing millions of automobiles in hopes of slaying me with carbon monoxide. And researchers on all continents were rushing to discover a cure for AIDS so I would become a mortal statistic in one of the many crises caused by overpopulation.

Bottom line, I soon realized, is that if everybody else on earth doesn't learn how to keep it simple, I'm doomed anyway. Unfortunately, my well-being is a collective effort. It does no good for me to mellow out if Lee Iacocca continues on his rampage.

Obviously, I can't just kick back, it

doesn't work that way. To save my own life, I gotta save yours too. If you're not willing to take responsibility for your own health (and mine), then I'll probably have to defend myself by making you very uncomfortable about your habits and actions.

According to John Muir, "Whenever we try to pick out anything by itself, we find it connected to everything else in the universe."

To me, understanding that statement seems like Step One on the road to recovery. Everything is interconnected, and the damage to any one small aspect of the overall picture (like me) usually threatens the entire picture. For example, look what happened tonight when I flicked on a light switch in order to write this article. A bulldozer started up in Arizona and stripmined a few tons of soft coal. Water was cut from a river into a slurry line to carry the coal to a generating plant in Page, Arizona. The generating plant fired up, turning the turbines that made electricity for my house. Smoke pollution spewed into the atmosphere, and prevailing winds blew it over my hometown of Taos and into the mountains and rivers near me. The pollution fell to earth as acid rain. Poisonous water came downstream into my irrigation ditch, and thence into my "organic" garden, which is full of beets and carrots. But when I ate a carrot it was contaminated by poisons which originated at Page, Arizona, whose raison d'être, of course, is millions of people like me who use lights at night, or run a refrigerator, or maybe watch a little TV to mellow out after a hard day at the office trying to save the planet.

The message is painfully clear. I love life, so I'm fighting like hell to make mine (and yours) more simple. I recycle everything possible, and try not to consume much to begin with. I buy all my clothes second hand, real cheap. I try to eat only what I need to survive. (How much of the planet do you think was destroyed by Orson Welles before he died?) Mostly, I don't need things so I don't buy them. If somebody turns on an air conditioner in my presence, I threaten to punch them, because they are personally attacking my well-being by adding to the greenhouse effect.

I have published four photo/essay books, and I still take pictures. But, frankly, I'm worried about photography. What happens to all those chemicals? How much poison, needed to print every beautiful image that I create, comes back to shorten my life?

And what about the pulp mills creating the paper upon which this chipper little article is printed?

No matter what, we all do damage. Nevertheless, it's real easy to reduce the damage we do.

Yes, I take a lot of time now to smell the flowers. I photograph them also. I'm training my eye to the simplicity in things, in order to move differently through the world. I always hope that by sharing a vision I'll gain other souls as allies. For in the end, only everybody else can save me.

In the meantime, my world has calmed down a lot, and I can tell the end of my life is receding.

*John Nichols, best known for his Southwest trilogy—*The Milagro Beanfield War, The Magic Journey *and* Nirvana Blues, *faxed this from his home in Taos on his 50th birthday.*

A. *20 percent*
Source: 15 Simple Things Californians Can Do To Recycle, *by the Earth • Works Group*

Ecofeminism

- By Irene Diamond & Gloria Feman Orenstein -

Today, more than 25 years after Rachel Carson's *Silent Spring* first raised a passionate voice of conscience in protest against the pollution and degradation of nature, an ecofeminist movement is emerging globally as a major catalyst of ethical, political, social and creative change. Although Carson was not an avowed feminist, many would argue that it was not coincidental that a woman was the first to respond both emotionally and scientifically to the wanton human domination of the natural world. Carson's 1962 text prefigured a powerful environmental movement that culminated in the nationwide Earth Day of 1970, but the notion that the collective voices of women should be central to the greening of the Earth did not blossom until the mid to late 1970s.

Ecofeminism is a term that some use to describe both the diverse range of women's efforts to save the Earth and the transformations of feminism in the West that have resulted from the new view of women and nature. With the birth of the Women's Movement in the late 1960s, feminists dismantled the iron grip of biological determinism that had been used historically to justify men's control over women. Feminists argued that social arrangements deemed to be timeless and natural had actually been constructed to validate male superiority and privilege. They asserted that women had the right to be full and equal participants in the making of culture. In this process writers and scholars documented the historical association between women and nature, insisting that women would not be free until the connections between women and the natural world were severed.

But as the decade advanced and as women began to revalue women's cultures and practices, especially in the face of the twin threats of nuclear annihilation and ecocide, many women began to understand how the larger culture's devaluation of natural processes was a product of masculine consciousness. Writers as diverse as Mary Daly, Elizabeth Dodson Gray, Susan Griffin, Carolyn Merchant, Maria Mies, Vandana Shiva, Luisah Teish and Alice Walker demonstrated that this masculine consciousness denigrated and manipulated everything defined as "other," whether nature, women or third world cultures. In the industrialized world, women were impelled to act, to speak against the mindless spraying of chemicals, the careless disposal of toxic wastes, the unacknowledged radiation seepage from nuclear power plants and weapons testing, and the ultimate catastrophe—the extinction of all life on earth. In the third world, women had still more immediate concerns. For women who had to walk miles to collect the water, fuel and fodder they needed for their households, the devastation wrought by patriarchal fantasies of technological development (for example, the Green revolution, commercial forest management and mammoth dam projects) was already a daily reality.

In many ways, women's struggle in the rural third world is of necessity also an ecological struggle. Because so many women's lives are intimately involved in trying to sustain and conserve water, land and forests, they

Q: *How many various chemicals are routinely added to food?*

understand in an immediate way the costs of technologies that pillage the Earth's natural riches. By contrast, in the industrialized world, the connections between women's concerns and ecological concerns were not immediately apparent to many feminists. Community activists such as Rachel E. Bagby, Lois Gibbs and Carol Von Strom, who were struggling to protect the health of their families and neighborhoods, were among the first to make the connections. Women who are responsible for their children's well-being are often more mindful of the long-term costs of quick-fix solutions. Through the social experience of caretaking and nurturing, women become attentive to the signs of distress in their communities that might threaten their households. When environmental "accidents" occur, it is these women who are typically the first to detect a problem. Moreover, because of women's unique role in the biological regeneration of the species, our bodies are important markers, the sites upon which local, regional or even planetary stress is often played out. Miscarriage is frequently an early sign of the presence of lethal toxins in the biosphere.

Feminists who had been exploring alternatives to the traditional "woman is to nature as man is to culture" formulation, who were seeking a more fundamental shift in consciousness than the acceptance of women's participation in the marketplace of the public world, began to question the nature versus culture dichotomy itself. These activists, theorists and artists sought to consciously create new cultures that would embrace and honor the values of caretaking and nurturing—cultures that would not perpetuate the dichotomy by raising nature

over culture or by raising women over men. Rather, they affirmed and celebrated the embeddedness of all the Earth's peoples in the multiple webs and cycles of life.

In their hope for the creation of new cultures that would live *with* the Earth, many women in the West were inspired by the myths and symbols of ancient Goddess cultures in which creation was imaged as female and the Earth was revered as sacred. Others were inspired by the symbols and practices of Native American cultures that consider the effects on future generations before making any community decision. The sources of inspiration were many and varied and led to a diverse array of innovative practices— from tree-planting communities, alternative healing communities, organic food co-ops, performance art happenings, Witchcraft covens, and the retelling of ancient myths and tales to new forms of political resistance such as the *Chipko* (hugging) tree actions and women's peace camps. Through poetry, rituals and social activism that connected the devastation of the Earth with the exploitation of women, these activists reinvigorated both feminism and social change movements more generally. The languages they created reached across and beyond the boundaries of previously defined categories. These languages recognized the *lived* connections between reason and emotion, thought and experience.

Ecofeminist politics does not stop short at the phase of dismantling the androcentric and anthropocentric biases of Western civilization. Once the critique of such dualities as culture and nature, reason and emotion, human and animal, has been posed, ecofeminism seeks to reweave new stories that acknowledge and value

A. **More than 3,000**
   Source: Silvercat Publications

the biological and cultural diversity that sustains all life. These new stories honor, rather than fear, women's biological particularity while simultaneously affirming women as subjects and makers of history.

We can discern three important philosophical strains from the many paths that people in the West and postcolonial societies are taking in their efforts to defend the Earth against the encroachments of life-denying imperialism:

1. One position emphasizes that the Earth is sacred unto itself, that her forests, rivers and different creatures have *intrinsic* value. The abstract "whole Earth" is not posed as being superior to or more valuable than the particular life of any one of her individual creatures.

2. Another strain emphasizes that because human life is dependent on the Earth, our fates are intertwined. Social justice cannot be achieved apart from the well-being of the Earth—we must care for the Earth as our survival and well-being are directly linked to her survival and well-being.

3. Finally, from the perspective of indigenous peoples, whose connection to native lands is essential to their being and identity, it is both true that the Earth has intrinsic value and that we are also dependent on her. Thus, we are led to understand the many ways in which we can walk the fine line between using the Earth as a natural resource for humans and respecting the Earth's own needs, cycles, energies and ecosystems.

The presence of these different strains indicates that ecofeminism is not a monolithic, homogeneous ideology. Indeed, it is precisely the diversity of thought and action that makes this new politics so promising as a catalyst for change in these troubled times. The planet is in crisis, as evidenced so clearly by the impending greenhouse effect and the concomitant droughts and loss of crops, the vanishing of rainforests and the extinction of so many species, the pollution of rivers, lakes and beaches, and the poisoning of the food chain. One response to this crisis is to reduce all these problems to one by arguing that there are simply too many people. Others say we are on the brink, that doomsday is at our door, and that only Draconian measures of control will see us through. Ecofeminist politics stands against any such monological, reductionist, apocalyptic thought processes. In contrast, this tapestry in green embraces heterogeneous strategies and solutions. While ecofeminism recognizes the severity of the crisis, it also recognizes that the methods we choose in dealing with problems must be life affirming, consensual and nonviolent. The process of creating new cultures that honor the Earth and her peoples is not something we can postpone. Moreover, because the creation of new images of living with the Earth is viewed as an essential element of the process of transformation, creative artists are an integral part of this new constellation. In short, ecofeminism radically alters our very notion of what constitutes political change.

Irene Diamond teaches at the University of Oregon in Eugene.

Gloria Feman Orenstein teaches at University of Southern California in the Study of Women and Men in Society Program.

Reprinted by permission from Reweaving the World, edited by Irene Diamond and Gloria Feman Orenstein, Sierra Club Books, San Francisco, 1990.

Q: *How many children are born throughout the world every minute?*

Biosphere Politics

- By Jeremy Rifkin -

In every culture, concepts of security are inextricably intertwined with human beings' relationships to the natural world. Securing sustenance, securing the state and securing peace of mind are always bound up, in one way or another, with securing the environment. Strangely enough, in much of contemporary scholarship concepts of security and concepts of nature have been treated as separate realms. Questions of security are generally relegated to the fields of political science, economics and military history. Questions involving the environment and nature are most often the preserve of the biologists, chemists and physicists, and secondarily the philosophers and poets.

Today the public is becoming increasingly aware of the connections that link politics, economics, war making and the environment. Still, national governments have yet to integrate environmental principles and concerns into their foreign policies, and business leaders still prefer to think of the environment merely as a "resource" or "externality."

Now, however, a new series of environmental problems has emerged that are global in impact and threaten the continued existence of planetary ecosystems and the future of civilization. Global warming, ozone depletion, acid rain, deforestation, desertification and species extinction are forcing our species to turn its attention, for the first time in our history, to the question of global environmental security. Questions of personal and national security, economic and military security, which have dominated the affairs of modern man and woman, have suddenly become dwarfed by the magnitude of environmental changes that threaten to alter the very biochemistry of our planet.

A younger generation is beginning to understand that preserving global environmental security is essential to guaranteeing the political and economic security of each human being and every community and nation. Despite the new ecological awareness, society has repeatedly shied away from a frank and open discussion of the roots of the contemporary environmental crisis.

The environmental threats facing the planet are not simply the result of scientific miscalculation. Nor are they merely the consequence of ill-conceived management decisions. Ironically, it is the notion of security upon which our entire modern worldview is based that has led us to the verge of ecocide. A thorough understanding of the current ecological crisis will require a vigorous examination of the social forces and philosophical currents that underlie our contemporary views of economic, political and military security. More important still, saving the Earth will require a fundamental change in our thinking about security and a new worldview that is more compatible with our species' awakening ecological consciousness.

The past several centuries have been dominated by the mechanistic thinking of the Enlightenment, with its emphasis on the privatization and commodification—the perception of things as economic goods—of nature and man; detachment and isolation from the natural world; and a near pathological obsession with creating a secure, autonomous existence, independent of the forces of nature. The nation state and its appendages, the modern business corporation and the professional military establishment, have emerged as the primary institutional vehicles for implementing the modern notions of individual and collective security. Geopolitics, in turn, has evolved as the primary political expression of nation-state ideals and objectives.

In less than a century, the practice of geopolitics has pushed the world to the brink of both nuclear Armageddon and environmental catastrophe, forcing us to reconsider the basic assumptions of security that animate the modern worldview.

Fortunately, the elements of "a new way of thinking" about security have been in the making for nearly a quarter of a century and are now steadily edging forward from the margin to the center of human consciousness, providing the context for a wholesale challenge to the existing world order. A new political vision is beginning to take shape and form, offering both hope and inspiration for the first generation of the 21st century.

Biosphere politics is the culmination of a 25-year odyssey of intellectual discovery and political activity that has begun to change the thinking and redirect the sociality of a generation of human beings around the planet. The term "biosphere" was coined at the start of the 20th century and refers to the thin chemical envelope, extending from the ocean depths to the stratosphere, that sustains all the various forms of life on the planet. The new politics envisions the earth as a living organism, and the human species as a partner and participant, dependent on the proper functioning of the biosphere and at the same time responsible for its well-being.

Biosphere politics unites the thinking of three great social currents of the post-World War II era into a unified philosophical vision. First, the movements for participatory democracy and economic justice, including the anti-colonial struggles of the third world, the civil rights, student and women's movements in the first world, and the newly emerging human rights and pro-democracy movements in the Soviet Union and Eastern Europe; second, the movements to preserve and sustain the environment, including the various environmental struggles, the animal rights and sustainable agriculture movements, and the new environmentally oriented peace movements; third, the movements centering around therapeutic consciousness and transformational politics, including the many new forms of personal therapy, the human potential movement, holistic health and the new spiritual awakening taking place both inside the Judeo-Christian communities and outside, in nontraditional religious and spiritual practices.

Each of these three social currents has been inspired by a deep human yearning to reestablish a sense of community: the political community and institutional life of the body politic; the spiritual community and the inner life of the soul; and the community of nature and the outward life of the environment.

The struggle for direct and intimate participation in the communities of life has been accompanied by the beginnings of a fundamental shift in human consciousness—first among the generation of the 1960s and now among their sons and daughters coming of age in the 1990s. The new consciousness eschews the strictly utilitarian thinking of previous generations that turned human beings into mere factors of production and consumption and that reduced nature to resources and commodities to be exploited in the marketplace.

Q: *The burning of fossil fuels, a nonrenewable resource, provides the US with how much of its energy?*

Champions of the new consciousness believe that human beings and other creatures we share the Earth with embody an intrinsic sacred value, not just utilitarian value, and deserve both our respect and stewardship.

The twin ideals of intimate repartication in the communities of life and deep spiritual resacralization of nature form the cornerstone of a new vision of security. When combined with the idea of the Earth as a living organism, the three concepts form a powerful trinity and serve as a foundation for a new overarching worldview for the 21st century.

The new biosphere politics offers a strong antidote and alternative vision to the politics of the modern era. Unlike geopolitics, which views nature exclusively as strategic resources, biosphere politics views the environment as a unified field and the irreducible context that sustains all of life and sets the conditions and limits for all other human thought and activity. In the biospheric era, the exploitation of nature gives way to a sense of reverence for the natural world and a sustainable relationship with the environment.

The conventional geopolitical idea of spheres of influence becomes an arcane concept in a biospheric framework and ultimately an obstacle in the way of achieving any kind of lasting peace. The idea of securing an autonomous existence, independent of the forces of nature, becomes increasingly suspect in a world defined as a living organism. In the new era, security is found in deep participation in the various communities of life that make up the body politic and the body of nature. Indeed, the transformation of private and public life from concepts of security based on self-interest and autonomy to those based on cooperation and the reestablishment of community distinguish the biospheric politics of the coming era from the geopolitics of the past.

The transition into a biospheric culture will spell the end of the nation state as the dominant political institution and the multinational corporation as the primary economic institution.

The biospheric era will spawn new political and economic arrangements more in keeping with our new ecological understanding of the earth as a living organism. New forms of governance will be grounded in the local biome and regional ecosystems. At the global level, the biosphere itself will become the governing region of the human species.

For too long, discussion of the mounting environmental problems facing the planet and civilization has been separated from the main currents of intellectual thought. Reorienting the various intellectual disciplines toward a biospheric perspective is an essential intellectual task if we are to create an ecological worldview to guide future generations.

It is my firm belief that a new ecological sensibility is emerging among the younger generation. A new commitment to the environment and the welfare of future generations needs to be accompanied by a well-reasoned critique of both the existing world order and the conventional geopolitical thinking that has accompanied it. At the same time, human civilization is in need of a bold new biospheric political vision that is strong enough to unite present and future generations in the formidable task of healing the Earth.

Jeremy Rifkin, author of Entropy, *is president of both the Foundation on Economic Trends and the Greenhouse Crisis Foundation in Washington, DC.*

Reprinted by permission from Biosphere Politics: A New Consciousness for a New Century, by Jeremy Rifkin, Crown Publishers, Inc., New York, 1991.

A. *90 percent*
  Source: Nontoxic, Natural and Earthwise, by Debra Lynn Dadd

Earth Day's Ebb

- By Andre Carothers -

In April 1990, in the midst of the Earth Day frenzy, no one would have predicted that a short 12 months later, environmental groups would be laying off staff, cutting programs and facing their most difficult financial crunch in a decade. Yet this is exactly what is happening. This year, almost every organization devoted to arms control, social justice and the environment in the US has seen its revenues drop as much as 20 percent.

Money is short. America, for economic and other reasons, has put environment on the back burner. The economic piece of the equation is fairly straightforward; it is the "other" that concerns us. We are worried that the economy is not the only problem, that just as the environmental decade is beginning, a curious complacency is descending on the leadership of the industrialized nations. It's not that we expected the banks, governments, corporations and institutions responsible for the environment's decline suddenly to do the right thing. But is is unnerving to see public support for groups like Greenpeace appear to decline just as the global leadership's green rhetoric is drying up as well.

And it is drying up. Three years ago, the Western democracies blithely signed off on the recommendations of the Brundtland report, a United Nations document on environment and development that, while not satisfactory to all environmentalists, certainly called for some significant reforms. Though agreed to in principle, the report was promptly ignored. Last year's meeting of the seven leading Western democracies, known as the G-7, was called the Green Summit because of the hefty proportion of environmental rhetoric. This year's G-7, the portion of the proceedings devoted to the environment lasted 13 minutes. And George Bush, the self-proclaimed environmental president of three years ago, has proved no friendlier to efforts to protect the planet than his predecessor.

It bears repeating that these global institutions will not change willingly. The interests of President Bush and his colleagues in the G-7 and the interests of the international banks, lending institutions and corporations that are responsible for the lion's share of our environmental problems are the same. In fact, they are often the same people.

To make matters worse, many businesses and their allies in government are organizing to preserve the status quo, creating what could be called an anti-environmental movement. Industry-funded groups with friendly names like the Information Council on the Environment, the Coalition for Vehicle Choice, the National Wetlands Council and People for the West are working to reverse two decades of hard-won victories for the environment. Several corporate public relations firms, once charged with defending the reputation of their clients, are now under a new assignment: to destroy ours by painting a picture of an environmental movement that is asking too much, that has less than the whole planet's interests in mind.

Reforming this array of interests is an overwhelmingly difficult task, and for all the successes of the environmental movement in the last decade,

Q: *Where is the most pristine US tropical rainforest, that supports five distinct types of rainforests: coastal, lowland, mountain, ridge and cloud?*

the overall trend is not encouraging. The rate at which new problems emerge and older ones become more intractable is still far outpacing the implementation of effective solutions. And the anti-environmental movement is splitting the country, casting ordinary people in pursuit of clean air and water as traitors or terrorists.

Under the circumstances, it is tempting to put a happy face on everything, quietly cut programs, wait out the recession, and content ourselves with some form of the organization that is determined by the vagaries of the economy and the public mood. But that's not our way. The environmental movement cannot be satisfied with being smaller. While we are as entranced by anyone by the myth of David and Goliath, it is clear that we don't have the luxury of seeing which way the legend turns out this time. There is one planet, and perhaps two decades to turn it around.

We must continue to try to lead the environmental movement in demanding changes that serve the planet, not public relations. We want every citizen to be part of the environmental movement. This is a plea, admittedly, not just for Greenpeace. It is a plea for everyone to understand that the survival of the planet is dependent on the health of the public interest movement. Any decline in support for groups pressing for social change means a proportionally larger concentration of power in the hands of institutions that, by their very nature, cannot have the public's and the planet's interest in mind. Civic society is not a luxury. It is essential to the functioning of the nation, and essential to the protection of the natural environment.

Andre Carothers is Editor in Chief at Greenpeace *magazine.*

Reprinted by permission from Greenpeace *magazine, October/November/December 1991.*

The New Conservation Movement

by Dave Foreman

Events ofttimes unfurl down different lines from those their authors plan. In 1981, when James Gaius Watt saddled up as Ronald Reagan's prissy paladin to head the conservationists off at the pass, neither the Secretary of the Interior nor Reagan's handlers (*nor* environmental groups, for that matter) could have predicted the outcome from Watt's pot shots at "environmental extremists."

The public, in reaction to the bewitchingly creepy Secretary of the Interior, joined groups like The Wilderness Society, Sierra Club, National Audubon Society and National Wildlife Federation in droves. As memberships soared to unprecedented heights, cash flow too welled up, allowing the organizations to hire more staff, trot out more programs and cover more ground.

My first wife's father—a crusty old fart who provided ranchers with government loans—once scoffed at me that environmeddlers were against all growth except their own. Being a slow, dense fellow (that's why my father-in-law liked me—I was easy prey), it took me some years before I appreciated his gibe. Not until the early 1980s did I

A. *American Samoa, which is just 76 square miles*
  Source: *Natural Resources Defense Council*

fathom that even for do-gooders fat carries much cholesterol. The new Watt members of the Sierra Club were "soft;" that is, they were less committed than the old members, often having joined on impulse after some particularly droll Wattism, and when their membership renewal came due a year later they were likely to drop. The Sierra Club administration, though, had immediately grown to count on the dues from the swollen membership and, indeed, had expanded the club's infrastructure to reflect (and require) that new level of funding. A treadmill was thus created, a treadmill in pursuit of members and their dues. Because the rate of renewals declined, more direct mail pleadings for new members had to be sent out just to stay even, much less forge ahead—as any entity must do when it comes to depend on planned growth. Of course, other environmental organizations (as well as other progressive social change groups) were taking advantage of the Reaganauts by climbing on the same growth/direct mail treadmill. To compete against allies in the membership run, each group had to redouble its efforts. More money was needed to raise more money. The proportion of each group's budget devoted to fundraising and membership solicitation increased faster than did contributions and memberships. The treadmills twirled faster and faster and no one had the *huevos* to jump off.

With more and more soft members, the percentage of active members decreased. This sociological imbalance led to power being concentrated in few hands and the grassroots being ignored in the high councils—soft members sent their money to national headquarters, strengthening the officers, without contributing to local efforts. A new breed of professional manager had to be hired to manage multi-million dollar budgets and corporation-sized staffs. A conservation group hooked on growth, with a CEO from government or industry, does not want to turn up the heat. Rash or controversial actions could lose soft members, and the foundation and corporate grants that the groups increasingly depended upon to fund top-heavy staff and high-profile programs.

The ultimate result of fattening the conservation movement with Brie and Chablis was to cause a New Conservation Movement to push up from the old roots, like green shoots of bunchgrass following a wet spring.

My views are shaped by my own experience of the 1970s—going from the original anarchist group, Black Mesa Defense; to Washington, DC, as lobbying coordinator of The Wilderness Society in 1977; to finally burning my bridges with the establishment by founding Earth First! in 1980.

Let's sit down here by these two different anthills (the conservation movements of the 1970s and 1990s) and worry them each with a stick and see what we can provoke.

It seems to me that the Old Conservation Movement of the 1970s had the following characteristics:

Nationals present solid bloc. During the 1970s, national conservation groups worked to present a solid front. It was crucial, strategists like Doug Scott of the Sierra Club believed, to show unanimity on legislation, in proposals for Wilderness Areas and National Parks, and in positions on agency initiatives. There were exceptions, of course. The National Wildlife Federation opposed the conservation mainstream on wilderness and wildlife protection as often as it supported it. Friends of the Earth and new groups spawned during the first Earth Day tested independent and more radical positions early in the 1970s, but by mid-decade were brought into line as part of the solid bloc of the conservation establishment.

Locals follow nationals. Complementing the solid front of the national groups, local chapters of the Sierra Club and independent grassroots groups like the Montana Wilderness Association and the New Mexico Wilderness Study Committee followed the lead of the big national groups. In campaigns for wilderness there was always "The Conservationist's Alternative," endorsed by national and local groups. There was never a wide spread of proposals ranging from moderate to visonary.

Conservationists support multiple use. In the 1970s, conservationists were tub-thumpers for the concept of multiple use. No group would have considered opposing timber cutting, livestock grazing, mining, oil extraction, motorized recreational developments, off road vehicle use, and other extractive uses on the public lands.

Conservationists use anthropocentric arguments for wilderness. In the 1970s, Wilderness Areas, National Parks, National Wildlife Refuges and other protected areas were still viewed primarily as recreational and scenic resources—not as ecological reserves. Areas proposed for Wilderness status were those with a vigorous constituency of hikers, packers, climbers, fishers, hunters and such. In most cases, it was the high country with glacial tarns, mountain meadows and imposing peaks above timberline that drew the support of recreationists. To gain protection for a popular alpine core, conservation groups willingly whittled off from their proposals the surrounding lower elevation lands desired by timbermen—even though these forested areas were far more valuable ecologically than the highlands.

The arguments for National Parks followed a similar theme. From the beginning, with Yellowstone in 1872, it was not wilderness being preserved but the spectacles and curiosities of nature—the wonders of the world like the Grand Canyon, Yosemite Valley, Carlsbad Caverns and Crater Lake.

National Wildlife Refuges were in most cases established to provide breeding grounds and other habitat for huntable waterfowl or big game; seldom were refuges set up for critters like whooping cranes. Even after scientists recognized the necessary ecological role of predators, conservationists did not dare advocate restoration of gray wolf, grizzly bear or cougar to areas where they had been exterminated.

For all of the protected areas, another anthropocentric rationale was what Alfred Runte, the preeminent scholar of the National Parks, calls the "worthless lands" argument. We could afford to set aside these areas and restrict full-blown multiple-use exploitation because they didn't have much in the way of resources. This approach, of course, reinforced the willingness of conservationists to exclude rich forestlands, grazing areas and mineralized zones from their proposals.

Additionally, 1970s conservationists saw Wilderness Areas, National Parks and Wildlife Refuges as islands—discrete, separate *units*. They were living museums, outdoor art galleries, backwoods gymnasiums, open-air zoos.

By 1980, these philosophical and organizational foundations were experiencing cracks. The zany excesses of Jim Watt helped the 1980s become a transition period for conservation, but

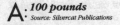

A. *100 pounds*
Source: Silvercat Publications

four other factors were essentially more important in cracking the old foundations.

Academic philosophy. During the 1970s, philosophy professors in Europe, North America and Australia began to look at environmental ethics as a worthy focus for discussion and explication. Sociologists, historians, anthropologists and other liberal arts academics also began to study attitudes toward nature. By 1980, enough interest had coalesced for an academic journal called *Environmental Ethics* to appear. Also, several university faculty members, particularly Bill Devall and George Sessions, were popularizing in the US the Deep Ecology views of Norwegian philosopher Arne Naess.

At first, little of this big blow in the ivory towers drew the notice of working conservationists, but by the end of the 1980s, few conservation group staff members or volunteer activists were unaware of the Deep Ecology-Shallow Environmentalism distinction or of the general discussion about ethics and ecology. At the heart of this discussion was the question of whether other species possessed intrinsic value or had value solely because of their use to humans.

Conservation biology. Despite the example of early-day wildlife scientists like Aldo Leopold and Olaus Murie, few biologists or other natural scientists were willing to enter the political fray in the 1970s. In the 1980s, however, two groups of working biologists appeared who were willing to provide conservationists with information, to speak out in public, and even put their reputations on the line over preservation issues. One group consisted of agency scientists: ecologists, botanists, zoologists, soils scientists and other researchers who worked for the Forest Service, National Park Service, Fish & Wildlife Service and Bureau of Land Management. These research scientists studied old-growth forest ecosystems, investigated the needs of endangered and sensitive species, and calculated the impact of resource extraction on a variety of ecosystems.

The other group of ecologists joining the movement were university researchers largely working in tropical rainforests and other exotic locations who suddenly became aware that the natural diversity they were studying was fast disappearing. As their data accumulated, a growing number of them could not deny the inescapable conclusion: Due to the activities of industrial human beings, the earth was in the throes of an extinction crisis greater than any revealed in the geological record.

These facts were so shocking—like the sudden buzz of a rattlesnake in tall grass—that a covey of biologists flushed into action and formed a new branch of biology. This "crisis discipline" (a term coined by one of its founders, Michael Soulé) was named Conservation Biology. The new field had dozens of books and a quarterly journal by the end of the 1980s. The warnings of conservation biologists were being heard through the national media. Even some politicians began to listen. By the decade's end, biodiversity had become a common term and a major issue.

Independent local groups. A third factor in rearranging the conservation movement was the growing independence of local wilderness groups. Such groups had begun to appear in the West in the 1960s, but their real development came about in the 1970s.

Earth First! In my book, *Confessions of an Eco-Warrior*, I discuss the

Q. *What food term has no legal meaning and may be used on almost any food? And which term may have a legal meaning, depending on where you live?*

whelping of Earth First! out of the mainstream movement, what the accomplishments of that remarkable phenomenon were during the 1980s, and why I felt it had largely achieved its practical goals by the late 1980s. Here, I want to emphasize something that rarely percolates to the surface in all of the volumes of media hype about Earth First!: The anti-establishment stance of Earth First! was a deliberate, strategic decision designed to effect certain defined goals. We founders of Earth First! did not believe that Earth First! was a replacement for the rest of the wilderness movement. In many respects, it was a kamikaze operation.

In the last chapter of *Confessions*, I sum up the accomplishments of Earth First!:

"Earth First! has led the effort to reframe the question of wilderness preservation from an aesthetic and utilitarian one to an ecological one, from a focus on scenery and recreation to a focus on biological diversity.

"We have effectively introduced nonviolent civil disobedience into the repertoire of wildland preservation activism. We have also helped to jolt the conservation movement out of its middle-age lethargy and re-inspire it with passion, joy and humor."

It was necessary for a group to consciously step outside of the system, to eschew the temptation of political access, to deliberately try to stir the stew; to bring biocentric arguments for wilderness to the fore; to emphasize biological diversity values over recreational and utilitarian values; to help prepare the soil out of which could sprout a necessary spectrum of groups within the wilderness movement; and to make possible the serious discussion of previously taboo subjects such as predator reintroduction, wilderness restoration and outlawing of timber cutting and livestock grazing on the public lands.

A different situation exists today in the wilderness preservation movement than ever before. There is an obvious spectrum of groups with differing positions on a variety of issues, and there is no centralized general staff able to dictate national strategy. Things are in a happy boil, and a new vision is challenging old ways of thinking and doing. The cutting edge of wilderness preservation has passed from well-established, wealthy national groups with large memberships and guaranteed political access, to struggling, hungry grassroots organizations with their feet and hearts planted firmly in the wildwood.

Any attempt to stuff dynamically evolving organizations, ideas and individuals into neat cubbyholes is as fruitless as trying to devise a mathematical rating scheme for wilderness quality. Such categorization, like any verbalized worldview or scientific theory, can only be a crude and temporary device for putting events into context. It must continually be updated. That said, when all the various elements of the current movement to protect the beauty and abundance of the living Earth are put into a boot, shaken and dumped out on the ground, these scorpions seem to arrange themselves into several reasonably distinct groupings.

One such collection is the National Mainstream Groups (the "Gang of Ten"): wealthy, powerful, but increasingly the followers (and sometimes, unfortunately, the thwarters) of new, more dynamic organizations. An unexpected irony is that the most slumbery groups of the 1970s—the National Wildlife Federation and the National

A. *Natural and organic, respectively*
   Source: Silvercat Publications

Audubon Society—are today more brash and farsighted than the old gladiators—the Sierra Club and Wilderness Society. On the telling issue of ancient forests, a leading Oregon activist ranks them (from strongest to most willing to compromise) Audubon, National Wildlife, Wilderness Society and Sierra Club. He predicts that will be the order in which they shake out on the public lands grazing issue as well.

The next batch is that of the state or regional Mainstream Groups, including those with paid staff—e.g., Greater Yellowstone Coalition, Idaho Conservation League—and those that are entirely volunteer, like the New Mexico Wilderness Study Committee.

Some of these groups have moved into another category—that of the Tough Mainstream. These guys and gals are still operating within the general confines of the mainstream, but are kicking sand in the faces of the buccaneers out to plunder our land.

Next, not quite fitting on a linear scale, but spreading out parallel to it, are the New Professionals, including the Society for Conservation Biology, and a loose colloquium of environmental ethicists grouped around journals like *Environmental Ethics* and *The Trumpeter.*

Our last wild bunch consists almost entirely of organizations formed within the last several years—Visionary Groups. These new groups proceed from a biocentric philosophy that argues for the intrinsic value of native ecosystems. They also come from a visionary political approach that dares to demand what was once off-limits and that applies the new understandings of conservation biology to practical, on-the-ground preservation proposals and land management questions.

The New Conservation Movement has largely turned its back on the old concept of Wilderness as primarily a recreational resource. Their arguments are solidly based in conservation biology, and recognize biological diversity as the fundamental value. Articulated and further developed by the visionaries, such ideas and reasoning are trickling down into the National Mainstream. No longer are Wilderness Areas and National Parks viewed as islands of solitude for harried urbanites, but as core preserves in an unfinished North American system of ecological preserves linked together to provide necessary habitat for viable populations of sensitive and wide-ranging wilderness-dependent species, like spotted owl, gray wolf, Florida panther, ocelot, grizzly and many less "charismatic" species.

It is a steep, rocky trail the New Conservation Movement must travel through the coming decade. Alongside it, behind rocks and trees, skulk goblins—some are terrifying things while others are delightsome sirens. The goblins I know about are these:

Invitation to the smoke-filled room. As the biocentric, biodiversity ideas of the New Conservation Movement are debated, they will trickle down into the rhetoric and platforms of mainstream groups and finally down to the nether depths of government agencies and politicians. When this happens, we will be invited into the smoke-filled rooms to cut deals and join in "management." We will be sorely tempted to compromise for such political access, such credibility. We need to guard against this and recognize the fundament of conservation activism: Our job is to argue for the natural world. We speak for Wolf. It is not our task to make the ultimate political compromises but to push those who do (politicians

Q: *Every day, how many newspapers are printed in the US?*

and bureaucrats) as far as we can to-ward our positions.

Siren song of the true believer. When we fall prey to this goblin, we lose patience with others, lose toler-ance for approaches different from ours, and begin to believe that those less strong are miserable sell-outs and traitors. Not only is this not fair, it is counterproductive, and it is damaging to our personal mental health.

Confrontation forever. It demands that we demonize all those we disagree with. We must carefully gird ourselves against allowing the need to sometimes be confrontational and uncompromis-ing take over our entire lives.

Marathon of burn-out. Being a wilderness activist is exhausting. Unless we follow Ed Abbey's advice and enjoy the wilderness we are trying to save, we will turn into bitter, ineffective little cinders. "Joy, shipmates. Joy!" Get out there and stare into sunsets, perfect your fly cast, learn how to differentiate Empids and woo the Big Outside.

Maw of fear. Violent reaction to our efforts to defend the wild will come from G-men trying to railroad us into court and prison, and from industrial goons who will intimidate us, beat us and even kill some of us. The weather will grow nasty before it clears. If we effectively campaign for the preserva-tion of the natural world, we will step on the toes of somebody trying to make a fast buck, or somebody enjoy-ing an ersatz sexual sensation by rip-ping the wild apart. These people are violent. Fear will well up inside us as we see others threatened, or are our-selves threatened. It will not be an easy ride.

Despair of destruction. As more great trees crash to the ground with a sickening shudder, as more species march into that long, dark night that has no dawn, as the fever in the body of the Earth climbs yet higher, we will become victims of despair. We, who are willing to open our souls to love this glorious, luxurious, animated plan-et, will be mightily bruised as that glory is tarnished, that luxuriance is shorn, and that animation is mechanized. Per-haps only the true knowledge that the destruction would be much worse without our brave efforts will buoy us through the dark days ahead.

Doubtless, there are goblins squat-ting silently next to the trail ahead about whom I have not yet dreamed. It is a long, rocky, fearful trail. But there is no other.

Dave Foreman is a founder of Earth First!, author of Confessions Of An EcoWarrior *and executive editor of* Wild Earth.

Reprinted by permission from Wild Earth, *Summer 1991.*

Bibliography

15 Simple Things Californians Can Do to Recycle, The Earth•Works Group, Earth Works Press, Berkeley, CA, 1991.

30 Simple Energy Things You Can Do to Save the Earth, The Earth•Works Group, Earth Works Press, Berkeley, CA, 1991.

50 Simple Things Kids Can Do to Save the Earth, The Earth•Works Group, Andrews and McMeel, Kansas City, MO, 1990.

50 Simple Things You Can Do to Save the Earth, The Earth•Works Group, Earth Works Press, Berkeley, CA, 1991.

50 Simple Things Your Business Can Do to Save the Earth, The Earth•Works Group, Earth Works Press, Inc., Berkeley, CA, 1991.

1990 IUCN Red List of Threatened Animals, World Conservation Monitoring Centre, Cambridge, England, 1990.

1991 Conservation Directory, 36th ed., National Wildlife Federation, Washington, DC, 1991.

1991-1992 Green Index: A State-By-State Guide to the Nation's Environmental Health, Bob Hall and Mary Lee Kerr, Island Press, Washington, DC, 1991.

The Ages of Gaia: A Biography of Our Living Earth, James Lovelock, Bantam Books, New York, 1990.

Antarctica: Private Property or Public Heritage?, Keith Suter, Zed Books Ltd., Atlantic Highlands, NJ, 1991.

Atlas of the Environment, World Wildlife Fund, Geoffrey Lean, Don Hinrichsen and Adam Markham, Prentice Hall Press, New York, 1990.

Backyard Composting: Your Complete Guide to Recycling Yard Clippings, Harmonious Technologies, Harmonious Press, Ojai, CA, 1992.

Balancing on the Brink of Extinction, Kathryn A. Kohm, ed., Island Press, Washington, DC, 1991.

Biodiversity, E. O. Wilson, ed., National Academy Press, Washington, DC, 1988.

Biosphere Politics: A New Consciousness for a New Century, Jeremy Rifkin, Crown Publishers, New York, 1991.

Buy Recycled! Your Practical Guide to the Environmentally Responsible Office, John Ortbal, Services Marketing Group, Chicago, 1991.

Chemical Deception: The Toxic Threat to Health and the Environment, Marc Lappé, Sierra Club Books, San Francisco, 1991.

CO_2 Diet For A Greenhouse Planet: A Citizen's Guide For Slowing Global Warming, John DeCicco, et al, National Audubon Society, New York, 1990.

Consumer Guide to Solar Energy, Easy and Inexpensive Application for Solar Energy, Scott Sklar and Kenneth G. Sheinkopf, Bonus Books, Chicago, 1991.

Design for a Livable Planet: How You Can Help Clean Up the Environment, Jon Naar, Harper & Row Publishers, New York, 1990.

Design for the Environment, Dorothy Mackenzie, Rizzoli International Publications, Inc., New York, 1991.

Dictionary of the Environment, 3rd ed., Michael Allaby, New York University Press, New York, 1989.

Dying Planet: The Extinction of Species, Jon Erickson, Tab Books, Blue Ridge Summit, PA, 1991.

Earth Book for Kids: Activities to Help Heal the Environment, Linda Schwartz, The Learning Works, Santa Barbara, CA, 1990.

The Earth Report: The Essential Guide To Global Ecological Issues, Edward Goldsmith and Nicholas Hildyard, eds., Price Stern Sloan, Inc., Los Angeles, 1988.

Earthfacts, Bo Gramfors and Siv Eklund, Earthbooks, Inc., Denver, 1990.

Earthship: How to Build Your Own, Michael Reynolds, Solar Survival Press, Taos, NM, 1990.

Eco Vacations: Enjoy Yourself and Save the Earth, Evelyn Kaye, Blue Penguin Publications, Leonia, NJ, 1991.

Ecology Begins At Home, Archie Duncanson, Archie Duncanson, publisher, Manhattan Beach, CA, 1989.

Ecology Cookbook: An Earth Mother's Advisory, Nan Hosmer Pipestem and Judi Ohr, Celestial Arts, Berkeley, CA, 1991.

Ecopreneuring: The Complete Guide to Small Business Opportunities from the Environmental Revolution, Steven J. Bennett, John Wiley & Sons, Inc., New York, 1991.

Embracing the Earth: Choices for Environmentally Sound Living, D. Mark Harris, The Noble Press, Inc., Chicago, 1990.

The Endangered Kingdom: The Struggle to Save America's Wilderness, Roger L. DiSilvestro, John Wiley & Sons, Inc., New York, 1991.

The Environmental Address Book: How to Reach the Environment's Greatest Champions and Worst Offenders, Michael Levine, Perigee Books, New York, 1991.

Environmental Data Report, 2nd edition, United Nations Environment Program, Basil Blackwell, Inc., Cambridge, MA, 1989.

Environmental Vacations: Volunteer Projects to Save the Planet, Stephanie Ocko, John Muir Publications, Santa Fe, NM, 1990.

EPA Journal, US Environmental Protection Agency, Washington, DC, Vol. 16, 1990.

The Frail Ocean, Wesley Marx, The Globe Pequot Press, Chester, CT, 1991.

The Fuel Savers: A Kit of Solar Ideas for Your Home, Apartment, or Business, Bruce N. Anderson, ed., Morning Sun Press, Lafayette, CA, 1991.

The Gaia Atlas of First Peoples: A Future for the Indigenous World, Julian Burger, Anchor Books, Doubleday, New York, 1990.

The Global Ecology Handbook: What You Can Do about the Environmental Crisis, Walter H. Corson, ed., Beacon Press, Boston, 1990.

Global Warming, Stephen H. Schneider, Sierra Club Books, San Francisco, 1989.

The Green Consumer, John Elkington, Julia Hailes and Joel Makower, Penguin Books, New York, 1990.

The Green Consumer Supermarket Guide, Joel Makower, Penguin Books, New York, 1991.

Green Earth Resource Guide, Cheryl Gorder, Blue Bird Publishing, Tempe, AZ, 1991.

The Greenhouse Trap: What We're Doing to the Atmosphere and How We Can Slow Global Warming, Francesca Lyman, Beacon Press, Boston, 1990.

The Green Pages: Your Everyday Shopping Guide to Environmentally Safe Products, Bennett Information Group, Random House, New York, 1990.

Guide to Recycled Printing and Office Paper and Papers With Postconsumer Content, Californians Against Waste Foundation, Sacramento, CA, 1991.

Guide to the Management of Hazardous Waste: A Handbook for the Businessman and the Concerned Citizen, J. William Haun, Fulcrum Publishing, Golden, CO, 1991.

The Healthy House, John Bower, A Lyle Stewart Book, Carol Publishing Group, New York, 1989.

Home Ecology: Simple and Practical Ways to Green Your Home, Karen Christensen, Fulcrum Publishing, Golden, CO, 1990.

Household Ecoteam Workbook, David Gershon and Robert Gilman, Global Action Plan for the Earth, Olivebridge, NY, 1991.

How to Make the World A Better Place: A Guide to Doing Good, Jeffrey Hollender, William Morrow and Company, Inc., New York, 1990.

Imperiled Planet: Restoring Our Endangered Ecosystems, Edward Goldsmith, et al, The MIT Press, Cambridge, MA, 1990.

Indoor Pollution, Steve Coffel and Karyn Feiden, Fawcett Columbine, New York, 1990.

Kids Can Save the Animals: 101 Easy Things To Do, Ingrid Newkirk, Warner Books, Inc., New York, 1991.

Kid's Guide to How to Save the Planet, Billy Goodman, Avon Books, New York, 1990.

The Living Earth: The Coevolution of the Planet and Life, Jon Erickson, Tab Books, Inc., Blue Ridge Summit, PA, 1989.

Making Things Happen: How To Be An Effective Volunteer, Joan Wolfe, Island Press, Washington, DC, 1989.

Managing Planet Earth, Scientific American Magazine, W. H. Freeman and Company, New York, 1990.

The Mother Earth Handbook, Judith S. Scherff, ed., The Continuum Publishing Company, New York, 1991.

The Nature Directory: A Guide to Environmental Organizations, Susan D. Lanier-Graham, Walker and Company, New York, 1991.

Nature Tourism: Managing for the Environment, Tensie Whelan, ed., Island Press, Washington, DC, 1991.

The Next Step: 50 More Things You Can Do To Save the Earth, The Earth•Works Group, Andrews and McMeel, Kansas City, MO, 1991.

Nontoxic, Natural, & Earthwise: How to Protect Yourself and Your Family from Harmful Products and Live in Harmony with the Earth, Debra Lynn Dadd, Jeremy P. Tarcher, Inc., Los Angeles, 1990.

One Earth, One Future: Our Changing Global Environment, Cheryl S. Silver and Ruth DeFries, National Academy Press, Washington, DC, 1990.

Only One Earth, Lloyd Timberlake, BBC Books, London, 1987.

Our Planet: The Magazine of the United Nations Environment Programme, United Nations Environment Programme, Nairobi, Kenya, Vol. 2, 1990.

Ozone Diplomacy, New Directions in Safeguarding the Planet, Richard Elliot Benedick, Harvard University Press, Cambridge, MA, 1991.

Permaculture: A Practical Guide for a Sustainable Future, Bill Mollison, Island Press, Washington, DC, 1990.

Plantworks, Karen Shanberg and Stan Tekiela, Adventure Publications, Inc., Cambridge, MN, 1991.

Preserving Our World: A Consumer's Guide to the Brundtland Report, Warner Troyer, Warglen International Communications, Inc., 1990.

The Rainforest Book: How You Can Save the World's Rainforests, Scott Lewis with the Natural Resources Defense Council, Living Planet Press, Venice, CA, 1990.

Ranger Rick's Nature Scope; Pollution: Problems & Solutions, Editor Judy Braus, National Wildlife Federation, Washington, DC, 1990.

The Recycler's Handbook, Simple Things You Can Do, The Earth•Works Group, Earth Works Press, Berkeley, CA, 1990.

Reweaving the World: The Emergence of Ecofeminism, Irene Diamond and Gloria Feman Orenstein, eds., Sierra Club Books, San Francisco, 1990.

Save the Animals: 101 Easy Things You Can Do, Ingrid Newkirk, Warner Books, Inc., New York, 1990.

Saving Our Ancient Forests, Seth Zuckerman with The Wilderness Society, Living Planet Press, Venice, CA, 1991.

A Shopper's Guide to Cruelty-free Products, Lori Cook, Bantam Books, New York, 1991.

Shopper's Guide to Recycled Products, Californians Against Waste Foundation, Sacramento, CA, 1991.

Shopping for a Better World, 1991, Ben Corson, et al, Council on Economic Priorities, New York, 1991.

The Simple Act of Planting a Tree: A Citizen Forester's Guide to Healing Your Neighborhood, Your City, and Your World, Treepeople with Andy and Katie Lipkis, Jeremy P. Tarcher, Inc., Los Angeles, 1990.

The Smart Kitchen: How to Design a Comfortable, Safe, Energy-Efficient, and Environment-Friendly Workspace, David Goldbeck, Ceres Press, Woodstock, NY, 1989.

The Solution to Pollution: 101 Things You Can Do to Clean Up Your Environment, Laurence Sombke, MasterMedia Limited, New York, 1990.

Southern Exposure: Deciding Antarctica's Future, Lee A. Kimball, World Resources Institute, Washington, DC, 1990.

The State of the Earth Atlas, Joni Seager, ed., Touchstone/Simon & Schuster, Inc., New York, 1990.

The State of the Environment, Organization for Economic Co-operation and Development, Paris, 1991.

State of the World 1991: A Worldwatch Institute Report on Progress Toward a Sustainable Society, Lester R. Brown, et al, W. W. Norton and Co., New York, 1991.

The Student Environmental Action Guide, The Student Environmental Action Coalition, Earth•Works Press, Berkeley, CA, 1991.

Sustainable Communities, Sim Van der Ryn and Peter Calthorpe, Sierra Club Books, San Francisco, 1991.

Thorsons Green Cookbook, Sarah Bounds, HarperCollins, Hammersmith, London, 1990.

Travel and Learn: The New Guide to Educational Travel, Evelyn Kaye, Blue Penguin Publications, Leonia, NJ, 1990.

Trees of Life: Saving Tropical Forests and Their Biological Wealth, Kenton Miller and Laura Tangley, Beacon Press, Boston, 1991.

Two Minutes A Day for A Greener Planet: Quick and Simple Things You Can Do to Save Our Earth, Marjorie Lamb, HarperCollins Publishers, New York, 1990.

The Universal Almanac, John W. Wright, ed., Andrews and McMeel, Kansas City, MO, 1991.

Why Wait for Detroit?: Drive the Car of the Future Today, S. McCrea, ed., South Florida Electric Auto Association, Ft. Lauderdale, FL, 1991.

The Wood User's Guide, Pamela Wellner and Eugene Dickey, Rainforest Action Network, San Francisco, 1991.

World Resources 1990-91, World Resources Institute, Oxford University Press, Oxford, 1990.

Your Resource Guide to Environmental Organizations, John Seredich, ed., Smiling Dolphins Press, Irvine, CA, 1991.

Index